Retrieving Freedom

CATHOLIC IDEAS FOR A SECULAR WORLD

O. Carter Snead, *series editor*

The purpose of this interdisciplinary series is to feature authors from around the world who will expand the influence of Catholic thought on the most important conversations in academia and the public square. The series is "Catholic" in the sense that the books will emphasize and engage the enduring themes of human dignity and flourishing, the common good, truth, beauty, justice, and freedom in ways that reflect and deepen principles affirmed by the Catholic Church for millennia. It is not limited to Catholic authors or even works that explicitly take Catholic principles as a point of departure. Its books are intended to demonstrate the diversity and enhance the relevance of these enduring themes and principles in numerous subjects, ranging from the arts and humanities to the sciences.

RETRIEVING FREEDOM

*The Christian Appropriation
of Classical Tradition*

D. C. SCHINDLER

*University of Notre Dame Press
Notre Dame, Indiana*

Copyright © 2022 by the University of Notre Dame
University of Notre Dame Press
Notre Dame, Indiana 46556
undpress.nd.edu

All Rights Reserved

Published in the United States of America

Paperback edition published in 2024

Library of Congress Control Number: 2022935751

ISBN: 978-0-268-20370-2 (Hardback)
ISBN: 978-0-268-20371-9 (Paperback)
ISBN: 978-0-268-20372-6 (WebPDF)
ISBN: 978-0-268-20369-6 (Epub)

For my father

hanc ex diverso sedem veniemus in unam.
tu, genitor, cape sacra manu patriosque penatis.
—Virgil, *Aeneid*, II.716–17

*Alles Gute ist Erbschaft: was nicht ererbt ist,
ist unvollkommen, ist Anfang...*
—Nietzsche, *Götzen-Dämmerung*, §47

Τῇ ἐλευθερίᾳ ἡμᾶς Χριστὸς ἠλευθέρωσεν.
—Galatians 5:1

CONTENTS

Preface ix

Acknowledgments xv

Part I. Prolegomena

1 Christian Freedom and Its Traditions 3

Part II. Late Antiquity

2 Plotinus on Freedom as Generative Perfection 51
3 Augustine and the Gift of the Power to Choose 82

Part III. The Patristic Period

4 Perfectly Natural Freedom in Dionysius the Areopagite 115
5 Maximus the Confessor: Redeeming Choice 137

Part IV. The Early Middle Ages

6 St. Anselm: Just Freedom 163
7 Bernard of Clairvaux: Liberating Love 189

Part V. The High Middle Ages

8 Bonaventure on the Trinitarian Origin of Freedom 203
9 Thomas Aquinas: A Fruitful Reception of the Whole 225

Part VI. The Late Middle Ages

10	Godfrey of Fontaines: The Absolute Priority of Act	281
11	John Duns Scotus and the Radicalizing of Potency	297

Part VII. General Conclusion

12	The Givenness of Freedom	331
	Abbreviations	343
	Notes	347
	Bibliography	496
	Index	523

PREFACE

The present book is the second part of a projected trilogy on the nature of freedom. Volume 1, *Freedom from Reality: The Diabolical Character of Modern Liberty*, was a diagnosis of the condition of the contemporary understanding of freedom and the deleterious cultural forms it generates. That book connected the inherently self-subverting character of modern liberty to a reduction of freedom to indeterminate potency, which has a definitive expression in John Locke's interpretation of the will as the paradigm of power. This *pars destruens* will eventually be complemented by a third volume, the *pars construens*, in which a comprehensive and positive theory will be developed in the light of the failings of the contemporary notion, in part by drawing on the great sources of thought on freedom in the West. This final volume will seek to tie together the dimensions of the question that are typically treated separately—the anthropological, the social and political, and the theological—in relation to a metaphysical core, which rarely gets addressed at all in studies on freedom. The hope will be that the long exploration of freedom in its current state of disorder and in the history of its rise and fall will enable a perspective that allows a genuine contribution to our philosophical understanding of this central human reality.

The present volume, the second in the projected trilogy, is an effort to lay bare the deep sources of the notion of freedom as it developed in the principal current of Western thought, namely, in what is often called the classical tradition. The first volume began with the study of John Locke, taken as a paradigm of the modern interpretation, and ended by contrasting that dialectical vision with the original notion that emerged from the pair of figures that founded the classical tradition, Plato and Aristotle. The current book covers more or less the same ground in the opposite direction, from the period of the inheritance of Plato and

Aristotle in late antiquity to the period that preceded, and in a certain respect prepared the space for, early modernity, namely, the late Middle Ages. But it needs to be said straightaway that this book does not intend to be a genealogy, which traces the lines of a particular problem's growth and thus reads the past specifically in its direct relation to a contemporary concern; still less is this meant to be a work of intellectual history, which studies the complex development of an idea with an aspiration to be as thorough as possible in uncovering sources and influences. Instead, the methodology governing this book does not fit in any obvious way in the conventional categories dominant in the academy. It is meant to be *a work of tradition*. This implies, on the one hand, the assumption of a time-transcending truth that is nevertheless conveyed concretely in time, through the actuality of history. On the other hand, it implies that the truth thus conveyed, transcendent and so "perennial" by nature, is nevertheless radically affected by this actuality of its realization. The effect of history on truth goes, so to speak, in both directions: while our contemporary understanding must be recognized as, most basically, a fruit of the past, a recipient of the tradition that has preceded it, it is also the case that this tradition is not an abstractly fixed quantity but is itself transformed by the particularity of its reception. Inheriting a tradition, in other words, is not a mere repetition of the same but a genuinely "poetic" act. From the vantage of the contemporary age, one can bring out novel dimensions of the thought that preceded, and indeed one *must* do so if one's own thinking is to be properly traditional. Gabriel Marcel once spoke insightfully of what he called "creative fidelity," which in fact is the *only* kind of fidelity, properly understood. As we are going to argue over the course of this book, the "creative" realization of tradition, in the sense just indicated, is not simply one possible way to approach the question of freedom but is essential to the very core meaning of freedom. Tradition and freedom cannot be separated.

Such, in a nutshell, is the aim of the present book: to re-source the meaning of freedom by seeking to enter into the heart of the idea in a number of the landmark figures in the classical Christian tradition. Perhaps the best image for the methodology adopted in this book is the oil drill: rather than scouring wide swaths of the surface laboriously, accumulating little pockets of the sought material here and there amid the slag, the drill penetrates directly into the core at a particular location. If several drills are placed at representative spots, one can achieve a fairly accurate picture of the geological stratification of an area and project an approximation of the topography, the nature of the soil's mineral content and of the various formations, and even perhaps a rough history of the geological shifts that brought them about. But these discoveries are incidental to the principal aim, which is to open access to the rich resource that lies beneath. Similarly, here, following in the spirit of our study of Plato and Aristotle that concluded volume 1, after an introduction that sketches the contours of the Greek and Jewish contribution to the notion, we will take a pair of figures as representative of the notion of freedom in five basic historical periods, which trace out what we might refer to as the rise and fall of the Christian appropriation of the classical tradition: late antiquity, the patristic period, the early Middle Ages, the High Middle Ages, and the late Middle Ages. The reason we treat two figures in each period is to set up a certain polarity in which those figures' mostly irreducibly different stances on freedom are considered as the ends of a spectrum. The idea is that a "stereoscopic vision" of this sort allows a depth dimension to emerge that would not come forth as clearly inside of a merely monocular view. This is one of the things that marks the distinction of a philosophical work of tradition from a more customary intellectual history. Apart from the section on the High Middle Ages, where the order is in a certain sense reversed, we have generally found it was possible first to present a more intellectualist and ontological account of freedom and then to complement it with a somewhat more existentialist perspective, which highlights the personal drama of choice. It will become evident, nevertheless, that what these complementary poles mean is analogously different in each period.

A word about the specific figures chosen to illustrate each major period is appropriate. **St. Augustine (354–430)** is often, and with good reason, taken to be the founder of the Western notion of freedom. It would of course have been possible to present him as one of the primary inaugurating figures of the long Middle Ages, in which the anthropological dimension of the notion was elaborated with such detail and logical sophistication. This more typical approach is legitimate and yields many insights into the later medieval thinkers. But we have chosen instead to interpret Augustine retrospectively, as it were: to pair him with **Plotinus (204/5–270)** and thus to take him as an essential representative of the first effort to receive, and "baptize," the pagan philosophical tradition. For his part, Plotinus has been unjustly neglected in the mainstream study of philosophies of freedom in the West. Paired with Augustine, he stands out as a kind of culmination of Greek thought and as preparing that resource, so to speak, for the Christian appropriation. If Augustine introduces a relatively novel emphasis on the drama of personal choice, Plotinus brings out more clearly the ontological depth from which such a choice is made.

Arguably *the* towering figure from the patristic period on the nature of freedom (if Augustine is included in the late ancient period) is **Maximus the Confessor (580–662)**, in whom the many strands of thought from the various pre-Christian and early Christian thinkers come together in a conceptual unity. To complement Maximus, for whom no apology is necessary, we made what is perhaps the most surprising choice in this study, namely, **(Pseudo-)Dionysius the Areopagite (ca. 500)**. We selected him, rather than, say, Gregory of Nyssa, for whom a strong case could be made, not only because of his evident influence on Maximus (which does not distinguish him from Gregory), but also because he articulates so clearly and definitively the metaphysics that underlies Maximus's reflection on freedom. At a more profound level, we have chosen him because in our view he represents more brilliantly than any other thinker in history the sense of being as superabundant generosity that lies at the heart of our effort at the retrieval of freedom.

In the early Middle Ages, there are no more influential figures in the development of the notion of freedom than **Anselm (1033/4–1109)** and **Bernard of Clairvaux (d. 1124 or shortly thereafter)**. In that regard, no apology for their selection is necessary. Though, as we will see, neither of these thinkers can be said to provide an ontological conception of freedom, properly speaking, the pair complement each other in a manner similar to the others insofar as one represents the "intellectualist" current in a more evident way, and the other the more "voluntarist" current. More specifically, they represent an illuminating polarity *within* a generally "existential" perspective between freedom ordered to justice and freedom ordered to love, both aspects of which are essential for a fully Catholic view.

Thomas Aquinas (1225–74), no doubt the key figure in the philosophy of freedom in the High Middle Ages, is a self-evident choice for this study, both as one in whom the Christian appropriation of the classical tradition can be said to reach a culminating moment and also as one who gathers up most completely the preceding sources (though not without a certain foreshortening, as we will see). **Bonaventure (1221–74)** is the appropriate complement in this matter—just as he is in so many other matters, as the tradition has generally recognized—insofar as he brings out more directly the voluntarist current but does so in the spirit of integration that is not so clear in the Franciscans after him.

John Duns Scotus (1265/6–1308) is of course the classic "philosopher of freedom" of the late Middle Ages. One could perhaps justify including other figures, who have been receiving more attention in this field recently, such as Henry of Ghent or Peter Olivi, not to mention Walter of Bruges, but one could not justify, in a study such as this, treating such figures *instead* of Scotus. Moreover, these figures do not represent a clear polar complement to Scotus, since they lie more or less within the same basic voluntarist current. **Godfrey of Fontaines (ca. 1250–1306 or 1309)**, by contrast, though he is not well known beyond the sphere of medieval studies, serves our purposes perfectly, and not only because Scotus himself used Godfrey as a foil against which to develop his own positions. The Belgian philosopher represents in an illuminating way a kind of "hardening" of the intellectualist current, just as Scotus does of the voluntarist one. If each of these subtle thinkers serves to bring out novel depths from these currents, they also foreshadow the fragmentation that will set the horizon for modern thought about freedom. In this respect, they bring the present volume to a fitting close.

Though this study is substantially limited by the fact of having had to be selective in its approach, the figures studied here, with the exception perhaps of Dionysius, would all be recognized as central, if not *the* central, figures in the development of the notion of freedom in classical Western thought. Major contributors to this development, nevertheless, have inevitably been excluded from this study: perhaps the most significant are the Stoics of late antiquity, certain figures from the patristic period decisively important for the interpretation of freedom, such as Origen and Gregory of Nyssa, and perhaps above all the teeming array of scholars and monks in the high and late medieval period, when the question of freedom exploded onto the center stage of theological anthropology. However that may be, the figures we have chosen prove—as the reader will discover—to illustrate the basic arc of the drama of the tradition of freedom, in its successes and failures, opening up in the end to the work still to be done.

ACKNOWLEDGMENTS

I would like to thank the gracious and conscientious staff at the University of Notre Dame Press, especially the director, Stephen Wrinn, who is always a pleasure to talk to, and Elisabeth Magnus, for her patient and thorough copyediting. I would also like to thank Fr. Anselm Ramelow and an anonymous reader for the press for having raised helpful questions and offering many suggestions on how to improve it. Whatever deficiencies remain in the text are my own responsibility.

PART I

Prolegomena

CHAPTER 1

Christian Freedom and Its Traditions

Every scribe who is trained for the kingdom of heaven is like a householder who brings forth from his treasure things both new and old.

—Mt 13:52

Setting the Horizon

Friedrich Nietzsche claimed that "free will" was invented simply to justify punishment.[1] One might initially smile at what one takes to be yet another instance of the German philosopher's mischievous wit, but a patient survey of the discussions of freedom in the different periods of church history, and perhaps even more of contemporary scholarly discussions of those discussions,[2] cannot help but introduce a worry that he may have been onto something. Explicit reflection on the theme of freedom more or less coincided with Christianity's reflective self-appropriation, and the theme virtually always presented itself in these original reflections within the context of sin and eschatological judgment.[3] There can be no doubt that freedom lies at the center of the Christian vision of man and his relation to the divine order; indeed, we will be proposing here that it is the very essence of Christianity. If there were seeds of a notion of freedom in ancient Greek thinkers, these seeds came to a full flourishing in Christian thought, where this notion moved to the center and became the object of relentless investigation and eventually systematic exposition, to the point that we can fairly say that—at least from a classical perspective—to deny that man is free is to reject Christianity *in toto*.[4] The question that arises at the outset, then, is whether the evident significance of freedom in Christianity is due to the fact that Christianity is centrally concerned with human sinfulness.

To enter deeply into the matter, let us take a step back and put the question in more positive and fundamental terms: What role does freedom play in the Christian vision, which is to say, what special connection does it have with the way God has revealed himself in Christ? The most immediate and obvious response might seem to be that Christianity is indeed basically about sin and redemption, which is a drama that presupposes human freedom. There can be no sin unless man has the capacity to do good *or* to do evil, and the final responsibility for determining that capacity must fall to man alone. The notion of redemption, moreover, makes no sense without the reality of perdition as the consequence of sin, which would be inevitable but for God's saving intervention. From this perspective, everything would thus seem to revolve around choice: man, at least *originally* if not in perpetuity, can choose to sin or not; God, too, then has a choice to make, since man's choice presents him with alternatives, either to save man from the choice he (inevitably?) makes or to damn him. Taking this approach to the significance of freedom eventually brings us to face a more fundamental set of questions: What is the relationship between man's power to choose and God's? Can the almighty God *really* be affected by the actions of one of his finite creatures, actions that can ultimately have no other source but some God-given power, however that power may be proximately used? If the answer is yes, then we would seem to reduce God to a mere character in a drama that encompasses both him and his creature; if we instead more reasonably deny that God waits on his creature in some such way, we would seem to turn what presents itself in scripture *as* a drama into a mere farce, or perhaps just a puppet show. In this, God pulls all the strings, and he plays out a story before no real audience, not even himself, since he has always already known not only how it turns out in general but every detail along the way. The assumption that freedom is essentially the power to choose seems to force us to choose between the nihilism of God being in control of everything or the nihilism of God being in control of nothing, since he too is at the mercy of the arbitrary moments of history. But if the outcome is all the same in either case, there is ultimately no real choice to be made. Making choice supreme undermines choice itself.

The point in describing this conundrum is not to entangle ourselves in the dilemma in order, then, to work through the various dimensions of the problem as we think our way out of it. The point is rather to identify a typical set of concerns that we will *not* adopt in the present study. It is astonishing to see just how much of the discussion of freedom in the Christian context is dominated by two problems: the problem of sin or the Fall (whether of man or more basically of the angels), which is essentially how and why man has the power to do evil,[5] and the problem of predestination, which is the problem of reconciling (finite) human freedom with (infinite) divine freedom, the uncertainty of future choices with absolute divine foreknowledge of what is to come, or human will with God's causal power. These are of course profound, and profoundly important, problems. We do not mean here to dismiss them. Nevertheless, we wish to suggest that focusing the discussion of freedom principally on these is already itself a problem. These two problems concern a single aspect of freedom, namely, the power to choose between alternatives. If we allow the problems of sin and predestination to set the horizon for our understanding of freedom, we turn this single (and, as we eventually hope to show,[6] derivative) aspect into the essence of the matter. But this reductive approach fixes an ultimate dichotomy as the *archē*, the governing principle, of all things, which locks us inside the radically unintelligible cosmos of Gnosticism in its endlessly recurring and ever-variant forms.

Where, then, ought the horizon for our investigation into the Christian interpretation of freedom to be set, if not on the problems of sin and predestination? In the previous volume, we sought to retrieve a notion of freedom more fundamental than the power to choose between alternatives. Our aim in the current volume is to see how Christianity appropriates and deepens this more fundamental notion of freedom, while integrating within it the drama of choice that is an essential part of the Christian vision. The point, thus, is not to eliminate things such as the potency for choice and self-determination but rather to set the most basic horizon as amply as we can so that these dimensions may be seen as far as possible in their truth. If we isolate these aspects in themselves, we cut the notion of freedom off from its source, which renders it sterile. If, by contrast, we view these aspects from inside the relation to the origin, they flourish and bring forth life.

Two basic themes will emerge as we explore some of the pivotal figures in the Christian appropriation of the classical tradition and the development of the distinctively Christian conception of freedom. On the one hand, we will see that some of the basic insights we discovered at least *in nuce* in Plato and Aristotle were made explicit or radically deepened, and taken up into a new context that recast them and brought out new and unsuspected dimensions. On the other hand, we will see the ways in which this appropriation failed, and how this failure gave rise to what we called in volume 1 the "diabolical" conception of freedom. If freedom is indeed a superabundant source, as we have suggested, then the question of how Christianity appropriates the classical source is not an indifferent one with respect to the quality and character of the freedom it offers, but turns out to be decisive. Nevertheless, it bears remarking that the present book does not intend in the first place to be a genealogy, to trace the historical roots of the problematic view of freedom in the contemporary world. Instead, the theme of relation to sources will emerge inevitably in the course of the fundamental project, which aims to bring out the positive development in the notion of freedom first and foremost. A failure makes sense, after all, only in relation to the positive aim it was unable to bring about.

A note regarding methodology is in order here before we begin. The aim explains what may seem unusual in how we are approaching the subject matter, above all in this first chapter. We are seeking to expose the roots of freedom, so to speak. A typical approach to the origin of an idea is to start with the smallest and least controversial claims about what defines the concept and then to seek traces of the definition in one text or another.[7] This is a reasonable approach in certain circumstances, but it is not appropriate for the project we pursue here or indeed arguably for any fundamental philosophical inquiry. The ultimate principle of freedom, we suggested in volume 1, is the priority of actuality over potency. If this is true, it requires that we do not begin with what is least significant and build up, which would imply a certain priority of "potential" parts out of which we then construct a whole. Instead, the priority of actuality demands that we set the horizon with what is highest, most basic, and most ultimate. In the present case, it means identifying what is most essential to Christianity and viewing the various aspects of freedom in relation to this horizon. The "test" of the truth in the modern approach is rigor of method and consistency of application, but we have argued that a radically impoverished conception of freedom stands at the basis of this approach.[8] A priority of actuality over potency implies a priority of real object over method (only an abstract conception of method would take this to be a rejection of method or a lack of rigor). A priority of object over method means that the test of truth is to see what results: you will know by their fruits. How do we know what counts as fruits? In the end, the measure cannot simply be set in a univocal way beforehand, because this would again grant priority to method over object. Instead, the fruits will have to be *ultimately* good, true, and beautiful in a *self-evident* sense.[9] And this means that the reception of truth, goodness, and beauty is in itself a free act, not compelled by anything extrinsic. Note that the model of inquiry differs from the standard one. We are not positing a claim and then unfolding the logical implications in a *deductive* way (which would be circular and would warrant the charge of theologizing philosophy). Instead, we are setting the horizon and then attempting to read particular figures on their own terms against this background. Thus, the explanation of the Christian notion of freedom demands that we set the horizon, not with some partial aspect or some general definition of a term, but with what is most basic to Christian revelation and how this bears on the notion of freedom. We will start with a basic sketch, to set the horizon, and will then explore individual figures inside the context thus opened up.

Tertium Datur

At the core of Christianity lies the grateful reception of what is given, a reception that takes into its depths (in-carnation) what is given and does so in what is inevitably a new way, allowing what is given to bear fruit that is unsuspected in some sense because it goes beyond what was present in the original gift.[10] Thus, a kind of *excess*, as it were, marks the Christian ethos, but it is an excess that grows from within rather than descending from "out of nowhere." The basic Christian image is the seed. It is not just the case that a single seed—a mustard seed, for example (Mt 13:31–32; Mk 4:30–32; Lk 13:18–19)—bears implicitly in itself, in its present, tiny reality, a massive tree incomparably greater than the form from which it springs. It is also the case that a seed contains an infinite *past* and an infinite *future*. As Bonaventure, speaking about the inexhaustible fruitfulness of scripture, exclaimed in wonder: "Who can know the infinity of seeds, when in a single one are contained forests of forests and thence seeds in infinite number?"[11]

Christianity is itself a tradition, but it is a tradition that takes into itself, and so unites and transforms, traditions that preceded it. The cross on which Christ hung bore an inscription, written authoritatively by the ruling power ("Quod scripsi, scripsi"; Jn 19:19–22) but bearing a meaning that radically transcends the *mens auctoris*:[12] "Jesus of Nazareth, the King of the Jews." The inscription was written in three languages, Aramaic, Greek, and Latin, and was thereby meant to communicate in principle to the whole world.[13] We fail to understand Christianity properly if we do not recognize it as taking up into itself the Jewish, the Greek, and the Roman traditions as a kind of novel synthesis of the three.[14] Because our focus here will be the philosophical dimension, which is inevitably metaphysical, theological, and anthropological, we will attend principally to the Greeks and the Jews, which in any event have represented a traditional pairing in Christian thought.[15]

To simplify in order to start the discussion, we might say that, with respect to the essence of freedom, the "Greeks" represent *nature* as an ideal standard, while the "Jews" represent the power of *will*, above and beyond nature.[16] These two traditions may seem to stand in direct opposition to each other, and it is not uncommon to take them to be fundamentally incompatible. It is striking, after all, to consider that the classical Greek thinkers had no notion of will[17] and that on the other hand there is no Hebrew word for "nature."[18] Regarding the contrast between Athens and Jerusalem, which Tertullian made famous ("What has Athens to do with Jerusalem?"),[19] Leo Strauss once wrote in a letter (to Eric Voegelin), "One reaches no plausible aim by covering up this contrast, by denigrating the *tertium non datur*. Every synthesis is in fact a choice *either* for Jerusalem *or* for Athens."[20] There is a certain logic to

Strauss's claim, which it behooves us to appreciate. If we accept the general view that nature represents a kind of necessary order, and will represents a certain arbitrariness, then there is no clear way to integrate these notions into a greater unity, since in such an integration one of the two would have to be subordinated ultimately to the other. If nature is taken to be ultimate, the will cannot be permitted to disturb the order, which means that it will at some point have to be reduced to something else, typically to reason or desire. On the other hand, if we make personal will ultimate, then the order that would be established by nature cannot but represent a mere contingency, something that the will happened to choose at this moment but that can be in principle changed in the next. Nature can thus no longer be a necessary order. They cannot *both* be ultimate. And so it would seem that we have to sacrifice one or the other. Strauss would appear to be right to reject any third possibility.

But Christianity *just is* this *tertium*; it just is a genuinely novel synthesis that does not reduce simply to the one or to the other but represents a transformation of both. It is not an accident that Strauss, who is known for having generated the energy of his own thinking by exacerbating the friction between Athens and Jerusalem, nature and will, should have systematically neglected anything properly *Christian* in history, as Rémi Brague has observed.[21] Our proposal is that one of the principal tasks of history, understood in the light of Christian faith, is the fruitful reception of revelation as the flowering of the deepest truths of the Greeks (and Romans) and the Jews, the "book of nature" and the "book of scripture," the intrinsic goodness of the world, which manifests the being of God, and the *holiness* of the God who infinitely transcends the world and acts according to his good pleasure,[22] the mysterious hiddenness of the "unknown God" and the positive manifestness of the God who has made known his glory through the world as his magnificent instrument,[23] the God who is perfect goodness and so without envy[24] and the God who is supremely and deservedly jealous.[25] If any one of these aspects is lifted out and isolated over against the other in detachment from the paradox of the whole, we get a distortion, which has profound cultural implications. As we will suggest at the end of this book, the "diabolical" conception of liberty arises when the tradition is not received in full but shattered into fragments that appear so opposed it is impossible to imagine that they could ever have belonged together.[26]

We are suggesting that the Greeks and Jews are best interpreted in light of each other and that just this is demanded by the Christian tradition. Given the limitations imposed by the present context, we can do scarcely more than draw some of the simple lines that will indicate the basic shape. Needless to say, the project would be enriched immeasurably by a careful study of the Roman contribution and a more thorough exposition of the Jewish than we can offer here. A sketch is at least a beginning. Because we have already spent a significant time on the classical Greek thinkers, Plato and Aristotle, in the previous volume, we can simply summarize what was developed in that volume, now specifically in relation to the discussion to come.

The Wisdom of the Greeks

According to the interpretation of the original sense of freedom as taken up and developed by Plato and Aristotle presented in part 3 of *Freedom from Reality*, we can say in sum that, for the ancient Greeks, *liberty* has the basic shape of *liberality*; it is a superabundance that streams forth with a noble indifference to cost. As we saw in some detail, this generosity is not exclusive of the moment of receptivity but integrates that moment. The virtue of liberality, according to Aristotle, is a mean between (otherwise abject) receiving and (otherwise extravagant) giving, though of course the giving remains the dominant note (at least from one perspective—we will return to this point). The activities that are properly called free are those that concern objects that are received into the soul precisely in the form of proceeding *from* the soul. The fundamental importance of this point cannot be overstated if we are to understand the Greeks properly. If such a basic shape was evident in the classical tradition (as we will see in Plotinus and all the way into High Scholasticism), it has become quite difficult for the modern mind to conceive, insofar as this particular paradox is essentially excluded by the materialist metaphysics that largely dominates our imagination. For the Greeks, the objects of contemplation most perfectly proceed from the soul in their being contemplated, since the actuality of the ideas is not an empirical fact that one may or not encounter but an eternal truth into which the mind rises up in its participation. Actions are free, by analogous extension, according to the degree to which they contain truth, which is to say, to the degree to which they present an intrinsic, and not merely relative, goodness. This is why virtuous action (*praxis*), which has its end in itself, is the most free, and why, for Aristotle, productive activity (*poiēsis*), which has its end outside of itself or in other words concerns the bringing about of something *external* to the soul, always occurs under the shadow of servitude.[27] The basic shape of free activity is an *exitus* and a *reditus* from and to a governing origin.

Now, the reader will certainly note that this description of free activity *exactly coincides* with Aristotle's definition of nature, which is "an internal principle of motion and rest."[28] In this regard, far from introducing some capacity to change, some intervention into nature, that would direct it to some end other than what is essentially inscribed in it by and from birth, as it were ("nature," *natus*, etc.), freedom presents nothing but the *perfection* of nature. If man is the only properly free being, it is not because he can transgress his nature but because the *rational* soul is the only sort of soul that can truly return to itself in its outgoing activity, or, as Aquinas would eventually put it, the soul, precisely qua spirit, is capable of a *reditio completa*.[29] The "self-knowledge" recommended by Greek wisdom is a call to be true to what makes man human. If man is the only being that is properly free, it is thus because man is the only being that is properly natural. What man *is*, all other kinds of being approximate in their own way.[30] It is not surprising, then, that one looks more or less in vain among the classical Greek philosophers for an independent human faculty—namely, the "will"—that would introduce its own set of potencies and actualities over and above the supreme actuality of the soul and its unity with its objects in knowledge.[31] There is no "separate" order of the will; there are simply the various powers, the desires and habits, that serve the realization of nature in truth.[32]

To say that freedom always remains within the bounds of nature, however, does not at all imply that, for the Greeks, nature remains simply trapped within itself, so to speak, as one almost inevitably assumes from our "postclassical" perspective. Here we see the importance of recognizing the distinctively *Platonic* contribution to the Greek conception of freedom, namely, what we might call the "immanent transcendence of the Good." The *exitus-reditus* in relation to a principal source, which characterizes genuinely *free* activity, is nothing but a moving image of the Good, an expression at the level of the externality of *natural* being of the absolute perfection that the Good *simply is*. Freedom is a participation in the Good. According to a properly Platonic interpretation of participation, to say that free action is the natural expression of the perfection of the Good does *not* simply mean that nature "looks like," that is, *externally resembles*, the original; more profoundly, it means that the Good is causally present in natural activity, which is to say that free action is always a "begetting or giving birth in Beauty." In this respect, though the note of generosity is indeed the dominant one in liberty-cum-liberality at the human level, this generosity rests on, or indeed more adequately put, results from, a more fundamental receptivity, not with respect to any particular object (i.e., in an "ontic" sense), but with respect to the transcendent source of all generosity (i.e., in an ontological sense).

Because this source is not ontic but ontological, which is to say because the receptivity with respect to the source is specifically *metaphysical*, it necessarily remains hidden or implicit: φύσις κρύπτεσθαι φιλεῖ.[33] This is the *nature* of nature, and it presents the basic horizon within which Greek thinking unfolds. But the very depth of the source makes nature an inherently ambiguous reality, which may be interpreted in two different directions (to keep matters relatively simple). On the one hand, the hidden source may be simply covered over, so that the imaging of the Good in freedom gets increasingly reduced to a mere external resemblance and the movement comes to be interpreted as a kind of wholly autonomous self-determination. We will see examples of this, briefly, in the Hellenistic period of Greek thought, which is in some sense a more resolutely—one might say, "resentfully," in the etymological sense of the word[34]—materialistic return to the pre-Socratic shape after the rise of classical form, the bourgeoning of the Good, in Plato and Aristotle; in the early Middle Ages, when the pagan (and Muslim) world appeared basically as a threat to Christian civilization; and also in the late Middle Ages, when Christianity began to be cleansed of its Greek inheritance and so the modern era dawned. On the other hand, nature might be opened up more radically and reconceived in the light of its transcendent First Cause. In this respect, Plato's reflection on nature in the light of the forms, and the forms in the light of the Good, can be seen as representing a certain *kairos* moment, in which the ambiguity of nature presents itself for decision. Heidegger, it seems, resented Plato for having given away the "secret" of nature by bringing it out into the light of the Good,[35] and so betraying the early Greeks, with their profound insight into the rhythms of coming to be and passing away that define nature. But whereas Heidegger was no friend of the Jews, we wish to see Plato as opening the Greek world up to the biblical vision, and *precisely thus* bringing the Greek insight into nature to its full flourishing.

As we saw in part III of the previous volume,[36] according to its etymology, freedom is an originally *organic* notion: it refers to belonging to a common stock, or in other words having the blood of the family line course through one's veins. More specifically, the unifying source seems to be, not the blood first of all, but the seminal fluid, which, to be sure, is not self-contained but transcends the individual[37] and is meant to be poured out and so multiplied beyond itself. If the first usage of the word tends to designate political membership (as extended family), the sense expands. The Greek philosophers' recognition of the source of freedom as not a natural substance but a "super-natural" principle, the Good, opens up an interpretation beyond the mere biologico-political boundary of the family, the clan, the tribe, or even the polis, to the universal dimensions of human nature as such: because its reference point is no longer merely relative but now genuinely absolute, the freedom of friendship in the Good cannot exclude anyone simply in principle.[38] Of course, though this opening to the universal was clearly seen,[39] it is not obvious how it could be realized without departing altogether from the concrete particularity that may not be eliminated from the *rootedness* of the organic notion. Nature remains the ultimate Greek horizon, so that even the "super-natural" principle of the good tends to reside within it. We will come back to this point.

The Wonders of the Jews

Formal Features of the Will. The Jews are a people set apart. The movement of "election," that is, the selection of one from the many as a distinct act of the divine will, is not at all incidental to the identity of the people. If *freedom* is not a word that appears often in the Greek world, and if it appears still more rarely as a central notion, it represents a decisive concept for the Jews.[40] To be sure, the word that gets translated as "will," *ratson*, does not in the first place refer to the spiritual power to make decisions or issue commands. Instead, it is connected to pleasure, delight, and favor.[41] If this connection reveals the proximity of the Jewish concept to the Greek association of the appetitive power and the good, interpreting it in relation to the Old Testament presentation of God's acts and man's response casts a significantly different light on the matter. One might say that the difference between the Greeks and Jews on the notion of will does not rest in the first place on the content of the notion (appetitive relation to what is good and so what causes delight) but is due to its principal *subject*: for the Jews, the will belongs above all to the supracosmic agent, Yahweh. As we will see, everything else in the understanding of will follows from this point.

What stands out in the Jewish notion is not first the (receptive) movement of desire but the (preceptive) movement of the bestowal of approval.[42] God is presented as an agent who makes a definitive difference in the world; his intervention marks a permanent "before" and "after." The Jews in fact understand themselves precisely in relation to such a difference. The decisive event in the history of the people is the Exodus from Egypt, which the Jews understood not simply as a discrete moment left behind in the past but as the abiding definition of who they are: the Jews are a *liberated* people.[43] As Brague has shown, this liberation is, moreover, not a mere means for some further end but so fundamental as to be itself the purpose;[44] the Jews are meant to live *as* liberated people, and their law is an articulation or codification of this freedom. It lays out what the life of freedom looks like, which is specifically *set apart* from the life that belongs to slaves.[45]

This being "set apart" is a sign of the presence of God, because God is, as it were, the One who is radically—indeed, *absolutely*—set apart. The word for "holiness," *qds*, appears to come from the verb *qd*, "to cut";[46] a holy thing is what is separated out from the profane and granted a special status.[47] If other religions tend to use the word *holy* for objects and rarely for God, in the Old Testament it is just the opposite. God is holiness itself because he is absolutely transcendent.[48] This transcendence coincides with power. Because God transcends all things, he has power over all things, which is to say that they are subject to

God's *will*. This will thus presents itself as the ultimate reference point,[49] which is not to be understood (i.e., subordinated to discernable reasons)[50] but obeyed (i.e., conformed to by the human will, which is, so to speak, called into existence by God's will; cf. Ps 40:3).[51] Given this absolute priority of God's will, it is not surprising that one does not directly encounter in the Bible the notion of nature in anything like the Greek sense of eternal essences or an order that defines the cosmos in its entirety and so comprehends both God and men. If, on occasion, the regular order of nature is indicated as a sign of God's wisdom, this is not meant to be a revelation of the divine itself, as it is in Greek philosophy; instead, when God reveals himself in nature in the biblical world, it tends to be in the form of a disturbance of the peace of order—in the thunderstorm or in fire, which are natural expressions of power.[52] The most direct revelation of God in the Bible, and so the most potent of all realities, is the proper *name* of God, which conveys his *immediate* presence, that is, his "person."[53] God is principally known, not *in* nature, but *above* and *beyond* nature.

If nature, with its intrinsic, self-related, and cyclical rhythm, is not the principal mediator of relation to God,[54] what takes its place is *history*, meaning in this context not simply a sequence of recorded events in time, which we might say is the merely formal sense of history, but the narrative of God's intervention into the world that he created.[55] Note that there is a direct connection between an emphasis on the *will* of God and the centrality of history in a people's self-understanding. If we except the distinctly Roman contribution, with its sense of temporal, worldly mission,[56] Voegelin is right to speak of "the creation of history by Israel,"[57] because it is with the Jews that we have a recognition of God's transcendence as a real "agent" whose seat lies outside of the cosmos, and who can therefore "break in" to it, so to speak.[58] This "inbreaking" can *only* take a narrative form, that is, can only be *history*, because an articulation as a strictly natural order would reduce it, as it were, back to the cosmological.[59] A mythological narrative, it is worth pointing out, while capturing something of a personal presence beyond nature in an analogous sense, does not suffice in this regard insofar as its very nonhistorical character tends to allow it to be reduced to the "merely metaphorical," as an articulation of eternal truths in the medium of images, and so to bring us back once again inside the cosmological horizon.

Let us pause in our general observations to gather together some of the essential features of the Jewish conception of the will and fill them out more explicitly in philosophical terms. Each of these features could be elaborated to a much fuller extent than we have the space for here, but our primary aim is in a fairly succinct fashion to present a general picture rather than to undertake an in-depth study. It goes without saying that the following list of features represents a philosophical interpretation of what is presented in scripture, and indeed one offered from a self-consciously Christian perspective. We will, moreover, focus on the clearest sense of will exhibited by divine action and will consider the human sense only in relation to this. In this first subsection, we are laying out only the *formal* aspects of will, which will be radically transformed when we consider their historical realization in the subsection that follows.

(1) There is a connection in the Bible between the will and transcendence, insofar as the will designates a capacity to act *on* what is other, with the source of this action thus lying outside or beyond what is acted on. This connection explains why the notion of will is not a generic term in the Bible which is then used in reference to God, but belongs absolutely to God. It is God, we might say, who *is* the will, because God is the Holy One *tout court*, that is, the absolutely transcendent one: "Our God is in the heavens; he does whatever pleases him" (Ps 115:3; cf. 135:6). To be sure, man, too, has a will,[60] but this, again, is not a generic anthropological datum. Instead, from its very origin it appears to bear specific reference to God's will: it is, so to speak, the organ of response—in *history*—to God's will, an organ that is, so to speak, *breathed* directly into man at creation.[61] Man can exercise his will over other creatures—"dominion" (*radah*)[62]—because he transcends them in a unique way as God's image.

(2) The will is that by which God manifests himself in a direct and nonmediated way. In contrast, say, to the Greek notion of the world emanating from God's nature, the Jews relate to God, not first *through* nature, but directly in response to God's discrete acts over and above the natural order, which come from God alone. Thus, the will is revelatory, indeed, *theophanic*, and represents what would come to be called a direct, *personal* presence. The Jewish God is not a hidden First Cause but "a God who acts" and thereby makes his reality known.[63]

(3) The acts of will therefore inevitably have something of an "interventionist" character. This is to say that, for the will to operate at all, it cannot but introduce into what was already there something new, something never before seen.[64] There is something essentially "miraculous" about the will, in the sense of bringing about something extra-ordinary, something not already given, and so always anticipated in the normal course of things. This character follows necessarily from the transcendence of the agent "behind" the activity.

(4) Because of the transcendence of the agent, and therefore the "otherness" of that on which the agent acts, the will's activity is essentially "transitive," in the sense that it expresses a movement across a distance (at least metaphorically). This "transitivity" does not in principle exclude the immanence of the acts of will, or in other words the fact that the act of will remains *within* the agent, is *self-referential*, even in its going out. In fact, the revelatory dimension of the act of will, or in other words the direct personal presence of the agent in the will, brings to light the essential immanence of its activity. Nevertheless, the more obvious dimension is its "out-going" character, the will's acting *on* what lies outside of itself.

(5) Bringing together the transitive and the interventionist aspects of the will, we can say that the Jews conceive the will essentially as a matter of power,[65] understood in the active sense as the capacity to bring about a change in what is other. Connected with God's absolute transcendence, this power is by its very nature "overwhelming": it is in no way limited by what stands over against it, because such resistance would imply a denial, or at least a compromise, of its transcendent agency. It is thus the very nature of God's will "to overcome." One is not surprised, then, that the activity of God's will in the Bible should so often be associated with a destructive force (e.g., thunderstorm or fire).[66]

(6) Tied essentially to the historical dimension described above, the activity of the will is always in some respect particular and "event-like," or even "event-full." Explaining an insight from G. E. Wright, Jon D. Levenson says that "the religion of Israel was a religion of recital, in which the highest spiritual level consisted of narrating the mighty acts of God. The key term is *event*."[67] As breaking in and intervening, precisely in the mode of introducing a change, the will "makes happen," it causes something (new) to occur. An event is the result of

an inter-vention; an e-vent is something that "comes from" and so has a source beyond, a source that thus makes itself felt in its effects. If what is inter-vened into is a given order or situation, the event cannot be a general state of affairs but must occur at a particular time and place, concerning some reality that is *unique* in the sense of being thereby *set apart* from what came before.

(7) Finally, the sense of *freedom* that is associated with the will so conceived will always bear the trait of being a separation, a *liberation from*, at least in some analogous sense. There are in fact two words for "freedom" in Hebrew. The first, *chupshah*, appears only once in that form and means literally "loosed";[68] the second, which is somewhat more common, *deror*, is strikingly similar in its origin and early usage to the Greek *eleutheria*: *deror* most basically means "free-flowing," like a liquid poured out, but was used first in a *political* sense to describe a people who had been taken out of the state of slavery.[69] The most obvious reference is the literal one we mentioned earlier as the defining event of Jewish identity, namely, the Exodus, the liberation, by God, of the Israelites from the condition of slavery in which they had lived under the Egyptians. But this sense is not limited to the particular event; it pervades the whole of the Jewish relation to God. This follows, as we saw above, from the nature of God as absolute "holiness": According to the Jewish understanding, "it is God's job," Brague says, "to liberate."[70] The Israelites are holy, that is, "set apart," or in other words "set free," *because* God is holy: "Say to all the congregation of the people of Israel, You shall be holy, for I the Lord your God am holy" (Lev 19:2).[71] God's election of Israel is the objective way his holiness is expressed *in the world*. Thus, the constitution of the people is an election that sets apart; the law that codifies their freedom as the people of God is a set of prescriptions that sets off a particular kind of behavior from what would otherwise be considered a normal way of acting. Indeed, an essential part of the law consists precisely in the separation of one thing from the rest that are like it (kosher laws) in a manner that transforms one's relationship to all of it, insofar as it allows one to live the whole, not as a merely natural reality, but as an expression from start to finish of the will of God.[72] For example, in this regard, the institution at creation of the Sabbath, which is holy, is a liberation of work through the liberation of one day from the rest.[73] In general, then, remaining in the freedom of the People of God means continually

turning back to the origin (*re-ligio*), freeing oneself from the old ways into which one has fallen in order to live freely in the will of God even now: "today."[74] Mercy thus bears a close association with freedom because it indicates the abiding presence of God, who is never simply finished acting in the liberation he has already granted.[75] It is the *will* of God that is absolute rather than any particular expression of it, and man finds his freedom in conformity to this holy will through the laws it institutes.

A More Concrete Consideration: Will as Bond. Now, given this initial description of God's will as presented in the Old Testament, it is not surprising that the Hellenistic Greeks who encountered this view through their interaction with the Jews, however superficial, should have found this conception of God so fundamentally foreign. Galen, for example, used the Jewish view of God as a foil against which to set what is distinctive about the Greek view into greater relief: "For Moses thinks that all things are in God's power, even if He wished to make a horse or cow from dust."[76] The general assessment is that the God who is *will* is arbitrary and whimsical, an ungodly God. *Prayer*, as an attempt to change God's will, is insulting of the divine nature, since it assumes that God has not always already, from eternity, determined what is best.[77] One finds a similar sense of the Jewish God as essentially *arbitrary* not only in the ancient world but still in the modern one, whether one champions this arbitrariness as the distinct origin of the modern conception of freedom as power to choose (i.e., a "libertarian" notion of will)[78] or laments it as threatening the *deep* conception of nature that would seem indispensable for the very possibility of philosophical contemplation, among other things, since philosophy can exist only in an intelligible world.[79]

But it should be noted that the perspective from which the Jewish view of God seems essentially arbitrary tends to have its place simply outside the Jewish tradition, which casts this view as the "opposite" of the view rooted in nature. If we start more concretely from *within* this tradition, and attend more precisely to the particularity of its history, a profound and thoroughgoing qualification of the preceding characterization begins to take shape. This shape, which we will sketch momentarily, is not the simple opposite of the Greek view but plays a remarkably similar melody regarding freedom, even if it plays this melody in what is clearly a radically different key.

If we do not satisfy ourselves with the general observation that God intervenes in history as an essentially transcendent agent, but instead begin concretely from within that intervention with the particularities of its history, one thing stands out immediately: God does *not* break into the world in a random way through a series of unconnected "irruptions" of destructive will, which seem to do nothing more than express sheer power, or better: to *vent* it. Instead, God's power is revealed as essentially *effective*; it enters into history only to *accomplish* something, to bring a reality *into being*.[80] For this reason, the interventions are meaningful, and their report has the form, not just of a linear history, but specifically of a dramatic narrative, which is to say they exhibit form simply, an order, a beginning, middle, and end, that gives them a wholeness.[81] If one were to ask, from this perspective, after the "plot" of the story of Israel, the answer would be quite evident. The central concept, or indeed reality, around which the whole of the Old Testament turns is that of *covenant—berit* or διαθήκη.[82] This is profoundly significant for the theme of this book. God does not simply act *on* the world from the outside; rather, his acting *on* the world takes the paradigmatic form of entering *into* the world, of binding himself to the world and binding the world to himself.[83] This is why his action does not crush the human will but, quite to the contrary, "liberates" it to respond in a free manner.[84] Let us enter into this crucial point in more depth.

According to Frank Moore Cross, an "oath and covenant is . . . a widespread legal means by which the duties and privileges of kinship may be extended to another individual or group, including aliens."[85] This extension of relation can take three distinctive forms, depending on its manner of institution: when it occurs between equals (kinship covenant), when a superior imposes it on an inferior (treaty covenant), and when a superior imposes it on himself in relation to an inferior (grant covenant).[86] Though there are different degrees and qualities of asymmetry in these various types, it remains the case that covenant essentially includes a certain reciprocity:[87] it is a relationship permanently established between two parties, which entails henceforward a particular way of behaving with respect to the other. To say that covenant is an extension of kinship means that the blood relation is the paradigm,[88] and the covenant thus represents a bond that is analogous to this original relation, not a substitution for it but an enlargement of it, so to speak, so that it can include more than was initially given.[89] As J. A. Davies explains, "It would appear that the fundamental image behind each of the applications of *berit* is the use of familial categories for those who are not bound by ties of natural kinship. By legal or quasi-legal process, people become 'father,' 'son' or 'brother' to one another for a range of purposes."[90] Marriage is a paradigmatic instance of covenant,[91] and it is not surprising that the covenant between God and Israel should eventually be presented in nuptial terms.[92] In marriage, one enters into communion with one who is not immediately part of one's family (incest taboo) but who lies beyond one's immediate family (note that Adam leaves his mother and father and cleaves to his wife; Gen 2:24), and yet the covenantal union is understood, henceforward, as belonging to the family (or indeed both families), now thereby enlarged (and open to getting larger and extending in number, in space, and in time, through progeny).[93] The covenantal bond was, for the Jews, a fundamental reference point, providing the organizing principle of existence generally, without which there would be no order: "One is born of a covenant and into a covenant, and wherever one moves in life, one makes a covenant or acts on the basis of an already existing covenant.... [The covenant] is the presupposition of all life."[94]

We spoke above about the central importance of the *will* in the Jewish vision of reality, and this importance is reinforced by the reference here to covenant, which comes into being only through an oath, an act of will. But this reference reveals the danger of contenting ourselves with a merely formal characterization of the will, namely, as an essentially "inverventionalist" and transitive power, which operates, so to speak, only episodically from the outside. Although all of the formal aspects we laid out above remain essential, the very emphasis on history that they imply requires us to interpret them from the beginning in a concrete way. The power of the will is not principally a power to disrupt or destroy, or even a power to choose, though of course these are part of it. The principal power of the will is rather the power to effect a covenant, to bind oneself to another, to recognize that bond, to fulfill it, and to remain faithful to it. Contrasting the Israelites with other nations, with whom God has not entered personally into relation, Moses says, "Did any people ever hear the voice of a god speaking out of the midst of the fire, as you have heard, and still live? Or has any god ever attempted to go and take a nation for himself from the midst of another nation, by trials, by signs, by wonders[?]" (Deut 4:33–34). Note that, in this formulation, God "goes" out to Israel, to take her *for himself*, that is, to enter into a personal relation with the people through the establishment of a covenant. God still becomes present *to* the world through fire, but this fire is no longer merely a destructive force; instead, God *speaks* through the fire, and so makes himself present in a specifically personal way. His will is thus no longer merely "*outside*," which would make it a crushing power, but is (already) "*inside*," in the midst of, Israel through the self-pledging bond. The biblical notions of love (*ahabah*), loyalty or kindness (*hesed*), and faithfulness (*emeth*), principal characteristics of God in his action toward Israel, are not in the first place discrete acts of will exercised by an autonomous power but *en*-actments of a bond already established.[95] It is, to be sure, a particular, historical act of will that gives rise to a covenant; this historical particularity is *crucial*, insofar as the act of will is equally an event, an intervention, that introduces something new. Nevertheless, it is equally crucial to see that the act of will that initiates a covenant does not come from *nowhere*, nor does the will remain "outside" in its operation, as an individually self-directing power.

Let us unfold this point more fully. On the one hand, the establishment of a covenant is, as we observed, an extension of kinship, which means that it originates with a bond that is already given, that is, preexisting. In this case, the novelty that is introduced is not "tacked on" in a merely external, accretional sense; instead, we might describe it as a creative rediscovery of the old, as it were. The "novelty" is in fact a taking of the other as (already) included in the kinship relation—*already* included, because kinship just means a relation that is "already given" rather than brought about by a distinct, deliberate act. On the other hand, as we hinted at already in the formal description of the will as *personal*, the will, even in its "transitive" activity on what is other, always also reveals the self. In the covenant, this takes the *decisive* form of a pledging of oneself: the self is quite really im-plicated, folded within, this act, which thus by its nature cannot be taken back, insofar as such a power would assume an agent that remained outside of it and so to that extent would be uncovenanted. A covenant can be broken or betrayed, but it can never be revoked.[96] The oath that is exchanged at the origin of a covenant is a *pledging* of the self specifically with divine sanction,[97] which is to say underwritten by divine power. It is thus an act of will that draws on, and so gives expression to, Will itself.

If *covenant* is the paradigmatic expression of will in the Old Testament, and covenant means *bond* or the extension of kinship, then the most basic meaning of will for the Jews is not the autonomous power of individual agency but the expression of the unity that holds together individual agents. It is significant that the first instance of a deliberate will in scripture comes in a grammatically plural form—"Let us make man in our image"[98]—and that the notion of "human agency" tends to be ascribed in the Bible not principally to individuals but to families or to the people (which is in part an extended family).[99] As Joseph Atkinson has shown, in the Old Testament personal agency is *corporate* agency, the agency of persons (literally!) incorporated into a greater whole, which is the specifically *organic* unity of many individuals.[100] This unity comes to expression in the whole acting with a particular will, meaning not just that many individuals come to agreement on a single item, or choose a single person to represent them with his single will, but that the ontological reality of the will is a unity participated in by many, sharing indeed in a *single soul*.[101] As Johannes Pederson puts it, "When souls are united, they get a common will and thus form a psychic unity. The mutual point of gravity lies in the whole."[102] Speaking, for example, of the unity of David and Jonathan in friendship, he writes: "Two souls enter into a union and form one whole. It means that they are ruled by a common will, this being the substance of the covenant."[103] The covenant is a substance with a single soul and a single will:

> The covenant must always contain a certain community of will, for the soul is determined by will. Those who are united have a common aim. The one becomes "whole with" the other (*shālēm*, Gen 34:21; 1 Kgs 8:61; 11:4; 15:3.14). The more intimate the union, the more they communicate to each other of their being, and then it becomes the stronger who imparts his character to the fellowship. For the stronger it is a question of making covenants in order to carry through one's aims; for the weaker to make a covenant with the strong in order to enjoy his strength.[104]

Will, in short, is not principally a power of individual agency but the expression of the soul of a community of persons.

Now, covenant does not describe only the basic relationship among human beings; it also, and indeed *most* fundamentally, describes the relationship between God and man. God is, by definition as it were, *omnipotent*; to say that he is pure power means that his acts of will are supremely and unfailingly *effective*. What it means to be effective is not, as one might perhaps initially think given our formal description, to be able to destroy at will, that is, to introduce a change and so to disrupt some preceding reality, for such a change as disruption can only ever be secondary, and so *not* fundamental. Instead, the most effective act of will is the establishment of a covenant, especially of the "grant" kind, since it is not dependent on the capacities of the partner but is first of all God's self-obliging. It is effective because it is in fact an unshakeable foundation that is definitively established, not within the confines of a single historical moment (as would be, for example, a destructive event), but, by its very nature, in such a way as to include "ahead of time" all future moments so that it may be said to "contain" time. The covenant is *eternal*. In this respect, it is essentially comprehensive, though in a nonreductive way, insofar as it does not short-circuit, as it were, the drama of the "encounter of freedoms" that will subsequently play itself out in history.[105] Walther Eichrodt is thus right in a general sense to say that "the unique character of the picture of God in ancient Israel is derived in essence from the attempt to hold together the ideas of a divine *power without limitation* and of a divine *act of self-limitation* in the establishment of a *berit*—an act whereby God makes himself known as *sovereign and personal will*."[106] This is profoundly true, and illuminating, but it is also misleading in the sense that it gives the impression that a power and the pledging of self in covenant are opposites that are then somehow brought together, however paradoxical or even simply *irrational* that union might seem.[107] What we are suggesting is that there is no basic friction between these two ideas, which would be the case only if we thought of power as having its proper reality in itself outside of any realization,[108] and thus thought of covenant as a mere instance of that (thus extrinsic) power, and so always relative to it in the sense of constantly in danger of being annulled.[109] Instead, the Bible reveals that will as power and will as self-binding in covenant are ideas that belong essentially together. Power just *is* the capacity effectively to bind oneself.

The fact that the effecting of covenant is not simply one possible exercise of will among others comes to expression in the thoroughly pervasive presence of covenant throughout the Old Testament.[110] One can justifiably say that covenant represents the very form that God's will takes in its operations in history. To be sure, innumerable discrete acts of the divine will depicted in scripture are *not* the establishment of a covenant; but our point is that all of these are, so to speak, parts of the "grand narrative" of covenant; we might call them chapters of that unifying story, which have their proper sense precisely as moments in that overarching plot. To think otherwise would be to trivialize the power of God, since it would render the acts of that power merely episodic, and therefore ineffective, that is, fruitless.

It might be objected that there are in fact many covenants in the Old Testament—we have the Noahic, the Abrahmic, the Mosaic, and the Davidic, to name just the most prominent—which would itself already seem to imply a certain impotence: Why, if covenant is definitive, would not *one* suffice? But we have to recall that the nature of covenant is not to replace a bond that was previously established, and thus to render that prior bond obsolete, but to affirm the given bond and extend it beyond its previous limits. In this respect, it is significant to note that the covenant God makes with Abraham, which, after St. Paul, we are inclined to read as the *essential* Old Covenant par excellence, is enacted in language that suggests, not the invention of something altogether new, ex nihilo, but the *renewal* and further specification or development of a covenant already established.[111] From this perspective, the various covenants may be read in a progressive manner, which we do not have the space to lay out in all of its exceedingly rich detail, but which we may nevertheless simply indicate in a simple way:[112] the Noahic covenant is established with all mankind (but—it is important to note—through a particular individual and his family) with the promise not to destroy the world (at least not by water!); the Abrahamic covenant is a promise to people the earth with Abraham's progeny (which again indicates a universality *through* a particular line);[113] in the Mosaic, God binds to himself in an exclusive way the People of Israel (and so the people sent out are called back); and the Davidic is an extension of the covenant to its eschatological dimensions.

If "covenant" has the form of affirming and extending what is previously given, an interesting, and indeed weighty, question imposes itself: How can there be a *first* covenant? And if there *is* one, what would it look like? Would it not necessarily have the form of an invention from out of the blue, and wouldn't this then call into question the description of covenant as an "extension of kinship" or the "expansion of a given bond"? There is a certain ambiguity here that will find a resolution only within the Christian reception of the Old Testament, as we will see. But in the meantime we may observe that, significantly, it is difficult to give a simple answer to this fundamental question within the horizon of the Old Testament alone. As it turns out, the first *explicit* covenant, namely, the Noahic, is not presented as an arbitrary "Deus ex machina" but seems to be enacted as an explicit and newly specified formulation of a general commitment already implicitly in place.[114] The "first" covenant, and so the origin of the commitment, turns out to be the very act of the creation of the world itself, which scholars have observed is presented already in covenantal language, even if it is not yet fully a covenant in the strict sense.[115] As we have been proposing, covenant is the very form that God's will takes in history, and so, if the creation of the world is a decisive expression of God's will, it is unsurprising that it should bear the traces of covenant: the establishing of a relationship (which is in some mysterious way already an extension of kinship) that imposes a bond, an abiding *form* of relationship, to which both partners are meant to conform in their behavior.[116]

A First Rapprochement between the Jews and the Greeks. Having given the Jewish conception of the will a more concrete substance, in however rudimentary a form here, we may now revisit the apparent contrast we laid out with the Greeks, in order to see that the difference between the two is not as radical, or at least not as exclusive, as it initially seemed. Most basically, we have noted that there is no Hebrew word for "nature" as such, and the formal description of the divine will gives the impression that there *cannot* be one, insofar as nature indicates a stable, if not an eternal, order, with an integrity of its own, while the Jewish conception sees all things as subject to God's omnipotent will at every moment.[117] While it is indeed true that, for the Jews, nature has no significance independent of the will of God,[118] it makes all the difference whether we conceive that will principally as a power that hovers, so to speak, over nature, making only incidental and episodic "contact," or as having created the natural world with an absolutely and perfectly effective pledge, in the spirit (if not the letter) of a definitive and everlasting covenant. In this case, we see in the Old Testament an appreciation of the order and constancy of nature, which, if in one sense it grows and becomes evident above all in the late Greek-influenced wisdom literature, simply bears witness to the truth expressed in Genesis 1 and 2: the world is good, and its creation proceeds according to a supremely dignified order, reminiscent of the beautiful rhythms of a liturgical rite (Sirach 42:21–25). The Sabbath rest represents from this perspective a respect for the intrinsic integrity of the world, in something like its "given nature."[119] The Greek and Jewish worlds cannot be said in fact to stand opposed on this point, even if the basis of their affirmation of the integrity of creation is fundamentally different.

At a deeper level, the shape of the movement that we said was so centrally important for the Greeks, namely, the reception or taking-in that has the form of a procession forth, which corresponds, objectively, to the classic "*exitus-reditus*" from a first principle, resonates, too, with the concept of covenant. There is here an outward pledging of self, which binds the other "back" to the self. This basic movement is especially clear in the procession of creation from the creative will of God, which is then called back to him.[120] The point is that the activity of the will does not principally have the form of what Hannah Arendt memorably described as "natality," namely, the irruption of something altogether new, which sets in motion a totally unpredictable sequence of events off into the essentially unknown future.[121] Instead, the shape of the will's activity is less like a line or indeed an infinitely extending ray, and more like a(n ever-expanding) circle, though it is clearly more essentially dramatic than the natural motion affirmed by the Greeks.[122] Nevertheless, it expresses an overarching and intelligible form.[123] If, as we saw, the Greeks affirmed a reception of the good in the mode of proceeding from the soul, and thus gave predominance to the intellect, we might say that the Jews affirm the going forward, though one that includes a destination as a return to what was originally given. If the Greek form emphasizes the internal dimension of the soul—the reception *into* the soul in the mode of proceeding *from* its inner depths—the Jewish form emphasizes the external dimension of the body: the establishment of a *new* relationship, in the mode of extending the bond of kinship.

Moreover, the Jewish sense of what Hans Urs von Balthasar described as the essential drama of the encounter of freedoms—most basically between God and man[124]—might initially appear to present a stark contrast to the Greek notion of freedom as perfect, not to say "automatic," unity with the Good. This unity is what scholars sometimes refer to as "Greek intellectualism," which would seem the opposite of "biblical voluntarism." But just as we saw in the previous volume that unity with the Good did not simply exclude the drama of something like spontaneous and responsible choice,[125] so too the reflection on the centrality of covenant has revealed that the drama of encounter, for the Jews, does not exclude unity. Quite to the contrary, the drama makes sense only inside the unity of will that is the very substance of the bond that is covenant. The "pact" of a covenant is not simply the *result* of two independent wills, which are more original than the bond, to which that bond remains subject.[126] Instead, it is *presupposed* by them in their encounter: *the bond of covenant is more basic than the individual wills that enact it*.[127] This prior unity does not compromise the "flesh and blood" reality of the individuals or the significance of the historical novelty of the act of will as it is individually exercised. Nevertheless, those individual acts always occur within the presupposed context of unity and receive their sense from this context. This is true to such an extent that the Old Testament presents the bond of covenant as liberating individual will: "'On the basis of a covenant I will set you free.' So he made a covenant with him and set him free" (1 Kgs 20:34). Even more significantly, the *end* of individuals in their encounter with one another is in the most ideal sense "one will," which we saw is constituted by a *real* joining of hearts, a union in one soul, of the members of the covenant. If the Greeks conceived of freedom as unity with the Good, we could say that freedom for the Jews is the unity of will with God—hence the fundamental importance of obedience to God's law, which is his will made objectively real.

Most profoundly, and most significantly for our purposes, we find a remarkable echo of the dynamic relation between potency and act, which has been and will continue to be one of the guiding principles of our entire investigation into the nature of freedom, in the biblical pattern of promise and fulfillment, a pattern that lies at the heart of covenant. This resonance is not just a superficial likeness. A key implication of the act-potency relation is that what comes about is not simply the introduction of an unprecedented novelty but the "re-newed" expression, as it were, of what was *already* given, a more inclusive or more specified recapitulation of a preexisting condition or arrangement. It is a creative *realization*. Similarly, realization quite obviously is an essential part of the promise-fulfillment relation: the deed accomplished is not a sheer "invention" or "fabrication" but a "making-good" on a pledge already given. The event is therefore meaningful; it serves a purpose that is, so to speak, pregiven. In other words, in technical language, the "promise-fulfillment" aspect of covenantal will introduces a properly *teleological* dimension into the Jewish sense of reality. To the objection that the initial promise, at least, represents a novel act of will even if the fulfillment does not, we recall the importance of the specifically Jewish sense of covenant as an extension of kinship, which is to say of some already given (natural?) relationship. Every fundamental covenant in the Old Testament has the form of the renewal of a pledge previously made.[128] Most decisively, we see that covenant implies the priority of actuality over potency, which we have argued marks the essential difference between the premodern and the modern worldview. As we saw above, a covenant, as a pledge given *now* that bears on all that is to come *after*, is *comprehensive*; it conveys a meaning, it gives form "a priori" to all future events. The acts of will that occur in history are therefore not arbitrary, as we would necessarily be led to think if we took each discretely, isolated from the whole, and thus in abstraction, according to the merely formal notion of will; instead, inside the comprehensive embrace of covenant, concretely speaking one wills only what one has already willed, which is just what we saw at length in the analysis of Plato and Aristotle in volume 1.[129] Every act of will is meaningful because it is a recollection of what was always already willed. Willing in each situation that presents itself in history what one has always already willed is what the Jews mean by *fidelity* (*emeth*).[130]

Let us turn, finally, to the Jewish notion of freedom, which we initially presented within the discussion of the formal characteristics of will in the Old Testament. There we said that freedom, for the Jews, takes the form of a "freedom from," in the specific sense of being liberated from a negative state (slavery), or more generally elevated above a normal condition (cf. kosher laws or Sabbath laws). Interpreted from within the concrete context of covenant, we see that "freedom from" represents only one part of the matter; the rescue from captivity is for the sake of inhabiting a "land flowing with milk and honey," which is to say that the "freedom from" plays a function within a more basic "freedom for."[131] In this respect, the Jewish sense of freedom is not simply the opposite of the Greek sense of belonging to the Good, though the emphasis is different insofar as more weight is placed on the achievement than on the fact of belonging. The covenant that God established with Abram coincides with the gift of what came to be called the "Promised Land" (see Gen 15:18–21; 17:1–8). It is to be noted that the land descendants are promised is one in which they already dwell but do so as foreigners. The promise changes the relationship.[132] It remains the case, however, that they come into possession of the land only *after* the experience of captivity. Though the rescue from Egypt was not an end in itself, terminating, so to speak, in the no-man's-land of the desert,[133] which would be implied if we absolutized the "freedom from," the "transition period" in the desert is not immediately passed through but endures for the symbolically significant span of forty years (Nm 32:13; Jo 5:6).[134] The Jews enter the Promised Land as a *liberated* people, and this liberation marks them indelibly. Their freedom is not, in short, an immediate function of their given nature but is and always remains a *gift*, something achieved over above a native condition.[135] The Jews are *granted* freedom, in other words, by an other, specifically by the Almighty who is holiness—that is, "set-apart-ness," or *liberation*—itself. Their freedom is not a natural property but a result of the relationship with the one whose "job it is to set people free," to use Brague's phrase once again. Nevertheless, it remains the case that that freedom is *lived* exclusively within the bond of covenant and so has the form of belonging for the Jews as much as it does for the Greeks. In the classical world, freedom is either a belonging to the Good or a belonging to God, but in any event it is a belonging.

Thus, we may say that there is no fundamental opposition between the Greeks and the Jews regarding the meaning of freedom or the will if we consider the concrete sense of man and his relation to reality and to the divine principle rather than the particular words used.

At the same time, there are what we might call mutually enriching differences that we ought not to neglect or trivialize. If the Greeks come to the will and freedom from inside nature, the Jews come to nature, we might say, from inside the will and freedom. These are not incompatible, but they are not simply the same, and each sets into relief an aspect of the meaning of freedom that will prove to be indispensable. Connected with this difference is a radical emphasis on intrinsic goodness in the Greeks and on personal, self-expressive power in the Jews, an emphasis on eternity and circular form in the Greeks and on history and progressive development in the Jews, an emphasis on the inner being of soul in the Greeks and on the external life of the body in the Jews. Again, all of these are essential, and, as we will see, from the Christian perspective to which we now turn, they ought to be interpreted in light of each other. That is to say, we need to avoid positing a simple dichotomy between them or reading them as two separate halves, that is, fragments, that are brought together into a whole: instead, viewing them in light of each other shows how the contribution that each brings is already anticipated in inchoate forms on the other side.

In Christ There Is No Greek or Jew

One sometimes hears Western civilization described as a convergence of the distinct influences of "Greco-Roman" antiquity, on the one hand, and the "Judeo-Christian" tradition, on the other.[136] While it is certainly true that Christianity bears an essential and intrinsically necessary connection to the Jewish tradition—the Christian Bible *includes* the Hebrew Bible, and the New Testament is simply unintelligible without the Old Testament, to such an extent that the attempt to divide them from each other has been formally condemned as heresy—it is misleading to connect Christianity with Judaism in a manner that leaves "Greco-Roman" antiquity simply outside as other. It is virtually impossible to overestimate the importance of this relationship for the question of freedom and everything that is at stake in getting this delicate and multifaceted matter "right." We can hardly do full justice to it here. Nevertheless, it is crucial for our larger project to stake out a basic position in simple terms.

In line with a notion found in the church fathers,[137] not to mention a figure like Philo, who makes a similar point from within the Jewish tradition, we propose to see the Greeks and Romans as playing an essential role within salvation history, now more broadly and actually conceived, beyond what is directly revealed in scripture: Christianity, though founded on the *Word*, is not principally a "religion of the book."[138] If the movement of the divine will in the Jewish conception is, as it were, from above, *into* the world, as we have been suggesting, the contemplative reflection on nature, the (explicitly philosophical) inquiry into the intrinsic meaning of things for their own sake, would seem to represent something like a fruition of this movement. Even more, if the notion of covenant, as the extension of kinship, entails an affirmation in some sense of what is (already) *given*, what is already there, it is not too much to suggest that the very fact of the Greeks presenting an extrabiblical source is itself demanded by the Bible. Scripture's relation to what lies outside of scripture is not foreign to scripture.

While this may not be as immediately clear in the Old Testament, it becomes absolutely clear in the New Testament, which features St. Paul alongside St. Peter. Paul is not only the apostle to the Gentiles—and appears to have his clearest "success," incidentally, with the Athenians, who raise questions and ask him to say more rather than attempt to shut him up in prison[139]—but he is also drawn from outside the original circle of the disciples who were called by Christ directly in the flesh.[140] To say that the Greeks figure providentially in Christianity is not to deny the historical contingence of the encounter but simply to say that, no matter how contingent this encounter certainly is, it reveals itself to be exceptionally fitting, and in this respect to show something of the *intrinsic essence* of Christianity, even if it is not as immediately connected as the Jewish tradition is. The excess beyond the Judeo-Christian tradition is *part* of the Judeo-Christian tradition. Or we might also say that the difference bridged between the Old Covenant and the New Covenant is large enough to include the whole Gentile world without breaking apart the original unity.[141]

We are making this claim in a rather schematic way here at the outset of this study.[142] The meaning of the claim will require a more concrete exploration of some of the major figures in the Christian tradition, to see how their interpretation of freedom gives expression to this twofold source and to evaluate the extent to which it does the source justice—a source that is literally *exceedingly* rich, since it abounds as the fruitful union of two radically different sources. To conclude this opening chapter, we may nevertheless make a number of general points, which will guide the studies in the chapters that follow, though mostly in an implicit way. The first point is a return to the observation we made at the beginning. To understand the distinctively Christian "contribution" to the meaning of freedom, it is decidedly *not* adequate to allow the discrete problems of sin, the Fall, and predestination to set the horizon. Instead, as we explained at the outset, if actuality precedes potency, we need to begin with what is most basic, not in the sense of crudest and most trivial,[143] but in the sense of *most complete*. It is only proper, then, to begin first positively (i.e., not with a formal problem, to which we respond), or in other words to begin by laying out the intrinsic nature of the reality, which provides the proper context for a *subsequent* exploration of the particular problems that present themselves. In short, we need to begin with the concrete doctrines that are properly Christian, that is, with what is specifically Christian about Christianity. Without any doubt, though Christianity may rightly be said to have a distinctively Christian take on *everything*,[144] and to have a wealth of doctrine about theological matters—eschatology, soteriology, sacramental theology, and so forth—the two doctrines that are fundamental for everything else are the Incarnation and the Trinity. To be sure, there is a particular connection between freedom and the doctrine of creation, which, as David Burrell has shown, bears a certain similarity in the three traditions of Judaism, Christianity, and Islam.[145] But the doctrine of creation itself reflects in subtle ways the nature of the God who creates, and that nature is revealed in the Christian tradition in a manner that is distinct from the revelation of God in Judaism or Islam. And so our fundamental question runs thus: What do the Incarnation and the Trinity reveal about the nature of God and creation, and therefore of freedom?[146] In the remainder of this chapter, we will approach this very large question specifically in the light of our discussion of nature and the will, goodness and covenantal love, in the Greeks and Jews, in order to suggest in very basic and general terms how the Christian vision represents a "creative synthesis" of the two, understood most radically in terms of the decisive Christian notion of gift: *tertium* datur because tertium *datur*.

We saw in volume 1 that, at its deepest root, freedom is associated with fertility; the original political sense of freedom was, accordingly, belonging to a common stock, or in other words membership in a family or tribe connected by blood, though the most basic etymological root sounds through even here in the note of the generativity that this membership implies.[147] Freedom is connected with *flourishing* and the "novelty" of superabundance. We proposed that the classical philosophical tradition, represented by Plato and Aristotle, took up, deepened, and transformed this original sense by rooting freedom, not in blood simply, but in the even more fundamentally and comprehensively *binding* reality of the *Good*,[148] and by defining the proper and fundamental relation to goodness basically *as nature*.[149] This transformation elevates freedom beyond the crudely physical to the level of intelligible meaning, the level of *logos*, which at least in principle universalizes it, even if the universality was never actually realized.[150] It may be that freedom is given in the logos of nature, which is in some sense available to anyone, but in fact membership is possible only for those able to "speak the language" (*legein, logos, logikos*). This means at first that "barbarians" are excluded but eventually comes to mean on the surface that freedom includes only the educated citizens and even more profoundly only those who are capable of leading a life strictly and explicitly according to reason; in this case, freedom belongs, not to "the many" (*hoi polloi*), but solely to the philosophers, who in some sense set themselves apart from membership in common humanity. There is a tendency for nature to become "unnatural," that is, for the *truly* natural man to be a relatively rare occurrence that requires an existence set in systematic opposition to normal human inclinations (Stoics).[151]

In Christianity, however, the *Logos* does not (merely) remain "above" as a transcendent ideal—though we ought not to forget that it *does*, also, remain "above" (ὁ Λόγος ἦν πρὸς τὸν Θεόν, Jn 1:1); it makes *itself* available, and indeed does so unto the very lowest: ὁ Λόγος σὰρξ ἐγένετο (Jn 1:14). The Greek principle of a naturally superabundant liberality, a "begetting and giving birth in the beautiful," becomes in Christianity ultimately a super-natural fruitfulness: "She conceived by the Holy Spirit" (and, note, this event has a "Jewish" historicity, not only because Mary is Jewish, but because it is an event that is said to occur, not in an eternal, mythological past, but in history). There would be many, infinitely many,[152] things to say about this divine fruitfulness, but we wish in the immediate context to point out an aspect that will be crucially important for the explorations in the chapters that follow. Though the principle of properly divine fruitfulness even more radically transcends nature than the Good from which all things emanate (as we shall see), it does not at all eliminate nature, as one might initially think, or render it irrelevant. Instead, nature is given a new ultimacy here. In the Incarnation, God enters *into* human nature, in a twofold sense, as the early Christian doctrine sought to make clear: on the one hand, in a radically intimate way, the Son assumed human nature in comprehensively *all* of its proper dimensions (everything but the sin, which represents a *betrayal* of human nature rather than an *expression* of it);[153] on the other hand, this nature was received *from* and *through* Mary, to such a real extent that we are required to call her, however paradoxical the phrase may seem, the "Mother of God." The doctrine of the *Theotokos* will turn out to have a fundamental importance for the interpretation of freedom because it establishes, as what we might call an unshakeable foundation or a necessary first principle, that the ultimate superabundance of freedom, the most complete transcending of nature, nevertheless always happens *within* and *through* nature (not to mention *as* a covenantal bond, the fulfillment of a promise *already* given): *Non coerceri maximo contineri tamen a minimo divinum est*.[154] The Logos that the world cannot contain first "comes to be" within the confines of a human womb. A basic principle of freedom as taken up and transformed in Christianity is that the excess *beyond* nature that freedom represents nevertheless always occurs in and through nature. It is for this reason that what we might call the "Greek" element remains indispensable in the Christian vision.

The Jews also give evidence of the "belonging to a common stock," that is, the "kinship," dimension of freedom,[155] though they too expand it beyond its most immediate natural sense. Whereas the Greeks deepen and elevate the blood relation in terms of the transcendent principle of goodness, the Jews extend kinship beyond blood by covenant. As we saw, while there is a "kinship covenant," which is formed between those naturally related, the usual sense implies an extension to one who would otherwise be a foreigner, or even a slave: consider Abraham's circumcising all those in his household, including the servants not related by blood, in the original covenant made with God (Gen 17:23). Here the act of will, the historical deed of making a pledge, acquires a special prominence, which it does not generally have among the Greeks to the extent that the horizon for the Greek vision is set by nature.[156] Christianity, quite obviously, takes up and transforms the Jewish notion of covenant: the "New Covenant" does not obliterate or simply replace the "Old Covenant" but unexpectedly fulfills the Old Covenant even according to its own terms more completely than that covenant fulfills itself.[157] As we have seen, no covenant is made in the Old Testament that does not have the form of a *renewal* of a promise already given. In this respect at least, the *radical* renewal of the Old Covenant in the New is perfectly continuous with the ancient tradition. Indeed, if the essential "reciprocity" of covenant did not exclude asymmetry or even unilaterality—the "grant" covenant was a relationship established by a superior who imposed an obligation on himself first of all, which the Old Testament bears witness to above all in God's not abandoning Israel because he is faithful first of all *to himself*—the Incarnation represents, so to speak, God's taking the reciprocity of covenant *into himself*. Christ is not just one party in the relationship over against the other but the perfect mediator because he is fully God and fully man. He thus takes upon himself the obligation imposed on the partner.[158] In a way that simply cannot have been anticipated—Who could imagine that God would not only become man but specifically "take the form of a slave [μορφὴν δούλου]" (Phil 2:7)?—the Son of God and the Son of Man fulfills in his very person the various elements that belong generally to covenant.[159] The "exchange" of oaths that typically accompanies the establishment of a covenant is found in the "annunciation" made to Mary, who is not imposed on as some passive material but gives her active consent.[160] Moreover, the blood sacrifice often performed in relation to the covenant becomes a literal reality in the crucifixion,[161] and the common meal that tends to seal the covenant appears in the Last Supper and the daily Eucharist that is its sacramental extension. With the New Covenant, God himself fulfills all of the conditions of the covenant—with the sole exception of the act of will, the moment of consent, of the covenantal partner: Mary's fiat.[162] Christ does not abolish the conditions of the covenant or render them obsolete (Mt 5:17); instead, he *accepts* them as given to him, as already established, and then fulfills them all in himself. As the Easter Liturgy says, Jesus Christ is not only *himself* the priest *and* the victim but *also* the altar![163]

Let us look at the nature of the New Covenant more precisely here. We saw that the Jewish conception of the will, formally considered, is revelatory, or in other words essentially self-expressive insofar as it is an act of a *personal* agent; materially considered, we see that the paradigmatic mode of this self-expression is the self-gift of the pledge by which one binds oneself to the other and the other to oneself. In the Incarnation, the form that the pledge or the revelatory gift of self takes is the shockingly real form of the entry of God himself (and not just in his power) into history in the "flesh and blood" of human nature. In this case, God does more than reveal his personal will as a distinct agent who remains radically outside the world (in heaven) and reveal just his supremely holy name, that is, as one most radically "set apart"; the eternal God *himself* enters into history ("I AM" is "Emmanuel"). Jesus Christ is the revelation, the making present or manifest, not just of the divine will or divine name, but of the divine *nature* (through the *divine person* of the Son). Here we see again how, in Christianity, the Jewish dimension opens up to the Greek: in Christ, God makes available his *being*.[164] It is just this radical revelation that institutes the New Covenant, as a transcendent fulfillment of the Old, in which God binds himself to man and man to himself (*admirabile commercium*!) in a definitive and never-to-be-surpassed manner.

Covenant is an extension of kinship, with all of the rights and privileges attendant upon membership in this bond of intimacy. This membership is freedom. When Christ says to the apostles that they are no longer slaves but free (Jn 15:15), it is because he has "revealed to [them] what the master is doing"; liberating membership consists in receiving this revelation, which means that the status of freedom includes a certain understanding—not, in the first place, the grasping of a universal principle (though, as we shall see over the course of this book, it is essential not to *exclude* this aspect), but the reception of a personal disclosure, the revelation of a *person*. Christians therefore understand freedom along the lines of a special kind of kinship: that of being "adopted" sons and daughters of God, an adopted sonship that can also be called "friendship" ("no longer slaves but friends"). As Paul put it, "For you did not receive the spirit of slavery to fall back into fear, but you have received the Spirit of adoption as sons" (Rom 8:15).[165] Note that both notions, that of friendship and that of adoption, imply a distinction from a simply *natural* state.[166] Friendship is not *given* in the manner of a family relation, and adoption implies a being taken *into* kinship from a previous condition outside of that kinship. But they are both strictly *analogous* to natural kinship: adoption quite clearly is the granting, and so the institution, of a family bond,[167] while the classical understanding of friendship, in clear contrast with the modern view, as we saw in volume 1, takes the relation to be a sort of imitation of a blood relation, or more specifically recognizes the family bond as the paradigm of *philia*.[168]

Let us consider, finally, how this retrieval of the Christian tradition as itself a recollection (*anamnēsis*) and remembrance (*zikkaron*) of the Greek and Jewish traditions casts a new light on the two problems that we said have dominated the discussion of freedom, namely, the problem of choice and the problem of predestination. We saw above that freedom, for the Jews, means in one respect a liberation from a prior condition of slavery and in another respect a form of existence in the place that is given and in accordance with the law, so that the people share one will with the Liberator. The Promised Land of Canaan, flowing with milk and honey, is, we might say, the *Realsymbol* of a free existence. This sense of freedom resonates in the Christian notion of "adopted sonship," insofar as adoption implies an elevation beyond a prior condition, not for the sake of change, or mere negation—not essentially a liberation *from*—but for the sake of the positive reality of community, a liberation *for*: "For freedom you were set free." There emerges here a point of crucial importance most directly for theology but also for our current endeavor to understand the *essence* of freedom: the *adoption* is most basically an elevation beyond the first gift of nature, which is itself already essentially positive, rather than a removal from a condition of slavery, that is, from the state of sin. Freedom, in other words, does not have its essential reality solely in the contingent and conditioned context of the fallen world, as a ransom from a negative condition. Freedom does not have sense only in relation to sin, as capacity for sin or a redemption from it. We might be inclined to see it as such if we isolated the Jewish roots of Christianity from the Greek tradition, for although the goodness of the original creation is certainly part of the Old Testament, the intrinsic goodness of creation *precisely qua nature* is not as evident.[169] Keeping both dimensions in view, we see that freedom is first of all, and most basically, positive and essential: while nature is already itself a gift, freedom is a gift beyond natural existence, a gift that is not just a condition into which one is simply born but requires moreover a "personal" involvement.[170] At the same time, it represents the flourishing of nature, the fulfillment of the promise given so to speak at the outset:[171] grace does not destroy nature but elevates and perfects it. If in the historical condition of the Fall the gift of freedom becomes also a rescue from sin, this is not the essence of freedom but only the form that freedom takes with respect to sin and evil. This redemption is then a surprising, novel, even more perfect and fitting following through on what was promised from the beginning (O happy fault!).

An elevation *from* the goodness of created nature—but *into* what, exactly? Here we see perhaps most clearly the extension in Christianity of what is initially given in Judaism. In a discussion of the Jewish notion of covenant, we noted a certain ambiguity: it is not, so to speak, a purely spontaneous act of will that originates from nothing but always the extension, through the will, of what is already presupposed as given, whether that be an already-existing bond of kinship or a promise that was previously made. The difficulty appears when we come to creation, which as an act of divine will has an original covenantal quality, but which is strictly ex nihilo, presupposing nothing (on the side of the creature) as given. As we indicated earlier, if we do indeed take the act of creation as absolutely spontaneous in this sense, the deep implication is that this most original covenant will have a noncovenantal form, which is to say, using modern language, covenant will have a tendency to model itself after *contract*, the deliberate institution of a relation by an autonomous agent who remains in some sense outside that relation and so always "free" to render the relation void.[172] The relation in this case becomes an only-apparent reality, always subservient to a will, which is now interpreted, no longer as an ability to give oneself, but as power in an abstract and indeterminate sense.[173] We will be suggesting that such a distortion lies at the origin of the modern conception of freedom. The alternative here is to see the Jewish notion of covenant taken up and fulfilled in the Christian: the kinship that is "already given" as a reality in itself and then "covenantally" extended in creation is the community that is God himself, who is the perfect unity of Father, Son, and Spirit. In this respect, creation is the fruit of a love that is already perfectly actual in itself, and not the realization of a merely potential love, which would be the case if God had no Other already in himself. Actuality precedes potency and makes it possible (so to speak!). As a fruit, creation has freedom at its roots; it is already, in some sense, perfect in itself: the world, that is, nature, is *good*, and it is essentially defined by its relation to ultimate goodness. But it is also invited "by extension" *into* the "kinship" of the *inner life* of God, which, as inner life, can be entered into only through personal disclosure and personal response to this disclosure (because only a *person* can respond to what is offered *personally*).

We wish to suggest that the God who creates the world, the God, so to speak, "of nature," is the absolute Good that represents the ultimate horizon for the Greek conception of freedom, a horizon that, it bears remarking, does not cut off the transcendent dimension as if it were a *ceiling* that capped things off and sealed everything below in a strictly enclosed space, but that, precisely because it is good and because it is a horizon, opens up to the possibility of a revelation of what lies beyond: the sun *breaks in*, from above, only into a world that is defined by a horizon. The Good discloses its inner reality as love in the gift of the Son, which means that divine love is not something simply new, juxtaposed, as it were, to the Good, but is "nothing but" the truth of the Good, its inner reality as personally revealed. We propose that the need for a personal response to the personal disclosure is the ultimate foundation, and thus the most profound essence, of choice, prior to any distinction between good and evil. In this respect, we could say that the matter of choice is central to the Christian notion of freedom precisely because Christianity is a "synthesis" of the Greek and the Jewish traditions.

Along similar lines, the other major question of "predestination" ought to be understood in the first and most basic sense as referring to the "a priori" kinship *into* which the Christian is granted entry through an invitation that is itself the constitution of freedom.[174] As Paul puts it, "He chose us in [Christ] before the foundation of the world, that we should be holy and blameless before him. In love he predestined us for adoption to himself as sons through Jesus Christ, according to the purpose of his will" (Eph 1:4–5).[175] Note that the adoption occurs, not as an abstract legal arrangement, but *through* Jesus Christ, which is to say through the *incarnation* of God, his entry into human nature, and this is what it means to occur according to the divine will. The Trinity is both the infinite perfection of self-diffusive goodness and covenantal bond, both a matter of being/nature and a matter of person/will, of pure act always already realized and the infinite surprise of gift, and thus the Trinity lies at the heart of the distinctively *Christian* conception of freedom. It is often recognized that, in Christianity, the (Greek) Neoplatonic "emanation of the Good" gets personalized, so to speak;[176] but we have to recognize at the very same time that the (Jewish) personal dimension also acquires here a genuinely metaphysical substance. Actuality is revealed as *both* highest excellence (*to kalokagathon*) and supreme love (*hesed*).

Perhaps most surprisingly, the universalizing of the kinship that defines freedom, which is achieved in the perfect goodness/personal love of Christ given in his incarnation and made fruitful in the personal act of self-sacrifice of the cross, is not a definitive move *away* from the particular reality of matter, as it seems to be in the Greek notion of transcendence into intelligibility, and in the interpretation of the Jewish outward rite as a physical, eternal symbol that must be replaced by the inner disposition of the heart, where God is now worshipped not in flesh but in "spirit and truth" (Jn 4:21–24). Instead, the universalizing of kinship is a *return to the particular reality of matter*. The etymological root of the word *freedom* in Hebrew (*deror*), Latin (*libertas*), and Greek (*eleutheria*) is free-flowing liquid. The kinship of freedom is offered precisely in the blood and water (the Greeks and the Jews?) that poured forth from the side of the crucified Christ,[177] which the church fathers understood to be the sacramental extension of the definitively liberating reality of the cross. The blood that God received from man in Mary's womb is returned to man, having coursed through the essentially transformative divine *nature*, and having poured forth as the fruit of the supremely divine *deed*. The freedom of communion—now freely available to all, not just those who are able to live according to the logos above and even against the flesh—is not a matter of pure spirit but once again an essentially fructifying share in the blood of kinship, a being grafted onto the vine so as to bear fruit, a being adopted as sons in the Son:

> But now in Christ you who once were far off have been brought near by the blood of Christ [ἐν τῷ αἵματι τοῦ Χριστοῦ]. For he is our peace; in his flesh [ἐν τῇ σαρκὶ αὐτοῦ] he has made both groups [Jews and Gentiles] into one and he has broken down the dividing wall, that is, the hostility between us. He has abolished the law with its commandments and ordinances, that he might create in himself one new humanity in place of the two, thus making peace, and might reconcile both groups to God in one body through the cross, thus putting to death that hostility through it. So he came and proclaimed peace to you who were far off and peace to those who were near; for through him both of us [Jew and Gentile] have access to one Spirit in the Father. (Eph 2:13–18)

What we claim to have done in this chapter is not so much to have defined or established the Christian conception of freedom and catalogued its essential features as to have "staked it out"—to have provisionally set, with rope and wood, the parameters of a plot of land on which one intends to build. To say that these are the parameters of a Christian conception is not meant to imply that they were ever consciously understood in precisely the terms in which we have sketched it, though it is important to add that we do not wish by contrast simply to deny the possibility *tout court* either. As we observed at the outset, much of the explicit discussion of freedom in the Christian thinkers of the patristic period or the Middle Ages tended to focus on just one aspect or another—for example, the moral question or the eschatological one. These aspects have to be considered in their proper place. To say it again, our point in setting out these parameters is to begin from as ample a foundation as we can manage, in order to be able to "see the form" of the figures we will explore from the vantage that allows their fullest profile to emerge, as it were. As Michael Polanyi has so insightfully shown, one can thematize and bring into focal attention one idea or aspect of a reality only *from* a particular perspective, which is to say from inside of a form in which one "indwells," and which therefore remains necessarily, in that particular act of knowing at least, implicit: every time we attend *to* one thing, we attend *from* something else.[178]

The problem with a great deal of contemporary scholarship on classical figures regarding the issue of freedom is that it tends, unsurprisingly, to attend to ancient ideas from the contemporary conception, which is taken for granted as the background, and therefore as a sort of implicit norm, whatever one's final judgment of the particular figure or idea turns out to be.[179] What we have sketched in these opening pages is meant to give form to the imagination, to shift the horizon of vision, so that we do not simply view the classical Christian tradition from a detached distance, as a modern spectator, but attempt to enter into that tradition, so to speak, from the inside.

The Christian conception of freedom is most obviously, and most directly, the heir of the Jewish conception. This is no doubt why the initial accent lay on the themes of sin and redemption. By contrast, the Greek dimension of the flourishing of nature under the light of the Good is one that required much more time to unfold and be properly appropriated: the missionary movement of the early church was, as it were, *from* the Jews, *to* the Gentiles. The drama of the development of the Christian conception of freedom thus lies most directly in this endeavor, which is why the appropriation of the classical Greek tradition is the background concern for our present study. The specifically *philosophical* dimension, after all, is our principal focus.[180] We will see that the act of appropriation, this reception of the Greek tradition, begins with a certain fullness, thins out in a certain respect in the early Middle Ages, and reaches a kind of culmination in High Scholasticism, only to fragment at the end of that period.[181] The rich paradoxes of freedom, radically present at the beginning, however implicitly, and variously reflected throughout the tradition, harden in the end into a tension between straightforwardly opposed positions. What stands at the beginning of the modern era, which arguably defines itself precisely *as* the fragmentation of tradition, are so many pieces of a now-forgotten whole, *symboloi* that are no longer recognized as belonging together but are now isolated as contradictory moments of a dialectic that thwarts resolution. In volume 1, we started with a modern representative of this fragmentation and ended with an appeal to the sources of the classical tradition in Plato and Aristotle. In this book, we make the passage in the opposite direction, picking up with the culmination of the classical tradition in Plotinus and following the thread to the late Middle Ages, in the figures that announce the dawning of the modern age. By surveying the whole, we hope to see how the parts fit together, to recall their original place and purpose, so they can be made fruitful again.

It is good, here at the outset, to state more directly in philosophical terms what we mean by the culmination of classical Greek thought on the matter of freedom in Plotinus, which opens up to a convergence with the Old Testament tradition integrated into the Christian vision, since this will present a kind of guiding norm for our study. In a decisive way in Plotinus, the Greek sense of perfection as an *end* reveals itself to be at the same time an ever-fruitful *beginning*, as we deepen our understanding of the inner truth of God. This requires a revision of the relation between act and potency, and indeed of the nature of actuality itself, which introduces a radical paradox. This paradox, which we propose constitutes the very essence of freedom (as we will see in the study that follows), is first, but barely, glimpsed by Plotinus, even if he lacks the theological sources to sustain it. In the Christian thinkers after him, aspects of the paradox are drawn out and deepened, but sometimes at the cost of the integration of the whole; this is especially the case where freedom is separated from its divine source, and that source is no longer conceived as *both* the Creator and the Redeemer, beginning and end, who reveals himself in both nature and history. This is why freedom is so originally *Christian*. To put the paradox in a rather abstract formulation, which will need to be unfolded through the thinkers that develop it, the actuality at the beginning and end of all things has to be interpreted, not in a simple polarity with potency, as it is more or less in Aristotle (though we have highlighted the paradoxes even there at the end of *Freedom from Reality*), but as prior to that polarity, or—to use the language of Erich Przywara's formulation of the *analogia entis*—as both in and above the polarity. What is at issue here is a kind of "superactuality," which is at the same time a "superpotency," and so revealed in both sides (though asymmetrically) of the polarity. Such a superpotent actuality, we will see, can be properly interpreted only as a radical *generosity*, and ultimately only in terms of a Trinitarian and Incarnate God. We will work out this dimension much more extensively in philosophical terms in our third volume, but we state it here in this bald way to help illuminate the perspective from which the study of the various figures that follow in this volume has been undertaken, and so to help the reader interpret some of the otherwise obscure judgments made.

It is worth pointing out here that the position that emerges by the end of the study affirms in a general way the traditional Catholic story, which sees Aquinas as the summation of classical thought and sees the later medieval thinkers (especially Scotus) as an unraveling of his achievement and therefore as the beginning of the end, so to speak. But the position differs from this traditional story in three basic respects. First, it gives great emphasis to Plotinus, and the (Christianizing) Neoplatonic tradition following him, as displaying a kind of original perfection of the notion of freedom; second, while it does indeed affirm Aquinas as a culmination, it attends to what we take (in light of the paradox summarized above) to be deficiencies in his thought in relation to this original perfection; and, third, it therefore not only sees Scotus as a decline and in fact a kind of betrayal of the classical view but at the same time argues that Scotus ought to be read as reacting to a dimension lacking in Aquinas's thought, at least in its most evident interpretation. Thus, the full Christian appropriation of its traditions, the full development of a Christian vision of freedom, is (in *one* respect, but not in another) something for which we are still waiting.

Let us conclude our "setting of the horizon" with two overarching claims, which we offer as proposals for a particular way of understanding what is at stake in the issues under discussion in this book. The first claim is that *freedom is Christianity's gift to the world*. All three parts of this claim need to be highlighted: (1) It is the gift *of Christianity* because, as we have been suggesting, freedom is the very substance of Christianity. Freedom has its roots in a doctrine of creation as a giving of being that is and remains distinct from the source of that being, even inside of a profound and abiding ontological unity with its source; the reception of this gift requires a personal appropriation that involves a "dramatic encounter" between the divine and human will; and the drama of this encounter, along with the integrity of the original gift that is implicated in it, is preserved, healed, and elevated to a new perfection in the work of redemption through the incarnate Son and the mission of the Holy Spirit. (2) It is *a gift*, which means it does not remain within the origin, with "strings attached," but is truly *given away*, so as to belong truly to the recipient, to bear fruit outside of itself.[182]

A gift that is given does not demand a constant and explicit reference to the giver but invites the recipient to become, as it were, a reference point for the gift also in himself. (3) It is a gift *given to the world*, in the sense that the freedom thus given away, as it were, has become, and will become, a constitutive property of the world as such *in principle*[183] — though this principle will be realized to varying degrees in different cultures and different periods of history. Freedom does not exist simply inside of the institutional, visible church but exceeds its borders ("excess" is, after all, a sign of freedom). Note that the general claim that freedom is the gift of Christianity is not meant as a comparative claim, in the sense that freedom is thus being denied of other religions. A comparative claim of this sort cannot, in any event, be logically proven or disproven.[184] Our claim, instead, represents simply an interpretation of the inner substance of Christianity considered in itself.

The second claim concerns the continued existence of freedom. Regarding (3) above, the fact that freedom belongs to the world does not mean it is simply an established fact. If, as we have suggested in *Freedom from Reality*, and will develop further in this and the following volume, freedom *just is* a reception of the source so as to be fruitful thereby and therein, then the reality of freedom, the *real*-ization of the principle, depends in some basic sense on the proper reception of this gift. The unavoidable implication — however inconceivable this will sound to the liberal mind, since liberalism takes itself to be the guardian of liberty, if not its inventor — is that the fate of freedom in the world is at some level bound up with the fate of Christianity. If freedom really is a *gift* in the manner described, it means that, if we cannot simply say that there is no freedom outside of Christianity, we nevertheless must say that the reality of freedom will be threatened to the extent that Christianity is explicitly rejected. Indeed, we must even say more: if freedom is the reception of the generative source, and if Christianity is itself a "generative" reception of its sources, namely, of the traditions of the Jews and the Greeks (and Romans) (gathered up and surpassed in Christ, who then hands *himself* over), the fate of freedom hangs on the recognition of what we might call the "traditionality" of Christianity.[185] The de-Hellenization of Christianity, or indeed the severing of its Jewish roots — not to mention the rejection of Roman institutions — would thus imply a threat to the reality of freedom more broadly. This does not mean that every individual Christian must himself master Greek philosophy and learn the whole of scripture—though it *does* mean that doing so would deepen and lend substance to his Christian faith. The bodily and cultural dimension that belongs inseparably to tradition implies that all who are members receive the fullness of its gift, even if they never become conscious of that fact in a direct way. But those to whom it *has* been given to think, to take the reality into consciousness in this way, do indeed have a positive responsibility to receive the whole of the tradition as far as they can: "Whoever cannot give account of three thousand years is condemned to remain in darkness, and live just day by day."[186]

PART II

Late Antiquity

CHAPTER 2

Plotinus on Freedom as Generative Perfection

The Basic Approach

Plotinus's *Ennead* 6.8, to which Porphyry gave the title "On Free Will [ἑκούσιον] and the Will of the One," simply towers over everything written on freedom in the ancient world. Indeed, it is arguably not until the High Middle Ages, in the work of Thomas Aquinas, a full thousand years later, that we meet its equal in speculative depth and systematic completeness.[1] In this text, written at the height of his powers,[2] Plotinus not only displays his wide reading of the preceding philosophical tradition—which is not in the least a mere "polymathy" in the sense criticized by Heraclitus[3] but a truly integrated and integrating vision that finds the proper place for all the disparate insights of the various thinkers in relation to an ultimate principle—he also demonstrates an almost uncanny capacity to raise essential and fundamental philosophical questions at exactly the right point. He therefore serves, like no other, to gather up the classical tradition,[4] to open it into its own depths according to its own inner logic, and to introduce, now at the highest level, the very problems that will occupy us over the rest of the book.

Plotinus's basic question in this treatise is whether we can say that God is free, what it would mean to say this, and what the implications of God's freedom are for the meaning of freedom in general.[5] But God is not present in the world like other beings, and so we cannot simply describe his nature and action directly, as we can for them. Instead, we must proceed according to the figure of what the tradition will eventually call "analogy," turning first to what is near at hand and inferring therefrom what must be true about the divine, according to the strictures of reason, albeit a reason that takes its bearings from above rather than simply from itself.[6] Thus, Plotinus says, after presenting his essential questions about divine freedom at the outset, "We must postpone these questions for the present, and first enquire about ourselves, as is our general custom [ἔθος]."[7] What results is a treatise that falls into two distinct parts, first a rich but compact inquiry into human freedom (chapters 1–6), and then a patient and profound reflection on the freedom of God (chapters 7–21).[8] We will refer to these as "parts I and II." Leroux describes part II as developing, uniquely in the pagan world, what we might properly call a "theology." If theology, *strictu sensu*, is an interpretation of God specifically on the basis of his self-revelation, and so cannot exist in the *most* proper sense outside of God's *direct* communication, we may nevertheless say that Plotinus's treatise is as close to theology as one can get outside of the biblical tradition, for he "dares" (τολμητέον, 6.8.1.9) something never undertaken anywhere else in the ancient world, namely, to go beyond the question whether God is free with respect to the natural world, the cosmos, and to venture into the "inner life" of God himself, to peer into God's internal self-relation, so to speak.[9] Let us record already here that there is a connection between free will and interior life (a connection we will develop at length in the next chapter). If Plotinus is the first thinker in the world to offer a *metaphysics of freedom* in the thematic sense, it is not accidental that he is also the first to reflect on the First Principle specifically *in* itself, and not just in relation to its effects. There can be no more basic starting point for the theme of freedom; in this regard, Plotinus's inquiry is literally *id quo majus non potest cogitari*, and so he is the perfect figure to frame our own endeavor.

As it happens, Plotinus addresses the question of freedom precisely in terms of the relation between act and potency, terms that he draws directly from Aristotle.[10] Essentially following Aristotle's own interpretation of their meaning,[11] he nevertheless dramatically recasts these notions explicitly in the light of the Platonic Good. He begins the treatise by taking up a central theme of Stoic thought, namely, the question concerning "that which lies within one's power" (τὸ ἐπ' αὐτῷ),[12] and immediately connects this theme with the nature of power more generally (both in the *substantive* sense, ἡ δύναμις [6.8.1.6], and in the *verbal* sense, τὸ δύνασθαι, "to be able" [6.8.1.11]), which in turn ought to be understood specifically in relation to *actuality* (ἡ ἐνεργεία, 6.8.1.13–14). We will come to understand the meanings these terms have for Plotinus as we unfold the treatise.

As we begin the study, it is helpful to see that Plotinus enters into his inquiry in this treatise in a dialectical manner, in the Aristotelian and *not* in the Hegelian sense of the term: he begins uncritically with a common notion—in this case, the Stoic *to eph'hēmin*, being "up to us," that is, "in our power"—as a starting point of reflection, without, however, allowing the common notion simply to set the terms, once and for all. Instead, Plotinus takes what is typically meant by the phrase, he identifies the truth it aims at, so to speak, and then, by raising precisely targeted questions, he reveals the ways in which the affirmation in its typical interpretation falls short of the very thing it seeks to affirm, so that a new foundation and a deeper understanding are required. Plotinus follows this procedure, step by step, but quite succinctly, over the course of his discussion of human action until he reaches the highest possible point, what he refers to as the "noblest" or "most beautiful principle" (εἰς ἀρχὴν ... καλλίστην, 6.8.3.22), and therefore that beyond which it is not possible to go. Although he does not mean it as a technical term (which is what it will eventually become), Plotinus describes the procedure as an ἀναγογή, literally a "re-ductio," a "reduction" or a "tracing back."[13] The *anagōgē* culminates already at the end of chapter 4 with the Good, the absolute first principle of all things, while chapter 5 goes on to compare the human activities of action and contemplation in relation to what was discovered in the preceding analysis (ἀνά-λύω, literally a resolving up or back to a more fundamental principle), and chapter 6 draws more general metaphysical conclusions about freedom, before Plotinus embarks on a reflection of the freedom of the Good itself in part II.

We will follow out the steps of the *anagōgē* in part I more precisely in a moment, but before we do it is helpful to reflect on the significance of the procedure itself, which provides such a perfect contrast to the methodology of modernity we mentioned in chapter 1. Plotinus's *anagogē* is the classical reduction of potency to actuality: power is essentially teleological, which is to say that it is itself something like an *appetite* or a *desire* to attain something or bring something about.[14] This aim, however, is not simply a future possibility, projected from an as yet simply undetermined basis, such as we saw in Locke's conception of power, which was defined in *just* this way.[15] It is not a simple "Yes, We Can!" without any determinate referent. Plotinus's procedure is not a "pro-jection" forward (προβάλλω, which is incidentally the etymological root of the word *problem*) but a tracing *up or back*, *ana*-gogē. The actuality of the end is in a certain sense (which will be discussed below) presupposed as enabling the potency for it. The aim (τέλος) is the starting point (ἀρχή), which is to say that teleology is archaeology. Instead of beginning with what is empty, incomplete, or partial and literally "building up" to completion in the sense of adding on additional parts, or taking further and further steps into an emptily open future, Plotinus interprets the incomplete and partial *as such* in the only light that makes it genuinely intelligible, namely, the light of what is most perfect and complete (καλλιστή). To explain all of this, Plotinus gives crystalline expression to an axiom that governs all classical thinking, namely, "It is necessary [δεῖ] for the principle to be better than everything that follows from it" (6.8.9.9–10).[16] In this regard, Plotinus represents perhaps *the* paradigm of what we mean by the "classical" tradition.

The Form of Human Freedom

It is this single-hearted view toward the *kallistēn*, that which is noblest and most beautiful, that carries Plotinus so quickly through the surfaces of human activity to their depth, moving from perfection to even more comprehensive perfection until he reaches what one would simply assume would be perfection itself, but which turns out to surprise expectations and require a rethinking of everything. The *anagogē* is not a simple series of logical inferences but, as we will see, reveals itself to have a genuinely dramatic character. Because the *kallistēn* itself is the heart of the matter, and we have a long book ahead of us (!), we will be brief ourselves regarding the intermediate levels. Every human action intends to *accomplish* something, however trivial that thing might be in a given case. We speak of a thing being "in our power" to the extent that there is nothing to obstruct the transition from intention to accomplishment. Now, whereas both a standard modern or indeed a standard Hellenistic approach would be more or less content with this purely formal description of what is *eph'hēmin*,[17] Plotinus immediately points out the importance of what we might call "concrete content," which is the obvious move inside the Platonic tradition.[18] To say that action intends to accomplish something means that it necessarily aims at some good, or at least what the agent takes to be good. Once we recognize this, we see straightaway that some judgment is involved, which means that the will operates in conjunction with *reason*, λόγος. Whereas one might be tempted to interpret this statement in the rather banal sense of extrinsically connecting the two separate activities of thinking and willing—*first*, I reason about something and come to a conclusion, and *then* I decide to carry it out through the exercise of my will—it is clear that Plotinus means this conjunction in the strong, Platonic sense we elaborated in *Freedom from Reality*:[19] the will at bottom "really is" nothing but a judgment concerning what is good, or in other words βούλησις is λόγος and vice versa. This profound identity becomes apparent as Plotinus continues the *anagōgē*: logos is not really logos unless it is *orthōs logos*, right reason, and right reason is not really right reason unless it is *epistēmē*, genuine knowledge. And knowledge will turn out to be not really knowledge unless it is actual possession of the Good in the soul. It is worth quoting Plotinus at length as he sums the first series of inferences up, which he does explicitly as a way of opening into the true subject of the discourse, *God's* freedom (part II):

> We must therefore enquire about these matters; for [in doing so] we are already also coming near to our subject of discourse, the gods. Well then, we traced back what is in our power to will, and then placed this in the context of reason, and then of correct reason—but perhaps we ought to add to "correct" that it belongs to rational knowledge; for if someone had a right opinion and acted on it he would not indisputably have the power of self-determination if he acted without knowing why his opinion was right but was led to his duty by chance or some imagination. (6.8.3.1–8)

To illustrate all of this, let us take for an example the one Plotinus introduces already in chapter 1, so that we can have a more concrete sense of his argument. In order to bring to light the connection between knowledge and freedom, Plotinus presents the man—clearly Oedipus, though he does not name him explicitly—who accidentally kills his father (6.8.1.36–38). On the surface, this might seem to represent a free act in the specific sense of an act carried out in the power of the agent, without anything introducing an obstacle to its exercise, but it does so only if we limit the meaning of power to its formal character, in this case to merely physical ability. This man evidently has the physical capacity to kill another, or in Plotinus's words, he has "mastery over the act of killing" (κύριος τοῦ ἀποκτεῖναι) (we will come back to the word *kurios*, "lord" or "master," in a moment). But the example of Oedipus shows that mere unobstructed physical capacity is insufficient for freedom. No one would say that his killing of Laius was an act of freedom in the sense of being an action that accomplished his intention, because not only would he never have killed the man if he *had known* it was his father, but in fact the act ran perfectly contrary to his intention. According to Sophocles's most famous telling, Oedipus was actively doing everything he could to *avoid* this act, which had been foretold by an oracle.[20] Not only did the concrete content of the deed contain more than he intended, but that "more" implied the very opposite of what he intended. Here we see the importance of, not only logos, but *orthōs logos*.

Now, as Plato showed relentlessly in his dialogues, the moment we introduce the standard of the *orthōs*, which indeed is not an extrinsic addition but simply a clarification of the meaning of *logos*, the perspective shifts and the measure is no longer merely immanent to the agent. Instead, the agent is now required to conform to a standard outside of him,[21] though as we will see below this does not in the least make it "heteronomous" in a banal sense. We no longer ask (subjectively) what a person thinks he wants but (objectively) what is good, that is, what the person wants more profoundly than he perhaps realizes. Once we make this shift, there is nothing that can prevent us from going all the way to the end, so to speak. It is not enough to be accidentally correct; knowledge is *better*. And if what is good has become the standard, the less good cannot justify itself against the better. What, then, is best simply? The truth of the Good itself. When we ask whether Oedipus's act is a free act, it is therefore not enough even to ask just whether he knew what he was doing—unless, that is, we give *know* the full Platonic sense that we elaborated in *Freedom from Reality*. Plotinus takes for granted the Platonic view of man as rooted in and ordered to the Good. In this case, it is simply impossible for him ultimately to desire what is straightforwardly contrary to the Good. Genuine knowledge is insight into the reality that corresponds to deepest desire. To discover whether the man is free in his action, we therefore have to ask not simply whether he is able to kill as he wishes, or even whether he is in fact killing precisely the man that he *intends* to kill; rather, we ask whether the deed itself is intrinsically good, an actual participation in goodness itself.

There are two remarkable things to highlight in this context before moving on. The first is that Plotinus moves to the ultimate perspective of goodness itself, not by correcting an inadequate view through external supplementation, or even simple contradiction, but by unfolding the truth already inevitably contained in the partial perspective. In other words, he does not say: "You think that freedom is having things in your own power, but you are wrong: freedom is something completely different." Instead, he says, "You are right"—indeed, a common opinion is virtually *always* right in some basic sense—"that freedom is having things in our own power. Now, let's think for a moment about what this actually means." This is the *anagogē*. The "completely different" truth discovered at the end turns out to be a fulfillment of what was initially being affirmed without one's realizing it. The other remarkable thing is the brilliance of his choice of Oedipus as an illustration of the partiality of the (initial) human perspective. Oedipus is the very exemplar of power; he is *kurios* in every *worldly* respect possible, both in the literal, regal sense and in the broader sense of physical and mental capacity. Sophocles presents him as the quintessential *wise* man—wisdom, *sophia*, understood here specifically in what we might call the "pre-philosophical" sense as "omnicompetence."[22] There is nothing within the horizon of the world, so to speak, that he cannot do, over which he is not master and lord, like no other person on earth. And yet he is not free, because the measure of his true desire does not lie within the confines of material nature; it is the essentially transcendent Good. If the point of Greek tragedy is to (re-)view human action from the ultimate perspective of the gods, classical philosophy might be seen as an appropriation of tragedy *in thought*.

All of what we have presented so far can be found in Plato, and less obviously perhaps but no less truly in Aristotle, as we showed in the previous volume. But in gathering up the insights of both, Plotinus will take a significant step forward in his inquiry. In our discussion of Plato in volume 1, we considered a common reaction to Plato's insistence on the necessity of the Good and the invincible power of knowledge, namely, that it seems to make man a mere puppet, an automaton.[23] There we proposed a possible response but admitted that Plato himself did not explicitly engage the question. Plotinus, by contrast, does face the question "head on," as it were, no doubt in part because of the widespread conversations regarding fate and free will among the Peripatetics, Stoics, and Epicureans, with which he was directly familiar,[24] but possibly also because of the biblical sense of will that would have been generally present in the Hellenistic milieus, from both Jews and Christians.[25] His direct engagement puts Plato to the test and allows a dimension to emerge that, we will argue below, is both dramatically new and perfectly consistent. Both desire and intellect, Plotinus observes, appear to compromise power because they subordinate power to something outside of itself. Desire implies deficiency, a need for some real thing that one *does not* possess, so that the presence of desire coincides exactly to that extent with the absence of power (6.8.4.1–4). To desire is inescapably, we might say, to be *led* by what is other (ἄγεται).

The same problem stands forth even more profoundly at the level of intellect: "And a difficulty must be raised about Intellect itself, whether, when its activity is what it is by nature and as it is by nature, it could be said to have freedom [τὸ ἐλεύθερον] and anything in its power, when it does not have it in its power not to act" (6.8.4.4–7).[26] Note the inseparable connection between *nature* and *intellect*, which will remain the fundamental presupposition of every thinker we will treat in this book. Plotinus concedes that intellect does not have the power *not* to act in conformity to nature. But he does not infer from this that the intellect therefore lacks freedom. There are three parts to his argument on this score. First, to be compelled to the *true good*, as the intellect is by nature, to what one really wants, seems like slavery only to a superficial regard. Second, and more profoundly, the objection falsely supposes that nature is extrinsic to the intellect itself, so that the intellect's conformity to (its) nature would represent subjection to a heteronomous law. But if something like this might be the case for lower-level beings,[27] the higher and thus simpler kinds of being, such as intellect, simply *are* their nature, which means that conformity to nature is freedom itself (insofar as we define freedom here as self-determination or self-possession: τὸ αὐτεξούσιον).[28] Third, and most profoundly, the Good at which the intellect aims is, we might say, even more intimate to intellect than its own nature, and so presents a heteronomous imposition even less than nature does.

In this immediate context, Plotinus does not elaborate a theory of the Good, but it is of course the principal theme of all his philosophy, and we will see that what he goes on to say about the Good in part II confirms the importance of the point he makes in a straightforward way already here.[29] In this particular context, he simply observes that, while goodness is indeed different from the intellect—he refers to it as a principle that is *other* (ἄλλην ... ἀρχὴν, 6.8.4.33)—it is nevertheless also the case that what is good *does not lie outside* the intellect (οὐκ ἔξω αὐτοῦ, 6.8.4.34). He does not spell out here why this is the case, but the most obvious interpretation is that it is the nature of the Good that is the ultimate cause of the intellect to be both inside and outside of the intellect. In more technical language, the Good is *simultaneously* transcendent and immanent. To be good means to be other than the agent in one respect, meaning that the ultimate origin of the agent's act is not the agent himself simply but comes from *beyond* the agent as another principle (ἄλλην ἀρχὴν); at the very same time, however, the origin is also the agent's acting *from* himself rather than from anything simply external to himself (οὐκ ἔξω αὐτοῦ). If Aristotle had shown that it is possible for a principle of action to lie outside oneself and inside oneself at the same time,[30] Plotinus makes it clear that this is not only *possible* when one does what is good but *necessary* because that is the essential nature of goodness. This simultaneity of transcendence and immanence may seem mystical—and it *is* indeed paradoxical—but it is also a perfectly normal experience: when I desire something, which is just another way of saying, "When I take something to be good" (in the classical rather than the modern sense of the term *good*),[31] I can say either that it moves me or that it is really *I* who want it. Both are equally true. Goodness by its very nature lies both within and without at once.

Plotinus's formulation of this last point in the final sentence of chapter 4 represents the culmination of his *anagōgē* of human action, and it brings to a head what we have been calling the classical view of freedom.

It is the clearest and most explicit expression in all of ancient literature (to our knowledge) of what we said in the previous chapter constitutes the essential insight of the Greeks, namely, that, in free activity, that which is received into the soul is possessed as something that proceeds forth from it.[32] This is the very *form* of Greek freedom. In Plotinus's words, "εἰ [ὁ νοῦς] οὖν κατὰ τὸ ἀγαθὸν ἐνεργεῖ, μᾶλλον ἂν τὸ ἐπ' αὐτῷ· ἤδη γὰρ ἔχει τὸ πρὸς αὐτὸ ἐξ αὐτοῦ ὁρώμενον καὶ ἐν αὐτῷ, ὃ ἄμεινον ἂν εἴη αὐτῷ ἐν αὐτῷ ἂν εἶναι, εἴπερ πρὸς αὐτὸ" (6.8.4.37–40).[33] Armstrong's translation is, to put it gently, confusing.[34] Corrigan and Turner present a more lucid rendition: "So if [the intellect] acts in accordance with the Good, it would be even more in its own power [and free];[35] for it already has in itself too the object of its vision toward which it is directed and from which it has come, which is better for it to be in it, if indeed it is directed to it [the Good]."[36] Whether we read the text as saying that one already has in oneself the object of vision (ὁρώμενον), toward which one moves and from which one proceeds, or, according to a commonly accepted correction, that it is the movement itself (ὁρμώμενον) that one already possesses in oneself, the essential point for us remains the same: if something is *good*, that is, "in the Good," it is something *toward* which one is moving (πρὸς), something *from* which one proceeds (ἐξ), and something *already* (ἤδη) in one's possession. It is all of these *at the same time*. There is a yet deeper paradox here: Plotinus begins by saying the Good is in the intellect (the intellect has in itself that toward which it is moving) but ends by saying that the intellect is in the Good (it is good for the intellect to be in the Good). Indeed, the grammar of the text, and the logic of what it affirms, allow us to flip the perspective and say that, when one does what is good, the Good itself proceeds toward one, comes from one, and abides within one.[37] The ambiguity of which is in which is part of the point here; either of these readings is possible, and they amount for Plotinus to the same thing. This taking in of what arrives from one, as an abiding with it and so participating in it, is the "logic" of free activity, and it is precisely *goodness* that permits this trifold unity.[38]

We will treat the matter of chapters 5 and 6 very briefly, because we will have to spend more time on part II, to see what happens to the "form" of freedom in God. In chapter 5, Plotinus demonstrates what we already saw in Aristotle,[39] namely, that the more intrinsically good an action is, the more free it is, because it more properly emanates from the soul in the enactment. This means that virtuous action (*praxis*) is freer, at least *prima facie*, than external production (*poiēsis*),[40] and ultimately that the immediate unity of act and end in intellectual contemplation is the freest activity of all. In chapter 6, he elaborates this point by using the Platonic schema to show that productive activity is a lower-level expression of will proper (βούλησις), that will is an imitation of intellect, and, finally, that intellect must be an image itself of the Good. This opens up a reflection on the Good directly, which will occupy the rest of the treatise. But in drawing out this schema, Plotinus makes an observation, which seems to be a commentary on the Hellenistic philosophers of his age but is equally illuminating for us in the modern era, who generally espouse a similarly materialistic metaphysics. It will also be crucial for our later explorations. Plotinus says that only that which is "immaterial" can be free (τὸ ἄυλόν ἐστι τὸ ἐλεύθερον, 6.8.6.26–27).[41] This simply follows from the description of freedom we just gave. If freedom is essentially connected to the Good, which is by nature *both* transcendent and immanent, simultaneously *other than* and *interior to* the free subject, then materialistic metaphysics cannot allow freedom for the simple reason that a wholly material thing cannot be in two places, so to speak, at the same time. Physical things by their very nature *displace* each other because each takes up a *particular* place and time. To the extent that we remain within a materialistic horizon, we will not be able to affirm the freedom of self-movement inside of being-moved by another but will rather be forced to negotiate between these *opposed* movements, either reducing one to the other or figuring out some sort of compromise ("libertarianism" or "determinism," on the one hand, or some form of "compatibilism" on the other).[42] The "fate and free will" problem haunted the Hellenistic philosophers (but not the classical philosophers) precisely because of their materialist metaphysics, which is something Plotinus insists on when he specifically addresses this problem.[43] Plotinus was very familiar with these discussions as well as with the problem of sin and the Fall, but, significantly, neither of these problems come up even as an aside in his principal discussion of the meaning of freedom. His view is more basically ontological.[44] The perspective Plotinus offers is a consideration of the intrinsic goodness of freedom in itself, rather than an approach to freedom as the solution to some extrinsic *problem*.

Having Freedom and Being Freedom

And so we move now to consider divine freedom, wherein freedom in itself is most basically to be found. If we recall that Plotinus is seeking the *ultimate* meaning of freedom, and so asks not principally about God's freedom with respect to the world that is his effect,[45] but, even more fundamentally than this already quite basic question, about God's "immanent" freedom with respect to himself, our own beginning question runs thus: Granted that freedom has the threefold form of procession, return, and abiding, what could the word *freedom* possibly mean for the *absolutized* simple "nature" of the One itself? The form of freedom is displayed at the level of intellect, which in Plotinus's general schema represents the perfect image of the One,[46] the closest proximity to unity possible without being absolute simplicity itself. If the language of procession, return, and abiding makes sense for intellect, which does indeed present at least a "logical" difference, if not a "real" difference, to use the Scholastic terminology, between intelligence qua subject and intelligence qua object,[47] does this language make sense for absolute simplicity? Is there a self-relation in the One? Can there be freedom at all *without* some kind of relation?

In one sense, the answer to these questions is just "no." Plotinus thus says repeatedly that it is not strictly proper to speak of the freedom of the One; at this level, we have to move beyond the typical formulations of freedom—having something in one's power, self-determination, unobstructed activity, and acting according to nature—since all of these formulations take for granted some sort of relationality and so otherness. On the other hand, however, Plotinus does not rest content with a simple negation, because freedom is clearly a perfection, and all perfections derive from the One. The source of freedom cannot simply be lacking in freedom (6.8.7.42–46). Plotinus thus presents in simple outline what later comes to be called "analogy": we first affirm "pure perfections" in the real things of nature; we then "remove" (ἀφαιρέω), or "put away" (ἀποτίθημι),[48] whatever is opposed or inappropriate; and we are finally left with "something like" (οἷον) the worldly perfection in the First Cause.[49] If freedom is essentially relation to the Good, the Good cannot be without "something like" freedom, for what could be more related to the Good than the Good itself? If we deny that the

Good is *free*, perhaps we ought to say instead that the Good *is* simply *freedom itself*, recognizing that this latter is an analogous term. When Plotinus begins to elaborate the meaning of freedom in the One, he appropriately cautions that the entire discussion is "improper" in a certain respect,[50] but this is not at all to say it is false. "Improper speech" is, rather, an essential and even necessary expression of truth that appropriately recognizes it is not simply truth itself, which lies beyond any particular and thus relativizing expression.

A profoundly interesting and important question confronts us before we begin to elaborate what Plotinus presents as divine freedom: What prompts Plotinus in the first place, not only to recognize freedom as a perfection of human existence, but indeed seemingly to take that perfection for granted as something obvious, so much so that he would be driven to raise the difficult and previously unheard-of question of God's own internal freedom? This question becomes even sharper if we recall that the notion of freedom did not appear thematically in Plato and Aristotle, the founders, so to speak, of the classical tradition that arguably culminates in Plotinus. As we have mentioned already, it is common for scholars to observe that the theme of freedom and free will begins to enter philosophical reflection in a direct way in the Hellenistic thinkers, above all the Epicureans and Stoics, with whom Plotinus begins his own treatment. The question of freedom is, so to speak, "in the air" around this time. It has also been suggested that Plotinus developed his own view of freedom precisely in response to ideas he encountered among Jews and Christians,[51] or at least in Gnostic perversions of Christianity. By contrast, the great Plotinus scholar Georges Leroux and the Norwegian scholar Asger Ousager insist that Plotinus did not come to his reflections on the question of divine freedom as a result of the influence of Christianity, arguing instead that this question arises as a natural Neoplatonic development of ideas already found in Plato.[52] There is no apparent way to resolve the question of Christian influence on the basis of textual evidence, since Plotinus curiously never makes any explicit allusion to Christian notions in his writing.[53] The most reasonable position on this question seems to be that articulated recently by John Rist, who simply leaves it open, but with good reason. Whether or not there is a Christian influence on Plotinus, he says, the fact of the matter is that the view Plotinus develops can be shown to be perfectly consistent within his philosophy as a whole.[54] We will explain how in just a moment, but it is crucial to see the way in which this position confirms the general argument we are making in this book: while freedom is central to Christianity, whatever the novelty that the notion may represent (which we discussed in chapter 1 and will elaborate over the rest of the book), this novelty is not at all a simple *reversal* of pagan thought but can be shown to bring that thought to completion in itself. To put the claim as clearly as possible: if Plotinus represents a certain culmination of the classical tradition, if the treatise on freedom represents, as Vincenzo Cilento claims, the crowning of Plotinus's thought,[55] and if freedom is the heart of Christianity, it follows that Christianity brings classical thought to completion, or in any event that the novelty it brings represents an elevation of classical thought that does not do violence to it but "perfects" it, allowing it to flourish.

To show how the question of divine freedom is consistent with Plotinus's thought—interpreted as an integration of Aristotle but also of the whole of the tradition of Greek philosophy, into an essentially Platonic conception of the Good as First Principle—brings us directly into the "substance" of Plotinus's notion, so it is good to follow out the details. As Ousager has convincingly shown, the argument Plotinus makes in the "theological" section of 6.8 (not his word but ours) is essentially a careful, systematic response to the great question Plato introduces in the *Euthyphro*, a question that remains a perennial one in the Western tradition: Are things good because God wills them, or does God will them because they are good?[56] These seem to present exclusive alternatives, and yet the age-old dilemma is that neither can be denied without disastrous consequences. As we will see by the end of this book, only when the tradition is fundamentally fragmented does this dilemma present itself as a Greek view (God wills things *because* they are good by their own independent essence, which subjects God to a cosmic principle) *versus* a (Judeo-)Christian view (things are good simply *because* God wills them, which evacuates intrinsic goodness and subjects the cosmos to a fully arbitrary God).[57] At the origin of the tradition, no such stark opposition exists.[58]

Plotinus sharpens the *Euthyphro* dilemma and gives it its *ultimate* form: Does God will *himself* because he is goodness itself, or is he goodness itself *because* he wills himself? While this formulation may be taken to be a philosophical event of the highest order (if such things even exist!), it is illuminating to see how naturally this question arises when one returns, as Plotinus does, to Plato *after* Aristotle (and to a lesser extent after the Stoics and Epicureans). In his own version of the *anagōgē*, Aristotle had—on the basis of the classical principle that potency always derives in some sense from act—reduced all natural potencies to the absolute actuality of self-thinking thought, that is, the perfect unity of thinking thinking thinking.[59] This *nous* is in one respect a completion of nature, in the sense that nature in its movement from and toward an intrinsic principle in which it rests is a kind of imitation of the *nous*'s perfect unity-in-logical-difference, now spread out, "discursively," in the temporal order. At the same time, though this is more implicit in Aristotle and becomes explicit only in Plotinus's Platonic appropriation of his thought, *nous* transcends nature, insofar as it is not itself a *thing* extended in time and space. With *nous*, we have a transition, as it were, from nature to *being simpliciter*.[60] But, as is well known, Plotinus criticizes Aristotle for failing to see the difference between perfect unity, a subject being identical with its object and thus identical with itself, and absolute simplicity, which is the *principle* of intellect's unity. Here he points to Plato's Good as beyond being and intellect as its cause.[61] But Aristotle is not simply a fall from this Platonic height, so to speak; his insight into the perfect self-relatedness of *nous* allows in turn a *deepening* of Plato beyond Plato's own thinking (in its exoteric form, in any event). To put the matter simply at first, if being (as *substance, ousia*) is, at its heart, the pure actuality of self-thinking thought, what sort of "self-relation" constitutes the Good that is the principle of knowing and being? What sort of actuality does the *Good* as such represent, if indeed the notion is even possible here?

It is in response to these sorts of questions that the will—or more precisely, "something like" (*hoion*) the will—turns out to have its proper place. We observed in the last chapter that there is a general tendency in Greek thought to reduce anything like will or the appetitive order *finally* to the order of intellect, and so to the nature that is bound to reason. This we see in Aristotle's anagogical culmination in self-thinking thought, which is the object of *both* knowing *and* desiring.[62] But if there is a principle "beyond" thought, there must be an "activity" or "actuality" (ἐνέργεια) beyond thinking. What is that activity? According to Plotinus, "The nature of the Good is in reality the will of himself" (ἔστι γὰρ ὄντως θέλησις αὐτοῦ) (6.8.13.38). It is significant that Plotinus uses the word θέλησις, and not only βούλησις, for this activity, though he does not in the least oppose these terms.⁶³ Βούλησις is the more common word in the classical Greek thinkers and tends to have an "intellectualist" note, if the term may be allowed, while θέλησις is more "voluntaristic,"⁶⁴ in the sense that it suggests a more spontaneous activity, which is not *simply* reducible to some form of understanding. If Augustine is often referred to as having "discovered" the will insofar as he seems to recognize a "power" of the soul with its own potencies and actualities, irreducible to those of intellection,⁶⁵ it is perhaps more accurate to point to Plotinus as having preceded him in this, as, for example, Leroux does.⁶⁶ If the Good is a strictly supraintellectual principle, then the "activity" it exhibits in analogy to *noēsis* must be likewise "supraintellectual," and this is *thelēsis*.

This affirmation of course immediately raises the concern of irrationalism,⁶⁷ which has often been the worry more generally of those who judge Neoplatonism to fall more in the realm of theology than philosophy in the strict sense,⁶⁸ so it is important to see why this objection to Plotinus, though certainly understandable, can be answered. The response is simple and incontrovertible. "Irrationality" is the opposite of rationality, and opposites necessarily lie within the same order (hot and cold are opposites within the order of temperature, for example). But the Good is not at all the opposite of intellect. Instead, it *transcends* the intellect precisely as its principle. But to say the Good is the principle of intellect means that, if intellect is denied, the Good is denied, according to the strict logic of *modus tollens*. There can be no rationality without the suprarational Good, and if the whole of intellect in the integrity of its specific mode of existence is not affirmed, then human beings have no access to the Good.⁶⁹ We might say that the Good transcends intellect in a way that includes the whole of it.⁷⁰ If Plotinus affirms a will beyond the intellect, his notion of freedom remains *maximally* "intellectualist."⁷¹ The "irrational" lies *below* reason; Plotinus's Good lies *above it*, which means his philosophy aims at *all of intellect, plus more*. Indeed, there is no genuine transcendence that is not fully inclusive of what it transcends.⁷² The truth of this judgment will be borne out as we proceed.

This clarification allows us to see, moreover, how Plotinus is able to affirm a transcendence of being that is not nihilistic and a transcendence of nature that is not unnatural. The Good that is *beyond* being is not *opposed* to being as nothing but rather precedes being as its source. Thus, if the Good is not "real" in the strict sense, because reality for Plotinus, as a definite being, is always finite,[73] it is not less than real but more than real. Similarly, if the Good has no nature, which implies an existence specifically in time, it is not in any respect against nature (*contra naturam*), but is rather essentially supranatural. This means that the activity of the Good, *thelēsis*, does not transgress nature but fulfills it in relation to a principle that nevertheless lies beyond nature's intrinsic capacities, so to speak. It is thus, with his deepened reflection on the Good, that Plotinus achieves the "kairos" moment of a *transcendence* of what we said in chapter 1 is the ultimate Greek horizon, namely, nature, but nevertheless does so precisely *from within* that horizon, and so *as a Greek*. In other words, in Plotinus's insight into freedom, *Greek philosophy transcends itself*.

In the light of these elaborations, let us look at a summary statement about the freedom of the One that Plotinus (significantly) presents already in the first chapter of part II of the treatise. Here he describes the Good's self-relation, noting the constant qualification of "something like" (*hoion*), which indicates analogy, and noting too the description of the Good's simplicity as an identification of its essence and its existence, or in Plotinus's (not yet technical) terminology, his hypostasis and his actuality (or energy):

> But when [the Good's] hypostasis, so to speak [*hoion*], is the same as his energy, as it were—for one is not one thing and the other another if this is not even so with intellect, because its activity is more according to its being than its being according to its activity—so that it cannot be active according to what it naturally is, nor will its activity and its life, so to speak, be referred to its substance, so to speak, but its "quasi-substance" is with and, so to put it, originates with its activity and it itself makes itself from both from eternity, for itself and from nothing. (6.8.7.46–54)

There are three things to highlight in this passage. First, Plotinus clearly has Aristotle's *Metaphysics* 12.7 in mind here, referring as he does to this highest actuality and including reference to *nous*, substance, life, and eternity, all of which occur in Aristotle's famous passage, not to mention the allusion to Aristotle's claim that, in the unity of being and knowing, being has a relative priority to the act of knowing in the sense that thinking does not *produce* being but conforms to it (we will come back to this crucial point at the end of the chapter).[74] Second, Plotinus spells out the steps of the transcendence as we laid them out above: the Good's actuality is not "according to nature" in the immanent sense,[75] which is why we cannot simply describe it as *life*, except analogously;[76] nor is its activity according to substance (*ousia*). The *subject* of the will is not nature per se or substance per se but simply *the self* (τὸ αὐτὸ), which lies beyond both.[77] But this does not in the least imply that the self-constituting activity is opposed to nature or substance, in the sense that these are first *given* and that the activity then must either conform to it or diverge from it. Instead, Plotinus says what we take to be the third point to highlight, namely, that its "quasi-substance" and its "quasi-activity" emerge at the same time. *The Good is what it wills to be, and it wills to be what it is.* This, in the most compact nutshell, is Plotinus's theory of divine freedom.[78] It is also a succinct expression of the paradox that constitutes the essence of freedom.

The Will of God, or the Will as God

By describing God as absolute self-will, or indeed absolute will-self—the meaning of which we need yet to unpack—Plotinus explicitly rejects what he calls "a bold discourse" (τις τολμερὸς λόγος), which turns out to represent what would seem to be the only alternative, namely, that God does not will himself *to be* (and to be will!) but first "just *is*" and *then* wills himself as a kind of recognition of what he already has been.[79] Because God is by definition, so to speak, absolutely first, there can be nothing "prior" to him to which one might appeal to account for him; regarding God, he explains, it is not possible to ask the two most fundamental philosophical questions, the "why" question concerning final cause, and the "what" question concerning formal cause,[80] but this is due to an overabundance of intelligibility rather than an absence of it. And this is precisely the point: if we interpret the inability to comprehend the One as an *absence* of intelligibility, an opaque darkness, and say that there is simply *no reason* for God, he just simply *is*, this amounts to saying God just "happens" to be, which reduces his reality to something like "chance" (*tuchē*) or "accidental event" (*sunebē*).[81] Not only is this contingency supremely inappropriate for God, it is also logically impossible insofar as contingency presupposes a prior necessity, and, moreover, if we were thus to divinize randomness, so to speak, the entire cosmos would be meaningless. This would ultimately undermine all human freedom.[82] The extraordinary genius of Plotinus comes to expression in the fact that he does not simply oppose this absolute contingency by positing an absolute necessity over against it,[83] because, as every good Platonist knows, (abstract) necessity is also unintelligible.[84] Plotinus responds to absolute contingency instead with absolute freedom, which transcends both contingency and necessity as *essentially good and beautiful*.[85] Thus, we could say that Plotinus elevates will and its essential activity to the highest, not in the least to denigrate intellect, but rather to saturate the First Principle with intelligibility. God is absolute freedom because he is absolutely meaning-ful:

> For something like what is in intellect, in many ways greater, is in that One; it is like a light dispersed far and wide from some one thing translucent in itself; what is dispersed is image, but that from which it comes is truth; though certainly the dispersed image, intellect, is not of alien form; it is not chance, but each and every part of it is rational principle and cause, but that One is cause of the cause. He is then in a greater degree something like the most causative and truest of causes, possessing all together the intellectual causes which are going to be from him and generative of what is not as it chanced but as he himself willed. And his willing is not irrational, or of the random, or just as it happened to occur to him, but as it ought to be, since nothing there is random. (6.8.18.33–44)

To a modern ear, absolute freedom as absolute self-will sounds like the very limit of arbitrariness and blind power: consider Schopenhauer, Schelling, or Nietzsche, not to mention Jean-Paul Sartre.[86] But this is simply because the modern ear has lost its capacity to hear the melody of the good and beautiful, so to speak, that constitutes the music of freedom. For Plotinus, it is simply impossible to conceive of the will apart from its relation to goodness; the very "discovery" of the will in Plotinus's philosophy is a result of reflection on the "nature" of the Good. It is crucial to keep this in mind when we read Plotinus's regular assertion in this part of *Ennead* 6.8 that the Good, as Freedom, makes or produces itself.[87] The connection that Plotinus makes between *thelēsis* and *poiēsis* is stunning, insofar as he earlier subordinated *poiēsis*, with the relation it implies to some external end, to the "immanent" activity of *praxis* in chapter 5, and finally to the "nonpraxis" of intellectual contemplation. Suddenly, at the "supreme" level, *poiēsis* is redeemed as higher even than intellection. Plotinus himself does not draw attention to the apparent reversal we witness here, but it is clearly an implication of God's radical transcendence of nature and being. The self-production in God here may sound like the Spinozist *causa sui*, which Heidegger famously criticized as the heart of the technologized ontology that defines the modern age.[88] But the modern technological form of production is an essentially violent imposition of form on meaningless stuff. Plotinian "production" is radically different. As a general principle, production, for him, is conceived essentially as a fruit, the overflow or superabundance (ὑπερερρύη καὶ τὸ ὑπερπλῆρες), so to speak, of internal perfection.[89] Thus, it is not at all opposed to contemplation but instead is always the "flip side," as it were, of contemplation, which he understands as reception of the Good.[90] By analogy, the self-production of the Good is not an imposition on a void, the bringing to be of something not already there. Or rather, if it is in *some* sense the self-generation from nothing, as we saw in the passage quoted above (ἐξ οὐδενός), because otherwise it would not be generation at all, this self-generation nevertheless coincides "equiprimordially," we might say, with a radical self-reception. Let us see how this is so.

Though (for reasons we will discuss at the end) this self-reception does not receive the same emphasis as the self-production, not only is it necessarily implied in the paradox of God's *both* being what he wills (self-production) *and* willing what he is (self-reception), but it comes to direct expression in one of the most astonishing affirmations in all of ancient philosophy: "And he, that same self, is lovable and love and love of himself" (6.8.15.1), or in other words, if Aristotelian *nous* is thinking thinking thinking, the Good is loving loving loving.[91] God is at once subject of love, object of love, and loving union of the two. As Plotinus explains in his treatise on love (see *Ennead* 3.5.1), eros is essentially a *being-moved* by the beautiful, or, in other words, by desire for the good.[92] The fact that desire implies some sort of incompleteness, some not-yet-ness, is of course why Plato famously denies eros of the gods,[93] and Plotinus echoes this denial in that particular treatise, which is after all a commentary on the *Symposium*. But in 6.8 he goes so far as to affirm, not just receptive eros, but other-dependent *desire* in God: in God, substance and desire are one and the same (6.8.15.8). The boldness of this affirmation becomes apparent when we recall that Plotinus earlier denied freedom of desire because desire implies the passivity of being led.[94] Rather than simply *deny* desire of God for this reason, he affirms it and "removes" the imperfection it entails by making it simultaneous with *being*, which implies a "need" that has always already been perfectly met; but the identification of being and desire nevertheless means that Plotinus recognizes some kind of perfection in reception. To be sure, Plotinus prefaced all of this with the "disclaimer" that it was all going to be "improper" speech. It nevertheless remains the case that this description of God's freedom as self-will in self-love and self-desire brings to imperfect expression *something nevertheless true*. Again, it is simply the implication of absolute goodness as the first principle of all things.

To the objection that the paradox that God's production of himself is at the very same time a loving reception of what he already is is nothing more than a logical contradiction,[95] we can give a brief answer, though we need to flag the importance it will turn out to have for our discussions in later chapters. It is obvious that two relatively opposed states of affairs cannot come *before* each other at a single moment of time, or even more obviously in successive moments. It is not uncommon to distinguish in this case between chronological and logical priority, or between chronological and metaphysical dependence, to say that a thing can be *metaphysically* dependent on some thing that nevertheless comes *after* it chronologically (i.e., merely physically). The temporal exclusivity is avoided by positing a metatemporal reference point.[96] But Plotinus goes even deeper than this. The "problem" implied in the paradox he affirms is not *only* a chronological one but *also* a logical one. Each "horn," so to speak, of the paradox *logically* presupposes the other. Plotinus's powerful solution to this problem is to recall that the Good not only transcends *nature*, and therefore time, but also transcends *being* (as *ousia*) and therefore eternity: the Good, beyond being, is "before eternity" (πρὶν αἰῶνα, 6.8.20.25). It is absolute *firstness*; nothing at all exists, in nature or in being or in logic, that is not preceded by the Good.[97] This absolute transcendence, once again, is not at all contrary to reason in the sense of falling into both sides of a mutually exclusive dichotomy at once, and thus falling into contradiction, because it precedes the very distinction. It is important to recognize this absolute firstness if we are to grasp the crucial point that follows.

We have suggested that the most basic metaphysical issue at the heart of the meaning of freedom is the relation between potency and act. The absolute transcendence of God has profound implications for the meaning of act and potency and their relation to each other, and thus profound implications for the meaning of freedom. Here, too, we have a couplet, a set of relatively opposed notions. As we discussed at length in *Freedom from Reality*,[98] for Aristotle, whose permanent philosophical achievement it is to have introduced the notions, potency and act are inseparable from each other: potency is the ability to bring about act (or, passively, the ability to allow act to be brought about), and act is the realization of potency. The two are reciprocally dependent on each other, but the dependence is asymmetrical. If potency has a relative priority to act in one respect,[99] act has an absolute priority to potency. Plotinus adopts this Aristotelian understanding, but at the same time he transforms it from within,[100] just as he transforms the meaning of intellect (pure actuality), and for the very same reason: he rereads these in light of the absolute transcendence of the Good. To make the point as clearly as possible, he does not reject the Aristotelian notion of perfection as pure act but rereads that affirmation from a perspective that exceeds Aristotle's vision, at least in its explicit articulation—namely, from the perspective of the (Platonic) Good. In other words, the point is not to deny that God is pure act but to insist that this be interpreted truly *purely*, and not in any simple opposition to potency as passivity. As we have constantly affirmed from the beginning of volume 1, the heart of the classical vision of reality is the priority of actuality over potency. Plotinus affirms this point unequivocally (which is, again, why he can be seen as a culmination of the classical tradition),[101] and this leads him to posit the first principle as most perfect,[102] that is, not imperfect or unfinished at all. He goes so far as to describe the Good as something defined, definite, or determinate:

ὡρισμένον (6.8.9.10)—literally, being circumscribed by a horizon.[103] The Greeks, as Heidegger among others has brought so powerfully to light, identified perfection and finitude, because the "infinite" is formless and so incomplete.[104] This classical affirmation leads Plotinus to describe God's freedom as absolute actuality, the highest act to which any and all subsequent potency can be reduced (*anagogē*).[105]

But at this point we encounter once again a wonderful mystery. Plotinus's reflections raise two difficulties regarding the conception of divine freedom as pure act, at least insofar as that is simply *opposed* to potency as its contrary, without further qualification. First, insofar as act is generally interpreted in relation to potency, it implies a kind of realization of what (as potency) is not yet realized, which means that the notion cannot be separated in reason from some sort of in-completeness. In more concrete terms, we cannot think of actuality without at least implicitly thinking of something *happening*—if not an actual change, at least a fulfillment or an exercise . . . of power. But this conception of fulfillment requires a reduction to a higher actuality that is not the realization of any potency.[106] In this respect, "pure act," if that actuality is simply isolated from all potency without qualification, cannot be ultimate. Aristotle's God cannot be the "godly God." Making act, as the contrary to potency, supreme, again without qualification, would lead to an infinite regress. What we need to affirm is not an actuality that is the absence of all potency in the sense of being exclusive of it (which would then be its contrary) but an actuality that transcends this opposition—and therefore a kind of "superactuality." Aristotle himself says, after all, that "no contrary is the first principle of all things in the full sense; the first principle is something different."[107] Second, actuality implies determinateness, as we just affirmed, but while this determinateness is perfectly fitting for (Aristotle's) intellect, as it were, it is not fitting for the *principle* of intellect, (Plato's) Good beyond being. Determinateness is finitude, and the absolute origin of all finite things cannot be itself finite.[108] The Good must therefore be, not exactly infinite and thus indeterminate (which would *oppose* it in the problematic way we have just described to finitude and determinacy), but rather suprafinite and supradeterminate. Though the Good is what the reduction of potency to act leads to, Plotinus affirms this role and yet sees that the best description for the highest is not (just) "pure actuality" but "all power" (δύναμιν πᾶσαν, 6.8.9.45–46). For this reason, Plotinus can affirm—recalling, of course, that the terms are understood analogously—*both* that God is pure actuality *and* that God is pure potency,[109] because he is prior to the distinction between them. Aristotle's vision of God as *nous* is both indispensable and inadequate. We will come back to this point in our discussion of Aquinas, below, to see that the medieval thinker is closer to Plotinus on this point than is generally recognized.

This insight radically transforms the meaning of each. Thus conceived, absolute actuality is an energy that does not accomplish anything, or, lest this sound like radical frustration and vanity, that accomplishes nothing but itself as, so to speak, pure accomplishment, or better as the constantly surging energy of accomplishing (which thus does not simply come to a rest as finished). Plotinus distinguishes between actuality as a completion (ἐνέργημα, 6.8.16.17–18) and the abidingly active actualizing (ἐνέργεια μένουσα, 6.8.9.16) that belongs most properly to the One.[110] And potency is thus not a void, an emptiness waiting to receive or an imperfection awaiting completion, but now an overfullness that is essentially productive, a superabundance that does not simply produce, as we will see in a moment, but *allows* to come to be.[111] The freedom that God *is* is not an empty power to accomplish what it will, or by contrast the already-completed accomplishment itself, but the perfection of both at once: potent actuality or superactual potency. If it is true that Plotinus tends most often to refer to the One as the productive potency of all things,[112] it nevertheless makes sense that, in this treatise on God's freedom, he speaks more often of God as actuality, for in contrast to the more common reflection on the One from the perspective of its effects (a reflection that follows the *via negativa*), in this treatise, as we remarked at the outset, Plotinus ventures a unique inquiry into God's inner life. The "positive" language of actuality thus dominates here. But, again, there is no opposition between these different emphases.

Freedom Granted

Plotinus's radical reconception of potency and act on the basis of the absolutely transcendent Good has extraordinary implications for the meaning of freedom "beyond" the Good, so to speak, though we have to draw on texts outside of 6.8 to see it. The ultimate unity of act and potency, or more precisely their sharing in a common principle, implies a living and radiant complexity in the causal structure that organizes the Plotinian hierarchy of being. If actuality were nothing more than already-accomplished fact, and potency were nothing more than purely passive availability for the imposition of form, then we would have a simple "top-down" schema, with no contribution whatsoever "from below," as it were. The lower levels would be nothing but a *fall from* the higher. Now, to be sure Plotinus's philosophy is indeed radically "from above" in character, the notion of the lower as a fall from the higher is a central theme, and he insists on the utter passivity of matter, in contrast to Aristotle, for whom matter and form enter into a kind of composition, so that for Plotinus matter represents pure absence and thus in a fundamental respect *evil*.[113] Nevertheless, if this were all we could find in Plotinus, we would fundamentally misunderstand him. There is also a "divine" potency, which is at the same time a superabundant actuality, in relation to which actual act as accomplished reality represents a kind of restriction.[114]

This is an extraordinarily subtle and weighty point, so it is crucial to be precise. The reason δύναμις πάντων is a more proper description of God for Plotinus than simply "pure act" is that it signals precisely a superabundance: *dunamis* in the One means containing all things already in a kind of nonactual condition, a preformed state.[115] The upshot of this conception is not at all to divinize incompleteness but to radicalize generosity. Actuality remains an ultimate perfection, but now the One may be conceived precisely as *giving* that perfection,[116] as it were, to what is *not* the One—in the first place, to intellect, but from there to all things that have form at any level. This is why Plotinus's "retrieval" of the Platonic Good is not an overturning of Aristotle and his affirmation of the ultimacy of the pure act of intellect, but a transformation of it literally *from within*. The actuality of intellect is not a once-and-for-all accomplishment, or better it is not *only* this, but an *ever-actual* desiring and being satisfied.[117] We also see that a fundamentally positive reading can be given of the notorious "disinterestedness" of the One, which is turned simply to itself "rather than" to the world, as one often hears.[118] The One does not "actively" perfect what is other than itself, like some maddeningly omnipresent Helicopter Parent,[119] but allows and en-ables things, as it were, *to perfect themselves*, giving them the "dynamic energy" that makes such self-creation possible.[120] Or, to put the point more adequately, he interprets the One's perfecting of all things *as* their (participated and so received) self-enacting self-perfection. In this case, then, the perfection that any given being enacts, because it is a particular sharing in a higher, "overfull" potency,[121] is always and at every level *more* than mere self-perfection; one's very own actuality is in every case without exception an actuality that exceeds one's own borders,[122] and so is at the same time a productive power that generates even more: "Actuality everywhere reveals completely hidden potency" (4.8.5.33–34). (This, incidentally, is why matter has to be radical nothingness without any actuality at all, or we could say why complete nothingness plays the ultimate role of matter, without which we would end with an infinite regress.)[123] The generosity, or generativity, of perfection is the essential "ethos" of Plotinus's philosophy.[124]

It is a recognition of this "ethos" that allows us to make sense of a profoundly illuminating series of chapters from *Ennead* 4.8, "On the Descent of the Soul," which presents Plotinus's understanding of human embodiment. Given the standard view of Plotinus, one expects to find here a view of this descent as a *fall* from perfection, and one finds what one expects. But one finds much more.[125] While Plotinus's philosophy is indeed a radically "top-down" philosophy, we discover here that this is a top-down movement that is *truly* and *radically* generative, to such an extent that we can speak of the lower making a contribution (which of course turns out to be always already anticipated), that is, representing something positive, a real manifestation of abundance rather than a falling short of an ideal. Thus, Plotinus says that, if the One were to remain simply in itself, it would represent a kind of *deficiency*, because it would indicate a kind of stinginess (4.8.6.1–17).[126] There is a kind of revelation in this movement of what would otherwise remain unknown and in a certain sense unreal. It is important to see that this is not, however, a movement from the imperfect to the perfect; instead, it is a "looking back" from superabundant perfection to the "earlier" perfection that has been, as it were, superabounded.

The positive movement of real revelation becomes especially clear in the soul's relation to the body. According to Plotinus, the powers of the soul are able to be *manifest* in the body, to bring about works and productions (ἔργα τε καὶ ποιήσεις) that would otherwise remain hidden and indeed would otherwise not exist (4.8.5.27–36).[127] Thus, there is a sense that the higher not only gives to the lower but also in some sense *receives* from it (4.8.7.7–9); the soul becomes *even more* by virtue of its embodiment: it acquires a *history* (ἱστορίαν), Plotinus says (note the term!), which teaches it better what eternity is.[128] Something good happens by virtue of the soul's life in the body, something good that can happen in no other way. This dramatic engagement introduces "sights and experience" the soul could not have received simply through contemplation of eternal being.[129] The Soul thus can be said to possess not only what is above but also what is below, that which it really produces as something that did not previously exist in reality.[130] Again, it is crucial to note that this movement is not a mere movement from potency to act in the normal, Aristotelian sense, which would turn God into an imperfection that needs creation, so to speak, to find realization, to complete himself, and which, by extension, would turn the soul into an imperfection that the body thus "fulfills."[131] It is, rather, an overfullness that discovers the genuine novelty of the fruit it bears as nevertheless an expression of what it always already is in itself. The Good is perfect, not by being (statically) the best, but by being constantly "ever greater."

Let us return to Plotinus's interpretation of human freedom in 6.8, now on the basis of this insight into the superabundance of actuality. We saw that a free act is a participation in the Good, which is simultaneously transcendent and immanent—that is, both a heteronomous and an autonomous power. The *more* an act is done *in the Good*, the more it is *in one's own power* (6.8.4.37–38). The generosity of the Good, as "productive power," now allows us more clearly to see why this is so. As Plotinus explains in 6.8.13.21–24, in subjection to the Good, three things happen, so to speak, at once: a thing wills precisely *itself*, its substance receives perfecting definition, and the thing *belongs* properly to itself. Plotinus goes so far as to say that, to the extent that a thing is, it possesses, along with its substance, the very cause of its existence (!) (τῆς ὑποστάσεως τὴν αἰτίαν, 6.8.14.21–22), which nevertheless does not imply that the Good is not the cause.[132] Quite to the contrary. The absolute and total causality of the Good does not *exclude* the self-causality of everything else but "necessarily" *includes* it. It is the implication of the Good being simply what it is, the productive power of all things.

78 LATE ANTIQUITY

This becomes especially clear in Plotinus's discussion of (the Stoic problem of) fate and divine providence in *Enneads* 3.1, 3.2, and 3.3. Here he insists that the total comprehensiveness of divine providence must nevertheless include true human initiative—or else there would be nothing to "provide" for (3.2.9)! We are reminded here of the absurdity of God pulling puppet strings without any audience, which we mentioned at the outset of this book. Note the echo, in this text, of what we called the Jewish sense of the drama of the encounter between divine and human freedom. The human soul, indeed *each individual human soul*, is not just the endlessly repetitive expression of a pregiven form, like a seed that simply unfolds what it simply already *was* in the past, but a self-initiating, literally "pro-active" (προτουργοῦ) *first principle* (ἀρχή) of its own (3.1.8.6–9).[133] Thus, it is not just the *Good* that is ἀρχή: "Men are first principles too" (3.2.10.19), they are moved to noble actions by their own nature, and this principle is free and independent, master of itself: αὐτεξούσιος (3.2.10.21). In doing the good, the human soul wills itself, receives definition, possesses itself . . . and becomes itself a *first cause*, a production of what is "new." It brings about new events in history. The frequently repeated saw that Plotinus denies freedom, both human and divine, is a caricature.[134] It is truer to say he is the first Greek thinker to see freedom in its glory.[135]

CONCLUSION

Let us, in conclusion, attempt to summarize Plotinus's conception of freedom and its significance and then set into relief a latent difficulty. The classical conception of freedom entails a reduction of potency to actuality, an approach that, for all its benefits, would seem to reduce the other-directed appetitive movements of desire and will ultimately to the perfect self-possession of intellect. By tracing this intellectual self-possession *itself* back to an even more original principle, Plotinus opens freedom up to what we might call an "ecstatic" dimension, thus offering room, so to speak, in principle for the novelty of the externality of desire, the body, history, and spontaneity, to find its proper place in a whole that remains nonetheless intelligible. In the course of the treatise, Plotinus presented common notions of will and freedom—

as self-possession, as power, as self-determination, as intentionally directed will, as the contentedness of intellectual contemplation, and as capacity to choose between alternatives—all of which he showed to be less than ultimate, but without rejecting any of them altogether. Instead, they turn out to have their best sense as rooted in a most ultimate kind of freedom, which we might describe as the power to generate, indeed, to *originate*, new and good things, precisely as the fruit of a perfection that is both received and actively achieved. The creativity of the will is radicalized in Plotinus's thought insofar as its "poetic" dimension is revealed as more fundamental than its merely "practical" dimension, so that, if it remains true that immanent activity (*praxis*) is freer than that which is directed to some merely external end, it is nevertheless true that praxis itself is more poetic the more it is a participation in God, the poetic power of all things. If choice and thus power and control are a *kind* of freedom, this radical generosity is a superfreedom: in this self-originating participation in superabundant goodness, one is "more than free and more than autonomous" (6.8.15.23–24).

Nevertheless, having said that, we must also mark a fundamental ambiguity or even a tension in Plotinus's formulation. We noted the astonishing affirmation of eros and desire in God, which implies a kind of receptivity in God himself. The boldness of this insight cannot be overlooked or dismissed. Nevertheless, it is also necessary to acknowledge that Plotinus is unable to sustain this insight, given the (Greek) resources of his thinking, which is why scholars have regularly suggested that, in his treatment of freedom, Plotinus straightforwardly deviates from his usual philosophy.[136] The tension can be formulated thus: while contemplation, the inferior's radical self-reception from the superior, generally represents the principle of production, it would seem that, precisely because of its receptivity, the contemplative moment would have to be eliminated at the highest level, *even though* we have here the most perfect productivity. This elimination, however, not only threatens the perfection of contemplative reception below but also denies the principle that Plotinus regularly affirms, namely, that everything good in a thing derives from its causal source, which implies that it is there in that source *in some respect*.[137] To formulate the tension from the other direction: the absolute "firstness" of God (even, paradoxically, with respect to himself!) is an indispensable part of freedom and the will, the priority of full actuality and generosity. But this "firstness" seems to require a reduction of freedom, in the end, to the sheer power to produce, and so beyond any intelligible conformity to the pregiven good. The *Euthyphro* problem thus reappears at the level of God's absolute will: if the will is simply responsive to the Good, we have empty potency at the origin; if it is *not* responsive, but simply productive, we have absolute power at the origin. In either case, the good is replaced by will as potency, in the dual form of *potentia*.

Thus, Plotinus relentlessly eliminates any receptive dimension to the Good's "self-relation," so much so that this "self-relation" cannot actually be relational. The *poiēsis* he identifies with will can be a pure *making*, he says, but not in any sense something *made*, insofar as this would imply what we might call some kind of "secondary," incompatible with the absolute *firstness* of the One.[138] It is only at the level of *intellect* that we discover a perfection of contemplative reception, but intellect is decidedly and unambiguously subordinate, that is, inferior, to the One.[139] If priority of the object—being—predominates in intellect, priority of the *subject* predominates in the One, which is *principally* self as (producing) power. Here we have the absolute priority of *self* (*to auto*) as productivity over being and nature.[140] The One, Plotinus states categorically, is not able to receive in any sense at all from what is other (6.8.17.27), for it would thereby cease to be the One. But how can it in fact generate itself in an eternal generation (γεννήσει ἀιδίῳ, 6.8.20.28) if it is not in any respect at all *generated* by itself? To put the problem in a nutshell, is it possible for what is secondary to be first without ceasing to be secondary? This is what the internal logic of Plotinus's position appears to require but does not succeed in delivering.

It is worth noting that, in Plotinus, we come upon a deep dilemma that is analogous to the one we saw at the heart of the Jewish vision of covenant. As we saw in chapter 1, covenant is an extension of relation, and covenant is the essential expression of God's will, so much so that even the creation of the world has a covenantal form. But how can the *original* expression of will be an *extension* of relation, an expanding of what is already given? There is a danger that thus radicalizing covenant undermines it, because the most basic instance of will becomes a sheer imposition from outside or from above. Similarly in Plotinus: freedom can be a communication of goodness only if it is in some respect a reception of goodness as (already) given, and this does not seem possible at the origin. But if this is not possible, then relation simply cannot be ultimate, nor can belonging to what is other, or receiving what is good rather than generating it from first to last.[141] Receiving qua receiving cannot be essential, here, to the deepest meaning of freedom. If there is a kind of encounter between freedoms in Plotinus's account of providence,[142] in the end it is simply impossible to speak of any genuine exchange, and so any love as reciprocal bond, between God and his creatures. Instead, what is ultimate is finally a dissolution of relationality *tout court*: as Plotinus famously puts it at the very end of all the *Enneads*, the proper end of life is "being alone with the Alone."[143]

This does not mean, however, that one cannot do with Plotinus's thought what Plotinus does with Aristotle, namely, take it up, affirm its fundamental truth, but then nevertheless transform it from within, bringing out possibilities that were unforeseen by the insight itself and at the same time bringing it to surprising fulfillment (this is freedom!). To see whether and to what extent this happens is the point of our investigation into the Christian appropriation of the classical tradition.

CHAPTER 3

Augustine and the Gift of the Power to Choose

Baptizing Classical Thought

If Plotinus argued that the total comprehensiveness of divine providence does not eliminate the genuine originality of human action, Augustine *demonstrates* this truth, so to speak, from the inside. In his attention to the drama of human freedom, the call to make a choice in the concrete circumstances of human history, he draws out the existential reality that complements Plotinus's more "epic" ontological account, and does so with a new, biblically inspired sense of God's actual, personal involvement. The two figures together, Plotinus and Augustine, thus offer, in their polarity, a deep and textured insight into the spirit of late antiquity, in which the Western notion of freedom may properly be said to have been born.

Augustine may not be the "discoverer" of the will, as many have suggested and many more have disputed, but his fundamental importance for the development of the will and its freedom in Western thought ought not therefore to be overlooked. Augustine is especially significant for our study insofar as he is one in whom the transition from the classical world to the Christian world, and the reception of the classical world into the Christian world, takes place, so to speak, in the flesh. He was classically educated—indeed, formed to be a classical *educator*—

and, though not very proficient in Greek, read widely and deeply in the philosophies of the Hellenistic age, according a special status to the Platonists.[1] But his conversion was radical, and led him to immerse himself in the world of the scriptures, which initially provoked a resistance in him precisely because of their foreignness to the glory of the classical world.[2] His acquiescence in this matter did not force him to leave behind his classical learning but prompted him instead to think it all through anew in the light of the central Christian mysteries. In John Rist's apt phrase, Augustine represents "ancient thought baptized."[3] As it turns out—and not incidentally, we suggest—one of the most prominent fruits of this baptism is a deep and rich vision of freedom.

We do not intend here to offer a complete exposition of Augustine's notion of freedom, concerning which there is quite an abundance of scholarly literature.[4] Instead, we will proceed in a more synthetic fashion and attempt to take stock of the extent to which the particular perspective we have been developing in this book allows us to cast a new light on relatively familiar themes. Let us begin with a general characterization of the sources of Augustine's notion of freedom. It is typically observed that Augustine's notion represents a convergence of Stoic and Platonic elements:[5] on the one hand, we see the imprint of the Stoic psychology on the decisive emphasis Augustine gives to things such as impulse, assent, and deliberate choice, as well as his profound sense of the importance of the *eph' hēmin*, the will as concerned with what is *in our power*. As we will unfold below, for Augustine, our choices and our actions come in an irreducible way, and whatever else is said, *from us*. On the other hand, recognition of this responsibility and self-determination ought *not* to lead one to suppose, as the libertarian interpreters do,[6] that Augustine posited a detached "faculty" of will as a power under the deliberate control of the "sovereign" self, interpreted as one who chooses *ad libitum*, so to speak, between the more or less equally possible alternatives of good and evil.[7] Rist has argued that the notion of will as a "faculty" is a much later "invention," falsely attributed to Augustine by those who are ignorant of the sources of Augustine's thought, which include, not only the Stoics, but even more basically the Platonists.[8] The reason these latter are especially important is that the recognition of their influence allows us to appreciate the fundamental role of *love* in Augustine's understanding of the will. Indeed, as we will show in a moment, Augustine ultimately *identifies* will and love.[9] The reason this is crucial is that love is inconceivable apart from a being-moved by another,[10] which means that, if Augustine *embraces* Stoic self-determination, as he clearly does,[11] he nevertheless affirms this self-movement as having its place only *inside of* the receptivity of attraction to the good, in a manner that will require more detailed exposition. The will, for Augustine, is not a separate and discretely operational faculty of a soul wholly in its own power but the *whole soul* considered in its relation to what is other than itself.[12] Failure to grasp this fundamental dimension of the Augustinian will, according to Rist, is one of the deep sources of the modern sense of freedom as sheer power to choose.[13]

Fundamentally in agreement with the basic description of the Augustinian notion of freedom as integrating Stoic elements into a Platonic vision, we nevertheless wish to point out that it begs a basic question: Why does Augustine synthesize these particular philosophical streams? Is it just because these philosophies happened to be current at the time, that these are the philosophies he happened to find particularly interesting? Without denying the historical contingency that is part of the constitution of every thinker, we nevertheless propose that the elements stood out for Augustine because of their *truth*, first of all, but also because they seemed especially apt for the Christian interpretation of the human person in relation to God, or more specifically in relation to the "theodrama" of creation and redemption.[14] To put the point succinctly, more fundamental than the synthesis of Stoics and Platonists, what distinguishes Augustine's vision of freedom is the synthesis of Greeks (and Romans) and Jews that represents the conceptual heart of Christianity. Only from this ultimate perspective do we find the proper place for the great variety of affirmations Augustine makes in his admittedly unsystematic account.[15] While we cannot offer a full exposition of the currents of the classical and Jewish traditions as taken up and transformed in the light of Christian revelation in Augustine's work as a whole, which would require a book of its own, we may nevertheless attend to pivotal moments in his account of freedom and consider the particular fruits that the Augustinian synthesis bears for the meaning of freedom more generally.

WILL AS TRINITARIAN LOVE

We do best by beginning, so to speak, *da capo*. The doctrine of the Trinity, we have suggested at several junctures, lies at the heart of the Christian synthesis of Greek and Jew, absolute goodness and personal will, that is decisive for the proper understanding of freedom. Augustine was of course one of the foundational figures in the development of Trinitarian theology,[16] and his interpretation of this mystery is an indispensable reference point for understanding what he means by will.[17] The connection between the notion of God as Trinity and the nature of freedom becomes evident when we recall the difficulty that the absence of a Trinitarian notion of God poses for Plotinus: his "subordinationist" sense of the "Three Hypostases" entails a radical tension between his general affirmation of contemplation at the root of all creative action, that is, all freedom, and the absolute unoriginateness of the One, who is "freedom itself." In Plotinus's vision, God in his absolute nonreceptivity threatens thus to become the simple *opposite* of everything else, which is defined by radical dependence. But this runs contrary to the constant drift of Plotinus's thinking. The One's "loving loving loving," which radically transcends the "thinking thinking thinking" of *Nous*, will cease to have any recognizable analogy to love to the extent that it is emptied of all receptive desire, which it must be if it is affirmed as sheer productive will, a making without a made. The ascription of love to God will tend to be, not only a *mere* metaphor, but a straightforward mistake. But Trinity implies that God is absolutely unoriginate *and also* that God is begotten, and indeed that God is the perfect unity of the two. Ironically, it is Augustine who is able to do more justice to (the Greek) eros than Plotinus to the extent that he recognizes the *receptive* dimension of "being from" as *coequal with divine fontality*.[18] As Lewis Ayres has put it succinctly, the doctrine of the Trinity—absolute simplicity of divine nature coinciding with radical affirmation of really (and not only notionally) different Persons—allows Augustine to attribute to *God* what Plotinus has to distribute between the One and the *Nous*, so to speak.[19] Augustine's God is thus One who is *both* "loving loving loving" and "thinking thinking thinking," which means not only that his notion of love does more justice to the Platonic insight into receptive desire but also that it is more mind-ful, more thoroughly intelligent in principle, than Plotinus's notion—or at the very least less ambiguous on this point—and so, again, more fully *Greek*.[20]

We ought to consider, in this context, how Augustine's conception here represents a solution to the *Euthyphro* problem that differs in an important respect from the response given by Plotinus. Robert-Henri Cousineau observed that Augustine's "Deus-Amor," drawn from Christian revelation, is a synthesis of the Deus-Bonus (of the Greeks) and the Deus-Volens (of the Jews), which overcomes what might otherwise have presented an unsurpassable dilemma.[21] We saw that, for Plotinus, divine freedom ultimately means that God wills what he is and is what he wills, so that there is no aspect of God's selfhood that is not willed. And yet, to make this point, Plotinus apparently has to transcend God's being and intellect in a unilateral way to reach a pure will, which is productivity without product. Augustine, by contrast, is able to carry through Plotinus's insight into the reciprocity of will and being more completely by giving will substance, so to speak. Intellect and being are, for Augustine, not secondary, but coequal with will. Will, in this case, is not productivity without production, a notion that will have a tendency to reduce simply to potency, but instead productivity *and* production; in other words, it is also complete and perfect even in its infinity. Will is love *as already perfect*, and so not just endless aspiration but also contemplative delight. Thus, we might say that there is not the tiniest "part" of the being of God that is not willed, but also that there is not the tiniest "part" of God's will that is not "full" of being and truth. Being is "shot through" with will, and will is "shot through" with being. The transcendence is no longer unilateral but now always also bilateral. This means that a fundamental place will be opened up for reciprocity, beyond what could have been anticipated with Plotinus's view of the absolutely unoriginate "One."

This reciprocity shows itself clearly in Augustine's vision at both the beginning and the end, so to speak, of the journey of the human soul. To illustrate by means of a comparison: it would be too much to say that the Platonic good is a merely passive object of the soul's aspiring eros, always just "there" and available, for Plato shows an acute sense of the drama that begins when the soul is *suddenly* (*exaiphnēs*) *struck* by beauty, which breaks into the soul, as it were, and draws it upwards.[22] But after this initial moment, the drama cannot be sustained in the Platonic world, since it becomes entirely one-sided; the good may be a "mover" of the soul but only by remaining itself altogether "unmoved." It is crucial to see that Augustine does not at all deny the "immovable" perfection of God[23]— in other words, he does not at all reject the Greek insight into the absoluteness of goodness, truth, and beauty—but he nevertheless affirms the dramatic encounter, not as incidental to eros, but as essential in it. The dramatic moment of encounter between the soul and God does not lie *only* at the beginning but also continues all the way through to the end. We note that Augustine personally *addresses* the Good all the way through the *Confessions*; the soul's introspection is altogether dialogical. The initial "moment" of the encounter is not simply the sudden realization of what was already the case, the discovery of an eternal object *to be pursued* (though it is of course always *also* this), but more profoundly a recognition that he himself is being pursued, so to speak.[24] The initial encounter itself is an invitation into relationship, which means that the love that results does not *first* originate in the soul, as it does in Plato,[25] but is first *offered* to the soul as something *already perfect*. This is to say that it is not (only) the distant Good that calls forth love but the actual presence of love that does so: "There is no greater invitation to love than prevenient love."[26] The *end* of the pursuit, for Augustine, is therefore not the absolute nonrelation of being "alone with the Alone" but retains forever the character of relation: Augustine refers to this highest fulfillment as an "adherence to God," or as a "clinging to God," or even as a "friendship with God,"[27] an expression one cannot imagine in Plotinus. Goodness in general is not (only) an object that allows friendship, as it is in Aristotle, but is ultimately identical with the order of harmonious relation in communion; Augustine famously argues that goodness, at whatever level it subsists, simply *is* peace.[28] Eschatological fulfillment is therefore a *fellowship* (*societas*) with God. Because of the absoluteness of relationship that this implies, this fellowship is nonexclusive (in one respect at least): fellowship with God is, at once, fellowship with all others in God.[29] The final state of completeness is not (only) utter solitude; it is a *City*.

In short, Augustine both takes up and transforms Greek thought by "personalizing" the Good, so to speak, in the light of the Trinity, bringing out more directly its *social* character: "The [pagan] philosophies hold the view that the life of the wise man should be social; and in this we support them much more heartily!"[30] We see this inherently social character of goodness come out perhaps most directly in book 8, the central book, of Augustine's *De Trinitate*. There he first presents God as absolute Truth, in chapter 1, and then in chapter 2 as the Goodness of all good things. We might see these descriptions as gathering up both Aristotle and Plato. But book 8 culminates in the insight, beyond these aspects, that God is love, the "personal" integration of all goodness and truth.

This recognition of God as personal helps us, moreover, to see how Augustine's conception of the Trinity brings the Jewish sense of God to a transforming fulfillment. First, we need to see that the Trinity reveals the perfection of what we have described as the "covenantal" sense of will. Love, which Augustine identifies as a proper name in the Trinity for the Holy Spirit, has the character not in the first place of appetitive motion but of "already" established *bond*, though this does not exclude desire but essentially includes it.[31] Moreover, insofar as this love, or will in its most perfect form, is itself *God*, and not simply God's activity *ad extra*, it reveals will to be most basically the actually given relationship, rather than the mere capacity to establish one—that is, the power to effect a relation. Augustine does not have a principally "dynamic" notion of the Trinity, such as one finds in the Chaldean Oracles in one sense,[32] and in Victorinus in another,[33] which implies a transition from unformed potency to formed actuality. Instead, Augustine's notion of the Trinity is always already *relational* (Pierre Hadot's term). To return to the point we made in chapter 1, the act of creation is not the introduction of relation from an utterly unrelated monad, so to speak, "ex nihilo," but comes from relation already eternally established: God *is* love.[34]

This leads us to a second point. Covenant, as we saw, is understood as the *extension* of kinship, which means it is not just a bond but a bond that communicates itself, that is open to broadening its scope, as it were. Self-communication, as it turns out, is the very essence of goodness, as Plotinus showed at the summit of Greek thought. Freedom as the generous sharing of a bond is crucial to Augustine; he observes that the proper name of the Spirit is not just *love* but also *gift*.[35] He thus sees the (already-)related-ness of love as not exclusive but open to being ever more inclusive.[36] One of the most immediate ways this dimension "turns up" is in Augustine's notion of the love that God is as something *given* away to man, to such an extent that the love that God is reveals itself to be the love (also) that binds people to each other. The Jewish covenant between God and man, which is reflected in the covenants human beings form with each other, is revealed to be the very "essence" of God,[37] so that the reflection no longer simply points to a transcendent reality but marks an immanent presence. Human love thus comes to present a unique analogy—not, again, as simple desire or disposition, or power to establish relation, but in the covenantal form as lover, beloved, and bond between them—that makes God in principle as universally accessible as the Good in itself. Indeed, even more so: if eros is the mediation between the human and utterly transcendent divine, and the Jewish Covenant is mediation from above, Christian love is the accomplished relation "in our midst."[38]

THE RECIPROCITY OF EROS AND OBEDIENCE

Let us unfold this last point more fully. Rist has called our attention to the way Augustine's reflection on the Trinity reveals the essence of will, not just as self-determining power, but as love. We have complemented his observation by pointing out that, if the Holy Spirit is the personal disclosure of the meaning of will, the proper name of the Spirit is not only Love but also Gift. This suggests that "gift" also reveals a fundamental truth about the nature of the will and so the nature of freedom. The etymological roots of freedom ring out in this name, to be sure: freedom as creative self-outpouring is freedom as gift. But Augustine's sense of Gift as the proper name, not of the unoriginate Father first of all, but of the Third Person as *from* the Father *and* the Son—brings out the reciprocity of gift, and so also the receptive dimension.

Let us turn at this point in a more focused way to the human experience of freedom as Augustine describes it to see further how its gift character integrates Greek and Jewish dimensions. In the Christian vocabulary, "gift" is signaled in the term *grace*, and grace is of course a fundamental theme in Augustine's reflections on freedom, especially in his more mature writings. Rist has proposed that, in order to understand the significance of grace in Augustine's understanding of freedom, we need to interpret grace in light of Greek thought; as he puts it, in Augustine, "Grace has come to perform the role of Platonic eros."[39] But we suggest that to see the full scope of the significance of grace on this score requires a recognition also of the Jewish note that is struck in Augustine's notion, namely, the role of obedience to God's commands, and indeed how these roles become inseparably joined. In general terms, Augustine's Trinitarian conception of God casts a new light on the Jewish sense of obedience, which is, we might say, the reflection in the human will of the absoluteness of God, as we argued in chapter 1. But just as Plotinian generativity threatens to become distorted into pure productivity unless it is redeemed, so to speak, by a Trinitarian concept of God, so too Jewish obedience threatens to turn into sheer heteronomy. The absolute "unilaterality" is overcome when we recognize that the obedience demanded is not simply imposed but, like love itself, *given* as something that has already been brought to completion. Augustine does not simply replace this Jewish theme with something else but embraces it even while transforming it. While affirming the essential coequality of Son and Father (and indeed Holy Spirit), each of whom is wholly God, Augustine presents the Son as exercising a *perfect obedience* toward the Father: obedience to God belongs not (only) to creatures, as the Jews supposed, but even more radically to God in himself.[40]

There are two implications of this Trinitarian overcoming of merely unilateral obedience. The first comes to light as a result of the radical immanence of God in creation. For Augustine, obedience to God and his law is never a mere heteronomy, the subordination of the self to an extrinsic law, but (paradoxically) a subordination of the self to the innermost principle of the self, which is to say, a subordination of the self to the self (in image of the Son's obedience to the Father, which is *both* a subordination and *not* a subordination):[41] disobedience to God is *always* and *necessarily* a disobedience to oneself.[42] This is because God is not (merely) a transcendent *other* but, as Plotinus also emphasized, at the very same time "more interior to me than I am to myself."[43] Obedience in this respect acquires a teleological depth, which is to say that obedience presents itself as *good*, in philosophical terms, or in other words reveals a convergence with eros.[44]

The convergence of obedience with eros leads us to the second implication, which is that Augustine's notion moves beyond heteronomy without simply collapsing into autonomy. On the one hand, it sustains more clearly the *paradox* of God's simultaneous transcendence and immanence: he not only moves the will from within but simultaneously commands it from without, though of course, as we just observed, the command is itself ultimately *desirable*, which indicates it is not pure heteronomy. In this case, the will is not simply moved *by* the good that it desires but is at the same time responsive to a personal will that is other, an agency of its own.[45] Reciprocity, so to speak, goes all the way down. On the other hand, to speak *only* of eros would incline one to see this movement as nothing but attraction, nothing but a *being-moved*, which is to say that one can come to understand the movement as merely passive.[46] For Augustine, however, this is unambiguously an *active* self-moving in being moved. It is precisely obedience that brings this dimension of eros more clearly to light. One cannot obey passively, whereas one *can* desire in a merely passive way. To obey is to exercise an act of will from within oneself in conformity to something *presented to* one, and thus to direct oneself in a fully engaged way. In this respect, the law as a matter for the will, something that stands before the will with a clarity and an objectivity, is crucial for its freedom. In the law, the will is given an object, *on* which to act, in a full "agential" manner. Here we find the philosophical basis for the theme of "merit" in the classical Christian conception of man's relation to the gift of salvation.

In one of the more accomplished texts from his later period, *On the Spirit and the Letter* (ca. 412), Augustine shows in a particularly illuminating way how grace gives freedom along just these lines. In this response to the Pelagians, Augustine reflects on the way grace gives the soul its very own movement in both its receptive dimension as attraction to goodness and its active dimension as fulfillment of the law in obedience. These two dimensions are not just balanced against each other but shown to be flip sides of the same coin, so to speak. We might say that grace converts eros into obedience and obedience into eros, and this reciprocal conversion is precisely why graces *gives* freedom. There have always been readers of Augustine who interpret him as having surrendered his early position on free will, which was formulated against the Manichees, as a result of his polemics against the Pelagians.[47] From this perspective, Augustine's emphasis on the radical priority of grace in *On the Spirit* would seem to threaten the soul's self-movement. But our exploration of Plotinus in the previous chapter allows us to read this text in a different light, insofar as it shows in principle that causality from above and from below, so to speak, can be reconciled. We saw that, for Plotinus, the *power* of God that comes from above is at the same time an *enabling* power rather than a (mere) self-imposing one; it provides the ability of the *nous* (and by analogy every kind of thing, to the extent that it is an actual being at all) to *bring itself* to perfection. There is thus no necessary opposition between the determination of the Good and self-determination. This is just the point Augustine is making in the text: grace does not eliminate free will but makes it both possible and real: "Do we then by grace make void free will? God forbid! Nay, rather we establish free will. For even as the law by faith, so free will by grace, is not made void but established."[48] The Pelagians assume a fundamental competition that forces them to negotiate between relatively opposed forces; for them God can help only by giving instruction and command, which then leaves the will on its own, outside and over against this help, to exert its own effort and bring about its own work.[49] For Augustine, by contrast, God's help is *interior* to the will, without "nonrelationally" eclipsing it, which is why the *more* God gives aid, the more the will acts from itself. Again, this is not fundamentally different from Plotinus. At the same time, however, and beyond Plotinus, the aid is not merely interior, but also exterior;[50] the gift of movement is not an action *on* a merely passive receptor but a gift of active *consent*. The active dimension of the will comes to expression in the pervasive theme of grace as not eliminating the law (which might be the case if we affirmed eros in an exclusive way) but enabling the will to fulfill the divine will in obedience. Augustine thus clearly uses the language of obedience in this text: grace heals the will "that our will may fulfill the law"[51] and interprets the doing of the law—"works"—as *taken up* into the freedom of grace. The Good, in short, is not just a (passive) mover of the (passive) will; rather, the true Good "*belongs to human agency to accomplish*, yet it is also a divine gift."[52]

The sense of freedom as the simultaneity of obedience and eros sets into relief the fundamental importance of *choice* in Augustine's conception, but it also gives choice a distinctive character. In general terms, choice for Augustine is either *free consent* to God as good, or disobedience, which is inevitably a failure to be free. We referred above to the observation that Augustine's notion of will is a synthesis of Platonism and Stoicism: from Plato, he gets the love of the Good, which is the more comprehensive theme; from the Stoics, he gets what we might call the mechanics of choice. For the Stoics, sentient beings are the constant recipients of impressions that enter into the soul from the surrounding world as "presentations"; some of these presentations, when joined with the soul's appetites, acquire the character of *hormai*, impulses, which Sarah Byers, for instance, has defined as "psychic prompts toward action."[53] What was initially *passive*, the registration of presentations, begins to take on a spontaneous energy, eventually issuing in some active motion. If animal psychology is constituted by the interplay of presentations and *hormai*, the human soul adds the further elements of reason and assent. The human being not only passively receives stimuli, which trigger a response, but *reasons* about possible responses and finally acts according to that to which he gives intellectual assent. It is the assent that converts the energy of impulse into action proper. Much of Stoic ethics consists of the wise restriction of such assent to that over which one has control.[54]

The radical unity of obedience and eros, and of will and being, which we presented above, allows us to see just how fundamentally Augustine transforms the Stoic psychology in his appropriation of it. Perhaps most fundamentally, Augustine's perspective allows a vision of the *unity* of the person, which is arguably threatened by the Stoic conception. The basic Stoic psychology tends to break the person up into relatively opposed components; it encourages a sense of the self as a sort of passive spectator, which watches the display of the body's passions from a "safe" distance and pronounces its ultimately dispassionate judgment (at least to the extent that it achieves philosophical wisdom), which is then carried out. Augustine, by contrast, describes the passions, not simply as mere passive "impressions," but already as *wills*, "*voluntates*,"[55] which means that the very reception of the movement from without is already inchoatively an active engagement, a kind of consent. Indeed, he highlights the role of the will in the very act of perception,[56] which makes clear that perception is different from a purely passive registration of some object acting on the soul. For Augustine, perceptions and passions already belong to the inner being of the self; they are not mere intrusions from the outside world on which the rational self initially gazes, so to speak, in detachment. The reason this is important is that the consent the soul finally gives, if and when it does give consent—which is not a merely intellectual "assent" but an act including intellect and will together[57]—is not an imposition of one part of the self (the purely rational soul) on another part of the self (the active, bodily part) but a gathering up of the *whole person*, body and soul, in relation to what the person takes to be good. This point becomes especially clear when we recall Augustine's understanding of the ultimate coincidence of being and will, his suffusing of the Good with Love. The soul does not simply *act on* itself from the outside, so to speak, but *is* in its *acting*, which is to say its will is an expression of the *whole* of its being, all the way down to its foundations in the bodily affections.

This means, however, that, while consent is necessarily a deliberate act, it is never only a deliberate act, or in other words the act is never wholly circumscribed within the soul's conceptual grasp—as it is, for example, in the Stoics. Instead, the act of consent wells up, we might say, from a depth of the soul that is more profound than its explicit awareness.[58] It is the unity of eros and obedience that sets this dimension into relief. The soul's deep movement does not make consent in any sense *irrational*, however; instead, it deepens what we mean by reason, beyond the merely conceptual.[59] Our reason, just like our will, lies more deeply in us than we realize. If being is suffused with will, it is also the case that will is suffused with being. We might recall, in this context, the importance that Augustine gives to memory in his psychology,[60] which suggests that the acts of intellect and will are not wholly circumscribed within themselves in their discrete operations but act from out of their rootedness in what precedes them.[61] When we consent, therefore, it has the form, not of a purely spontaneous choice between alternatives, before which we initially stood in indifferent detachment, but of a discovery that we are already under way; we consent precisely *as already consenting*. This is simply what Augustine means by speaking of our free will as a gift: it is *given* to us to consent, and even this gift of consenting is one to which we have consented,[62] which is why the consent is both desire (which is already moving us) and obedience (which is responsive to what we are willed to will, as it were). Aristotle argued that self-motion is possible only if one is moved by another, because a self-mover that moves itself exclusively by itself necessarily falls into two parts, a part that is moved and a part that moves.⁶³ The Stoic psychology—precisely to the extent that it remains within a materialistic metaphysics—cannot avoid fragmenting in this way, which means that its sense of choice will be limited. One might say that the choice that originates from a power entirely in one's rational control is by definition superficial; it is not a movement of the soul in itself. For Augustine, by contrast, the soul can move itself *wholly* precisely because its very movement, the work that it accomplishes by itself, is (also) a *gift* it receives.

We see the drama of the will that wills to will in a wholehearted way in the famous depiction of Augustine's actual conversion in book 8 of the *Confessions*. Here Augustine describes the dramatic moment in which he discovers that he intensely desires to turn away from his earlier life of sin and to turn toward the Good—or more accurately, to hand the whole of himself over, once and for all, to God.⁶⁴ The reason for the great drama is that he found himself, paradoxically, unable to will the very thing he willed to will: "I longed [to devote myself entirely to You, my God], but I was held fast, not in fetters clamped upon me by another, but by my own will, which had the strength of iron chains."⁶⁵ As Plato had observed, centuries before, the mightiest prison is the one in which the soul is its own jailor.⁶⁶ The modern libertarian is wont to read this chapter of the *Confessions* as evidence of Augustine's discovery of the will as a power that is independent of the intellect: Augustine's mind says one thing, but his will insists on another and does not simply respond obediently or automatically to the mind's command. But this way lies nihilism,⁶⁷ and in any event it is quite clearly not true to what Augustine is describing. The conflict, for Augustine, is not between the will and the intellect but between the will and itself. In explicit contrast to the Manichees, who have a fragmented anthropology, believing that the soul is the site of encounter between two separate wills, a good one and an evil one, and who thus make the self a passive victim of an external force along the lines we described above,⁶⁸ Augustine is able to recognize real division precisely because he has a deeper insight into the soul's unity: "It is the same soul that wills both [eternal bliss and temporal pleasure], but it wills neither of them with the full force of the will [*non tota voluntate*]. So it is wrenched in two and suffers great trials."⁶⁹ As he had put it a few pages earlier, "My inner self was a house divided against itself."⁷⁰ Let us note that, like

Plotinus, Augustine identifies the will with the *inner self*.[71] Unlike Plotinus, however, he also identifies the will with the soul, considered, evidently, as a complex whole that remains truly one in the midst of its complexity. The passions, which are due not only to the reality of the soul's life in the body but also to the actual *history* of that life, which takes shape in habit, are all part of the self, and so part of the will. We will come back to this particular point, but we note here that the will is not presented as a mere faculty alongside other faculties of the soul; instead, the will is the whole soul, from the loftiest heights of the mind to the lowest depths of the most basic passions, considered with respect to its movement toward an object of desire. When Augustine speaks in *Confessions* 8 of making an act of will, he means, not issuing a command from a separate control center, as it were, but moving the whole of his self in one direction or another. This, again, is evidence of his vision of the unity of being and will.

But it is just this (self-)moving of the whole soul that poses the problem; Augustine describes in existential terms the very dilemma formulated by Aristotle that we mentioned above. Self-motion is impossible if it is *only* the self that moves itself, because this would imply a division between the subject and object of motion. On the one hand, Augustine observes that, even in this state of internal conflict, he is perfectly able to will bodily motions. If this is true, it is because the body is not simply the soul itself, and so can be the recipient of a motion that the soul initiates qua (relatively distinct) will. On the other hand, the soul cannot move itself unless it is already fully in motion, but it cannot be in motion unless it fully moves itself:

> The mind commands the hand to move and is so readily obeyed that the order can scarcely be distinguished from its execution. Yet the mind is mind and the hand is part of the body. But when the mind commands the mind to make an act of will, these two are one and the same and yet the order is not obeyed. Why does this happen? What is the cause of it? The mind orders itself to make an act of will, and it would not give this order unless it willed to do so; yet it does not carry out its own command. But it does not fully will to do this thing and therefore its orders are not fully given. It gives the order only in so far as it wills, and in so far as it does not will the order is not carried out. For the will commands that an act of will

should be made, and it gives this command to itself, not to some other will. The reason, then, why the command is not obeyed is that it is not given with the full will. For if the will were full, it would not command itself to be full, since it would be so already.[72]

It is finally only grace that can resolve this dilemma, as Augustine indicates in 8.12, because grace is a being-moved, not just by some other, but by *God*, who is able to move the will specifically in the form of enabling it to move itself.[73] This insight, which we will find repeated, though with a significant difference, by Anselm, and in a more hidden way, perhaps, but no less truly by Aquinas, does not in the least contradict the more apparently Stoic reflections on the will's being ultimately in its own power, which we find for example in *De libero arbitrio*, but provides an indispensable context for interpreting that work properly, as Augustine points out at the end of his life in his *Retractions*.[74]

We ought to note how Augustine's notion of grace enabling freedom once again represents a beautiful convergence of Greek and Jewish themes. On the one hand, Augustine affirms freedom as the capacity for the good, while on the other hand he recognizes that this capacity has to be enabled from above. In the context of a state of sin, which Augustine represents as slavery, this enabling is a deed of liberation. Indeed, Augustine sees this liberation in decisively historical terms, as an event that unfolds in time, though this "salvation history" concerns not (only) a People but (also) the individual soul. The *history* of the soul's enslavement, which is at a profound level an enslavement to itself as much as to some foreign ruler, belongs to the story of its freedom.[75] The self-enslavement is that from which the soul is liberated, and this deed of liberation occurs as a particular event. The free soul is a *liberated* soul, which has been enabled to gather the whole of itself—not just its rational mind but its entire embodied history—and set itself, once and for all, on the Good.[76]

GLORIFYING CHOICE

Indeed, the will's power to move itself, its power to choose by itself and of itself, is not a marginal dimension, which Augustine concedes only reluctantly—unwillingly, so to speak—as far as he *must*, but which he quickly relativizes by introducing a series of basic constraints. Instead, it is *central* to his thinking. Nevertheless, the centrality of the spontaneous, self-originating will for him does not at all imply a form of "voluntarism," much less "libertarianism" in the modern sense. Instead, it remains perfectly compatible with the classical tradition we saw culminate in Plotinus, even if it brings out a genuinely novel dimension only implicit in this tradition. The power to choose, is, for Augustine, nothing but a power to do the good.[77] To understand this claim properly, we need to see that this is not, as it were, an arbitrary limitation, as if the soul were presented with two basic alternatives, good and evil, of which its will was equally capable, and then some lawgiver designated, in a merely positive way, only one of these options as legitimate.[78] Instead, Augustine has a classical sense of power, which is essentially ordered to actuality and thus to perfection. This means that power *in general* is nothing but the ability to bring about the good. For a person with proper insight, the phrase "power to choose the good" is a redundancy, which does not add anything that is not already implied in the phrase "power to choose."

This point comes out most clearly in Augustine's well-known description, in the *City of God*, of the choice of evil in the most original instance—which is not the sin of Adam but even more basically the fall of the angels that made Adam's sin possible[79]—specifically as a *deficient* cause.[80] If power involves efficient causality, at least in some respect,[81] deficient cause implies a certain impotence, a *failure* of power rather than simply an exercise of power that happened to be directed at X when it should have been directed at Y. To be sure, Augustine lays great emphasis on the fact that sin is *due* to the will; it is an activity that is brought about by the will, so much so that in tracing the cause of sin, when we come to the will, we come to a stop: the creature's willing, and it alone, is the cause of sin.[82] Nevertheless, it remains the case that the will is a *deficient* cause of evil, which means that it is cause only in the analogous sense of being responsible, but not in the *strict* sense of being an *effective* source. Thus, it is true that there would be no sin if there were no free will, and in this sense it is free will that makes sin possible, but sin is nevertheless not an expression of the will's power; it is a failure of that power. Etienne Gilson formulated this subtle but absolutely crucial point with impressive precision: "Man is free, and by his own choice he does evil, but not by that which makes his choice free."[83] Since the point, which is perfectly obvious from the perspective of the classical metaphysics informing Augustine's reflections, has become so foreign to us, it is good to illustrate it with an analogy. Man, with his upright posture that distinguishes him from other creatures, has the *power to walk*, which is the ability to bring about a certain perfection, namely, the graceful motion that carries him from one point to another. But the exercise of this power introduces a possibility that is unknown to lower creatures: unlike a snake, for example, a human being can trip and fall. Note that the "can" here is only analogous to the same word in the sentence "Man can walk." It is entirely derivative, one might even say "parasitical." It is only *because* man can walk that he can trip, but if he *does* trip, this is not an effective expression of his capacity to walk; instead, it is a *failure* of that capacity. By analogy, we can say that man "can" sin because he has free will, but his sin remains a failure of his will rather than an expression of it.[84]

The force of this point becomes evident when we return to the dilemma Augustine described in the *Confessions*. There, as we saw, he spoke of the "full force of the will" (*tota voluntate*) as lacking in the sinful condition, which is quite clearly another way of describing *deficient* causality. We need not understand "force" in this context in merely "quantitative" terms, as if a will has more force the more it is able to overcome a countervailing force of resistance and so impose itself. Indeed, it is easy to imagine a sinful choice expressing itself more violently, and in *this* respect more powerfully, than the choice to acquiesce in some genuine good (and indeed the choice of the good—integrating eros and obedience—is *always* a kind of acquiescence), just as the act of tripping will often be more "explosive" than the tranquility of a graceful stride. But being more quantitatively forceful does not mean operating with "full force." The key term is *full*, meaning complete, involving the whole in a unified and harmonious way: a free choice is a "singlehearted" choice. This is why the choice of evil diminishes freedom, insofar as it fragments the soul, setting one part at odds with another: "The choice of the will, then, is genuinely free only when it is not subservient to faults and sins."[85] A soul cannot wholeheartedly choose evil, because "our hearts find no peace until they rest in you," that is, in God, which is to say that the soul is intelligible only as originating from God and so directed to God as its proper end.[86] In this case, however desirable some evil thing may appear to be at some level, it is not what the soul most profoundly desires and so can never be embraced by the soul as a whole.[87] It can be willed only in a *deficient* way, rather than as the fruit of the soul's concerted powers. It is a choice that the soul imposes upon itself and that precisely for that reason lacks full force. By contrast, the more a will chooses the good, the more fully and actively involved it is through its erotic obedience and obediential eros: created wills "have efficient causes, the higher their degree of reality, the greater their activity in the good, for it is then that they are really active; but in so far as they fail, and consequently act wrongly, their activity must be futile, and they have deficient causes."[88]

This description of sin as deficient, or ineffective, choice allows us to understand Augustine's well-known characterization of the sinful condition of the will ("will," in this case, as general disposition rather than particular motion) specifically as love of self,[89] or in some contexts love of power.[90] Outside of a context of classical metaphysics, one might be inclined to read this characterization in moralistic terms: "You shouldn't be so self-centered, but ought to think more about other people, and above all about God." Given this moralistic critique, one would then find Augustine's regular presentation of God as a supreme good that brings the self to fulfillment to be in tension with his general view of Christian charity as "self-less love."[91] But Augustine's critique of the love of power is not principally a moral one; it is an ontological one.[92] Power is by its nature ordered to actuality, the good. If power is not directed to what is good, to a real actually, it is directed, not to some other kind of actuality, namely, an evil one (which ultimately does not make sense), but to nothing . . . but itself, now precisely as undirected potency, as power *separated from actuality*. It is in fact just this lack of a *real* object that makes it *deficient*. Augustine's is thus not a perverse, resentful thinking, afflicted by self-contempt, but a consistent carrying through of a classical view of the nature of reality and the soul's relation to it. The "demonizing" of the love of self is nothing but a deepening, in an existential key, of the classical axiom that potency is potent only "inside of" actuality, that is, ultimately as love of God. "Idolatry" is another name for the subversion of act by (now impotent) potency.

An important question arises at this point: Does the interpretation of the "power to choose" as "power to choose the good" eliminate any genuine options, or at least the "ability to do otherwise," which we almost inevitably associate with choice? The answer is not a simple Yes or No but requires some qualification of the terms of the question. On the one hand, as we just saw, the very power to choose good entails the possibility of failing to do so, which means that a free will that is not absolutely perfect does include the "ability" to sin—though this is not in the positive sense of ability but only in an extended sense, which we just described. Tim Chappell may be overstating matters when he suggests that Augustine's recognition of the possibility of knowingly sinning, which biblical revelation requires him to admit, introduces something previously absent in Greek philosophy,[93] but he is surely right that Augustine makes this aspect central in a way that the philosophers generally did not. On the other hand, to understand Augustine's notion of will, it is necessary for us to consider his account of it in the will's *final perfection*, which reveals something of its deepest nature. Describing the saints in heaven, who have been finally redeemed and so no longer have even the *possibility* of sinning, he writes the following, which is worth quoting at length:

> Now the fact that they will be unable to delight in sin does not entail that they will have no free will [*liberum arbitrium*]. In fact, the will will be the freer in that it is freed from a delight in sin and immovably fixed [*indeclinabilem*] in a delight in not sinning. The first freedom of will, given to man when he was created upright at the beginning, was an ability not to sin, combined with the possibility of sinning. But this last freedom will be more potent [*potentius*], for it will bring the impossibility of sinning; yet this also will be the result of God's gift, not of some inherent quality of nature. For to be a partaker of God is not the same thing as to be God; the inability to sin belongs to God's nature, while he who partakes of God's nature receives the impossibility of sinning as a gift from God.[94]

Note that, in perfect accord with the interpretation offered above, Augustine describes the will's eschatological perfection as "more potent" than the original power to choose, which may or may not succeed.

He describes this infallible, or indefectible, power as a gift from God, which is what it *must* be, as we have seen, if it is to be a power of total self-determination. It is crucial, with respect to what we will see in later chapters, to recognize that this does not mean that God controls the will from the outside, vigilantly keeping it from going astray, like a Divine Curler brushing smooth the path that keeps it on track. Instead, God gives perfect freedom by enabling the will to do unfailingly what it wants all the time. To refer to the earlier analogy, a redeemed soul would be like a person who has become so perfectly strengthened in his power to walk that there is nothing that could cause him to trip, no pathway so treacherous he would be prevented from following it if he would.

Do the saints in heaven, then, no longer choose between "options"? It may seem so, since Augustine describes the perfectly free will as "immovably fixed" (*indeclinabilis*) in the good. But let us be precise. What exactly is excluded from this definitive attachment to the good? Only evil. The alternative "either good or evil" no longer has any sense for the perfectly free will, but this does not mean that there are no alternatives *simply*. Instead, we might say that the redeemed will is no longer able to choose *anything but* what it wants; the only choice impossible for it is the choice to surrender its capacity to choose, which is to say, its freedom. In other words, the will can now choose any good *ad libitum*, and choose it perfectly, in a wholehearted and fully effective way. At the risk of making too much of an image, we might ask what limitations are placed on the man who walks perfectly, unable to trip and fall. Is he not now, for the first time, able to go absolutely anywhere he wishes, without fear and the self-conscious anxiety that accompanies it? Augustine is clear that the perfect goodness in heaven is not the inclusion of free choice *only* within the relativizing presence of infallibly imposed constraints but rather the full flourishing of free will as the power to choose, a power that has finally been liberated from any constraints. "Love, and do what you will!"[95] In Augustine's notion of redemption, we see the Greek (spontaneously doing the good) and the Jewish (liberation from slavery) themes converge. Though Augustine wisely avoids trying to describe eschatological fulfillment in too much detail, what he does say makes clear that the "fixity" in the good is anything but static: "I am not rash enough to attempt to describe what the movements of such [redeemed] bodies will be in that life, for it is quite beyond my power of imagination. However, everything there will be lovely [*species*] in its form, and *lovely [species] in motion and in rest*, for anything that is not lovely will be excluded. And we may be sure that *where the spirit wills there the body will straightway be*; and the spirit will never will anything but what is to bring new beauty to the spirit and the body."[96]

The reason it is important to note that the exclusion of evil is *not* the exclusion of choice simply is that it helps steer a course between two tempting misinterpretations of Augustine, one in the insightful book by Timothy Chappell, *Aristotle and Augustine on Freedom*, the other in the "Kantian" interpretation offered by Hannah Arendt.[97] Chappell correctly contrasts the good will, which is caused in each of its acts by the good, and ultimately by God, to the evil will, which is ultimately "caused" by nothing but the will itself in its self-assertiveness. We are wrong, Chappell says, to think that the will, in its choosing, must represent an "extra component in every good or bad action,"[98] in the sense that its causal power would have to be *added* to the components of action already present, which are in their sum insufficient to account for the action. In this respect, there would be something finally inexplicable about every human action, attempts to account for which would ultimately be reduced to saying that the person willed it because he willed it. While Chappell judges that Dihle, for example, ultimately holds such a misunderstanding, and there is a lot in Augustine that would apparently justify it, a more attentive reading, Chappell insists, reveals that such inexplicable willfulness is found *only* in sinful choices. Good choices can be explained entirely by the good thing aimed at, a good that suffices to account for the choice. Only for bad choices is there finally no reason other than sheer act of will. Chappell concludes that there is no "mystery of the will" per se, but only of the bad will; the good will, which is the will properly speaking, is totally explicable by the good.[99]

In her interpretation of Augustine, Arendt, apparently in perfect contrast, ascribes inexplicability, as it were, to the will *simpliciter*, in all of its actions, whether they be good or evil. The reason the will is essentially a surprise is that, even in its most perfect form, the will is never a mere link in a causal chain but is itself the *first* in any causal series, preceded by nothing but its own spontaneity. As we mentioned before, this is Arendt's celebrated notion of "natality," which she takes

Augustine to have introduced with his notion of man as the *initium*, the "efficient cause" of action, and thus the maker of history.[100] The will, in the final analysis, can never be explained by any cause outside of itself, whether good or evil, but is itself the ultimate cause; it is itself the source of its action.

So Chappell would make only evil choices ultimately inexplicable, while Arendt would accord this character to all acts of will. Which of these apparently opposed interpretations is correct? We propose that each of them identifies a fundamental insight in Augustine but that each also leaves out a complementary point that would profoundly qualify their respective conclusions. Chappell affirms that the good will can be explained because it has a sufficient cause, namely, God[101] — but he does not see that this does not exclude the will's also *being* a cause, which is the point we have highlighted above. This failure seems to be due to the assumption of a certain competition between God's causality and that of the human will, which is why Chappell accepts the will's causality (deficient though it is) in the case of sin, that is, precisely when God is *not* causing the choice. We can agree that, to the extent that a choice is good, it can be explained entirely by the good at which it aims. But we have to recognize that to refer to the will as an efficient cause, as Augustine does, is to say that the will brings something about that did not previously exist: to ef-fect is to bring into being.[102] In *this* respect, the good that will perfectly explain the choice made of it ... does not exist until the choice is made![103] This means that, prior to the will's effective choosing, it is not possible to determine what a perfectly good will is going to choose, unless it is choosing between good and evil in a straightforward way. The fact that the particular good that a good will chooses is a sufficient cause of the choice does not mean it is the only such good possible. Augustine, to be sure, tends to discuss free will principally in terms of the great choice between "love of God to the point of hating the self or loving the self to the point of hating God," but this does not mean that the only choice is between good and evil, so that the elimination of evil is the elimination of choice. Instead, Augustine clearly recognizes the need to choose from among many "incommensurable goods"[104] and *insists* on the "unpredictability" of the will, as we see in the famous account of the identical twins who make fundamentally different decisions.[105] Given his sense of choice as *efficient* causality, we can say that, for Augustine, every act of will is a novelty, a true surprise. At the same time, this surprise will have different qualities, depending on the quality of the will at its source: while the sinful will is unintelligible, the good will, even in its unpredictability, will be totally radiant with intelligibility. There is no reason why intelligibility and unpredictability need to be opposed or posited as mutually exclusive. We can give a *complete* account of a proper choice made in terms of the good that is chosen, without necessarily having to refer to the will explicitly as a cause (since a will that is perfect eros and obedience is perfectly transparent, one might say, to the good at which it aims). But the fact that *this* good suffices to account for the choice, rather than *that* good, which also would have sufficed had it been chosen, remains a surprise.[106] It is therefore not just the evil will that is a mystery—perhaps it would be better to call it a *problem*[107]—but the good will even more so because it is a positive mystery, a *luminous mystery*, more mysterious the more it is understood.

In this respect, we see the profound truth in Arendt's notion of natality, which is an essential implication of the will as an efficient cause:[108] the will cannot operate at all without being in some sense the *beginning* of a series of events, and so always a surprise. But we also see what is profoundly lacking in her conception. For Arendt, to be a first cause means not to be preceded by anything. For Augustine, by contrast, the will can be an *effective* first cause only as a *gift* from God and only to the extent that it is thereby "fixed" as a whole in the good. This fixity necessarily precedes and makes possible any particular choice. If the will's spontaneous action is, thus, *first* in a certain respect, as we just described, it is always nevertheless first only as responsive to the goodness of the good it chooses, and so in this sense always preceded ontologically by a more comprehensive causality. The soul moves itself, and so is properly effective, *only as* being moved by God, and so being "preceded" by a more comprehensive causality. For Arendt, the will's spontaneous causality is a surprise *and therefore* ultimately inexplicable; she assumes the same opposition between surprise and intelligibility that Chappell does. But her celebration of natality, if we read it in these terms, leads to incoherence in the end, as we showed in the previous volume with respect to the same notion in Kant, from whom she derives it.[109] For Augustine, the movement of the will is essentially a surprise, good or bad, but it is all the more intelligible in relation to its causes, the more it is a genuine act of *freedom*. There is an extraordinary mystery in the capacity to respond, beyond the reach, so to speak, of purely material forces, to reasons, to take *into* the intimate depths of the self the ability to bring about something good, to receive the gift of the power to choose.

Conclusion: Augustine's Novelty

In the light of the foregoing, let us conclude by gathering up some of the distinctive characteristics of Augustine's conception of the will and its freedom in more general terms in order to appreciate his particular contribution to the Western understanding. Most generally, we have seen that Augustine radically expands the content of the will, though he does so completely from inside of the classical understanding. If Plotinus had opened up an ultimate depth of will as transcending intellect and being, Augustine opens up its breadth as inseparable from these.[110] The liberated will includes the whole person, body and soul, and so enables a new kind of spontaneity. More particularly, we may highlight three further features of the will, which stand out in Augustine's work.

The first is the connection between will and personality. Charles Kahn has observed that the reflection on the self-determining character of the will beyond the Platonic/Aristotelian νοῦς in later Stoicism coincided with the awakening of a sense of the "inner life" of the person, insofar as it implies a "personal" involvement, so to speak, in the constitution of one's identity, of *who one is*. This awakening, he says, also goes with a sense of *intimacy* with God.[111] We saw this already in Plotinus, whose reflections on divine freedom led him to an unheard-of inquiry into the inner life of God himself. In Augustine, this burgeoning sense of self comes to full bloom and becomes a permanent feature of the landscape of Western thought. If Augustine dwells so much on the problem of sin, we may now say it is not because of a Nietzschean *ressentiment* but in the first place because of the personal drama that the gift of freedom inevitably entails. The intimate depth of Augustine's personal reflection, the baptism — by immersion! — of the classical soul in the mystery of the self and its interior life, that one finds in the *Confessions* is startling with respect to ancient literature: one might, for example, read Homer's *Odyssey*, another journey and homecoming tale, in psycho-symbolic terms, but the difference between it and the *Confessions* is immense, for we never enter in a direct way *into* the interior life of Odysseus. On the other hand, however, the difference between Augustine's *Confessions* and the modern version one finds, for example, in Jean-Jacques Rousseau is, if anything, even greater, in spite of any surface similarities. It does not require a training in psychology to recognize the narcissism of Rousseau's *Confessions*, which is in fact a gazing fixedly at the self in quite explicit isolation from the real.[112] Augustine may have turned radically into the self, but it was from first to last the inside of a relationship with the real, with an already actual other. At the very core, even deeper than the core, of his interiority is, not pure self-relatedness ("alone with the Alone"), but the always prevenient love of the Wholly Other.[113]

This leads to the next basic feature: the will, for Augustine, is not only personal but *radically interpersonal*, which is to say that it has its own reality only within the reciprocity of personal relationship. We spoke earlier of the importance of the theme of obedience, a scriptural notion that he integrates with the Platonic eros. To say that he thus integrates it is in fact just to say that he recognizes a personal reciprocity right at the root of the will in its ordination and aspiration to the Good. Because of this recognition, he is able to elevate the significance of love of neighbor.[114] We recall that Augustine's notion of will is founded on his notion of God as Trinity. This implies, as we saw, that will is love, and love, in its paradigmatic form, is accomplished bond. Again, the Jewish vision of covenant, which we elaborated in chapter 1, resonates in this complex unity. Though the will is a fully *personal* reality, and though it designates, as Rist explained, a movement of the soul toward its beloved object or at the very least a disposition toward such movement, the Augustinian will is more than just movement or the disposition of a power to move. To reduce love, and thus the will that is ultimately the same, simply to an aspiration for an as-yet-absent good threatens to confine the will to an individualistic form. Whereas one might critique the Platonic eros as tending toward the instrumentalizing of all others for the sake of the soul's ultimate enjoyment of the absolute good and beautiful,[115] Augustine's notion of the personal reciprocity of love and the will, with the integration of eros and obedience it implies, keeps him from simplifying the soul's ascent in this fashion.[116] We noted that the soul's highest end is the reciprocity of friendship with God; this end is so radically relational, we might say, that it requires inclusion of all personal relations: "By this we know that we love the children of God, because we love God. How is this so? Aren't the children of God and God himself two different things? But one who loves God loves his commandments. And what are his commandments? 'A new commandment I give you, that you love one another.' You can't excuse yourselves from one love because of another. This love holds together! As it is itself joined together in one, so it makes all those who depend on it one single being."[117]

As Scott Roniger has observed, in stark contrast to the similar ascent of the soul to God in Plotinus, Augustine presents the ascent as occurring in and through a conversation—with his mother, Monica.[118] In other words, what lies at the end is not (only) the soul's "private" vision of the divine essence but a *community*, a *kingdom*: the City of God.[119] The freedom of will, as Augustine finally understands it, is not a solitary possession but a social form: "In the Heavenly City, then, there will be freedom of will. It will be one and the same freedom in all, and indivisible in the separate individuals."[120] This point warrants special emphasis: there is no submersion of distinct individuality in a "night in which all cows are black," or even a "twilight in which all cats are grey,"[121] but a vivifying of individual uniqueness in the brightness of the "eighth day"—and yet there is, here, a single will and a single freedom.[122]

Finally, we note the significance of *history* that emerges with Augustine's notion of freedom, which is such a distinctive contrast to what one generally finds in Greek thought. We pointed out in chapter 1, in our discussion of the Jewish notion of the will, that there is a logical connection between the idea of will as a power to make a change—freedom as efficient causality—and an appreciation of history as a sort of progression, a movement forward in time. The suggestion that Augustine presents a sense of will as *initium*, as the surprising introduction of a "new" series of events, finds confirmation in the fact that he is *also* recognized, next to Eusebius, as having brought history as a theme onto the stage of Christian thought, even if not as a central character.[123] His *City of God*, no doubt the most comprehensive exposition of his theological vision, is, among other things, an engagement with the question of the meaning of historical events.¹²⁴ Again, precisely because he too recognized the will as *archē*, Plotinus opened up the significance of history in a certain way in principle, as we saw in the last chapter, but he did not attend to the actuality of any particular history. Plotinus would never have written *The City of God*. Instead, the Greek philosopher explained the significance of history as a revelation of eternity, which is certainly an echo, as we observed, of Plato's profound characterization of time as a "moving image of eternity." Augustine gives more weight to the immanent unfolding of history, asking not simply what time teaches us about eternity but also, more dramatically, what light eternity sheds on existence in time. This gives time itself a new significance, because it implies that time not only reveals eternity but also in some basic sense *determines* it. We will return to this point, and discuss it in more depth, in chapter 5 on Maximus the Confessor.

Arguably, the entire argument of the present book turns on seeing this last point correctly. Karl Löwith is simply expressing a commonly held view when he describes the Christian sense of history as *linear*, which simply replaces the pagan view of history as *cyclical*, the eternal recurrence of the same.¹²⁵ We have been arguing, by contrast, that the Christian vision is not a substitution of the Jewish tradition for the Greek but a unity of the two. The Greek form of freedom, an *exitus-reditus* from a center, lies behind the "cyclical" sense of time, and it is, as we have been insisting, essentially connected with a recognition of the absolute primacy of actuality.¹²⁶ The rejection of this primacy, we will argue as the present book unfolds, constitutes one of the theoretical cores of modernity, and it begins to take place only as modernity dawns; it does not take place in Augustine. We see a profound sense of the intrinsic connection between time and eternity in Augustine's pervasive notion of history as *providential*, which is a notion that embraces the irreducible distinctness of potency, power, and possibility, and the surprising novelty it implies, fully within the ever-comprehensive primacy of actuality: God has eternally "foreknown" the deeds of history as particular acts of will, but he has foreknown them *precisely as acts of will*,¹²⁷ which means as essentially unpredictable expressions of the good, insofar as they are free, and as senseless failures of will insofar as they are not.

Two basic questions arise in this context regarding Augustine's notion of freedom, but we will have to turn to other thinkers in the tradition to find fruitful responses to them. Augustine's own reflections on both questions leave us with profound ambiguities, which in fact threaten his achievements in the development of the meaning of freedom. Both of the questions, as we will see, regard the radical God-centeredness of his thought. In the first place, his sense of the providential character of history, which we just described, entails a fundamental dilemma: How do we reconcile the significance of choice, of free self-determination in history, with the ultimacy of divine actuality? Does this actuality have an intelligible form? It is crucial that we appreciate the genuine dilemma that this represents, insofar as it makes *concrete* the tension regarding which Strauss had said, "*Tertium non datur*," namely, the fundamental dichotomy between the ultimacy of will or of intelligible order. To be sure, at a general level, Augustine affirms both a basic order and the reality of freedom by embracing what will be the common Christian reading of the fundamental form of the ages of history, which remain in some sense open-ended in the wait for the return of Christ;[128] but at the same time, he tends to give a more determinate resolution to the dilemma in the form of what will eventually be formulated as a "double predestination":[129] the saving of some and the damning of (the great majority of) others are both equally expressions of the absolute will of God, actual from all eternity. But this resolution would seem finally to give will, in its ultimate actuality, the form of arbitrariness.[130] There is absolutely nothing that accounts for one choice or the other, either before or after the choice is made. God's will is absolutely inscrutable, and there is nothing more to say.[131] We will return to this matter in our discussion of Maximus in chapter 5.

The second question concerns the gift character of freedom. If free will is wholehearted choice, it is possible only in response to the perfectly comprehensive good, which preveniently offers itself to the soul as love and thus sets the soul in self-motion. It is for this reason that freedom is a *gift*, and one that brings together eros and obedience, interpersonal love and the attraction of goodness. But granting that all of this is true and of permanent significance for the proper understanding of freedom, one may legitimately ask: Is the choice of God the only free choice? Is freedom in the end *only* theological, or does it also concern our daily interaction with created goods and created persons? Granted that freedom is a divine gift, in other words, can created things *also* be said to give freedom in some analogous sense? What is at stake here is in fact the very reality of human freedom, because a denial of the liberating character of reality in general entails a reduction of freedom to its sole source, which puts God, so to speak, in absolute "control" of all freedom. To be sure, the radically relational sense of the will we described above implies in principle that Augustine does not finally reduce the mediation of the "neighbor," and all the relative "others" to the soul that the word *neighbor* implies, to the im-mediacy of the soul's (now wholly privatized) relation to God. We also recall, in this context, his recognition of the possibility of incommensurable goods and, more fundamentally still, the importance of the *analogy of love* that Augustine affirms in book 8 of the *De Trinitate*. But it is nevertheless not a surprise that the absoluteness of God in Augustine's thought would make the tendency to read the "grace and free will" issue in a one-sided way a recurring problem.[132] Augustine, after all, presents God as the *only* good in the end to be affirmed for his own sake (*frui*) and every other good in the world to be affirmed, *not* for its own sake, but for the sake of God (*uti*).[133] This does not *have* to be read in the unilateral way that the stark formulation most immediately suggests,[134] but it raises the question of how the absoluteness of the divine good can be harmonized with the relative absoluteness of created goods. Let us be clear, the problem we are highlighting is *not* that Augustine ends up giving too much to God's causality and too little to man's, because there is in principle no competition between these. The problem is, rather, whether there is what we might call an insufficiently *analogical* sense of goodness, which would deprive created goods of their mediating role in human choice.[135] In this problem, again, the nature of freedom is at stake; but for a more fruitful engagement with it, we will turn to Dionysius in the chapter that follows.

A final remark. Simon Harrison has insightfully argued that Augustine does not present free will as a merely objective datum, so to speak, out there in the world to be analyzed in theoretical detachment.[136] Instead, he *offers* it, which means he invites his readers "into" the notion, an invitation that can be, itself, received only in freedom.[137] In other words, one can grasp the notion of freedom only *in* freedom, which is to say that the good of freedom objectively compels only in and through its being chosen. If we see this, we understand that the personal drama that he unfolds from within in his *Confessions*, for example, is part of the very meaning of the freedom he portrays: a gift from God, and a gift of God, which one receives as gift in the desire and docility of an open heart. It is not that freedom is something vague and elusive; it is, instead, given with decisive clarity. But it is a clear reality that one can properly see only from the inside, within a free engagement with it. Augustine might be fruitfully compared to Kant on this point. Kant recognizes the difficulty of proving the reality of freedom and responds by demonstrating it *indirectly*, deducing it from the necessity of moral punishment. There is a connection between this approach and his notion of freedom as a kind of power rather than most basically an actuality. For Augustine, by contrast, freedom is just that, an actuality, the beautiful form of the totality of souls in motion and in rest that constitutes the Heavenly City, and so his approach involves a knowing of freedom through active participation in a "prevenient" gift. Freedom is therefore something that must always be renewed, something ever again to be achieved, but this power itself is possible only because it has already been achieved—*pro nobis*. Augustine's work offers us an invitation into a gift that has been definitively given.

PART III

The Patristic Period

CHAPTER 4

Perfectly Natural Freedom in Dionysius the Areopagite

DIONYSIUS AS A CHRISTIAN THINKER

Dionysius,[1] the mysterious monk writing presumably around AD 500, does not typically appear in discussions of freedom in the premodern world, in spite of his massive influence on Christian theology, of both the East and the West, more generally. This is quite easy to explain on linguistic grounds, since the word *freedom* is scarcely to be found in his work;[2] but it also makes sense if we take for granted the conventional notion of freedom as the power to choose, since Dionysius not only fails to mention this power in his description of the harmonious activities of the creatures constituting the cosmos, from the lowest material elements to the highest spiritual natures,[3] but positively *denies* choice in the supreme activity, namely, God's creation of the world.[4] Dionysius's work appears in a radically different light, however, if we approach the question of freedom, not from the vantage of modern convention, but from that of the *roots* of freedom, such as we have sought to lay them bare here and in *Freedom from Reality*: liberality is the paradigm of liberty; freedom is generative superabundance. When we consider the matter from this perspective, we might say that Dionysius stands closer to the font of freedom than just about any other figure from the tradition that one could name. His work is simply saturated with the generative presence of superabundant goodness and beauty, and every question that Dionysius takes up drives him to this principle to find an answer. If freedom is generous self-communication, then we can say that, for Dionysius, it is not a marginal feature that belongs only to certain kinds of creatures but "goes all the way down." Freedom is coextensive with being.

To be sure, we have also drawn out a second tradition, which we have suggested converges with the first in the Christian—and so eventually the *Western*—conception of freedom, namely, that of the Jews. This tradition highlights the elements of the personal, the historical, the exercise of power, and the achievement of relation and unity of will, all under the sign, as it were, of *covenant*. The personal dimension is not as evident in Dionysius, and it is good to begin our brief presentation of his contribution to the conception of freedom by addressing the question that this relative absence presents. It is not uncommon to see Dionysius interpreted as corrupting the Christian form, so to speak, by forcing it, with some violence, to fit the Greek mold; as Luther famously put it, Dionysius bears a particular responsibility for what he takes to be the church's betrayal of the gospel for "Platonizing" at just the moment he should be "Christianizing" ("plus Platonizans quam Christianizans").[5] Let us note, straightaway, how strange this charge sounds from the perspective we just explored in Augustine, who identified the Platonists as proto-Christians. Of course, one could simply respond by observing that Augustine, too, already betrays symptoms of the Hellenistic contagion. But this response raises a prior question, namely, whether the Greek mind is simply foreign to the revelation in Christ, or, to put it in a different way, whether Christianity is an exclusively scriptural religion, *positively not* extrascriptural,[6] so that fidelity to scripture would seal it up into a strictly self-enclosed sphere.[7] We staked out a position on this question in chapter 1.

What, then, are we to make of Dionysius in light of the position sketched out there? The first thing to say is that he does not simply replace the Jewish tradition with the Greek one but is quite clearly a *Christian* thinker who brings these two traditions into a novel synthesis. The Jewish tradition is present, not only in the fact that he quotes scripture on virtually every page (admittedly the New Testament as well as the Old),[8] but also in the central importance he gives in his work to what might be called the "priestly" dimension in his love of hierarchy, the fundamental role he gives to office, law, prescribed rite, and so forth.[9] That being said, it is also clear that the Dionysian synthesis integrates the Jewish element into the Greek more fundamentally than it does the Greek into the Jewish—he is, after all (or at least *pretends* to be!), the *bishop of Athens*.[10]

But there are two observations we wish to make in this regard, the importance of which cannot be overstated with respect to our general project. In the first place, if Dionysius receives the Jewish form, so to speak, into the Greek, it is *also* the case that the Greek form is thereby transformed, as we hope to show below: the novel role he gives to *eros* develops the Greek form further by deepening the relation to the other as an expression of perfection. In other words, there really is a (Christian) synthesis here, so that the Jewish form is not violently distorted in order to fit a model that is simply foreign to it but also co-informs the mold into which it is received, bringing about something genuinely new. Second, though the more or less "one-sidedness" of the synthesis implies a certain limitation of the vision Dionysius offers, so that his contribution will need to be complemented in a significant way, it nevertheless remains the case that the dimension he brings to light is of permanent value. If it is not the most important dimension of freedom *tout court*, one could argue it is the most important given the way the meaning of freedom subsequently develops in the West. The impoverished concept of freedom that defines modernity can be described as a result of the oblivion of the vision that Dionysius represents perhaps more vividly than anyone else. But before we assess his contribution, we need to lay it out, at least in broad strokes.

The Saving Power of Nature

There would be any number of access points into Dionysius's conception of freedom; as in a hologram, the whole is imaged in each part. We will approach the matter here by taking up the theme already introduced, namely, Dionysius's reception of the Jewish spirit into the Greek form. The basic pattern of this reception comes to expression perhaps most clearly in his discussion of the (decidedly Jewish) name "Salvation" (σωτηρία) in chapter 8 of the *Divine Names*, his most influential work, which will be our principal focus. It is good to begin with this name because it will provide a reference point for the other dimensions of Dionysius's conception that we hope to bring to light.[11] "Salvation" is of course a major theme in scripture, both the Old Testament and the New, and it is closely tied to the Jewish notion of freedom: the most basic sense of freedom in the Old Testament, as we saw, is *liberation*, a being set free from a prior condition of slavery, the paradigm of which is the miraculous exodus of the Israelites out of Egypt. We argued in chapter 1 for an analogous interpretation of this liberation that would not make the fallen condition of slavery most basic but would instead see the gift of liberation in principle as the "gratuitous" elevation from an original perfection (created nature) to a superabundant perfection (grace). In contrast to this, however, Dionysius gives an unsurpassable ultimacy to *the original gift of nature* in what we might call a perfectly Greek fashion:

> If any one speaks of salvation as the saving power that plucks the world out of the influence of evil, we will also certainly accept this song of salvation, since salvation has so many forms. We shall only ask him to add that *the primary salvation of the world is that which preserves all things in their proper places* without change, conflict, or deterioration. . . . Indeed, it would be quite in keeping with the sacred Scriptures [ἱερᾶς θεολογίας] to say that this salvation, by means of the goodness that preserves the world, redeems all things, keeping them from falling away from the good that properly belongs to them, according to the receptive capacity of the nature of each of the things redeemed.[12]

Dionysius is seeking here to give a fundamentally *positive* meaning to the notion of salvation, and he does so specifically by insisting on the absolute quality of nature.[13] As this passage reveals, it is nature, the original reality of things given in their creation, that provides the final measure. This explains why salvation comes precisely through *goodness* (understood metaphysically rather than first morally), and indeed the specific goodness that belongs properly to each thing itself. Because the intrinsic goodness of nature represents the governing principle, salvation coincides both with the internal perfection of each particular thing and with the harmonious interrelation of all things in the whole, which forms the "cosmos." Liberation, in other words, is not from a (fallen) nature *to* a supranatural condition but in the first place a sustenance *in* nature, and then, in the event of disorder, a restoration *to* nature, which is to say, to the original and unsurpassable gift.[14] The final result is therefore a comprehensive order, an intelligible whole.[15]

Now, it is crucial to observe at once that "nature" is not itself a "closed" concept in Dionysius, as it will become in later Scholastics (*natura curvatur in se*), to say nothing of the early moderns.[16] Instead, Dionysius has a radically self-transcending notion of nature, which is why the supremacy of natural goodness does not necessarily imply a cramping of the Christian form. As in everything else, Dionysius interprets the meaning of nature specifically in relation to its absolutely superabundant source,[17] which we will characterize in a moment. More immediately, we catch a glimpse of the self-transcending character of nature already in the discussion of power, δύναμις, that represents the content within which Dionysius reflects on the name "Salvation." Before we look directly at the supreme name, that is, "the Good," let us thus first consider how Dionysius presents this attribute, which, like salvation, also bears a particular connection to the Jewish tradition. Following a similar pattern for all the other divine names, Dionysius says that God is power itself, that he is more-than-power, and that he is the source of all power, everywhere in the cosmos. God is power, not in the first place as imposing himself on what is impotent, thus causing it to change (or more accurately: passively *to be changed*). Instead, God is absolute power in the most essential sense as communicating himself, and thus his power, in an infinite variety of ways to things other than himself: "He is above all power and is power itself, and possesses that excess of power which produces in infinite ways an infinite number of other existent powers."[18] Since power, for Dionysius, just as for Plotinus, is productivity, that is, generativity, God's exercise of power gives rise not only to *things* other than God but to an infinite variety of generative activities; divine power does not (first) impose, but em-powers,[19] "powerifies," everything else, so to speak.

Where do we see this generative power in the cosmos? The short answer is: absolutely everywhere, without exception. There is no actuality that is not in another respect also a potency, interpreted as creative energy. One might initially think to look to the obvious instance of generativity in biological reproduction to find an ontological expression of the power of self-communication, but for Dionysius, power is a far more comprehensive "feature." As he sees it, the world is populated not so much by *things* as by *powers*, or better: the things that make up the world are also essentially powers. In discussing the distribution of divine power, Dionysius says that "there is nothing in the world that is utterly bereft of power"[20] and goes on to offer a list of types of power. What is striking about this list is that it represents a further differentiation of the classic Neoplatonic triad of "thinking-living-being" that is meant to sort into a basic hierarchy all the things that are. Dionysius's list runs as follows: knowing, reasoning, perceiving, living, and essential being (οὐσιώδη)—all the way to the very act of being, "to be" itself (τὸ εἶναι), which he likewise conceives as an exercise of power.[21] Let us highlight this acknowledgment of the act of existing that transcends the essential mode of being, which will prove to be so important for a proper conception of freedom, as we will see in our discussion of Aquinas. It is not so difficult, perhaps, to think of reasoning as a power, for example, but what would be the point of characterizing the *act of being itself* as an exercise of power? According to the modern conception of power, as an indeterminate quantity of energy that is stored in itself so as possibly to be applied to something outside of itself for the sake of effecting some change, this characterization simply makes no sense. But Dionysius does not have a modern conception of power. He offers an insight into what the notion means for him by the particular example he presents of the exercise of power, namely, the power of visibility of a physical object.[22] What power means in this case is evidently a kind of self-communication, the transference of sensible form. Far from presenting a merely extrinsic imposition of force, power proves to be relational, and indeed in an intrinsic sense. The power of visibility essentially depends not only on a corresponding power to see, which is exercised by an agent that is genuinely distinct from the visible thing, but more comprehensively still on the light, the divine power, that empowers the rest. Note that there is no competition between or among these powers; quite to the contrary, the strengthening of one strengthens the others.

If Dionysius thus describes both essential being and the act of being itself, from which nothing in the universe is separate, as a *power*, what he is saying is that to be at all is to exist in intrinsic relation to all others in the whole. This relativity does not compromise the substantial "in-itself-ness" of things in the least, any more than the power to see in one thing compromises another thing's visibility; instead, it brings to light that substantiality, so to speak, and the nature that defines it in every case has its proper place only *in* relation to what is other. The divine power, which empowers all things, at the very same time establishes them absolutely in themselves and inside relation to others in the cosmos: it "attracts to mutual harmony and concord [φιλίαν καὶ κοινωνίαν], and draws separate individuals into being, according to the natural laws and qualities of each [κατὰ τὸν οἰκεῖον ἕκαστα λόγον], without confusion or merging of their properties."[23] This simultaneity of self-relation and otherness may be especially evident in life, which involves quite evidently an "interchange" with the surrounding world that constitutes a thing's own reality, but Dionysius is clear that this kind of self- and other-relatedness constitutes being itself.[24] For Dionysius, the very elements, which are inanimate and unthinking, are nevertheless not mere "materials" lying inert, passively subject to external motion, but actively partake in the harmony of the whole by occupying their proper place;[25] Dionysius expresses this "active partaking" precisely as *power*. There is no quality of anything in the cosmos that is not an expression of power, which is to say a generous *self*-communication that coincides with its being properly, distinctly, unconfusedly its unique *self*.[26] Nature, then, is not a restriction in the sense of defining a thing merely in its self-relation, its self-seeking, over against all other things (which is how Spinoza, for example, will come to define nature).[27] Instead, nature is a principle of living exchange, of simultaneous identity and relation, a principle that solidifies a thing internally in itself and unites it with everything else in the cosmos.

This interpretation of nature as, so to speak, an open totality gets radically reinforced when we connect it with what is no doubt the principal theme of the *Divine Names*, namely, God as "the Good and the Beautiful." First, let us note that Dionysius binds nature indissolubly to goodness. This becomes especially clear when he addresses the question of the origin of evil. According to Dionysius, evil is strictly and unqualifiedly unnatural (οὐ κατὰ φύσιν),[28] or better, contra-natural (παρὰ τὴν φύσιν);[29] for the same reason it is altogether powerless, and so unable to generate.³⁰ Evil therefore cannot be found inherent in anything that exists at all, from the highest spiritual natures to the lowest nonessential existence of matter. Nor can evil be found in nature considered as a whole (ἐν τῇ ὅλῃ φύσει),³¹ in the natural world per se. One might be tempted to say that evil is therefore introduced by "free choice," by an act of will, which thus would represent a power that transcends what is given by nature.³² But Dionysius is even more resolute in his rejection of this notion than was Augustine. There is *simply no* power, for Dionysius, that transcends nature because nature, as we have seen, just is the fullness of power; even the intervention of God's providence is not such as to destroy nature.³³ The will, like all other things, is *wholly* circumscribed by the causality of goodness and beauty³⁴ (which, Dionysius insists, like the Neoplatonic thinkers before him, does not in the least compromise its self-originating activity).³⁵ Nature is defined strictly in relation to the good, and so every act of will, precisely insofar as it is an act of will, is always natural, always according to nature.³⁶ The good, Dionysius says, is "the source of will, power, and action."³⁷ It therefore follows that evil is altogether a failure of will, an *inability* to act from oneself as origin,³⁸ an impotence, which draws whatever power it exhibits in its resistance to the good paradoxically from the very good it resists.³⁹ For Dionysius, nature is so much a matter of goodness that not only is that which is natural ipso facto good, but we can also say that everything produced by goodness is natural.

What does nature look like as an expression of goodness? To answer this question, we need to consider more closely the nature of goodness. Doing so, we will see how Dionysius takes a decisive step beyond both Plotinus and Augustine. Like Plotinus, Dionysius presents God as absolute and, as it were, wholly unrestrained goodness, who pours himself forth in radical generosity, thus giving rise to the world. The generosity is literally radical, rising up from the very roots, so to speak, of God's being, so that there is no separation between God's being and God's giving⁴⁰ — a point to which we will have to return below. Here we wish to observe that this radical generosity is reflected in the world that, as the effect of God's causality,⁴¹ shares by analogy in his being.⁴² If God's being *is* his self-giving goodness, the being of creatures *is* their reception of this goodness, which is to say that, insofar as we define eros according to the classical tradition as the subjective correlate of

Perfectly Natural Freedom in Dionysius the Areopagite 123

goodness, the being of things *is* their eros. Plotinus also said as much.[43] But, more explicitly than Plotinus, though certainly in harmony with the basic "drift" of Plotinus's thought, Dionysius unfolds the complexity that follows once we accept this characterization: the more things desire the good, the more they receive it; the more they receive it, the more they become "like" the good they receive; the more "goodlike" they are, the more they too participate in the generosity that "founds" the universe, which means the more they too pour themselves out in generosity: "[God's] Goodness maintains them [the things that exist] and protects them and feasts them with its good things. Through desiring this they possess their being and their blessedness, and, being conformed to this (according to their powers), they acquire the form of goodness, and, as the divine law commands, pass on to those that are below them, of the gifts which have come unto them, from the good."[44] Eros, the reception of goodness, both establishes things in themselves and moves them in generosity toward others.

If we recognize the ontological depth of this "movement," in other words, if we see that it concerns not simply the *doing* of things but their *being*, or more accurately their doing only because it is already a matter of their being—goodness is in-nate, inscribed into their *nature*—we see that the moments of this movement are not sequential stages but are simultaneous and mutually implicating. It is not that I, as a creature, first receive (the good and myself), and then that I possess (the good and myself), and then, after that is settled, that I give (the good and myself).[45] Instead, my very being *is* my giving and receiving, and indeed receiving is a kind of giving, and giving a kind of receiving. One of the most profound ways to give to another is to lower oneself so as to be able to receive from him: to receive from the other is to give the capacity to give (which itself must be received). We will return to this below. This paradox of generosity as the very form of existence, which lies at the core of Dionysius's vision and shines through in every notion on which he reflects, is not so different from Augustine's radicalizing of the will, which we described last chapter, though Dionysius puts the matter more obviously in ontological terms, while Augustine's thought moves in a more directly moral line. In any event, the result is that a complex inner form is given to eros: it is no longer "pure ascent," as it may seem to be in Platonic thinking, but now includes, precisely *as* eros, both the

Greek immanent abiding of friendship and self-love and the "descent" of providential care, which is an echo of the Jewish tradition:

> All things must desire and have eros and agape for the beautiful and the good. Indeed, because of it and for its sake the inferior things have eros for the superior under the mode of attraction, and those of the same rank have eros for their peers under the mode of mutual communion; and the superior have eros for their inferiors under the mode of providential kindness; and each has eros for itself under the mode of cohesion, and all things are moved by a longing for the beautiful and good, to accomplish every outward work and form every act of will [ποιεῖ καὶ βούλεται].[46]

This passage presents quite clearly Dionysius's "twist" on the general Neoplatonic conception of love.[47] To say that a higher-order being has eros for a lower-order being means that the inferior represents a goodness and beauty *toward which* the superior can aspire; in this case, the superior relates to the inferior *as if* standing below him. The external completion of the act of will (*poiēsis* and *boulēsis*) is therefore not merely an epiphenomenon, so to speak, of an inward completion that arises as an indifferent aftereffect of that perfection, but presents the *locus* of that completion, which is why such activity can really be filled with "providential kindness." The receiving is a giving and the giving is a receiving.

This turnabout adds a new dimension to what we have described as the "Greek form of freedom," namely, the *exitus-reditus*, the reception into the soul that occurs in the mode of the procession out from the soul. When Dionysius turns to discuss explicitly the essential "movement" that constitutes spirit,[48] he insists on three distinct but inseparable shapes: there is not only the circular movement of *exitus-reditus* (κυκλικῶς), which is the movement, paradigmatically, of contemplation, but also the progressive linear movement (κατ' εὐθείαν), which he associates with the actual accomplishment of purpose,[49] and finally the spiral movement (ἑλικοειδῶς), which is the unity of the two.[50] This unity reveals both that the contemplative circle is not merely self-enclosed and that the linear movement forward is not aimless and so without intelligible form.[51] There is thus an opening up in Dionysius's conception of spiritual being, at least in principle, to history in the sense of the accomplishment of events in time (linear movement), but the image of the spiral suggests the ultimate "containment" of history within a pattern. Once again, we have an inclusion of the Jewish spirit within the Greek form, which expands that form from within and so without "breaking" it, so to speak. In this respect, though it is clear that nature represents the ultimate horizon for Dionysius, because the horizon is set, paradoxically, by what transcends it, namely, by the "supernature" of the Good, it is not a simple, closed nature (a circle) but an *open* one (a spiral, which incorporates the shape of linear progress).

It is fitting to compare this to Plotinus's discussion of the relation between will and nature in God and creatures: freedom represents the will's transcendence of nature, which nevertheless perfectly coincides with nature. But if the radical priority is given to will in God, this is *only* in God; in *all* other things, without exception, nature has a radical priority as the principle of reception of what is first. Without rejecting the paradox of the relation between transcendence and immanence, Dionysius deepens the analogy between God and creatures. The ecstatic, or self-transcending, character, the spontaneous self-giving generosity, which culminates in the *will*, is more generally constitutive of the very being of all that is (*to einai*), and, as we will see in a moment, this is mirrored in a deeper acknowledgment of receptivity *also* in the highest principle, God himself. The paradox is intensified.

Eros Incarnate

In our discussion of Augustine, we observed how his Trinitarian conception of God led him to see love, not as merely open aspiration, but as perfected bond that includes aspiration, and at the same time to see this perfection of love imaged in human relations: the love that is the perfection of will does not have its place exclusively in man's relation to God but is present also in the relationships among men: "neighbor love."[52] But, at the end of the chapter, we noted a certain ambiguity that has often been fretted over in the reception of Augustine, namely, whether his characterization of all created goods as *uti*, and God alone as *frui*, threatens to undermine the immanent exercise of love.[53] We also noted that the reality of human freedom depends on the recognition of the *proper* and intrinsic goodness of created goods. Whatever ambiguity there may be on this point in Augustine gets clarified in a breathtaking manner in Dionysius. It will become clear, in this context, just how crucial is his insistence on the absoluteness of nature, and the proper goodness that belongs to it, which even God's most dramatic liberation does not leave behind, for the theme of freedom.

The clarification occurs as an implication of Dionysius's transformation of eros. Again like Augustine, Dionysius conceives God as the perfection of love in a more than merely metaphorical sense; Dionysius famously affirms that "God is love," not only in the moralistically "pious" sense to which "agape" is sometimes reduced,[54] but specifically *as eros*.[55] Augustine, too, recognized the receptive dimension of love, which is essential to eros, as equally divine in the Trinity insofar as he highlights explicitly the "being from" of the Son and the Spirit.[56] But Dionysius is more radical than Augustine in his insistence that this dimension has its place not only *inside of God* but also, and therefore, in God's relation to creation *ad extra* (so to speak).[57] Apparently turning Neoplatonism on its head (but *only* apparently),[58] Dionysius makes the astonishing claim that God has eros for the world:

> And true reasoning will also dare to affirm that even the creator of all things himself has eros for all things, creates all things, perfects all things, conserves all things, attracts all things,[59] through nothing but excess of goodness. Indeed, the divine eros is nothing else than a good eros towards the good for the mere sake of the good. For the eros which creates all the goodness of the world, being pre-existent abundantly in the good creator, did not allow him to remain unfruitful in himself, but moved him to exert the abundance of his powers in the production of the universe.[60]

To understand why this is not simply a contradiction of the Greek order, which sees God as pure self-giving and everything else as "erotic" reception, we need to recall the interpretation of eros that emerged above: eros is not just a receiving but also and inseparably a giving; we saw it marks both the relation of inferiors to superiors *and* that of superiors to inferiors (and everything in between). If—again in a rather startling contrast to the standard "Greek" line—a superior can have eros for an inferior, this reveals an interpretation of eros that opens up the possibility of attributing eros to God, the absolute superior, in relation to all creatures, his inferiors. Eros for inferiors is a perfection; God, as summing in himself all perfections, turns out to be absolute Eros. This deep paradox opens up an analogy by virtue of which we may understand God's perfect self-giving precisely as including a kind of receptivity, insofar as eros implies receptive desire for another.

To be sure, this receptivity remains quite paradoxical; Dionysius is relentless in his insistence on God's perfect immutability, as the passage quoted above reveals. Dionysius does not deny, in other words, that God is absolute goodness, always already in himself, so absolute that it cannot, so to speak, get any better. Instead, he is unfolding in more depth what this absolute goodness *means*. We might interpret Dionysius's conception thus: when he describes God's goodness as, literally, "hyperbolic," he is first of all making the same point that we saw in Plotinus, namely, that God's perfection overflows his borders, so to speak. For Plotinus, this means that God gives rise to perfections outside of himself, enabling things to come to their own perfection. We might express this figuratively by saying God wishes to possess his own perfection only in the form of (also) giving it away to what is other than himself. But Dionysius takes the insight a step further. As we suggested above, one of the most radical forms of generosity is an openness to receive (back) from one's other; one of the most profound gifts a person can give to another is—contrary to the inevitably humiliating giving without reception that Nygren, for example, calls Christian agape[61]—to place oneself in humility *below* the other so as to be able to receive in a genuine sense *from* him. One thus lifts the other up. To understand Dionysius's point properly, we ought to take this lifting the other up by placing oneself in a position of receiving the other—the position of eros—as expressing the form of the act of creation, and so of God's relation to the world simply. According to Dionysius, God's perfect generosity, as perfect, does not exclude this most radical form: he gives to his creatures most perfectly in allowing them to give a gift in return. We see this giving by receiving not only in the remarkable statement that God is, as it were, "ecstatically" drawn out of himself by the beauty of the world[62]—which is just what it means to speak of God as eros in the sense of "hyperbolic goodness"[63]—

but even more directly in his brief, but extraordinarily profound, allusion to the mystery of the Incarnation:

> And since the supra-divine has in love for man [φιλανθροπίας] come down from thence into the state of nature, truly taken substance and assumed the name of man (we must speak with reverence of those things which we utter beyond human thought and language), even in this act he possesses his supernatural and superessential existence—not only in that he has without change or confusion of attributes shared in our human lot while remaining unaffected by that unutterable self-emptying as regards the fullness of his Godhead, but also because (most wondrous of all wonders!)[64] *he entered in his supernatural and superessential state into the conditions of our nature and being, and receiving from us all things that are ours* [πάντα τὰ ἡμῶν ἐξ ἡμῶν], *exalted them far above us.*[65]

Note that the Trinitarian and Christological mysteries here do not simply contradict the philosophical insight uncovered by Plotinus as the flourishing of the classical tradition from Plato and Aristotle but bring to light a hidden depth that would no doubt have been impossible to conceive otherwise. It is the light of this glorious transformation of classical thought that decisively clarifies whatever ambiguity there might be in Augustine. Things are so intrinsically good and beautiful that *even God*, the one who "has everything," desires them! He cannot rest until he has them—though of course this inquietude is due, not to an imperfect lack, but to an excess of goodness as ecstatic love,[66] and it is *also* true that he always already *does* have them.

Let us pause for a moment to cast this point in the terms of act and potency. We saw above that Dionysius readily ascribes the name of "Potency," δύναμις, to God. This is due in the first place to scripture—as we have discussed, the Jews associated God with power in a special way—but it is no doubt also due to the prominence of the notion in the Neoplatonic tradition, as was apparent in our discussion of Plotinus.[67] But this is not yet the "power" that will arise in nominalism, which is entirely dissociated from goodness and nature and is held together with these notions, if at all, only by force, so to speak. For Dionysius, power is altogether identical with goodness and nature; this indicates that power is not *empty* and indeterminate (ἀόριστον) (as is evil),[68] but coincides with the fullness we associate with actuality. When he discusses the title "Omnipotent" (ὁ παντοκράτωρ), for example, in chapter 10, he explains that God rules over all precisely by imposing the bonds, so to speak, of pure goodness. As we saw in Augustine, we have here a perfect synthesis of eros and obedience: "The supreme Godhead is called 'omipotent' because it is potent over all things, and rules with unalloyed sovereignty over the world it governs; and because it is the object of desire and eros for all, and casts on all its voluntary yoke [ἐθελουσίους ζυγοὺς] and sweet travail of divine all-powerful and indestructible desire for its goodness."[69]

Note that what is being "cast upon" all things, here, is the iron-clad constraint . . . *of eros*, sweet desire. Dionysius (significantly) draws less attention to the movement from without than does Augustine, but the note of obedience is nevertheless unmistakable here. It indicates that God moves not *only* from within but also from without—and this means, once again, that nature is not mere immanence but is open, as nature, to what transcends it. In any event, the expression of power can move in this way only by being a fullness, but one in which there is room, so to speak, for the other.

Moreover, when he speaks of "dominion" (κυριότητα) in chapter 12, he acknowledges the connotation of "lordship" with respect to inferiors—which is why Aquinas, for example, says God has the title only with respect to creation[70]—but, drawing on the Greek etymology of the term,[71] Dionysius insists on the positive and intrinsic meaning as the principal one: "And dominion is not only the superiority to inferiors, but is also the entirely perfect and comprehensive possession of beautiful and good things and is a true and steadfast firmness."[72]

The reason this is important is that it indicates, once again, an inner fullness of the potency, which implies a classical sense of the relation of potency to actuality, or internal perfection. To think of power, by contrast, in the *first* place as the capacity to effect a change "transitively," so to speak, to be able to act *on* what is other, implies an internal indeterminacy or emptiness. As we saw at length in volume 1, such a notion of power is "diabolical" in the sense that it requires the opposition of the *other* in order to define itself.[73] For Dionysius, by contrast, "power" is the result, so to speak, of an *excess* of inner perfection, which means that its exercise is not an (arbitrary) *acting on* the other but most fundamentally a self-communication, as we have seen. This becomes especially evident in his response to the classic sophistical objection that God cannot be strictly omnipotent if he is not able to be untrue, evil, ugly, and so forth.[74] Such things would be possible for omnipotence only given a wholly abstract and empty notion of potency, lacking all actual content (which eventually gets defined in purely logical terms as permitting anything at all except what is formally self-contradictory). This is nominalism in a nutshell. For Dionysius, by contrast, the divine omnipotence is a full potency, open not because it is empty but because it is over-full, and in *this* respect able to receive from the other without being changed in itself through an extrinsic agent. This is why Dionysius insists that God's being is not outside of nature in the sense that would make it unnatural or contra-natural, but is supranatural in a way that preserves the absoluteness, the never-to-be-surpassed-ness, of nature.[75] God is omnipotent because he is limited only by his boundless perfection. In this respect, he is not potency in contrast to actuality, but a superpotency that is at the very same time a superactuality.

Let us be clear regarding the paradox here: God is not simply *perfection*, actuality, which would imply a kind of limitation over against what is other, and so a kind of finitude;[76] rather, as we have seen, he is *infinite perfection*, an excess of perfection. *Power* is an especially appropriate term, insofar as it indicates, more clearly than *actuality* does, a connection to increase, and so an openness to what is to come. But a remarkable dimension comes into view in Dionysius that was only implicit in Plotinus: the subordination of potency to act coheres in a particular way with the distinctively Christian sense of humility, which turns out *also* to be implied, as we saw, in eros. Thus, to make the point in these terms, we can say that God's power is not just an imposition of force, but nor is it simply a communication of power that enables things to en-act themselves and so perfect themselves; instead, while being this latter, it is at the same time and for the same reason a capacity to receive from the very perfection belonging to things—a perfection that has always already been its own. This receptivity, in other words, does not at all imply that God did not have this perfection before—his lordship is, after all, the all-perfect and comprehensive possession of all things good and beautiful—but is simply a way of expressing God's extraordinary capacity, so to speak, to possess from all eternity in a way that *includes* a receiving from the other.

To sum up the essential point: God is absolute perfection, but this does not mean God is pure act *as opposed to* potency (as Aristotle, for example, is often thought to imply).[77] One might be tempted to eliminate potency from divine being insofar as potency generally implies an ordination to act, which, precisely to the extent that it is "not yet" actual, is precisely imperfect. Though it is true, and important, to see the ordination of potency to act, if we go no further than to affirm act and potency as relative opposites, we end up reducing the meaning of actuality itself to the realization of potency. In other words, act and potency come to represent qualities that lie, as it were, within the same order and so reciprocally supplant each other, in the way that the actuality of heat, for example, eliminates the mere potency of cold.[78] Dionysius avoids this by thinking of God, not simply as actuality (or, as he puts it more generally, as *ousia*, essential being), but as "superessential" (i.e., "superactual"), an excess of perfection rather than a perfection that has simply come to completion in a way that can be, so to speak, left behind as a "fait accompli." It is not enough simply to say that God is eternal actuality, an abiding perfection that is the simple opposite of the temporal coming to be and passing away that is bound up with potency.[79] For Dionysius, God does not lie "contained," so to speak, on one side of the distinction between eternity and time, but *precedes* the distinction.[80] We saw Plotinus make this same point and considered how it helps resolve the *Euthyphro* dilemma, whether God is good because he wills himself, or wills himself because he is good: this distinction allows him to say that both are true, even if they seem to be logically exclusive alternatives at bottom. Dionysius does not seem to be troubled by this particular problem (and we will come back to this point), but there is an analogous problem implicit in his notion of God's excessive goodness that is illuminated by the same paradox: Is God equal to himself (priority of goodness) or is he more than himself (priority of will)? The answer, which has to be simply "Yes," is possible because of God's transcendence even of eternity. This supratranscendence is precisely what allows Dionysius to affirm God's eros for the world without compromising his always already being complete perfection. God is not a potency that "needs" creation in order to reach his own perfection; nor is he a mere actuality that would leave the world, with its dynamic movement from potency to act and back again, simply outside of himself as a straightforward opposite. Rather, he is a perfection so excessive he is able to come out of himself into the world, to descend unto the lowest of all creatures, even to the extent of the pure imperfect potency of matter, and indeed to be *attracted* to the world, and receive its gifts, all without being in the least bit changed in himself:

> And we must dare to affirm, for the sake of the truth, that the very creator of all things, in his beautiful and good eros towards the universe,[81] is through the hyperbole of his erotic goodness, transported outside of himself [ἔξω ἑαυτοῦ] in his providential activities towards all things that have being, and is touched by the sweet spell of goodness, agape, and eros, and so is drawn down [κατάγεται] from his transcendent throne above all things, to dwell within the heart of all things, through a super-essential and ecstatic power whereby he yet stays within himself.[82]

One of the implications of God's radical *ecstasis*, his movement *outside* himself,[83] which nevertheless remains immanent, is that this introduces, as it were, a space *in* God for what lies outside of God, or in other words for what has its own being in itself. Dionysius prefaces this passage with a description of the *ecstasis* that is essential to eros, which he illustrates by referring to St. Paul's statement "Not I live, but Christ lives in me." According to Dionysius, this is a statement of the effect of eros. If *ecstasis* is indeed essential to eros, it follows that, to the extent that God is eros, his being "includes" the life of what he loves, namely, in this case the entire created cosmos. To say that God is love thus implies that the world he created lives, moves, and has its being in some basic sense *in* God. Dionysius does not hesitate to describe the world as having just this place: "God produces the universe out of himself as out of an all-powerful root, and attracts all things back into himself as unto an all-powerful receptacle, holding them together as their omnipotent foundation, and securing them all in this condition with an all-transcendent bond [κατὰ μίαν ὑπερέχουσαν] suffering them not to fall away from himself nor by being removed from out of that perfect resting place [ἑστίας] to come utterly to destruction."[84] We will now have to consider what all of this implies for the meaning of freedom.

Conclusion: No Choice but to Be Free

Let us conclude, then, first by attempting a summary statement regarding the shape of freedom in Dionysius and then by offering a brief general assessment of its implications. As we saw in the study of Plato and Aristotle in volume 1, the most original sense of freedom in the Greek tradition is superabundant source, which exhibits the paradox of generating what is new, but wholly from within itself. We saw expressions of this source, and this paradox, in Plato and Aristotle, and, in the present volume, quite powerfully in Plotinus, but this source achieves a certain perfection in Dionysius. By virtue of the Jewish tradition, taken up by Christianity, which enters deeply into his thought through scripture, Dionysius is able to affirm the otherness of what arises from the created source, and so a kind of reciprocity—let us use the biblical term, covenantal bond—between God and the creature that we have seen is essential to freedom. This reciprocity, to be sure, has its place *ultimately inside* of the expansive goodness of God, which means, we might say, that freedom, for him, exercises itself wholly within the given horizon of nature. For Dionysius, freedom is *perfectly* natural. In virtually the only appearance of the word *freedom*, *eleutheria*, in the *Divine Names*, Dionysius uses it to describe, not the restless movement between various options, but the resting in unchanging truth, in contrast to the aimless shifting in error.[85] Let us consider the positive implications of this conception of freedom first, and then, finally, raise a fundamental question.

First, we ought to recognize that Dionysius represents an extraordinary reception of the Greek form, which, by bringing it into the Christian, radicalizes it, giving it a depth it does not have in that tradition alone. Nature becomes, here, supreme in an unprecedented way. It does not at all represent a sphere of being that is defined, as it were, over against God and his supernature, as if it indicated an entity's closed self-relation that would have to be "broken into" by grace in order for the transcendence of redemption to be achieved. There is not the least hint of a liberation *from* nature in Dionysius, but only, so to speak, a liberation *of* nature. In the end, for Dionysius, even the most radical transcendence of nature, that which is "ὑπὲρ φύσιν," remains a fulfillment of nature and so never contravenes God's original gift; the elevation beyond nature in salvation never reaches the point of stepping outside of nature, so as to stand opposed to it. Evil alone is *contra naturam*, παρὰ φύσιν. This absolutizing of nature gives the things of the world a new weight. If there were more ambiguity about the status of relative goods in Augustine, there is no such ambiguity in Dionysius: it may be the case that all things point to God in their very being, so much so that there is no element of existence, however basic or crude, that is not *as a matter of its very essence* a *sign* of God;[86] but it is also the case that God, so to speak, in his *ecstatic* and therefore *erotic* goodness points back at things, and of course his pointing is definitive, never to be gainsaid. The goodness of the things of the natural world thus means they acquire what can legitimately be called an *infinite* value, because they are valued by an infinite power, the beautiful and good eros of God, though this also means that they do not have this value in some sense *separate* from their relationship to God. In this case, the *uti/frui* distinction remains in place, even if it gets paradoxically "spun."

Moreover, if the absoluteness of divine freedom required, in Plotinus, a radical transcendence of being and nature, in a manner that has led some scholars to identify Plotinus as having planted the seeds for what will eventually blossom into the wild growth of absolute voluntarism in modernity, Dionysius turns Plotinus, as it were, on his head — or perhaps it would be more accurate to say, puts him back on his feet. To be sure, God, for Dionysius, radically transcends cosmic being and created nature, just as he does for Plotinus. But Dionysius goes on to affirm something that Plotinus most certainly does not: the God who transcends being and nature also, so to speak, enters back into them — "He entered in his supernatural and superessential state into the conditions of our nature and being" — which is why nature remains an *analogous* concept that is never simply surpassed. Here we see that Dionysius is able to carry further the Greek sense of the absoluteness of nature than is Plotinus, ironically perhaps not by setting it in opposition to the transcendence that belongs to the Jewish tradition but rather by (re-)discovering that transcendence precisely *inside* the humble limits of nature. This is a decisive aspect of the Christian form.[87]

But it is nevertheless justifiable to ask whether this radical re-immanentizing of transcendence, so to speak, threatens to eclipse a crucial dimension of freedom. Is it sufficient in the end simply to reconceive freedom in terms of nature, or in other words, to receive the Jewish spirit simply into the Greek form, even as thus transformed? We noted that the dimension of history, though a radical foundation for it is established in principle, all but disappears in Dionysius's vision. He may make reference to the will and self-acting at decisive points, as we saw, but it remains the case that the explicit language of freedom is quite rare. The issue presents itself most directly in the matter of *choice*. The only time Dionysius alludes to choice, *prohairesis*, in the *Divine Names* is to deny that it occurs in God's creation of the world:[88] "For as our sun, through no deliberation or choice [οὐ λογιζόμενος ἢ προαιρούμενος], but by the very fact of its existence [ἀλλ' αὐτὲ τὲ εἶναι], gives light to all those things which have any inherent power of sharing its illumination, even so the Good (which is above the sun, as the transcendent archetype by the very mode of its existence is above its faded image) sends forth upon all things according to their receptive powers, the rays of its undivided goodness."[89]

Before any criticism is raised about the denial of choice here we must first underscore what is positive, and indeed essential. Dionysius denies deliberation and choice because he wants to show the *depths* of the act of freedom: it arises, not arbitrarily and therefore superficially, but from the very "to be" of God: we could say he puts his very being into this act of freedom. We saw earlier that Dionysius interprets the act of being, not as a simple fact of existing, but as an exercise of power, and power he interprets in turn as self-affirming self-communication. If he affirms this generosity as eros and describes it as a being-moved by goodness and beauty, it is to make clear the perfect totality of the act. The *Euthyphro* dilemma reveals the need to affirm *both* that the will is unconstrained and *also* that it *conforms itself* to what *precedes* it, namely, the good. Plotinus sought to include the whole of this paradox but gave far more emphasis to the supremacy of the will—in his treatise on freedom at least. Dionysius's achievement is to harmonize this supremacy with the absoluteness of goodness and beauty also in its objective dimension. With an extraordinary boldness, he affirms that God himself is *compelled*,[90] thus making the compelling force of the good an ultimate and unsurpassable perfection, and not something that characterizes only the imperfect creature. Augustine, we saw, does something similar with his affirmation of the perfect obedience of the Son of God, but the achievement of Dionysius is to have brought to light the ontological depths of this "responsive" dimension of freedom. This depth becomes apparent in Dionysius's recognition of the movement of love that runs through the whole of creation, from the most sovereign angels to the very "nothingness" of matter.

All of this said, we must nevertheless ask whether the spontaneity of freedom, which stems from eros and its consecration, so to speak, to the good and beautiful and the absoluteness of nature associated with it, makes *choice* and the deliberate movement of the will by the person simply a sign of imperfection. As we just noted, history holds little significance for Dionysius; the ultimate locus of the world lies in the history-transcending being of God. Though this radical God-centeredness of creation does not *exclude* the historical dimension in principle, as we suggested, this definitive establishment of the world would seem to eclipse the "open-endedness" that seems to belong essentially to choice, and to keep freedom ultimately "contained," as it were. Dionysius himself does not explicitly address the matter of the personal operation of the will in choice, but that theme emerges in a central way in Maximus the Confessor, to whom we now turn.

CHAPTER 5

Maximus the Confessor
Redeeming Choice

Introduction: Maximus and History

Maximus the Confessor introduces a dimension into the Christian understanding of freedom that we have not yet encountered among the classical figures, and it will prove to be a culminating point: not just historicity but the actuality of a historical event. He thus presents an illuminating polar complement to Dionysius. In Maximus's vision, the point of reference for the reality of the human will is no longer only a radically transcendent principle—the good and the beautiful—but also the perfect and comprehensive realization of that primacy *in time*. At the center of his vision, which is at once both philosophical and theological, lies the mission of the man Jesus Christ, understood as the historical extension of the procession of the Son in the inner life of the Trinitarian God.

This resolutely Christocentric form of thought places Maximus in a somewhat awkward position with respect to intellectual history as it is normally conceived. On the one hand, Maximus demonstrates an exceptional mastery of philosophical concepts (largely Stoic, to be sure, though transcending that particular school),[1] and integrates this patrimony in such an ample way that the scholar R.-A. Gauthier, for example, is rightly able to judge that he is the first thinker in history to offer an essentially complete theory of the human will.[2] On the other hand, the explicitly theological resource upon which his integrating vision ultimately draws would seem to place him *outside* of the philosophical tradition, to such an extent that other scholars deem Gauthier's judgment, without necessarily disputing the substance of it, "eccentric."[3] For our part, we will not directly engage with the methodological question of the use of revelation in philosophical reflection[4] but will simply weigh the philosophical implications of Maximus's contribution in light of the themes that have been emerging thus far in this book. We will see that, in Maximus, the "threads" of both the Jewish and the Greek traditions on the nature of freedom come together in a decisive way.

Maximus was concerned most directly with clarifying Christological doctrine with a view to its soteriological implications. To put the matter simply, following the patristic affirmation according to which "that which is not assumed is not saved,"[5] Maximus unflinchingly defended the principle that a distinct human will was included in the human nature Christ assumed in the Incarnation—and he did so at great personal cost.[6] It had been defined at the Council of Chalcedon (451) that Christ is one (divine) Person in two distinct, but united, natures, a divine and a human. Significantly, Maximus insisted that the question of the will was inseparably bound up with the judgment concerning nature. In spite of what might be the prima facie strangeness of affirming a single personal agent operating with two distinct wills—a strangeness that no doubt goes a long way in explaining the attractiveness of what came to be recognized as the heresy of monotheletism—Maximus clung to this idea in part because of his profound insight into its implications for our understanding of what it means to be human. It is clear that our interpretation of the theological revelation cannot but bear on our anthropology precisely in its *philosophical* dimension, since we cannot determine the theological issues without answering, whether implicitly or explicitly, certain philosophical questions. Does the will belong to man *by nature*, or is it rather a function of human personhood somehow over against, or in any event, *outside of*, our nature? If the will is essential to human nature, moreover, what exactly is essential to the will?

The contours of this line of questioning stand out especially clearly against the backdrop of our discussion up to this point. In Plotinus, we saw a notion of will arise precisely as a transcendence, not only of nature but also of being, though we argued that this transcendence need not be interpreted in an exclusive way (as it will essentially be in modernity) but can be understood in a way that *includes* nature in its integrity. We then saw in Augustine that the inclusion of nature does not in turn exclude the spontaneity and even unpredictability of free choice, though this point remains ambiguous in Augustine (and so it is not uncommon to interpret him as *denying* it), insofar as he tends in a unilateral way to relativize all created goods, which would be the normal objects of human choice, to what is ultimately the *only* genuinely free choice, namely, the choice for God. In Dionysius, God's paradoxical subordination of himself to the goodness and beauty of the created order, which has its paradigm in the Incarnation, in which he receives *from* his creatures the particular good of human nature, implies a new ground for the absoluteness of nature. But for Dionysius, this absoluteness threatens to eclipse the spontaneity of free choice, especially in its "unpredictable" historical dimension. It is precisely in this context that we see Maximus's contribution: like no other before him, he embraces *both* the historical novelty of free choice *and* the absoluteness of nature, and these apparently opposed aspects have their surprising unity in the historical person of Christ. Let us see how he formulates this remarkable synthesis.

Free Movement

The first thing to state is that Maximus affirms a distinct faculty or power of human *will* (*thelēsis*) in as unambiguous a manner as one could wish.[7] Although it is inseparable from the intellect, the will nevertheless represents a distinct causal order. His definition of the essence of the will becomes the definitive one in the classical tradition: it is the "rational appetite" (λογικῆς ὀργέσεσθαι),[8] which, though essentially rational, does not concern specifically the soul's *understanding* of its objects but rather its movement toward them. Thus, the will represents the unifying seat, as it were, of all of the components of this movement:

> For the rational nature has the natural ability and rational appetite [proper to it]. This is called the "faculty of will" [θέλησις] of the

rational soul. It is according to this [faculty] that we consider when willing, and in considering, we choose the things which we would. And when willing we also inquire, examine, deliberate, judge, are inclined toward, elect, impel ourselves toward, and make use of a thing. As has already been stated, if the rational appetite, in other words, willing and consideration, be proper to our nature, then so are deliberation, inquiry, examination, choice, judgment, inclination towards, election, and the impelling of ourselves toward [something], the natural actions of rational things, and these are not subject to compulsion.[9]

It is precisely his gathering together of these various aspects, which, for example, remain separate in Aristotle or in the Stoics, under a single notion that warrants the judgment that Maximus is the first figure with a full-fledged notion of the faculty of the will.

The full weight of Maximus's description of the will becomes evident only when we interpret it alongside his account of spiritual motion, which he offers in his justly famous *Ambiguum 7*. According to the standard interpretation, in this text he presents an inversion of the general "Neoplatonic" schema that one finds for example in Origen (though the "reversal" of Neoplatonism that Maximus carries through here turns out to be a fulfillment of the Neoplatonic insight, such as we have been interpreting it in this book, rather than a straightforward contradiction of it), according to which *rest* is the original, spiritual condition of spiritual souls, which introduce *movement* in their turning away from God, and this fall leads to the "coming to be" of the created, material world.[10] For Maximus, not only does this view make the sinful fall away from God an absolutely irrational principle that can never be finally exorcised (since the new "rest" of redemption will remain just as vulnerable to the possibility of a new transgression), but it casts an indelible shadow on the material world and all its relative goods. These cannot be seen as *created*, that is, as a gift positively willed by God, but are instead at some fundamental level the products of sin. Maximus insists, to the contrary, that the *coming to be* is the first moment, as God's original gift of the world; *movement* remains the second moment, but instead of having its essential ground in a departure from the absolute good (as in Neoplatonizing Origenism), it now represents *most funda-*

mentally a sharing in that good, a real-izing of it. *Rest*, then, is not the point, literally, of departure but instead a gift given at the end.[11] But because movement has shown itself to be essentially positive, this rest is not the *absence* of movement; instead, it coincides with movement. Maximus makes this point, which we sought to bring out from between the lines, so to speak, in Augustine, with all desired clarity: for him, the final beatific fulfillment may be described equally as an "ever-moving repose" (στάσις ἀεικίνησις)[12] or a "stationary, self-identical motion" (στάσιμος ταυτοκινησία).[13]

There is a direct connection between this "reversal" of the Origenist schema and the special significance Maximus gives to the will, as well as his interpretation of it specifically as *rational appetite*. To say that it is rational is to say that the soul *first*, and most fundamentally, *receives* the truth of things into itself (as what governs all of the soul's own self-directed movement). But because what it receives exceeds its capacities to appropriate, the very reality that enters, so to speak, into the soul draws the soul outside of itself and toward the reality, which the soul ultimately desires not simply to embrace but to be *embraced by* (a point to which we will return below). This is why the rational soul is appetitive precisely by virtue of its being rational. Maximus presents this dynamic in a striking way, worth quoting in full:

> If an intellective being is moved intellectively, that is, in a manner appropriate to itself, then it will necessarily become a knowing intellect. But if it knows, it surely loves that which it knows; and if it loves, it certainly suffers an ecstasy toward it as an object of love. If it suffers this ecstasy, it obviously urges itself onward, and if it urges itself onward, it surely intensifies and greatly accelerates its motion. And if its motion is intensified in this way, it will not cease until it is wholly present in the whole beloved, and wholly encompassed by it, willingly receiving the whole saving circumscription by its own choice, so that it might be wholly qualified by the whole circumscriber, and, being wholly circumscribed, will no longer be able to wish to be known from its own qualities, but rather from those of the circumscriber, in the same way that air is thoroughly permeated by light, or iron in a forge that is completely penetrated by the fire, or anything else of this sort.[14]

The soul *loves* what it *knows* because what it knowingly takes into itself exceeds its capacity to appropriate it. Moreover, because this movement beyond, this self-transcendence, is incited, so to speak, by what is already present *in* the soul, Maximus describes it in terms of love—rather than, say, simply in terms of a spontaneous, self-initiated power of self-determination. This latter conception would dominate, by contrast, to the extent that the object of the will were *not* already present in the soul. In this case, the movement of transcendence would be a movement from absence, imperfection, or empty indeterminacy, to determinate perfection. But for Maximus, the movement is an expression precisely of the *excess* of perfection. We hear an echo of Dionysius here, now in a new, temporal register.

At the same time, there is *genuinely* a movement in this perfection, the significance of which becomes clear in the contrast with the Origenist conception of the primacy of rest. The simple primacy of rest would imply on the one hand both a simple intellectualist conception of freedom, and on the other an irrationalist voluntarism, which turns out to be its flip side. In this case, the highest actuality is possession of the good, and the most perfect possession of the good as a totalizing embrace, so to speak, is the merely intellectual appropriation of goodness in its truth. It follows, then, that the movement of will can at its best be nothing but a "catching up" to this a priori perfection. If the will "adds" anything of its own, over against the pure intellection, it can only be a movement *away* from this static possession, or in other words a completely *senseless* fall. The will therefore does not represent a genuinely positive dimension, an order irreducibly distinct from that of the intellect, but is essentially negative, whether that be the negativity of a simple rejection of the good or the merely apparent positivity of a negation of the negation: one wills not to set the will in motion on its own. If, by contrast, movement is something perfect, then the various aspects of the will—deliberation, judgment, choice, pursuit, and so on—stand forth as genuinely positive components of human nature.

That Maximus views them as such is clear in the unprecedented importance he gives to the act of *choice*, *prohairesis*, in his philosophical anthropology. The act of choosing represents for Maximus an indispensable moment in the perfection of a rational nature. To see this, we must place it in the context of his overall vision. As is his general wont, Maximus distinguishes three modes of being (τρεῖς τρόπους) which are three degrees of perfection: that of simple being (τὸ εἶναι), of well-being (τὸ εὖ εἶναι), and of eternal being (τὸ ἀεὶ εἶναι). In *Ambiguum* 65, Maximus explains that the first mode of being is given to rational creatures "according to essence," the second is given to them "according to choice, insofar as they are self-moved," and the third is given to them "according to grace."[15] It is tempting, initially, to read these three degrees as successive stages of perfection, each "building on" the other, which is to say, each picking up where the other left off, thus adding to what was lacking in the antecedent. From this perspective, one would take the first stage to be a relatively empty condition of possibility, being as *merely* given, the meaning of which is yet to be determined. The second stage, then, would be the elevation of being as given through the exercise of choice, by which one surpasses the merely natural and arrives at a properly rational existence. But this remains a finite perfection, limited by its own power, which means that the perfect fulfillment of eternal beatitude must be introduced from without as a wholly gratuitous gift, one that therefore supplants the mere rational self-determination. To read Maximus in this way, however, though it is not absolutely false, betrays the basic thrust of his vision. It implies a sense of movement as the overcoming of a deficiency or a merely extrinsic addition, rather than as an overflowing of perfect goodness.

Maximus himself provides a much more subtle reading of the relations between these three degrees. He states succinctly that the first condition contains the "mode of potency" (τὸν... δυνάμεως), the second that of "actuality" (τὸν... ἐνεργείας), and the third that of "rest" (τὸν... ἀργίας).[16] But he makes it clear that we ought not to see these as three discrete stages, layered on top of each other, so to speak, or following upon each other in mere succession, so that each begins simply where the other ends and so each increase leaves the previous moment behind. Instead, Maximus presents the moments as implicated *in* each other in different ways and so as interpreting each other successively. Thus, far from leaving the previous mode behind, the higher modes in fact fulfill the earlier ones, bringing them to be most properly what they are. Following this approach, let us first note that Maximus does not simply identify each stage in an exclusive sense with a particular characteristic (potency, act, and rest) but instead says more precisely that each *contains* (περιεκτικόν) the particular characteristic, which suggests that the characteristic may define the particular mode, but not in a manner that excludes the characteristics of other modes. When he goes on, then, to explain the particular relationships that obtain between the particular modes, their mutual inherence becomes altogether evident. The natural potency is not an inert passivity upon which actuality adventitiously supervenes but a potency *for* the actualization, which is to say it is positively disposed toward the actualization, even if the actualization does not arrive except through the exercise of choice. In this case, the first mode is already the *beginning* of choice, so that the actual choosing is not a foreign addition. Instead, choice is the condition that brings about what was in some sense already there. It is the *potency* that actualizes itself through choosing. The actuality, then, which comes about only through the rational appropriation (*gnomikōs*),[17] is nevertheless always an actualization *of* a natural potency and so can never itself be "without the natural."[18] There is, in other words, a reciprocal dependence between the first two modes. Finally, the third condition transcends both: it is neither included in the given natural potency nor achieved through choice. At the same time it does not simply leave the anterior modes behind but "wholly contains those that precede it," namely, the natural potency and its rational fulfillment, for reasons we will indicate below.[19] What we have here in all of this is not a mere transition from one mode to the next but a movement of enhancement that intensifies each preceding mode rather than leaving it behind, since the lower is in some sense already the beginning of the higher.

It is illuminating—and crucial for the general argument of our book regarding the development of the notion of freedom—to see this paradoxical relation of act and potency in Maximus's interpretation of the modes of being as a kind of mirroring in the immanent, created, and temporal order of the ultimate principle of goodness, apparent above all in Plotinus and Dionysius, which transcends the difference between act and potency so as to be able to integrate them properly. This was the key to the freedom of God, and it turns out to be, in Maximus, the key to the freedom of the creature. There can be no doubt that it was the reflection on Christ, who is the perfect unity of God and creature in person, that opened Maximus's vision to this interpretation, beyond Origen, for example, who remained still too close on this score at least to the schema of a standard Neoplatonism. What we have here is genuinely a mirror imaging in time, not of eternity simply (as in Plotinus), but—again, paradoxically—of supraeternity: whereas the absolute principle in Plotinus and even more thematically in Dionysius *precedes* the polar distinction between time and eternity, and the related polarity between potency and actuality, in Maximus the emphasis is on the "rest" that *supersedes* potency and actuality, though not, of course, in the sense of temporal sequence. Let us explore this point further.

Maximus had expressed the same three modes in *Ambiguum 7*, where he presents their interrelation in a similar but more differentiated manner and reveals the cause of their unity-in-difference. In this context, he clarifies further that the potency that is inscribed in being "by nature" is not therefore an empty passivity but already a "being-moved," specifically a being-moved by the *archē*, which is to say, by God understood as first principle.[20] Because this movement is inscribed precisely *in our nature*, which is universal, it has at root a generic quality (τὸ ἁπλῶς κινεῖσθαι). This movement, however, cannot actually comprehend the rational creature unless that creature actively appropriates it through repeated acts of will (*prohairesis*), which through their regularity acquire the status of a fundamental disposition (*gnomie*).[21] This appropriation, which we might call "personal" or "hypostatic," in distinction from the natural, even as it is contained within it, is necessarily an enactment *in history*, which means that it "particularizes" the "generic" movement in relation to the telos, God as the end, according to a specific mode in every case (τὸ πῶς κινεῖσθαι).[22] Note that to say that it *particularizes* the movement that belongs to nature simply means that the actualization it accomplishes is in some respect already precontained in the nature. In this sense, though the act of choice accomplishes something that the merely natural potency *as such* cannot accomplish on its own, what it accomplishes nevertheless lies, not outside nature, but inside it as an expression of one of its given potencies.

The end, which represents the third mode, however, precisely because it is also the *original source* of the creature's being, is not the good as a discrete object that the creature can lay hold of simply through the act of choosing; instead, Maximus explains that the creature desires *to be comprehended by the good that it chooses, namely, God*. But this can happen only through *God's* act, an act initiated from beyond the creature and its natural capacities and deliberate choices. In *this* respect, Maximus says, both creaturely potency and act reach their limit, and the whole is taken up into eternity,[23] which of course exceeds the creature's own resources, even as it requires them. Eternal being is therefore a kind of *rest*, beyond potency and act. It is illuminating that Maximus associates this rest with the super-Sabbath, as it were, the "Eighth Day," and this illumination casts an important light on the relation between these three ideas.[24] The Eighth Day, as it is traditionally interpreted, is not a particular day of the week alongside the others as nothing but the last of a linear series but transcends them as both beginning and end: "The seventh and Sabbath is the dispassion that in succession follows practical philosophy undertaken according to virtue. But the eighth and the first day, being single and perpetual [μία καὶ ἀκατάλυτος], is the wisdom that comes about after cognitive contemplation."[25] It therefore bears on the meaning of all of them. The "rest" of the Eighth Day is not a *static* one in any simplistic sense: if it were nothing but the actualization of a potency, which came after the preceding condition as merely succeeding it, the act would represent a terminus, an *end*, that put a stop to the movement enabled by potency. The ultimate end that Maximus presents, however, is one that transcends the relativity of potency and act to each other, which is why he describes it not as a satiety that causes movement to cease, or as a constant striving,[26] but, as we indicated above, as an ever-moving stillness.

The key to the unity of the modes is the fact that each is relative to one and the same thing, namely, God, under a different modality. God does not enter into the picture, so to speak, only in the third moment, while the first two, potency and act, relate to each other in a merely natural-as-nontheological way. Instead, the potency aims not only at its corresponding act but also at God, because it is in the first place a being-moved *by* God.[27] Thus, we could say that the three basic modes of being are not simply a progression through successive stages but represent a gradual deepening of what is given at the outset: it is only *in* the actual choosing that the potency becomes fully alive, so to speak, *as* potency, and it is only in grace that the choosing fully realizes itself as choice (since the actual desire for God is ultimately a choosing *to be chosen*, as it were). In other words, the desire is ordered to what both precedes it and exceeds it, and so is a desire to be comprehended by the beloved on both sides; but the comprehension can be complete only if the rational nature also *takes* the beloved *into* itself (chooses) and is *taken in* by the beloved in turn. In Maximus's formulation, the fulfillment of choice is, paradoxically, a "voluntary surrender of the will, so that from the same source whence we receive our being, we should also long to receive being moved."[28] Note that, in this respect, the third mode returns to the first mode, being-moved, though now under a new aspect. The three modes are profoundly related because they are all relative to God. As Maximus puts it in *Ambiguum* 10,

> The two extremes [being and eternal well-being, which are the first and third modes] belong solely to God, who is their author, but the intermediate mode depends on our gnomie and motion, and through it the extremes are properly said to be what they are, for if the middle term were absent, their designation would be meaningless, for the good (i.e., well-being) would not be present in their midst, and thus the saints realized that apart from their eternal movement toward God, there was no other way to possess and preserve the truth of the extremes, which is assured only when well-being is mixed in the middle of them.[29]

If we step back for a moment and recall Dionysius, we note here a central role given to choice that is simply absent (or at least left unhighlighted in the background) in that other monk's thought. For Maximus, there is no rational participation in the gift of being, or any aspect of it, that is not either actually mediated or meant to be mediated by choice, that is, by an active and "deliberate" appropriation by the creature. What the creature initially possesses passively, so to speak, by suffering (τὸ πάσχον), he is ultimately meant to transform into a *doing* (τὸ ποιοῦν), through his *choice*.[30] One might therefore think that there is a decisive tension between Dionysius, who absolutizes nature, as we argued last chapter, and so downplays deliberate choice, and Maximus, who foregrounds choice and distinguishes the "well-being" it provides precisely from the mere being of nature. But as our exposition ought to be making clear, Maximus does not at all set the free choice of the will over against nature as a supervening causal order; instead, he identifies this power of will with the nature that is proper to a rational creature.

Thus, he coins the term *natural will* (*thelēma physikon*),[31] by which he means not only the will that is inscribed in our nature but even more fundamentally the actively choosing will that is informed, guided, and indeed in some sense *moved* by nature, operating *within* the order given by nature and with nature's own momentum, as it were. This is because nature is not mere (static) matter, to be taken up by will and set in motion, but potent source, which in some sense precontains the very motion initiated by the will. In other words, the reason Maximus can use the phrase *natural will*—which will become in the late medieval thinker John Duns Scotus a strict oxymoron, as we will see—is that *will*, properly understood, represents the fullest expression of the meaning of nature, rather than a principle that is at least logically if not also really opposed to nature; the "natural will" is for Maximus a kind of perfect recapitulation of the movement that defines nature rather than a simple step beyond nature. Here we see a more profound integration than, for example, even Plotinus was able to achieve, however much the drift of Plotinus's thinking may have moved in this direction.

Above, we distinguished the "generic" potency that is our nature from the actualization of that potency through *choice*, in view of our end, which specifies the generic motion according to a particular mode. But it is crucial to see that nature, for Maximus, is not just the point of departure but remains all along the way the abiding measure of freedom. In other words, nature represents a *perfection*; it is for Maximus, no less than for Dionysius, an absolute. The thrust of this point becomes most evident when we realize that what *natural* means for Maximus is nothing less than "being moved by God"—a point that resonates at an extraordinary depth when we recall that, as Augustine observed, the Trinity reveals that even God himself (as Son and Spirit) is, so to speak, moved by God (as Father). This point is revealed now in the reality of history, as we will see, in the Garden of Gethsemane. It is thus even clearer in Maximus than in Dionysius why "supernatural" beatitude is so fully natural, since the creature is never so fully and completely moved by God as when it actively participates in grace. If Maximus emphasizes free choice more than does Dionysius, he nevertheless means it as deepening the sense of nature that Dionysius affirmed rather than as adding to it in an adventitious way or indeed overturning it. Thus, for Maximus, a good choice is always and precisely a choice "according to nature."[32] Any choice that is not made according to nature is by contrast always a sin, a kind of disorder. This principle does not get overturned even in the radically novel order introduced by grace.[33] With his notion of *natural will and choice*, Maximus is arguably bringing to fulfillment an aspect left implicit in Dionysius's integration of eros, as receptive and appropriating movement, into goodness simply.

Let us unfold the point of Maximus's "natural will" more completely. The reason Maximus can affirm the absoluteness of nature so definitively is, again, that he recognizes God as *both* first principle *and* final telos and therefore as circumscribing the whole creature. Thus, what most originally sets things in motion is not "materially" different from that at which all things, of themselves, *aim*. In this regard, they may be said "passively" to be moved, all the way from the beginning to the end. It is precisely their nature that moves them, the nature given to them once and for all by God. Here we might see a development in the meaning of nature in Maximus's appropriation of Aristotle, a sort of integrating of the Jewish, theological dimension more directly into the Greek: while Maximus affirms the Aristotelian conception of nature as an internal principle of motion and rest, he brings out directly that this motion is at once the creature's own and *given* to the creature by God. Again, *natural*, for Maximus, ultimately means "being moved by God." Because it is being moved by what transcends it, nature is *essentially* desirous,[34] which means that it "naturally" transcends itself in pursuing an end that it has in some respect not yet attained, and yet at the very same time this end is not simply absent from it, which would make the end an abstract ideal toward which the creature would move *merely* by itself or not (i.e., pure potency in the Lockean sense). We might think, in this regard, of Plato's insight into the paradoxical unity of presence and absence, poverty and fullness, the already and the not yet, in all desire.[35] Instead, the end is already present in some sense from the beginning, which is why motion—not just physical motion but also and indeed *especially* rational, voluntary motion—is and remains something fundamentally *received*, and therefore abidingly *natural*. The receptive character of motion thus does not exclude spontaneous self-determination, and so receptivity, being moved by God, marks out the creature's entire trajectory, from beginning to end. The conversion of the passive to the active in the eschaton, which we mentioned above, is not the ceasing of the being-moved and the beginning of pure self-motion but the *full appropriation* into the self through the rational appetite, the will, of the natural being-moved, so that the being-moved can be seen truly as an act of the agent himself.[36] This is also why the act of will has the basic form of *obedience*.[37] We recall here the *fundamental* goodness of being moved, which Maximus interprets as a sign of the radical generosity of God's act of creation. We can think of nature as motion that is meant as a gift, which is to say it is given away to creatures in such a way that it is meant to become their very own (according to the analogous specificity of their nature). In this regard, choosing "according to nature" is not a slavish conformity to some extrinsically imposed measure but the reception of freedom, a reception that constitutes the freedom received. This is why Maximus is able to describe not only the original potency of our mere being as due to God but *also* the active realization of that potency through choice in our "well-being." The entire vision here comes to a culminating expression at a decisive moment in *Ambiguum 7*: "For the end of the motion of things that are moved is to rest within eternal well-being itself, just as their beginning was being itself, which is God, who is the giver of being and the bestower of the gnomie of well-being, for He is the beginning and the end. For from God come both our general power of motion (for He is our beginning) and the particular way that we move toward Him (for He is our end)."[38]

To put the matter "in a nutshell," the conventional judgment that free choice represents a step beyond nature, because in choice one is determining oneself, positing something new, beyond what is merely given, presupposes an impoverished sense of both nature and freedom. Nature, on the one hand, is conceived in this case in a materialist sense, wholly "from below," as it were. In his celebrated *Disputation with Pyrrhus*, Maximus sharply criticizes the identification of nature with "compulsion."[39] The succinctness of his argument against it ought not to cause us to overlook the depth of its implications: God has a nature, he points out, and yet no one would deny God's freedom; and the rational beings he creates have precisely a rational, and therefore a voluntary, nature. It is natural for them, therefore, to do things freely. There is a kind of *necessity* in this, to be sure, but not all necessity is a compulsion: God is good by the necessity of his nature, but that poses no external constraint on him.⁴⁰ If we consider the point made above, we can say that the unity of the *archē* and the telos implies that the potency is ordered from the beginning to the end, which is thus why the free realization of the potency will always be an unfolding in some respect of what was already given *in* the potency.⁴¹ This is, of course, simply another way of saying that the active choosing always remains at the same time a passive being-moved. But it brings more clearly to light the fact that nature is not a limited kind of being, which comes to a rather low-level end, so that free choice would be a self-moving power that takes nature only as a point of departure and is able to arrive further.

If the opposition of freedom and nature presupposes an impoverished view of nature, it also presupposes on the other hand an impoverished notion of freedom. Free choice *over against* nature would be nothing but a rejection of what God generously gives, which is to say it would represent a stepping outside the trajectory given in creation and so outside the fullness of being. To the extent that self-determination operates in detachment from one's being moved by God, it is empty freedom.

It is in this context that we can best appreciate Maximus's famous affirmation of a natural human will in Christ, along with his rejection of what he terms the "gnomic" will. Maximus, as we have seen, had given a positive meaning to *gnomie* as the particular mode of actualizing the potency of our natural movement. In the *Disputation with Pyrrhus*, he presents *gnomie*—a term, to be sure, that has a variety of senses: Maximus himself claims to have found twenty-eight different meanings in scripture⁴²—as the particular mode of willing characteristic of hypostatic human nature, which is de facto fallen.⁴³ In this case, *gnomie* refers to a specific mode of willing in the face of something that presents itself as good but that may in fact be good only in appearance. Something can *seem* good in a deceptive sense, it must be admitted, as a result of our ignorance, our disordered desire, our fears and anxieties, and so forth. Thus, "gnomic" willing, in this context, includes uncertainty, doubt, ignorance, and the possibility of conflict. Though these features are not sinful of their essence, they presuppose a fallen condition. They are of course a normal part of our experience of willing in the present state of the world, but Maximus means to show that what we take to be normal, and indeed often precisely a sign of the *freedom* of the will, does not in reality belong to the essence of the will as a power of self-determination (*autexousion*).⁴⁴ To think that such features are essential is to posit an anchorless freedom, without interior order or purpose. If deviation from purpose is possible for free will in the sense of abstract, logical possibility, it does not have to be possible in reality, and, indeed, to the extent that such deviation becomes real it represents a loss of freedom, a choice of emptiness, a surrender of the given fullness of being. It is by contrast possible to choose for oneself what is inevitably given, to inquire, deliberate, and examine in a manner that does not compromise certainty, immediate and spontaneous resolution. Indeed, it is only such a choice, only such an inquiry and deliberation, that, for Maximus, is truly and unqualifiedly free. This uncoerced, good necessity, evidence of active and deliberate participation, is what Maximus means by "natural will." In this respect, Maximus, for all his emphasis on choice, in all of its differentiated elements, does not contradict in any significant way what we saw in Dionysius. For both monks, freedom *is* (rational) nature, and nature *is* freedom.

Realizing Freedom

But this does not mean Maximus does not introduce something genuinely new. In truth, we have yet to consider Maximus's most decisive insight. As we have argued, the principle that governs and so guides the classical interpretation of the will and its freedom is the priority of act over potency, along with its correlate, that potency can be reduced to act only by something already actual. If this principle is affirmed in a simplistic way without any further qualification, there are two related implications for philosophical anthropology: on the one hand, we end with a kind of intellectualism, according to which the ultimate actuality to which the power of the will is reduced is the immediate unity of the soul and its object in contemplation, so that no reality remains so to speak outside or beyond the soul, *to* which it would be ordered in turn. On the other hand, the unqualified principle implies a kind of "eternalism" (to coin a term), according to which the movement in time and space would be *nothing more* than the unfolding of what is already actual in an "a priori" way, so to speak.⁴⁵ In this case, time as a sequence of moments following one upon the other would represent no positive contribution whatsoever to the meaning of things. Now, it must be said that none of the figures we have considered thus far offers an unqualified affirmation of the classical principle,[46] though it is equally important to insist that they *all* thus far accept it. We saw in Plotinus a revelation of goodness as the potency of all things, higher than but not in conflict with the pure actuality of intellect, a superabundant potency that reveals the bodily conditions of the human soul, in space and time, to be more than just a fall from perfection; we saw the positive affirmation in Augustine of the order of will, as distinct from the order of intellect, at the human level, with the concomitant affirmation of the historical *novelty*, the spontaneous unpredictability, of choice; and we saw the deep grounding of the *positive* significance of the created order in its material reality in time and space in Dionysius's rereading of divine goodness as eros, a seeking of creation and not only an object of creation's search. But what remains ambiguous in all of these developments is the fact that actuality tends to re-duce to what transcends time and so retains a principally (which is not to say exclusively) supratemporal character. From this perspective, the actuality of perfection, for evident reasons, is "a priori," something to which the "a posteriority" of time relates itself in the accomplishment of freedom. But this means that the historical dimension, *precisely qua historical*, has not yet been directly affirmed in the meaning of freedom. We might say that, in this case, the classical Greek notion has not yet been received in such a way as to have room for the properly *Jewish* sense of freedom, to the extent that the Jewish sense foregrounds the events of history. As a result, the historical is included in the form of a supratemporal pattern, as we see in Augustine (the ages of history) and in Dionysius (the spiral as integration of circle and line). To be clear, there is nothing problematic in principle in this vision of an eternal form instantiated in history—quite to the contrary, to lose this aspect would be to surrender altogether the classical conception of freedom, which it is the very purpose of the present study of freedom to recover. The point is simply that such an integration does not yet recognize the historical precisely in what is most distinctive about it, namely, its sense of the progressive, the novel, the open-ended, the as yet undecided or unrealized, and so forth.[47] It is just this dimension that Maximus opens up in principle, and so it is this that marks his lasting achievement. Let us explain.

The comparison with thinkers that precede Maximus serves to bring to light an extraordinary implication of the resolutely Christocentric character of his thought. The God who is the actual *archē* and telos, setting the horizon, so to speak, within which the free self-determination of the human will unfolds and finds its effective energy, is *not only* the transcendent good and beautiful but now the incarnation of absolute goodness and beauty in the Person of Christ. Let us note how this recapitulates in a historical register the very point we have been seeking to make clear metaphysically: suprahistorical nature is *given to be realized* in history *through choice*; the historical mission of Christ is the realization, in time, of what has "always been." We will see, in a moment, how Maximus foregrounds, beyond the simple fact of the Incarnation, the dramatic moment of choice that fulfills the divine mission and so makes manifest the full reality of human freedom. We saw the importance of the created reality in Dionysius, for whom the fact of the Incarnation represents a paradigm of the eros that expresses generous goodness precisely by *receiving* the other: in this case, the absolute God receives human nature from his own humble creature. In Maximus, this reception is crucial not only as an established fact, a permanent truth, but *also* as a dramatic event, a task, that has to be lived out in history. The human nature God receives in Christ is thus not only flesh and blood, so to speak, but nature as a self-realizing movement in the manner we have been describing, which is to say that it is nature also and indeed most fundamentally *as will*. We might say that, if Dionysius brings out the metaphysical and ontological implications of the mystery of Christmas, Maximus brings out the implications of Easter, or more specifically of the Triduum.[48]

It is in this context that we can appreciate the remarkable weight that Maximus accords to a simple event in the life of Christ, which proves to be a supreme moment of convergence of all of the themes we have been discussing so far. Maximus focuses his interpretation of the mystery of Christ in a decisive way on the "Agony of the Garden," the moment in Gethsemane in which Christ separated himself, not just from "the crowd," but in this case from his closest followers (Mt 26:36)—we ought to recall here the Jewish notion of the *holy*, which sanctifies that from which it is separated—and in prayer and suffering gave his assent to his mission, the saving deed of the cross. As repeated in the synoptic Gospels, Jesus gave his assent in a rather complex form: not a simple yes but a twofold response: "My Father, if it be possible, let this cup pass from me; nevertheless, not as I will, but as you will" (Mt 26:39; cf. Mk 14:36, Lk 22:42; cf. also Jn 6:38 and 18:11). The yes is a willed surrender of his own will and the acceptance of the will of another—indeed, *the* Other. In contrast to those who would interpret this passage as the triumph of the perfect divine will *over* the sinful human will, an interpretation that would place the divine and human at odds in a dualistic fashion and so compromise the very principle of the Incarnation at the heart of the Christian vision, Maximus insists that Jesus is a single, Divine Person with two irreducibly different and yet perfectly united natures.[49] In this regard, Jesus's affirmation of the goodness of his natural life ("Let this cup pass") is not some sort of concession to weakness—an interpretation that would call into question the definitiveness of creation and so the completeness of nature—but an expression of absolute and comprehensive perfection, without a trace of sin.

Moreover, as Jonathan Bieler has pointed out, it is not just the natural human will that affirms the goodness of existence and then yields to the higher operation of the divine will. Rather, *both* operate in this twofold manner: the divine will *also* wills the good of natural existence, and the natural will *also* sacrifices that created good for the sake of the Father's mission.[50] This implies both a divine depth to the natural goodness and nature's "innate" capacity for radical self-transcendence—a perfect convergence of the Greek and Jewish dimensions. (We might recall here Maximus's appropriation of Aristotelian *physis* as a being-moved by God, which opens nature from the beginning.) We mentioned earlier that for Maximus, no less than for Dionysius, nature remains in some sense absolute, to such an extent that any act of the will that is not *kata physin* is sinful and a departure from freedom. What has come to be called Christ's "deprecation" at Gethsemane is an act of will that is *kata physin* but at the same time more than that, so that in this act the affirmation of the goodness of nature is taken up into an assent to the *historical* will of the Father beyond (though not outside of) the givenness of nature. If there is some ambiguity in Augustine, who seems in the end to allow only the choice of God to be a free choice, Maximus shows that the choice of God does not at all exclude, but in fact necessarily *includes*, the affirmation of the good belonging properly to nature, even in some sense over against God, though of course the willing of the will of God is ultimately ultimate, so to speak.[51] We emphasize that the goodness of nature is not simply permitted in relation to transcendent perfection but positively willed *in history* by God himself. We saw earlier—in the discussion of nature and freedom—that distinction does not necessarily imply opposition or conflict but can coincide with perfect unity; here Maximus presents a single agency with an irreducibly twofold will, which does not compromise difference but overcomes dualism once and for all.

Before concluding, it is worth pointing out here the ultimate ground for Maximus's integration of nature and the person, which is an irreducibly distinct subject of action: namely, the mystery of the Trinity, which "is truly a Monad, for such it is; and the Monad is truly a Trinity, for as such it subsists, since there is one Godhead that in essence is a Monad and in substance a Trinity."[52] Thus, as he observes in the course of his refutation of the Arians in *Ambiguum* 24, on the one hand, will is not a generic power, which operates on its own, but is only ever active through "the consent of a willing subject . . . who possesses it and exercises it."[53] On the other hand, however, in the Trinitarian God, in whom there are three Persons, there is only *one will*, which Maximus identifies with the "one substance and one nature" of God.[54] Here, at the highest and most decisive level, namely, in the inner life of God, we see, not a transcendence of nature in the will, as Plotinus seems to have thought in the end, but *an identification of will and nature*. This implies both an "expansive" notion of nature, sufficient to include the full meaning of will in its perfect operation, and a truly substantial notion of will that, even in its most radical transcendence, remains an expression of nature. If Maximus insists on the *perfection* of the will *as nature*, not only in Christ but in all creatures, it is because there is in the end nothing higher than the simplicity of the triune *nature* of God.

Conclusion: Maximus and History

To use the words of T. S. Eliot, Jesus's affirmation of his created nature inside of a consent to God's will is not a final vanquishing of the mutability of history in any simplistic sense but rather an "overcoming of time *in* time." History receives its sanctioned meaning, so to speak, from within itself, rather than from a measure that stands simply outside of it. To be sure, the redemptive event is not simply a particular historical moment, which occurred and then receded into the past, but represents the "fullness of time," as St. Paul says (Gal 4:4), and it is such because it is a kind of unity of eternity and time. But it is nevertheless *also* a particular event in history, and this has profound implications for the meaning of freedom. We will close this chapter with a focus on just two of these implications before ending with a remaining question prompted by Maximus's synthesis.

First, we have seen that the nature of human freedom is determined by the relationship of the will to the transcendent good, which eventually proves to be a relationship between man's will and the will of God. The recurrent difficulty in the classical conception of freedom is the absoluteness of a priori perfection, which would seem necessarily to render the finite and temporally bound human will finally meaningless by implication. What Maximus shows is that the absoluteness of perfection does not exclude movement in time and space. This particular problem of freedom has a dramatic resolution in Maximus's vision; it is one that is achieved, so to speak, on the stage of history, and one that is achieved by God himself, to be sure, but—and this is decisive—not simply qua God, but also qua *man*. This is the crucial point that Maximus heroically refused ever to surrender. What this means, then, is that the order of redemption, on which freedom ultimately depends, is not simply an eternal form but can include what is sometimes called the "messiness" of history, the series of events that unfold in an infinity of unpredictable ways, none of which is simply a priori excluded from the outset, even if the choices involve the disorder of sin and evil, as they of course generally do in the fallen world. In this case, the "vagaries" of man's free action in history are not of their essence a falling away from an original rest of perfection;[55] instead, the order of perfection, present from the beginning as *archē*, can be present *also* at the end, the telos, in a new way, which means that the original presence of that perfection does not in principle and of necessity exclude the real drama of movement that is the hallmark of Maximus's vision.[56] Order reinstitutes itself at the far end of freedom's activity, and indeed in some sense as an expression of that identity. Here we have the essential Christian contribution to the meaning of freedom, the reason why freedom is essentially Christian: the drama of the incarnation of the personal Goodness that defines freedom overcomes the exclusive dichotomy of historical reality *or* the good as such, the a priori *or* the a posteriori.

Though we cannot unfold it at any length here, we see the implication of this point in Maximus's distinctive account of the passions.[57] If Augustine was able to affirm the goodness of the passions in principle, beyond Plotinus or even more so the Stoics, as revealing the relation to a goodness in some sense *outside* of oneself, Maximus takes a step further. He distinguishes in fallen man the passions that belong to us *by nature*, and so are *essentially* good, from those that represent a departure from our nature. But *even these* are not simply excised from the meaning of genuine human existence. Referring to St. Paul's interpretation in the Letter to the Romans, Maximus speaks instead of the "Gentile" passions, which were not *originally* included in the given nature (the plan of perfection) but intruded on the original order as it were from the outside.[58] Because of human sin, the improper use of freedom, which draws man away from his natural goodness, these distorted passions that have come to present themselves in this contingent way can nevertheless also be brought into the proper meaning of the whole and can become themselves genuine instruments, so to speak, of redemption.[59] They are (dramatically) included in the plan as surprising, that is, unanticipated, opportunities to show how the original plan included more than originally apparent. In a word, for Maximus, the "disorder" of history thus does not of necessity simply lie outside the goodness of a priori perfection. Of course, this also means that the perfection is not imposed in a unilateral way, but involves freedom, which is to say that the historical resolution of the drama of human freedom is at the same time an opening up of the drama. The end is a beginning.

The account of the passions points to the second implication, namely, the reconciliation of the Jews and the Gentiles, or more specifically the union in Maximus of the Jewish and Greek conceptions of freedom. We have seen that Maximus absolutizes nature in a manner that would rival any Greek philosophical interpretation of existence.[60] And yet what he offers is not simply a Greek interpretation of nature. The *logoi* or natures of things are at the same time divine *wills* (*thelēma*), Maximus says, citing Dionysius.[61] The nature that defines the horizon of human action is a radically dynamic nature that is able to include the movement of history in a dramatic fashion, rising all the way up to sacrificial obedience to the will of the Father. And so it is a Jewish transformation of nature. At the same time, Maximus's conception is "more than Jewish." As we saw in chapter 1, history is decisive in the Jewish understanding of freedom: freedom is a particular *event* of liberation, namely, the exodus from Egypt, an event that becomes a permanent form of existence, which has its articulation in the law and the priestly rites of commemoration. For Maximus, there is also a particular liberating event that essentially constitutes freedom. But this event is also a revelation of the good and beautiful, and so the establishment of the proper meaning of (universal) nature. The good that is revealed is a comprehensive one: it is not just the goodness of God, as transcendent principle, but at the same time, and inclusively, a revelation of the irreducibly distinct goodness of the created order, precisely in its *difference* from God ("Let this cup pass") and its finite conditions in space and time. Insofar as this synthesis—the absoluteness of the good and the beautiful, and the particularity and "open-endedness" of history—is essential to the full meaning of freedom, we see that the reality that Maximus describes is the real gift of freedom, which lies at the core of Western civilization (though not limited to this particular history, of course, by its very nature), even if it is not acknowledged as such.

If there is a question to raise regarding Maximus's contribution to the understanding of freedom, it lies in his somewhat notorious rejection of a "gnomic" will in Christ. The word *gnomie*, as we have seen, is not univocal. Maximus uses it in some contexts in an altogether positive sense as the act of deliberate choice, which specifies a natural movement to a good according to a particular mode: in other words, *gnomie* "personalizes" the natural will. In his earlier writings, he posits such a will even in Christ.[62] When, in his most mature writing, he comes to *deny* that Christ had a "gnomic will," insisting only that Christ possessed a *natural* human will, he makes it clear that *gnomie* in this particular context means the specific modality of *sin*: "Those who say that there is a gnomie in Christ . . . are demonstrating that he is a mere man, deliberating in a manner like unto us, having ignorance, doubt, and opposition, since one only deliberates about something which is doubtful, not concerning what is free of doubt."[63] The question that arises here, however, is whether uncertainty, the time lag between the presence of goods and the choice made, the need to deliberate between goods that in some respect exclude each other, and even the need to distinguish between what appears to be good in a particular respect and what is in fact best are all *necessarily* bound up with sin. To be sure, to have to bring about in oneself a resolution to do the good when faced with a less good, or even an evil, alternative that exercises a powerful attraction is inconceivable apart from the disorder due to sin. But is there not a possibility of being faced with equally good, or even incommensurably good, possibilities, which requires a kind of unpredictability or ignorance of how a thing might turn out, a venturing, which is due to the altogether-good particularities of historical existence, and has nothing to do in principle with sin? Shall I surprise my beloved with *this* gift, or rather with *that* gift, knowing that either one will no doubt please her best, because she knows that I have picked it out especially for her from a number of good possibilities? In this case, we recognize the gratuity of the act, which would have its own particular kind of uncertainty—not, of course, a worry or doubt, but a certain joyful desire to wait, to allow an interval of time to elapse, to see how she will react—as something that belongs to the *perfection* of the will.[64] The danger, in Maximus, is that the very proper denial of a gnomic will in Christ in the sinful sense implies an identification of *gnomie* with the conditions of sin simply, which implies in turn a separation of historical particularity from human perfection. In this regard, Maximus threatens to undo what seems to be his most significant achievement. The clarification of this particular dimension, without surrendering the centrality of nature and its being moved by goodness and beauty, is something that will require centuries to unfold and first takes a questionable turn in the early Middle Ages, as we will see in the following two chapters, in which we see how the Christian reception begins to separate from the founding principles of the classical tradition.

PART IV

The Early Middle Ages

CHAPTER 6

St. Anselm
Just Freedom

At first glance, despite the great distance in time and place, there appears to be a striking thematic continuity between Anselm (1033–1109) and Maximus the Confessor.[1] Maximus insisted on *two wills* in the Person of Christ and presented their perfection as a hierarchical unity: Christ's will to preserve his "natural" life was affirmed but subordinated to his will to obey the Father: "Not as I will but as you will." Similarly, Anselm presents the essential drama of freedom as a choice between *two wills*, the affection for advantage or benefit (*commodum*), which is a natural will (*voluntas naturalis*), and the affection for justice (*justitia*), a will given by God beyond the gift of nature, to which the affection for advantage is meant to be subordinated. From the perspective of this apparent continuity, Anselm might be interpreted simply as universalizing Maximus's insight. Thus, what Maximus presented as a singular historical event in the mission of Christ, Anselm presents as a sort of suprahistorical event—namely, the "fall of the devil"—a drama that reveals, through contrast, the model for the attainment of freedom generally for all rational creatures. Instead of an absolutely unique relation between two irreducibly distinct natures in a single divine person, we have a universalized principle, which as such institutes a drama that all rational creatures are meant to enact in their realization of their single nature. One might thus see this freedom as won by Christ and communicated to human nature.[2]

But in fact the differences between the two understandings are quite profound and turn out to bear in a significant way on the meaning of freedom simply. As we will see, if Maximus introduces a novelty that still remains within a continuity with the classical tradition, St. Anselm marks a decisive moment in the development of the Western notion of freedom, introducing an ambiguity that will be fateful in the centuries that follow him. One notices a clear shifting of horizons in this early part of the Middle Ages regarding the way the question of freedom is approached: the reflection is not evidently rooted in *being*, the nature of reality, and it no longer takes its bearings so fully from the meaning of freedom in God.[3] Thus, the interpretation of freedom becomes decidedly intramundane, focusing above all on man's moral condition. In the present chapter, we will first present an interpretive summary of Anselm's understanding of freedom, then highlight the personal deepening that the notion of freedom undergoes in Anselm's work, the genuine contribution we receive from him inside a continuity, and, finally, suggest how Anselm's reconception of the will and its freedom emerges as a kind of crack in the Christian synthesis of its traditions, if not an actual break.[4]

The Essence of Freedom

Anselm develops his notion of freedom principally through four works, spanning from the beginning to the end of his writing career, with each book disclosing a different aspect, but without representing any basic evolution in the sense of a change of mind on any fundamental idea.[5] In *De veritate* (1080–86), he worked out the notion of *rectitude*, which would become the pivotal notion for the rest of his thinking; he formulated the essential definition of the freedom of the will in *De libertate arbitrii* (1080–86); he brought out the concrete meaning of this definition through the most basic "test case," namely, the fall of the angels, in *De casu diaboli* (1080–86); and, finally, in his last completed text, *De concordia praescientiae et praedestinationis et gratiae dei cum libero arbitrio* (1107–8), he defended this notion of freedom as compatible with divine foreknowledge, predestination, and the effective power of grace.

Let us begin directly with what is already a major achievement, namely, Anselm's formal definition of freedom. This definition is in fact the first one we have encountered in such a direct and explicit form so far in our investigations. According to Anselm, "Freedom of choice is the ability [*potestas*] to keep uprightness-of-will [*rectitudinem voluntatis*] for the sake of this uprightness itself."[6] In the *De veritate*, Anselm had defined justice as "uprightness-of-will kept for its own sake."[7] We may thus condense the definition and say that *freedom is the capacity for justice*. This definition is evidently what has come to be called a "normative" conception of freedom, which is to say it is a conception of freedom, not as an indeterminate power, which can be used for good or ill, but as a power that is so fully meant for proper use, so to speak, that the standard is built into its very definition. Anselm presents this formulation as an alternative to what was often (misleadingly) designated among medieval thinkers as the "Augustinian" view of freedom, namely, *the power to sin or not to sin* (*posse peccare et non peccare*).[8] The reason to prefer the normative definition, according to Anselm, is that only such a definition allows us to recognize God and the redeemed saints, who are incapable of sin, not only as free, but as paradigmatically free, as freer than those still vulnerable to temptation. A definition, says Anselm, needs to cover all cases.[9] Now, we saw in chapter 3 that Augustine, too, had a normative conception of freedom, and we explained it there in just the same terms that Anselm does in his account: "Each sinned by his own choice, which was free; but neither sinned by means of that in virtue of which his choice was free."[10] According to Anselm, if it is freedom that allows us to sin, the act of sin is never an expression of freedom: "'To be able to sin' does not pertain to the definition of 'freedom of choice.' In fact, the ability to sin does not constitute either freedom or a part of freedom."[11] Anselm and Augustine are in perfect accord on this point, as we saw in chapter 3. As Stanley Kane has correctly observed, Anselm consciously avoids ever saying that one can sin *freely*.[12] A potency aims at an end. If this aiming entails—at least in its not yet perfected instances—the possibility of failure, this possibility nevertheless does not define the potency as such and in its essence. Defined simply as a *power* for justice, freedom can be found both in the sinner, who for a variety of reasons that we will shortly investigate cannot manage to accomplish justice on his own, and in God, who is supremely potent in his acts of justice and so represents absolute freedom. Importantly, the reason the definition can span such extremes without shattering is that a *potency* does not need to be realized, and indeed does not need to be *actually* realizable, in order to be what it is. We will return to this point below.[13]

Anselm fills out what it means to will justice in his reflection on the possibility of a spiritual creature, created without a trace of disorder, nevertheless turning away from its creator, a possibility that seems to be entailed by the traditional notion of the fall of Satan. To understand Anselm's interpretation of this fall, it is helpful to draw on an illuminating distinction that Anselm makes explicit in his last work but that is already clearly, if implicitly, operative from the beginning in his thinking about freedom. In *De concordia*,[14] Anselm explains that the single word *will* can designate three different things: (1) the faculty of will, taken in itself, or in other words the *instrument* (*instrumentum*) by which one wills; (2) the fundamental disposition of the will (*affectio*), a kind of inclination, which is present whether or not the agent is aware of it; or (3) the discrete, deliberate act, the agent's "occurrent" use of the instrument (*usus*). Thus, we may say succinctly that my will (1) is disposed, that is, has a will (2), to will (3) a particular act. This distinction will prove to be fundamental to everything else in Anselm and already represents a decisive novelty in Anselm's anthropology in comparison, for instance, to that of Augustine.[15] With respect to the fall of the devil, the distinction helps to clarify Anselm's difference from Augustine, who also reflected in depth on the question of angelic freedom. As we saw in our discussion of this event in chapter 3, Augustine inferred a *deficient cause*, that is, the will's otherwise inexplicable allowing itself to lapse, to fail to participate fully in the good in the manner it was given to participate. According to Anselm, by contrast, a power cannot be deficient considered in itself, *as* power; instead, it is only the particular *use* of a power that can be more or less strong in relation to its object. To illustrate what he means, Anselm presents the man who had once held a bull immobile being seen in another instance allowing a ram to get the better of him: it was not that he became less strong but that he exerted himself less in the second instance.[16] Similarly, for Anselm, the will may be weak or strong in one of its particular acts, but considered *simply in itself*, as a mere power in abstraction from any particular realization, it is never more or less powerful: "The will which I call the instrument-for-willing is always one and the same thing regardless of what we will; but the will which is the instrument's activity [*opus eius*] is as multiple as the number of things we will and the number of occasions upon which we will."[17] It is revealing (for reasons we will present at the end of the chapter) that Anselm ascribes a kind of absoluteness to the will thus conceived as a separate instrument: as a pure power, the will "has an inalienable strength, which cannot be overcome by any other force."[18] If it is overcome by anything, then, it can only be by its own choice.[19]

This isolation of the will as instrument actually intensifies rather than resolves the problem. If the will has a native power that cannot be overcome, what would cause it to thwart itself, or more specifically to allow itself to be thwarted? In one respect, such a choice will be inexplicable, as Anselm eventually concedes. The movement of the will is ultimately due to nothing but its own causality; the will is ultimately self-caused. The will of the devil in this case "was an efficient cause of itself—if this can be said—and its own effect."[20] But Anselm nevertheless believes we can give an account of how such a choice is at least *possible*. To explain how the will, in its original pristine goodness and fresh from the Creator's hand, so to speak, can sin, Anselm insists that we must posit *two* wills in any free agent, each of which is originally, if not equally, good, and presumably each of which is invincible in itself. It must be noted that, when Anselm uses the word *will* in this context, he no longer means it in the first sense (instrument)—that is, he is not suggesting that the creature has two separate *faculties* of will—but now in the second sense, namely, will as disposition, aptitude, or affection.[21] God originally gave the angels an affection for benefit (*commodum*), which is essentially a desire for happiness. Whether this affection is genuinely *native* to the will is ambiguous in an interesting way. On the one hand, Anselm once uses the phrase *natural will* (*voluntas naturalis*) to describe it[22] and explains (in *De concordia*) that this affection is inalienable, impossible to forfeit no matter the agent's historical condition or circumstances.[23] On the other hand, he asks his interlocutor initially to envision the faculty of will—even if this is actually a *per impossibile* hypothesis—as mere instrument, prior to the affection for what is advantageous, so that his interlocutor can understand that disposition, namely, the inclination to enjoy goodness, specifically as something that has been implanted at a subsequent moment by God: "I am asking about a state where there is no willing and about an ability which precedes an occurrence."[24] Anselm is in this case isolating will in the first sense from will in both its second and third senses. If this isolated sense of will is nothing but a hypothetical abstraction, rather than an actual reality, it nevertheless implies that the power in itself, as *instrumentum*, is intelligible apart from an ordination to its realization.[25]

However this may be—and we will return to this point again at the end—Anselm goes on in the present context to distinguish this first affection from a second one. In addition to the affection for the beneficial or advantageous, God also gave the angels an affection for justice, which is to say, an inclination to preserve justice for its own sake. This, Anselm makes clear, is emphatically a *superadded* gift, beyond the original scope of the will, and so as such implies an *obligation* (*debitas*) that would not otherwise have been there.[26] There is a distinction here—revolutionary with respect to the classical tradition—between nature in its most originally given condition and in its ordering to the good. If this is the first clear step inside the classical Christian tradition toward what we called the modern "diabolical" conception of freedom in volume 1, it is quite suggestive that it arises specifically in the attempt to account for the fall of the devil. To be sure, obligation does not imply (as it will for the moderns like Kant and arguably already even for Scotus, as we will see in chapter 11) an ordering to a simply absent good, because such a view would take for granted an original indifference, a notion of the will as empty power, that Anselm evidently means to avoid. Thus, he describes this justice, not as the achievement of something new that has not yet been given, but, as we have seen, as the fidelity, so to speak, to what is already there—the *preservation* of *original* justice, which is given and so already exists, even if it is not given in the faculty of the will as such.[27] In contrast to the first gift that is made beyond that of the will as instrument, namely, the gift of the affection for benefit, which is inalienable, the second gift can be lost through sin, in which case the agent ceases to have any positive capacity for freedom, even as it retains the will as the ability to make choices regarding benefit. Freedom can be restored, just as it was originally given, only through the deed of another: in this case the redemption of Christ.

Now, to take a step back for a moment in order to see the significance of what is going on here in Anselm's account, we may recall that for Plato (who will turn out to be an essential "foil" to clarify Anselm on several points), the soul is ordered to the good *as such*, to such an extent that it is defined by this ordination.[28] If Plato distinguishes three "parts" of the soul, which correspond to different aspects of goodness (as sensible, as honorable, or as good in itself),[29] it is nevertheless one and the same goodness that presents itself in each of these aspects, so that we can say that the love of sensible pleasure is *in reality*, in its deepest truth, a love for the good itself (which is why that love can be elevated beyond itself to the good in its truth). Anselm is concerned, by contrast, not first with the unity, a single goodness that manifests itself (formally) in different ways, but above all with the difference between the affections in the will itself. To ask why he insists so resolutely on the difference will bring us into the essential core of Anselm's vision of freedom.

As Sandra Visser and Thomas Williams have pointed out,[30] there seems, on the surface, to be a tension between the way Anselm characterizes freedom in *De libertate arbitrii* and the way he presents it in *De casu diaboli*: the former, normative description of freedom, as "power for justice," does not seem to require possible alternatives, while the latter does; to put the issue in modern language, *De libertate arbitrii* seems to espouse a "compatibilist" notion of freedom (one can be free even if there is no possibility of acting otherwise than as one does) while the notion in *De casu diaboli* is libertarian (freedom is inconceivable without the possibility of acting otherwise).[31] According to Visser and Williams, the apparent tension, however, disappears the moment one looks beneath the surface in *De casu diaboli* and sees *why* Anselm insists on the angels' having to choose between benefit and justice. The point is not because freedom necessarily entails the capacity to do otherwise than one does (which is the libertarian principle) but more fundamentally because freedom is a power that belongs to the subject to such an extent that its use can be ascribed *properly* to the subject rather than to some cause outside of the subject.[32] To understand the connection between freedom as self-determination and the presence of original alternatives, we need to take account of the argument that Anselm makes in *De casu diaboli* 12, to which we just alluded. Apparently recalling Augustine's dilemma in the *Confessions*, in which Augustine realizes he cannot will himself to will the good that he does not yet will, because if he could it would imply that he already wills the good, which is precisely what is lacking—a realization that opens him up to the absolute priority of the grace of God[33]—Anselm shows that the will cannot set *itself* in motion unless it is already moved. This is a version of the classical argument that potency can be reduced to act only by that which is already actual. As Anselm himself puts it, it is not possible for an agent to "have his *first* willing from himself [*a se*]."[34] Instead, to will at all, he must already be willing to will; *that* will, which wills to will, cannot be the result of his own act of will but must be given to the will. According to Anselm, this "first will" is implanted by God. Drawing implicitly again on the tradition we have unfolded in previous chapters, Anselm identifies this being-moved by God with nature: the first will is the "natural will," by which the will moves itself to everything else: "No one is compelled by fear or by a sense of any disadvantage, or attracted by the love of any benefit, to will anything, unless he first has a natural will to avoid disadvantage or to possess what is beneficial."[35] This interpretation of nature as being moved by God echoes what we saw in Maximus.

But the fact of the first will's being given by God, and so, for Anselm, precisely *not* originating from the creature, presents a dilemma. If everything the agent subsequently willed, it willed literally by *virtue* of this first will, that is, out of the power of its affection (which, we recall, is strictly invincible in itself in abstraction from any actual occurrence of will), then all of its acts would be attributable to God alone; the agent would be able to do nothing properly *per se*.[36] Therefore, Anselm says that this initial affection for happiness is a desire for an as yet undifferentiated good. Goodness, in fact, has two fundamentally different meanings: on the one hand, there is benefit, on the other there is justice. When God gives the natural will to the good, he does not determine the precise aspect in which that will will be actualized but leaves that determination, so to speak, to the created agent. Thus, the created agent is able to be the author of *this* aspect of the will, if not the *original disposition to happiness*, which means that the agent is able to *act* (third sense of will) properly *per se*. If God gives the creature the will ordered to the good, which includes both the ordination to benefit and the ordination to justice, the creature decides himself how this will is actually realized. To put the matter more precisely, God does not give a mere potency for the good, which is then actualized by the creature, for this would imply an impossible movement from potency, qua potency, to act. To compare again to Augustine, we do not have a potency that fails in itself (deficient cause), but now a positive choice (efficient cause) between two wills, either of which is actual in some sense in itself, and indeed either of which is in principle invincible: "[The sinner] abandons uprightness-of-will not because the ability to keep it fails him (which ability constitutes freedom of choice) but because the will to keep it fails him. The will-to-keep-uprightness is not deficient in itself but ceases because another will expels it."[37] For Anselm, God gives *two distinct actual wills*, a will to benefit and a will to justice, the relative order of which is left up to the creature. The presence of alternatives is not due to the ability to act otherwise being a sine qua non condition of freedom; it is instead a function of the more basic need to secure self-agency. If God had given only the inclination to benefit, as he did to all nonrational creatures,[38] then there would be no freedom, because all activity would be determined by one's given nature, which is to say it would be determined ultimately by God in a unilateral fashion. But such wholly natural determination would also follow from a single inclination to justice, since that too is given by God. Anselm says that an automatic will to goodness for its own sake could not be called just *or* unjust in the strict sense.[39] As Anselm puts it, without the capacity in this case "to will otherwise" (*aliter velle*), the act would not be free but would proceed "of necessity" (*ex necessitate*).[40] What is needed here is the *drama*, we might say, of the decision for or against the good in itself; what is needed, in other words, is the original possession of two distinct wills and the task of choosing between them.

We will not, here, concern ourselves with the profoundly mysterious problem of determining on what basis the creature chooses between the two wills, which Anselm raises briefly at the end of *De casu diaboli*.[41] Given his account, we may presume that either will would suffice in itself to make the choice, and the decision as to *which* will one follows is thus in a basic way gratuitous and not traceable back to any single cause apart from the act of will itself. Anselm ends the infinite regress problem by affirming that the will finally causes itself, which is a resolution by way of praxis, we might say, rather than by theory.[42] But because the matter figures so prominently in our general discussion, we *do* have to concern ourselves, at least for a moment, with a second problem, which Anselm does not address in any direct way. If a basic alternative is necessary for genuine self-agency, does God also need to have the drama of this decision in order to be supremely free? It is curious that Anselm does not raise this question, since as we saw his argument for what we called the "normative definition" in *De libertate arbitrii* turned on the fact that the definition had to accommodate both God and the sinner. Along these lines, we need to ask whether agency in general *essentially* requires the difference between two wills, and so the alternatives of subordinating one to the other or vice versa. If it does not in the case of God, that would certainly have implications for the notion of freedom *simpliciter*, and so also in the case of the creature. And so it is a question that has to be addressed.

The first point to make in this regard is to recall Visser and Williams's argument that alternative possibilities are not *essential* to freedom but only enter into the meaning if such possibilities are required for the self-agency that *is* essential to freedom. In the case of the creature, the foundation of the will, its *natural* dimension, is not *per se* but *per aliud*, which is to say it is given by God. *This*, the fact that the inclinations of the will are *per aliud*, and not due to the creature itself, is what opens up the need for alternatives in Anselm's view. In God, by contrast, *everything* is *per se*, and *nothing* is *per aliud*,[43] which would imply that God cannot help acting from himself, so to speak, and so does not need alternatives to choose from in order to be free. Now, this response to the question, which we have derived from Anselm's principles, is quite illuminating, but it raises in turn a more subtle form of the problem, which is profoundly significant for our general discussion. If everything in God is *per se*, and so everything is due to his will, does this mean that his nature is a function of his will, so that God *is* only what he wills to be? Here we discover the return of the *Euthyphro* problem, determining whether God wills a thing because it is good or it is good because he wills it. In chapter 2, we suggested that this problem, in its most radical form concerning the goodness of God's very self, is perhaps the most basic problem there is in reflection on the nature of freedom, and we saw that Plotinus sought to answer the dilemma paradoxically by affirming both sides, even if he tended to the former: God's nature is a function of his will *and* his will is a function of his nature.

Dionysius and Maximus, we saw, are more balanced on this point. Anselm by contrast seems to affirm one *but not* the other. Is this a correct interpretation of Anselm, and if so what are the consequences?

THE GRATUITOUS JUSTICE OF GOD

We said that Anselm does not directly address the problem of whether God requires the possibility of doing otherwise than he does in order to be free in *De casu diaboli*; but he does imply an answer in *Cur Deus homo* (1094–98), and it is a subtle one. *Cur Deus homo* is a novelty in the Christian tradition, and the precise reason why it is a novelty bears directly on our discussion, both in this chapter and in the book more generally. What Anselm is doing in this text is a particular kind of apologetics: he means to offer here an argument, from a standpoint relatively *independent* of the Christian tradition, for a central truth *of* that tradition,[44] namely, the incarnation of the Son of God and his redemptive suffering and death. Although we cannot enter into a full exploration of this text, its influences, and its methods,[45] it is necessary to observe here that the very form of the task Anselm sets himself is already relevant to the question we have raised, and this in two respects: On the one hand, the reality of salvation, the singular act by which God enters into history and definitively transforms it, now appears in a new light with respect to the church fathers. Instead of being taken as a kind of absolute, an unsurpassable reality that represents the reference point in relation to which one thinks of everything else (which we might say is the approach seen in Maximus and Dionysius),[46] the argument asks one to think of this event as one of the possible ways God could have acted, which tends to detach God in his essence in some respect from his self-revelation *ad extra*. To put the point simply, using Pascal's language, the "God of Abraham, Isaac, and Jacob" at least threatens to become a merely contingent face of the "God of the philosophers."[47] On the other hand, given this starting point, Anselm seeks to show precisely the *necessity* of the Christian mystery, which means that the question now becomes whether God is compelled by some extrinsic principle to "choose" a particular option from an array of possibilities. We see here that the theme of the relation between potency and actuality in God acquires a new prominence in Anselm and that this theme both illuminates and is illuminated by the nature of freedom simply. Let us first consider, *in nuce*, Anselm's answer to the question of this relation, which is of course a variation on the central *Euthyphro* problem, and then reflect on its implications.

Anselm is clear that there is nothing higher than God's will, which is the absolute to which all else is relative.[48] In the strictest sense, God is omnipotent, so that, if there are any impossibilities with respect to God's will, these are properly interpreted as deficiencies on the part of the object, not on the part of God's will.[49] As Anselm makes explicit in *Cur Deus homo*, all necessity and all impossibility are subject to God's will.[50] Now, while this position clearly anticipates later voluntarism, it is crucial to see that Anselm decisively avoids taking a radical form of this position in two respects.[51] First, Anselm insists that God's will is by no means arbitrary. Indeed, the point of *Cur Deus homo* is precisely to show that God is supremely *just*, that his gratuitous action on behalf of the human race satisfies the demand that is essential to justice.[52] To the crucial question "Whence comes the standard implied by justice?" Anselm says it is not *simply* God's will, in the (purely voluntarist) sense that whatever God wills is thereby just;[53] instead, Anselm explains, while it *is* true that whatever God wills is thereby justice, this is only because his acts of will are always and only "befitting" to him, never "at odds" with who God is.[54] We might say (though this is not Anselm's language) that the will is not compelled by God's nature, as if God's nature were extrinsic to it, but the will nevertheless is always and inevitably expressive of God's nature. As Balthasar puts it, Anselm may be in some evident sense a "pure voluntarist," but this is not at all irrationalism insofar as God's freedom penetrates the whole of his being and embraces it.[55] In this way, there is always a fundamental correspondence between God's will and nature: "We ought to explicate these notions [of freedom, will, and kindness] so in accordance with reason that we do not seem to oppose His dignity."[56] The second way Anselm avoids radical voluntarism is by insisting that God's acts of will are not whimsical, liable to change at any moment, but necessarily have a permanent, indeed, eternal quality. To illustrate his sense of the essential stability of God's will, he compares God's acts of will to the fidelity to a *promise* or a *vow*: "Let us say that it is necessary that God's goodness—on account of its immutability—accomplish with man what it began, even though the entire good which it does is by grace."⁵⁷ Here we have a kind of necessity, but it is a necessity that is, so to speak, saturated with freedom, insofar as the necessity never precedes the will but conversely has its own ground in an act of will. There is a constraint on God's will, but that constraint is self-imposed. Thus, Anselm does not want to set necessity and freedom over against each other as opposites but seeks instead to integrate them in a unified vision. The integration, however, stands quite clearly on the side of freedom, which takes necessity into itself, or in other words it is the will that interprets nature, *rather than the reverse*. One can raise the question here whether it makes sense ultimately to speak of God's action as "*befitting*" him unless it is action in some sense in conformity *to* the divine nature, and then whether one can speak of conformity if there is no sense in which the nature "precedes" the will,⁵⁸ but—noting a kind of impoverishment of the preceding tradition here—we will not engage the question at this stage, because Anselm himself does not go any further.

The point we nevertheless wish to draw out here is that there emerges a fascinating analogy between Anselm's description of freedom with respect to the creature and his interpretation of freedom just briefly sketched. The angels are free insofar as they are able to conform (or, more properly speaking, to adhere) to a justice that exceeds the necessity of their nature, and God's freedom too is manifest in the fact that his will is not constrained by the necessity, so to speak, of his nature. There is something essentially gratuitous in both cases, a gratuity that is generally contrasted to the necessity that now appears to define nature. The difference is that, for the creature, the standard of justice is imposed from outside its nature in a way that liberates the will's capacity to take its bearings from the self-exceeding obligation of goodness; for God, by contrast, justice is, as it were, the result of his radical transcendence, a gift that expresses an order that is intrinsic to him rather than extrinsic. We might say that, in his omnipotent freedom, God "outdoes" himself in the deed of redemption, but this turns out to be the most glorious revelation of who he has always been.⁵⁹ This would represent a way of interpreting *Cur Deus homo* that differs from the usual one, but it has the advantage of introducing a profound connection between the creaturely freedom articulated in his other texts and the divine freedom expressed in *Cur Deus homo*.

The Irreducibility of Wills

It will be necessary to weigh the implications of the apparently one-sided resolution of the *Euthyphro* problem for the meaning of freedom, but we must first take stock of Anselm's achievement. On this score, the three things that stand out most clearly are Anselm's radicalizing of interiority, his corresponding recognition of a kind of "plus" in the order of goodness as essential to freedom, and his bringing to light the centrality of personal reciprocity for the meaning of will—centuries before, we might add, the dialogical philosophy inaugurated by Fichte and Hegel.[60] As for the first point, Anselm introduces a distinction in his interpretation of human action that sets into relief what we might call a new interior depth. Perhaps most explicitly in his early text *De veritate* but running through the whole of his work in his account of freedom, Anselm explains that "every will has both a *what* [*quid*] and a *why* [*cur*]. Indeed, whatever we will, we will for a reason."[61] In the Aristotelian account of action, the most basic distinction is that between the means and the end for which the means are chosen, which at first glance resembles Anselm's distinction: the means are the particular object, the "what," of choice, and the end is the *reason* it is chosen, the "why." But Anselm's distinction is of a different order. To be sure, his distinction is anticipated most directly by a similar distinction drawn in Plato's *Gorgias*,[62] a text Anselm would not have known, and it also lies within the field sown by the Stoics,[63] in their exploration of interiority, which reached a certain flourishing in Augustine, as we saw in chapter 3. Anselm's formulation, nevertheless, introduces a novel lucidity. We discussed above his notion of two wills, which designate two different dispositions rather than two different instruments,[64] namely, the affection for benefit and the affection for justice. It is crucial to see that this difference lies within the *final* rather than the *formal* order; it is a matter of the *why* in the use or particular exercise of the will, not of the *what*. In other words, we would misunderstand Anselm if we interpreted the two wills as aiming at two different goods, two different objects of choice. Instead, they represent two different *aspects* under which potentially one and the same choice might be made, one and the same means ordered to one and the same end.[65] In other words, there is in principle a distinction here between a given *end* and a chosen *reason* it is pursued.[66] I can choose a particular good (whether that be a thing as good or a means to some end) either principally because it will make me happy or principally because it is what I ought to do. What eventually comes to be called "intention" thus becomes a decisive category. This does *not* mean that the content of the choice is simply irrelevant: the primacy of intention is not a "subjectivizing" of action, to use the modern term. As we saw in the previous section, even the most perfectly unconstrained divine will never acts in a merely arbitrary way. But there is nevertheless a new register in this vision of the will that Anselm offers, which becomes most clearly apparent in comparison with the ancient tradition in which the crucial measure of action is the good accomplished. With Anselm, we have a decisive moment in the transition from the ancient "extramoral" ethos to the medieval "moral" one, to use Nietzsche's categories.[67] When we enter the horizon set by freedom, for Anselm, a radically new dimension opens up "beneath the surface" of things, so to speak. The moral "self" emerges, and does so in response to the call to come out beyond himself in justice, the obligation to *choose* a good that is not simply drawing him passively along.[68]

This leads to the second point: to the new depth of the spiritual subject, the rational, moral agent, there corresponds a new and essentially personal depth of goodness. As we saw especially in the previous two chapters, freedom always implies, not exclusively but nevertheless indispensably, a kind of movement; it designates a novelty, a superabundance, a "more-than," which means that there is some sort of boundary or limit established that is at the same time exceeded. The difference we just mentioned between benefit and justice is not a juxtaposition between two equal but opposed purposes. Instead, there is a hierarchy between them: the first is meant to be subordinated to the second,[69] which means that they are meant to coexist within an order. That order, however, is not something simply posited by the will but a reality to which the will responds, which is why the emphasis on what we have called intention is not at all "subjectivistic."[70] We might best think of the difference between the two affections as a sign, in the spiritual subject, of the excess in the goodness of reality. This point is made most clearly in *De casu diaboli*, when the "teacher" attempts to respond to the student's question, asking him to identify the additional benefit (*commodum*) that the good angels received in contrast to the fallen angels: "I do not know what it was. But whatever it was, it suffices to know that it was something toward which they could grow and which they did not receive when they were created, so that they might attain it by their own merit."[71] The drama of freedom is possible only if there is a superabundance in what is given, a first gift (creation), and so affection for goodness, which nevertheless, even in its completeness, does not exhaust what is meant to be given, so that a growth, an inner self-transcendence, can occur on the part of the subject as a result of the second gift (the affection for justice).[72] From this perspective, we ought to complement Visser and Williams's claim that the alternatives are necessary for the creature's self-determination and say that they are, even more profoundly, necessary for the genuine self-transcendence that the will represents. We may, in short, interpret the distinction between benefit and justice as a distinction between the original gift, given once and for all,[73] and the gratuitous surplus, which is offered to the subject in a way that requires the subject to come out of himself *by moving himself* (merit) so that he can receive it. Justice is *more* than benefit, and as such indeed is not opposed to benefit, but represents its excess, as the text just cited shows. Justice is surplus benefit.[74]

It is important to note, however, that this *excess* is due precisely to the presence of the omnipotent God. This is a subtle point, but the details are crucial, as we will explain in the section below. Anselm defines justice as "willing what God wills that we will."[75] In contrast, for example, to Plato, who draws a distinction between relative and absolute *goodness*,[76] Anselm makes a distinction between goodness determined relative to created nature, and goodness determined relative to nature-transcending divine will. The "excess" is not principally an excess *of* nature, as it is for example in Dionysius and Maximus, but lies specifically *beyond* nature. It is true that the subject's relation to justice is described as an *affection*, which is an internal inclination and so implies something like an attraction[77]—a note that will come to disappear in Scotus's appropriation of this Anselmian idea—but the principal note, in a certain contrast to Augustine, is *not* desire but *obedience*.[78]

Before we consider the implications of this point, we need to mention the third contribution. The heart of freedom, and so the essence of the will, is an interpersonal event for Anselm. Freedom is ultimately "willing what God wills that we will," which is to say it consists of a reciprocity of wills. This becomes especially clear in Anselm's last completed work, the *De concordia*. As Balthasar has shown in great depth, the highest point of the good in Anselm is an "inner penetration of wills," namely, the will of the creature with the will of God, so that man's relation to the good has an essentially "dialogical" character.[79] This character represents, we might say, a new recollection of the *Jewish* form of freedom beyond the Greek form. We need to feel the full weight of this point, for it will end up being a decisive one for the general argument of this book: accounting for the movement of the will *simply* in terms of the attractive power of the good will tend to reduce the will to the good without remainder (we need only identify the reduction with ad-traction to visualize this point). The dominant note of obedience implies a spontaneous self-movement of the will that is *distinct* from the movement of desire.[80] The result is an irreducibly "personal" reciprocity of wills even in a perfect unity (willing what God wills that we will = being of one will with God). Freedom, however, just *is* preserving justice for its own sake, which means then that there is no freedom apart from the intimate reciprocity of wills that Balthasar describes as a "nuptial" mystery.[81] The human (or indeed angelic) will makes a positive contribution of its own (hence Anselm's use of the word *merit*) to the highest good it receives from God. The good toward which the created will grows is something it attains through its own action. To show this as clearly as possible is the basic purpose of *De concordia*.[82] As becomes clear in this treatise above all, reciprocity does not at all mean simply symmetry: Anselm is unequivocal that the absolute priority in the relation lies with God, an insistence already clear in *De casu diaboli*, where he describes the actuality of the first will, given by God, as what enables the potency of the creature's self-will. But the point is that the absolute priority of God does not eliminate the creature's own self-causing activity "inside" of that priority. We can see here indeed a kind of universalizing of Maximus's argument regarding Christ, whose divine will never absorbs his human will. Freedom, for Anselm, in the end is *love*,[83] and love is ultimately unthinkable without a kind of interpersonal reciprocity.

The Rise of Power

Now, having brought out the permanent contribution of Anselm, which presents an element that will remain indispensable in all further reflection, it is nevertheless crucial to see that there are the beginnings of a certain "break" with the classical tradition in this interpretation of freedom, which will prove fateful. The essential issue can be put rather simply, but we will elaborate it in five points. Put simply: in Anselm we have the repetition of a classical theme—namely, freedom as a doing of the good for its own sake—but within a new order, which entails a reconception of the nature of freedom from the ground up. Or, more precisely, it is a severing of freedom from its ground, a vision of freedom no longer nourished, we might say, by ontological roots. When the ontological level is, so to speak, leapt over, basic aspects of divine freedom get reinterpreted on the basis of created freedom rather than the reverse. Moreover, it is the deep theological and ontological originality of freedom that allows the essential paradox, which we have suggested constitutes the heart of the classical inheritance, namely, the ordered unity-in-difference of potency and act in the superabundant superactuality of divine generosity. That this horizon has receded in Anselm becomes apparent in the tendency to separate potency and act out from each other in a sequential fashion. Thus, instead of seeing freedom in an "organic" sense, as representing a flourishing of nature, an inward transcendence of nature that remains "of nature" even in its transcendence, as we have seen in some form in each of the figures we have thus far studied (including Plato and Aristotle in volume 1), Anselm conceives of freedom as an essentially spiritual power in a strictly nonanalogical sense.[84] This restriction will of course have radical implications in the eventual birth of the modern world.

(1) We start with what we might call an "ontological evacuation" of the concept of nature, which we see in the tendency to juxtapose person and nature in such a way as to place the will and freedom more basically on the side of person over against nature.[85] Maximus presents an illuminating contrast on this point.[86] As Kristell Trego has shown in a magnificent study,[87] Anselm's novel conception of freedom can be best understood within his novel conception of being more generally. We cannot rehearse the complexity of her argument in all its documented detail but will simply point to conclusions that bear most directly on our study. The simplest description of Anselm's novelty with respect to metaphysics is that he tends to remove the substantial foundations of things in themselves; as Trego puts it, he "desubstratalizes" being ("une désubstratalisation"), and this, we add, would include a

similar desubstratalization of nature.⁸⁸ Thus, for instance, one of the most basic distinctions in Aristotle is that between *kath' auto* and *kath' allo*, a distinction that indicates the difference between substance and accidents and so manifests the textured complexity that resides *in* a thing, which has a center, a deep inner being, that radiates or sends forth its particular properties. The corresponding fundamental distinction in Anselm is that between what is *per se* and what is *per aliud*, a distinction between one being and another, most fundamentally between the creature and God.⁸⁹ Indeed, this distinction includes a certain "dynamic" note (consider the difference between *a se* and *per se*), which is fitting if one absolutizes the divine will, as we have seen Anselm does. The metaphysical focus, as it were, has now shifted from the interior dimension of being (substance and accidents) to what lies over against it (a thing constituted by itself or constituted by another). We note that the interior depth that we described in the previous section is specifically a moral one, pertaining to the spiritual *subject*, rather than an ontological one residing in the *substance*.⁹⁰ *Ousia*, which in the classical tradition means *both* an individual thing and its general nature, thus gets translated in Anselm, not as *substantia*, that which underlies a thing and so, we might say, represents its inward depth, but as *essentia*, that is, the universal whatness that defines a thing.⁹¹ There is in other words a shifting from the ontological to the logical order. In Anselm's thought, Trego shows, nature ceases to mean the same inward depths it meant in the classical tradition but becomes instead something one *possesses*, a (universal) "property" that remains other than the *self*.⁹² Trego argues that in Anselm the whole creature becomes a gift from God, and what she apparently means by this is that the creature ceases to belong to itself *ontologically* as a result of this dependence.⁹³ But it is necessary to qualify Trego's characterization here: we ought rather to say that the opposition between what is *per se* and what is *per aliud*, and the resultant opposition between independence from the other and dependence on the other, is evidence that the category of gift is no longer decisive. In the radical dependence on God, which is now opposed to independence, the creature in fact *ceases* to be a gift if *gift* means the definitive handing over of a thing,⁹⁴ since the lack of *ontological* selfhood, real substance, is a sign that a gift has not truly been made—*to* the creature and *from* the Creator—in the act of creation. In any event, the upshot is that the rational creature no longer has its center in its substance or nature; instead, selfhood tends to be transferred, so to speak, to a will that is juxtaposed to nature. Nature thus ceases to be genuinely *analogical*, which is to say open from within itself to what transcends itself, and so it can no longer be seen as an abiding *wellspring* of freedom.

(2) It is therefore not an accident that Anselm emphasizes potency, understood not in the first place as ordered *to* act and as fruit *of* act but, so to speak, as first a kind of reality in itself. We are suggesting that this isolation of potency and act from each other is an expression of the loss of a certain ontological depth. Many commentators point out his preferred use of the term *potestas*, rather than *potentia*, a term that indicates a privation or in any event a radical ontological dependence. *Potestas* has less of a "privative" sense and more of a sense of a thing that is complete in some respect already in itself.[95] To be sure, the primacy of actuality, which characterizes the classical tradition, remains in Anselm in two obvious ways, with respect to the beginning and to the end of this power in its particular use: as we explained earlier, he acknowledges a first *actual* will, the natural will given by God, as the necessary precondition for any subsequent exercise of the potency, and he posits an actual end, justice, for which it ought to be exercised, an end that the agent already possesses from the outset, or is given through the restoration effected by Christ's vicarious death, so that it does not have to be created, so to speak, out of nothing. And yet an inner transformation occurs inside of this continuity with the classical tradition.[96] Without the ontological dimension of substance and nature, indicated above, the ordination of potency to act can only be a "moral" one, which is to say a connection in the order of action between things separate in their substantial nature, rather than always already given ontologically. Thus, the first will is not understood as causally present in all subsequent acts, but each of these is sufficient cause of itself, even if made possible by the first,[97] and the justice of the end tends not to be an actuality that draws the potency precisely from within but is principally an obligation, as we saw.[98] We have here, in the relation between potency and act, something like a succession of individual moments. This presents a perfect contrast to the paradoxical integration we witnessed in Maximus.

The tendency to isolate potency in itself, as a real power, becomes apparent concretely in three ways: first, Anselm insists that the will remains essentially free even if its concrete historical conditions are such that it lacks any capacity to realize itself in the choice of justice. As we saw Anselm arguing, the will remains essentially the same, regardless of context.[99] Note that this implies a univocal, rather than *analogical*, conception of will (such as we find, for example, in Augustine, who conceives of the will *principally* in terms of its actual differentiations by nature, habit, history, and grace). To say that the will retains its potency even when it does not have an actual possibility means that its potency is *principally* self-referential rather than first relative to some more basic actuality. As we recall, Anselm presents the will as like the wrestler who has an inner store of power, which he may use more or less in any given circumstance, and in fact characterizes that strength as absolute precisely insofar as it is considered (abstractly, univocally) in itself rather than relative to reality. Second, the actuality thus relates to the potency in a basically extrinsic sense, rather than as moving the potency from within. Thus, Anselm presents the actuating element of the will as something like a mountain that stands before one's vision: prior to its presence, the capacity to see a mountain cannot be realized, but when the mountain is present, it can.[100] The power remains exactly the same in the two cases; the actualization of the power depends wholly on the presence or absence of a separate object external to the power. The potency becomes, thus, impotent in itself, a lifeless capacity that finds its realization through a reality that acts upon it. We might compare this to Plato, who, using a similar image, admits that the power to see remains in some sense in any person, regardless of context, but nevertheless says that its realization requires a "turning around of the whole soul"[101] and indeed a movement up through the levels of the cave out into the bright skies of the really real. For Plato, this movement is an image of education, understood as the formation of the soul. In this case, the reality, the good, is always already *there*, and the realization of the power requires an inner transformation of the subject.[102] For Anselm, by contrast, what is always already there is an isolated power, which in one sense is self-sufficient and in another respect depends wholly on the object that moves into the power's sphere. The power is thus not informed but just turned on, so to speak, or left off. Third, because the will is defined as a spontaneous power in itself (rather than as principally receptive potency), it is not an accident that Anselm tends to describe its exercise in terms of quantities of *force*.[103] The will exerts itself as an effort to *overpower*: Anselm describes the will's struggle with temptation as an effort to "subject" or "overcome" an "alien force," an externally imposed power, or else to "*be* overcome" or "subjected" by that force. He finally describes the will's free choice as its being "overcome only by *its* own power" (*non aliena vincitur potestate sed sua*).[104] Even the ultimate relation to God tends to be interpreted as an act of obedience of a power that in every other case is meant to *command*.[105]

(3) More briefly, it is significant that Anselm characterizes the ultimate end of the will as *justice* rather than as goodness. There is a certain ambiguity on this point, since Anselm introduces his novelty precisely from within the classical tradition. Thus, he presents justice as a supreme good, and as such a reality that brings happiness.[106] At the same time, however, the emphasis shifts decisively away from what we might call the appetitive order. In the two basic definitions of justice that he formulates — "uprightness-of-will kept for its own sake"[107] and "willing what God wills that we will"[108] — the essential referent is not goodness or nature but the will's relation to will, whether that be to itself or to God's will. Once again, a comparison between Plato and Anselm is helpful to bring out the significance of this point. For Plato, goodness has an essentially twofold character, both an "in-itself-ness" and a "for-others-ness," which is to say it is an intrinsic quality that also communicates itself beyond itself. Thus, something that is good in itself will *also* bring happiness to the one who possesses it — one could say "by necessity," but this turns out to be a kind of gratuitous necessity.[109] In order to preserve the drama of freedom, as we saw, Anselm separated these two Platonically inseparable dimensions into that which is sought for happiness *rather than* because it is right, and that which is sought simply because it *ought* to be sought, *rather than* for the happiness it brings. Significantly, this latter is no longer conceived in a basic sense as the intrinsic goodness of a thing, a goodness that belongs to that thing by nature, which would make goodness not merely formal but also material and would for that reason inevitably enter into the order of desire and happiness. Instead, it is essentially formal in what is now a more abstract and so extrinsic sense, something introduced most basically "from the outside," as it were. Thus, while Plato presents justice as *exceedingly good* from the beginning, and unfolds that as a goodness first in itself

and then also in its consequences, Anselm insists that the goodness of justice be initially veiled so that a properly free choice can be made.[110] The obedience of the will requires, it seems, a certain blindness in order actually to be obedience. It would be possible to envision this blindness in a principially positive sense of a personal trust rather than in the essentially negative sense of ignorance, but Anselm himself does not cast it this way.[111] Nevertheless, we note that the "plus" of justice that we discussed above is due, for Anselm, essentially to the *personal* element, and most specifically to God beyond the (natural) good, so to speak. For this reason, Anselm argues that there is no concrete reality that is essentially just or unjust in itself; the only thing that can be just in the strict sense is the *will*.[112] We will return to this in the last point below.

(4) Without the *mediation* of natural goodness, there turns out to be an ineradicable "competitiveness" in the relation of wills, even in their coordination. This is the negative flip side, as it were, of the essential "reciprocity" of wills we presented above as one of the real contributions of Anselm. To be sure, the whole point of the *De concordia* is to show the harmony, in principle, between the divine and human will in their cooperation. Two wills can, in fact, be identical, and so intrinsic to each other, in their object.[113] But the question is whether this intimacy of wills is genuinely *ontological* or is instead merely *moral*. The point we made above regarding the "desubstratalization" of being speaks against an ontological interpretation. If will is understood to be a power that already has a kind of reality in itself (*potestas* rather than *potentia*), independent of any actual context, relation to what is other will inevitably be extrinsic, conceived as an acting *on* the other from the outside. Thus, it becomes apparent in the *De concordia* that, though the point is harmony, that harmony is interpreted as a kind of negotiation between separate powers, a division of jurisdictions, as it were. Preserving the power of the human will requires discovering a gap in the activity of the divine will, the particular space, no matter how small it turns out to be, in which the will causes itself *rather than* being caused by God.[114]

More subtly, but perhaps even more profoundly, we recall in *De casu diaboli* that Anselm insisted on a lack of knowledge as essential to the created will's autonomy: if the angel *knew* the greater benefit of justice, the angel's will would be naturally, and so necessarily, *moved by* that goodness rather than moving itself. Thus, an ignorance of consequences is required for free choice.¹¹⁵ We see here a basic departure from what we have been calling the classical tradition: for this tradition, knowledge is a reception into the soul of what lies beyond it; the insistence on the rootedness of the will in the intellect is a recognition that one can move oneself *only by* being moved by what is other than the self. To present a kind of ignorance as a decisive element of freedom is to reconceive the will's movement in a one-sided way as originating from the self alone rather than from the self and from its other simultaneously and inseparably. If the drama of freedom requires ignorance, this implies an original opposition, outside of unity, that precedes and sets the terms for any subsequent "coordination." In other words, reciprocity, even positively conceived, rests on something like an ontological competition, *either* one *or* the other, so that the possibility of affirming *both* demands a kind of opening of neutral space.[116]

(5) Finally, we return to the severance of the moral dimension from the ontological dimension. If freedom does not arise from the depths of being in nature, as we saw in point (1) above, it also does not arrive at its flourishing end in the depths of being in nature. As Trego has pointed out, the language of virtue is largely absent in Anselm.[117] In the classical tradition, there is a connection between *virtue* and *intrinsic goodness*; freedom means *being* good, taking goodness into one's nature so that one's very substance is ordered and productive of ever-greater order. For Anselm, by contrast, it is not the substance of the creature that becomes good but simply the *will* that becomes *just*, that is, acts in conformity to an external standard.[118] To be sure, this does not make justice merely forensic, which would imply a complete indifference toward the nature even of the will.[119] But it remains the case that the will is not a *potentia* that resides within a substantial being and remains at the service, so to speak, of the teleology of the whole; instead, the will serves its own teleology, namely, the ultimate *intention*, radically interior to the person, that determines the moral quality of the act, precisely in abstraction from the order of the whole, that is, the fulfillment of the nature. This sense of the will ought to be compared, for example, to Maximus's definition, which so evidently strikes the ontological note: for him, the will is "a faculty desirous of what is in accordance with nature, which holds together all the attributes that belong to a being's nature."[120] We have by contrast a tendency in Anselm to subordinate the end of the *man* to the end of one of his *faculties*.[121]

Conclusion: A Step Outside the Tradition?

St. Anselm represents a pivotal figure in the development of the notion of freedom in the West. On the one hand, he brings to the fore a distinctively Christian element, the irreducible reciprocity of wills in love and obedience as essential to the very meaning of the will and so of freedom. On the other hand, he casts this element in a new light by beginning to take it out of what we might call its *native* context, insofar as the Greek form, which gets eclipsed in this respect, emphasizes nature.[122] This point stands out most clearly if we consider it from the perspective of tradition, as we have been presenting it in this book. We argued (in chapter 1) that freedom concerns a novelty that springs from within what is given, rather than arriving wholly from without. Accordingly, we suggested that Christianity, which is simultaneously deed and doctrine, as the conceiver and liberator of freedom, arrives from *within* the Jewish tradition and appropriates the Greek form as one that in some sense (along with the Roman form) was being prepared for it. Christianity thus represents a transformative synthesis, which receives and interprets these two traditions in light of each other, and in a way that brings each to a surprising fulfillment. From this perspective, Anselm stands in an ambiguous light. As scholars have recognized, he explicitly engages with Jews and nonbelievers, most specifically Muslims, who in their intellectuals represent a certain continuation of Greek philosophy.[123] What is novel here is that he confronts these, not most basically from the perspective of Christianity as a transformative fulfillment of what is *given* in them, but rather as *others*, as, so to speak, alternative religions or at the very least alternative traditions. But simply to recognize other traditions is to undergo a certain change in one's relationship to one's own, which becomes respectively *a* tradition and so ceases to be Tradition *tout court*. It is not surprising, then, that, as we saw above, to confront these others Anselm sets aside Christian dogma, the specifically Christian tradition (which thus becomes what is *other* to these alternative traditions), and makes an argument in some sense from a neutral standpoint, using putatively neutral means.[124] His principal resources are not the authors of the tradition but the text of scripture and the power of logic.[125] To be sure, there is no need to oversimplify the evidently rich and subtle view of faith and reason, which has rightly been admired in Anselm, and the details of which have always remained a matter of some controversy. But we mean here simply to set into relief an aspect of this view that bears on the notion of freedom.

The Jewish and Greek elements nevertheless remain in the Christian inheritance, but we may see them undergo a certain transformation in Anselm. They acquire a more abstract form, rather than emerging, so to speak, from within each other. Thus, the Greek element of reason now stands forth without its rootedness in nature and begins to become instead a more pure power, which in this abstractness consists essentially of logical consistency inside of external parameters.[126] Similarly, the Jewish elements of obedience and justice reappear in terms of power, newly conceived in isolation from actualization, so that they tend to take a principally formalistic shape.

The more general question that emerges here is whether the Christian element of personal love can be affirmed without the sacrifice of its inherited form. If not, Christianity will tend to be distorted into something essentially revolutionary: its novelty will inevitably require *breaking* with tradition. Centuries will pass before this distortion sets in, and there will be an attempt in the High Middle Ages to re-collect the tradition in its diversity, which will bear great fruit in the conception of freedom, but in the meantime we will consider the other major thinker of freedom in the early medieval period who shares with Anselm a certain forgetfulness of tradition: Bernard of Clairvaux. To him we now turn.

CHAPTER 7

Bernard of Clairvaux
Liberating Love

Drawing on Anselm,[1] Bernard of Clairvaux can be seen both as radically deepening the interpersonal dimension of the will and at the same time as even more decisively isolating and absolutizing the potency of freedom. We shall elaborate each of these developments, beginning with the personal dimension as setting the proper context for everything else that concerns the will in Bernard's thought.

Whereas Anselm, in affirming the essentially "dialogical" character of freedom and seeking to establish an ultimate harmony (*concordia*) in the interaction of the divine and human wills, nevertheless left in place at the core a kind of extrinsicism of reciprocal displacement of acts wherein God's and man's contributions are "added" together to produce a whole, Bernard presents one of the boldest interpretations of the mystical union between the soul and God yet known in the Christian tradition. If Maximus showed that a unity between the divine and the human does not eliminate their duality, Bernard shows that an irreducible duality does not preclude a profound unity. Etienne Gilson was right to say that it is easy to distort Bernard's doctrine if one attempts to make sense of what he says in a piecemeal fashion.[2] To avoid this, we must begin at the end, take the consummation of his teaching on freedom as a reference point, and think backward from there.[3] And so we begin, here, with Bernard's notion of the unity of the divine and human will, though we approach this not as a theme in itself, which would require a full exploration and detailed account of Bernard's rich doctrine of love, but specifically from the perspective of the meaning of freedom, which, as many have pointed out, lies at the *center* of his mystical theology.

The union between the soul and God, which Bernard presents as the aim of human existence, the purpose for which man was created,[4] is not a (pantheistic) unity of substance but a unity of wills. This unity, which Bernard sees as the core of *charity*, is in its ideal form so complete that we may refer to it as a singular reality: he speaks, not of a harmony between separate wills, but of a *single* will, the *voluntas communialis* or "common will," which is common between God and man. Now, for Bernard, there is a clear echo in this notion of the Jewish "covenantal" sense of the will. This will, more specifically, is the presence of the Holy Spirit in the soul, which is to say that the achievement of charity is becoming "one spirit" with Christ.[5] This unity in spirit, however, is not the annihilation of the distinct particularity of the human will, since it is not a consubstantiality;[6] if, according to Bernard, charity requires the elimination of the *propria voluntas*, "self-will," this is not the will that belongs to the self as a created and free agent but is meant to be understood as the self precisely in opposition to the common will, the self conceived as resisting and rejecting charity.[7] The highest unity, in short, is for Bernard never an absorption into an undifferentiated One but always and decisively *nuptial*.[8]

The nuptial union of the soul and God, which represents the crowning of Bernard's mystical vision, also comes to expression in a certain sense in his doctrine of freedom (even as this doctrine, in turn, is essential to the meaning of the mystical union).[9] Bernard's treatise *De gratia et libero arbitrio* (ca. 1128)[10] culminates in a description of the "cooperation" between God and the soul that seems, once and for all, to overcome any trace of the competitive extrinsicism we saw in Anselm. Thus, where Anselm sought to preserve the reality of the human will inside of the comprehensive act of the divine will by locating a gap and then describing even this gap as permitted, and so willed, by God, Bernard affirms in a more paradoxical way the perfect simultaneity of both wills in their fullness and thus recovers something of Augustine's insight into the noncompetitive nature of God's grace:

What was begun by grace alone, is completed by grace and free choice [*liberum arbitrium*] together, in such a way that they contribute to each new achievement not singly but jointly; not by turns, but simultaneously. It is not as if grace did one half of the work and free choice the other; but each does the whole work, according to its own peculiar contribution. Grace does the whole work, and so does free choice—with this one qualification: that whereas the whole is done *in* free choice, so is the whole done *of* grace.[11]

Let us note how simply and elegantly Bernard here solves at a stroke the perennial question of interpreting the free involvement of the human will within an encompassing causal order; but let us note, too, how much this integration turns on the specifically personal quality of the event, which we will have to explore further: it is an integration not of the will with *goodness* but of one will with another will, or in other words an integration not of subject and object but of two subjects. The specific question of the ontological character remains open, even if the personal and existential achievement is evident. However this may be, we will at this point simply observe that there is no trace of extrinsicism in his description of the interaction of divine and human freedom, wherein each will would contribute a part so as to constitute a whole by their addition, but there is a single reality in which both wills coincide at once, though in a radically asymmetrical fashion. The saving act is altogether given by God, but it is given to the human will, which is to say it is received *in* the will. In other words, there is a cooperation, not in the sense of a harmonizing of two separate and more or less extrinsic operations,[12] but rather in the sense of a single act, which can be numerically one because it is constituted of a relation between radically differentiated orders of causality.

Now, the standing here of the human soul as what amounts to material causality (as the substrate of a change) does not at all mean that the soul is completely passive; this is evident insofar as the will is not acted *on* but acted *in*, and there cannot be a taking in, a receiving, without the "active" willingness of the soul. Better than *passive* is the word *receptive*, but better still is the word that represents a kind of hallmark of Bernard's vision: the very essence of the will is *consent*, and if we understand what Bernard means by this word, we will have understood

Bernard's doctrine of freedom. It is to be noted first of all that Bernard uses the terms *consent* (*consentire*), *free choice* (*liberum arbitrium*), and *will* (*voluntas*) interchangeably, without making any distinction between them. The simple fact that Bernard uses the word *consent* as a synonym for *will*, which is exhaustively characterized by the function of "free choice," is already profoundly significant, for it sets into relief just how thoroughly "interpersonal" Bernard's notion of will is. *Sentire* means to perceive, to feel, to experience, or to think; more generally, it means to be disposed or to dispose oneself in a particular way toward something, to make up one's mind about a thing.[13] *Con-sentire* means to do so jointly with another mind, another agent. To call the power of the will "consent" is thus to conceive the human agent from the beginning and at its core as involved in a dialogue, as it were. This dimension is not initially made explicit in Bernard, but its significance will become apparent as he proceeds to work out in detail the nature of the will's operation. But we must first ask directly how Bernard himself explains the meaning of *consent*.

Bernard begins his treatise by identifying "consent" as the defining essence of the *liberum arbitrium*, which we will translate here as "free choice" in spite of the ambiguities of that translation.[14] *Consent* he defines as a "self-determining habit of the soul" (*habitus animi liber sui*), though, as Goffredo Venuta has pointed out, the term *habitus* here does not have the technical sense it would for the Scholastics after the reception of Aristotle's substantial works but simply means something like a fixed property.[15] It is, for Bernard, precisely the will—and, nota bene, *not* the intellect—that distinguishes human beings from animals.[16] While animals are governed by powers—life, sensibility, and natural appetite—that operate in an automatic fashion, the very essence of the will is its opposition to any necessity: "Its action is neither forced nor extorted. It stems from the will and not from necessity, denying or giving itself on no issue except by way of the will."[17] Its determining cause is the self as agent or author. If man is different from the animals, it is because he moves himself and they do not. Though Bernard does not say so explicitly here, and curiously does not mention the intellect in this context, it seems that the reason the intellect does not distinguish man from the animals is that we are not so fully the author of our thoughts as we are of our acts of will.[18] In any event, to say that man is the cause of his acts of will does not necessarily mean he is the *sole* cause, as we will explain further below.

Although Bernard does not include reason initially in his list of powers of the soul—life, sense perception, natural appetite, and consent—he does mention it immediately in his elaboration of the will's operation. The will, he says, in this regard following the tradition, is a "rational movement" (*motus rationalis*). But Bernard is notoriously unclear about exactly how the will and reason are related.[19] In one moment, he presents reason as preceding the will as the will's instructor, in another he presents reason accompanying the will as its companion, and yet again he says that reason *follows* the will. All on the same page! It is not possible to determine the relationship more precisely, given the little Bernard himself offers to explain his meaning; the most one can say, it seems, is that, for Bernard, the will never operates alone, but always with reason, even though reason never eliminates the will's spontaneity.[20] As Venuta puts it, the two are ontologically distinct but joined in their operation—so closely joined, in fact, that we can explain the will's ownmost activity as constituted by both the will (*liberum*) and reason (*arbitrium*)[21] and can describe the will's proper movement as an essentially *rational* movement, as we just mentioned. However this may be, it is crucial to see that reason plays a radically different role in relation to the will in Bernard than it does in the tradition (as can be seen in all of the other figures so far discussed in this book, and in Plato and Aristotle, discussed in the previous one). In the tradition, the subordination of the will to the intellect, however this was formulated in each case, always indicated a basic ordering of the will to the good. In Bernard, we have a reversal of sorts. In the first place, as we will be explaining in a moment, the will for Bernard is *not* ordered in any essential and constitutive way to the good, and therefore the judgment of reason tends to be a post hoc evaluation of the moral quality of the action; it operates principally in the mode of conscience.[22] This is a novelty. If will had been conceived typically in an "intellectualist" view in the tradition, the intellect is here interpreted moralistically.[23] This makes sense, of course, if it is now free will and not reason that represents the noblest power in man.

We thus approach the heart of Bernard's distinctive conception of the will. In the previous chapter, we saw that Anselm separated out *conceptually* the power of the will (*instrumentum*) from any particular inclination (*affectio*), though he noted that there could never be any actual *exercise* of the will (*usus*) except on the basis of an inclination, which must therefore be present from the start in reality. Bernard takes this development one step further, separating out the power of the will from any inclination, no longer as a *per impossibile* hypothesis, as in Anselm, but as an operative reality in all man's acts. For Bernard, the will is essentially indeterminate;[24] it is not ordered either to the good or to evil.[25] The will can be not only perfectly spontaneous (as Anselm also admits) but also perfectly *free* even in sin (which Anselm explicitly rejects).[26] Because the essence of the will is just uncoerced self-determination, its freedom remains *full* (*plenum*) whether doing good or evil. This does not mean, however, that freedom includes the capacity to sin in its definition; like Anselm before him and (as we will see) Aquinas after him, Bernard excludes the "capacity to sin" from his definition of freedom. But he does so for a reason that is radically different from that in the other two thinkers: it is not because the will is essentially ordered to the good but because it is not essentially ordered to anything at all.[27] If Bernard excludes the capacity to do evil from the definition of the will's *native* freedom, he also excludes the capacity to do good. As Jean-Luc Marion has observed, Bernard conceives free will in a perfectly *univocal* fashion, as a kind of unaffected, impassible, and indeed inalienable core that remains exactly the same in essence regardless of the concrete circumstances of its existence or where it stands in the hierarchy of being: free will is more *orderly* in the saints, and it is more *powerful* in God, but it remains exactly the same in its essence regardless of its concrete reality or where it is found.[28]

Now, this claim, namely, that the sinner is perfectly free in spite of his sin, would seem to run contrary to Bernard's principal, not to say exclusive, source, the New Testament—and specifically Paul's Letter to the Romans.[29] If we cannot help but be free regardless of our condition, then what could it possibly mean to point to Christ as our liberator? Here Bernard introduces a distinction, which turns out to be his most influential insight in medieval theology with respect to the understanding of freedom.[30] According to Bernard, there are in fact three very distinct kinds of freedom. The first is freedom from necessity, which is our natural freedom. This freedom defines the essence of the will, which cannot be removed insofar as there is a will at all, and represents the distinctive way that the human soul images God. The second is the freedom from sin that Christ wins for us by enabling us to choose the good that will bring us happiness, ultimately the good that is God himself. This freedom concerns the soul's (acquired) *likeness* to God, beyond its (natively created) being as image.[31] And the third is the freedom from sorrow, which is the perfect enjoyment of God in love, a state that is finally achieved only in the eschaton.[32] We thus have created freedom, redeemed freedom, and glorified freedom, which Bernard associates respectively with judgment, counsel, and pleasure.[33]

It is to be noted that to connect the ultimate, glorified freedom with pleasure is to identify it with actuality, the real possession of the good that one most profoundly desires, rather than the mere *potential* to receive it. In fact, Bernard goes on to distinguish two degrees in these two latter kinds of freedom, in contrast to the first, freedom from necessity, which (revealingly) admits of no such internal differentiation.[34] The freedom from sin is either being able not to sin or being not able to sin, while the freedom from sorrow is either being able not to be disturbed or being not able to be disturbed.[35] This acknowledgment of the task of deepening freedom is a trace of the classical tradition and its sense of freedom as interiorizing order, but it presents a complication for Bernard that he does not attempt to resolve. In one sense, the first freedom, as pure potency, is already full; in another sense, it is not full until it is fully realized.[36] We will come back to this point.

We are now in a better position to understand Bernard's notion of the soul's cooperation with God. It is precisely his notion of will as *pure consent*, abstracted from all intrinsic ordering to the good (or evil), that allows him to posit a complete unity here. The will is absolute receptivity, we might say, because it has no "substance" of its own, which would come from its inherent teleology.[37] The specification or determination of the will, in this case, comes wholly from the outside; there is nothing inside, so to speak, but pure willingness. As Venuta puts it, the will gives the whole of itself in its consent because consent is all that it is.[38] In Bernard's words:

> To will lies in our power indeed as a result of free choice, but not to carry out what we will. I am not saying to will the good or to will the bad, but simply to will. For to will the good indicates an

achievement; and to will the bad, an effect; whereas simply to will denotes the subject itself which does either the achieving or the failing. To this subject, however, creating grace gives existence. Saving grace gives it the achievement. But when it fails, it is to blame for its own failure. *Free choice, accordingly, constitutes us willers: grace, willers of the good.* Because of our willing faculty, we are able to will; but because of grace, to will the good.[39]

To be sure, Bernard does not present the determination to evil or to good in the same terms as if they were simply equivalent options: "It is our own will that enslaves us to the devil, not his power; whereas, God's grace subjects us to God, not our own will,"[40] but he does not offer here any real reason for the asymmetry. If the will is not ordained to any object, but has its essence as pure willingness, it would seem to make no essential difference to the will itself whether grace or the devil happened to advene upon it in any given instance. For a reason for the difference, we will have to look briefly in a moment at his discussion of love. In his treatise *On Grace and Free Choice* we are left with something like a parallel: "Free will makes us our own; bad will, the devil's; and good will, God's."[41] To use the notions we developed in our discussion of Locke in volume 1, the will appears as pure form, without any content, nothing but "willingness" abstracted from any content. We might think of its willingness as perfectly transparent in its "irreality," and so able to be laid over any image without affecting line or color. The content comes, then, wholly from without. In this case, there is a radical ambiguity, a kind of reversibility of pure voluntarism from within and pure determinism from without: free will, Bernard says, need have nothing at all to do with choice, since we can affirm free will of both God and the devil, neither of whom can do otherwise than they do,[42] while, flipping the image, we can say that the pure core of free will as totally spontaneous self-determination remains even inside this definitive and so absolute determination: "Whether we belong to God or to the devil, this does not prevent us from being also our own."[43] It may be that the will has no other possible option, but precisely because it is not itself ordered one way or the other, this "necessity" does not need to exclude an affirmation of the will's pure, free, self-determination: *liber sui*.

So, it seems the will is fundamentally indifferent in itself, and for this reason it makes no difference to the will what happens to impose itself from outside. But as Gilson and others have insisted, the will taken thus in itself is an abstraction, and Bernard does not think in abstractions. He will be fundamentally misunderstood if we isolate his formulations and so remove them from their concrete context.[44] The matter looks a good deal different if we view it from within the context of his celebrated doctrine of love (even if he himself does not allude to this within his treatise *On Grace and Free Choice*, which is not an insignificant point, as we shall see). Bernard had presented *spontaneity* as the essence of consent, and so the essence of the will. But the question of whether a particular choice is spontaneous is not in fact a purely formal one. In reality, because of our fallen condition, our choices tend to be made out of fear or cupidity. But in either of these cases, the thing chosen is not chosen simply for its own sake; instead, it is chosen for the sake of something else (i.e., to avoid pain or to obtain pleasure), which is to say that the thing itself is chosen qua means. If spontaneity indicates a self-caused act, an action that justifies itself because it is undertaken for its own sake, then choices driven by fear or cupidity are precisely not spontaneous. It is, for Bernard, finally only *charity* that drives out fear and transforms cupidity, only charity that enables us to choose something for its own sake, which means it is only in love that the will is genuinely free: love "is sufficient by itself, it pleases by itself, and for its own sake. It counts as merit to itself and is its own reward. Besides itself, love requires no motive and resulting fruit. Its fruit is its exercise of itself. I love because I love; I love in order to love."[45] As Gilson puts it, it is love that makes a will spontaneous, and so love that makes a will, the essence of which is nothing but this spontaneity, properly itself.[46]

At a deeper level, which is not made explicit in Bernard but can be discovered in a sense just below the surface of what he says directly, it turns out that the love that liberates the will, so to speak, from a purely indifferent freedom does so once again by virtue of its interpersonal character. As we saw at the outset, love is the *will* shared *in common* between the soul and God. We might therefore see the indifference of the will, in its innermost core, not as a sort of "windowless monad" that is unaffected by any relation, but rather as a radical relatedness that comprehends the will from the beginning. The will, we recall, is essentially *consent*. This implies at least the possibility of interpreting the will's own indifference in personal terms as a kind of a pure trust, an unwillingness to anticipate what the other will decide. The will is in this case not predetermined in one direction or another because it awaits determination from an other; in the meantime, so to speak, it presents itself as pure willingness . . . for whatever happens to be given.[47]

Another image that suggests itself to describe this particular form of freedom is self-transcendence. The common will that the soul assumes in love is common, not only in the strict sense of being shared with God, but in the broader sense of being extended to all things in principle, even to itself. The common will includes a love for the goodness of all things for their own sake, which is to say a genuine spontaneity toward all things, because it is a relating to all things, so to speak, from God's perspective. If the self-will, in its *resistance* to such spontaneity and so its "unwillingness" (*invitus*) to affirm the goodness of things in themselves, is a *curvature* of the will back upon itself, and so a complete restriction, love is the expansion of the will beyond this restriction.[48] The will can thus escape its being bound to its own need—whether originating in fear or cupidity—and can come to rest in things themselves, out "beyond" the self (*ecstasis*). This relation is spontaneous precisely because it is its own reward. Thus, it is pure freedom.

In this, we have something like the classical understanding of freedom as a love of the good for its own sake, a love that is an *ecstasis*, a transcendent movement beyond the self, put into new, more directly personal, terms.[49] But it would be too facile to interpret Bernard simply as continuing in this line, which after all is founded precisely on a notion of the will as intrinsically ordered to the good. In fact, Bernard breaks from this tradition even more radically than does Anselm in his isolation of a core of freedom as pure potency. If Bernard suggests that fear and cupidity compromise freedom in one respect, he nevertheless insists that the will's pure spontaneity can never be compromised, so that even sin remains the will's *active forcing of itself*, rather than its being moved by something outside of itself, and so it is in this case still an act of perfectly spontaneous freedom.[50] Gilson insists that one not separate out elements from his doctrine but read Bernard concretely *from the end*, that is, from the perspective of the perfection of charity; but the fact that there is a particular tendency to read him in a fragmentary way is not accidental.[51] We might say that the beginning in Bernard does not *of itself* point to the end, which would make such a concrete reading natural. Instead, Bernard is unequivocally clear that the will in itself is *not* ordered to the end, because it is not, of itself, ordered to the good. Bernard insists on this point in order to be able to affirm both that one can sin *freely* and that one *always* remains free, and so capable of choosing the good and avoiding evil, no matter *how* immersed the will may be in sin, or indeed how totally moved by grace. But the implication is that such a will cannot in truth even be properly redeemed, except in a superficial sort of way: unless the will is intrinsically *ordered* to the good, it cannot find completion in the good. Instead, its spontaneous selfhood can but remain a kind of indigestible element, an untouched and indeed untouchable core inside the person.[52] Thus, even the "interpersonal" interpretation proposed above ultimately rings hollow, for an indifferent will achieves nothing in being united (*consentire*) with another will, if will as such in its most essential core is empty indifference. Absolutizing the will is in this case an absolutizing of emptiness.[53]

Given the absence of intrinsic ordering in the will, it is not an accident that Bernard characterizes freedom, in all three of its forms, in essentially *negative* terms, as a "freedom from . . ." Here, we have a (one-sidedly) biblical view of freedom as liberation, severed entirely from the Greek sense of the naturally given good. But without a positive sense, which is given at the start, the first meaning that freedom can have is a form of rejection, separation, opposition, negation. What is *most basically* rejected? "Necessity" is the clear answer Bernard gives to this question, but what is not clear is whence this necessity comes. Even Gilson admits that Bernard is ambiguous as to whether the necessity is *natural* or *due to sin*.[54] In fact, one will lose a solid ground to distinguish these without a priority of actuality and so intrinsic order. It is thus also not an accident that Bernard has some difficulty in distinguishing nature per se and fallen nature, and that there has always been confusion whether the "self-will" from which charity liberates us is the will that defines our nature or, to put it another way, whether the love of God that represents man's end is present from the beginning in human nature or whether that place is occupied first by love of self.[55] However this may be, what is clear is that the freedom of self-transcending love is contrary in its basic shape to the shape that belongs essentially to nature.[56] We recall that at the very outset Bernard characterizes the most basic power of *life*—in contrast here to the classical tradition[57]—as wholly circumscribed within itself.[58] In this case, the self-transcending movement of freedom will be the opposite of the soul's most natural movement. With Bernard, we have arrived at a complete reversal of the sense of nature apparent in the fathers, for whom nature, which itself already expresses God's generosity, tends to represent self-exceeding bounty, the superabundance of goodness. This sense is present to an extreme in Bernard's incomparable account of love, but this latter now bursts forth suddenly from above, without roots in the substance of the world.[59] It is surely not accidental that this separation of Christian love from what thus becomes the self-enclosed realm of nature occurs precisely in the midst of the Investiture Controversy, or in other words at the moment in history in which the church is separating herself most forcefully from the ingrown structures of the world—a movement to which Bernard contributed his extraordinary personal energies. Love turns out, in this new and somewhat triumphalistic context, to be in a rather startling way a freedom from nature and the institutions belonging to it. Ironically, by conceiving freedom in radically "theological" and so personal terms—it is to be noted that Bernard's treatise is called, not simply "On Free Choice" (Augustine) or "On Freedom of Choice" (Anselm), but "On Grace and Free Choice"—he has opened the door to its radical secularization.

PART V

The High Middle Ages

CHAPTER 8

Bonaventure on the Trinitarian Origin of Freedom

The thirteenth century stands out for being a kind of harvest time of the Christian inheritance; the contribution of this period is very much a "*con-tributio*" in which the swelling tributaries converge to produce a mighty river. In this moment of convergence, the two most prominent figures are of course Bonaventure and Aquinas, the "'two olive trees and two candlesticks' illuminating the House of God,"[1] whose philosophies represent, according to Etienne Gilson, "the two most comprehensive interpretations of the universe as seen by Christians."[2] In according them this special status, it is nevertheless important not to oppose them in a simplistic way to their contemporaries or to the streams of thought that they accrue from their forebears. Rather, the most fruitful way to read them is as representative, which is to say as figures in whom the truth of the tradition, in which all share, comes to a certain fruition. Indeed, what is especially distinctive about both is their gathering of influences, the remarkable balance of their thinking, the capacity to hold on to unity in relation to difference, and the depth and goodness of heart to allow paradoxes to stand as such. As we will see, the remarkable balance that these two hold in their different ways is not so obviously retained by their successors.

We will explore Aquinas's account of freedom in the next chapter, but it is worth signaling right at the outset a basic difference between Aquinas and Bonaventure on the reception of tradition, which will prove to have deep significance for their respective interpretations of freedom. While Bonaventure affirms a kind of superabundant self-sufficiency in the Christian tradition—expressed perhaps most directly in his judgment that any philosophy not centered in Christ is thereby *false*[3]—Aquinas sees the tradition as open in some sense to receiving from what lies outside itself. It is difficult to decide, on the face of it, which attitude is more properly Christian, since the affirmation of what is other can be a sign of either generosity or a lack of generosity that requires some compensation. Perhaps the truth lies in holding both the poverty and the wealth of the tradition together, as we intend to argue, finally, in the projected third volume.[4] However that may ultimately be, the difference between Bonaventure and Aquinas stands out most directly in their respective responses to Aristotle, and specifically with respect to their interpretations of the nature of freedom. If, in contrast to the older scholarship that tended to present Bonaventure as "anti-Aristotle," the general consensus now is that Bonaventure integrated a good bit of Aristotelian thought and rejected only the interpretation of him *outside* of the faith,[5] it nevertheless remains the case that Bonaventure did not take over the Aristotelian *act-potency* distinction to illuminate the notion of freedom.[6] Instead, he made fundamental the categories and concepts he had received from the Christian thinkers who preceded him,[7] producing a beautiful synthesis without adopting a particular position on the specific terms of *act* and *potency* in this regard. In what follows, we will briefly identify the foundation of Bonaventure's view of freedom and consider how that foundation gives Bonaventure's notion its unique coloration; then, we will elaborate the nature of free choice in Bonaventure's thought; and, finally, we will weigh the possible dangers in his view against its evident achievement. Because Bonaventure's *ex professo* treatment of freedom is not extensive,[8] our discussion here will be shorter than our treatment of Aquinas, but the notion Bonaventure articulates nevertheless warrants a special focus because of the way it brings to a culminating point a central current in the Christian tradition.

Liberality as an Actual Infinity

What distinguishes Bonaventure most decisively is the absolute primacy he accords to the self-diffusiveness of the good, which he is able to interpret in radically personal terms as generosity or liberality by virtue of his thoroughly Trinitarian sense of God.⁹ The significance of God as Trinity for Bonaventure's thought in general and in particular for his interpretation of freedom cannot be overstated.¹⁰ Because the Trinity is, along with the Incarnation, *the* distinguishing mystery of Christianity, we may say that the distinctively Trinitarian inspiration of his thinking is evidently what makes Bonaventure one of the two culminating figures in the development of the Christian notion of freedom. To see the significance of the Trinity in this regard, it is helpful to return to Plotinus, who likewise recognized the self-diffusiveness of the good as fundamental to his conception of freedom, but without being able to interpret it with the benefit of Christian revelation. As we recall, Plotinus's great achievement was to move beyond Plato, who interpreted the self-diffusiveness of the good principally with respect to the good's relation to the world, understanding this latter term to designate collectively everything distinct from the first principle. Plotinus, by contrast, ventured to inquire into the inner life, so to speak, of the good itself, so as to be able to interpret God's relation to what is *other than* himself in light of his nature *in* himself. We identified this decisive move in Plotinus as the reason for his robustly ontological conception of freedom, which represents the heart of the Greek contribution. But in Plotinus, the absolute originality of unity means there can be no difference without subordination. This makes unity a purely generative or productive potency (ἡ δύναμις τῶν πάντων), because what is generated is thereby determined in its secondariness. Plotinian transcendence therefore tends to get identified with an essential indeterminacy. This foundational indeterminate productivity is why, as we have seen, some have pointed to Plotinus as the deep source of the stream of irrational voluntarism one finds in the Western tradition.¹¹

Bonaventure's distinctiveness stands out in contrast to Plotinus. For Bonaventure, difference in God has always already been hypostatically appropriated by coequal divine Persons. There is thus a taxis in the inner-Trinitarian life, but without a simplistic subordination. The Father is the absolute origin, though he is never isolated from the Godhead even in his absoluteness.¹² The first procession within the life of God is that of the Son, which is a procession in the mode of the intellect or the mode of nature.¹³ But in his interpretation of the traditional name "Verbum" for the Son,¹⁴ which highlights the intellectual character,

Bonaventure typically emphasizes the name "Expressio," which includes the intellectual dimension but highlights the dynamic movement of generosity that always already coincides with the procession of the Son: *expressio* in contrast to *verbum* can mean both the act and the passive result of the act.[15] The Son is the Word as the Father's generous, self-giving self-expression. Interpreting the matter in this way, Bonaventure does not separate the natural procession of the Son from the free procession of the Spirit in a simplistic manner, as for example Scotus will do.[16] Instead, the natural generation of the Son is *also* an act of love,[17] whereas the Spirit's procession, while being in the mode of liberality, is at the same time perfectly natural, so to speak. As Bonaventure puts it, in the Son, freedom concurs with nature, and in the Spirit, nature concurs with freedom.[18] The unity of God is the unity of each Person, and also the unity of the divine being *simpliciter*; the Persons are not parts of a greater whole, or mere modes of an otherwise impersonal absolute Godhead. To the contrary, the being of God is always already perfectly personalized, even if this personalization is not a Hegelian unilateral movement from substance to subject but a bilateral movement: the Persons rest in turn in the absolute unity of the divine being, which is to say that the personalizing of the essence does not leave us in the end with any sort of Tri-Theism.[19] This is the mystery of the Trinity.

We may grasp the significance of this orthodox interpretation of the Trinity, and its implications for the meaning of freedom, if we set it against the foil of the radical philosophy of freedom developed in the nineteenth century by the German thinker Friedrich Wilhelm Joseph von Schelling, who appears to have drawn from the well of the Franciscan tradition.[20] For Schelling, thinking God in terms of freedom requires a positing of the dramatic interplay of three pure potencies, which begin, so to speak, abstractly in perfect opposition to each other and then achieve the actuality of genuine Personhood only through the overcoming of the real opposition of evil, introduced through the creation and fall of the world.[21] God is love in himself, for Schelling, only as having actively *become* love by triumphing over the resistance of sin. As a result, Schelling does not so much recover the ontological roots of freedom as subsume being into the power of the will, and so ends up conceiving freedom in a rather anarchic fashion as the (positive) power to do good *and* evil.[22] For Bonaventure, by contrast, God is always already perfect love in himself; he is always already the perfectly free communion of Persons in whom potency (divine essence) and actuality (hypostases) have never not perfectly coincided and in some sense implied one another. We may see Schelling, thus, as a resurrection of Plotinian absolute dynamism after Christian revelation. Bonaventure, instead, presents a reception of this ontological energy, so to speak, but *from within* the full reality of revelation.

To transpose this feature of Bonaventure's Trinitarian theology more fully into the language of act and potency, we may say that God the Father expresses himself totally and completely in the generation of his perfect image in the Son, so that there is nothing "left over," no part of his being that is "waiting" unexpressed. This is to say that there is no dimension in God of a *potentia absoluta* that is not always already, from all eternity, *ordinata*.[23] But this *ordinatio*, as a loving and beloved *expressio*, is a superdeterminateness, in the sense that it is not finite, not a secondary contraction of something more original (as one might infer from Plotinus, for example, who, as we saw, essentially subordinates the Intellect to the One): in the Son, God is an actual Infinity, however contradictory the notion might appear in Aristotelian categories.[24] Bonaventure explains that the infinity of God is indeed an *excess* but specifies that it is an excess "of perfection and nobility" rather than an excess "of superfluity" (*superfluitatis*).[25] The excess of perfection, the superabundance of God's "determinacy," his *potentia ordinata*, becomes most apparent in the Spirit, who proceeds from the Father and the Son as Love, as Gift, and so specifically in the mode of liberality.[26] It is crucial to see that the Person of the Spirit does not come about as a result of some deficiency in the procession of the Son, in the sense that the Son would represent an imperfect image that failed to give expression to the whole infinity of the Father. The Son is wholly and perfectly God, just as the Father is. And yet it is also the case that the procession of the Spirit is not simply arbitrary, so to speak. This procession must in some sense correspond to a need, even if it is, so to speak, a gratuitous one. To navigate this delicate point, Bonaventure draws on the profound insight of Richard of Saint Victor,[27] who argued that the only thing "lacking" in the absolutely perfect loving expression of the Father and the Son is the joint love, *condilectio*, with another, an act that is not the accomplishment of something yet undone but a further manifestation of something complete. If supreme goodness implies absolute sharing, the con-spiration of a third Person is essential to goodness (we might say that it is *necessary* to the *gratuity* of goodness) because only a third Person allows each to communicate what is most precious to himself, namely, his being (already perfectly) loved by the other. The procession of the Spirit is thus not the completion of what was imperfect but the superabundance of perfection. In this way, Bonaventure reveals the inherently surprising logic of the Anselmian "that-than-which-nothing-greater-can-be-thought," bringing out more emphatically the dynamically "expressive" or "communicative" dimension of God's perfection than does Aquinas, who, as we will see, emphasizes more basically its completeness.[28]

Disclosing the ultimate roots of freedom in the inner being, so to speak, of God's personal existence allows Bonaventure to take up the insights into the humanly personal reality of freedom developed by those who preceded him, above all Anselm and Bernard, but in a way that gives these insights a new ontological depth by connecting freedom to the insights from the earlier tradition we explored (Plotinus and Augustine, Dionysius and Maximus).[29] In so doing, he is able to overcome what could be called a tendency to one-sidedness in these more personalistic thinkers; while he affirms what has now become the distinctively Christian notion of the radical centrality of freedom in the interpretation of existence, this affirmation does not imply a problematic voluntarizing of ontology as it threatens to do in the preceding thinkers and most definitely does in some of those who come after.[30] And if he gives priority to the free will in his anthropology, this is not voluntarism, not even of the merely psychological sort in contrast to full-fledged ethical voluntarism,[31] because, as we will explain, the free will, for Bonaventure, is most basically not a single faculty of the soul set over against the intellect and the other powers; rather, it gives expression to the whole soul in its fulfillment of love.

Before we enter into the detail of Bonaventure's view, it is good to make a summary statement regarding his relation to the prior tradition. In the last point mentioned, we see a carrying forward of the Augustinian insight into the will as an act of the whole soul, but now with a greater differentiation by virtue of the intervening developments in Trinitarian theology. We have, as we have already indicated, a full appropriation of the Dionysian spontaneous and natural self-communication of goodness on more directly Trinitarian terms, and a recovery of Maximus's distinction between the will as natural and the will as deliberative, though, as we will explain below, Bonaventure reverses their order. His gathering up, and transformation, of Anselm and Bernard is even more direct. Bonaventure affirms Anselm's insight into the will as supreme power (*summa potestas*), and as ordered, beyond mere sensible appetite, to justice, that is, to what is good in itself (*bonum honestum*), but like Augustine he integrates this Jewish form more fully with the Greek ontology and eros: as we will explain, the act of justice is not an act of will indifferent to desire (as it tends to be in Anselm) but represents the highest fulfillment of desire. Finally with Bernard, Bonaventure takes over the radically nuptial insight into the centrality of consent and the degrees of freedom that arise from a deepening relationship with God, but, again because of the ontological rootedness of his conception, he foregrounds the will without the suspicion of hostility toward reason. To glorify love does not require one to disparage reason. At the end of this chapter, we will raise some concerns regarding Bonaventure's extraordinary achievement, but let us first expound his interpretation of the will in more detail.

INTEGRATING FREEDOM

At the very center of Bonaventure's vision of man and his relation to God, which is to say at the center of his vision of Christian existence, lies the Augustinian *liberum arbitrium*. We will see how this centrality distinguishes Bonaventure significantly from Thomas Aquinas, but we will fail to grasp the particularity of Bonaventure's vision if we interpret him on this point through a Thomistic lens, or even principally in terms of the Franciscan thinkers that followed him; doing so would inevitably cast Bonaventure in the role of voluntarist over against Thomistic intellectualism. For Bonaventure, the reason *liberum arbitrium* stands at the very center of existence is that God created man ultimately for relationship with him, a relationship of love that cannot be without a personal reciprocity, which requires the unforced consent of the other.[32] If this is the original purpose, and so meaning, of freedom, it makes sense that Bonaventure would follow Bernard in emphasizing what we have called the Jewish element of the divine liberation from slavery, most formally as freedom from coercion, but in its deeper appropriation as freedom from sin and freedom from suffering.[33] But these are all interpreted in principally positive terms: the freedom from coercion (*libertas a coactione*) is a freedom of choice (*libertas arbitrii*), which in this new context means the capacity positively to posit an act of will in cooperation with the intellect;[34] the freedom from guilt (*libertas a culpa*) is a freedom of counsel (*libertas consilii*), which is the positive capacity to direct the act to the good; and the freedom from suffering (*libertas a miseria*) is a freedom of complacency (*libertas complaciti*), which is the ability to choose the good with ease and take delight in one's choice.[35] Note that while Bernard and Anselm tend to define the will first in itself as potency, and then consider the realization of the potency in particular acts relative to the defined capacity, Bonaventure posits the actual fulfillment at the foundation, the will understood in its realization in and with the good, interpreting the capacities relative to their fulfillment.[36]

This positive approach to the will explains the integration of intellect and will in the *liberum arbitrium* that is no doubt the most distinctive and original aspect of Bonaventure's conception of freedom, and so it warrants a fuller exposition. Without going into the details here,[37] the nature of the *liberum arbitrium* was a matter of particular debate among the Scholastics, specifically whether this power belonged to the intellect or to the will, or instead represented a distinct faculty in itself. Any one of these three options presents profound difficulties; Bonaventure avoided them with a unique proposal. According to him, the *liberum arbitrium* is not a distinct power unto itself set over against the intellect and will but is distinct precisely as the coincidence of the two, just as the act of ordering a household is a coincidence of the activities of the father and the mother.[38] It is thus a "faculty," but specifically in the sense of a facility or habit, or in other words of a "capacity" understood as positive ability.[39] To explain the point, Bonaventure uses the example of the lifting of a heavy stone, which is not possible for either of two men acting alone but is possible in their acting together.[40] What is interesting in this example is that the act is one, namely, the lifting of the stone, but it is a single act with two genuinely distinct agents, both of which are active.[41] In one respect, there is nothing added to the two in the sense of some third power over and above the power each has in himself; and yet the convergence of the two gives rise to a whole that is in some sense greater than the sum of its parts. For Bonaventure, the act of free choice is a power, a positive capacity, that arises from the distinct contributions of the intellect and will, though as more than a simple sum of the two conceived as operating separately. The act of choice possesses a real unity in itself.

Now, the acts of the two rock lifters can be joined together in a single activity of lifting because they are in fact powers of the same order; by analogy, the intellect and will are able to cooperate in one and the same active choice because they enjoy what we might call an original unity. In contrast, for example, to Peter Olivi, who rejects the possibility of intellect and will acting together in a genuine sense as one,[42] Bonaventure affirms this possibility because he affirms a real unity at the foundation. To understand this properly, we need to consider the distinctive position Bonaventure takes on the disputed question concerning the relationship between the soul and its faculties. Bonaventure rejected the view that would deny any real difference between the faculties, principally of intellect and will, as failing to recognize the distinctiveness of these powers in themselves, and yet he also rejected the notion that these faculties could be mere accidents inhering in the substance of the soul.[43] In the first case, there would be an insufficient affirmation of the difference of the faculties from the soul; in the second case, there would be an insufficient grasp of the unity between the soul and its faculties. Similarly to Aquinas on this score, but as we will see in terms that differ from his,[44] Bonaventure attempts to steer a middle course. What is especially interesting about his approach to this question is the light he draws from the mystery of the Trinity to resolve the problem. Just as, in the Trinity, the absolute simplicity of God is not compromised by the "plurality" of Persons,[45] so too, by analogy, the distinctiveness of the particular faculties does not have to be set in opposition to the simple unity of the soul. As Bonaventure very carefully formulates the matter, the soul *is* its faculties, which are *consubstantial* with each other, in the one essence of the soul: "The soul's powers are consubstantial with the soul and are able to be reduced back to the same genus in which the soul lies."[46] The faculties are thus really distinct from each other (just as are the Persons of the Trinity), but this does not imply that they each have a distinct essence of their own, as they would if they were accidents. Instead, they each share the very same essence, which is the soul itself, even as they remain distinct precisely as powers: "Differere essentialiter in genere potentiae."[47]

The extraordinary upshot of this interpretation is that the whole soul can remain present as a whole in its acts.[48] The real distinction of the faculties lies in the order of potency, but the consubstantiality lies in the essence, on the one hand, and the acts, on the other. More properly put, the original unity of the soul comes to expression in the soul's activity, and this is nowhere more true than in the central act of choice, which can be said to be the quintessential act of the soul precisely because it brings together so perfectly the soul's various "parts." The act of the *liberum arbitrium* is not simply an act of will, which has been for example conditioned or modified by the other faculties, namely, the intellect and the sensible passions. Instead, the act of free choice, for Bonaventure, is the culminating expression of the soul in its totality, a manifestation of its ordered wholeness in relation to what is other than itself. As Marianne Schlosser puts it, free choice is not so much a power as it is the whole soul under the aspect of freedom, which is to say its moving of itself to the other.[49] In Bonaventure's words (citing Augustine), "When we speak of *liberum arbitrium*, we are speaking not about a part of the soul, but about the whole soul."[50] This is, of course, another word for love.[51] And thus we may say that the act of free choice is a gathering up of the whole soul, a gathering that exceeds the sum of its parts just as the whole soul exceeds the distinction of its faculties, in the liberality or generosity of self that affirms the other.[52]

It is in relation to the *liberum arbitrium* thus interpreted that we can understand the central importance that Bonaventure gives to beauty in his interpretation of existence within the horizon of revelation.[53] It is beauty that awakens the soul's love, gathering up the whole of the person, and draws it upward, through the world, toward its final destiny, not simply in *God*, but in Christ, who is, so to speak, God made beautiful. There are three aspects here worth highlighting. First, regarding the gathering of the whole soul, we see the crucial importance that Bonaventure gives to the spiritual senses in the movement of love; as a genuinely ecstatic act, in particular in the *status viatoris*, the affective dimension of the relation has a privileged place, even in some sense higher than the specifically cognitive (which is a point Bonaventure shares not only with Dionysius but also with Aquinas).[54] Second, Bonaventure also recovers the Platonic insight into the essentially hierarchical sense of beauty and love: though it is found everywhere—all things are essentially their forms, and every form is in a certain way beautiful[55]—beauty represents a kind of call, which draws the soul ultimately to its final end. By virtue of this teleological dynamism of beauty, we can say that Bonaventure makes clear once again the Augustinian notion that freedom can be had finally only in relation to God. And, third, while the act of freedom is most fundamentally ecstatic, its origination in beauty underscores the reciprocity of this movement; the ecstatic act, in other words, also includes an immanence, or intimacy, insofar as the generosity of love implies a transformation of the lover into the beloved through beauty: there is an *impressio* that corresponds to the ultimate *expressio*,[56] and in its highest sense that free act reveals itself to be a taking over of a likeness, an active reenactment, or in other words an *imitatio*.

But this dimension of love and beauty lies more implicitly within Bonaventure's notion of freedom. At this point, let us take a step back and consider the role the distinct faculties play in this unified act of *liberum arbitrium*, since this will bring insight into the nature and structure of the act. The distinct contributions of intellect and will become clear when we consider the basic elements of freedom, according to Bonaventure. For him, an agent is properly said to be free with respect to his activity if he possesses full power over both his objects and his act: "Liberty is opposed to servitude; and only that power is said to be free that has full power [*dominium . . . plenum*] as much over its object as over its own act."[57] For Bonaventure, the word that captures the essence of freedom is *dominion*, meaning mastery, control, or "power over." Note that Bonaventure's opposition of freedom to slavery is reminiscent more of, for example, Bernard and the Jewish, biblical tradition than of Dionysius and the Greek philosophical tradition. We will come back to the implications of the word *dominion* below, but first we need to see how such power is the fruit of the cooperation of intellect and will. Odon Lottin explains Bonaventure summarily thus: "A faculty dominates its object if it is capable of more than its object. And it dominates its act if it is capable of producing the act or not, according to its wish."[58] With respect to the object, the soul is capable of more than any given object because reason expands the will's options, so to speak.[59] An irrational creature, Bonaventure says, is limited in its pursuits to useful or pleasurable goods; but the rational soul is able to direct itself, not only to such goods, but also to what is good in itself (*bonum honestum*). We see here, of course, a reflection of Anselm. Whereas this latter, however, presents these as opposite kinds of relations—either desire or a desire-transcending act of obedience—Bonaventure sees more of a continuity between the kinds of goods and the soul's relation to them without denying the moral difference: "Will is not essentially different from the concupiscible or irrascible power, but names that power insofar as it is deliberate [*rationatus*] or conjoined with reason."[60] Thus, pleasure, utility, and intrinsic goodness are all objects of desire, and the desire is in every case a free one because, if one chooses a pleasurable good, this does not exhaust the soul's possibility, since it could have chosen an intrinsic good. Presumably, the converse is true: if the soul chooses something intrinsically good, what makes that choice free, for Bonaventure, is not specifically that it is an intrinsic good, as Anselm affirms, but that the soul also could have chosen a pleasurable good instead and opted not to.[61] In other words, freedom is defined not as obedience but as dominion, though of course Bonaventure would ultimately affirm obedience as the purpose of freedom understood as consent to God's will.[62] It is proper, Bonaventure affirms, to refer to the act of freedom as *liberum arbitrium* rather than as *liberum judicium*, "free judgment," because the judge conforms to a pregiven rule, while the free act posits of itself what is to be done, or in other words, the will essentially commands.[63]

With respect to the act itself, the dominion is twofold: first, there is the positive capacity to produce its act, which is to say, to set itself in motion,[64] and, second, there is the capacity to refrain from doing so, namely, the power of self-restraint (*potest actum suum refrenare*).[65] The former is due principally to the will, which is, so to speak, natively motive, while the latter is due to reason: self-restraint implies the capacity to judge one's prospective actions, which is why nonrational creatures are incapable of self-restraint.[66] But it is important not to divide these aspects from each other, as two separate parts that combine to form a whole. Instead, the act of judgment on which self-restraint depends is, of course, an act, and so itself set in motion, while—and this point is of decisive importance for Bonaventure—self-motion requires reflexivity to be genuinely a movement of the self. Self-motion, in other words, is more than just the Aristotelian origination of motion from an internal principle, that is, more than simple spontaneity, which is something even animals are capable of. More precisely, self-movement is the capacity to gather oneself up entirely and put oneself in motion of oneself. This is an act that is possible only by virtue of the perfect self-possession of complete reflexivity, a quality that belongs exclusively to spiritual being.[67] As Bonaventure puts it, "For the will in rational creatures not only restrains the exterior hand or foot, but it also restrains itself and reins itself in, frequently beginning [*incipiens*] to hate what it had previously loved; and it is just this that gives it command and control [*imperio et dominus*]. Though appetite moves a creature from within toward what is without, because it is not able to reflect on itself beyond its act, it is of course not able to restrain itself, and it therefore does not possess dominion."[68]

In the spiritual, and so essentially self-reflexive, creature, the intellect is what allows the will to will, and the will is what allows the intellect to reason. Thus, if, as we will discuss in more detail next chapter, the reciprocity between intellect and will leads Aquinas to God, a principle that transcends the soul altogether, as a way of resolving the infinite regress, Bonaventure avoids the problem by affirming the essential self-reflexivity of spirit: the soul is, as spirit, able to set itself in motion at will, though of course the act of will in doing so is always simultaneously, and not subsequently, an act of intellect. In other words, spontaneous self-movement is an act of the whole soul, meaning both the subjective and the objective sense of the genitive at once. This is just what freedom, *liberum arbitrium*, is.

There are (naturally!) three acts that constitute the one act of *liberum arbitrium*, each of which is itself a single act (*unicum actum*), but one composed of the actualities of intellect and will working conjointly (*necessario duos includit*): *intendere*, *eligere*, and *consentire*. It is interesting to note that, though intellect and will operate conjointly in all of these acts, there is nevertheless an order, just as there is in the Trinity: intellect always comes first,[69] and in that sense can be said to be primary, but the will is that in which the act comes to completion, and in this sense may be said to be ultimate. In the analysis of these three acts, we thus see Bonaventure's integration, which makes him appropriately difficult to place in the eventual split between voluntarists and intellectualists. First, most basically, there is the act of intention (*intendere*), which Bonaventure interprets, in what we might call, in contrast to modern subjectivistic versions at any rate, an objective sense, as the ordination to (*in-*) possession (*tentio*) of the highest good, God.[70] This basic appetite is prior to all of the soul's movements, but it is nevertheless *rational* from the beginning: if this ordination to the possession of God precedes deliberate thought and explicit conceptualization, it nevertheless follows a "vague" intellectual grasp, simply because for Bonaventure there *is* no appetitive or affective movement that is not subsequent to cognition. The act of intending, which directs the whole soul to God, is therefore essentially an act of both intellect and will: "Quod in nomine intentionis clauditur simul actus rationis et voluntatis" (The acts of both reason and the will are simultaneously gathered together in the word *intention*).[71] Within this ordination to the end, the soul then makes a choice or selection (*eligere*) of particular means to the end. This act is likewise a single act composed simultaneously of intellect and will: "Eligere . . . includit in se rationis iudicium et voluntatis appetitum" (Choice includes in itself both the judgment of reason and the appetite of the will).[72] Finally, in sum, there is the act of consent (*consentire*), which is directed to the concrete action that affirms the means to the intended end: "Consent is nothing other than the concord between will and intellect regarding the particular thing to be done [*unum aliquid faciendum*]."[73] If (as we will see in the next chapter) Aquinas restricts the *liberum arbitrium* to the choice of means (what Bonaventure calls *eligere*), Bonaventure sees all of the dimensions of the act of freedom we have named here—intention, choice, and consent—as acts of *liberum arbitrium*, precisely because this means they are acts of the whole soul working in the consortium of its powers.

This same comprehensiveness leads us to see how Bonaventure presents what might initially seem to be a dramatic reversal of Maximus the Confessor but on closer inspection of each proves to express a similar insight, even if the point of emphasis is different in the two cases. As we recall, Maximus distinguishes between the will as nature and the gnomic will. This distinction finds an echo in Bonaventure's distinction between the will qua nature (*voluntas naturalis*) and the deliberative or elective will (*voluntas deliberativa*).[74] The natural will is the movement of the soul according to synderesis, which is the soul's native motion toward the *bonum honestum*, while the deliberate will is the soul's self-motion through choice, which is exercised properly when it accords with the natural will.[75] While Maximus gives priority to the natural will over the gnomic as more or less indicating the priority of what is given by God over the creature's own achievement, Bonaventure gives primacy to the deliberative will, which he says indicates will in the proper sense.[76] The point is not at all to diminish the significance of God and his absolute role in human action[77] but, rather, to highlight that the whole reason for the existence of the faculty of will, beyond the simple activity of nature, is personal cooperation.[78] If this is just what will means, it makes sense to affirm that the will fulfills its purpose more adequately the more fully it involves itself in cooperation, and it is capable of so involving itself by virtue of its self-mastery, its perfect self-possession and deliberate self-reflexivity.

We thus arrive at the heart of Bonaventure's vision of freedom, which is the heart of his anthropology.[79] We note that this is specifically a doctrine of freedom rather than simply a doctrine of the will, which is, as we will see in the next chapter, Aquinas's principal concern.[80] Freedom lies at the heart of things because, to say it again, what is at stake for Bonaventure is not just the character of one of the faculties but the whole soul, interpreted according to its ultimate created purpose, which is a taking hold of God and a being-taken-hold-of by him. This relationship constitutes beatitude.[81] The totality is not incidental; the self-involvement of the whole soul is the very point of freedom. But if freedom is a matter of the whole soul rather than merely the will, it is nevertheless an especially affective affair. As we have shown, freedom is for Bonaventure principally a matter of movement, the soul's directing itself toward its other, and it aims finally at love, which transcends all knowledge (though importantly this is a transcendence that emphatically includes, rather than excludes, knowledge, bringing the knowledge in its comprehensiveness beyond itself to the other) and in which the soul finds rest.[82] Because this relationship of love is the reason for creation, the reason there is a world at all, there is nothing greater than human freedom: the *liberum arbitrium* is the highest power (*summa potestas*) in the created universe, subject to nothing other than to God himself.[83] It is properly characterized as a superabundant potency, not in the sense of a mere indeterminacy that would be empty in itself, but in the sense of an overfullness of actual ability, which has dominion because it is able to act out of its internal wealth, unconstrained by external need.[84] From self-diffusion as a principle of nature, we have come to the fontal plenitude of personal love: human existence thus proves to reflect in its inner structure the ultimate defining characteristic of God's own inner life. Freedom is the sublime generosity in which what one gives is above all oneself in the supreme exchange of love.

Generosity and the Question of Receptivity

The very thing that shines out as the glory in Bonaventure's notion—liberty as liberality—harbors a certain danger, and while we ought to reiterate the paradigmatically Christian element that stands forth in this indispensable achievement, a proper reception of the tradition requires a judgment on this count. The question must be raised whether the notion of freedom as dominion, in the way Bonaventure presents it, offers sufficient room for the receptivity toward the other, which is part of the full meaning of generosity. As we will explain more fully in the next chapter, while Aquinas affirms that the will is an active power, its activity is qualified by a prior, radical passivity insofar as the will is defined as an intellectual appetite, and the intellect receives the desirable form from its object, which is one of the things that sets the power in motion. This is why, for Aquinas, the soul is not sufficient of itself to actuate its powers. For Bonaventure, by contrast, the soul *is* sufficient unto itself to actuate its powers.[85] This capacity is one of the implications of his teaching that the will's self-reflexivity, as spirit, suffices to account for its motion in any given case. The will does not need an object to move it: it can move itself. As Bonaventure insists, "Not every movement from within produces a free power [*potestam liberam*]"—because even nonrational animals, moved to pursue an appetible object, are moved from within—"but specifically that motion by the motive power of which it moves itself."[86] If the will is sufficient to move itself, it would seem to follow that, when the will moves, it is not moving *by virtue* of the good, but instead the will is *moving itself* in pursuit of the good. It may be the case that the will can move itself only in relation to the good, as we have seen, but this does not make the good a contributing cause of the will's motion.[87] And if goodness itself is not a contributing cause, then that means that no particular good is a contributing cause, or in other words no particular good can be said to move the will. A particular good, instead, appears to present the occasion for the will to move itself, according to its own determination and reflexive capacity.

Let us spell the point out a bit further by comparing Bonaventure to Aquinas, in anticipation of our fuller treatment of the latter in the next chapter. While both Aquinas and Bonaventure define the will as *essentially* related to the intellect, their formulations of that relation differ in a subtle but profound way. For Aquinas, the will is "intellectual appetite," which is to say the will (as we will see) is in a certain sense contained within the intellect and pervaded by it. For Bonaventure, by contrast, the will is defined as *affectus sive appetitus ratiocinatus*, which means it is a faculty that operates alongside reason, in tandem with it, so to speak, or conjoined to an activity that is different from its own (as one rock lifter is a different agent from the other, who collaborates with him). Bonaventure does not expound the point in any detail, and we will have to consider Aquinas's position, and then even more directly those of Godfrey and Scotus, in order to see the full stakes of the matter, but we may observe that, while reason always precedes the act of the will for Bonaventure in the conjunction that constitutes the *liberum arbitrium*[88]—just as, in the Trinity, the procession of the Son is prior in the eternal taxis to the procession of the Spirit[89]—the act reaches its proper end in the will, and this final resolution of the act has a relative independence from the reason.[90] While the relative independence is only relative, and far more conditioned than in Bernard or the later Franciscans,[91] the key is that the intellect does not comprehend the whole of what follows from it, as it does in a certain respect in the "intellectual appetite." Instead, it presents principally what will eventually be called by the strict voluntarists a *conditio sine qua non* for the will to act of itself. The will takes its cue from reason, as it were, but does not *arise* from reason as its root. This is what it means to characterize the will as *entirely active*, as complete dominion (*plenum dominium*) and supreme power (*summum potestas*): it is not in any sense "pulled" in its act, but the soul reasons about what is to be done and then "pushes" itself, so to speak, in and through the will. Although Bonaventure insists on *consent* as an essential dimension of free will, he explains the "concord between two things" that consent implies, not as taking place between the soul and the objective good it encounters, but as "the coincidence of reason and will in a single act."[92] Creatures enter into human freedom not principally as intrinsic contributions to its power but, less intimately, as either persuasions or impediments, which incline the will, but do not force it, by presenting to the reason possibilities for the action that it generates of itself.[93] It is significant that Bonaventure prefers the Anselmian term *affectus* to the more Aristotelian *appetitus* to describe those powers of the soul that are divided against the cognitive:[94] both terms refer to the soul's movement toward its other, but while *appetitus* emphasizes the lack, the soul's need for what it strives after, *affectus* emphasizes the soul's own motive energy.[95]

This observation acquires a metaphysical resonance when we recognize it as extending a general principle of being in Bonaventure's interpretation of reality. As we have noted, there is an extraordinary dynamism in Bonaventure's thought, due above all to the notion of God as absolute liberality. Things do not just "sit there" as inert objects but radiate their presence—in the first place as beauty, but in and through their beauty in their action. The dynamism "built into" things is a reflection of God's dynamic actuality, and *reflection* is the proper term: if things move, it is not in the first place because they are empty, which is to say they seek the divine goodness in a receptive and appetitive mode, in order to achieve the perfection that they possess as creatures only by dependently receiving. Instead, while they are also centrally moved by desire, their principal impetus is a fullness, the goodness that radiates. Creatures "mirror" the divine goodness by expressing in their own way the divine liberality. Bonaventure highlights what he calls "the fullness of things" unforgettably in his *Itinerarium*, unpacking the elements of reality to find more and more fullness: "Matter is full of forms because of seminal principles, form is full of power because of its active potency, power is full of effects because of its efficiency."[96] It is not an accident that, with the Franciscans, the *imitatio Christi* comes to expression in a newly literal (*sine glossa*) way. Here is a reflection of God's perfection at the highest level.[97] At the base level, we see that Bonaventure resists an identification of matter with *privatio* or pure potentiality: if matter moves toward form it is because it has a kind of positive actual form already within itself.[98] In between the highest and lowest, we have the paradigm of causal power, the direct extension of God's creative goodness, namely, the human soul gathered into the unity of the free will.

In the glory of this vision of freedom, the ambiguity becomes clear. Gilson has insightfully characterized the most basic difference between Bonaventure's and Aquinas's metaphysics and anthropology as turning on the question of "innatism": while for Aquinas matter is pure potency and receives actuality from form, for Bonaventure form awakens a potential form already in matter; while for Aquinas there is nothing in the intellect that was not first in some respect in the senses, for Bonaventure the intellect ultimately receives the intelligible from a radically interior divine source that transcends the senses altogether; and while for Aquinas the will acquires its natural virtues through exercise, for Bonaventure the natural virtues are already present in the will in general and need only be awakened by grace.[99] In short, there is a paradox here: Aquinas (as we will explain in detail in the following chapter) affirms a more radical dependence of nature (*appetitus*), but this turns out to coincide with a greater natural sufficiency, whereas for Bonaventure there is a more spontaneous independence of nature (*affectus*), which cooperates with the divine, but this turns out to require constant completion from above, specifically from grace.[100] We return here to a point made at the beginning, but we are now able to see its deeper implications. Bonaventure insists on the fullness of Christ, to whom all things can ultimately be re-duced,[101] and interprets this to imply a certain resistance to the novelty represented by Aristotle regarding the immanence of natural goodness. What might be offered in Aristotle is in fact already present in the tradition that flows from Christ. In other words, we see here a kind of inchoate gesture of exclusion of what we have called the Greek contribution to the notion of freedom.[102]

The implications of this metaphysical decision come to an especially clear expression on the one hand in Bonaventure's interpretation of the body-soul relation, and on the other hand in his interpretation of freedom essentially as dominion. For Bonaventure, the soul is not principally, but only incidentally, the form of the body, because the body has its own form already: the body is already its own complete substance in itself. In one respect, this seems to give the body a special importance and integrity; indeed, the Franciscans were known for the special attention they gave to all things bodily, an ethos we discover, for example, in the new naturalistic turn in Franciscan aesthetics[103] or in the decisive role of the spiritual senses in beatitude.[104] But this very point entails by implication a relative independence of the soul, which is likewise a complete substance in itself in independence from the body. If the two come together in Bonaventure—and they most certainly do[105]—they come together in a certain sense as two separately acting things, like two men lifting a rock or the mother and father jointly ruling a household: their relation is not a completion of their substance but results rather from what we might call the gratuitous overflow of the substance of each.[106] Does this compromise their unity? In one sense, there is certainly a danger here: Bonaventure does not emphasize the unity of the human substance in the same way as Aquinas,[107] and for example in his interpretation of the virtues he insists that they lie exclusively in the will (rather than lying also in the sensible appetites, which is the part of the soul more obviously connected to the body).[108] On the other hand, however, we need to recall that, for Bonaventure, gratuity is, so to speak, not simply gratuitous; it is instead the very nature of reality. Bonaventure grants a supreme importance to God's *condescenio* to the world, a condescension revealed all the way down through creation in the positive significance accorded to poverty and humility.[109] The danger of overemphasizing the personal and spiritual over substance and nature, which is reflected in the central importance given to will with respect to intellect, is that freedom will tend to reduce to a kind of disruptive possibility set in a certain opposition to the actual reality of the world in its givenness. Bonaventure avoids this danger himself by virtue of his properly Trinitarian conception of God: the Son is the perfect expression of the Father, an expression that does not lack anything, even if the "additional" procession of the Spirit, the liberality of God, reveals that perfection in an even more perfect way. This sense of an always already perfectly ordered potency is reflected in Bonaventure's grateful affirmation of the reality of this world, which does not ask whether God might have created some other.[110]

What becomes apparent in our exposition of Bonaventure is the illumination of the inner meaning of freedom provided by the revelation of the Trinity as the inner life of God, which is not only the analogous model of freedom but its ultimate Source. At the same time, we see how everything turns on a proper reception and interpretation of this revelation, along with a recognition of how this reception is implicated in turn in our interpretation of freedom. On this score, we cannot help but see a tension in Bonaventure's notion of freedom as *dominion* in the sense of a full power over one's objects and acts. The Father, who represents *power* in the traditional interpretation of the Trinity, does not cling to a dimension of potency over against, and so in excess of, the Son, but expresses himself *completely* in the Son, which is why divine power is totally *ordinata*, as we saw above. Similarly, the goodness of liberality represented by the Spirit is not juxtaposed to this *expressio ordinata* but discloses its meaning even as gratuitous superabundance.[111] This perfect coincidence of "open" generosity and "closed" perfection is reflected in a rather distortedly one-sided way in the dominion of the *liberum arbitrium*, even if this power brings out the depths of the generosity of freedom in a manner that remains decisive.

It is generally recognized that Bonaventure had a profound influence on the notion of freedom in the Middle Ages.[112] But if this is true, one cannot but be surprised at the dearth of studies on the matter. What quite possibly accounts for the apparent lack of interest among scholars is by contrast the very thing that makes him stand out for us. Scholars who are interested in the development of freedom and the deepening significance of the will tend to neglect Bonaventure because he appears as one who opened the door but did not enter, or, to use the more biblical image, he appears as a Moses figure who discovered the Promised Land but never settled in it.[113] Bonaventure is not a voluntarist as Peter Olivi and Henry of Ghent, for example, very clearly are (and, as we will see, Scotus is too but in a more complicated way) because of his profoundly balanced approach, his integration, his sense of the unity of intellect and will, nature and freedom, ontological depth and personality. It is to be noted, for example, that Bonaventure does not *oppose* freedom and necessity, and even concedes that there is more of a tension between freedom and *contingency* than between freedom and necessity. He affirms this in light of the fact that God and the angels are perfectly free even though none of their actions are contingent, and so are fruits of deliberation (here is an echo of both Dionysius and Maximus).[114] Bonaventure's exquisitely sensitive attention to the paradoxes involved in liberality interpreted in the light of the Trinity leads him to respect complexity and allow a highly nuanced sense of *liberum arbitrium*, which is a multifaceted unity-in-difference. This delicate balance makes Bonaventure less "sensational" than his more radical followers, one of whom we will study in conclusion, but this very thing makes him more properly representative of the full Christian sense of freedom.

CHAPTER 9

Thomas Aquinas
A Fruitful Reception of the Whole

Anselm, Bernard, and Bonaventure, like many of the Christian thinkers on freedom before them such as Augustine or Maximus, tended to approach the theme from the perspective of the theological question of redemption. One of the contributions Thomas Aquinas makes is — perhaps more like Plotinus and Dionysius in this regard — to conceive of the question most basically (though of course not exclusively) in terms of a metaphysics of creation, and indeed an astonishingly rich one. Aquinas represents a culminating point of sorts in the Christian appropriation and development of the classical tradition. Not since Plotinus have we witnessed such a thorough attempt to gather up all that has been given into an integrated whole, an effort to leave nothing out, no matter how apparently incidental, that might bear on the theme under consideration, and to find the proper place for each part in relation to a principle of unity ample enough to accommodate them all.[1] For Plotinus, it was the Platonic notion of the Good that allowed one to overcome the growing eclecticism of the late ancient period without compromising the diversity of discovery, and indeed to reach back through the "divine Plato" to recover even Plato's own "ancient" sources. For Aquinas, who is similar in this respect to Bonaventure, the principle is *also* the Platonic good, now revealed as the Trinitarian God of love, an inexhaustible revelation taken up and developed through centuries of tradition. Such a work of tradition, of integral reception and handing on, is possible only inside a vision of radical generosity, which brings new from old but always in a way that displays, no matter how "unprethinkable" in certain aspects,[2] an ultimate and unsurpassable order. The *trust* in the loving order of the whole naturally extends to a trust in its channels of communication, so to speak. In this regard, the poverty of sources we witnessed in the early medieval period on the question of freedom is philosophically significant no matter how much it may also be a function of historical contingencies.[3] So too, then, is the fact of the foregrounding of sources, evidenced in the extraordinary, indeed utterly unique, fortunes of an otherwise unremarkable "book," namely, Peter Lombard's *Sentences* (or better translated: *Opinions* or *Authoritative Judgments*), which sought to do nothing more than receive the preceding theological (and in a certain respect philosophical) tradition according to some modicum of order.[4] The *floruit* of this book just happened to coincide with a renewal of interest in, and attempt to recover a fuller sense of, nature[5] — and the most complete and comprehensive sense of freedom we have yet encountered.[6]

In Thomas Aquinas, we discover the legacy of all our previous figures, whether explicitly or implicitly cited, along with an attempt to integrate them within a whole, which involves both a locating of their contributions in the proper place, so to speak, and always to some extent a correction that results from relativizing them with respect to the whole. Thus, to mention, without any effort here to be complete, some basic points that will require some elaboration, we have the Plotinian absoluteness of the Good, now affirmed as, not just participated, but fully and effectively communicated;[7] we have an Augustinian sense of the radically theocentric character of freedom without any danger of eclipsing the love of natural goods;[8] we have a Dionysian sense of the infinite superabundance of goodness, but now with a clear recognition of the particularity and historical novelty and contingency of choice;[9] we have Maximus's unambiguous affirmation of the distinctive integrity of the human will with respect to the divine, but now without the shadow of doubt cast over the fact of having to choose;[10] we have the Anselmian affirmation of justice as *essential* to the will, but without any juxtaposition of justice to nature as competing opposites;[11] we have Bernard's affirmation of the inalienable "freedom from necessity" as definitive of *liberum arbitrium*, without allowing the *liberum arbitrium* to stand for the whole of the will simply, but seeing that dimension as one element within a greater whole;[12] and finally we have his contemporary Bonaventure's notion of *liberum arbitrium* as *self-moving* in cooperation with the intellect and the other parts of the soul, but with a more evident integration of one's *being moved* by the good.[13] Whether there is anything essential to freedom that Aquinas leaves out in his account of the will is something we will have to consider at the end of this chapter.

Free Creation

Expositions of Aquinas's notion of freedom often confine themselves to a precise analysis of some aspect of the human will in its operation, whether they focus on a single text[14] or show a development across many texts in succession.[15] This is understandable, both because Aquinas treats the question of the will and its freedom in discrete places *ex professo* in an apparently exhaustive way—very much unlike Augustine, for example—that attempts to draw out each significant aspect in response to the most trenchant objections from authoritative sources, and because he has so much in fact to say in these minitreatises. But rather than follow that procedure, which has been done often enough, and well (though of course without ever definitively resolving all of the controversial questions), we will here attempt something a little different. One of the central ideas that has been emerging in this book is the necessity of a principle that transcends the simple act-potency polarity—a "superactual" and at the same time "suprapotential" principle—for an adequate conception of freedom that is able to bring together (to oversimplify a bit) the "Deus-Bonus" of the Greeks and the "Deus-Volens" of the Jews, or in other words the radical generosity of goodness and gratuitous, bond-forming personal love. It has become clear that such a view of freedom requires an interpretation of the human soul specifically in the light of the inner life of God and the nature of being. We will attempt to show, in this chapter, how Aquinas, above all with his insight into the "superessential" act of being, offers an exemplary form of this interpretation.

Let us thus begin by setting the widest horizon we can. Because the will is ordered to the good, in order to grasp the nature of the will we need to take our bearings from the nature of the good; but the created goods that form the object of the human will are profoundly determined by their being created, and indeed as such they are reflections of the *ultimate* "object" of the human will, God, who not only is goodness itself and the source of all goodness but has revealed himself as goodness precisely in the form of the absolute unity of three really distinct divine Persons, which is to say revealed himself as *love*. As we saw already in our exploration of Augustine's thought, the most adequate way into the question of human freedom proceeds by way of a consideration of creation as an expression of the freedom of a Trinitarian God of love.

Aquinas sets into relief the distinctively Christian vision, in both its continuity and its novelty, through an engagement with the Greek philosophical tradition in the *Summa contra Gentiles*, and so it is good to start our discussion with this text. We recall that the basic Greek focus is goodness as perfect procession and return, which is analogically "mirrored" at the human and divine levels. Thus, the human soul receives what is good precisely in the mode of its procession from within, which is why the purely intellectual act of contemplation is the highest, and why emphasis lies on the interiority of the motive force. Nature clearly represents the center here. Divine freedom is thus the absolute contemplative act, thought thinking itself, which does not exclude, but necessarily includes, a "natural" procession of goods from the perfectly immanent intellectual act as its fruit: God creates what is other through the thinking of himself. What tends to be excluded in the Greek tradition, however, is any sense of relationship between the fontal goodness and the individual beings that constitute the cosmos specifically in their uniqueness and individuality.[16] It is just this form that undergoes a transformation in the Christian appropriation, which we have seen in principle in the various figures we have studied, especially those with a more ontological approach to the theme of freedom.

This transformation comes to direct expression in Aquinas. According to this latter, God is not only pure intellect; he is also—and indeed *therefore*—pure will, of his very essence.[17] Aquinas's reasoning is profoundly significant in relation to what we just described as the basic Greek form: one of Aquinas's general claims, which he derives ultimately from Aristotle, is that "knowledge is of things as they exist in the knower; but the will is directed to things as they exist in themselves."[18] He explains in the *Summa contra Gentiles* that intellect implies will precisely to the extent that what is understood by intellect has its own existence "outside" of the particular mode of existence it has in the knower.[19] To conceive of God as pure intellect would thus be to conceive of the world as ultimately reducible back to God simply, so to speak, so that there is no definitive distinction between the world and God, or in other words the world does not enjoy any being *that is properly its own*. By contrast, to say that God is not only pure intellect but also pure will is to say that, however much the world may have its being *in* God, it remains the case that this being is its *own*, and not (only) God's.[20] Considering God specifically as *Creator*, we may say: If the divine intellect is the relation of things to God, the will is God's relation *to* things, his affirmation of things in themselves, his extension of himself toward them, as it were.[21] If God both knows and wills all things in knowing and willing himself, not just their universal ideas, which are (analogously distant or proximate) imitations of the divine essence, but also as singulars and in their own natures, in their innermost being, it is precisely because he simultaneously and inescapably *both* knows them and wills them.[22]

To speak of the divine will, then, is to set into relief the *generosity* of God's creative causality, its character as a *communication of being* ("Creare est dare esse"),[23] which is at the same time a self-communication, *from* God and *to* the creature. This character will determine everything else in Aquinas's notion of freedom, as we will see. Though it does not disrupt the *unity* of the Greek form, it nevertheless does open it up beyond a mere self-containment. We do not have, simply, a reception of the other in the form of proceeding from the self, but in principle also a movement from the self toward the other. This openness beyond a mere self-containment, this transcendence beyond the self, shows up, so to speak, also on the side of the object. Here, too, we see a distinctively Christian modality: the good at which the will aims is not just a fixed quantity, an object that is simply there, in relation to which the will is passive recipient, which actually correlates to an object that merely proceeds *from* the self in a wholly immanent movement of contemplation. Instead, the will aims at more than the mere good: it aims at the multiplicity of the good, at its *fruitfulness*: "The things that we love for their own sake we want to be most perfect, and always to become better and be multiplied as much as possible."[24] The will aims at the good *and at the increase of the good*. Goodness is, indeed, by its nature something "superadded" (*secundum actum supervenientem*) to the essence of things, and so something that exceeds what they are simply in themselves.[25] Again, this increase is a reflection of the will as entailing a kind of transcendence or excess: to receive what is given merely in its antecedently complete givenness is, we might say, to reduce the will to intellect and so to pure interiority/immanence; to receive in a way that fructifies is by contrast to give as well as to receive, to receive in a way that is generative and so extends beyond the receptive self, comes to rest in what is other than the self. We will come back to this point later, and once again at the end.

It is helpful to think of this superabundance of goodness, which we might refer to as a kind of "suprateleology,"[26] specifically in terms of fruitfulness because its unity of internal perfection and self-transcendence provides a way to avoid falling into the dilemma we have encountered in different forms in the course of our study. On the one hand, it is the nature of the will (even the divine will, though by analogy) to be ordered to the good, which resides in things themselves (*in rebus*), and so God's creative will would seem to terminate in the created order, such as it is. At the same time, Aquinas affirms that, because God's will is his essence, and because God's essence is infinite, his will is infinite. But the created world is finite. To speak metaphorically, the created world, in its natural limitation, would seem inevitably to *frustrate* God.[27] Now, the most obvious step to take to avoid this problem is no doubt to affirm that creation does not, so to speak, have to bear the infinite weight of God's will on its own: the *principal* object of God's will is not creation but God himself; God wills creation inside of, and we might say as kind of a spontaneous fruit of, his will of himself.[28] Here the principal object does indeed correspond perfectly to the subject, and so the secondary object is relieved of this impossible burden.

As straightforward as this solution to the dilemma may seem in one respect, we should note that it leaves open further questions in another. Is there some analogy between God's will of himself and the willing of the world? The will, as we have seen, represents transcendence, a "movement," or at least relation, of the self to what is other than the self. There is a clear self-sameness in form in the order of intelligence;[29] but to characterize God's self-relation, his *essence*, as will is to "introduce" a radical kind of otherness into the being of God.[30] We saw Plotinus struggle with this question, a struggle that generated some extraordinary insight. But it is not at all evident how one would reckon with this point outside of a notion of God as Trinity.[31] Plotinus is forced to say that, for all of the insight gained in thinking of God as loving himself (and so of God as free will with respect to himself), the language remains merely metaphorical, and indeed what Plotinus means by this is that it is strictly speaking not true.[32] Aquinas, by contrast, can acknowledge a *real* differentiation within God that does not compromise his simplicity,[33] and so can say that God *loves himself* in the most proper sense—and even that this self-love is inclusive of real otherness, and so in this respect at least is generative.[34] Thus, Aquinas can even speak of God "seeking himself" as an end, and mean this analogously, to be sure, but not in the sense of "not strictly speaking true."[35] If Aquinas concedes that a notion of God as Trinity is necessary for creation,[36] one of the reasons, no doubt, is that only a Trinitarian God *finally* allows us to understand creation as an act of God's free will.[37]

Nevertheless, even this affirmation does not yet solve the dilemma we presented above. The fact that God wills himself principally in willing his creation, does not, as it were, simply relieve creation from the task of conforming to God's infinite will. To speak more technically, God's (creative) will *ad extra* cannot simply be unrelated to his will *ad intra* because this extrinsic difference would compromise God's simplicity. Just as God's knowing the world in knowing himself implies an analogy between the divine essence and the essences of created things,[38] so too does the willing of the world in God's willing of himself mean that the creative will bears some resemblance to the will that constitutes God's essence, even with the infinite difference of analogy.[39] One of the implications of "locating" the will to create *inside of* God's self-will is that the will to create the world becomes, as we already suggested above, a genuine *self*-communication. In other words, if God's will is his essence, his will *ad extra* cannot but be an analogous extension of God to what is other than he, which is to say that, conceived thus in terms of generosity, the world in its own being is not just an external effect of God's adventitious will but in some respect *a revelation* *of God's nature.*⁴⁰ Thus, there must be an analogous infinity even in the will that generates the finite world.⁴¹ The world cannot exhaust the divine will to create, because there will always be an infinite difference between God's power and the necessarily finite, created world,⁴² but *this discrepancy must also itself find some expression in the nature of the world itself*. Aquinas invariably insists that God could always have created a better world, not only than the world he in fact created, but in principle better than any he might have happened to create, and this is simply because no finite reality can possibly exhaust the infinite power of God's creative will.⁴³

Our question is therefore the following: In what sense does the world itself positively *express* (and not *only* negatively fall short of) the infinite power of God? It is necessary to reflect on this question with some care because it turns out to bear in a radical way on the meaning of freedom. What exactly is the relationship between the infinite potency of God's will and the finite actuality of creation? We might say that this is the ultimate, concrete form of the question of the relation between act and potency generally.⁴⁴ The roots of this question, as regards the divine will, can be found in a debate that arose in the early Middle Ages, since it sets into relief what is at stake. The question, which eventually became the great question of the relation between *potentia absoluta* and *potentia ordinata* in God, was originally put quite concretely: Does God actually do all that he can? In other words, does the created order, such as it is, that God has in fact willed exhaust all of the possibilities of his will?⁴⁵ Even if one takes for granted that God is *omnipotent* in the sense that there is nothing at all that can limit God's power, we nevertheless stand before a genuine dilemma: if we say that God does in fact do *just* what he wills, and that he *wills* all that he can, we seem to subordinate the infinity of his power to the finite actuality of its result; if we say that his power *exceeds* his achievement, this not only seems to imply a kind of impotence, since it would mean that God is incapable of achieving what he might have, that is, that his reality will always fall short of his potential, but implies that there is a kind of empty potency in God, which would compromise his simplicity and perfection.⁴⁶ Clearly, one of the things in question here is the essential meaning of power: Does it mean *most* basically the capacity to effect a change (which we might call "extrinsic power"), or the capacity to communicate oneself effectively ("intrinsic power")?⁴⁷ The very fact that the emergence of the debate occurred when it did may itself be a sign of a shift beginning to occur in the way power was coming to be understood.⁴⁸

However that may be, Aquinas's response to this dilemma, which we can draw from statements made in the *Summa contra Gentiles*, is both subtle and profound, and bears on the essential meaning of power. On the one hand, he says that God's will includes not only what actually exists but even "nonexistents," which means that his will in some sense transcends the finitude of the actual created world in what we might call its empirical reality. However, he adds what turns out to be a crucial qualifier. Infinite possibility *as such* does not "really" exist (because if it did it would be finite actuality; a created infinite actuality is strictly speaking impossible).⁴⁹ If there *is* something beyond finite actuality, which is to say if there is infinite possibility, it would seem to have its location in the infinity of the divine intellect. One might think, therefore, that God's creative will is ultimately directed to the infinite possibility of things as those possibilities exist in his mind, from which he picks and chooses.⁵⁰ But this is *absolutely not the solution that Aquinas takes*. We recall that the will implies a relation to what is other in its own reality. To resolve God's creative will back into his intellect in this way would be to undercut the very essence of the will. Aquinas is unequivocally clear that God's creative will does not terminate in his intellect but only in the actuality of the created world: "The relation of the divine will, therefore,⁵¹ is to the non-existing thing according as it exists in its proper nature at a certain time, and not only according as it is in God knowing it. The thing that does not now exist God wills to be at a certain time; He does not will solely the fact that He understands it."⁵²

In other words, God's will does not exceed the actual world by being directed to God's (infinitely possible) *ideas* regarding the world but by extending to everything that actually *will* be at some point, whenever that might be. And this, we might add, would include whatever may bring it about—which is to say includes all of the natural and free causes as both natural and voluntary.⁵³

This is, however, only part of the response, since it transcends the finitude of the actual created world horizontally, so to speak, in the endlessness of history in its complexity and extension. There is, in addition to this, a more profound dimension Aquinas does not mention in his discussion of the infinity of the divine will in relation to its created object[54] but that we can draw from other texts in his corpus: Aquinas affirms a kind of analogously infinite actuality of the created world not only in a horizontal or an extensive sense but also in a vertical or intensive sense.[55] Extensively, there is an in-principle endless multiplicity of things in the cosmos; there is no a priori limit to the number of things that can exist.[56] But at a deeper level there is a certain indeterminateness that is, so to speak, "built into" things as created. This becomes apparent in Aquinas's explication of the essential contingency of the created world. When Aquinas speaks of creation as *contingent* rather than *necessary*,[57] it is important to see that, as he observes in *Summa contra Gentiles* 1.82.6, the primary meaning of the term is positive rather than negative, that it is an expression of perfection rather than imperfection (though of course imperfection is included in its meaning in a secondary sense).[58] Thus, he explains, the "openness" (*esse ad utrumlibet*) or indeterminacy of contingency can be, on the one hand, an expression of imperfection, as when a finite intellect doubts which of two options to take: this is a potency that lies below actuality, so to speak, to which the as yet undetermined power aspires to rise through decision. Aquinas says this is an openness due to the power taken in itself, and so in abstraction from the power's completion in a concrete act. But openness, he says, can on the other hand also be due to the object, that in which the power terminates (*ad quod*), when for example an artisan has the capacity to make a particular thing in any number of different ways. This is a superdeterminacy rather than a subdeterminacy, or, as Aquinas puts it, it is an indeterminacy due not to imperfection (*ad imperfectionem*) but to eminence (*ad eminantiam*).[59] It is a kind of potency that transcends, rather than falls below, actuality. More specifically, we see that Aquinas interprets potency here in the intrinsic sense of an overflow of already-willed perfection rather than an extrinsic sense that relativizes the perfection of what is actual to an array of as yet unreal alternatives.[60] The contingency is more like a positive quality of a thing's actual being than like a shadow cast on it in its relation to what lies outside of it. A thing made by a consummate artist radiates a certain gratuitousness, not in the sense of being arbitrary, but in the sense of being unconstrained, and this freedom coincides with an evident necessity.[61] Such a gratuity, which is again perceived *in* the thing, in the work of art itself, differs from the sort of arbitrariness ("It could have been otherwise, and there is no reason why it should be such as it is") one perceives in the work of an imperfect and uncertain artist, which is opposed to necessity.[62] From this perspective then, to say that there is an essential contingency or non-necessity to creation means that there is a kind of wealth of possibility that lies *within* its actuality, and that reflects the essentially gratuitous power of the divine will, as an implication of that actuality.[63] In other words, this intrinsic potency or contingency in the positive sense is compatible with the definitiveness of things being such as they are. This point will prove to be enormously significant when we consider Scotus's notion of "synchronic contingency" in the last chapter of this book. Just as *creation* is not a change (*mutatio*) (from idea to reality, for example) but a quality of the creature,[64] so too is contingency not a reference to some prior necessity, to which it is opposed, but in the first place an inner quality: the (superabundant) perfection of created being.

Let us elaborate this last point further. The superdeterminacy of God's creative power appears not simply in the power of the divine will—though of course it *does* lie there[65]—but also in a certain analogous respect in the creature itself as the terminus of the will (*ad quod*). One of the ways to understand what this "inner wealth" means, and therefore what genuine potency means, is by reading these notions in terms of Aquinas's famous elaboration of divine causality in *Quaestiones disputatae de potentia dei* 3.7 (and also *Summa theologiae* I.105.5). In these passages, Aquinas is attempting to show, contra the Muslim "occasionalists" above all (as he interprets them), that there is no competition in principle between the "transcendent" or primary causality of God and the "immanent" or secondary causality of creatures.[66] God's power em-powers. It exercises itself by *effectively* in-vesting itself in what is other. Far from positing an inverse relation between divine and creaturely power, or a "zero-sum" game, whereby whatever causally efficacious power is given to creatures would have to be drawn from God's account, Aquinas shows that the truth is just the reverse: the *more* God causes the creature, the *more* the creature causes itself (in a certain respect).[67] Interpreted in the light of our previous discussion, what this means is that to speak of the *contingency* of creation in relation to the necessity of God is not in the first place to say that God has power over creation (which of course he does) and that the creation therefore stands under this power in complete subjection (though of course it does), so that its existence or nonexistence depends entirely on literally *nothing other* than the arbitrariness of God's will; instead, it means principally that God has given the world the power to determine itself in particular respects, in ways that are not simply set *prior* to the creature's own actuality.[68] In other words, created things themselves possess contingency in the eminent sense, a kind of superdeterminate fullness that *belongs* to them and that allows them to generate something other than themselves in some respect, and so in this sense to produce something really new. This intrinsic power as an expression of an inner fullness will differ according to the kinds of being, as we will see below, and so will be diversified analogously, but the point is that this power does not, so to speak, hover over things as that to which they will never fully measure up. Instead, the power dwells in created things first of all as their own *actual* (and so active) potency: "God confers upon all things their being, their form, their movement and their efficacy; and yet this efficacy belongs all the same to them, once they have received it, and it is they that perform their operations. Even the lowliest being acts and produces its effect."[69]

Now, if we were to ask more precisely after the "location" of this power in creatures, we might first look to Aquinas's famously *active* sense of nature, but in fact it is necessary to go deeper: however potent nature is, in Aquinas's understanding, it remains essentially finite—that is, determinate and determined—and thus, in that respect at least, not a direct expression of the inexhaustibility of the creative will. Even more basic (although, as we will explain, it is not at all in opposition to nature) is, as Aquinas puts it, rather uncharacteristically alluding to himself, "what I call being," *esse*, the act of being, which he revealingly describes as the "first of created things."[70] We characterized the contingency-as-perfection in creatures as a kind of "superdeterminacy," and it is not an accident that Aquinas presents *esse* in just these terms: it is not just an actuality or a perfection (as for example Greek *form* is)[71] but the "actuality of all acts and the perfection of all perfections," which is to say that it is an actuality and perfection that transcends the essential order of form. To say that it transcends the essential order of things, however, does not mean that it hovers over this order as a kind of "superform." Instead, Aquinas says that *esse* is "most interior" to things, more basic even than form, and that this internal "fontality," so to speak, is just what is *given to* things in the act of creation: "Creare est dare esse."[72] We might say that the free act of creation is the inscription of a kind of superdeterminacy in things themselves. What this means, in short, is that, in creating things, God does not simply make them to be in such and such a way (by, say, allowing them to participate in that which he himself is by his essence) but gives them *to be*, which is to say he gives them the source of their own being and so allows them, again in a certain yet-to-be-determined respect, to be authors of themselves, to arise from their own ground, so to speak. As Gilson puts it, "The universe then, as conceived by St. Thomas, is not a mass of inert bodies passively set in motion by a force transmitted through them, but an organism of active beings each one of which enjoys the efficacy which God has delegated to it at the same time as its being. At the first beginning of such a world, we must therefore postulate not so much a power that exercises its force, as an infinite goodness that communicates itself to the world: Love is the deepest spring of all causality."[73]

This, incidentally, is the ultimate reason for Aquinas's privileging of *being* as a name of God over "the Good."[74] God does not simply share his goodness with creatures, as the Neoplatonic schema of emanation has it. He does this, but there is something still more fundamental: the specific way he shares his goodness is by giving to creatures their own "to be," so that what is given to creatures can truly take root *in* themselves, as we will elaborate below.[75] At the same time, Aquinas describes *esse* as "most common":[76] the giving of being to things in their unique reality is not an isolation of individual items over against the collective whole but, as we will see in the next section, precisely the principle of unity that allows the cosmos to be a "one-many" without any external limit in principle to the multiplicity.[77] A sense of *being* as *inherently* gratuitous is the proper perspective from which to consider the action of creatures. We thus have here an answer to the dilemma we posed above regarding the question whether the finite actuality of creation "frustrates" the infinity of God's power: the world in fact betrays in itself a certain, analogous reflection of that infinity, both extensively and intensively, because the power that has created it (and in some sense continues to do so)[78] is a generative power, a principle of fruitfulness.

We may thus circle back to the point we began with in this section and sum up our initial reflections. Conceived as intrinsically bound to intellect rather than as a "free-floating" power, will, in general, is essentially relation to goodness, but as will it is at the same time related to goodness specifically qua other. God's creative will *ad extra*, which lies within his will *ad intra*, is ordered to the goodness that lies *in* creatures (*in rebus*), which includes a decisive affirmation of creatures as "singular," individual beings, belonging to themselves and acting from themselves. The goodness the divine will posits in creatures is not in the first place a goodness for God, because to make this claim would imply that God pursues an end outside of himself, or in other words that he "uses" creation to fulfill himself, which would be possible only for an incomplete being, and it moreover compromises the basic sense of will that is essentially directed to a reality "outside" the self.[79] Out of his perfect goodness, he wills things altogether for their own sake.[80] On this score, it is interesting to note that, when Aquinas asks whether goodness is convertible with being, his positive response requires him to face a further question: if goodness is essentially a relative term (goodness is always a "goodness *for*"), to say that goodness is universal, which is what convertibility implies, means that there must be, so to speak, a universal recipient of, or referent for, the goodness of things, someone or something for whom all things are desirable. While one might guess that the referent would be God, or perhaps the human soul,[81] Aquinas says that all things are good because they are first of all desirable to and for themselves.[82] He elaborates this, in fact, by saying that all things desire first of all their own "to be."[83] God's creative will, thus, does not stop at the goodness given to things as a property in which they share but reaches, so to speak, all the way to their "subjectivity," their self-relatedness as *subjects* of being: not just what they have but what they are, and not just *what* they are but their very own "to be," their arising from themselves. If God's creative will is infinite, that infinity finds its expression in the endless array of creatures in their "unpredictable" interactions, and even more basically in the inner depth of things, which is a kind of supradeterminate wealth of possibility.

This line of reflection opens up a notion of divine freedom that is quite different from the typical one: a free act is a contingent one (rather than a necessary one), but not in the sense that it is an uncoerced choice from among a given set of options, which would presuppose only the imperfect sense of contingency described above. Instead, a free act is most basically an act of *liberality*, a generosity that aims at the multiplication of the good, its essential fruitfulness, both in the extrinsic sense of ever more multiplicity and diversity and in the intensive sense of empowering one's other to be himself fruitful in himself. The power of such freedom is most basically the power to communicate in a perfectly effective manner, in a way that establishes a reality in itself, with a life of its own.[84] In other words, the first sign of the freedom of God's act of creation is the very opposite of what one typically thinks: it is not contingency as arbitrariness, an instability and uncertainty about things that could always be somehow different or not at all, but rather the *definitiveness* of the things in the world, which are so fully and perfectly themselves that created contingency is most basically the creature's capacity for self-expression, a kind of self-authorship, a manifestation of novelty from one's own being. God's act of creation is *perfectly free* in just this sense.[85]

Creative Freedom

Let us now explore the matter from the side of the creature, looking first at the implications of God's freedom, thus conceived, for the "dynamics" of creaturely being in general, before focusing on the human will in the next section. God's creative act is free, we have said, because it is, so to speak, an infusing of potency into the actual being of creatures, or in other words because it is contingent in the ontological and perfect sense of the word. By virtue of the freedom of creation, creatures possess their own proper, and so limited, share of God's "active power."[86] Note that this "active power" is worlds away from the active power that Locke ascribes to the human will (and it alone), which, because it represents in Locke the complete reversal of the classical primacy of actuality, amounts to the capacity to effect change through the imposition of some kind of force or energy.[87] Locke's sense is anticipated already by Anselm, Bonaventure, and, as we will see in chapter 11, even more evidently by Scotus. For Aquinas, by contrast, active power is active precisely because of the primacy of actuality. Leaving aside the question of the relationship between act and potency in God,[88] with respect to the creature we can say that there is an active *potency* because the primacy of actuality refers most fundamentally to the primacy of being, *esse*, which is a principle that on the one hand *exceeds* the determinacy of essential actuality, since it is the actuality *of* all acts, and yet is ordered to such determinacy, since, again, it is precisely the actuality *of* all acts, not a kind of free-floating energy, outside of and indifferent to all specification, but always in, of, for, by virtue of, and for the sake of such specification.[89] The possibilities given to things are therefore not abstract options that have a kind of independent existence in some logical space — in the sense, for example, of eternally "preexisting" "Platonic" forms in the mind of God, as we will see in our discussion of Scotus — but are instead as yet unrealized possibilities *of* the given nature in every case. The primacy of actuality means that, whatever primacy *esse* has as a superessential, superdeterminate principle, it does not displace the primacy of actual, finite nature as a principle but transforms it, or in other words elevates and enhances the primacy of nature.

Perhaps the best way to describe this transformation is to say that, in Aquinas's vision, nature comes to possess (and *really* possess, as its "very own") an actuality that exceeds its own limits. This *ecstasis* comes to expression in the fact that nature not only designates for Aquinas, as it always does in the Greek tradition, an existence *in* itself but at the very same time comes from beyond itself and extends beyond itself, and both of these in a truly radical way.[90] If Aristotle defined nature principally in terms of the "in-itself," or substance as standing under oneself (nature is an *internal* principle of motion and rest), we saw that Maximus brought out the "from-beyond-itself" dimension by reinterpreting this same sense of nature radically theologically as perfectly coincident with a being-moved by God. This dimension in Maximus is resolutely taken up by Aquinas in his regularly repeated notion that God is the absolutely *first* agent, which acts principally, though transcendentally, in every act of nature:[91] nature's being itself a genuine principle of activity is invariably an expression of God's principality *simpliciter*. We will come back to this point specifically in relation to the movement of the will below.

What receives a distinctive emphasis in Aquinas is the third dimension, namely, that nature extends beyond itself, a dimension that stood out centrally in Dionysius, as we saw in chapter 4. As Norris Clarke has observed, a basic but somewhat forgotten theme in Aquinas's metaphysics is the "self-communicative" character of being.[92] According to Aquinas, everything that is actual tends to communicate itself precisely to the extent that it is in act.[93] It is natural to form, we might say, to communicate itself,[94] or in other words nature, as essentially good, is essentially generous. For Aristotle, nature does indeed pass beyond itself insofar as it is a principle of motion, but it moves beyond itself, for him, ultimately to return to itself as rest. By speaking of *communication*, Aquinas introduces into this Aristotelian notion something decisively new, or more specifically integrates the novelty that Dionysius introduced,[95] namely, a recognition that this movement does not simply return but genuinely arrives out beyond itself *in* an other.[96] It is not at all an accident that we hear an echo here of our discussion of the act of creation (and the other-directed notion of *will*, which is not to be found in Aristotle). There is a profound integration of the Greek and Jewish elements here. God does not only allow a share in what he is by nature, in the sense of not excluding others from what he is in himself,[97] but "actively" gives it, through a will that is directed to what in some sense lies "outside" him, so that it can arise from within things themselves as their own. Interestingly, Aquinas does not describe the inner tendency to self-communication in things as a sheer imposition of force from the outside, in Lockean fashion, so that there is no ontological unity whatsoever between the subject and the object of the communication, but neither does he say, in what one might describe as a "merely" Neoplatonic fashion, that the same, numerically one, *form* passes from agent to recipient, which we might judge would imply *too much* ontological unity (or at least too simple a conception of such). If it were numerically the same form without any qualification, we would have to say that it does not truly enter into the being of the other as its own, and so in this sense there is no genuine communication but only a simple return to self (which would be reflected in a merely intellectual movement, without will, as we explained above with respect to the simple Greek form). Instead, Aquinas says that the agent *generates* its *likeness* in what is other than the self: "Omnes agens agit sibi *simile*."[98] "Likeness" indicates an analogically differentiated unity. The example Aquinas uses to illustrate the natural activity of being's self-communicability is fire, which communicates its own heat to something other than itself. It does not simply pass on its own accidental form, as if it were transferring some detachable, self-contained *thing*, which would then lie, as it were, on top of the self-contained substance of the other, but passes on the form along with the power to generate that form, so that the heat that it gives comes to radiate *from the recipient*.[99] In a particularly striking passage, Aquinas says that the heat that fire generates in its other is in fact the other's *own* good, which coincides with the good of the fire: "For fire has a natural inclination to communicate its form to another thing, wherein consists *this other thing's good*; as it is naturally inclined to seek its own good, namely, to be borne upwards."[100] (This intimate exchange in being, incidentally, is one of the ontological bases for the pervasiveness of analogy in Aquinas, beyond the extremes of equivocity and univocity.)

Now, the tendency of nature to communicate itself may seem to be simply an axiom, a self-evident truth that we can therefore not get "behind" in order to understand it.[101] This is true, and important precisely because this status is a reflection of the absoluteness of nature. Aquinas's metaphysics nevertheless allows more to be said on this point. Nature, as substantial form, and so as actuality and perfection, would seem to come to a final completion in itself, so that there is no transcendence *beyond* nature that would not be for that very reason an act *against* nature, that is, simple violence.[102] But Aquinas's principle of *esse* is a transcendence of nature that is nevertheless *not* "contra naturam."[103] There are all sorts of paradoxes that arise from this apparently simple point. Specifically in relation to the matter under discussion, we can see that nature's self-communication to what is genuinely other than itself in a manner that gives rise to the other's generation from itself can nevertheless be in some respect also and at the very same time a fulfillment of its own principle, a pursuit of its own actuality. To quote the passage cited above, "Natural things have a natural inclination not only towards their own proper good, to acquire it if not possessed, and, if possessed, to rest therein; but also to spread abroad their own good among others, so far as possible. Hence we see that every agent, in so far as it is perfect and in act, produces its like. It pertains, therefore, to the nature of the will to communicate as far as possible to others the good possessed; and especially does this pertain to the divine will, from which all perfection is derived in some kind of likeness."[104] And "in the ordering of the universe, as a result of the outpouring of God's goodness, superior creatures have not only that by which they are good in themselves, but also that by which they are the cause of goodness for other things."[105] Likewise, the recipient of the form that is communicated can really and truly receive the form *into* itself (rather than simply having it imposed upon it) because of its inherent ontological wealth, the superdeterminacy of its own act of being. The communicated form does not actualize itself by itself, as it would if it remained numerically one; instead, it is the act of being that is the *actuality of all acts*. This means, as we have shown, that the communicated form arises in some basic sense *from* the recipient, as actualized within its own act of being. This is simply a different way of putting the point made above, namely, that possibility (as potency or power) does not exist by itself like some sort of abstract entity but has *its* reality even as unrealized potency only *in* real, actual beings. In this book, we have described "Greek" form as receiving from the other precisely in the mode of procession from the self.[106] Without overturning this Greek form, the radical self-communicativity of actuality brings to light a complementary dimension, which we may properly describe as "Jewish," insofar as it reflects a sense of power as *blessing*, as rendering fruitful: freedom is also giving to the other precisely in the mode of generosity, allowing what is given to arise *from* the other. As we will see shortly, this generative and self-communicative dimension will cast a new light also on the meaning of receiving in the mode of proceeding from the self.

The tendency that things have to move out beyond themselves is utterly pervasive in Aquinas's vision of the world. The general word he uses for this movement is *appetite* (*appetitus*), which he interprets according to its etymology: "To desire or have appetency [*appetere*] is nothing else but to strive for something [*ad aliquid petere*], stretching, as it were, toward something which is destined for oneself."[107] Whereas, first of all, we conventionally think of desire or appetite as belonging exclusively to persons, that is, human beings, or at most sentient creatures, animals, and, second, we tend to envision appetite principally as a "taking in"[108] — the filling of an empty stomach, for example — Aquinas (along with the Neoplatonic tradition generally) gives the notion a decidedly "objective" and ontological sense. One might say that the two reductive tendencies in the conventional contemporary sense are both forms of a "subjectivizing" of appetite. However that may be, for Aquinas and the classical tradition he represents, there is absolutely nothing at all in the universe that is not characterized by appetite. Every single thing that exists, by virtue of what it is by nature,[109] has a tendency to move toward *something other* than itself (*ad aliquid*, i.e., *aliud quid*).[110] Not only sentient beings but even nonsentient ones, all the way down to the most basic material realities, the elements, express *appetite* in some analogous fashion.[111] Now, the precise nature, shape, and causes of this movement are complex; we will only gesture toward that complexity here, deferring the more elaborate explanation for the specific case of the human will. It is particularly interesting in relation to our general theme to note that Aquinas uses two different terms to describe this movement outward. In the context of his description of "active power," he describes the movement as communication, which suggests a kind of giving of oneself to one's other.[112] His much more common term, however, is *inclination*, which suggests a kind of attraction, and so a being drawn out of oneself toward what is other (*ad-trahere*).[113] Intriguingly, Aquinas—exactly like Dionysius in this respect—does not draw any strong distinction between these two interpretations of the movement, active communication or passive attraction, that is, being drawn. For example, as we saw earlier, to illustrate inclination in its most basic natural form, he presents fire's tendency to be drawn upward to its proper place (attraction) and its tendency to generate its like in what is other (communication).[114]

So we ask: Is appetite a movement of *giving* (*communicatio*) or of *receiving* (*inclinatio*: a being bent toward)? The matter is quite complex, though of course our study of the classical tradition has already prepared us for these paradoxes, which are nothing new in principle. On the one hand, Aquinas says that the object of appetite causes the movement, relating to the appetite as mover to moved.[115] On the other hand, he says that things are not simply "led" to their proper good, as so much passive matter on which motion is imposed from without, but instead the movement that carries them to their good arises from a principle interior to them.[116] The good that one seeks is thus not imposed on the seeker as an external form but communicated *into* the seeker. Let us deepen this mysterious exchange: Aquinas says that the higher a nature is, the less it is inclined by what is other than itself, and the more it inclines itself.[117] At the same time, he says that it is precisely higher natures that are *receptive* to what is other than they, and so in this respect capable of being genuinely moved by what is other to them.[118] So, are higher things *more* moved by what is other, or *less* moved? Do they *give* themselves more than they receive, or do they *receive* more? Are they more principally communicative or more principally receptive? To bring the matter to a point, he says that appetite is the movement from potency to act, which would indicate the movement to acquire a form one does not yet have,[119] and that nevertheless this movement is possible only if one already has the form, at least in some respect.[120] Here we stand once again before the classic Platonic paradox, whether it is interpreted in the terms of *eros*, which implies a kind of simultaneity of presence and absence, *poros* and *penia*, or in the more logical form of the Meno problem, namely, that one can really seek something only if one has already found it.

We will look more closely at the details of Aquinas's take on this paradox when we lay out his understanding of the will below, but we will first end this section by making a couple of general observations. First, although, as mentioned above, we have encountered this paradox regularly from the beginning of our investigation of the classical tradition,[121] Aquinas's introduction of the principle of *esse* as the act of being that transcends the determinate actuality of the essential order—which is to say, transcends the polarity between essential act and potency—permits a new clarity. It reveals that one can possess an actuality that is nevertheless "not yet" realized in substance, without that actuality being empty, a "mere" potency. The good at which all appetite aims is not just a simple, abstract form, one among others, which one either already possesses or does not possess. If those were the only two alternatives, the paradox we are at this point still gesturing at would degenerate into a simple contradiction, which could be "solved" only dialectically.[122] In relation to *esse*, a thing can be moved to communicate that whereby it is in act as something that both belongs to it and exceeds it, and thus also to be drawn to an act that both belongs to it and exceeds it, and this reveals the reason that giving and receiving cannot be so simply distinguished from one another.[123] The pursuit of the good will always be in some sense both a giving to what is other and a receiving from what is other: the active giving correlates to the actuality, the "already givenness" that sets appetite in motion, while the receiving correlates to the "potency" of the "not yet," without which there would be no motion, though what is not yet will always come about as in some sense already there.

Having said this, we must also acknowledge straightaway that the simultaneity of giving and receiving is nevertheless an asymmetrical unity: one of the *backbone* principles of Aquinas's thought, the removal of which would cause the whole to collapse into a formless heap, is the primacy in a given power qua power of passivity or receptivity with respect to the act to which it is ordered. As Aquinas puts it succinctly with respect to the will in the *De malo*, "To will is to undergo" (Velle est pati).[124] This is an expression of the ultimacy, indeed, the absoluteness, of nature, which is always taken as *given* with respect to the exercise of the particular power. Nature always comes first: "Since nature is first in everything, what belongs to nature must be a principle in everything."[125] In other words, since a power is a potency ordered to act, which is primary for Aquinas, then that power is always relative to act, in relation to which it is fundamentally passive or receptive. Aquinas's affirmation of the primacy of *esse* is not in the least like Sartre's priority of existence over essence, which leads Sartre to affirm that human beings have no essence that they do not actively determine for themselves through their own, ultimately wholly arbitrary choices.[126] For Aquinas, though *esse* is really distinct from essence, there never is any existence without an essence;[127] *esse* does not exist as such in the created order but *is* only as inhering *in* a given substance, a given nature. As we already suggested above, the possibilities of a thing's moving beyond itself, its interaction with other things as part of a whole greater than itself, its capacity thus to be intrinsically affected or in-fluenced by what is other than itself, are nevertheless always *rooted* in and in some (yet to be specified) sense *circumscribed by* what it already is by nature.[128] The novelty of any and all appetitive movements is never an arbitrary spontaneity but always in its most basic sense responsive to what is already given; all change is relative to something unchangeable.[129] This is due to the fact that, whatever paradoxes might emerge from his notion of *esse* as superdeterminate actuality, Aquinas holds fast to the classical principle that potency can be reduced to act only by that which is in a state of actuality. The decisive question, which Aquinas does not address directly, and which introduces the basic ambiguity in his thought on this point (an ambiguity we will discuss at the end), is the following: Where is the most actual actuality? Does it lie in being precisely in its transcendence of essence, or does it lie in substance as being that is made real? We will not explore this question here[130] but will leave this ambiguity intact, so to speak. However this may be, it is clear that, for Aquinas, if *esse* exceeds the determinate actuality of natures, it nevertheless does not ever have actuality except in and through natures, which means that *esse* can be a causal principle of action only in and through the givenness of some nature, a givenness that characterizes, as we will see, both the subject and the object of the action. The notion of fruitfulness that we signaled at the outset is relevant again here to characterize the point we are making: the transcendence emerges from within immanent perfection, rather than opposing itself to the completion of natural form.

To see how all of this works more precisely, we need to take a particular natural agent as an example. The evident choice for this is man, both because the appetite that defines human being specifically, namely, the will, is the highest and most comprehensive appetite, which means that this example will shed light on all others, and also because our general theme is of course the meaning of freedom. So let us turn now to an investigation of the operation of the will against the backdrop of the metaphysical and theological reflections we have just presented, which will allow us to bring out dimensions of human freedom that are not often noticed in studies of Aquinas.

THE HUMAN WILL

The comprehensiveness that we noted at the start of this chapter, the attempt to gather together whatever is relevant, the refusal to see the whole except as the unity of all the parts and aspects, comes to a particularly clear expression in Aquinas's discussion of the operation of the human will. Following the classical Aristotelian tradition, which we saw already in Maximus but which was significantly absent in both Anselm and Bernard (and present only marginally in Bonaventure), Aquinas defines the will as "rational appetite," or sometimes (and arguably in a more technically correct way) as "intellectual appetite."[131]

In a certain sense, the whole of Aquinas's understanding of the will can be drawn out of an explanation of this definition. As we have seen, appetite is a movement out toward what is other than the self. For Aquinas, what causes such movement is the good, because this causality is just what makes goodness good.[132] What distinguishes the will from any other appetite is that, while every other appetite—whether that belonging to subhuman natures or that belonging to the human soul but nevertheless lying "below" the will—is set upon goodness in some limited, that is, determinate, sense, or in other words goodness in a particular respect that would distinguish it from some other respect that it is not, the will is set upon goodness *simpliciter*, or, as Aquinas puts it, the *bonum in communi* or the *bonum universale*,[133] which is goodness in its unlimited sense. For Aquinas, this is just why the will warrants the definition "*intellectual* appetite": goodness *simpliciter* is goodness in its truth, goodness perceivable only by intellect insofar as it is goodness that transcends any particular instance of goodness, whether material or immaterial. Notice how different this understanding of the intellect's relation to the will is from what we saw, for instance, in Bernard, for whom reason is a separate power that operates in and with the operation of will, or in Anselm, who has to isolate the essence of the will from its ordination to some end, since there are two relatively opposed ends equally possible to the will.[134] For Aquinas, precisely because the will is *appetite*, there is no power of will except as ordered to an end, and that ordering thus defines its essence; the will, for Aquinas, is nothing but a desire for unlimited goodness, and, because goodness in this respect—or in fact this "respectlessness"—is goodness as grasped intellectually, the will is *essentially* intellectual, from the ground up, so to speak.[135] It is worth pointing out that there is nevertheless a latent tension here, since intellect denotes a taking into the soul while appetite denotes the soul's moving out from itself, in which case "intellectual appetite" is a paradoxical unity in opposition that resonates with the complexity we just discussed in the prior section. However that may be, if intellect is contained in the will, insofar as it constitutes an essential part of its definition, it is because the reverse is also the case. As Aquinas will put it, the will is "contained" in the intellect ("Voluntas tamen proprie in intellectu est"),[136] which is to say it is embraced by the intellect on all sides and indeed "pervaded" by it.

But this does not at all mean that the will is simply a function of the intellect. Aquinas is unequivocally clear about the irreducible difference between the two powers—just as he was clear about affirming God *not only* as intellect but *also* as will, which brings out a dimension that is not simply contained in the mind: "It belongs to one faculty [namely, intellect] to have within itself something which is outside it, and to another faculty [namely, will] to tend to what is outside it."[137] The difference results from the *nature* of the reality to which the soul relates, and the nature of the relationship.[138] For Aquinas, the will is a distinct power of the soul, which operates according to its own principles. The will covers, so to speak, a distinctive causal order, with a specifying principle and an end—the causal order, that is, of the good, which is irreducibly distinct from the true, the intellect's proper object, even if the two are convertible with each other (because they are convertible with being).[139] The "intellectual" character of the will is not a limitation placed on it, a kind of external constraint or discipline imposed upon it, whereas, absent such a constraint, it would be essentially boundless and unruly.[140] The intellect is not an extrinsic check on the will's power but is the intrinsic *medium* through which the soul enacts its will.[141] (The interpretation of the "two powers" as acting *on* each other in their *inter*action tends to be assumed in the controversy over whether Aquinas is an intellectualist or a voluntarist, which we will address below.) No, the boundlessness of the will is due precisely to its intellectual character,[142] for it is just this that allows its essential relation to goodness in its *unrestricted* sense; it is what gives the will its "superdeterminate" character, as Yves Simon has argued.[143] Because it is intellectual, the will is openness to goodness, we might say, wherever it might be found, without any a priori limitations.[144]

One of the most revealing ways this *comprehensiveness* of the will comes to light is in Aquinas's discussion of "what moves the will" in question 9 of the *Summa, prima secundae*.[145] To see the significance of his discussion here, it is helpful to recall the basic problem of the freedom of the will that earlier thinkers struggled with, as we have seen: To what extent is the will determined by something outside itself—say, fate, or the passions—and to what extent is it self-determining? In this particular question, Aquinas attempts to gather up all of the possibilities that have been considered in the tradition and devotes a particular article to each. In a nutshell, he asks: Is the will moved by the intellect (article 1)? Is it moved by the passions (article 2)? Is it moved by itself (article 3)? Is it moved by some external object (article 4)? Is it moved by the heavenly bodies (i.e., astrological fate) (article 5)? Is it moved by God (article 6)? And his answer is simple: Yes. But the will's simplicity is a unity in diversity.[146] All of these things represent in principle some aspect of the good, and so they *all* enter into the question of the will in some respect. The will is disposed by the passions, it receives its specification from the intellect, it moves *itself* in its choices, it is always at the same time moved by some good external to the soul, it is moved in some quite distant and indirect way by the planets,[147] and, finally, it is totally and completely moved by God.

We do not have the space to enter into the very rich details of this "symphonic" causality of the will's operation in relation to the role each particular part plays. Instead, we will have to content ourselves with a more general characterization. The first thing to note is what we might call the "textured complexity" of the act of will, even in its proper unity. The act of will is not the abstract simplicity of a (pure) power that has been isolated from all possible contexts, as it appears to be in Anselm, even more decisively in Bernard—and perhaps most emphatically will be in Scotus. This kind of simplicity would tend to oppose the will's native spontaneity to every other causal influence. For Aquinas, all of the aforementioned causal contributions *belong to the will's own operation*, without ceasing to be "*in-fluens*" strictly from outside the will. In other words, the will's act is not simply the act of choice (wherein it is indeed *causa sui*),[148] which is then "negotiated" over against other causal inputs. Instead, to take only the most extreme dimension, the very movement of the planets, for instance, is *part of the will's own act!*[149] The self, in Aquinas, is not an isolated monad but has its per se unity only *inside of* a whole web of relations, which are thus at the same time *inside of* the self.

Even more profoundly, we may look at the "objective" side of this interpretation of the will. What we just referred to as the "symphonic causality" of the will's operation ought to be connected to the previous point about the will as openness to the good as unrestricted, which allows us to see the complexly unified causality as a sort of "distribution" of the causal energy of the good, the supreme mover of the will.[150] Indeed, looking at the same point in relation to our initial reflections in the first section of this chapter, we might speak of this as a kind of analogous participation in the radiant freedom of God, which stretches, so to speak, into the very being of things and establishes their intrinsic goodness, not as imposing a numerically singular form, but as analogously generating the "same" goodness in the thing itself as belonging to it, and making it fruitful, that is, both good in itself and for others.[151] Because this freedom is generosity, it does not exclude, but generatively includes, the nonreducible goodness of even the lowest dimensions of being—such as materiality. As we saw, there is an essential intensive and extensive infinity in God's creative will, which means it comes to expression, or better, to fruition, simultaneously in the interior depth that makes things belong irreducibly to themselves and the multiplicity of things, the "unpredictable" infinite diversity of their connections to each other.[152] Goodness "exerts" its causal power, not through the external thrust of force or the univocal imposition of form, but ultimately through a *final* causality, understood precisely as gathering up into itself every other kind of causality.[153] In sum, God communicates goodness to the creature, man, not only in his being but in his action, and the diversity of the aspects of the will's movement is the full articulation of the goodness of God's creative and providential will in this case.

Let us look concretely at what happens when we make a choice.[154] As intellectual appetite, the will is desire for unrestricted goodness,[155] which is a natural desire and so far necessary in an absolute sense: there cannot *be* a will without such desire, which in fact means that it is *natural* to the will to desire God above all things, even itself.[156] Now, the inescapable necessity of this desire does not necessitate the will in each of its acts in the sense of imposing a particular choice; instead, this necessity can be said to liberate the will, to open up its range of possibility in a certain respect as far as it can go.[157] The goodness that the will desires, *because* it is unrestricted—that is, infinite—necessarily transcends every possible good that we encounter in our existence in the world.[158] Faced with a multiplicity of goods, I *cannot but* choose one at any given moment, which typically implies leaving the others behind, at least in this moment. The will is not a sovereignly indifferent power, standing unmoved before these goods until it decides, purely spontaneously, to move itself. We might say that, as appetite, the will always already finds itself in motion. When it moves itself, it does so "inside" of a being-moved that precedes it: most radically a being-moved by God in the manner we described above. Ultimately, then, there is a necessary desire for the unrestricted good,[159] but this desire will have always already "distributed" itself through the arrangement of the cosmos at this moment, the history of the world that brought me here, and my particular history, according to which I have developed certain dispositions and predilections, in part through particular choices I have already made. Moreover, there are certain goods that move me necessarily, at least in a hypothetical sense, given my nature as human and the nature of things around me, and given certain conditions of possibility (I cannot pursue unrestricted goodness without *existing*, without *living*, without exercising my human faculties, and so forth), which means that these will *necessarily* be part of whatever I will at some level.[160] But these necessities remain in most cases rather general: the particular choice required of me cannot be sufficiently determined by any of these *outside* of my will, because none of them are identical with the unrestricted goodness that defines the will's object. Thus, the particular choice remains ineluctably in *some respect* "up to me," as the Stoics say, and as the "champions" of free will in the tradition have always affirmed.[161]

What finally accounts for the choice that I make in this particular moment? It is not enough to say that the desire for God (too general) or my historical circumstances (too superficial) or my immediate inclinations or imaginations or passions (too particular or indirect) suffice, in the convergence of their motivational power. We want to know the positive reason for the choice I make here and now, in light of the equally possible choices I thereby forgo. To begin to try to answer that most mysterious of questions, we first have to consider more precisely what it *means* to make a choice. As Aquinas explains, following Aristotle, if my will is necessarily directed to an end,[162] in most cases the will to the end leaves open a variety of possible means to attain it.[163] Free will, for Aquinas, is the power that determines the means.[164] It is a power *of* the will, but one that operates always *inside of* the will directed to the end, in just the same way that *ratio* operates inside of *intellectus*.[165] As we have seen, in most cases (prior to the eschaton), no particular object of choice of itself suffices to move the will, because no particular object corresponds simply to the appetite that defines the will.¹⁶⁶ There will thus be a kind of "contingency" in the choice in the positive sense we laid out above as the will's superdeterminacy, but now also in the "imperfect" sense of contingency as an aspect of indetermination. What I am doing, then, when I choose is determining that this particular thing is most conducive to the end I am pursuing, or, to speak more adequately, the most desirable means to that end, given all of the circumstances in which I find myself at the moment.

But it is important not to lose sight of the "big picture" here. We said above that, in any given case, the will is necessarily ordered to the end and contingently ordered to the particular means. But in fact the end moves only by a "hypothetical" necessity in most cases: that is, in deliberation I have to take *something* as given, and so as an absolute with respect to which my options in the situation that now faces me are relative, if to deliberate is to make any sense at all. The only end that moves the will "unhypothetically" by necessity is the good *simpliciter* (as Plato saw). But this means that it is only the unrestricted good that can finally set the will in motion qua will, even in its particular choices. No particular good suffices to move me unless I view it in relation to an end,¹⁶⁷ but no end in turn suffices unless it too is seen in relation to the *final* end. This means that every choice we make is not simply an expression of arbitrary "preference," as we often say today; at the very same time and by the same token in fact it is (however implicitly) an *interpretation*. When I make a choice, I am in effect "making a statement"; I am situating this particular thing in relation to the whole and the ultimate end. Whether explicitly or not, consciously or not, I am saying, "X or Y is the closest I can come to God, that is, the best way to realize my desire for infinite goodness, in *these* particular circumstances." While this may seem an extreme formulation, it is simply an explication of what it means for an intellectual appetite to move itself.¹⁶⁸ There is no choice of the will that does not draw its power from the desire for God.¹⁶⁹

Setting into relief here what we might call the "hermeneutical" dimension of the will raises one of the classic questions regarding Aquinas's understanding of freedom and the powers of the soul. Indeed, it is one of the classic questions regarding freedom simply. Does my understanding of a particular good as *best* in a given set of circumstances *of itself* and qua understanding necessitate that I choose it? This is the question of the relationship between the will and the intellect, specifically the question of which has primacy in this relation. Aquinas's answer to the question is not entirely obvious, which is why scholarship has been divided—however unevenly—over how properly to interpret him.[170] Aquinas is most generally taken to represent an "intellectualist" position, by which it is meant he follows the Greek philosophical tradition in affirming that whatever choice the will makes will always turn out to have been an (intellectual) judgment of what is best.[171] Not a few scholars, however, have pointed out that certain ecclesial pressures in reaction to thirteenth-century currents of naturalism and intellectualism, due in part to the influx of a new Aristotelian materialism, ensured that he was decidedly "voluntarist" by the very end[172] and so came to acknowledge more directly what we have indicated is a "Jewish" element in the interpretation of the will. The most balanced position on the question of a possible shift in understanding seems to be the one that Anselm Ramelow has described as the "growing consensus," namely, that Aquinas neither changed his position nor merely his terminology but rather evinces a growing clarity about what his position is.[173] As Yul Kim puts it, Aquinas came to adopt a more concrete perspective in the end, which was more sensitive to the self-causing activity of the will but which nevertheless remained perfectly compatible with his early position. However that may be, it still leaves the question of *what* his position is, and in this regard it seems that neither "intellectualism" nor "voluntarism" does full justice, though perhaps the former is closer than the latter.

Aquinas describes the relationship between the two powers in terms of what we might describe as a kind of reciprocal causality.[174] The reason this reciprocity is not contradictory is that it is asymmetrical: each causes the other according to a radically different order.[175] As he articulates in his late text on the matter, the intellect is concerned with the order of specification, and the will is concerned with the order of execution.[176] The example Aquinas uses here in the *prima secundae* to illustrate how all of this works is the eye and its sight. Just as the will is ordered to goodness, the eye is ordered to color. If a colored object is presented to the eye, it can only see color if it is to see at all, and indeed only the color that is in fact present: the color "specifies" the eye's vision, and does so in this case with a certain necessity. But Aquinas observes, first of all, that the eye can nevertheless look away; it does not *have* to execute the act of vision. Moreover, if an object is colored only in one respect and not in another, Aquinas says, the eye can look at the uncolored part, and so is again not "compelled" by the color that is present in this case.[177] By analogy, the will is not compelled by the intellect. As the illustration suggests, even if the intellect's specification entails a certain inescapability in the sense that it cannot properly operate without grasping the form that is in fact there to be grasped, the will is not constrained to act unless it so wills, as it were. But the will's contribution in fact turns out to be broader than a mere "yea" or "nay": Aquinas says that, if the given object is not "good universally and from every point of view," the will can direct the intellect to thematize one aspect rather than others. If, in the *prima secundae*, Aquinas emphasizes reason's role in directing the will to one aspect or another of the object, in the *De malo* he allows that the will itself has a significant part to play: "The cause that makes the will will something need not necessarily achieve this, since the will can present an obstacle, whether by removing the consideration that induces the will to will it or by considering the contrary, namely, that which is presented as good is not good in some respect."[178] Note that, though he is careful not to ascribe a positive causal role in this specification of choice (we will come back to this point at the end of the chapter)—he presents its contribution as introducing an obstacle to the otherwise sufficient causality of the object given by the intellect—he nevertheless does indicate something like a positive role by suggesting that the will is what considers an aspect or another of the object presented. In this respect the will can direct the intellect to whichever aspect it happens to choose. Here, suddenly, the seat of power seems to shift: the intellect specifies the will, but the will apparently "gets to decide," so to speak, which formality of the object the intellect will specify the will with.

Aquinas acknowledges the potential infinite regress, namely, the fact that the will's decision in this regard will be itself the result of the intellect's prior specification, which in turn results from the will's direction, and so on, and so comes to the following conclusion: "There is no need to go on indefinitely, but we must stop at the intellect as preceding all the rest. For every movement of the will must be preceded by apprehension, whereas every apprehension is not preceded by an act of the will; but the principle of counseling and understanding is an intellectual principle higher than our intellect—namely, God—as also Aristotle says (*Eth. Eudemic.* vii, 14), and in this way he explains that there is no need to proceed indefinitely."[179]

While the appeal to God here certainly solves the logical problem in principle, since it identifies a principle that is absolutely first and so not determined by anything preceding it, what Aquinas states is put rather baldly and calls for further reflection. *Pace* Lawrence Dewan,[180] what Aquinas means here cannot simply be a linear sequence: first God, presumably qua intellect, moves the will, which moves the intellect, which moves the will, and so on, up to the point of the choice I make now. God's causal activity cannot be reduced to the same order as the human intellect and will so as to form a series with them.[181] Instead, David Gallagher is no doubt right to insist that the reciprocal co-action of intellect and will is not most basically *successive* but simultaneous.[182] If intellect ultimately "precedes" the will, this does not mean that it acts first alone, by itself. What we saw in Bonaventure on the inseparable reciprocity of intellect and will in their operation at every level can be ascribed as well to Aquinas.

But Gallagher draws a curious inference from this simultaneity: he seems to think that, if we do not have to go back chronologically, we can simply stop at the will's directing the intellect's specification.[183] In other words, Gallagher takes Aquinas finally to be a voluntarist regarding the will's freedom.[184] The problem with Gallagher's position on this point, however, is that he does not recognize that the act of the will that directs the intellect is itself responsive to an act of intellect, which is to say that he assumes that to deny that choice has *an anterior reason*, that is, a fully articulated reason that precedes it, is to affirm that the choice is made without a reason. But its being "without a (prior) reason" does not have to mean that a reason that could have been there is lacking (the privative sense of "without"). Instead, as we will explain in a moment, it can mean that the fully adequate reason for making a choice comes to be in the *making of the choice*. Aquinas's basic point is that there is *no* act of the will *whatsoever* that is not always already specified by intellect,[185] just as there is apparently no act of understanding that is not also willed.[186] He insists on the priority of intellect, absolutely speaking, even if he concedes a *relative* priority to will in particular cases, not just because he happens to like intellect more than he likes will (!), but because there is a certain metaphysical necessity to this. Potency can be reduced to act only by what is *actual*, which is to say that the will cannot simply move itself, actualize itself as a potency, except in relation to an actuality that is already *given*, and as first given is first received—and reception, the taking into the soul of what is outside, is just what defines the intellect.[187] For Aquinas, it is finally only the good that can actualize the will. But here is the rub: it cannot be the good merely as a possible object, "out there," to which the soul has no relation. To conceive the matter thus would be to require the will, so to speak, to cross the distance between the soul and the good simply by its own power, which is to say it would require the will to actualize itself precisely qua potency, which is a contradiction.[188] Instead, the actuality of the good has to be what actualizes the will; but it can do so only as in some sense already present in the soul. And the reception of an object into the soul is just what Aquinas means by "intellection," as we said. Thus, it is not the *good* that moves the will but the goodness *as apprehended*, and so as present in the soul by the mediation of the intellect.[189]

To say that it is the *apprehended good* that moves the will does not, however, mean, that the act of will is first preceded by a discrete act of intellect that comes to completion on its own prior to the beginning of the will's involvement. Instead, we may say, as Yul Kim does, that, in choice, the activity of intellect and the activity of will are *moments* of a single act.[190] Here we come upon a paradox, which we will sketch briefly in this context and then deepen in the next section before coming to a fuller formulation in the conclusion. In a remarkable little book from the early twentieth century, *The Eyes of Faith*,[191] Pierre Rousselot presented the moment of faith, and indeed any genuine *insight*, as involving a paradoxical interdependence of intellect and will: it is simultaneously true, he explains, that we do not properly believe until we understand and we do not understand until we believe.[192] The same paradox appears here in the act of choosing: we do not will something unless we understand it as good, and at the same time the considering of *this* as the good sufficient for choice (rather than *that*, which would also have been possible), or in other words the recognition of this object as not only generally good but specifically *suitable to me*,[193] is due to the will. In other words, it is the apprehended good that moves the will, but that apprehension occurs in some respect *inside of* the act of will that moves itself reflexively in being moved by the apprehended good.[194] To put the matter another way, the apprehended good to which the will *responds* comes about as a result of the will's act, or in other words, the intellectual grasp of the good both precedes and follows from the will's exercise; the will does not exercise choice until the intellect apprehends the particular good that specifies the will (because the will never acts blindly), and the intellect does not apprehend the good until the will exercises its act (because the will directs the intellect to its object).[195] Now, however difficult this paradox may be to envision—and we will come back to it and try to provide a concrete example toward the end of the chapter, after we fill out more of the constitutive aspects of the act—it is worth noting right away that this is simply an implication of the principle that act is prior to potency; this priority means that the potencies (of the intellect and will in this case) have to be "reduced" to the actuality of the choice that is in fact made, rather than the reverse, namely, reducing the choice to the discrete powers involved in making it, as a result of their activity.[196] In other words, we do not *begin* the account of the free act with the potencies of intellect and will as discretely actual first as such and then apply these to one case or another;[197] instead, we work backward from the actual choice and so begin the account from the actual actuality of what is chosen, considering the constitutive elements on its basis.[198] The absolute priority of *esse*, which we introduced earlier, reinforces this insistence on the concrete reality of the free act in its paradoxical complexity and reveals why the accounts, for instance, in Anselm and Bernard, lacking this ontological dimension, tended to isolate the potency of the will in a problematic way. But this priority of *esse* means there will be something "unanticipatable" about any free act in the sense of its being irreducible to antecedent conditions, at least prior to the event, without this implying (as Gallagher seems to assume) a kind of arbitrary spontaneity.

Nevertheless, we do indeed need to ask after the nature of the soul's relation to the actuality of the good, which is also an apprehended-as-to-be-chosen good, in which the soul's will, its intellectual appetite, is rooted. If this good is already actual, this would seem to eliminate the potency of the appetite and make any *movement* of realization null.[199] But Aquinas says it is not the realized good that we pursue in our action but the "bonum agibile, quod est bonum applicatum ad operationem."[200] To get at this question, it is helpful to reflect more profoundly on the apprehended good that moves the will. We note first of all that Aquinas does not say it is the *true* that sets the will in motion but the "apprehended good." It is not the *concept* of the good he has in mind here. The formulation is significant. The true is the proper object of the intellect. If Aquinas had said it was the true as such that moved the will, we would be justified in labeling him an "intellectualist." But, again, he identifies the final cause that sets the will in motion as the "apprehended good."[201] We observed above that the will, as intellectual appetite, is ordered to the good in its truth, and we explained that this meant goodness in its unrestricted sense (and also pointed out a curious tension, insofar as truth means reception and goodness means *ecstasis*). It does not mean good simply as the object of understanding. To put the point more existentially, it is never enough for us simply to understand *that* something is good to be able to will it, that is, to be sufficiently moved by it so as to be able to choose it. Instead, more than understanding its goodness, we have to "feel" that goodness.[202] And so we can raise the question: Is there a way for true goodness to be present *in* the soul other than simply as an object of intellect? As we will come to see, addressing this question will bring us more insight into the paradox we just mentioned.

Love, Affection, and Imagination

Here we come upon a dimension that is typically left out of the debates concerning the relationship between intellect and will, though it turns out to be an utterly indispensable piece of the puzzle—indeed, quite literally *foundational* to Aquinas's doctrine of freedom.[203] Its absence from discussions can be explained by the fact that Aquinas himself does not highlight it in his own *ex professo* treatments of the will and its operation,[204] but its place in his understanding becomes apparent the moment the proper connections are made. Ultimately, for Aquinas, it is not simply *reason* that is the "whole root" of freedom[205] but arguably *also love*, once we understand love properly.[206] To see why, we will briefly have to unfold three things: the meaning of love, the connection between love and the perception of goodness precisely in its unrestricted sense, and finally the role that God plays in this, not just as first and formal cause but as personal, providential presence, or in other words as solicitous generosity.

It is curious that the theme of love arises so rarely in scholarly discussions of the will's freedom, since Aquinas himself says clearly that love is the first movement of the will ("primus motus voluntatis").[207] It is not first in a merely horizontal sense as the initial item in a series, which moves beyond that item as the series progresses. Instead, it is first in a literally foundational sense. Every act of will, just like every act of the appetite in general, is a *seeking after* (*ad* [*aliquid*] *petere*). But this movement cannot be merely a movement from potency to act, since potency cannot actualize itself. Instead, it has to be actualized by the nature of what is *already* actual. Whereas the intellect (qua agent intellect) *can* actualize itself (qua possible intellect), the will can actualize the power of choice only in relation to the actuality of goodness *present* to the soul—not simply as a possible object qua possible, or even as the actuality simply of desire.[208] Instead, the good that moves the soul has to be *apprehended*, which is to say in some sense *already in the soul*. It is often assumed that Aquinas means by these assertions simply that every act of will is governed by intellect because we cannot will something without *knowing* what we will; the will cannot will blindly, without some object, and this is supplied by intellect. While this is certainly true, we get a better sense of the relationship when we consider the matter not simply in terms of specification but in terms of exercise, or, in other words, because exercise is a movement from potency to act, in terms of the relation between act and potency, which has implications for what we might call "motive force." The reception of the form of goodness that moves the will, or indeed allows the will to move itself, is not just a taking in of intelligible species in the order of cognition: the form has actually to enter into the appetite.[209] But it is just this particular kind of apprehension, the reception of specifying form into the appetite, that Aquinas defines as love. According to Aquinas, love is a reception of the form of the other so as to dispose the soul to that other.[210] Because the soul cannot move at all toward the other except as first antecedently disposed, there cannot be any movement of the soul, whether that be appetitive or cognitive, insofar as the cognitive act qua act is itself moved by appetite, that is not founded in a prior love.²¹¹ Love betrays a curious complexity: it is something like an intellectual movement of a reception of the form of the other into the soul, but it is also something like appetite, insofar as it is a movement of the soul *to* the other in its reality, specifically as a con-formity.²¹² There are some grounds for distinguishing this complexity as an order of beauty, as distinct from (though of course profoundly related to) the order of the good.²¹³ In any event, Aquinas intriguingly defines love as a *co-aptatio*, a reciprocal adjusting of the soul and its object to each other.²¹⁴ The term *co-aptatio* recalls Aquinas's basic affirmation that it is *native* to the human soul to come to *agreement* (*con-venientia*) with all things.²¹⁵ We will come back to the "reciprocity" indicated in the terms *co-aptatio* and *con-venientia*, but for now the point is that the soul cannot move itself toward its other appetitively without first having received the other into itself. Love indicates a principial movement of the will (objective genitive) that allows every other movement of the will (subjective genitive).

It is significant that love is most generally characterized as a *passion* of the soul—indeed, the first of the passions.²¹⁶ We saw above that the will operates always within a context that precedes it as given, in relation to which it is fundamentally receptive, though without this precluding its activity. But it is also significant that love has a universal scope: while on the one hand it is a passion, and so a matter of the sensitive appetite—to such an extent that one can speak of love as "natural," expressed not only in animals but even in the elements in their self-communication and pursuit of what is fitting to them—on the other hand it passes through human existence from its basest to its noblest form (friendship in the good) and extends all the way to the pure spirit of "separate substances" and even God himself.²¹⁷ We might say that it has a "simple infinity" just as do the good and the true, the will and the intellect.²¹⁸ The highest end of man is friendship with God, that is, charity or love, because God is love in himself: this friendship is a being taken up into God's inner life, an entry into the charity that God *is*. The reason love has such a universal scope is that it is an always-prior reception of form. As *prior*, that is, as preceding the (subjective, deliberate) act of will, it takes the form of a passion of the soul; but as a reception *of form* it is not principally a matter of matter, so to speak. If the problem of the will's operation, specified as the problem of locating the actuality that enables the reduction of the will's potency, is ultimately a question of how a self can in fact move to the other as other, love presents a solution: it is a "bridge" between the subject and the object, the self and the other (*co-aptatio*), insofar as it is a communication of actuality that allows a pursuit of the actuality communicated: love literally in-forms the appetite.

So, what is the precise nature of this actuality? As we already noted, the communication of form in love is not an intellectual act, which is a taking of the likeness of a thing into the form of the knower as an appropriation that terminates in the soul[219]—a conversion of the known into the knower, so to speak—but rather an act in the appetitive order, which is why Aquinas describes it in the *opposite* sense as a conformity of the lover *to the beloved*.[220] And yet it is like an intellectual act because it is not simply the realization of the appetite, its satisfaction in the reality of its object, but implies a kind of contemplative distance insofar as it is a communication that is already complete in itself, prior to, and in an order that is distinct from the realization through appetite.[221] The act of love is more theoretical/essential than appetite and more practical/existential than intellect. To understand the kind of actuality we are dealing with here, it seems that we need to take a speculative step beyond the letter of Aquinas and make some connections that he himself does not explicitly make.[222] Let us recall that the will is an intellectual appetite, which means that it is ordered to goodness in its unrestricted sense. It is just this "sort" of goodness that is capable of moving the will, that is, of in-forming it in a manner sufficient to allow it to move itself. This unrestricted goodness is, as we have seen, connected to the *act* of being, which inheres *in* particular beings, but which in some sense transcends their particularity.[223] Whenever the human will makes a particular choice and moves itself to a particular reality, it cannot but do so in relation to this appetite for unrestricted goodness, which we have come to see must be already actual *in some respect*, even as it remains also a *bonum possibile*.

There are three different, but equally fundamental, dimensions to the particular goodness that represents the object of the will in its actual operation. First, the love at the root of freedom, because it is a reception of form under the aspect of the *bonum in communi*, is grounded in the *truth* of the good, which is to say in the intrinsic goodness of things, rather than in the relativity of the thing to the particular act of appetite. Prior to and more fundamental than any benefit that may be derived from things or any use to which they might be put, there is in the love that moves the human soul always an implicit, if not also explicit, affirmation of their goodness simply with respect to themselves, or else the appetitive act would lie more within the order of abstract sensibility than within that of the will (as *intellectual* appetite). Anselm seemed to take for granted that a desire for benefit is aimed simply at a good in relation *to me* (*commodum*): that is, the desire is essentially self-interested, rather than at goodness in its truth (*justitia*). Aquinas's notion of the will recalls the deeper Platonic tradition that recognizes a desire for justice *inevitably* at the heart of the desire for any good, no matter how apparently "self-interested."[224] To be sure, Aquinas draws a distinction between love of desire, which is the relation between (unrealized and so imperfect or incomplete) potency to act, and love of friendship, either for oneself or for another,[225] which is a reciprocal relation between actualities. We will come back to this point, but it is crucial to see that, precisely because the will is an intellectual appetite, and so directed to the *truth* of the goodness of a thing, and because the truth of a thing concerns its essence in itself and not simply its practical implications, so to speak, for what is other than itself, it means that at the basis of all of the will's acts will be something like a love of friendship, something analogous to the generous and ontologically affirming relationship of actuality to actuality, whether the will is directed in any particular instance to a person or to an object.[226] The fact that Aquinas does not highlight this point himself, however much it may be implied in what he does say, is not insignificant, and gives expression to an ambiguity that we will have to attend to at the end of this chapter. But we may nevertheless see that, in this notion derived from Aquinas, if not stated by him, we recover Anselm's sense of freedom as the power to choose true goodness, but now with a genuinely ontological foundation.

The second dimension concerns the self-transcending character of goodness that we discussed above. Here we will see not only why love of desire cannot be separated from love of friendship but also conversely why love of friendship can never be separated from love of desire. Aquinas makes a distinction between mere goodness in a relative sense (*secundum quid*) and goodness in the absolute sense (*simpliciter*),[227] coordinating this distinction with that between first and second actuality: *relative* goodness, which is to say goodness in its analogous or extended sense, is the goodness of a thing in its substantial being, its being what it is according to type. But goodness in the strict and proper sense concerns the actual *subsisting* of a thing, its self-achieved being, its enactment of what it is from out of its own self through its operation, and so its manifestation of its proper reality or being.[228] Thus, we might say that a thing is not properly desired in an abstract sense that would isolate its given quiddity from its concrete reality (as occurs, for example, in the intellectual grasp of essential form), but rather that a thing *gives itself* to be desired, which is to say that it achieves "appetibility" in its self-expression in its accidents, or, in higher-level beings, in its operations.[229] But note, it is in just this way that a thing enters into relation with what is other than itself. We saw above that the actuality of things is greater than they; it belongs to them only in their extending out beyond themselves in interaction with others,[230] taking up their proper place as members of a community, a greater whole that exceeds them. This is *decisive* for the theme of freedom, which is why Aquinas presents the movement of the will as a symphonic unity in diversity, ultimately involving the whole cosmos in each of the will's acts.

As we explained earlier, the divine will in the act of creating terminates in a kind of "positive indeterminacy" in things that arises from their superabundant perfection: this "yet-to-be-determined-ness," which is not an empty potency but an overfullness, is the goodness that corresponds, so to speak, with God's freedom. This superabundance gives rise to possibilities, but these possibilities, as expressions of perfection, result from the inner reality of what things actually are (*resultare*: they "bounce back," or "leap up" from what is already there). If we connect this with the theme of love, interpreted as the communication of act that principially moves the will, we can see that what the soul receives in the *co-aptatio* that constitutes love is not an actuality as a discrete, realized act of appetite that has already reached its termination *in re*; instead, because it is founded on the intrinsic being of the beloved thing, this is actuality as the real opening of always-particular possibility, which *enables* distinct acts of will specifically as intellectual appetite in the sense that these acts are aspiring receptions (appetite) of the truth (intellectual) of things. As we have already suggested, there is good reason to think of the object's in-forming of the soul in this respect as presenting its form under the aspect of the beautiful, interpreted as the manifestation of a thing's being in appearance, or in other words its self-revelation in its accidents, rather than under the aspect of the true, as a grasp of a thing by means of a concept.[231] What moves the soul in other words is the *apprehended good*, the object that combines the true and the good—namely, the beautiful. Aquinas himself connects the "apprehended good" with beauty.[232] However this may be, what we have here is thus a kind of reciprocal fructification: the will does not impose its possibilities on things wholly from the outside but dis-covers its possibilities *from* things, even while things receive in the human will an opportunity, so to speak, to express themselves in a more profound way—specifically, in the truth and goodness of their *own being*—than in their natural interactions with other things in the cosmos.[233] We see in this a dimension of the significance of the reciprocity signaled in the word Aquinas uses to define love, namely, *co-aptatio*, a reciprocal disposing of two things to each other. Free human action *on* things is simultaneously a "coaxing" *out of* things a possibility that is not yet expressed and perhaps lies beyond the power of things to realize themselves (*praeter intentionem naturae*).[234]

At the beginning of this chapter, we spoke of God's creative will as a kind of infinity ordered to the goodness of things, not simply as a kind of definitive form, already established, which is then imposed on things from above, but as a kind of "hyperbolic" affirmation:[235] as we saw, the divine will aims not just at goodness but at its propagation, its never simply limited a priori multiplication and increase, both extensively and intensively. We see that there is an analogy between love as God's creative will and the love of the human soul that affirms its object, that is, receives its actuality into the soul, precisely in the form of an openness to what is "yet-to-come" from the thing,[236] which is why it is properly characterized in this case not as a *comprehensio* but as a *dispositio*, even if it is born into the soul from the beginning.[237] Thus, the love of friendship is always also necessarily a love of desire: an affirmation of the other that always wants *more*, specifically that the other flourish, grow, enact more fully its own goodness by being increasingly good for others.[238]

Though we cannot elaborate the point in any depth here, it bears remarking that, from the perspective we are developing, themes like *affection* and *imagination* turn out to have a much more fundamental place in the meaning of freedom than is typically recognized. The attachment to things in love is what provides the proper context *within which* to make one's decisions and direct one's attentions.[239] We recall in this context the Jewish theme of *covenant*, which takes on a particular depth when viewed within the context of Aquinas's metaphysics of creation.[240] The antecedently given attachment to things implied in the notion of affection corresponds to the "passional" character of love, its entrance into the soul, as it were, prior to the soul's deliberate operations.[241] The role of imagination, perhaps even more surprisingly, takes on central importance.[242] The apprehension that moves the will, as we have said, is not "merely" intellectual in the sense of receiving a likeness of a thing into the soul but is an apprehension of goodness precisely *as good*, in the form of a kind of *being-moved*: "Just as the imagination of a form without estimation of fitness or harmfulness does not move the sensitive appetite; so neither does the apprehension of the true without the aspect of goodness and desirability."[243] We ought to interpret this act of imagination as a thing's communicating its actuality — or, given the point above, we may now say its "superactuality" — into the soul as a kind of radiating of its reality *and* its inner possibility at once. This particular perception is not only of the thing in itself but at the same time in relation to goodness *simpliciter*, which both includes it (and so implies a completion of the perceptive act) and transcends it (and so implies an openness to greater possibility). We have been suggesting that this radiance seems best characterized as beautiful, but in any event it bears a relation to imagination in two different respects: as "receptive" imagination, insofar as it is a *concrete* form, related to sense experience and to nature,[244] or in other words having its place not just in the soul but specifically in the *embodied* soul, which is naturally inclined to material realities;[245] and as "productive" imagination, insofar as the actuality received is not a cognition but a *coaptatio* and *complacentia*, that is, a "superactual" *disposition*, and so coincides with a recognition of as yet unrealized possibilities, pointing toward the essentially contingent future (first in the perfect sense of contingency and second in the imperfect sense). The point is that the possibilities with which genuine freedom is concerned are not abstract options but *real* possibilities that emerge from the prior natures of both subject and object, in the concrete reality of the complexly ordered actual world.[246] Freedom, we might say, requires a deep affection and an expansive imagination—an affection and imagination that are rooted in love of reality and take their measure from the *truth* of the goodness of things.

The third dimension concerns God. It is not just common goodness (*bonum in communi*) that accounts for the will's movement, or in other words the "Greek" good, but the *self-subsistent, transcendent cause* of goodness, the *bonum universale*, God himself, that is, the "Jewish" dimension, which is inseparable from goodness in the sense of what is most common.[247] We now come full circle in our exposition. It is often recognized that God is central to Aquinas's anthropology: he affirms, of course, the church's traditional teaching of man being made in the image of God.[248] But he interprets the "structure" of the human soul more basically in the light of the nature of God, revealed as Trinity, than scholars often acknowledge who see him merely as recovering an essentially Aristotelian schema in his interpretation of human nature.[249] The procession of the Son and the Spirit from the Father have a likeness in the procession of intellect and will from the essence of the soul. But the imago, for Aquinas, is a matter not simply of essence (the soul "looks like God") (first actuality) but also and more decisively of existence and operation (second actuality): the soul can operate in its proper sense only by virtue of the actual presence of God.[250] In other words, God comprehends the human soul, not just as its exemplary cause, but as the beginning and end of its operation. Thus, God is not only the First Truth, and so the ultimate object of the intellect, but at the same time gives the created intellect the very light by which it knows what it knows.[251] Similarly, God is the *comprehensive cause* of the activity of the will, as Aquinas makes clear in *Summa theologiae* I-II.9.6: the will is moved by *God alone* (*a solo Deo*). The most obvious dimension of this causality is the reality of God as the supreme good: if the will cannot will anything except *as* good, to say that God is ultimate goodness is to say that whatever moves the will can finally be traced back to God. Goodness is final causality, and final causality comprehends all of the other causes. But Aquinas says more than just that God himself *is* the good that the will seeks in all of its acts, which is the main point he makes in the body of the text that responds to the question. In his reply to objection 3, Aquinas clarifies that God also moves the will in what we would call an "efficient" sense.²⁵² The argument is straightforward, even if key premises are left unstated here. It is only the universal good that is sufficient *actually* to move the will, but in this life the universal good is never actually present *as such*, as the explicit object of the will's choosing. Aquinas clarifies in the *prima pars* that "to will is nothing but to be inclined towards the object of the will, which is universal good. But to incline toward the universal good belongs to the First Mover, to Whom the ultimate end is proportionate."²⁵³ Therefore, God himself must actually dispose the will to this good that exceeds man and yet is necessary to him.²⁵⁴ The passage in the *prima secundae* may seem to suggest a kind of piecemeal cooperation (such as we saw in Anselm): God disposes the will to the universal good, but by contrast man disposes himself to particular means toward that end. Aquinas makes it clear, however, that each and every particular act is also moved by God as First Agent. God operates in each act of will comprehensively, in the order of efficient, formal, and final causality all at once.²⁵⁵ Again, while it may seem that, for the most part, God moves the will in general but man moves himself in particular cases,²⁵⁶ in fact because the disposition to the universal good is involved in every single act without exception, God's causality includes even particular volitions in their particularity. There is no dimension of the human act of freedom that is not from the beginning and all along the way a participation in God's freedom. The order of execution, which God operates as first cause, is always particular. No less than does Augustine or Maximus, Aquinas affirms God as the cause of each choice made without God's causality making it any less a self-originating choice.

One of the ways we may interpret Aquinas's understanding of God's relation to the human will is in terms of one of this book's theses, namely, that the Christian vision is a transformative synthesis of the Greek and the Jewish forms. God does not move the human will simply by presenting himself to the will in the Greek form as the eternal good, qua object of appetite. Instead, he does this, but only as at the same time "actively" (*effectively*) disposing the will to the universal good, precisely in the concrete context of actual history. We recall that in general what disposes the will to the good for Aquinas is *love*, as the reception into the appetite of a certain aspect of the form of that to which the appetite is directed. We have argued that this form is not simply the abstract species but the *manifestation* of the actual being of the concrete reality, and we now see that this also necessarily includes implicitly both the relation to universal goodness (*bonum in communi*) and the active presence of God (*bonum universale*). We may thus say that God moves the will not simply as good but also and more comprehensively *as love*, an internally effective spontaneity perfectly coincident with attractive power. In this sense, we have, along with the Greek form, a distinctively Jewish element of power, of action, of history, but all as a fruit of divine love. Above, in the account of the operation of the will, we alluded to the classic "conundrum" of the reciprocal causality of the intellect and will, which would appear to imply an infinite regress. As we saw, Aquinas solves the problem by pointing to God, as the ultimate cause, the subsistent good that causes universal goodness, though somewhat curiously he sometimes takes this to show that *reason* is the absolute beginning.[257] Elsewhere, however, drawing on the same text from Aristotle's *Eudemian Ethics*,[258] he says that God moves the will through *instinct* (*instinctus*), which translates the Greek *hormē*.[259] Cornelio Fabro suggests that a better word here might be "impetus" (*impulsion*),[260] since it more clearly suggests an im-putation of movement from without, but we suggest that a *far* better term is *love*: love includes a kind of bodily affection, like instinct or impetus, but is not mere physical motion as they are, which would run the danger of introducing a fundamentally *irrational* note into Aquinas's understanding of the basic motion of the spiritual powers. Instead, love may reach beneath reason in one respect but also exceeds it in another, and is thoroughly rational in principle in between, insofar as it is precisely the reception into the appetite of *form*. Thus, God moves the will to the good not simply by presenting the good in reality, or deferring it as always beyond, but rather by presenting it inchoately, we might say, in the sense of a superactual disposition that suffices in itself for the choice made, even if it does not compel any particular choice. Even more basically, God grants the reality of the choosing *in* the choosing, with the actuality of the good chosen, without supplanting the will's own active power. In every one of its proper acts, the will fulfills Anselm's definition of justice: it wills what God wills that it will, just as it integrates the Plotinian/Dionysian suprarationality that is not irrational and the transcendence of nature within nature, and the Augustinian/Maximian sense that even what is most natural is also a gift from God.[261]

To see why God's being the all-comprehensive cause of the will's operation does not eliminate the will's own activity or impose on it a necessity from without, we ought to connect the point just made with our discussion of God's creative will at the beginning of this chapter. God's will is not just general but absolutely particular, and we can now say it includes not just the bringing to be of all things that are but, in one and the same will, also the causing of all the operations of all things: God is lord of nature (Greek) and of history (Jews). But as Aquinas insists at many reprises, God does not cause the operation of anything by imposing a pregiven form on something just there, as it were, adding it to that thing from the outside. Instead, he causes operation by introducing *into* things their own internal principle, by making them the origin of their own acts, which he also causes.[262] He is not just the good that draws all things to himself; he also *gives* the good to things, as love, which enables them to realize the very good that is caused in some sense also *of themselves*. The fruit of God's freedom is the novelty, the "fontality," of creatures' being free.

We are now in a position to return to the paradox sketched out earlier in this chapter, now elucidated specifically in terms of the human will. The question raised previously was whether the movement toward things (*ad-petere* as *quasi quodam motus ad rem*),[263] designated as appetite, is a giving or a receiving. The best answer is that, founded in love, it is always inseparably both, though in creatures the priority lies of course with the receiving. Though Aquinas contrasts God's love, which *causes* the good in creatures, to man's love, which principally *responds* to the good it discovers in creatures, he does not leave these as opposites but suggests that man's love *does indeed* cause the good in creatures, at least in a certain respect.[264] Thus, the human will is not *merely* a receptacle for the good placed before it but in some sense participates in God's creative will, which effects that good. To illustrate this, we ought to connect this point with some of the other themes we have elaborated: the will aims not at the good simply but at the propagation of the good, not at the actual qua already realized but in and through the actual also *to the possible*.[265] This is because the will cannot operate without realizing something that was in some respect not there before; it is ordered specifically to the *bonum ad agibile*. We explained that the possibility lies most basically in the act of being, which in some sense exceeds the order of essences. Whenever I make a decision, whenever I move my will at all, I bring something into being, something absolutely unique, which never existed before and will never exist again in quite the same way. According to Aquinas, "All created causes have one common effect which is *being* [*esse*], although each one has its particular effect whereby they are differentiated: thus heat makes a thing *to be* hot, and a builder gives *being* to a house. Accordingly, they have this in common that they cause *being*, but they differ in that fire causes fire and a builder causes a house. There must therefore be some cause higher than all others by virtue of which they all cause being and whose proper cause is *being*: and this is God."[266]

This being that I (co-)cause as a free creature was a dimension of goodness that was, prior to my decision, only possible, and now it is real.[267] We might call this a "vertical" novelty, as distinct from the "horizontal" sort of novelty that the contemporary libertarian-determinist debate invariably has in view. To be sure, for Aquinas, the novelty always at the same time concerns possibilities given *in* things by their nature, and in me by nature; in this sense, the possibility I realize is always in some fundamental sense at the same time a possibility I receive from the reality I transform. In other words, my giving of reality to a thing in choice is inseparable from my receiving it from the good I am choosing, articulated in the complex way we outlined in the previous section.

Let us look at what this means concretely. I am trying at this moment to describe the reality of freedom. I am using words, most of which are centuries old; I am using my intellect, will, hand, a notebook, a pen, all with their own natures. Even more than this, I am attempting to describe a reality, the reality of freedom, not just "making things up" about it, but to the best of my ability describing what I actually see, regardless of what I may *want* to be the case.[268] Dante describes the perfect vision (*perfetto veder*) as one in which the apprehension coincides with a being-moved to pursue.[269] Nevertheless, in spite of the preexistence of every element involved, phrases are emerging in this moment, here and now, that have never before been spoken or written, heard or read. With these phrases are particular judgments, which the formulation of words gives a certain shape, color, tone, and so forth. But here is the important thing: it is not simply the case that I first understand and then write. In a certain sense, I understand the ideas only as I write them down: the apprehended good that moves my will is apprehended *in* that movement, I know *what* I am going to say only *when* I say it.[270] This does not make speaking or writing an irrational act. It is in fact the actualization of reason. But the point is that this actualization does not simply take place in my soul and then receive a kind of mechanical reproduction externally on the paper: I come to understand something that takes shape *before me*, in every sense of that word, and its taking shape is something I am doing but at the same time of course something that I am re-cognizing, "in-venting" only in the etymological sense of "coming upon" or "entering into." While my most banal, least inspired thoughts and actions might have the character of a mechanical reproduction, the "linear" execution of a preplanned idea, my best and freest ones I dis-cover (in-ventio), simultaneously producing them and finding them as *given*. This coincidence of generation and discovery, this *gift*, in both senses, which realizes a particular good even as it receives it, is a paradigm of a free act. And it is a paradigm of freedom because it is an analogous reflection of the supremely free act of creation, whereby God *gives* being to creatures, which is to say presupposes them as recipients in his very giving.[271]

A Conclusion and a Critical Question

What we have sought to present in this chapter may be called a "speculative development" of Aquinas in the sense that it goes beyond the letter of his *ex professo* treatments of freedom and the will, or at least beyond the most immediate sense of those treatments, though it does so on the basis of texts drawn from other parts of his work. The aim here has been to interpret what Aquinas says about freedom in light of his metaphysics and understanding of God, and, moreover, to do so in a way that is guided by the themes that have been developing thus far in this book. Such an approach has given rise to a reading of Aquinas on freedom somewhat different from "standard" ones, though to be sure there has never been a single, accepted interpretation. In this concluding section, we will briefly summarize the vision of freedom we have sought to articulate over the course of this chapter in a succinct statement, since this represents what one might justly call the culminating philosophy of freedom of the classical Christian tradition, and then present the difficulties that arise from a more typical view of Aquinas.

To say that God's creative act is free is to say that it aims at and produces the "proliferating" goodness of things in the world: liberty as liberality. The free activity of creatures is a participation in God's freedom, and so a reception of the good, that is, of the generative will, that is also itself generative in its own way. Fire affirms itself in its heat, and there is no heat without things that are hot; fire communicates itself in the pursuit of its proper good and at the same time gives its good to what is other than itself. The human will—as Maximus the Confessor so clearly saw—is the perfect expression of what occurs generally in nature.[272] To the extent that it operates successfully, a free act of the human will is in every case a reception of a good but simultaneously gives rise to the good received. To describe it from the other direction, the act of will achieves a good by bringing it about, calling it forth from the *nature* of the things with which it concerns itself. There is a simultaneity of reception and generation, which means that even the *apprehension* of the good occurs most basically in the actuality of the act of freedom (this does not exclude its being ontologically prior to the will's contribution to the act, which thus always takes a principally responsive form even in its self-giving). The *novelty* of the act of freedom, then, is more basically a vertical novelty, an effecting of what was not there before, than it is a horizontal novelty (indeterminate and so unpredictable), which is why it can be *perfectly* rational and explicable in terms of the causes that are realized in the actuality itself. The dimension of *esse*, which transcends the essential order, and indeed the presence of God, who radically transcends the created order in its entirety,[273] are what allows the paradox of the reciprocity between intellect and will that characterizes genuine human freedom. A free act is a solicitation *from* the natures of what is given of the good that, as appetible, gives the reason for the act; it is simultaneously a giving and receiving, a creative realization of the good.

Outside of this more comprehensive theological and metaphysical context, the act of will tends to be interpreted in tension with the extravoluntary aspects that constitute freedom. This tension comes to expression, for example, in the classic debate between "intellectualism," in which the will is subordinated to the intellect, and "voluntarism," in which the intellect is subordinated to the will. Vernon Bourke once observed that most modern Thomists tend to have a Scotistic view of Aquinas's notion of freedom.[274] What he seems to mean is that, however much one affirms the good as the final end of human action, one tends to see the will as choosing indifferently among various options toward that end. A more faithful reading of Aquinas, for Bourke, would see that in fact the will is not indifferent but remains subordinate to the intellect in all of its choices. Our claim has been that the framing of the question as an either-or between intellect and will, rather than a recognition of their simultaneity in love, as a generative participation in being, fragments the paradoxical synthesis that is Christian freedom, whichever side of the debate one takes.

Inside of this modern interpretive fragmentation, it is clear that, whether or not Aquinas becomes a voluntarist in the end, the bent of his thought goes the other way. We might say that the Greek inheritance in this regard finally seems to set the measure for the contribution of biblical revelation.[275] There are five points in particular where Aquinas seems to embrace a one-sided intellectualism.

First, as we have noted, Aquinas tends to describe the apprehension of the good that precedes the will as an act of intellect rather than an act of love.[276] The reason Aquinas offers for giving priority to the intellect over the will is precisely that act precedes potency.[277] But we have argued that love *also* presumes the priority of act, and form, without being reducible to the order of intellect simply. The kind of actuality prioritized in love includes a greater integration of potency into actuality than does the simple order of intellect, set as it necessarily is on truth as *what (actually) is*. Though an affirmation of love at the root of freedom can be drawn from Aquinas's work, he himself roots freedom principally in intellect.[278] However it may be subsequently complexified, the act of apprehension, according to Aquinas's explicit treatment, is in itself and essentially the intellect's *own* act, operated on its own terms, even if that act is set in motion by the will. Thus, if the simple priority of intellect is qualified in the way we have seen, by showing the reciprocal "directing" influence of the will on the intellect, as Gallagher for example has argued, this is not so much a solution as an example of falling off the other side of the horse. One does not overcome dualism by affirming intellectualism in one respect and voluntarism in another.

In any event, however much the will may have primacy in particular contexts, Aquinas himself gives an absolute primacy to the intellect.[279]

Second, though command is an *exercise* of power, which would seem to locate it in the order of the will, Aquinas ascribes it instead to reason, and he does so precisely because what commands is highest.[280] The way in which he makes the argument is especially curious, since Aquinas admits at the same time that the intellect has the power to command only by virtue of the will, whose act precedes the act of intellect in this case.[281] In response to the objection that this seems to make the intellect follow the will, Aquinas affirms that even this prior act of will must itself follow an act of intellect.[282] In the end, the intellect is not commanded by anything other than itself, while the will is commanded by the intellect, and this by its own power.[283] Whatever reciprocity may exist seems finally to be resolved on one side.

Third, Aquinas notoriously characterizes the highest human act, namely, the beatific vision, as *essentially* an act of intellect.[284] To be sure, he does not exclude the will, which *delights* in the completion of the intellect's act, but it remains the case that this act is subordinate to the essential one, which is why it is identified as a speculative act, because "man's highest operation is that of his highest power in respect of its highest object," and the highest power is intellect, specifically in its speculative aspect.[285] But there remains a fundamental tension, insofar as God exceeds the soul even *in* the vision, and Aquinas associates the soul's relation to what lies beyond itself with the appetitive order.[286] We have argued elsewhere that the tension might be removed by developing love and beauty, along the lines we have sketched briefly here, but this is again not a standard interpretation of Aquinas.[287]

Fourth, Aquinas insists, for good reason, that, just as will is "contained" in the intellect, freedom has its place within *nature* without reciprocally including nature within freedom.[288] The realization of possibility always occurs within a given horizon. There is something essentially and importantly true in this, as we have already stressed repeatedly in this book (in our discussions of Dionysius and Maximus, for example); but there is also here a danger of one-sidedness. The absolute and unchangeable, which is the necessary condition for every act of will, does not have to be "pregiven" in an extrinsic sense. There can be a recognition that nature will always show itself in a unique way in every instance—that the end that precedes and makes possible every contingent choice nevertheless will always turn out to present itself in a unique, surprising way in the light of the choice, or more precisely in the *reality* chosen. Even the nature of happiness, the absolute that precedes all absolutes in the appetitive order, will always turn out to mean something both surprising and fulfilling.[289]

Fifth, that Aquinas does not foreground and develop the dimension of the novelty and so the inescapable interdependence between intellect and will, even though basic principles in his thought seem to open this up, comes to ultimate expression in his interpretation of the relations in the Trinity, which is the highest possible "instance" of the relation of freedom and nature, intellect and will, and act and potency. In his interpretation of the Trinitarian taxis, Aquinas says that the procession of the Spirit cannot precede the procession of the Son in any sense at all because will cannot operate except in relation to what is absolute, in relation to a pregiven necessity. Alternative possibilities arise *only ever* in relation to an absolute given prior to the distinction. To be sure, Aquinas does not conceive the priority of the Son in temporal terms, which would make the natural necessity simply unfree. But he nevertheless insists that there is *no sense* in God in which the Spirit precedes the Son, in such a way that one might say love is a *cause of knowledge*. Instead, it can only be a *sign* of the knowledge already there.[290] And so we are left in the end with what is perhaps the most radical question that can possibly be asked: Does not the supraeternity of God, to which we have repeatedly alluded in our book thus far, imply that such a reciprocal priority would *have* to be the case?[291] And would this not mean that, given the *permanent* and *indispensable* truth of Aquinas's insistence on the essential passivity of the will, there nevertheless has to be a sense in which the will is also active with respect to the intellect and the object it mediates, that the passivity and activity are more paradoxically bound together than is typically realized?[292] Where, we may ask, has the *communicative* aspect of operation gone, why is there no analogy between the fire that gives heat as the good of the other, "spreading abroad" its goodness as far as possible, and the operation of the human will? Why no emphasis on the fact that the will is not just intellectual appetite but as such also what we might today call a kind of generous self-gift, which not only takes something in but also effects a change without?[293] What happens to

Aquinas's assertion that "it pertains . . . to the nature of the will to communicate as far as possible to the others the good possessed" in the context of his general presentation of the will as ordered to the reception of the good?[294] While it is true that we love only what we in some sense know, it is also true that we know only what we in some sense love, and this paradox ought to find expression and illumination in the supreme paradox of the Trinitarian life of God. As we will see in the chapters that follow, if there is a potentially fruitful ambiguity and tension in Aquinas's thought, which we can bring interpretatively to the fore, this complexity tends to disappear in the discussions of freedom after him, and we begin to see lines open up in both directions, setting up the modern dialectic between determinism and libertarianism, which have become the comprehensive horizon for the understanding of freedom in the contemporary world.

PART VI

The Late Middle Ages

CHAPTER 10

Godfrey of Fontaines
The Absolute Priority of Act

Godfrey of Fontaines (ca. 1250–1306),[1] the Belgian secular master at the University of Paris, is perhaps the least generally familiar of the figures we feature in this book, and the only Christian we treat in this book not recognized as a saint, or at least a blessed.[2] But, given his participation in the trenchant debates regarding freedom and its place in the Christian vision of man, which arose during the crisis of tradition provoked at least in part by the encounter with Aristotle conveyed by Muslim thinkers, and which reached a decisive point in the final quarter of the thirteenth century,[3] Godfrey plays an indispensable role in our study. In our account of the nature of freedom, we have repeatedly insisted on what we have referred to as the classical priority of act over potency, and the related principle that potency can be reduced to act only by something in a state of actuality. What is distinctive about Godfrey is the perfection of his conviction regarding this classical principle. As the foremost scholar on Godfrey, John Wippel, has shown, the act-potency axiom is the backbone of Godfrey's thought; it is the final criterion he uses to resolve nearly every fundamental question in theology, metaphysics, and psychology.[4] It thus lies at the heart of his interpretation of freedom.

In his unreserved affirmation and defense of this principle with respect to all of the questions regarding the nature of freedom, Godfrey may be taken to represent a rather emphatic instance of the effort to appropriate the classical tradition into Christian thought.⁵ In this respect, he is typically taken as one who continues in the Thomistic line, in spite of the paucity of direct reference to Aquinas in his *ex professo* discussions of freedom;⁶ but Godfrey affirms the classical principle without the dimensions of the specifically Christian vision that would complexify it—the Trinitarian nature of God, the relation between time and eternity in the Incarnation, and even the paradoxes generated by the notion of *creatio ex nihilo*. It is not at all that he denies these mysteries; it is just that, as we will see, he does not allow them to introduce paradox into the classical principle, in the manner we witnessed, for example, in Bonaventure and Aquinas. This means that, for all of its authority in Godfrey's philosophy, the classical principle does not penetrate into the Christian notion of freedom here in as profound a manner as it might initially seem. Because of the stringency of his application of the act-potency principle, Godfrey presents what one might call a "pure position" on the question of freedom, which brings to perfection a certain line within the Western tradition. Doing so, he offers a unique opportunity to consider what the Christian notion of freedom looks like as reconceived strictly within the boundaries of the classical Greek horizon. We will see that Godfrey ends up with a more rich and textured view of freedom than scholars often give him credit for, but at the same time one that presents a fundamental problem. And it will be in relation to this problem that we can best make sense of Scotus's epoch-making position.

The distinguishing mark of Godfrey's philosophy of freedom is his apparently novel claim that, in every act of will, it is the object that moves the will, and indeed does so in the order of efficient causality: "Obiectum effective movet voluntatem."⁷ Thus, when I say that I will to do something, grammatically I appear to ascribe agency to myself, as a subject acting on an object; but the reality is more complicated. If we consider the matter at the metaphysical level, we recognize that the act of will is like an act of apprehension or perception. When I say that the eye sees a stone, it may look, grammatically, as if the eye is the agent and the stone the recipient of the action, but in fact it is the other way around. Similarly, when I say that I will something, my will is not *exerting* an activity *on* an object but is *receiving* that activity *from* the object.⁸ To be sure, it would be too simple to say that the grammar expresses the truth of the matter. The act of willing establishes a relation between the will and the object, and the relation is *real* from the perspective of the will but *not* from the perspective of the object.[9] In this relation, the object represents the *terminus* of what we might call the "intentional" act of the will,[10] and a terminus is in a certain sense passive, according to Godfrey, with respect to the relation.[11] Godfrey says that it is therefore correct to express the will's agency in the grammatical form, though this does not overturn the first and most basic point, which is that the will, even in its intentional relation to the object, remains wholly the recipient of the object's causal force. In this sense, the will is radically passive with respect to its objects—in every single case without exception.

If the will is radically passive with respect to its objects, it is nevertheless not *simply* a passive power. Godfrey accords the will an active dimension, specifically in relation to the other powers of the soul. In this, he appears to align with Aquinas, who likewise characterizes the will as the faculty that moves the powers of the soul to their own act. But there are significant differences in how the two thinkers interpret the nature and scope of this activity. For Aquinas, the will moves *all* the (nonvegetative) powers of the soul without exception in the order of exercise, and this means it moves both itself and the intellect.[12] For Godfrey, the will, strictly speaking, moves only the "subspiritual" powers, and it does so with a kind of borrowed energy: the will does not have in itself the capacity to initiate motion, but because the efficient causality, introduced into the soul through the intellect's grasp of the object, reaches its completion in the power of the will and, from there, sets the other powers in motion, we can say that this motion in a certain respect originates from the will: "Because the active source by which man . . . moves himself is completed in the will, to move is attributed to the will rather than to the intellect, although they at bottom concur to move."[13] Godfrey thus does indeed speak of the will's moving the intellect,[14] but when he explains precisely what this means, it turns out to be not *per se* but only *per accidens*: the will does not move the intellect directly but (through the efficient causality mediated by the intellect) moves the body and the sensitive powers, which then, by means of the phantasm they contribute to form, dispose the intellect to a particular motion.[15] The *per se* cause of the act of intellect, not only (as for Aquinas) with respect to specification but also (in contrast to Aquinas) with respect to exercise, is the object rather than the will.[16] Godfrey also speaks of the will's moving itself,[17] but again this turns out to be only *per accidens*: the will (indirectly, as we just saw) moves the intellect to consider the object, and its consideration is what sets the will in motion.[18] Thus, the will moves itself only through the mediation of the intellect, and so it moves the intellect, too, only through the same mediation.

The reason the will cannot move itself in a direct way (as *causa sui*), according to Godfrey, is that the will is a potency, and what is in potency can be brought to act only by something in a state of actuality. This is the metaphysical principle behind Aristotle's observation that everything that is moved is moved by something other than itself: "Omne quod movetur ab alio movetur."[19] And it is indeed a metaphysical principle for Godfrey, which means it applies not only to physical being, as Bonaventure thought, but also to spiritual being. It is strictly universal and brooks no exception at any level.[20] The will would have the capacity to move itself, thus, only if it were already actual, which is to say already in motion, and if that motion is to begin at a certain moment it has to be introduced into the will by something outside the will. What introduces the motion into the will is the intellect, and what the intellect introduces is the object, the desirability of which suffices to initiate the process.[21]

We noted at the end of chapter 8 that Bonaventure's conception of the will as pure self-moving activity and his conception of freedom as dominion threatened to exclude the causal influence of the good in general, and any individual good thing in particular, on the soul, which turns out to act on things external to itself in what tends to be an exclusive or impositional sense. This problem, which was only an implicit possibility in Bonaventure, becomes quite real in many of the Franciscans after him, as well as in the secular master Henry of Ghent, Godfrey's contemporary at the University of Paris. In order to protect freedom, Henry believes it is necessary to minimize the object's causal influence on the will, and so invents a novel kind of cause, what he calls "sine qua non" causality.[22] Recognizing that it is the intellect that receives the formality of the object, Henry claims that the intellect is required only to present the will with alternatives, without which it cannot act. The object thus does not "enter in" to the will's activity but only presents the necessary occasion for it to move itself in pure spontaneity.[23] It is specifically in response to the problematic implications he sees in Henry's formulation of the nature of the will and its operation that Godfrey articulates his own view, but the significance of his view exceeds this particular debate. Indeed, as we have observed already, it represents a pure position on the relation between intellect and will, one that allows us to see clearly the implications of a strict intellectualism. The influence of the object is not only safeguarded in Godfrey's thought; it is radicalized. We saw in Aquinas an acknowledgment that, whenever I act, it is always the case that a world of things is acting with me, and indeed within me, as a kind of symphonic unity, of which, however, the soul remains, so to speak, the conductor. The question is whether Godfrey brings the reality of things so radically into the soul as to displace the soul as principle, to eliminate its agency altogether.

Before we engage that question directly, we need to allow Godfrey's position to unfold more fully so as to avoid any oversimplification. For Godfrey, the axiom that potency can be actualized only by virtue of what is already actual implies a clear dichotomy between potency and act, which stand opposed to each other in a strict sense; *potency* means the capacity to receive something that is now absent, and *act* means possession of the same: "Moreover, act and potency are contraries, and so cannot coincide in the same thing in the same respect. For that which is in a state of receptive potency because a particular thing is absent cannot be in act, as it would be if the thing were present. And if it is in act with respect to something, and thus possesses that thing, it is not able to be in receptive potency with respect to it, as it would be if the thing were absent."[24]

Here we witness in as clear a fashion as one might wish the absolutizing of the act-potency polarity that we have claimed inevitably problematizes the nature of freedom. Act and potency are, for Godfrey, opposed to each other as much as being and nonbeing are. For him, therefore, to deny the absoluteness of the dichotomy is to contradict the most universal and fundamental principles in existence.[25] With respect to the soul, this axiom implies a radical passivity in relation to the world. First of all, the soul is passive with respect to its powers. Because the act-potency axiom, as Godfrey interprets it, requires one to deny that a substance—which is the passive receptacle, so to speak, of all that inheres within it—can be the cause of its accidents (which brings the substance to its second actuality), it follows that the soul cannot be the cause of its powers, for example, of the intellect and the will. Instead, it can only be their passive substrate.[26] Here we see that Godfrey rejects not only Bonaventure's sense of the intellect and will as "consubstantial" with the soul but also Aquinas's notion that the powers emanate from the essence of the soul as proper accidents.[27] Second, the powers are in their turn passive subjects with respect to the objects to which they relate, as we already suggested above. This is true not only for the will but also for the intellect. The intellect is actualized by receiving the object into itself, and the intellect subsequently actualizes the will, which goes on to actualize the other powers in performing the action. There is, here, a kind of transfer of energy, from the object into the soul and back again, and it is a transfer that takes place in a strictly unilateral direction. In this transfer, the will is totally subordinate to the intellect, just as the intellect is totally subordinate to the object.[28]

Godfrey's unqualified acceptance of the act-potency axiom leads him to adopt what has come to be called an "intellectualism" in as bold a form as we can find in the Middle Ages.[29] According to Godfrey, the will always and without exception chooses what the intellect determines—rightly or wrongly—to be best in a given case. We can explain this by observing that, if the will chooses something other than what the intellect presents as best, it will inevitably be *for some reason*, which is to say, it will do so in passive subordination to some other judgment about what is best. The notion that "I will just because I will," Godfrey says, "is something only children would say."[30] Godfrey's explanation of this point can be reinforced metaphysically by the recognition that for the will to choose something other than what the intellect presents as best would require that it draw the energy for this choice from some object, because it cannot generate it, so to speak, ex nihilo, and it can receive this energy from the object only through the mediation of the intellect. There is simply no way for the will to act except as actualized by the intellect, and this means that the will is bound to follow the intellect by an absolute necessity. To the retort that the will directs the intellect to the object by which the intellect actualizes the will, Godfrey affirms this point wholeheartedly but then points out that it nevertheless always does so in response to a prior intellectual judgment.[31]

Now, we must avoid the temptation to dismiss Godfrey's intellectualism as a straightforward betrayal of the Christian inheritance—or to put it in medieval language, an ultimate subordination of Augustine to Aristotle—in contrast to the voluntarists, who would be the true champions of freedom.[32] What Godfrey represents is not a betrayal of Christian freedom but a safeguarding of a basic truth harbored within this tradition. We will nevertheless need to ask whether it is the whole truth. Before we do so, it will be helpful to consider his responses to the evident objections to his position. First, there is the worry that Godfrey is affirming notions that were clearly targeted in Etienne Tempier's 1277 condemnations, which sought to protect the Christian inheritance from the threat of pagan ideas, a central focus of which was the problem of freedom. In particular, Godfrey seems to hold two propositions that Tempier rejected in the name of the Magisterium, namely, that the will necessarily follows the judgment of reason and that an error in the will necessarily coincides with an error in the intellect.[33] Regarding the latter, Godfrey argues that Tempier was wrong to condemn the proposition, because it is indisputably true and, moreover, has been recognized as such by significant theologians even after the condemnation. It thus stands as a condemnation that has been effectively rescinded.[34] Regarding the former, Godfrey claims that his interpretation of the relation between the intellect and will can be reconciled with it as long as we make a further distinction: one can act against the basic judgment that something ought not to be done if one concedes that this action coincides with the contrary judgment, which eclipses the fundamental judgment for one reason or another.[35] In other words, one can act against one's better judgment, but not because the will acts independently of judgment *simpliciter*, which according to Godfrey (and indeed according to the truth of the matter) is simply not possible, since this would require the will to actualize itself. Instead, we would have to say that, if one fails to do what one knows one ought, one is making, and so carrying out, a judgment, here and now, that goes against one's more considered position on the matter. One is *judging*, in this case, against one's *better* judgment. Along these same lines, Godfrey shows how his position, thus articulated, can be harmonized with some of the most apparently voluntaristic claims one can find in the Christian tradition, in particular those found in Saint Bernard.[36]

But how does Godfrey's notion that the will follows reason with absolute necessity not simply destroy freedom altogether? It is in response to this question that we see what is no doubt Godfrey's most significant insight. Drawing explicitly on Anselm, but in clear accord with Aquinas on this point, Godfrey affirms that freedom not only is compatible with a certain kind of necessity but in fact necessarily coincides with it. The only kind of necessity incompatible with freedom is external compulsion or coercion. But external compulsion is possible only in the order of physical being. Spiritual being cannot be externally compelled. If the will is therefore free by virtue of its spiritual nature, we would have to say that, if anything, the intellect, which determines the will in a necessary mode, is even more free than the will: nothing can externally compel it to grasp what it grasps. To explain what freedom is, Godfrey proceeds in a properly ontological manner, which befits the view that properly recognizes the priority of actuality. Rather than defining freedom in terms of potency, which would require giving an undue prominence, ultimately, not only to the multiplicity of alternatives but eventually also to the capacity to sin, Godfrey defines freedom most basically in terms of the actuality of being: "Actus liber est qui egreditur a libera potentia; et potentia liber est quae est naturae liberae," that is, a free act is an act that arises from a free power, and a free power is a power that belongs to a free nature.[37] What, then, does it mean to be free? Godfrey offers a positive definition, drawn from Aristotle (and, we might say, one that represents a perfect contrast to the Jewish sense of dominion as mastery, which we saw in Bonaventure):[38] "Liber est causa sui," or as he interprets the saying, that is free which exists for its own sake.[39] And it is precisely spiritual being that not only exists for its own sake but can properly perform an action simply for its own sake. What distinguishes free rational creatures from unfree animals—or plants and minerals, for that matter—is not principally that they can act contrary to nature or to law but precisely the opposite: a rational creature is free because it can act with understanding. It is different from these other creatures in nothing other than in the fact that its action follows judgment. From this perspective, freedom is inseparable from the necessity of truth. For Godfrey, we might say, in short, a free action is one that is as completely as possible compelled by what is true.[40] With this, we see that Godfrey takes his place within the line of all of the great figures of the classical tradition we have presented in this book (with the possible exception of Bernard on this point).[41] That he nevertheless problematically *narrows* this tradition in which he stands will become apparent in a moment.

Let us summarize Godfrey's explanation of how an act of will necessarily bound by the intellect can nevertheless produce an act that is free. In quodlibet 15, question 4, Godfrey lists the following things that bring about freedom in the act of choice: (1) the universality of the good that initially moves the will; (2) the immateriality of the spiritual powers; (3) the will's capacity to move the other powers; and (4) reason's indifference to contraries, which is to say the soul's openness to diverse possibilities in every case.[42] By gathering these factors together, Godfrey is attempting to show how his pure intellectualism avoids a facile determinism, which would destroy moral responsibility, and how he can accommodate contingency, even while he founds the act of will on a certain necessity. Essentially, by virtue of its spiritual nature, the soul is ordered to the universal good (*bonum in communi*), which is not fully realized in any single object in this life. The will is therefore not compelled, either physically or logically, by any single option among a given set. But what makes the soul free, for Godfrey, is not most basically the fact of contingency and the diversity of options but the capacity to choose the best, a capacity that includes within its meaning a diversity of options, even if it does not simply require that diversity (a capacity to choose the best would not be frustrated in principle by a single option, which is what the beatific vision ultimately represents). It is indeed precisely the intellect that opens up the diversity of options: as *intellectual*, the soul is able to grasp its end in a *perfect* manner, which implies a grasp of the various means that enable its achievement.[43] In other words, while an animal can be aware of the end it pursues, it grasps this end imperfectly. Man grasps that it is an end, and so simultaneously sees the different ways it may be attained. It is in a certain sense, therefore, up to the man himself to choose one of the means, and the judgment that determines the choice can be a good one, true to the nature of the object, or a bad one, swayed for example by man's concupiscible or irascible passions. But in each case his will necessarily follows his judgment, and this subordination to judgment is just what makes the choice free.[44]

Above, we suggested that Godfrey's position contains an essential truth and in this sense must be accommodated in any adequate interpretation of freedom. He might be said to bring completely to the fore the "golden thread" inside the classical tradition that reaches all the way back to Plato,[45] namely, the liberating necessity that the good in its truth grants by virtue of its intrinsic relation to the soul. But in bringing this thread to the fore in the particular way that he does, Godfrey in fact begins to unravel the whole, and as we will see in the book's conclusion, this unraveling will present in the modern era something of a threat of entanglement or a strangulation hazard. It is generally agreed that Godfrey in some sense follows his master, St. Thomas, but in doing so goes beyond him even without ultimately betraying him.[46] Indeed, the description of the free act in Godfrey that we just offered is one that Aquinas himself would accept in principle. In our discussion of Aquinas in the previous chapter, however, we attempted to show the relevance of a dimension in Aquinas's thought that remained implicit in his discussion of the will but helped to explain certain nuances present that kept him from representing a simple, one-sided intellectualism. We wish to argue, in conclusion, that Godfrey explicitly rejects this dimension, which entails an impoverishment in his conception of freedom, and indeed a fragmentation that calls forth further fragmentations. Godfrey is right to connect freedom most basically with actuality, but in order to absolutize actuality in the way he does he has to restrict its scope, so to speak, and this leads him to exclude certain elements that are essential to a proper conception of freedom. Reflecting on this problem in Godfrey will therefore help deepen our understanding of freedom by bringing more directly to light its full dimensions.

Let us spell this out. In spite of the clarity of his conviction regarding the mutual exclusivity of act and potency as metaphysical principles, the sheer passivity of the powers of the soul that this implies, and, further, the serial unidirectionality of their interrelation, Godfrey makes some claims regarding the psychological act that appear to render the matter more complex and interesting. On the one hand, Godfrey insists, as we have seen, that the will is absolutely incapable of moving itself, since this would require the *per se impossibile* supposition of a self-actualizing potency; and yet, on the other hand, he does concede that the will moves itself in a certain respect, namely, through the mediation of the intellect, or more fundamentally through the mediation of the object. In fact, he seeks to give this self-movement as strong a sense as he can within the horizon he has set. As he puts it emphatically in quodlibet 8, question 6, "The will is moved *per se* by the object, though it is so moved by the object that [the will] also moves itself in such a way that its movement is said to be from itself and unqualifiedly voluntary."[47] Note that to say that the will moves itself, and that this movement is properly said to arise from itself (*ab ipsa*), is to ascribe a real agency to the will. This would seem to imply that the will does indeed possess a kind of self-generating spontaneity. As it turns out, Godfrey affirms just this, and does so explicitly acknowledging that such a notion of the will is an essential part of the Christian tradition.[48] To justify this affirmation, he observes that, by willing the intellect to consider the very object that sets the will in motion, the will has been in operation from the beginning of the soul's movement and not only subsequent upon the movement of the intellect. In quodlibet 10, question 11, in fact, he makes explicit the fact that, if the will follows the intellect in one respect, it nevertheless precedes the intellect in another.[49] This reciprocal involvement *ab initio* in the production of its own movement permits us to ascribe efficient causality in a certain respect to the will in its own motion.[50] We thus have—in some tension, to be sure, with his emphatic insistence on the absolute priority of intellect—a deep recognition of the reciprocal interdependence of the soul's faculties, which leads Godfrey to affirmations that approach what we saw in Bonaventure. Neither faculty suffices unto itself to generate action, he says; any genuinely human act requires the concurrence of both the intellect and will.[51] If there is an absolute priority of the intellect in relation to the will, the act of intellect and the act of will are also in a certain sense the same *secundum rem*, which gives them, if not a real unity in a single co-act, as Bonaventure affirms, at least what appears to be a temporal simultaneity: "One and the same object, *secundum rem*, brings about a double action in the order of nature, the one [naturally] prior to the other, but at the same time and in the same subject, that is, the soul, by reason of its powers, the intellect and will."[52]

But we saw in our discussion of Aquinas that the reciprocity of the powers is a paradoxical phenomenon, or indeed a paradoxical *reality*, because the paradox implicates the nature of being itself. Godfrey's ideas about freedom allow us to bring out a further dimension of the point. As we have just seen, Godfrey recognizes the need to ascribe a certain self-causality to the will in order to be able to say that the will moves itself from itself, and so with some sort of spontaneity. But his interpretation of the act-potency axiom strictly excludes this ascription in principle. Nothing can act on itself because nothing can be in act and in potency at the same time and with respect to the same thing.[53] If it is one, it cannot be the other. The will may "*be said* to move itself," but it cannot move itself in reality; this can be only metaphor. Godfrey affirms the Christian inheritance on this point only *superficially*. If act and potency are mutually exclusive in this way, they cannot be present together "at once" but can only follow each other. This means that the reciprocity of the powers can unfold only in a strictly linear sequence, one after the other: "prius unum quam alteram."[54] Given such a sequentiality, the will does not move itself but moves the intellect, which then, in its turn, moves the will.[55] This sequentiality, of course, raises the question of an infinite regress. Bonaventure avoids the regress by (implicitly) denying that the act-potency axiom applies to spiritual being; but unless this claim is clarified and qualified, it amounts to a rejection of the axiom as a properly metaphysical principle, and this would entail a flood of problems, a few of which we raised at the end of our chapter on Bonaventure specifically with respect to the theme of freedom (and which we will elaborate in the next chapter). If the will moves itself immediately, then mediation becomes superfluous, and freedom comes to mean dominion as pure "power over." Godfrey, in perfect opposition to this, denies that the will moves itself immediately and says instead it is only by mediation, which effectively means that the will does not really move itself except *per accidens*. The sharpness of this dilemma, thus, points us directly to what has to be the truth of the matter: a proper sense of freedom requires us to affirm that the will moves itself immediately, but only through the mediation of what is other than itself, namely, the object—though, as we saw last chapter this means also by the mediation of God, the good, the intellect, the passions, and the material world. In other words, what is mediated to the will by this profoundly and comprehensively rich object is, along with everything else, the will's relation to itself, its immediacy.[56] To put the matter simply, given the choice of the apparently exclusive alternatives, either immediacy or the necessity of mediation, we have to insist, like Plato's obstinate child, on both at once.[57]

Now, we saw that, when Aquinas faces the question of infinite regress in the reciprocity between intellect and will, he simply, and without any explanation at all, points to God as a transcendent first principle.[58] While this might look like a literal *deus ex machina* solution, it is crucial to see that the essential point is affirmed therein: genuine reciprocity is possible only in relation to a principle that transcends the order of the relation.[59] What transcends the simple opposition between act and potency, in Aquinas, is not only God but also the *actus essendi*, *esse*, which is not itself an actuality in the order of essence (whether substance or accident) but gives actuality to all such acts. As we discussed last chapter, *esse* is not determinate in the way essential act is, but neither is it indeterminate in the manner of potency; it is, rather, "supradeterminate." Now, because he rejects the real distinction, and so ultimately identifies essence and existence, as Wippel has shown,[60] Godfrey effectively closes the horizon of philosophical reflection to this supradeterminate dimension of being. This has profound implications for his view of freedom. While we cannot develop the point in detail here—it will await our third volume, which will aim to think through a constructive, speculative account of the nature of freedom— it is good to register in principle what Godfrey's restriction of the meaning of act (i.e., his rejection of the supra-actuality of *esse*, which transcends the act-potency polarity)[61] implies and what it excludes. We have seen from the beginning of this book how indispensable it is for an adequate notion of freedom to recognize a principle that transcends the act-potency polarity, which mediates the two to each other and so introduces a fundamental dimension of paradox into their relation. This stood out with all necessary clarity in Plotinus and appeared in different ways throughout the classical tradition, reaching a kind of culmination in Aquinas's notion of *esse*. Godfrey confirms the importance of this point by revealing what happens to the act of freedom when there is no "superessential" horizon and the opposition between act and potency becomes absolute, so that each by definition excludes the other. Again, though we cannot work out the details of this point in a systematic way in this context, we can nevertheless mention, without elaboration, three points for future reflection:

1. The affirmation of *esse* as presenting a dimension of being that transcends, without opposing, the essential order opens up paradoxes of *time* and *order* that are necessary for a proper understanding of the interrelation of the subject and object, and, within the subject, of the powers of the soul, required for freedom.
2. The transcendent superactuality of being opens up the possibility of a kind of *presence* that is distinct from the already-realized essence of substance, a presence that would outwit, so to speak, the simple dichotomy between presence and absence that Godfrey makes absolute by virtue of his reduction of the sense of being. Thus, the soul can be present in its act, the object can be effectively present in the soul prior to its realization, and, most fundamentally, God can be fully present in human freedom without eclipsing it.
3. The transcendent dimension of being allows a more comprehensive and *dramatic sense* of order, which mediates within itself the spontaneous movements of history and the surprise of potentially contingent interrelations that those movements imply. We saw such a "largess" in both Aquinas and Bonaventure, both of whom deny the simple separation of *potentia absoluta* and *potentia ordinata* in God. Godfrey, by contrast, and unlike intellectualists in general, is happy to reify God's *potentia absoluta* over against his ordained power and to attribute to that potency a set of activities unto itself.[62] This implies a tendency toward essentialism, which would leave history, and the free acts that constitute it, wholly in the realm of a pure positivism.

The implications of Godfrey's rejection of the "superessential" dimension of being, and the resultant absolutizing of the act-potency axiom are far more dire for the meaning of freedom than one might initially anticipate. While one might be tempted to judge that Godfrey's sense of freedom is reductively Greek, or in other words that it sheds the distinctively Christian dimension, in fact in shedding the Christian it represents a reduction of the Greek inheritance too. As we have argued in this book, the *heart* of the Greek form is a reception of the object in the mode of its procession from the soul; Godfrey's impoverished sense of being (i.e., his reduction of *esse* to the essential order) undermines *both* of these aspects of the paradox. On the one hand, his notion of freedom eliminates the Bonaventurean sense of freedom as generous self-gift; not only does the will not move itself immediately in its act for Godfrey, but the powers do not proceed immediately from the essence of the soul.[63] Thus, we cannot say that the soul is really present in its powers, and a fortiori in its acts. This implies that the soul does not manifest itself in its deeds; it does not so much perform its actions as suffer them. However much one may try to argue for the person's "control over," and therefore responsibility for, his actions, the bottom line is that there is no metaphysical resource for any spontaneity with respect to the things of the world. The person simply does not *initiate* any of his operations in any meaningful way; he does not *take action*.

But, on the other hand, while this would seem to shift all of the causal weight to the side of the object, in fact and contrary to initial appearances, the object, too, ultimately gets deprived of the effective power that, for example, Aquinas gives to it.[64] Godfrey recognizes that the *object* of the act of freedom comes to realization only through that act. Prior to this act, the object is, therefore, simply not actual, which means it can only be potential. Godfrey therefore concludes that the object as end can move the will only metaphorically.[65] What *actually* moves the will, then, must be, not the object, which is merely potential, but the intellect's conception of the object.[66] We made an argument, in Aquinas, for the real presence of the object in the imagination as causally effective in the act of freedom, but such an interpretation is excluded by Godfrey's formulation of the act-potency axiom: for him, the metaphorical presence of the object in the imagination is strictly not real; what is merely potential cannot be actually present and so cannot act. The very principle that makes the object the efficient cause of the motion of the will deprives the object of just that causal energy. In the end, it is neither the subject nor the object that can account for the act; neither provides the genuine spontaneity that characterizes the action that introduces in an irreversible way some novelty, some new being, into the world.

Thus, in Godfrey, we find a radical fragmentation in the conception of freedom, which renders the object, and even more evidently the subject, fundamentally impotent. This fragmentation is due to a particular metaphysics, a reduction of the act-potency axiom to what we might call a purely immanent horizon. It is interesting to note that, in contrast to every other figure we have studied in this volume (and we may include in this judgment the study of Plato and Aristotle in the previous volume), Godfrey does not affirm the presence of God as an essential feature of human freedom. Thus, while he aimed to adapt Aristotle to Christianity, and so to take up the classical Greek tradition into the Christian vision of reality, in fact the Christian aspect of that vision gets marginalized—and it is no accident that the notion of freedom, which we have said is essentially Christianity's gift to the world, suffers dramatically. If Godfrey represents an impoverishment of the Thomistic synthesis, what is left is the development of an impoverishment of the Bonaventuran synthesis.[67] We thus turn to John Duns Scotus, who, we will see, begins with a fundamental rejection of Godfrey's intellectualism, and subsequently a radicalizing of the personal involvement in the act of will, understood now as the opposite of actuality, which then imposes itself as a fundamental reinterpretation of the nature of being simply. In the polarity between Godfrey and Scotus, we therefore discover the distant seeds that eventually grow into the dialectic of the modern conception of liberty.

CHAPTER 11

John Duns Scotus and the Radicalizing of Potency

Revising the Tradition

An essential feature of a genuinely free act is that the cause or causes that account for it not be exhaustively traceable back to the set of conditions that precede the act; instead, they must arise and present their effective force somehow in and with the act itself. We suggested how Aquinas's metaphysics of *esse* allows for just this sort of freedom in an inclusive way that permits a reciprocal dependence of the distinctive causal contributions of intellect and will (among other things).[1] But Aquinas himself leaves this possible interpretation implicit and undeveloped. Lacking this particular sense of *esse* as "superactual," Godfrey attempts to include the whole, one might say, within the absolute causality of the intellect, an approach that leads to the impoverishment we expounded at the end of the previous chapter. We will now see how, in reaction to this one-sidedness, John Duns Scotus endeavors to account for the whole in a nonreductivistically comprehensive way on the basis of the will. In so doing he brings to a kind of perfection a basic current, which sought to foreground the distinctive significance of freedom in Christian thought, a current exemplified in our study by Anselm and Bernard above all, and perhaps also Bonaventure.[2] The reason we say this current comes to perfection in Scotus is that, instead of accommodating the spontaneity of freedom within a general vision of the world, he rethinks the world itself, and everything in it, on the basis of freedom, and the world is thereby transformed from top to bottom. As we will see, Scotus affirms the point that we began this book with in our discussion of Plotinus, namely, that if freedom exists at all anywhere, it must have its foundation in a First Principle interpreted as absolute freedom itself. And yet what this affirmation means in Scotus, along with the implications it has for all other things, is virtually the opposite of what it means in Plotinus. Scotus thus serves to bring the trajectory of our book's investigation to its proper closure.

William Frank has proposed that what lies at the heart of Scotus's thought, what makes ultimate sense of the notoriously subtle and sophisticated lines of reasoning that constitute it, is an insight into the absoluteness of divine love.[3] The love of God, or better the love that God *is*, is underivable from anything else and is that from which all else is derived. This insight itself is ultimately underived, which is to say that it arrives most basically as God's self-revelation, which cannot be subordinated to anything else. In this respect, it is a specifically theological insight,[4] one that Scotus takes to be the very thing that distinguishes Christianity from all other religions or interpretations of the world. For him, the affirmation that God is love coincides with the recognition of God as a Trinity of persons.[5] But if this essentially theological insight cannot be anticipated by philosophy, it also cannot be contradicted by philosophy, and so one can expect that philosophy will reflect insights congenial with this fundamentally theological point.[6] In other words, Scotus's Christianity is not the inheritor of traditions from within which it grows to surprisingly new heights, a discontinuous novelty inside of continuity. Instead, it is essentially underived: Christianity is the starting point, and the traditions that preceded are measured and reinterpreted in relation to *it*. Where this reorientation comes most basically to expression is no doubt the place of freedom in the created order; there can be no love, for Scotus, without freedom, and so any philosophical interpretation of reality that precludes freedom in principle will be false. The Greek legacy of the centrality of nature, which confronts the church in a newly dramatic way in the thirteenth century with the "rediscovery" of Aristotle's substantial works, requires a careful scrutiny and clear judgment.[7] One of the principal tasks for any Christian thinker is thus to conceive the world in such a way as to be open, so to speak, to the exercise of freedom, most basically that of God but in a secondary way the freedom of his creatures, called to love God in return. So, what does it mean to think of the world as essentially open to freedom?

Scotus offers a "groundbreaking" answer to this question, which unfolds in many aspects. More or less following the approach we took in the chapter on Aquinas, we will present Scotus's radical philosophy of freedom in several steps. We will look first at divine freedom *ad intra*; second, at divine freedom *ad extra* and the ontological implications of such a view of freedom for the structure of created reality; third, at the meaning human freedom acquires within this structure; and, finally, at some of the basic implications of this view. We will save an overall assessment of Scotus's transformation of freedom within the trajectory of the other authors we have studied for our General Conclusion, where we will consider his philosophy of freedom in relation to the classical tradition, on the one hand, and, on the other, in relation to the basic horizon of thought and action that has come to define the modern world.

FREEDOM IN GOD

As Ludger Honnefelder has shown, the crucial question in the task of affirming freedom concerns the nature of the First Cause, or indeed the First Cause of nature.[8] Scotus believed that the tendency of the radical Aristotelians, among whom he would place not only Godfrey of Fontaines but also Aquinas,[9] to embrace an intellectualism that excluded spontaneous freedom of will was not an accident. A God interpreted wholly within the horizon of nature, as Aristotle interpreted God and could not help but do since he had no access to a higher principle, is not free, and if God is not free, nothing else in the world can be free. In a world effected by a purely natural God, whatever might appear to be free and spontaneous activity will ultimately be reducible to a necessary cause. There is a certain circularity in this way of articulating Scotus's argument (nature excludes freedom because it is posited from the start as exclusive of freedom), and we will come back to this in the General Conclusion, but it is first important to lay out the substance of the matter more fully.

According to a certain view of Aristotle, what prevents the world from being a purely deterministic system is the element of chance, but chance finally amounts to nothing more than accidents that divert what would otherwise be necessary causality. Necessity presents the norm; the check on determinism is thus negative, a privation of some sort, rather than something positive. Any disruption of the system is ultimately due to matter, which introduces the possibility of a discrepancy in the full realization of form.[10] Behind this is a conception of the First Cause as pure form without matter, which is to say the absolute and unqualified necessity of fully realized act.[11] (Let us note here how different this characterization of God is from the one we find in Plotinus, which is taken up into the classical Christian tradition.) In relation to this first necessity, which governs the entirety of what proceeds from it and so determines accordingly the whole cosmos and everything in it, even chance, and the contingent accidents that occasion it, are ultimately necessary and determined: the chance event appears to be contingent in relation to a limited perspective, but in relation to God it is as necessary as everything else. God becomes the final seal on a perfectly closed system.[12]

To escape this total determinism, we have to posit the first principle as more than simply necessary and the cause of all necessity; we have to recognize it as capable of contingency, and this means as a willing power, a potency that wills.[13] But in contrast to the more standard "voluntarists" of the time who would simply assert theological freedom over against philosophical necessity,[14] and so lock in place a fundamental dualism, a "double truth," Scotus sought to draw from the well of Aristotelianism itself to open up this new dimension.[15] Pagan thought ought not to be contradicted in a simplistic way but reoriented. To a certain extent, Bonaventure had already begun this retrieval of a neglected dimension in Aristotle by highlighting the distinction between the order of nature and the order of freedom, which Aristotle had hinted at, if he did not develop it himself.[16] Scotus takes up this point from Bonaventure and others, develops it, and draws the implications out further than anyone did before and in a certain sense perfectly contrary to expectations. In book 9 of his *Metaphysics*, Aristotle made a distinction between a natural potency and a rational potency[17] by observing that, while a natural potency can produce only one effect, a rational potency is equally capable of contraries. Fire, a natural potency, can only communicate heat, for example; but one who possesses the rational power of the medical art is able both to heal and to cause harm. Reason opens up beyond what is factually given to its contrary; a rational power always contains both x and not-x within the scope of its capacity. As is well known, Scotus identifies the rational potency most basically with the will, which, as even Aquinas recognized, is indifferently capable of contraries in its activities.[18] While one might initially assume that the intellect is the paradigmatically rational power, Scotus points out that the intellect, because of its essentially intuitive and so passive character,[19] is more like a natural potency; it cannot but receive whatever is true to the extent that it functions properly at all, just as the open eye is not free to see anything but what lies in fact before it. Indeed, Scotus goes so far as to say that in its simplicity of effect, the intellect is in fact *irrational*.[20] Because of its essential indeterminacy, it is finally the will, and not the intellect, that qualifies as the rational power.[21]

Contingency is thus essential to the will, so conceived, and if Scotus intends above all to overcome what he takes to be a pagan cosmos that is governed by necessity because it lies wholly, all the way up to and including its First Cause, within the horizon of nature, he will have to liberate the will from this horizon in the most radical way possible. To do so requires recognizing freedom already—as Plotinus too had seen a millennium earlier—in God's relation to himself, for if freedom at its highest point is subordinate to nature, even if it is the divine nature alone, nothing else in the cosmos will be free: whatever appears contingent will turn out to be only apparently so; every event in the cosmos at its depths, which means in relation to God, will be an expression of unshakeable necessity.[22] It is crucial to note, straightaway, that Scotus has no intention of eliminating necessity;[23] instead, he aims to integrate it into freedom in such a way as to do justice to the necessity that has always been properly recognized. We see this, for example, in the sixteenth *Quodlibetal Question*, in which he states: "An intrinsic condition for a power, considered absolutely or in relation to a perfect act, cannot be opposed to perfection in acting. Now liberty is an intrinsic condition of the will, either considered absolutely or as regards a perfect act. Therefore, liberty can coexist with that condition in acting that is the most perfect possible. Such is necessity."[24]

But Scotus's great novelty with respect to the tradition is that, while previous thinkers generally sought to accommodate freedom within a primacy of nature,[25] an effort Scotus believed was doomed to failure, Scotus sought to recover necessity in nature from inside a more basic horizon given by freedom. We will come back to this point below, but let us first briefly lay out his reinterpretation of God along these lines according to three dimensions: the relation of the persons to the divine nature, the meaning of God's will of himself, and the meaning of God's will with respect to what is other than God.

From at least the time of Augustine, but in a more axiomatic way in the Scholastic Middle Ages, the procession of the Son has been associated with the intellect (*processio per modum intellectualis*) and the procession of the Holy Spirit associated with the will (*processio per modum voluntatis*). Moreover, the Son's procession has been recognized as natural—"begotten, not made"—which is what allows an affirmation of the consubstantiality, the oneness of nature, between the Father and Son ("God from God"). Spiration, by contrast, has never been so clearly defined: on the one hand, it must also imply a communication of nature, for the Spirit, too, is perfectly God, and yet on the other hand it cannot be simply another begetting, which would make the Spirit no different from the Son. Because Aquinas interprets the will as intellectual appetite, he is able to think of spiration by analogy to the will in such a way as to preserve the perfectly natural character mediated by the intellect, and yet to distinguish it from the Word by virtue of the appetitive dimension, the specific character of love.[26] But this is inadequate for Scotus, insofar as it subordinates freedom to nature in a manner that risks leading to the one-sided intellectualism we see, for example, in Godfrey. Scotus avoids this danger by separating intellect and will, nature and freedom, in a radical way, which is to say at the very root, and then subsequently reconnecting them in order to affirm an inseparable unity. Thus, Scotus takes for granted an absolute difference between will, considered in the performance of its proper activity, and nature. Referring to the phrase we saw originating in Maximus, Scotus says, "The natural will is really not will at all, nor is natural volition true volition, for the term 'natural' effectively cancels or negates the sense of both 'will' and 'volition.'"[27] Regarding the Trinitarian processions, this implies that a basic distinction must be drawn, *within* the procession of the Holy Spirit, between the communication of the divine nature and the act of divine self-love that is most proper to the Spirit.[28] (The Person of the Spirit is thus curiously twofold, representing a kind of perfect cooperation between divine nature and will.)[29] Here we see that Scotus is able to retain the traditional taxis—first Father, then Son, then Spirit—and yet resist a simple reduction of the Spirit to being a function of, or repetition of, the Son. As proceeding *per modum voluntatis*, the Spirit is not determined *extra se*, that is, by what lies outside of himself (mere nature), but is absolutely self-determining and so absolutely free. At the same time, however, this does not mean that the Spirit is self-determining in opposition to nature and the particular kind of determination that implies; instead, the Spirit affirms the necessity of the divine nature. But that is just the point: he represents the active *affirmation* of the divine nature, which is to say takes it into his freedom as an expression thereof. Necessity is added in this way, or, as Scotus puts it, is "annexed" to freedom, which is not in itself necessarily determined, even if the necessity that is "annexed" to freedom is not added simply from the outside.[30] This point is crucial for everything else in Scotus's thought: what determines freedom cannot in any sense *precede* the free act in a real or actual way without compromising it and so must be interpreted as arising *with* the act itself.[31]

This opens up Scotus's interpretation of God's will with respect to himself. As we have pointed out, what distinguishes Christianity from pagan thought, according to Scotus, is divine freedom, but this is not a simple alternative to the pagan notion. Instead, Scotus presents the revealed conception of God precisely as offering an insight into God that allows an integration of the pagan conception, but now on a radically new ground that implies a transformation of that conception from top to bottom. Thus, Scotus affirms the immutability of God, as do the pagan philosophers, but insists that God freely chooses to be immutable: "By the fact that it is rooted in the divine nature or essence, the [divine] will has annexed to it a certain natural force. From the 'naturality' or natural force working with it, it acquires a certain natural necessity, and thus becomes the elicitive principle of the notional act. There is in the essential will-act as ordered to what is supremely loved a necessity of immutability stemming from free will alone."[32]

In other words, immutability is not a constraint placed on God from the outside, by, say, a logical implication of the essentially finite nature of change, but emerges from God's free act of affirming himself and becomes an expression of the perfection of God's free will: "Something may well be necessary in itself with a necessity repugnant to freedom and still be accepted freely and even contingently."[33] As Walter Hoeres made clear, this is the most distinguishing mark of Scotus's philosophy of the will: perfectly, infinitely powerful self-determination entails a new way of conceiving the coincidence of freedom and necessity.[34] He saves the coincidence first by distinguishing a kind of necessity from nature: "The division of agents into those which act naturally and those which act freely is not the same as the division of those acting necessarily and those acting contingently."[35] The opposite of necessity is therefore not freedom but contingency, which means that freedom can be opposed to nature without being opposed to necessity. Necessity can therefore arrive, so to speak, from the inner strength of freedom rather than from the form of an external object. Only an imperfect will is arbitrary and indifferent to order. A perfect will, such as God's, is infinitely firm in its choices; it is permanent and unshakable in its resolve.[36] If the divine nature is necessary, we can nevertheless affirm a perfect coincidence of the divine nature and divine freedom insofar as freedom has now been shown to achieve its perfection in necessity; the will and nature coincide in necessity, but the necessity of the will is *not* the necessity of nature *as* nature. Rather, it is nature's necessity now taken up from a different principle: "The necessity [of God's self-love in the Holy Spirit] is a consequence of liberty's infinite [perfection] and there is no necessity of nature involved."[37] Necessity perfectly coincides with divine will, and it does so as an implication of the perfection of that will's freedom.

In the second chapter of this book, which presented Plotinus, we saw that Plotinus, too, insisted that there could be no nature of God that was not freely willed. But this implied, for Plotinus, a paradoxical response to the *Euthyphro* dilemma: Does God will himself because he is good, or is he good because he wills himself? Plotinus says *yes*, though he gives priority to will in God while at the same time, and in fidelity to the "Greek" spirit, maintaining a priority of the good for everything "after" God.[38] Scotus answers *yes*, too, and also gives priority to the will, but this priority reverberates even into the created order. If the priority of will is utterly unique to God in Plotinus, for Scotus this priority is in a sense "reproduced" in the spiritual creatures God created.

The good does not move the will, even in the created order (as we will explain below), as it does for Plotinus in the Greek tradition—a tradition that appears at any rate to culminate in Godfrey's claim that the object is the efficient cause of the act of will. For Scotus, in clear contrast to this tradition, the good presents itself to the will as that according to which the will *ought* to determine *itself*. In other words, instead of being an object of appetite, which moves the appetite from within, the good now represents an obligation, a purely extrinsic measure to which the will, in its freedom, chooses to conform itself.[39] There is a coincidence, in this case, of freedom and necessity, but that necessity is no longer a natural necessity that imposes itself on the will; instead, it has become what we might call a moral necessity. God's will is unqualifiedly perfect, and because it is perfect, he cannot, as it were, help but affirm himself completely, doing perfect justice to the good that he presents to himself: "The infinite will is related to the most perfect object in the most perfect way possible. The divine will is infinite. Therefore, it is related to the supremely loveable object in the most perfect way that a will can relate to it. But this would not be the case unless the divine will loved this object necessarily and adequately, and unless it spirated a love adequate to that object."[40]

But this inevitability does not in the least compromise freedom; to the contrary, the inevitability, as what we might call the expression of an absolute readiness to do the good, represents the most perfect expression of freedom. God cannot help but be perfectly free, he cannot help but exercise his will as perfectly as possible, and thus in just the way he is supposed to. In line with the classical tradition, Scotus affirms that the will is essentially ordered to the good, but this now has a profoundly different sense: it is no indication of passivity in the will.[41]

We have described, here, the perfectly active will in moral terms as a doing of justice to the good in itself—which of course recalls Anselm's definition of freedom (a definition that Scotus wholeheartedly accepts).[42] But we could just as well describe it as an act of love, and this perhaps fits better Scotus's deepest intention. As a description of the act of love, this characterization of the will recasts the classical notion of love just as it did the notion of goodness, which we might formulate in succinct terms as a shift from desirability to rightness.[43] Similarly, in Scotus, love comes to lose its character as being a matter essentially of appetite or desire and becomes instead an essentially "selfless" affirmation of the other as other.[44] Hoeres contrasts Scotus and Aquinas on just this point: for Aquinas, he explains, the will, as appetite, is essentially a desire to possess, whereas for Scotus the will is ordered to "loving in the proper way."[45] Thus, the will is not rightly conceived as a striving but rather as a joining in unity with its object. The completion of this act includes enjoyment, to be sure, but is most fundamentally an essentially ecstatic act of friendship, a willing of the good of the other for his own sake. According to Hoeres, Scotus's integration of desire into a principally other-centered act presents a perfect contrast with Aquinas, who grounds the ecstatic act of friendship in the fulfillment of desire.[46] Whether Hoeres gets Aquinas right on this point ought certainly to be disputed,[47] but he nevertheless captures the fundamental notion in Scotus: the heart of love, and so the heart of the freedom of the will, is a perfectly spontaneous movement, which is to say a movement that is not effectively caused by what is other than the will in such a way as to impose determination on it from the outside, whereby the will seeks the good of its other for itself. Instead, the will's proper movement is an unmotivated, which is to say perfectly gratuitous, affirmation of the other qua other. To say that God is love is to understand that his necessary will of himself has just this form.

Now, with respect to God's relation to the world, the will has of course an essential role. It is not the case, as a certain generation of scholars may have believed, that Scotus was a voluntarist in his interpretation of this relation, if that means that God wills in some sense independently of reason.[48] Scotus is unequivocally clear, not only that the will never operates independently of the intellect (at least in some respect), but even that its act always follows an act of the intellect.[49] As we will elaborate below, at least at one point in his development he conceives the act of freedom generally in a manner similar to Bonaventure, as a joint act of sorts, shared by the intellect and will.[50] However that may be, with respect to God's freedom in relation to the world, Scotus faces a certain dilemma. If God's knowledge precedes God's will,[51] and knowledge is governed by natural necessity, as Scotus insists it is, this would seem to contradict the line of argument we have just laid out, undermining the possibility of divine freedom and therefore all freedom.[52] On the other hand, however, one cannot give priority to the will over the intellect without overturning not only an apparently settled tradition but also the obvious data of experience—in addition to the decidedly ungodly arbitrariness such a reversal would imply. Scotus resolves the dilemma by characterizing the content of the divine intellect, which ontologically precedes the act of the divine will, in a new way. He denies, first of all, that God's knowledge is practical: if his knowledge were ordered to realization, the will would either surrender its freedom by submitting to this prescribed order or exercise its freedom by contradicting this knowledge.[53] Neither alternative is acceptable. So, instead of affirming any sort of essential connection between God's knowledge and the real as such, *Scotus severs the connection between the intellect and actuality.*[54] In other words, in perfect contrast to Aquinas, who, as we saw, affirmed an essential bond between God's knowledge and actual being (and therefore *all* knowledge and being), for Scotus the object of God's knowledge is existentially neutral by its nature: it has no reality but becomes instead pure logical possibility, the only ontological status of which is the barest minimum of being an object of God's thought (*esse objectivum, esse intelligibile*, or *esse cognitum*).[55] Regarding the truth of things that occur contingently in time, Scotus says,

> The divine intellect merely naturally apprehending the terms of some future contingent complex is indifferent or in itself neutral because it does not conceive the truth of a complex unless the truth of it is included in the notion of its terms or it follows necessarily from the truth of *complex* knowledge. But the divine intellect offers the terms of a future contingent complex to his will as neutral concerning it. . . . And so contingents of this kind are true because their truth is caused by an act of the divine will. It is not the case that because the contingents are true, the will wills them to be true, but rather the reverse is the case.[56]

What God knows are the infinite *possibilia*, all of the things that could be, objects constrained only by the requirement that they not be self-contradictory.[57] God's act of understanding comes to *completion* in the production of these possibles, and this act is separated from the act of will that produces them in reality.[58] Because of what we might call the ontological emptiness of the intellect, it is the divine will that essentially determines what *actually* is, choosing according to itself alone from among the infinite *possibilia*: "Possibile fiendum et non fiendum uniformitas et eodem modo respicientur ab ideis ante actum voluntas."[59] We can therefore say, as Tobias Hoffman does, that, strictly speaking, God does not know what he is going to do until he does it.[60] This also implies that the *possibilia*, because they precede the will absolutely, are strictly speaking uncreated;[61] they exist, insofar as they do, by virtue of themselves, by the nature of logic, as it were.[62] This implication is not meant to offend against the classical doctrine of *creatio ex nihilo* because the *possibilia*, severed absolutely from actuality, are effectively nothing (*nihil secundum rem*).[63] Thus, Scotus is able to preserve the antecedence of the divine act of intellect with respect to the divine will, while at the same time affirming that effectively nothing precedes the will, or in other words that the will acts with an absolute spontaneity, since nothing really bears on it prior to its act in any way that would actually constrain it.

To understand why this absolute spontaneity of the divine will does not imply an arbitrary voluntarism, we need to connect the point just made with the previous discussion. First of all, we recall that, for Scotus, the will is not an essentially irrational power that receives whatever rationality it may have from its relation to the intellect. To the contrary, the will is essentially rational of itself, and independently of its relation to the intellect.[64] Scotus conceives the will in a radically new way as a power that orders things itself, establishing its own kind of intelligibility. According to Scotus, the will can order things rationally because the will is a "collative power" just as the intellect is.[65] Instead of referring to an intrinsic meaning, a real "what" that would inform the spirit by communicating itself, intelligibility comes to be identified with the replication of a form, a similitude, in the intellect as a kind of mirror to the reality, which is generated by the concurrent efficient causes of intellect and object. Knowledge is severed from the actually real, not only in God's intellect, but also in man's. The object is a partial cause, according to Scotus, and does not inform the intellect, which is the other partial cause; rather, these two partial causes are brought together, without the one informing the other, simply by their fitting proximity.[66] As he goes on in another context to clarify the nature of the similitude that now comes to be in the intellect, "I do not want to say resemblance by communication of the same form, but resemblance by imitation, like the copy in relation to the idea."⁶⁷ Emmanuel Perrier helpfully summarizes the point thus: "The production of the representation is not a communication of the intelligible form but rather this same form reproduced or represented by concurrent efficient causes, which are the agent intellect and the object."⁶⁸ Understanding, in this new conception of intellect, comes to be reduced to the formality of relations between (possible) objects, coupled with an a posteriori empiricism with respect to material content.⁶⁹ It is possible now to speak of the will as rational because rationality now has to do with formal ordering rather than with insight into actual substance, with knowledge of real being.

In addition to the will's inherent rationality (thus reconceived), the other reason that the absoluteness of the divine will does not imply arbitrariness is that, as we saw above, the will can conform to moral norms, to a standard of justice and perfection—in short, to the good—without this compromising in the least its free spontaneity. The measure of the good does not bear on the will in an ontologically effective way but presents itself to the free choice of the will, as an option that the will can adopt or not as its own standard. In this way, the absolute freedom of the divine will is not a principle of disorder but one that brings order; it operates according to its own lights, but this simply means it illuminates the world.

Being Contingent

Having sketched out how Scotus is able to affirm a perfectly free First Cause of the cosmos without undermining natural order and necessity, or, to put the same point in other terms, to show how the Christian vision of God can take up and transfigure the pagan vision of the world without destroying it, we can now consider what this notion of freedom implies for the nature of reality. As we have already indicated, one of the basic implications of Scotus's philosophy is that it elevates the significance of contingency, and we now want to show that Scotus achieves this by radicalizing it, locating contingency not in the sphere of accidents floating about otherwise perfectly necessary substances, as it might appear to be in a "natural" cosmos, but in the very heart of being itself. To grasp this, we must briefly present what has come to be called Scotus's doctrine of "synchronic contingency."[70] According to the customary interpretation of Aristotle, what *is* necessarily is to the very extent that it is: if A exists, it is necessary that A exist.[71] This affirmation of the necessity of A does not deny its contingency in principle because it refers only to what is actually the case in a given moment: if A exists in moment m, it is impossible for A not to exist in moment m, which is to say that A exists in that moment by necessity. Note that this conception therefore takes the actuality of A as the "ne plus ultra" reference point for thought: if A is given, it is thereby absolute in that respect; one has no intellectual leverage, so to speak, outside of what is given to relativize it. But for Aristotelians, this absoluteness is perfectly compatible with the claim that A did not have to exist the moment before ($m - 1$) or that A will not necessarily exist the moment after ($m + 1$). A can be necessary in one respect and yet not necessary in another respect, specifically with respect to adjacent moments. This is what we can call "diachronic" contingency. In this case, we can describe certain kinds of being (material being) and above all certain states of affairs (historical circumstances) as essentially contingent and can contrast them with kinds of being (divine being) that are essentially necessary. But such a description of contingency is inadequate for Scotus, for, to his mind, it places a certain constraint on divine freedom, which ultimately undermines the heart of the Christian claim. If it allows God freedom with respect to the future, it nevertheless subordinates God's freedom to the actuality of the real in the present (not to mention the past). But in fact even this qualified affirmation of divine freedom is threatened.[72] If we add to this consideration the fact that, in relation to God's eternity, all of time is actual, which is to say that God sees even future events as if they were present, then the affirmation of merely diachronic contingency is incompatible with divine freedom *simply*.[73] To avoid this implication, Scotus introduces a radically new interpretation of the matter.[74] In order to preserve divine freedom, contingency has to be affirmed in a more fundamental sense as synchronic: in the very moment m that A exists, it is simultaneously possible for A not to exist. Thus, contingency becomes no longer just a historical fact, and so an accidental matter, but now an ontological reality; it lies more basically in the foundation of created being.

There is nothing more decisive in the thought of Scotus, and the claim is a momentous one for the development of the notion of freedom in the history of Christian appropriation of the classical tradition. It implies a radically new vision of reality from top to bottom. For the pagan intelligence of Aristotle, the horizon of the cosmos is absolute; there is nothing higher or more fundamental than what actually is, nothing that can "trump" the givenness of nature.[75] For Scotus, by contrast, freedom is essentially outside the bounds of nature, and so the freedom of God necessarily breaks open the horizon of what is, it refers that horizon to a power that transcends it, and so it casts a new light on everything without exception that lies within the horizon—indeed, on both sides of the horizon. The "ne plus ultra" quality of the given gets eclipsed; instead of potency always being relative to a more basic actuality, now actuality is itself relativized to a more basic potency, or more precisely, an active *power*, which exceeds any actual determination, and thus a reality understood as more fundamentally possible than necessary: "We are speaking now of contingency as a mode of actual being [*modus entis in actu*]."[76] Instead of ontological freedom as the inexhaustible *givenness* of the real in its actual determination, ontological freedom comes to mean that what is could always have been, and indeed could now be, other than it is. Of course, because what now is *in fact* is the way it is, the recognition of synchronic contingency is not the positing of some other reality in the place of the given one. Instead, one might say that, in this case, while the reality in itself may not change, what is real is being referred away from itself to what is unreal, or in other words to unrealized possibility, and so the reality is supplanted or in any event transformed by that unreality. What actually exists in this new context presents itself as an instance of a set of possibilities that are in themselves indifferently related to what is, because they are themselves altogether separate from actual reality. This indifference makes them at the same time in a certain respect even independent of God, whose creative act of will also becomes in some sense a mere instance of a prior range of possibilities that "precede" him insofar as they are absolutely "a priori."[77] Even something as abstract and apparently absolute as logic undergoes a transformation: "If A, then A" no longer presents itself as an absolute truth in a natural sense but henceforward represents only a purely formal constraint; the existential implication that governs Aristotelian logic is eliminated, and the path is opened to modern modal logic;[78] the categories of form and matter, substance and accidents, *esse* and essence, are no longer most basic in ontology but are displaced by the distinction between possibility and actuality.[79] Instead of the analogy of being as the governing principle of reality and therefore also thought, we have a univocity of being that governs thought in its formality coupled with analogy in the existential order of actual reality.[80] Metaphysics is thereby transformed into transcendental philosophy: *scientia transcendens*.[81] What is remarkable about this transformation of reality is that it opens up only by virtue of the theological order.[82] Synchronic contingency is not something that can be deduced from the world as it exists; quite to the contrary, within the horizon of what is, we cannot but identify actuality with necessity, as Aristotle did. It is only by virtue of recognizing an actual "reality" of infinite possibility that we can see the world as contingent to the core. For Scotus, this allows us to see the very being of things, in their innermost reality, as an expression of divine freedom and therefore a gift of divine love.

The notion of synchronic contingency does not only transfigure the nature of reality; it also casts a new light on the nature of freedom in God himself. Specifically, it implies a new interpretation of the relationship between God's absolute and his ordained power, which Scotus presents in *Ordinatio* 1.44. As Henri Veldhuis has shown, Scotus's novel interpretation of this relationship is the result of his viewing it in the light of the notion of synchronic contingency.[83] The ordained power is God's will considered in its actual exercise, and the absolute power is God's will considered in itself *simpliciter*. As we have seen in previous chapters, according to the traditional view of the distinction, the *potentia absoluta* is considered an abstraction, a merely hypothetical dimension that comes to light through speculation.[84] Scotus, who is like Godfrey in this respect, changes the distinction, by contrast, into a distinction between two different ways of acting, two different kinds of acts, both of which are real. In other words, he "operationalizes" the *potentia absoluta* as representing a particular kind of agency, namely, an agency that is able to operate beyond the limits of what is already given or "preestablished."[85] Concretely speaking, Scotus uses this distinction to illuminate the scriptural accounts of God's commanding of acts in apparent contradiction to established moral law, such as the killing of Isaac or Hosea's marriage to the harlot,[86] but more generally we can see that the granting of effective reality to the *potentia absoluta* harmonizes with Scotus's basic vision: what is actual is never simply absolute; actuality is always relativized with respect to a more fundamental potency, expressed in the ontological reinterpretation of contingency. No actual state of affairs, even that of the exercise of the divine will itself (at least from the perspective of the created result of the act), can overshadow the infinite reality of God's freedom. To be sure, this freedom is not opposed to actuality, necessity, and the rest. We have to keep in mind Scotus's integration of this dimension. Thus, he says that, if God's freedom springs from his *potentia absoluta*, his exercise of that freedom is always *ordinata*, always an expression of his perfect wisdom, justice, and so forth.[87] What this means is that, whenever God acts, it will always be a surprise, always something that could not have been deduced from prior conditions, never a mere implication of nature, even his own, and so anticipated (in some sense even by God!). But nevertheless, post factum, once we have witnessed the act, we will see it makes sense; it is not random or arbitrary but invariably expresses a fundamental *fittingness*, the free necessity of beauty.[88]

Scotus's radicalizing of contingency has a somewhat paradoxical "flip side." While on the one hand his view of freedom might seem to threaten to make reality, the things of the world, purely passive subjects of power by reducing their ontological density, so to speak, in the manner we have described (ontologizing, one might say, the "desubstratalization" that Anselm began from a more logical or semantic perspective), on the other hand the very absolutizing of freedom projects it *into* things, so that reality itself takes on the character of pure spontaneity. This becomes evident when we consider what happens to the Aristotelian dictum that "omne movetur movetur ab alio," which implies that all potencies need to be brought into act by a prior actuality. Bonaventure affirmed this condition only of material things and posited the spiritual reality of the will as an exception, insofar as it is capable of dominion, that is, proper self-determination. Aquinas affirmed the principle universally but in a qualified sense: potencies are actualized by act, but because the ultimate created source of this energy is the superactuality of *esse*, things can be said in some respect genuinely to actualize themselves even in being brought to actuality by another. Godfrey loses this specific qualification and universalizes the axiom in a univocal way, effectively rendering all things entirely passive in the way described.

And, finally, Scotus, in reaction to Godfrey, rejects the principle now in a universal way: "Virtual act and potency to formal act are not repugnant to each other, since if they were repugnant in principle they would be repugnant everywhere,"[89] which means that if we allow the axiom to hold in principle it would have to apply even to the will, which Scotus takes for granted is not the case, presumably because of Bonaventure's exception. Though he initially wavers on this point, as Yul Kim has shown, Scotus eventually decides that all potencies whatsoever are self-actuating[90] and that, if this does not imply that all things have the infinite power of God, it is not because of the passive nature of potency but because the potencies of creatures are finite and so subject to other constraints. We see the aspects that were held in a paradoxical unity in Aquinas—things actuate themselves only in being actuated by another—get split up and divided between Godfrey and Scotus. If Godfrey insists that all things move in an exclusive way *only* by the virtue of another, for Scotus all things by nature are able to move themselves, and nothing is set in motion essentially by something other than itself.[91] We are a surprisingly short step away here from Leibniz's windowless monads. The absolute contingency of a free world is thus to be understood in both the objective and the subjective sense of the genitive.

Human Freedom

The human act of freedom acquires radicalized significance in this context, both because everything with which it deals is, so to speak, saturated with freedom[92] and because its ultimate model, the freedom of God, has itself an absolute status. The will, though second to intellect, does not emerge from within a given reality, an understanding bound to nature, but now enjoys a more basic sovereignty. The point of Scotus's rethinking cosmology and the nature of the First Cause was precisely to open a place for freedom at the center. Thus, in contrast to the Greek tradition, typified by Aquinas, which recognized the intellect as the highest human faculty, for Scotus this status belongs decisively to the will. The will is the supreme power in human being;[93] its freedom, considered with respect to itself at least, is as infinite as God's is.[94] To be sure, man is not creator of the world, nor legislator of morality; his otherwise intrinsically unbounded freedom must act within certain limits, though these are set no longer by the nature of things but ultimately by divine decree.[95] But even in this constrained exercise, the power of human freedom always exceeds every particular realization of that freedom in its act. One of the novelties in Scotus is not only the operationalizing of *potentia absoluta* in God but the extension of the distinction between absolute and ordained power to every free agent, whether created or uncreated, precisely to the extent that it is free.[96] Freedom, even in the world, represents a wealth of possibility in relation to which every actuality is a kind of restriction, a relative poverty.[97]

To explain this, Scotus articulates explicitly something we saw was more or less implicit in Aquinas and Bonaventure and in doing so changes its meaning: the unique quality that characterizes the will is "superabundant sufficiency."[98] For Aquinas, the will is intellectual appetite, which means that it ultimately is passive with respect to the good mediated by the intellect. We suggested that for Aquinas it is *esse*, the act of being, that possesses a kind of abundance of actuality, which is, as it were, communicated to the will, able to choose freely among options because of the fullness it receives from its most basic relation to the good and ultimately to God. Scotus make superabundant sufficiency a quality of the will in itself, irrespective of any relationship to the good.[99] The superabundant sufficiency is the native power to achieve of itself any of a number of possibilities. It is an active potency: this phrase here does not indicate any sort of relativity by which the will would exercise a received power in a particular way but expresses rather its absoluteness.[100] This is why the will is specifically not an appetite but a power.[101] If it were essentially an appetite, it would lack any resource to move itself beyond the limits of what attracts it, which is to say that, according to Scotus's terms, the will would be incapable of love. As we recall, for Scotus, love is precisely the transcendence of appetite, since appetite, according to Scotus, relates to the good as its own fulfillment (*bonum sibi*) rather than as a good in itself (*bonum in se*). Liberty, for Scotus, is liberality; it is generosity rather than desire: "To love something in itself [or for its own sake] is more an act of giving or sharing and it is a freer act than is desiring that object for oneself."[102] To define the will in appetitive terms is precisely to bind it to itself and restrict it absolutely to self-relation: "According to the affection for what is advantageous, however, nothing can be willed save with reference to self. And this we would possess if only an intellectual appetite with no liberty followed upon intellectual knowledge, as sense appetite follows upon sense cognition."[103] As we have been suggesting, it is, for Scotus, just this restriction that the Christian notion of God allows us to transgress. It is just this restriction from which God frees us.

Now, one of the advantages, as we have seen in earlier chapters, of the definition of the will as appetite, which goes back to the earliest Christian reflection on the matter,[104] is the connection it establishes between the soul and the givenness of reality. There is a simple intelligibility in this vision of the world in which activity is conceived as the diffusion of actuality, which the soul takes up through cognitive acts that enable it to move in response, an intelligibility summarized by the Aristotelian dictum "Omne quod movetur ab alio movetur" and its correlate "Potency can be reduced to act only by something in a state of actuality." But a problem arises here, insofar as the principle seems to exclude all novelty, all of what Hannah Arendt meant by her term *natality*, which seems to be an indispensable feature of genuine freedom. It excludes, or at least appears to exclude, any real significance to the human act of freedom, the possibility that human freedom can contribute to the meaning of things.[105] We recall that just this problem emerged in Godfrey, as we interpreted him, as a result of his insistence on what might be called a univocal priority of actuality. We will come back to this critically important point in the conclusion of our book, but we see that Scotus, anticipated in this by Bonaventure and other Franciscans, solves that dilemma by rejecting the most basic premise. A potency, he insists, can actualize itself. This is just what it means to be free.[106] But this resolution of the problem entails a new one in turn: How do we save the significance of the object, the actual good in the world, in the face of the superabundant sufficiency that belongs to the will? If the object does not *communicate* itself to the intellect but merely coproduces a likeness of itself in the intellect, does the will that operates in consequence upon the intellect have any way of making true "contact" with reality? Is the good of the real object anything more than an extrinsic and accidental occasion, a mere "sine qua non" condition, for the will to exercise itself? Does freedom thus imply an impenetrable sphere of subjectivity set over against the outside world of mere objectivity?

In contrast to the more straightforwardly "voluntarist" thinkers that preceded him, who were content to allow the intellect to represent nothing more than a necessary condition for the will's self-contained exercise, Scotus initially sought to accommodate a deeper reciprocity between the act of will and that of the intellect, even if this endeavor presented him with continual difficulties. Recent scholarship has made increasingly clear that Scotus remained undecided about how exactly to negotiate the will's relation to its other, whether to the intellect,[107] or to the will of God,[108] in connection to its own act. If there was any development in his thinking, it seems to have been in the direction of the absolutizing of the will. However that might be, the theme of *reciprocity* stands out in his various reflections on the will, as a theme he sought to preserve, even if his presuppositions worked against it. In a manner reminiscent of Bonaventure, Scotus at one point conceives the act of freedom as a joint act, shared between the intellect and will, which co-operate in their irreducibly distinct orders of operation to give rise to a third that is more than the mere sum of its parts.[109] To specify this particular kind of cooperation, he distinguishes it on the one hand from the concurrence of two powers operating within the same order—such as two men pulling a mule—the unity of which would be purely accidental. Instead, intellect and will cooperate more like the male and female in the act of generation: this union is an *essential* coordination because each contributes an indispensable part of the whole that is of a different order than the other part so that the two can be properly conjoined.[110] On the other hand, and even more decisively, Scotus uses the same image to distinguish the kind of cooperation between the mother and father in the act of generation from the co-causality between the father and the energy of the sun.[111] This latter is a participative kind of cooperation, whereby the father receives into himself the generative power of the sun and expresses it through his own activity. Such a participatory co-causality would be apt to describe Aquinas's notion of the will, which receives its actualizing power, so to speak, from the good object itself as mediated by the intellect. For Scotus, by contrast, the will does not participate in the intellect so as to receive its actuating power therefrom; rather, it operates in an autonomous fashion, acting on its own, through its own actualizing power, in a manner that coordinates with the equally autonomous activity of the intellect. Each of these represents a partial cause of the whole, which is a single act composed of two independent operations. Scotus ends up more or less using a similar schema to describe God's role in human volition (and ends up with the same dilemma).[112] From this perspective, the will's act can be interpreted ultimately entirely in relation to itself, according to its own principles, its own order of act and potency, and then subsequently related to the equally self-interpreting activity of the intellect.[113]

To spell this cooperation out more fully, we can see that the intellect operates by grasping possibilities and offering these to the will as options. These options are essentially neutral in the sense that they do not contain within themselves a compelling power to move the will of themselves. To express the will's subsequence to the intellect, which is not thereby a passivity but remains a mode of act, Scotus coins a (relatively) new term to indicate a modality that transcends the distinction between act and potency: namely, *receptivity*.[114] We recall that, in order to liberate the freedom of the divine will, Scotus was led to sever the objects of the divine intellect from any connection to reality and thus to deny practical knowledge in God. Similarly, the objects of the human intellect are not in themselves dispositive; they stand forth as something like effectively inert *possibilia* for the human will. We saw that Scotus's "representationalist" epistemology eliminates the "in-forming" presence of the object in the intellect in its theoretical aspect; practically speaking, the objects likewise lack any capacity to move. Whatever dispositional power the objects might have is due principally to the will: what begins as a vague possibility for the agent acquires a kind of clarity and strength because of the special attention we happen to give it through the act of will.[115] What determines the choice in any given case is thus not the intellect but the rational power of the will: "The intellect grasps or knows of some possible action before the will can will it, but it does not apprehend it as something definite that must be done, as if 'to apprehend' meant 'to dictate.' Indeed it is offered to the will as something neutral; after the will makes a definite decision that this is to be done, the intellect consequently grasps as true that this is to be done."[116] So, if the act of intellect by its nature precedes the act of will, it precedes it somewhat in the manner that a servant carrying a lighted lamp precedes his lord as they travel through the dark: the lord would not be able to decide which way to go without the illumination provided by the servant, just as the will would be blind without the intellect, but the servant is finally entirely at the lord's disposal, responsive to his commands.[117] Ultimately, the intellect, for Scotus, even as a positive contributor to the whole act of freedom, is at the service of the will, which is decidedly the superior power.[118]

The will can be secondary—to the intellect, to the object it apprehends, and to God—without surrendering its absoluteness in its own order only if that which precedes it is "effectively nothing" with respect to that order.[119] According to the principal current of the tradition, as represented by Aquinas, there are a host of things that precede the will's own operation;[120] let us consider three of these in particular in order to set the distinctiveness of Scotus's notion in relief: the will's nature, the end of its operation in each case, and its desire for happiness. These three principles are clearly connected to each other in an essential way. For the classical tradition, the nature of all things is given as a kind of absolute. From this perspective, the will is defined by its nature, which is ultimately to enjoy the universal goodness that is God. In each of its acts, God is effectively present both immediately and through the mediation of the particular good that stands before the will, which thus moves the will in the will's moving itself. Scotus rejects this view, and he does so, we might say, in the name of love. To quote again the passage cited above: "To love something in itself is more an act of giving or sharing and is a freer act than is desiring that object for oneself."[121] This statement, which introduces not just a tension but an outright *opposition* between desire and generosity, necessarily implies a transformation of the status of nature.[122] Scotus admits that the will has a nature that precedes its operation, and that this nature is ordered to its proper perfection, but he denies that this nature has any *effective* significance in that operation.[123] Thus, following Anselm, he recognizes a twofold inclination in the will, an "affection for advantage" and an "affection for justice," and identifies the former as the "natural will," the will in its natural existence.[124] But this nature is not *real* in the strict sense, but only an abstraction: on the one hand, Scotus says the "natural will," as affection for advantage, is only the genus of the will, whereas what *specifies* the will is the affection for justice.[125] On the other hand, the inclination toward (one's own) perfection, or in other words the natural *affectio commodi*, is not itself an "elicited act," which is to say it is a tendency only in the sense of a generic description or an empirical fact (i.e., most people on average seek gratification).[126] The will itself *actually* inclines *itself*, either by following the natural inclination now of its own free will, in which case it is enslaved, or by generously affirming the other in itself in indifference to the natural inclination, in which case the will is free. As Scotus puts it, "This affection for justice, which is the first checkrein on the affection for the beneficial, inasmuch as *we need not actually seek* that toward which the latter affection inclines us, . . . is the liberty innate to the will."[127] In other words, the will is moved, not *by* its nature, but only by itself, whether that be according to its nature or according to its freedom. These are options, which have effective power only if the will so grants.

This effective "neutralizing" of natural inclination implies a new independence of the will with respect to its end, both in each operation and in general. With respect to each act, the tradition represented by Aquinas accords to the will a certain determinative power with respect to means (*liberum arbitrium*), always on the basis of an end that is given in each case (*voluntas*). The *power* to choose any given means is a participation in the attraction of the end, which is why that power is always relative and always operative in conjunction with the intellect. But Scotus, as we have seen, rejects the idea that the will's power is participative in this sense, because for him this would "trap" the will within its own nature. Thus, Scotus affirms that the will determines not only the particular means in relation to a given end in any operation but *both* the end and the means.[128] We recall here Anselm's sense of the ultimate motivation in the will's activities, which is always in the end up to itself: it may be that a particular object imposes itself more or less inescapably because of circumstances; it remains the case that the will is "free" to affirm that object either because of the satisfaction it might bring or for the sake of the thing itself, a choice that nothing can compel, not even God.

This brings us to the question of ultimate happiness, which, according to the classical tradition represented in a paradigmatic way on this point by Augustine, necessarily governs the will in all of its operations. The meaning of happiness, too, undergoes a revolution in Scotus. Happiness, for Scotus, *does* govern the will, but now in an extrinsic rather than intrinsic sense: specifically, it represents an outer limit, so to speak. Along with the preceding tradition, Scotus affirms that the will is ordered to infinite goodness, that is, to God, and this order defines the will. When presented directly with this happiness, therefore, the will cannot reject it, which is to say it cannot exercise a positive act of "nollition" in its regard, without contradicting itself.[129] But this negative constraint does not imply the positive necessity that the will assent to God in his presence. This position may seem similar to Aquinas's later admission, namely, that the will is not compelled to affirm even God because it can withhold its assent.[130] The difference is that, for Aquinas, the only way to withhold assent absolutely speaking is to refrain from willing anything at all, because the will cannot move without at some level being moved by God, and so, however implicitly, by giving its assent to God. For Scotus, by contrast, there is no ontological presence of God in the will's operation. The "desire for God" is only a possibility, an abstract and as yet unreal option, which the will can take up or not.[131] It is able to act in indifference to this desire, which is to say to disregard happiness in any of its acts. And while this indifference to God would appear from the perspective of the classical tradition to be an expression of sin, a disorder that represents a falling away from what is given in nature, for Scotus it is an original condition, which is ironically what precisely allows the will to love God in a genuine way.

We thus come back at the end to the point from which we started: the absolute primacy of love, which is for Scotus the essential, distinguishing mark of Christianity. The primacy of love in Scotus's interpretation determines the characteristic ethos of his notion of freedom. As William Frank puts it, "A free act must always be fresh and . . . the existence and nature of the act is neither prefigured in the will nor passively received by the will from the object."[132] Scotus's sense of a continually self-actuating freedom reverberates in the dying words of Goethe's Faust: "Yes—this I hold to without devout insistence, / Wisdom's last verdict goes to say: / He only earns both freedom and existence / Who must reconquer them each day."[133] For Scotus, nature—which has a central place in the tradition—is not *really* opposed to the will but only *formally* or *logically*: the will can, and indeed ought to, take up the order of nature into its act and *make* that natural order free by directing it beyond itself. In this way, the reconciliation of freedom and nature in the human will mirrors the reconciliation we saw in the Trinity: the freedom of the Holy Spirit is not *determined* by the divine nature, but that nature is rather taken up into freedom, now giving it effective force rather than intelligible form, so that the freedom wills what it wills without any prior determination that has not already become its own self-expression. As Hoeres has explained, whatever determines the will in its activity determines it only from inside the will's own self-determining act. This is what makes it "always fresh," utterly original in every moment. It is also what gives the will the form of a personal self-gift, a generosity beyond natural inclination, which is precisely what now constitutes the *personality* of man.[134] The ultimate freedom in the eschaton, then, is not finally a *resting* in the highest object of appetite, as it is for Augustine and for the tradition that follows from him, but a constant and ever self-renewing affirmation of God in love. Just as God's immutability is not a dead fixity but a *firmitas* of will in its self-originating activity, whereby God never fails to will what he actually wills, so too heavenly freedom is an unceasing choice for God, who is eternally new.

Conclusion

Scotus's aim was to vindicate the Christian celebration of divine love as that-than-which-nothing-greater-in-heaven-or-on-earth-can-be-conceived, and this entailed a reversal of perspective: rather than attempting to make room for this distinctively Christian reality inside of a "preestablished" cosmology, anthropology, and metaphysics, which would set essentially non-Christian terms for that reality, he turned the tables, so to speak. The preestablished is no longer absolute (if A exists, it exists necessarily) but is at every moment relativized by the sole absolute, namely, freedom as *potentia absoluta* (if A exists, it is no longer absolute in its givenness but has the character of pure contingency). The intention was thus to bring freedom into the very heart of being and thereby to open a space ample enough for the personal reality of the human being. Only in this way can the world in which we live do justice to the dramatic categories of scripture.

This intention failed. Contrary to the common critique of Scotus that would seek to limit the scope of freedom out of a concern that this absolutizing of freedom would introduce a principle of irrationality into the core of reality, it has to be said, first, that Scotus's notion of freedom is meant to be thoroughly rational, even if it is not essentially subordinate to intellect, and, second, that Scotus's aim represents the acknowledgment of a truth to which the preceding tradition did not do sufficient justice.[135] The problem Scotus's philosophy of freedom poses does not lie in its aim; instead, it arises because the aim does not succeed. Rather than disclosing freedom at the heart of being, as manifesting the ultimate truth of things, Scotus places freedom beneath being, so to speak, and then reflects that freedom back in the form of a universalized potency as self-actuating power. The consequences of this displacement of freedom are epoch-making. It sets the stage for the impossible dialectic congenital to the modern conception of freedom that we explored in volume 1.[136] To affirm freedom at the heart of the world would require a sense of freedom as interior to being precisely in its actuality, which would mean that being is analogously free already in itself. Instead of seeing freedom as always already present in being, however, Scotus posits a notion of being that, on the one hand, has its own intelligibility in itself and in essential indifference to freedom but that, on the other hand, is always already relativized to the freedom that is essentially external to it. This is the root of Scotus's well-known "essentialism,"[137] as well as his attempt to account for the complexity of unity in difference by means of a purely formal distinction, which always disappears in reality.

Etienne Gilson contrasted Scotus to Aquinas along these lines. For Aquinas, he explains, every being that exists has a causal efficacy intrinsic to it by virtue of the act of being that actualizes its essence from within.[138] We might say that things thus receive a productive potency differentiated analogously by virtue of the kind of being each thing is, by virtue of the act of creation, which implies a coincidence of the creature's power and God's own. This is the legacy of the Neoplatonic tradition, passing through Plotinus, Augustine, and Dionysius on the way to Aquinas, intensifying along the course of its transmission. For Scotus, by contrast, whatever dynamism there is in the cosmos arises, not through analogical distribution, but by virtue of God's direct conferral of power on forms—and indeed on certain forms in particular but not others. The effective potency, the ontological freedom, in other words, does not belong to the essences of things as an expression of their innermost actual reality but remains a kind of unassimilable *potentia absoluta*.

This freedom is God's, unless God specifically grants it, in which case it becomes the creature's over against God's, as an autonomous power that cooperates with God's power as separable parts of a whole.[139] Instead of infusing being, freedom reveals its absoluteness by either constantly intervening into being and so affirming itself—freedom as "always fresh," always having to achieve itself as freedom at every moment—or at least retaining the right, so to speak, to do so at any moment, irrespective of what happens right now to be the case: *potentia absoluta*, precisely in opposition to *potentia ordinata*. In this case, freedom gets defined precisely in its opposition to the givenness of nature, which means that this opposition becomes constitutive of freedom's essence. To be sure, this definition of freedom does not imply a simple incompatibility between the two, as a superficial consideration might think; the two, free contingency and natural necessity, are clearly combined in Scotus's thought, as we have explained above.[140] But combination is not the same thing as integration, and Scotus clearly rejects an integration that would see freedom and nature as intrinsically related to each other in their inner acts rather than merely aggregated together in the external accomplishment.[141]

The universalized self-actuating potency represents a kind of imitation of the integration of being and freedom. In one respect, it conveys a certain energy to all things in the world, somewhat like the abundance of forms we saw in Bonaventure. But it does so precisely *not* as the "superactuality" of the act of being, which is expressed more fully by what is in act than by what is in mere potency, even as it transcends all actuality of the essential order. Instead, it appears here in the form of what we might call a "superpotency," which gives priority to potency precisely in its as yet unrealized form as *potentia absoluta*. In this respect, it betrays a certain repugnance to actuality, which becomes a kind of immanentized parody of the transcendence of (essential) actuality. Things such as nature, order, form, idea, truth, and final causality present a challenge to freedom, which can be overcome precisely to the extent that the actuality of these things is neutralized and recast within the order of potency, which renders their reality a function of the will's own supersufficiency. In other words, the potency here is no longer the real potentiality of Aristotle but ontologically impotent logical possibility, which can be realized only by something external to itself.[142]

In the long run, the shift implies a revolution, not only in our understanding, but even more radically in our understanding of understanding: if in the modern era what it means to know is to grasp, not *what is*, but how things work so that we can determine what *can* be, the roots of such a reconception go back no doubt to the relativizing of actuality to (now empty logical) possibility.

Another way we could fruitfully contrast Scotus and Aquinas concerns Scotus's observation in his *Auseinandersetzung* with Aristotle: "If—to assume the impossible—the intellect and its subordinate powers alone existed, without a will, everything would occur deterministically after the manner of nature, and there would be no potency sufficient to accomplish anything to the contrary."[143] For Scotus, the intellect, on its own, is a faculty of necessity, and it is the will that, so to speak, adds freedom to the otherwise wholly determinate order that belongs to intellect. For Aquinas, by contrast, the proposition is not just existentially impossible but strictly unintelligible. There simply cannot be an intellect without a will,[144] and this is because the intellect is ordered, not just to formal necessities, but always through these to what is real, or in other words to actual being. Thus, as Maximus emphasized even prior to Aquinas, giving voice to the classical tradition in general, to understand is in a sense already to be directed "out beyond" oneself to something real, and the appetitive power in general, and the will specifically, *is* the faculty of this movement out beyond oneself to the other.[145] This is why animals, too, already display something of the reality of freedom in their appetitive movement out into the world, which brings them into a kind of essentially unpredictable interrelation with a veritable infinity of other things. Nature is *not* "deterministic." There is, in this vision of the world, a kind of ontological density in both our understanding and our freedom because the reality of the world is itself, in its very being, a real presence, or in other words an actualization, of the divine intellect and will in their generous unity. If nature is not simply the same as freedom, it is nevertheless an analogical anticipation of freedom, which in its turn is nature in its perfection.[146]

The authentic mark of freedom, once it is defined in opposition to nature, as it is in Scotus, cannot rest in the reality of a power already *ordinata* but must ultimately coincide with the *potentia absoluta* that lies "behind" it—a *potentia* that is ab-solute with respect to reality as it already is. This of course shifts the center of freedom in agency simply, away from the actuality of what is now to the possibility of what *can* be, what may or may not be realized in the future. But the realization is no longer the point; the decisive thing is the potency itself, in *this* moment, here and now. The *potentializing* of freedom that Anselm introduced thus gets ontologically radicalized in Scotus. Being thereby undergoes a profound change in *quality*; what is most basic in things is no longer a reality that, so to speak, overflows of itself, generating an ever-actual novelty of expression, a "superactuality," but now stands as a kind of "always-other-than-what-is" potency, which is nevertheless actual *as such* (synchronic contingency as a *modus entis in actu*); this means it can have expression only in the retrospectively projected unreality of what is real, a kind of recasting of actuality as a mere instance of what could have been, what could now be, and what could always turn out in the future to be otherwise.

A complex dialectic ensues here, both with respect to being and with respect to free will. Regarding being, we have, as Boulnois has observed, the paradox of the world being in one sense a mere shadow, a reality that can only hint at the infinite possibilities that transcend it, and at the very same time being absolute just as it is.[147] Thus, the actual world is eclipsed by God's freedom, which represents a kind of constant threat to change whatever happens to be *now*. To be sure, Scotus insists on the *firmitas* of God's will, as we saw, and argues that God cannot be capricious or irrational because he always necessarily enacts his will with perfect justice and wisdom. But this is ultimately a moral assurance rather than an ontological truth or a reality, because it turns on the moral reinterpretation of goodness as fulfillment of duty rather than ontological completion or perfection; it is a matter of rightness rather than desirability, and so remains an *external* standard, even if it is always necessarily met.[148] However firm God's will might actually (*ordinata*) be, the reality of God's freedom lies in his as yet undisclosed—and so in some basic sense ever-*dark*—power. But this points to the other side of the paradox. If it is in fact a contingency lying *behind* things, juxtaposed to their reality, rather than being an inner freedom *of* things, the reality becomes absolute in itself. There cannot *really be* a *potentia absoluta* by definition. Thus, not only does the world get populated in a certain respect by so many necessities of the essential order, but even history takes on a strangely fateful character. Scotus is not the only Christian thinker, of course, to face the profoundly difficult question of God's eternal foreknowledge of things and predestination, but this problem (which we will explore in more detail in our final volume) not only stands out with a novel urgency, it also proves essentially insoluble once God's freedom and man's are set in competition with each other as self-determining powers, neither of which can be determined by what is other. In this case, the conflict is essential and one side ultimately has to win. Given the alternatives, Scotus has no choice, so to speak, but to come down on one side or the other.

As for the will, we see a similar paradox. On the one hand, the whole point of Scotus's philosophy of freedom is to champion love in the face of "pagan" eudaimonism, which is essentially bound to a naturalistic determinism. The will is not definitively circumscribed by the self-referentiality of its given nature but can transcend itself in its affection for justice and affirm the other as other. This capacity for self-transcendence, however, because it does not in any fundamental way *depend* on the other, is unable to *attain* the other in fact. Motion always ends in some sense where it begins: if the motion of the will can begin nowhere but *in* itself, it cannot but end merely in itself.[149] We saw this danger emerge in Bonaventure, with his emphasis on the "dominion" of the will as *summa potestas*, but it reaches a culminating point in Scotus: the will is absolutely *self*-determining and can allow nothing into its own act that does not become an expression *of* the act; in its much more rigorously grounded superabundant sufficiency, its capacity for all things in principle, it is strictly *in*capable of being determined by the other qua other. One of the most "notorious" expressions of the problem here is the difficulty Scotus had in doing justice to the Christian notion of transformation in grace, and eventually in glory: because the will is defined as absolute, that is, as essentially nonrelative, in its operation, what ought to have been an ontological elevation turns out only to have been a further realization of the will's own native power. Grace does not enable the will to love anything but what it was already naturally able to love in principle.[150] The difference between the will on earth and in heaven can only be a difference of degree in operation of something univocally the same, the realization of a power already there.[151] Such a conception of the will simply *cannot* be integrated into anything greater than itself, which is why Scotus was never able to resolve the questions regarding its "integration" with the intellect or its integration with God's freedom. And if the will is the "supreme power" that defines man, and so defines human existence, eventually in all its institutions and cultural expressions, this impossibility of integration poses a truly *radical* problem. "Oppositionality" gets established at the foundation of all things. Scotus sought to make central love and all its demands, but if love does indeed include among all its other features an affirmation of the other qua other, he ends by eliminating its possibility in an a priori way.

And so we end with a strange inversion. No doubt more than any other major figure in history, Scotus sought to make explicit and essential an implicit theme in the Christian appropriation of the classical tradition, namely, *liberty as liberality*. But if this theme was mostly implicit in the tradition, one reason is that it was rooted in *being*, in the inner nature of things, and so did not need to be deliberately added, so to speak. Dionysius, for example, expresses the superabundant generosity of activity in every thought, every turn of phrase—and yet he virtually never uses the language of freedom. Scotus cannot stop using the word, and insisting on generosity, and yet sets the terms in such a way that there can be no *communication of being* in the world. We have instead what we might call a novel display of personality, but one that is precisely *not* a communication of being. Scotus is of course not a modern. But in formulating a notion of freedom that opposes integration in its logic, even if it accepts cooperation with its various "others" (the intellect, nature, the good, God's will, the object, and so forth), and in formulating a notion of freedom that lies in self-referential potency rather than unified actuality, even if it subsequently *affirms* this unity as its own achievement, he advances a philosophy in which what we have described as the "diabolical character of modern liberty" lies implicit like an ever-vanishing shadow behind the things of the world, a glimmer of the *potentia absoluta* that cannot but lurk under the veil of reality as an undisclosed, un-self-giving presence—in short, a power of darkness.[152]

PART VII

General Conclusion

CHAPTER 12

The Givenness of Freedom

Freedom has an origin. We have come to take freedom for granted as an evident fact, one of the obviously given realities of the world, or else we dispute that reality, just as we might dispute other ostensibly obvious things, such as the existence of nature or the existence of God. If the question of freedom has become in the past century one of the classics of philosophical controversy—"free will" versus "determinism"—it is a sign that the ground of its evidence has become occluded, just as it has for the other questions just mentioned, namely, those of the existence of nature and of the existence of God. And indeed the ground, in the end, is the same in all three cases. At the core of the question of freedom ultimately lies the question of God, who is the source of both nature and freedom. To the extent that we allow the question of God to be eclipsed, which is to say that we block the intellect's natural and essential access to God, whether we do so as individuals or as a culture, we do not simply begin to draw bad inferences regarding the existence or nonexistence of freedom; we become incapable of raising proper questions to begin with, incapable of thinking fruitfully about freedom and inquiring into its reality in a genuinely productive way.

To say it again, freedom has an origin. There can be no freedom if there is no God at the origin of all things, no God who is at once Creator and Liberator of the world, who is free of his very being, whose nature it is to be both free and freeing. To be both free and freeing, this God must be able to give rise to a world that has its own reality in itself, its own principle of self-originating self-motion, which exists in some fundamental way *in* itself and *from* itself. This God must not, then, stand in radical competition with this creaturely reality but must be able to share its reality himself, which is to say to enter into its history and to establish that history *tout court*, giving a liberating, theological sanction to what is in its essence a wholly natural reality. And this God must be able to do so because he is *already in himself, in his own inner being,* something like a reciprocity of wills, a reciprocity of freedom joined in love—a love that both generates and results from a nonreductive relation that can be perfectly, numerically one without being any less a reciprocity between abiding others.

If such a God is in fact the real origin of freedom, then the fate of freedom will be bound up with the fate of the self-revelation of this God in the actuality of created nature and of history. In this book, we have traced some of the key figures in the reception of this self-revelation, specifically in what concerns the nature and meaning of freedom. To be sure, there is no claim here to be exhaustive, even within the limits of this particular theme. God's self-revelation has been received by an effectively infinite number of people, and it has been analogously different, not only in every individual case, but more generally at different historical periods and geographical locations. Nevertheless, the figures we have chosen to study in some depth are paradigmatic and collaborate in their polarities, which span the extremes of the spectrum of possibility in a given period, to present an illuminating picture of the arc of freedom in the West, the rise and fall of the great classical Christian tradition. Plotinus represents a culminating point of the pre-Christian classical tradition, the point at which that tradition flourishes and allows its fruit to be taken up into the Christian form. It is not an accident that this bearing of fruit coincides with the first great insight into freedom, since freedom is exactly this fruitful generativity. As we saw, for Plotinus, the perfection of freedom is essentially a superabundant perfection, which has its own goodness always both in itself and out beyond itself. A key principle arose here, which proved to be crucial for the fate of Western freedom as it has unfolded in the figures we have studied in this book: freedom requires a principle that simultaneously transcends the act-potency distinction and establishes that distinction in its properly asymmetrical order. This simultaneity is the meaning of generosity, the essence of gift, which creates things as good and as fruitful in their goodness. Plotinus, we might say, inaugurated the Western tradition of freedom by opening up an insight into this radically original generosity, even if he ultimately lacked the theoretical resources to sustain it.

In Plotinus's vision we thus find the absolute priority of perfection, everywhere throughout the universe, both physically and metaphysically, with a single exception, a single instance of an excess of perfection, which is the absolutely unique source, or origin, of all perfection, namely, the One. Here there is an ambiguity. As radically generous, the One does indeed transcend the difference between act and potency and establish that distinction, but—perhaps because the One, for Plotinus, has not *actually* revealed himself in history and so cannot help at this point but be defined, so to speak, as the negation of such an actuality—there is an inclination to invert the order at the highest principle, as the simple reverse of all that follows. In the One alone, potency of a certain paradoxical sort has a certain priority over the perfection of actuality. *Because* of the primacy of potency in God, actuality can have a priority everywhere else. The potency of the origin comes to expression in Plotinus's tendency, *in fine*, to give the spontaneity of the will priority over the receptivity entailed by relation to the good in his interpretation of the free love that *is* God, even in his affirmation of both of these aspects at once as a response to the *Euthyphro* dilemma. A tension certainly lies in this point, which will return in a more aggressive form in the late medieval discussion of the relation between God's *potentia absoluta* and *ordinata*, but the pure generosity of the One in Plotinus, and the primacy of the tradition that springs from it, in a sense defer the problem this could pose. The perfection of freedom, and so the absolute primacy of actuality, is first received by all other things outside of the One because, in the One, it is nothing but given, nothing but gift. The nonreductive subordination of freedom to goodness turns thus on the absolute primacy of gift, which allows a universal priority of actuality that does not entail any restrictive limitation.

But this primacy of generosity, precisely to the extent it is given, must be received; it demands a personal response by virtue of being offered in a free way. The actual community of tradition that communicates freedom, in other words, has to be inherited; freedom can be possessed only in a real relation to its origin, in the ontological dependence of participation in the goodness of God as absolute first cause of all things, but a real relation that has been actually appropriated. We see once again that the quality and nature of freedom will depend in some fundamental sense on what is made of the claim that thus invitingly imposes itself. The priority of perfection holds sway throughout the whole of the classical tradition, but its meaning undergoes a development, a certain complexifying self-appropriation and simultaneous deepening and expansion of relationality, by virtue of Christian revelation and the synthesis it brings with the biblical tradition of the Jews. In Augustine, this synthesis reveals itself in the more directly "interpersonal" drama that unfolds from within the essence of freedom. The will for the good reveals itself to be a will for love—or indeed will *as* love—and love reveals itself to be as much gift as it is desire; it reveals itself as covenantal bond, and one that involves an evidently existential and dialogical drama of pursuit and choice. Dionysius then brings out the unsurpassable perfection of reciprocity: eros is not only a feature of creatures in ontological dependence on God, as in Neoplatonism generally, but, mysteriously, the reality of God in himself and (only) therefore also of God in relation to creatures. This implies a kind of immanentizing of the Plotinian paradox, so that the world itself comes to reflect God's goodness as its own and for that reason reveals an unsuspected depth of *nature*. In Maximus the Confessor, who may be seen as bringing the ancient tradition to a certain culminating conclusion, the absolute priority of nature, so conceived, can be understood as not excluding the drama of choice, the actual self-determining operation of the will, which it might seem to do if nature is interpreted as limitation. Maximus achieves this by appropriating the Aristotelian sense of nature (as internal principle of motion) more directly as a "being-moved by God," and recognizing God as moving, so to speak, in the actuality of history. He thus interprets the freedom of the will specifically in the concrete relation of God in the hypostatic union of Christ, and indeed in the historical deed undertaken by Christ. It is not a coincidence that he also recognizes the paradoxical relation between act and potency that freedom entails, a paradoxical relation now explicitly manifest *within* the temporal order of history. The Greeks and Jews, nature and history, come together in a fruitful way here.

The drama of freedom may be interpreted as shifting from its Christological source to a more general anthropological principle in the early Middle Ages, but at the same time it is just here that the basic thrust of the classical tradition begins to weaken. In the place of the absolute simplicity of divine goodness, as unadulterated generosity, we have a new division within goodness in St. Anselm: goodness in itself is no longer simply identical with goodness for another, in this case, the choosing self. There is a certain division here between the natural and the personal. The potency of the individual human will acquires a new prominence and finds itself now interacting with divine freedom in some sense as two "cooperating" agents, which encounter each other inside of what is no longer the given reality of nature but now a more empty, "logical" space of potency. We see here that the paradoxical unity (which would preserve the difference and asymmetry) of act and potency collapses into a sequential parsing out of the moments. Bernard recovers, and brilliantly foregrounds, the paradox in his account of the "nuptial union" of man and God in grace, but it is now a paradox of love *rather than* a paradox of nature. It has been displaced. Potency begins to take on a reality of its own, interpreted separately from the perfection of actuality given in *both* nature and history. Neither of these thinkers, it is worth pointing out, draws very extensively or profoundly on the tradition that precedes him but instead uses the more individually sourced "tools" of logic and rhetoric in a more unmediated encounter with scripture.

It is at this moment that the classical tradition experiences what is no doubt its most fulsome resurgence. In the high medieval figures of Aquinas and Bonaventure, we have an astonishing recovery of creation, the very principle of the being of the world, as radical gift, and indeed as the gift of the Trinitarian God of love, incarnate in Jesus Christ. Here we have the richest possible resources for a philosophy of freedom. But if the resources are present, they have arguably been as yet only partially tapped. In Bonaventure we have the opening up of a thoroughly Trinitarian notion of God and of being that provides the ground for a profound sense of human freedom as an active gathering up of the *whole* person—not just the faculty of the will—in love but one that does not eliminate in principle ontological substance and the primacy of actuality that comes with it; and in Aquinas, we have what is perhaps the most complete synthesis of the elements of an integral philosophy of freedom in history, an affirmation of choice and the potency of the will, the receptive spontaneity of human freedom in pursuit of the good to be realized inside of God's more comprehensive causal act, the metaphysical key to which is a reinterpretation of the absoluteness of nature in relation to the superabundant actuality of being as the *actus essendi* that perfects all perfections. Here we discover a perfect created reflection of the transcendence of the act-potency polarity that is the mark of generosity. A fully adequate philosophy of freedom would bring these two developments together and deepen the paradoxical unity of nature and person, actuality and potency, spontaneity and receptivity, and goodness and power. But this possibility remains a task to be carried out, and it will form a principal aim of our projected third and final volume. What we see in the waning of the Middle Ages, in any event, is a tendency to settle on one side of the paradox or the other, determination by the good or self-determination, and thus a tendency to leave in place a partial vision of freedom.

The partiality of the vision stands out strongly in our final two figures. Here, instead of a paradoxical simultaneity of nature and freedom, intellect and will, act and potency, we have a fragmentation that forces an accordance of primacy in a unilateral way to one aspect or the other. Godfrey represents a repristination of the classical axiom of the primacy of act over potency, but now *after* the complexifying of this axiom in the metaphysics of gift, from Plotinus to Aquinas and Bonaventure. Now the primacy of perfection no longer has the form of generosity, and so the phenomenon of freedom tends to find expression in the all-but-automatic self-imposition of goodness, within an a priori necessity, as it were, from above. The radical championing of freedom in the name of Christian revelation, which we find in John Duns Scotus, is almost inevitable as a reaction to the one-sided "intellectualism," "naturalism," and "actualism" of Godfrey. Scotus's understandable insistence on the absolute novelty of the active will, which can never be simply derived from its antecedent conditions but must arise spontaneously, from itself, is not the introduction of a foreign idea from out of the blue. He may be seen to be recovering a theme from the tradition that disappeared from the late-medieval horizon, namely, freedom as superabundant power, an ever-renewed source of novelty. But this effective power is no longer a reflection *in* human nature of the superabundant actuality of being, which is itself a natural reflection of God's infinitely free generosity. Instead, it becomes a compensatory reaction *to* and so *against* the lack of goodness in reality, which has now become ontologically poor.[1] The real world is a mere limited and limiting possibility of what could have been and could yet still be. If the richness of gift, if superabundant actuality, is still evident at all, it is now *outside* of the world that actually is, and demands to be made evident by means of man's own productive activity.

The four figures in our study who evince to varying degrees a problematic conception of freedom turn out to be those that do not receive the whole tradition, the Jews and the Greeks, and so do not fundamentally affirm the *givenness* of being as the very source of freedom. They foreground instead some essential *aspect* of freedom, which thus intensifies but also threatens to grow out of proportion. In Anselm, we have the normativity of freedom as a distinct power ordered to goodness; in Bernard, the perfection of freedom in love (which tends to eclipse the original gift); in Godfrey, the determination of the will by the object; and in Scotus, the subject's self-determination. All of these aspects are indispensable, but they introduce problems when affirmed in a fragmentary way, outside of a reception of the whole. This confirms the basic thesis of our book. *As* partial, the theories of Anselm and Bernard remain ambiguous, since these theories may be taken up into a more integrated view and transformed accordingly. This transforming assumption is something we arguably see in Bonaventure and Aquinas. But there is less ambiguity in Godfrey and Scotus insofar as they foreground a part with a new absolutizing tendency: Godfrey absolutizes the act-potency polarity in a relentlessly one-sided way, while Scotus overturns it *completely*. They thus *return* to partiality, post-integration, and offer it as the whole itself.

We have emphasized repeatedly over the course of this study the importance of the transcendence of the act-potency polarity that establishes their asymmetrical relation for the proper interpretation of freedom. It is crucial to see the connection between this primacy and the meaning of generosity, especially if we recall the link we have sought to recover between generosity and freedom: liberty as liberality. The key to this link is *the given*, that which always already is, that which is offered prior to any deliberation, choice, or action but which is at the same time offered *for* choice. If generosity is affirmed as absolutely first, that according to which every other aspect takes its bearings, then what is actually given will have a positive significance, prior to what might come later but now exists only *in potentia*. Two questions thus present themselves as decisive in this respect for the theme of freedom, both of which concern the meaning of the given: the question of nature and the question of tradition, both in terms of human history and in terms of God's self-revelation. We will sketch out these questions here, not so much to resolve the present study, but to prepare for the volume projected to follow this one.

The chasm that separates the rise of the classical Christian notion of freedom from its fall comes to expression perhaps nowhere so clearly as in the almost-perfect inversion that the concept of nature undergoes when we compare it at the beginning and at the end of our study. In the first part of our investigation, nature has what we might call an absolute status, which is not called into question in the Christian appropriation of Greek thought, and so the biblical reconfiguration of the terms of philosophy, but only transformed and in a certain sense radicalized. Nature, which represents the highest category in the Greek mind (as we witnessed in Plato and Aristotle at the end of our first volume), if it enters into a moment of ambiguity in Plotinus in his speculative ventures into the inner life of God, finds a kind of definitive establishment in the fathers, which is recalled in an even more systematic way in Bonaventure and Aquinas. To be sure, the gift of redemption offered in Christ exceeds the original gift of being in creation, but this ought not to be taken simply as the supplanting of nature by grace. Redemption is a kind of *re-creation*, a transformative renewal of the first, and so in some sense a new, surprising, and nevermore-to-be-surpassed establishment of natural goodness. Part of the question here concerns the precise definition of nature. For Maximus, we saw, the self-motion of nature is ultimately identified with a "being-moved by God." If this is the essence of nature, grace is not its simple opposite, and there is no principle in the world that could supplant nature and remain a principle of order. To affirm the absoluteness of nature is in this case nothing more or less than to affirm the absolute primacy of God, and so the givenness of nature is inseparable from the givenness of the gift of creation and redemption. For Maximus, it is the natural will that is in perfect conformity to the holiness of God, and so the natural will that is identical with perfect freedom.

One cannot but experience a certain intellectual shock to pass from this affirmation to that in John Duns Scotus, according to whom the natural will, far from representing the perfection of freedom, turns out to be perfectly opposed to it.[2] The natural will is essentially enslaved to the extent that it subordinates itself to the naturally given. The givenness of what is natural is no longer a sign of the absolute primacy of God but the denial of God, or at least the denial of the freedom that the presence of God necessarily entails if properly understood. What accounts for the transition from nature as the paradigm of freedom to nature as the perfect opposite of freedom?

It would be too much to say that the principle of nature has always represented something of an extrabiblical intrusion into the Christian spirit and that Scotus's assertion of freedom over nature represents a triumph of the biblical vision of reality over the pagan resistance to the reality of God. This view would see the primacy of the will and its capacity for spontaneous gift of self as the preferential option for the Jews and their notion of freely instituted covenant, over the Greeks and their idealizing of the *megalopsychos*. In fact, this interpretation of freedom does justice neither to the Greeks nor to the Jews, and a fortiori it fails to grasp the Christian notion of freedom. The Jewish notion of covenant is not a pitting of election over against natural givenness, which would tend to degenerate into a merely liberal notion of contract, but the establishment of a bond, which is in some sense an extension of kinship, and so expansion of the actuality of substance, so that two wills become one in reality and truth, without ceasing to be two. And the Greek form is a reception of the other in the mode of a procession from one's innermost self. Both of these forms turn out to be complementary in the one mystery of love as gift. It may be that the discrete agency of individual wills, the spontaneous and unpredictable decisions of the person acting in history, present a certain tension with the transcendence of eternal nature, undisturbed by the incessant changes of history. In this respect, the emphasis on the will as a power to choose among alternatives, in independence of prior restraints, which we discover in the nonmarginal figures of Anselm and Bernard, would have to be properly integrated within a deepened sense of nature and of being as gift. This represents a task still to be carried out in all of its dimensions, but we have to trust that the Christian vision must make such a thing possible. For at the heart of the Christian vision is an affirmation of the absolute compatibility of person and nature, spirit and substance: the reciprocity of Persons in the Trinity, each of which is definitively and absolutely itself and not the others, coincides with the absolute simplicity of the divine being; the unoriginate fontality of the Father is not a hierarchical priority that must subsequently be coordinated with the other Persons but is relational from the very origin; the procession of the Son, which is in some sense a "natural" begetting *per intellectum*, is no less absolute in God than the "free" procession of the Spirit, *per voluntatem*; and the incarnation of God in the hypostatic union is not only a reception of the actual flesh of human nature in the physical womb of Mary but a reception of human culture and tradition in the "spiritual womb" of the Holy Family[3] — and this reception of nature and tradition occurs without any diminishment or compromise of the absolute perfection of divinity. All of this, which we have glimpsed, so to speak, as a background horizon for the figures we have studied in this book, only occasionally being made explicit, will be worked out more systematically in our third volume.

The second question is the significance of tradition, of that which is given prior to any individual operation of the will. The Christian vision opens up the most radical dimension possible in response to this question as well: Hans Urs von Balthasar has observed that tradition has its beginning already inside of the Trinity, insofar as the Son does not possess the Godhead merely "of himself" but receives it from the Father, who "hands it over" to him (*traditio*).[4] With respect to the problem of freedom, we see that it is not a matter of indifference whether the Greek inheritance, as pre-Christian, is conceived as pagan thought that presents a problematic restriction, which must be overcome by the novelty of Christian revelation, or is understood as a positively given first insight into the nature of freedom, the significance of which abides even as it is taken up and transformed or made new. We have sought to demonstrate this by beginning the present book, not with Augustine, but with Plotinus. It is not possible to make a kind of indeterminacy *basic* in the notion of freedom, as Scotus does in his critique of the philosophical tradition, and at the same time to affirm the absolute generosity of God, from whom we receive the real world as given. If undecided indeterminacy is most basic, the identity of liberality and liberty is undermined, even if the connection between the two is then insisted on in a compensatory fashion in a second moment. If, by contrast, freedom is generosity, if gift is absolutely first, actuality has to precede potency as a perfection, and this means that the givenness of nature and the givenness of tradition have to be recognized as fundamentally positive elements of freedom. The internal principality of nature is the first movement of freedom, recapitulated in all subsequent movements, and the received forms of tradition liberate. Inside the positive significance of the given, freedom retains its participatory character; it subsists in ontological dependence on reality, in and through nature, and on its original source, in and through the tradition. The God that reveals himself already in Plotinus's speculative ventures thus introduces a drama of decision in the first Christian thinkers of the tradition. If the perfection of God's gift is recognized herein, this acquires a kind of normative character for all that follows. It is not possible subsequently to affirm the abstract content of the idea disclosed in Plotinus, now outside of the actuality of the Christian tradition in which that idea was actually received and developed, along the ways we have laid out in this book. To take the content outside of the actual concrete form of the tradition is in fact to distort the content in a radical way. It ceases to be an actual ontological dependence, or participation, and becomes instead a mere extrinsic imitation. As we have seen, the superabundant potency of God presented at the beginning of this book, which was shared by all things after the One in the form of the positive priority of actuality and so the radical primacy of receptivity in everything after God, becomes by the end of the book a multiplication of superabundant potencies: there are as many originally indeterminate and purely spontaneous powers as there are individual wills, and none of them participates in a more basic perfection first given in nature and tradition. (We recall that Scotus explicitly rejects a *participatory* account of the will's causality.)

The absolute primacy of indeterminate potency, which coincides with a radicalizing of contingency, a supplanting of actuality as the principal category or quality of being, represents a fundamental and definitive break, both conceptually and *in actu*, with the classical Christian tradition and its organically given reality. The connection with the prior tradition may henceforth be subsequently affirmed, and particular elements of the tradition may be recovered and safeguarded, but they will no longer be able to mean the same thing. What was originally given can now only be cobbled together in a manner that leaves in place the priority of potency. It *has* to give priority to potency because it does not *start* from the actuality of the traditional inheritance. This is why we cannot fully address the question of freedom, even at the "purely philosophical" level, without reckoning with the question of the hermeneutics of tradition, and more concretely without engaging the metaphysical and theological inheritance of the West. We will face the question this poses for the possibilities of the recovery of freedom in volume 3. Whatever conclusions we may reach there, it is necessary to recognize in the present context that what was a paradoxical unity of apparently opposed features inside the organic continuity of tradition cannot but devolve, outside of the givenness of truth, into a dialectical process, which attempts to compensate for the actual wholeness it replaces. We thus find the establishment, at the end of the Middle Ages when the classical Christian tradition founders and begins its long dismantling, of a pattern that reappears in the early modern thinkers of freedom we studied in the previous volume, *Freedom from Reality*. In the place of a paradoxical simultaneity and reciprocal (but *always* asymmetrical) dependence of act and potency, intellect and will, reception and innovation, being and doing, perfection and fruitfulness, and limitation and excess, we have constant self-subverting imitations. The greatest figures in this modern revolution in freedom are those who are neither mere rationalists nor mere voluntarists, neither simple libertarians nor simple determinists, but who attempt to hold all of the disparate elements together: Hobbes, Locke, Leibniz, Spinoza, Rousseau, and Kant, to name just some of the most influential. But none of these reflects the dawning light of freedom as purely and radiantly, as generously and generatively, as the original thinkers of freedom in the West, the central vision of whom we have sought to present in this book.

ABBREVIATIONS

Ad Thal.	*Quaestiones ad Thalassium*, Maximus the Confessor
Amb.	*Ambigua*, Maximus the Confessor
Brev.	*Breviloquium*, Bonaventure
C	*De Concordia Praescientiae et Praedestinationis et Gratiae Dei cum Libero Arbitrio* / *The Harmony of the Foreknowledge, the Predestination, and the Grace of God with Free Choice*, Anselm
CCSG	Corpus Christianorum Series Graeca
CD	*De casu diaboli* / *On the Fall of the Devil*, Anselm
CDH	*Cur Deus homo*, Anselm
CH	*On the Celestial Hierarchy*, Dionysius the Areopagite
Conf.	*Confessions*, Augustine
De civ. Dei	*De civitate Dei* / *The City of God*, Augustine
De lib. arb.	*De libero arbitrium* / *On Free Choice of the Will*, Augustine
De pot.	*Quaestiones disputatae de potentia Dei*, Thomas Aquinas
De red. art.	*On the Reduction of the Arts to Theology*, Bonaventure
De sc. chr.	*Disputed Questions on the Knowledge of Christ*, Bonaventure

De spir. creat.	*Quaestiones disputatae de spiritualibus creaturis*, Thomas Aquinas
De Trin.	*De Trinitate / On the Trinity*, Augustine or Richard of St. Victor
De ver.	*Quaestiones disputatae de veritate*, Thomas Aquinas
De ver. rel.	*De vera religione*, Augustine
DK	*Die Fragmente der Vorsokratiker*, Hermann Alexander Diels, rev. Walther Kranz
DN	*The Divine Names*, Dionysius the Areopagite
DP	*Disputatio cum Pyrrho*, Maximus the Confessor
EH	*On the Ecclesial Hierarchy*, Dionysius the Areopagite
FEDP	Fathers of the English Dominican Province
FFR	*Freedom from Reality*, D. C. Schindler
*GL*1–7	*The Glory of the Lord*, vols. 1–7, Hans Urs von Balthasar
GLA	*De gratia et libero arbitrio / On Grace and Free Choice/Will*, Bernard of Clairvaux or Augustine
Grg.	*The Gorgias*, Plato
Hex.	*Collations on the Hexaemeron*, Bonaventure
H/R	Anselm, *Complete Philosophical and Theological Treatises*, ed. Jasper Hopkins and Herbert Richardson. Minneapolis, MN: Arthur J. Banning Press, 2000.
I or *II Sent.*	*Commentary on Book I* or *Book II of Lombard's Sentences*, Bonaventure, Thomas Aquinas, or John Duns Scotus
In divin. nom.	*Commentarium in Dionysii De Divinis nominibus / Commentary on the Divine Names*, Thomas Aquinas

In VIII Meta.	*In duodecim libros Metaphysicorum Aristotelis expositio* / *Commentary on Book 8 of Aristotle's Metaphysics*, Thomas Aquinas
Itin.	*Itinerarium mentis ad Deum* / *The Journey of the Mind to God*, Bonaventure
LA	*De libertate arbitrii* / *On the Freedom of Choice*, Anselm
Leclercq	*Sancti Bernardi Opera.* 8 vols. Edited by Jean Leclercq, Charles H. Talbot, and Henri Marie Rochais. Rome: Éditions cisterciennes, 1957–77.
Leon.	*Sancti Thomae de Aquino Opera omnia.* Leonine ed. Rome: Ex Typographia Polyglotta S.C. de Propaganda Fide, 1882–.
Metaph.	*Metaphysics*, Aristotle
NE	*Nicomachean Ethics*, Aristotle
NT	New Testament
Opus.	*Opuscula theologica et polemica*, Maximus the Confessor
OT	Old Testament
PB	*Les Philosophes Belges.* 15 vols. Louvain: Institut Supérieur de Philosophie de l'Université, 1901–37.
PG	*Patrologia Graeca.* Paris: Jacques-Paul Migne, 1857–66.
Phdr.	*The Phaedrus*, Plato
Phys.	*Physics*, Aristotle
PL	*Patrologia Latina.* Paris: Jacques-Paul Migne, 1877–.
Q	*Quaestiones disputatae*, Godfrey of Fontaines
Q. in Meta.	*Quaestiones super libros Metaphysicorum Aristotelis*, John Duns Scotus

QQ	*Quaestiones Quodlibetales*, John Duns Scotus
Quar.	Bonaventure, *Opera omnia*. 9 vols. Ed. Fathers of the Collegii S. Bonaventura. Florence: Quaracchi, 1882–1902.
Rep.	*The Republic*, Plato
SCG	*Summa contra Gentiles*, Thomas Aquinas
Schmitt	Anselm, *Opera omnia*. Ed. Franciscus Salesius Schmitt. Stuttgart-Bad Cannstatt: Friedrich Frommann, 1968.
SL	*De spiritu et littera / On the Spirit and the Letter*, Augustine
ST	*Summa theologiae*, Thomas Aquinas
Symp.	*The Symposium*, Plato
*TD*1–5	*Theo-Drama*, vols. 1–5, Hans Urs von Balthasar. San Francisco: Ignatius Press, 1988–98.
Tim.	*The Timaeus*, Plato
*TL*1–3	*Theo-Logic*, vols. 1–3, Hans Urs von Balthasar. San Francisco: Ignatius Press, 2001–5.
Trin.	*Disputed Questions on the Mystery of the Trinity*, Bonaventure
TWOT	*The Theological Wordbook of the Old Testament*, ed. R. Laird Harris, Gleason L. Archer, and Bruce K. Waltke. Chicago: Moody, 1980.
V	*De veritate*, Anselm
WA	*D. Martin Luthers Werke.* 127 vols. Weimarer Ausgabe. Weimar: Böhlau, then Hermann Böhlaus Nachfolger, 1883–2009.

NOTES

CHAPTER 1. Christian Freedom and Its Traditions

1. "Wherever responsibilities are sought, it is usually the instinct of wanting to judge and punish which is at work. Becoming has been deprived of its innocence when any being-such-and-such is traced back to will, to purposes, to acts of responsibility: the doctrine of the will has been invented essentially for the purpose of punishment, that is, because one wanted to impute guilt." *Twilight of the Idols*, in *The Portable Nietzsche*, ed. Walter Kaufmann (New York: Viking Penguin, 1982), 499. Nietzsche's most immediate target was no doubt Kant, who derived the existence of freedom (for which he said there was otherwise no empirical evidence) from the necessity of moral judgment and the warrant for punishment; see Kant's "Critical Elucidation of the Analytic of Pure Practical Reason," at the end of the first book of the *Critique of Practical Reason*, in *Schriften zur Ethik und Religionsphilosophie*, vol. 4 of *Kants Werke in sechs Bände* (Wiesbaden: Insel, 1956), 212–34. But Nietzsche's claim has a broader scope: the claim is ultimately to be interpreted in relation to the argument in the *Genealogy of Morals* about the "slave morality," founded on *ressentiment*, for which Nietzsche takes Christianity to bear a particular responsibility. For Nietzsche, the culminating expression of the desire to punish comes in the apparently Christian picture of the happiness of the blessed in heaven being *enhanced* by their vision of the suffering of those damned—the glory of punishment—evidence for which he draws from Aquinas, and at much greater length from Tertullian; see sections 14 and 15 of part 1 of *Genealogy of Morals* (New York: Vintage, 1989), 46–52.

2. For example, John Rist observes that the later Christian tradition developed a notion of "free will" because these thinkers were "impelled as all Christians had to be to explain responsibility for sin"; *Augustine Deformed: Love, Sin and Freedom in the Western Moral Tradition* (Cambridge: Cambridge University Press, 2014), 26. For his part, Rist argues that the notion of a *faculty*

of will is not (yet) to be found in Augustine. We will return to this point in our discussion of Augustine in a later chapter.

3. One need only consider the central importance given to free will by Origen, who is no doubt the first figure in the early church to attempt a "speculative/systematic" account of Christian doctrine; see his *On First Principles*, chap. 1 of book 3, ed. G. W. Butterworth (New York: Harper, 1966), 157–210. Origen raises the question of free will in an effort to show forth the "righteous judgment of God, a doctrine which, if believed to be true, summons its hearers to live a good life and by every means to avoid sin—for it assumes that they acknowledge that deeds worthy of praise or of blame lie within our own power" (157). And, of course, the first Latin father to present a "systematic" interpretation of revelation, Augustine, was likewise fundamentally concerned with the notion of freedom as an explanation for evil, as we see in his *De libero arbitrio*, and he wrestles specifically with the Fall and the question of predestination in *The City of God*.

4. In contrast to the classical Christian tradition, the modern era is constantly haunted by the question of predestination in the form of God fixing one's destination, heaven or hell, beforehand without one having any say in the matter (so-called double predestination), even to the point of God more or less controlling all one's actions. Although the question of freedom and divine foreknowledge occurred in the classical tradition, heir as it was in part to the work of the Stoics (consider Augustine, Boethius, and Eriugena, for example), that question tended not to be addressed as the principal matter concerning the meaning of freedom (this is less clear, perhaps, in Eriugena, though, as we will see in our discussion of Anselm below, there was a certain impoverishment of the tradition in the early Middle Ages). The question moves distinctly to the center in the modern era. At the dawning of that era, we have, on the Catholic side, beyond the nominalism of the late medieval era, the massive *de auxiliis* debates, which began privately at the end of the sixteenth century and culminated in the eighty-five sessions of the *congregatio de auxiliis* in Rome from 1602 to 1607 (which nevertheless failed to resolve the question); and on the Protestant side, we have much more unambiguously the theses of Luther (his *De servo arbitrio* is implicitly a retort to Augustine's *De libero arbitrio*, while explicitly a retort to Erasmus; *The Bondage of the Will: A New Translation of De Servo Arbitrio (1525), Martin Luther's Reply to Erasmus of Rotterdam* [Old Tappan, NJ: Fleming H. Revell, 1957]) and John Calvin (who in the second edition of his *Institutes* may have attempted to integrate something like human choice but was nevertheless resolutely one-sided in his affirmation of predestination). We will propose reasons for this new anxiety about freedom and divine control in our subsequent volume. It is worth mentioning here that the image of God as a

monolithic power is a regular danger in Islamic and Jewish metaphysical theology; see David Burrell, *Freedom and Creation in Three Traditions* (Notre Dame, IN: University of Notre Dame Press, 1993), 86, cf. 197–98n24.

5. In more classical terms, this is the problem of *akrasia*, "weakness of will," designating the tendency to choose something *other* than what one really wants or knows is good for one. This approach to the question boils down to specifying the relation between intellect and will in choice.

6. We intend to reflect on this particular question at some length in volume 3.

7. This is the approach, for example, of H. J. Muller, who in his *Freedom in the Ancient World* (New York: Harper and Row, 1961) begins with what he takes to be the simplest or most obvious view of the will and its freedom and then investigates the appearance of this assumed view in the ancient world. Richard Sorabji has argued that one's judgments regarding ancient philosophy change significantly depending on the concept of will one takes for granted; see "The Concept of Will from Plato to Maximus the Confessor," in *The Will and Human Action: From Antiquity to the Present Day*, ed. Thomas Pink and M. W. F. Stone (New York: Routledge, 2004), 6–28. This argument is helpful, but it remains necessary in the end to offer reasons why one view of the will is more adequate than another. We aspire to filling this need in the present book, or more specifically in the projected trilogy, of which the present book constitutes the second volume. For his part, Sorabji clearly believes that, whatever else one might say about it, will is essentially a form of power, which is more truly will the more it exercises itself in independence of other factors. We have criticized that conception of will at length in volume 1 and will develop that critique in the current volume.

8. At the heart of the priority of (abstract and so universal) *method* over (concrete) object is the assumption of potency as prior to actuality, which we have argued lies at the root of the modern conception of freedom; see chap. 5 of *FFR*, 193–275, especially the discussion of *power*, 264–69.

9. To call the fruits "self-evident" is not to deny that reasons might be necessary to open one's eyes, so to speak, to be able to see what shows itself. As for the alternative, it bears remarking that even the strictly "methodological" approach cannot avoid justifying itself by appeal to some claim it takes to be self-evidently true or good. The only difference in this case is that such "self"-evidence lies *outside* of the application of the method it insists on and so stands in tension with it, if not outright contradiction.

10. Along such lines, Rémi Brague famously proposes "secondarity" as the character that defines (Christian) Europe, meaning by the term the fact that what is best in one is received from the other; Brague, *Eccentric Culture: A Theory of*

Western Civilization (South Bend, IN: St. Augustine's Press, 2002). Europe, he says, is *Roman* in the literal sense (because the Romans recognized their cultural treasures as inherited from the Greeks) but also eventually in the *Catholic* sense: the defining character of Christianity is reception of what has been "handed over" (*traditio*). At the root is the Son, who receives everything from the Father, and the Spirit, who is bond and fruit. It is the Spirit that makes all things new.

11. *Hex.* 13.2 (Quar. 5:388a), trans. Jay M. Hammond, *Collations on the Hexaemeron* (St. Bonaventure, NY: Franciscan Institute Publications, 2018), 236.

12. There is in fact a profound connection between authority and irony, which is impossible to see in the modern sense of these terms but which is evident in the ancient understanding: "authority," from the Latin, *auctoritas* and *augere*, indicates a fidelity to an order one receives and to which one bears witness, communicating that order to what lies "below" one in the sense that allows the order to grow and be fruitful. For a profound sense of the Roman understanding of authority along these lines, see Hannah Arendt, "What Is Authority?," in *Between Past and Future* (New York: Penguin, 2006), 91–141. (Cf. my forthcoming essay, "Catholic Politics and the Analogy of Authority," in *Communio*.) Authority thus expresses a principle that one *receives* and so does not *control*. Similarly, irony occurs when the principle of meaning of what a person says lies not in the person himself, and so under his control, but at a level that transcends him. In *this* sense, authority will always have something "ironic" about it. For a profound exposition of the meaning of irony along these lines, see Fr. Paolo Prosperi's unpublished manuscript on John the Evangelist.

13. Obviously, Greece and Rome are not the whole (ancient) world in a literal sense: indeed, contrary to their own self-understanding, they represented only the tiniest fraction of the world. But they may be taken to represent the whole world *symbolically*: the relation between the Jews and the Gentiles is the model that establishes the principle for the engagement with the entire world. See note 136 below.

14. This is a theme we have expanded on in *The Politics of the Real: The Church between Liberalism and Integralism* (Steubenville, OH: New Polity Press, 2021).

15. See, for example, Rom 1:16. Paul says there that the Gospel is "the power of God for salvation to everyone [παντὶ] who believes, first to the Jew, then to the Greek." By "the Greek" he clearly means all Gentiles—the Romans, after all, considered themselves the heirs of the Greeks. Thus, to include Jews and Greeks, that is, "non-Jews," is logically to include *everyone* (*panti*). The specifically Roman dimension is the political and institutional, which is evidently an essential part of freedom but lies outside the scope of the present

book. We touched on the political dimension in our discussion of Locke in *FFR* and intend to return to that dimension in more detail in volume 3. It is also a focus of *Politics of the Real*.

16. In this book, we will be using the referent "Jews" in the broadest and most undifferentiated sense to mean the people of what Christians call the Old Testament (and obviously not contemporary Jews)—in other words, the term stands for what some refer to as the "biblical Jews." We will not be making a distinction, here, within the accounts of the evolving history presented in scripture between Hebrews, Israelites, Jews, and so forth. The term is meant to be imprecise and therefore inclusive.

17. See Albrecht Dihle, *The Theory of Will in Classical Antiquity* (Berkeley: University of California Press, 1982), 18.

18. See M. C. Monteiro Pacheco, "Les transformations du concept de *natura* aux XIIe siècle," in *L'élaboration du vocabulaire philosophique au Moyen Age*, ed. J. Harnesse and C. Steel (Tournhout, Belgium: Brepols, 2000), 282. There is no need to exaggerate the differences here, which we will in any event qualify significantly below. Monteiro Pacheco, for her part, observes that nevertheless many words in scripture intend something like "nature," e.g., "earth," "works," and so on. For a similar observation, see Rémi Brague, "The Biblical Roots of the Western Idea of Liberty," in *Christianity and Freedom*, ed. Timothy Shah and Allen Hertzke (Cambridge: Cambridge University Press, 2016), 392 and 298. Moreover, we showed in volume 1 that the things we associate with the will's freedom generally were not absent in classical Greek thought, even if the formal notion of will was not developed explicitly.

19. Tertullian, *Prescription against Heretics*, chap. 7, in *Early Latin Theology*, ed. S. L. Greenslade (Louisville, KY: Westminster Press, 1956).

20. Emphasis added. Quoted in Rémi Brague, "Athens, Jerusalem, Mecca: Leo Strauss's Muslim Understanding of Greek Philosophy," *Poetics Today* 19.2 (1998): 236.

21. Ibid., 253.

22. See Abraham Joshua Heschel, *The Sabbath* (New York: Farrar, Strauss, and Giroux, 2005), 75: "There is much that philosophy could learn from the Bible. To the philosopher the idea of the good is the most exalted idea. But to the Bible the idea of the good is penultimate; it cannot exist without the holy."

23. Balthasar, in *Theo-Drama*, vol. 2, explains that God is so completely free in his self-expression he is not even constrained by his own nature (*TD2*, 191). This affirmation, of course, would have to be qualified, as we will see over the course of this book.

24. Plato, *Tim.* 29e.

25. Ex 20:4–5: "You shall not make for yourself an idol, or any likeness of what is in heaven above or on the earth beneath or in the water under the earth. You shall not worship or serve them; for I, the Lord your God, am a jealous God." On the surface, this prohibition seems the precise opposite of the Platonic cosmology of the *Timaeus*, according to which *everything* is an image of God, precisely on account of God's goodness.

26. We cannot pursue the theme here, but it might be interesting to consider whether the fragmentation of the tradition occurs generally through a "reintroduction" of part of what already exists in the patrimony, now from the outside, as if it were something foreign. It appears that this novel reappropriation of the tradition in nontraditional terms occurs in stages, proceeding backward from the most recent to the oldest. Thus, there is the "reintroduction" of Aristotle (who was already implicitly present in the tradition through the Neoplatonic legacy, which is expressed in the fact that the Proclean *Liber de causis* could have initially been mistaken for a text from Aristotle!); the "reintroduction" of Plato in the Renaissance; and the "reintroduction" of the pre-Socratic materialists (by way of Lucretius) in early modernity. We would thus have a kind of "peeling back" of the tradition, layer by layer.

27. In *Politics* 8.2, Aristotle calls those activities *not* performed for their own sake "illiberal," i.e., "unfree" (ἀνελευθερίος). In *NE* 6.4, he distinguishes *poiēsis* from *praxis* by saying that *poiēsis* is an action whose end lies outside the action (cf. *Metaph*. 9.8.105a23–1050b1). Philosophy is ultimately the *only* perfectly free activity since it is done purely for its own sake (*Metaph*. 1.2.982b24–27).

28. Aristotle, *Phys*. 2.1.192b14–15.

29. The phrase comes from the *Liber de causis*, prop. 15, and is derived from Proclus, *Elements*, prop. 83. See Aquinas's commentary on the *Liber*, in which he discusses this notion; *Super librum de causis expositio*, ed. H. D. Suffrey, 2nd ed. (Paris: Vrin, 2002), trans. Richard C. Taylor, *Commentary on the Book of Causes* (Washington, DC: Catholic University of America Press, 1996), 98–102.

30. We are leaving the gods (or, from the Christian tradition, the angels) out of the picture here because they have an ambiguous status for Aristotle: on the one hand, they transcend material nature, while on the other hand they remain within the sphere of nature in its most comprehensive sense.

31. Aquinas, to be sure, ascribes a notion of will to Aristotle without indicating he is inventing something that is not already there. (As Charles Kahn shows, the various elements that are scattered about in Aristotle under different names require the unity of a single word, the Latin *voluntas*, to become a full-fledged theory of will, which is why Aquinas's systematic interpretation of Ar-

istotle is so decisive in the development of a notion of will in the West. See Charles Kahn, "Discovering the Will: From Aristotle to Augustine," in *The Question of "Eclecticism": Studies in Later Greek Philosophy*, ed. John M. Dillon and A. A. Long [Berkeley: University of California Press, 1988], 234–59.) One might argue that Aquinas is simply bringing out a latent possibility in Aristotle's anthropology, for which there is significant warrant (just as he brings out a theme of *creation*, which is not so evident on the surface of the Aristotelian text). We have a certain sympathy for this judgment. At the same time, we will have to ask in the end whether Aquinas himself does full justice to the novelty of the will. There is no simple answer to this question, as we will see in our study of Aquinas below.

32. Aristotle's order of appetite does indeed seem to introduce an order different from the cognitive order, as we saw in our investigation in volume 1. This seems, though, to find a final resolution in the order of intellect, as demonstrated by the perfect actuality of *nous*, which lacks nothing whatsoever in its thinking on its thinking. But it is crucial to note this ambiguity—namely, that the appetitive order is *more* than the cognitive order but that it remains at the same time *contained within* the cognitive order—which is a major part of our argument regarding the internal openness of the Greek vision to the Christian.

33. "Nature loves to hide"; Heraclitus B123, DK. The whole spirit of the Homeric epic, Pindar's lyric, and Attic drama is the *test* or *trial* or *contest* that makes the hidden nature *manifest*, though without making it simply obvious in a superficial sense.

34. We have in mind Nietzsche's profound (if arguably misapplied) notion of *ressentiment*, which is not an original impulse (*sentiment*) but a *reaction* to (*re-*) what is original and authentic, a reaction that regrets the first impulse and so tries to reject it or bury it.

35. See Heidegger's interpretation of the Allegory of the Cave in his essay "Plato's Doctrine of Truth," in *Pathmarks* (Cambridge: Cambridge University Press, 1998), 155–82. For Heidegger, this "exposure," as it were, was a fateful move that connected truth with *correctness* and being with permanence, which, through the Roman (the people of Imperial Rome, then traditional Christianity [Roman Catholicism] and then the spirit of modernity [Romanticism]) mediation, came to define European humanism. Cf. "Metaphysics as History of Being," in *The End of Philosophy* (New York: Harper and Row, 1973), 12–13. Heidegger took Aristotle, with his organic notion of nature, to represent an attempt to recover the early Greek view after Plato's betrayal (see 9–10). We are proposing the opposite judgment, namely, that Plato opened up the deepest dimension of the original Greek vision.

36. *FFR*, 288–90.

37. As Richard Onians has shown, the seat of individual consciousness for the ancient Greeks was the chest area (he proposes specifically the *lungs*), while the head was taken to contain a "psychic" substance, a fluid, that belonged principally to the family or tribe (a fluid that pooled up, so to speak, also in the gonads, and, curiously enough, in the *knees*, which are etymologically related to the gonads, as well as to the "gn" roots connecting all these with "knowledge"). See *The Origins of European Thought about the Body, the Mind, the Soul, the World, Time, and Fate* (Cambridge: Cambridge University Press, 1951), 93–122, 174–86.

38. For Aristotle, the ideal relation is the virtuous friendship, into which one is not simply born (even if the quality of one's given family bears on one's capacity for virtue); see *NE* 8.3.1156b7–24. Plato, similarly, defines friendship as a loving of the Good (the *ultimate beloved*) in one's companion, which implies a principle that transcends the particularities of a "blood" relation; see *Lysis* 219d.

39. Significantly, the moment Socrates attempts to universalize, i.e., to "unrelativize," the principle of social relations in his discussion with Polemarchus in *Rep.* I, by appealing to goodness *simpliciter*, beyond the relativity of doing good to friends and harm to enemies, the sophist Thrasymachus violently intervenes and sends the conversation in another direction, from which it never explicitly recovers; see *Rep.* I, 335e–336d.

40. To be sure, the Hebrew words for freedom, *deror* and *chuphshah*, do not occur frequently in the OT. Nevertheless, it remains the case that the event that *defines* the Jewish identity, the Exodus, is understood to be essentially an event of *liberation*; see Brague, "Biblical Roots," 394. As we will see, it is significant that the Jews understand freedom in the first place as a particular historical event and not just as a generic condition. Freedom, thus understood, is essentially connected to God's *deliverance* or *salvation* of Israel (*teshuah*). See Strong's Lexicon, #8668. The word *teshuah* occurs much more commonly in the OT; one might say that the notion of freedom pervades the whole Bible, even if it is not always made explicit.

41. See *TWOT*, 859–60.

42. *TWOT*, 860.

43. Joseph Atkinson, *Biblical and Theological Foundations of the Family: Domestic Church* (Washington, DC: Catholic University of America Press, 2014), 73–74. Even the creation story of Genesis, and more obviously the election of Abraham, were read from the perspective of Exodus. As Sol Roth puts it, most of the Bible is concerned with the removing of shackles; "Two Concepts of Freedom," *Tradition: A Journal of Orthodox Jewish Thought* 13.2 (1972): 65.

44. Brague, "Biblical Roots," 400. Brague here ascribes this view of freedom as *end* rather than *means* to Christianity especially, but he interprets the Christian notion in continuity with the Jewish view. Cf., by contrast, the view offered by Roth, "Two Concepts of Freedom," 66, who insists that Jews conceive freedom as *only* a means (in comparison to the modern American view of freedom as an end in itself). Roth's point is simply that the Jews give priority to the particular bond of community over individual autonomy, but we will argue below that this priority constitutes the deep essence of freedom. David Burrell proposes that, in the classical tradition, the summit of freedom for Jews (as for Christians and Muslims) is not choice (means to an end) but union of the will with God (an end in itself); *Freedom and Creation in the Abrahamic Traditions* (Washington, DC: Center for Muslim-Christian Understanding, 1995), 4–5.

45. Brague, "Biblical Roots," 395. Note that the law stands over and above the *given* order of nature, or, to put it in Greek terms, the *nomos* transcends *physis*.

46. Walther Eichrodt, *Theology of the Old Testament*, 2 vols., trans. J. A. Baker (Philadelphia: Westminster Press, 1961), 1:270–71.

47. The essence of the sacred, according to Mircea Eliade, is that it does not belong to the immanent order of things but represents a radical *break* with that order ("das ganz Andere"), though precisely for the sake of giving that order a foundation and making it *real*; *The Sacred and the Profane* (New York: Harcourt Brace, 1958), 11–13.

48. Eichrodt, *Theology*, 1:272–73.

49. While one might say that the *law* is the ultimate reference point for the Jews, the law itself is understood finally as an expression of God's will: "Not only the cultic law, but the secular law derives its validity from being a direct command of Yahweh" (ibid., 1:75).

50. Job presents his perfect relation to God (Job 1:1) by finally renouncing understanding (Job 42:3) and simply accepting what God, the almighty Creator, wills.

51. In other words, as Burrell argues, the Torah given to the Jews is precisely what enables them to *fulfill* the divine will (*Freedom and Creation in Three Traditions*, 144). The power of will is not so much inborn as *given from above*. As Balthasar explains in his study of the OT (*GL6*, 164, cf. n31), "The one who acts may think that his deed lies in his own power, but in fact it is the deed that takes him into the sphere of its power." In this respect, the "deed" of responding to God's self-revelation is what brings the capacity into being. As a general principle, insofar as God both brings man into being (first actuality) and into relation with him (second actuality), theology has immediate implications for psychology. See Eichrodt, *Theology*, 2:269, for an explanation of the precise

connection between the way God reveals himself and the structure of the human being. Cf., more generally, 2:118–50.

52. Eichrodt, *Theology*, 2:16–17. See the extensive list of examples given in nn1–10.

53. Ibid., 2:40–45. Cf., also, 1:206. It has been observed that when Jesus responds to those in the Garden of Gethsemane who have come to arrest him with the statement "I am [he]" (ἐγώ εἰμι, which is mentioned three times: Jn 18:5–8), or in other words, with the name that Yahweh revealed to Moses, it knocks them off of their feet: "When he said to them 'I am [he],' they drew back and fell to the ground" (Jn 18:6).

54. The "covenantal" relation (which we will discuss below) is essentially a transcendence of the "naturalistic" relation one finds in other ancient religions, expressed in mythology. See Eichrodt, *Theology*, 1:48.

55. Ibid., 1:41.

56. See Arendt, "What Is Authority?," 120–28.

57. Eric Voegelin, *Order and History*, vol. 1, *Israel and Revelation* (Baton Rouge: Louisiana State University Press, 1956), 115, cf. 126–27: "Without Israel there would be no history, but only the eternal recurrence of societies in cosmological form." Eliade makes a similar point: "Judaism presents an innovation of the first importance. For Judaism, time has a beginning and will have an end. The idea of cyclic time is left behind. Yahweh no longer manifests himself in *cosmic time* (like the gods in other religions) but in *historical time*, which is irreversible. Each new manifestation of Yahweh in history is no longer reducible to an earlier manifestation" (*Sacred*, 110).

58. As Jon D. Levenson observes, "If Israel can be shown to be radically discontinuous with her environment, then the likelihood is increased that her identity is the result of supernatural intervention, just as the Bible says (e.g., Gen 12:1–3)." *Sinai and Zion: An Entry into the Jewish Bible* (San Francisco: Harper, 1985), 11.

59. On *history* as the locus of God's interaction with Israel, see G. Ernest Wright, *The Old Testament against Its Environment* (London: SCM, 1950), and *The Old Testament and Theology* (New York: Harper and Row, 1969).

60. The more common word in the OT for "will" is "heart," *lev*, which is not simply the physical organ but the *center* of man, the *soul*, wherein man is disposed in one direction or another (Strong's Lexicon, #3820). It is this disposition from which action originates, which is why the word gets translated as "will." See Johannes Pederson, *Israel: Its Life and Culture*, 2 vols. (London: Oxford University Press, 1926), 1:103–4.

61. Gen 2:7. Man becomes a living soul (*nephesh*) by virtue of God's breath or spirit (*ruah*). Soul is the breath of life as indwelling in a particular body; see Eichrodt, *Theology*, 2:133 and 136.

62. Gen 1:28. As Eichrodt explains, "Just as God himself is not a natural force, . . . so Man also sees himself as set over against the multitude of natural objects and forces as different in kind" (*Theology*, 2:119–20).

63. G. Ernest Wright, *God Who Acts* (London: SCM, 1952); cf. Burrell, *Freedom and Creation in Three Traditions*, 67.

64. Eichrodt, *Theology*, 2:162–67. Hannah Arendt suggests that all free action is a kind of miracle, insofar as it has an essential uniqueness and unpredictability: we can neither fully explain its origin nor anticipate its implications. See "What Is Freedom?," in *Between Past and Future* (New York: Penguin, 2006), 168.

65. Roth, "Two Concepts of Freedom," 63.

66. Fire and the thunderstorm are typical symbols of God's active presence precisely because of the "destructive force" that the thunderstorm makes visible (Eichrodt, *Theology*, 2:17) and, regarding fire, "the suddenness of its outbreaks and . . . the mockery it makes of all human defences" (18).

67. Levenson, *Sinai and Zion*, 42.

68. See Strong's Lexicon, #2668. The sole occurrence in this form is Lev 19:20; cf. *TWOT*, 312–13.

69. Strong's Lexicon, #1865. Cf. *TWOT*, 197–98.

70. Brague, "Biblical Roots," 395.

71. Immediately following this statement, as a sort of elaboration of the meaning of holiness, the text continues: "Every one of you shall revere his mother and his father, and you shall keep my sabbaths" (Lev 19:3). Here we see the meaning of freedom: a reception of one's origin (reverence for father and mother—and notice that the origin is referred to as both father *and mother*, whereas the Greeks consider only the father the origin, strictly speaking), and keeping the Sabbath, i.e., cleaving to the gift character of existence, which is essentially connected to the being "set apart" that is signified by the Sabbath rest.

72. Freedom lies in the conformity of one's existence, in all its aspects, to Torah; see Roth, "Two Concepts of Freedom," 62.

73. See Heschel, *Sabbath*, 27–32. In Judaism, Heschel observes, what is at issue is not the holiness of space first of all but the holiness of time (9). As Eliade explains, the *holy* thing, which is set apart ("non-homogeneity"), is so not in order to separate but, as we pointed out above, to found the reality of that from which it is separated (*Sacred*, 2–24).

74. As Balthasar puts it, Israel is not meant to rest in itself but to come to a place that is *given*, a place ultimately in God, which is to say that the rest lies *beyond* itself (*GL6*, 178). Israel "must live in relation to itself as a foreigner."

75. According to Eichrodt, the merciful love of God is constant, but it is not static; it is rather like the sun that "shines forth unalterably" (*Theology*, 1:256).

76. Galen, *On the Usefulness of the Parts of the Human Body* 11.14, ed. Helmreich, 2:158, quoted in Dihle, *Theory of Will*, 159n2. Dihle sums up the Jewish view thus: "Creation results from the power and the pleasure or will of Yahweh and nothing else. He can create, change, and destroy as He pleases, and it is only because of His benevolence towards His creatures that He has set some rules for the universe" (4).

77. Dihle, *Theory of Will*, 3. One of the most extensive discussions of this criticism of biblical religion from the Hellenistic Greeks, which responds to it from both the OT and NT, is of course Origen's massive work *Contra Celsum*, trans. Henry Chadwick (Cambridge: Cambridge University Press, 1980). Celsus complains, for example, that the Jews "worship angels and are addicted to sorcery, of which Moses was their teacher" (1:26).

78. An extreme version of this position can be found in the work of Lev Shestov, who spent his life attempting to show the absolute discontinuity between biblical freedom and the oppressively constraining "eternal truths" of Greece: see, e.g., "Parmenides in Chains," and "The Bull of Phalaris," in *Athens and Jerusalem*, 2nd ed. (Athens: Ohio University Press, 2016), 69–126 and 127–206 respectively. A much more sober and reflective argument for the essentially biblical origins of freedom (without which Greek philosophy would devolve into a kind of necessitarianism) can be found in Montague Brown, *Freedom, Philosophy, and Faith* (Lanham, MD: Lexington Books, 2011). Fania Oz-Salzberger has offered an interesting suggestion that the revolutionary modern political thinkers in seventeenth-century Holland, England, and France generally sought to retrieve the Hebrew political forms from the Old Testament outside of the Greco-Roman tradition mediated through Christianity, viewing themselves as promoting "the 'second Israel'"; see "The Jewish Roots of Western Freedom," *Azure* 13 (Summer 2002): 93–94. In nineteenth-century Germany, Spinoza was taken to represent the inevitable culmination of (Greek) rational thought, the only alternative to which was what Friedrich Heinrich Jacobi famously formulated as the "leap of faith" in Jesus Christ.

79. This is essentially the position adopted by Leo Strauss; see his originally unpublished lecture "Reason and Revelation," in *Leo Strauss and the Theologico-Political Problem* (Cambridge: Cambridge University Press, 2006). It is interesting to note that, in order to save the intelligibility of the world (or so he thought), Spinoza felt he had to deny above all the notion of the "will" of God as something that resisted total reduction to God's intellect; see propositions 32 and 33 of part I of his *Ethics* (Indianapolis: Hackett, 1992), 53–56.

80. Note that this was the initial sense of "efficient causality," drawn out of Aristotle's first cause (which did not exclude this sense, but which did not have the creativity of the first cause thematically present), specifically by the

faith traditions that recognized God as creator and not just as principle of order; see Etienne Gilson's "Notes pour l'histoire de la cause efficiente," *Archives d'Histoire Doctrinale et Littéraire du Moyen Age* 37 (1962): 7–31.

81. The groundbreaking work revealing the complex narrative structures that fill the OT is Robert Alter, *The Art of Biblical Narrative*, 2nd ed. (New York: Basic Books, 2011). Here we see an approach to scripture that recognizes the internal structure of divine action (and interaction) with man. For examples of a tracing of regularly recurrent narrative patterns in the OT, see David Daube, *The Exodus Pattern in the Bible* (London: Faber and Faber, 1963), David Damrosch, *The Narrative Covenant: Transformations of Genre in the Growth of Biblical Literature* (San Francisco: Harper and Row, 1987), and Robert C. Culley, *Themes and Variations: A Study of Action in Biblical Narrative* (Atlanta, GA: Scholars Press, 1992). Our claim is that this tendency for events to exhibit the form of a structured plot is not a mere literary device but reveals something of the "nature" of God's will (and so of will *simpliciter*). In general, on the mutual implication of drama and form, see my *Hans Urs von Balthasar and the Dramatic Structure of Truth* (New York: Fordham University Press, 2004), 17–25.

82. Eichrodt, *Theology*, 1:36, 65–66. Eichrodt suggests that συνθήκη may have been a better translation of the Hebrew, since it sets into relief the cooperation of the covenanting partners. But the *dia* need not imply opposition in the sense of any hostility; it can also indicate *reciprocity*, which is clearly the case here.

83. *TWOT*, 128. The word for "covenant," *berit*, etymologically seems to come from the Akkadian *birtu*, "bond" or "fetter." The Greek word indicates a reciprocal positing or establishing through will.

84. Burrell, *Freedom and Creation in Three Traditions*, 85.

85. Frank Moore Cross, "Kinship and Covenant in Ancient Israel," in *From Epic to Canon: History and Literature in Ancient Israel* (Baltimore: Johns Hopkins University Press, 1998), 8.

86. The typology and terminology are taken from Scott Hahn, *Kinship by Covenant: A Canonical Approach to the Fulfillment of God's Saving Promises* (New Haven, CT: Yale University Press, 2009), 28–29. We will not concern ourselves so much with the differences as with the unity that runs through all these.

87. See Joachim Begrich, "Berit: Ein Beitrag zur Erfassung einer alttestamentlichen Denkform," *Zeitschrift für die alttestamentliche Wissenschaft* 60 (1944): 1–11. Begrich presents an argument for the growth of reciprocity as the covenant evolves into its proper shape.

88. Hahn, *Kinship by Covenant*, 38; cf. W. Brueggemann, "The Covenanted Family: A Zone for Humanness," *Journal of Current Social Issues* 14

(1977): 18–23. On the centrality of the family in the biblical view more generally, see Atkinson, *Biblical and Theological Foundations*, 91–160.

89. Cross and Hahn represent an alternative to a commonly held view that the covenantal relation *replaces* the natural relation of kinship instead of extending it: for examples of this view, see Eichrodt, *Theology*, 1:39, and G. P. Hugenberger, *Marriage as a Covenant* (Leiden: Brill, 1994), 197 (according to Hugenberger, a covenant is "an elected, as opposed to natural, relationship" [215]). Our suggestion is that this view presupposes a more modern sense of will, which we will trace in its slow development over the course of the present book.

90. J. A. Davies, *A Royal Priesthood* (London: T&T Clark, 2004), 177.

91. See Hugenberger, *Marriage as Covenant*. In Mal 2:14–15, human marriage is referred to explicitly as a covenant, by which God makes man and woman *one*. To refer to human marriage as a paradigm is not meant to imply that God's covenant with Israel is modeled on marriage (which would tend to divinize sexuality, in the manner one finds in extrabiblical ancient mythology; Atkinson, *Biblical and Theological Foundations*, 19–32), but rather that the marriage depicted in the creation account is an as yet inchoate image of the covenantal relation first established at creation, which will finally be clarified with the coming of Christ (Eph 5).

92. This is principally in the prophets (Hosea, of course, but also Ezekiel, Jeremiah, and Isaiah), more often (but not exclusively) in the negative sense of an accusation of infidelity. We also see it in the Song of Songs. For a discussion of Hosea in this sense, see Gerhard von Rad, *Old Testament Theology* (New York: Harper and Row, 1965), 2:141–42.

93. Cross, "Kinship and Covenant," 7–8.

94. Pederson, *Israel*, 1:308–09, cited in Hahn, *Kinship by Covenant*, 39.

95. Cross, "Kinship and Covenant," 5–6. Cf. Hahn, *Kinship by Covenant*, 38, and Eichrodt, *Theology*, 1:232, 250 ff.

96. The permanence of covenant follows from its definition: extension of *kinship*. Membership in the covenant is literally cut into one's flesh with circumcision. It is significant that, for the Israelites in particular, the place of the sign is specifically the generative organ of the male, signifying the abiding presence of the covenant through the generations (see Atkinson's illuminating remarks, *Biblical and Theological Foundations*, 84–85). Those, like Eichrodt, who interpret covenant as a *substitute* for kinship will tend to see covenant (now more like a sheer act of will) as able to be *undone* by the instituting agent (see Eichrodt, *Theology*, 1:44; cf. 457). Even Eichrodt, however, recognizes that the form of the covenant develops into an *eternal* one with the Davidic covenant (1:458). The permanence of the divine covenant may not have been initially apparent, since at the Mosaic stage, so to speak, it bears some dependence on Israel's fulfilling of certain conditions, but it is eventually made uncon-

ditional in Abraham (Atkinson, *Biblical and Theological Foundations*, 216). Even if one concedes a developmental view of covenant, it remains the case that one cannot simply *define* covenant as a bond that can be made or unmade at will (which, as we will see, is eventually the way it is understood in late medieval nominalism). The permanence of covenant, we will suggest, gets finally sealed in the flesh, so to speak, with the New Covenant in the blood of Christ, as we will explain below.

97. Hahn, *Kinship by Covenant*, 51.

98. Gen 1:26. The other actions of creation are simply effective commands. This is the only time in which God "reflects" before acting and refers to the activity as his *own*: "Let us make" rather than simply "let there be." According to Atkinson, citing the celebrated Hebraist Genesius, the extremely unusual use of the plural is not the "royal we," as contemporary scholars are compelled to assume, since that is a form that appears in the language only later (and would appear to be self-contradictory, given the traditional emphasis on the absolute unity, the oneness, of God), but can finally be explained only as a "plural of self-deliberation" (Atkinson, *Biblical and Theological Foundations*, 53n71)—or in other words, a reference to the inner life of God, which "contains multitudes," so to speak.

99. Levenson observes, for example, "For 'deliverance' in the Hebrew Bible is in the main collective and historical, and not individual" (*Sinai and Zion*, 44).

100. Atkinson, *Biblical and Theological Foundations*, 161–82.

101. "The word *nephesh* rarely occurs in the plural, because souls which are together are generally taken as a unit" (Pederson, *Israel*, 1:65).

102. Ibid. Cf. "Soul is will. A community of souls must therefore mean that one will more or less prevails among the souls" (1:166).

103. Ibid., 1:279.

104. Ibid., 1:286.

105. As we pointed out above, Burrell offers a metaphysical argument for this point (*Freedom and Creation in Three Traditions*, 85). Here he shows that the drama of the biblical narrative of God's presence *enhances* human freedom.

106. Eichrodt, *Theology*, 1:286–87.

107. It is not a surprise, then, that Eichrodt characterizes God's love in the OT as "irrational" (*Theology*, 1:251): the "quite irrational power of love" is "the ultimate basis of the covenant relationship." Eichrodt seems to presuppose a concept of perfect love as *agape* specifically in the sense Anders Nygren eventually made popular. See Nygren, *Agape and Eros* (Chicago: University of Chicago Press, 1982). See also my critique of this view: "The Redemption of Eros: Philosophical Reflections on Benedict XVI's First Encyclical," *Communio* 33 (Fall 2006): 375–99.

108. This is what we characterized as an essentially "diabolical" notion of power in the previous volume (*FFR*, 264–69). W. J. Courtenay has definitively shown that the notion of what Eichrodt refers to here as "divine power without limitation," which came to be referred to in Scholastic philosophy as God's *potentia absoluta*, was never understood, prior to the late medieval period, as a "real" power on the basis of which God acts but only as an *abstract* consideration. It was only with the school of thought that came to be called nominalism that this abstract power was taken to be an *actual basis* of God's activity, in contrast to the *potentia ordinata*, which is bound to the real world that God in fact happens to have created. See the whole collection of Courtenay's essays entitled *Covenant and Causality in Medieval Thought* (London: Variorum Reprints, 1984), especially article IV, "The Dialectic of Divine Omnipotence" (the page numbers follow the original publication and not the appearance in the collection). We will be discussing this theme at many junctures over the course of the present book.

109. As we mentioned above, there may be oblique references to the possibility of annulment (cf., for example, Ex 32:10), but this possibility can hardly be said to define what a covenant is by nature. That nature gets displayed in its fullness over the course of the OT, when it becomes clear that the covenant is *eternal*, and even more clearly in the NT. The idea that a covenant is a "sheer" act of will, which can be eliminated by another "sheer" act of will, requires an "extrabiblical" conception of God—in the sense, on the one hand, of the influence of Islam, and on the other hand of a new, "purely logical" form of reasoning that simply abstracts from tradition. Regarding the Muslim influence, see the following: David Burrell, *Freedom and Creation in Three Traditions*, 77 (who notes that, in contrast to Judaism and Christianity, Islam presents God's revelation as unmediated by any covenant); W. J. Courtenay, essay V of *Covenant and Causality*, "The Critique on Natural Causality in the Mutakallimum and Nominalism," *Harvard Theological Review* 66 (1973): 77–94. Cf. Brague's comments in "Biblical Roots," 394, on the primacy of the will in the Muslim conception of God, which contrasts with the Jewish sense of this primacy, and his comments on the Muslim tendency to eliminate human mediation in the relation to God in "Athens, Jerusalem, Mecca," 247–49; and Etienne Gilson's well-known discussion in *The Unity of Philosophical Experience* (New York: Scribner, 1950), chap. 2, "Theologism and Philosophy," 31–60, in which Gilson explores the influence of this view of Christian thought. It bears remarking that Muslims also preserved the Greek inheritance in the early Middle Ages better than did the Christians, even if philosophy was not central to the life of the religion (in the way that it is, *in principle*, in Christianity, though not in Judaism). Burrell points out, moreover, that, as a *revealed* religion, Islam

presupposes at the very least sufficient human freedom to receive revelation (*Freedom and Creation in Three Traditions*, 163), which we see in the Muslim philosophical recognition that, if God *creates* all human acts, man at least has to *appropriate* them. Regarding the advent of a logic abstracted from tradition, we will see in a later chapter that, while this logic may find its most complete expression in Peter Abelard (see Gilson, the chapter "Logicism and Philosophy," in *Unity of Philosophical Experience*, 3–30), it arguably first appears in a significant way among the Latins (and in a very different form among the Greek-style thinkers in Eriugena) in St. Anselm. It is not an accident that the distinction between *potentia absoluta* and *potentia ordinata*, which will prove so fateful for the conception of freedom, emerges in embryo, so to speak, in Anselm's thought. On this, see W. J. Courtenay, "Necessity and Freedom in Anselm's Conception of God," in *Die Wirkungsgeschichte Anselms von Canterbury, Analecta Anselmiana* 4/2, ed. Helmut Kohlenberger (Frankfurt: Minerva, 1975), 49.

110. See Eichrodt, *Theology*, 2:98, who says that the central importance of covenant is the sign of a single, almighty will behind all things.

111. Hahn, *Kinship by Covenant*, 125. Cf. note 112 below.

112. Scott Hahn presents a brief account of how the principal covenants are related (*Kinship by Covenant*, 120–21); Burrell has shown how the relation is not a simple logical one but is essentially dramatic (*Freedom and Creation in Three Traditions*, 143 ff.) in the sense that the development occurs through successive betrayals and restorations, rather than through a simple unfolding of one from another. The essential importance of the "dramatic" development of covenant is presented in the classic text from St. Paul, the Epistle to the Romans, which shows that the inclusion of the Gentiles in the covenant occurs in response to the failure of the Jews, to whom God for his part remains faithful, but now in a wholly new way.

113. Atkinson provides a powerful account of this; see his chap. 3, "Abraham and the Family of Faith," in *Biblical and Theological Foundations*, 78–90.

114. The verb used for the first instance in the OT of the institution of covenant (Gen 6:18) may be translated either as "established" or as "confirmed" (note that it is translated in this latter way in the NET Bible and the New Living Translation). Cf. Hahn, *Kinship by Covenant*, 9, and Jacob Milgrom, "Covenants: The Sinaitic and Patriarchal Covenants in the Holiness Code (Leviticus 17–24)," in *Sefer Moshe: The Moshe Weinfeld Jubilee Volume*, ed. C. Cohen, A. Hurvitz, and S. M. Paul (Winona Lake, IN: Eisenbrauns, 2004), 91–101, cited in Hahn, *Kinship by Covenant*, 9. After studying the passage and its context in detail, William J. Dumbrell says: "The most natural interpretation of this verse is that an existing arrangement to be preserved is referred to, to

which no more specific appeal is required than the denomination of it as 'my covenant.' Of course, the manner in which it will be preserved may well be specifically designated in Gen. 9:8 ff; in this sense Gen. 6:18 could be said to be anticipatory. But both passages will then refer to some definite arrangement, prior to both, which is being upheld." William J. Dumbrell, *Covenant and Creation: A Theology of Old Testament Covenants* (New York: Thomas Nelson, 1984), 24. He concludes: "We may probably now surmise that what is being referred to in Gen. 6:18 is some existing arrangement presumably imposed by God without human concurrence, since it is referred to as 'my covenant'" (26).

115. Karl Barth insists that "Creation is not itself the covenant" (*Church Dogmatics*, vol. 3, pt. 1, *The Doctrine of Creation* [Edinburgh: T&T Clark, 2004], 97), but of course this statement occurs within a deep and extensive argument for their profound interconnection: if creation is "the external basis of the covenant," covenant is the "internal basis of creation" (those are the titles of major sections of this volume).

116. Note that, because the covenant originates through the absolute initiative of God's will, his conformity to the covenant is a conformity to himself and thus represents perfect divine freedom. It is precisely this point that Martin Luther misses in his rejection of vows in the name of God's abiding freedom; see my discussion of this in "The Crisis of Marriage as a Crisis of Meaning: On the Sterility of the Modern Will," *Communio* 41 (Summer 2014): 331–71.

117. Dihle relates a striking instance: "According to a legend reported in the *Talmud* (b. Sanh. 9a), the famous Rabbi Gamaliel tried hard to demonstrate to a Roman emperor how everything happens solely because of the will of God and why it does not make any sense to apply the categories of the possible, the reasonable, or the probable to anything that is caused by the will of God" (*Theory of Will*, 4).

118. Eichrodt, *Theology*, 2:156.

119. Even if "good" makes reference to God's will above all (ibid., 2:108; Heschel, *Sabbath*, 75, on good as penultimate in the Bible, subordinate to the holy, which is *directly* related to God), that suffices if will is genuinely understood as generative (the words are etymologically connected), or *effective* in the manner we have been describing. Brague explains that the Sabbath in Gen 1 is a freeing of the world, as it were, to rest in itself, which is effectively what the Greeks mean by *nature*; "Biblical Roots," 393. It is illuminating, here, to consider that the Sabbath is affirmed as the *sign* of God's covenant (Ex 31:16–17).

120. See Voegelin, *Israel and Revelation*, 135–36.

121. Hannah Arendt, *The Human Condition*, 2nd ed. (Chicago: University of Chicago Press, 1998), 8–9, 247. We do not mean simply to deny the

reality of what Arendt indicates here, only to suggest that it has its proper place as integrated into a larger order, which determines its character from the beginning.

122. Hegel contrasted the "bad infinity" of a line with the "good infinity" of a circle, which is infinite perfection, and so not exclusive of finite determination. See his *Elements of the Philosophy of Right*, §22 *Zusatz*, and my discussion of this image in *The Perfection of Freedom* (Eugene, OR: Cascade Books, 2012), 292–93. Schelling is right to observe that Hegel's view is precisely *undramatic* (his word is "monotonous"), since the unfolding never goes beyond what was given at the outset. See Friedrich Wilhelm Joseph von Schelling, *On the History of Modern Philosophy* (Cambridge: Cambridge University Press, 1994), 142–43. According to the Jewish view we are presenting, there is a certain sense in which the unfolding does not proceed beyond the origin, but the origin is precisely given *as a promise*, which requires (creative, concrete, historical) *fulfillment*, and so in another respect everything goes beyond the origin. This is why the creative renewal of covenant, the unprecedented extension and specification of what went before, is not a betrayal of the original or simply its replacement with a new arrangement.

123. For a more conventional view, which opposes (stable) form to (dramatic) movement, see Ben Quash, "Drama and the End of Modernity," in *Balthasar at the End of Modernity* (Edinburgh: T&T Clark, 1999), 139–71, and my critique in *Hans Urs von Balthasar*, 17–25.

124. Balthasar described the "opposition" (in the sense of dramatic encounter of freedoms) as the essence of Christianity (*TD2*, 190) but sees this drama as beginning in the OT, about which he says, "The foundation of everything is the idea of 'covenant' between Yahweh and his people" (*GL6*, 149).

125. See *FFR*, 311–13, 341–47, inter alia.

126. See our discussion of this point in Locke's *Second Treatise* in *FFR*, 98–109, 124–25.

127. See again Pederson, *Israel*, 1:308–09.

128. As we saw, according to Hahn, *Kinship by Covenant*, 120–21, the various covenants relate as anticipation and fulfillment in a clearly structured unity. To say this is not at all to deny the radical novelty of the pledge; we are proposing a more paradoxical view, which in contrast to a merely "additive" sense of novelty would integrate the newness with what came before: "Every scribe who is trained for the kingdom of heaven is like a householder who brings forth from his treasure things both new and old" (Mt 13:52).

129. See *FFR*, 308, 309, 444n91.

130. *Emeth* means reliability, stability, faithfulness, and truth: Strong's Lexicon, #571.

131. The word *deror*, as we observed above, originally meant "free-flowing"; see Strong's Lexicon, #1865. The "flowing" of milk and honey in fact resonates with the original etymology of the word for freedom.

132. This being transplanted into a land from elsewhere, rather than, so to speak, growing up natively from within it, is fundamental to the Jewish interpretation of man. We ought to consider that Adam, too, was created first and then subsequently *placed in* the Garden. Aquinas sets this point into relief and draws a basic inference from it for the meaning of created nature: "Paradise was a fitting abode for man as regards the incorruptibility of the primitive state. Now this incorruptibility was man's, not by nature, but by a supernatural gift of God. Therefore that this might be attributed to God, and not to human nature, God made man outside of paradise, and afterwards placed him there to live there during the whole of his animal life; and, having attained to the spiritual life, to be transferred thence to heaven" (*ST* I.102.4 [Leon. 5], trans. FEDP).

133. Levenson, *Sinai and Zion*, 19–23. Yahweh's mountain "home" is in the desert (which represents God's radical transcendence), but the Israelites were not meant to take up residence there: "Sinai is not the final goal of the Exodus, but lying between Egypt and Canaan, it does represent YHWH's unchallengeable mastery over both" (23).

134. According to the 1906 *Jewish Encyclopedia: A Descriptive Record*, ed. Isidore Singer (New York: Funk and Wagnalls), the number forty indicates a *generation*, which is to say a long period of time that is not precisely specified. It is often used to refer to a period of waiting or of trial.

135. Brague, "Biblical Roots," 396: "Liberty is nothing natural, but something that was vouchsafed by God."

136. It is important to note that we are speaking here in a limited way about "Western civilization," which forms the general horizon for our larger project. We are thus not addressing the civilizations of the East, or for that matter of Africa, of the indigenous peoples of the "new world," and so forth. This is the case for many reasons, not least of which is the author's lack of competence, but also because scripture itself appears to leave the encounter between Christianity and the people of the East as something for the future: note the curious fact that the Holy Spirit forbids Paul and Silas to evangelize Asia (Acts 16:6–10). A profound study of the encounter between the East and the West, and its implication for the meaning of freedom, for example, remains to be done and would enrich the limited perspective of this book immensely. But the perspective developed here would have to be recognized as an essential part of that larger study, insofar as we remain concretely in history: Christianity was born in the Middle East, but it "grew" first in the West and gave birth to

its own culture here, even if it may never be simply limited to any one civilization. By its nature, Christianity is global; it is meant to reach the ends of the earth, though to do so in a concretely historical manner, through the particularity of mission, and not as an abstract principle. The account of freedom that we proposed in volume 1 and are developing here recognizes the *novelty* of the encounter with what is other as essential to the integrity of freedom. The historical meeting of "East and West" may be seen as a paradigmatic instance of such an encounter (see John Wu, *Beyond East and West* [Notre Dame, IN: University of Notre Dame Press, 2018], for reflections along these lines. I am grateful to Tongxin Lu for bringing John Wu to my attention), and every other instance might be seen to bear an analogous resemblance to this one—which means it will also be irreducibly different in each particular case.

137. For example, Clement of Alexandria, who proposed that God had prepared the Greeks through Plato so that they might fruitfully receive the Gospel; *Stromata* 2.5.

138. Rémi Brague, *On the God of the Christians (and on One or Two Others)* (South Bend, IN: St. Augustine's Press, 2013), 15–22.

139. Acts 17:16–21.

140. Significantly, Paul ascribes his apostleship specifically to the "will of God" (κλητὸς ἀπόστολος Χριστοῦ Ἰησοῦ διὰ θελήματος θεοῦ: 1 Cor 1:1; 2 Cor 1:1; Eph 1:1; Col 1:1; 2 Tim 1:1), or the "command of God" (κατ' ἐπιταγὴν θεοῦ: 1 Tim 1:1), which is an essential expression of the will.

141. The dramatic inclusion of the Gentiles within the salvation given to the Jews is of course the theme of Paul's Letter to the Romans. The person of Christ, "in whom there is no Jew or Greek" (Gal 3:28), is the one who bridges the difference between them, embracing the whole in his universal mission. It is interesting to note that in John's Gospel the event that "triggers" the arrival of Jesus's "hour" is the Greeks appearing on the scene, asking to speak to him (Jesus's enigmatic response to the request to see him is not a simple yes or no but an apparent non sequitur, "The hour has come for the Son of Man to be glorified"; Jn 12:20–23). Jesus's decisive hour thus coincides with the Greeks' openness to receive.

142. A much longer argument can be found in my book *The Politics of the Real*.

143. This is the method proscribed, for example, by Descartes; see part 2 of his *Discourse on Method*, in which he proposes, after having divided problems up into as many parts as they allow, to commence "with those objects that are simplest and easiest to know, in order to ascend, little by little, as by degrees, to the knowledge of the most composite things." René Descartes, *Discourse on Method and Meditations on First Philosophy*, 4th ed. (Indianapolis:

Hackett, 1998), 11. The revolution of Cartesian philosophy is arguably nothing but the shift from a primacy of object to a primacy of method.

144. The notion of Christianity as providing a form that liberates all worldly and human realities has been a constant theme of the work of my father, David L. Schindler. See, for example, his "Is Truth Ugly? Moralism and the Convertibility of Being and Love," *Communio* 27 (Winter 2000): 701–28; "Trinity, Creation, and the Order of Intelligence in the Modern Academy," *Communio* 28.3 (Fall 2001): 406–28; and "Toward a Culture of Life: The Eucharist, the 'Restoration' of Creation, and the 'Worldly' Task of the Laity in Liberal Societies," *Communio* 29 (Fall 2002): 679–90.

145. Burrell, *Freedom and Creation in Three Traditions*, 96. Burrell observes that the idea of creation as free (and freeing) is not in principle different in these religions but that Christianity is best able to provide a ground for the freedom because of the (triune and incarnate) nature of God that is revealed.

146. This question has been pursued in extraordinary depth by Ferdinand Ulrich; see his *Gegenwart der Freiheit* (Freiburg: Johannes Verlag Einsiedeln, 1974), *Gabe und Vergebung* (Freiburg: Johannes Verlag Einsiedeln, 2006), and *Homo Abyssus: The Drama of the Question of Being*, trans. D. C. Schindler (Washington, DC: Humanum Academic Press, 2017). We intend to give an account of this approach to freedom in our third volume.

147. *FFR*, 287–90.

148. As we see in Plato, the Greeks understood the good as that which essentially "binds and keeps together" (συνδεῖν καὶ συνέχειν); see *Phaedo* 99c, my translation.

149. This is arguably one of Aristotle's primary achievements.

150. Consider, in this regard, Hegel's observation that the Greeks and Romans, who first grasped the reality of freedom, recognized only that *some* people were free, and that it was not until the appearance of Christianity, whose very principle is freedom, that freedom was universalized, i.e., it was recognized that man *as such* is free; see his introductory lecture in the *Philosophy of History* (New York: Dover, 1956), 18–19. There is a sense of the universality, no doubt, in Greek democracy, which extends the tribal relation through the capacity to deliberate and decide (Aeschylus's *Oresteia* is of capital importance in this regard: here we see the elevation of the principle of justice beyond blood relations [revenge] to the common good as commonly determined through deliberation). But of course among the Greeks democracy was limited only to citizens, i.e., male land owners (though the reason for this is more profound than is usually recognized and concerns the relation between freedom and being properly rooted in a place so as to belong organically to the whole and have one's "interests," so to speak, connected inseparably to that whole).

151. "Nature" is so rare that, in the end, the Stoics could find no one but Socrates or Cato to present as examples of beings who had succeeded in conforming to it.

152. As John wrote, if all the things regarding the event of Christ were recorded, the world itself would not be able to contain the books that would be written (Jn 21:25).

153. The common expression "To err is human" requires serious qualification, or else it is disastrous, insofar as it implies the *definition* of man in terms of his fallen condition. But every definition is ipso facto a norm. It thus follows in this case that the sinful condition is transformed into a sort of ideal. We see this in the early modern supposition of man's self-interest as the basis of political order, which may be seen as a secular reinterpretation of the Reformers' doctrine of total depravity.

154. "The divine is that which cannot be circumscribed by even the greatest of things, and yet can be contained in what is smallest." This has come to be known (erroneously) as the Ignatian Grabschrift.

155. As we pointed out earlier, the essential covenant made with Abraham is a gift of salvation to all those included in the bodily continuity of Abraham's family line; see Atkinson, *Biblical and Theological Foundations*, 204–6. Cf. Cross, "Kinship and Covenant," 5: "Kinship was conceived in terms of one blood flowing through the veins of the kinship group.... Kindred were of one flesh, one bone."

156. This is why the notion of free will that "pops up," so to speak, among the Hellenistic Greeks (the earliest appearance of the attribution of the adjective *free* to the "will" is in Lucretius, *De rerum natura*, book 2, and then is taken up by Cicero; this sense then gets projected, so to speak, back into the Greek αὐτεξούσιον, for example, by Tertullian [see Kahn, "Discovering the Will," 248, 250–51]) cannot be sustained and carried to term but instead tends to collapse into an inescapable dialectic with a natural (i.e., divine) determinism, as we see above all but not exclusively in the Stoics. In *this* respect, Dihle, in *Theology of Will*, is right to point to the Bible, which opens up a dimension beyond nature as such, as the genuine source of the notion of will. We will return to this point in our discussion of Plotinus in chapter 2.

157. We cannot enter into detail here, but we see a pattern in which God fulfills the obligations laid on his partner. As Balthasar puts it, when man fails, "the history of the covenant of God becomes a history of God with himself" (*GL*6, 222–23). This is perfected in the economic drama played out in the work of redemption between Father and Son in the Spirit.

158. We will argue below (especially in our discussion of Maximus in chapter 4) that this is what *enables* freedom of choice.

159. This is why Balthasar suggests that the notion of "covenant" by itself does not suffice; see *TD2*, 201.

160. Lk 1:26–38. The angel, to be sure, announces to her what *will* happen, without any restrictions or conditions. But, significantly, the meeting ends only once Mary has given her assent (Lk 1:38). For a profound meditation on the significance of this event, see Paolo Prosperi, "'Fixed End of the Eternal Plan': Rereading Cabasilas's 'Homily on the Annunciation,'" *Communio* 46.2 (Summer 2019): 207–36.

161. According to von Rad, there are three essential ideas in the OT sense of sacrifice: (1) gift, (2) communion, (3) atonement (*Old Testament Theology*, 1:253–54). It is clear how all of these are perfected in the sacrifice that establishes the Christian covenant.

162. This is not at all to deny that Mary's fiat itself is a fruit of grace that is also most fundamentally "caused" by God: we will address this point in due course later in the book.

163. This description occurs in one of the (optional) Prefaces to the Eucharistic Prayer for the Easter Season.

164. On the importance of this for a proper sense of the public objectivity (as distinct from exclusively private subjectivity) of the truth of faith, see the final chapter, "Being and God," in my *Love and the Postmodern Predicament* (Eugene, OR: Cascade Books, 2018), 149–66.

165. The chapter in Romans goes on to say that all of creation is groaning in anticipation, waiting for the moment that "the creation itself will be liberated from its bondage to decay and brought into the freedom [εἰς τὴν ἐλευθερίαν] and glory of the children of God" (Rom 8:21).

166. Another image of spiritual freedom is rebirth: a being born again, or being born "from above" (ἄνωθεν) (Jn 3:3). There is a radically new starting point (from above), but it remains analogous to the natural condition: a being *born* from above.

167. See Cross, "Kinship and Covenant," 7–11: "In the West Semitic tribal societies we know best, such individuals or groups were grafted onto the genealogies and fictive kinship became kinship in flesh and blood. In a word, kinship-in-law became kinship-in-flesh" (7).

168. See Aristotle, *NE* 8.1.1155a16–21. There remains a tension between the personal and the ontological, which will never simply go away: Are we closest to our family or to those with whom we share a love of the good, i.e., with the virtuous? Consider Jesus's question: Who is my neighbor? Aquinas asks whether one ought to love more a neighbor who is better (i.e., closer to the good) or one who is more closely united to one (i.e., a relative in blood). See *ST* II-II.26.7 and 8 (Leon. 8). The tension entails an abiding dramatic ambiguity.

169. If freedom is first described as a *liberation from*, there will be a tendency to identify the *original* state with a kind of slavery.

170. From Origen on (see *On First Principles*, III.6.1, ed. Butterworth, 245), classical Christian theologians drew a distinction between "image" and "likeness" (Gen 1), taking the former to refer to man's original, created condition, and the latter to an achievement, or additional gift, involving man's free response. As Augustine famously put it, "So while [God] made you without you, he does not justify you without you" (*Sermons* 169, trans. Edmund Hill, *Sermons* [148–183], The Works of Saint Augustine: A Translation for the 21st Century, part III, vol. 5 [New Rochelle, NY: New City Press, 1990], 231). It is important to see that this distinction appears *already* in the (Jewish) *creation* account, which thus promises from the outset what will only come about in a completely surprising way through the redemptive work of Christ.

171. The precise relation between nature and grace is one of the weightiest and most delicate in all of theology. We do not mean to "solve" the problem with these simple statements, or even to work out a particular position in any detail, but simply to trace out the basic shape.

172. We noted Eichrodt's tendency to interpret the covenant in this way (see note 82, above), which seems to stem from a modern concept of will. The notion of covenant, however, quite clearly develops into a reality that cannot be unmade precisely because of God's involving of himself—i.e., his very nature and substance—in it. In other words, the sign of the will's power is not its capacity to break in and break out but the permanence of what it effects, to which it is bound and in which it is involved.

173. From the perspective of such an interpretation, creation appears as the supreme expression of the capacity to change, exercised by the most autonomous agent of all. All actuality becomes a function of potency, absolutized *as* original: the actual world is a mere "instance" of many possibilities. We will discuss this at greater length below, especially in our presentation of Scotus. See Burrell, *Freedom and Creation in Three Traditions*, 111–18.

174. To be sure, a host of technical issues are embedded in the question of predestination, and they are not simply resolved by the shifting of horizon we indicate here but require some careful attention. We will address these issues—e.g., how to hold together the absoluteness of divine causality and the integrity of human freedom—at the appropriate times over the course of this book.

175. Cf. Burrell, *Freedom and Creation in Three Traditions*, 120.

176. Ibid., 87.

177. Jn 19:34. The water may also be read as an allusion to the "water of life," traditionally interpreted as the Holy Spirit (Jn 4:13–14). There is a significant echo in this crucial passage from John's Gospel of the Greek idea of truth

being received into the soul in the mode of proceeding forth from it: the living water is taken into the soul in the form of a wellspring that pours forth, welling up to eternal life.

178. See Michael Polanyi, *The Tacit Dimension* (Chicago: University of Chicago Press, 2009).

179. We have noted this in both Dihle and Frede; *FFR*, 286–87.

180. It would of course be possible, and even desirable, to develop a specifically theological account of freedom, which would present a different accent from the conception that we are developing over the course of the three intended volumes. Such a theological theory of freedom would no doubt draw more directly on the biblical sources and would complement the philosophy of freedom offered here.

181. Note that we are speaking specifically of the concept of freedom here, and not of the life of faith, or the condition of human culture, more generally (though of course there can be no absolute separation of these things). In other words, this brief characterization concerns not the state of the church in the world but simply the quality of the interpretation of freedom. The connection between ideas and culture is rarely immediate. A reality can be lived for centuries without being understood in a full and explicit way, while an idea that is first conceived may take centuries before its cultural implications are felt. As Nietzsche observed at the end of the nineteenth century regarding the death of God: "This tremendous event is still on its way, still wandering. Lightning and thunder require time; the light of the stars requires time; deeds, though done, still require time to be seen and heard. This deed is still more distant from them than the most distant stars—*and yet they have done it themselves*" (*The Gay Science* [New York: Vintage Books, 1974], 182). Thoughts are even more like stars than deeds are in this respect: it can be centuries before their light reaches the ground of earth, so to speak, or they may continue to glow on the surface for a time even if in reality they have already gone out.

182. See Ferdinand Ulrich, *Leben in der Einheit von Leben und Tod* (Freiburg: Johannes Verlag Einsiedeln, 1999), 63–79.

183. To say it becomes a "constitutive principle" is not a reduction of grace to nature but rather a recognition that the gratuitous event of redemption has implications for nature, implications that affect nature ontologically.

184. Evidence of freedom in other religions (which of course is there to be seen) does not itself logically constitute proof that this freedom does not ultimately come from the Creator God who reveals his Trinitarian Personhood in Christ and his redemptive deed.

185. We make this argument at greater length in *The Politics of the Real*. Brad Gregory has shown what happens, historically, when the organic conti-

nuity of tradition and all it implies is broken in *The Unintended Reformation: How a Religious Revolution Secularized Society* (Cambridge, MA: Harvard University Press, 2015). Gregory's diagnosis of the "hyperpluralism" of modernity, however, ought to be complemented by a recognition of the absolute monism that is tyrannically imposed by liberalism, which we detail in part 2 of *FFR*.

186. Goethe, from *West-Oestliche Divan*, book V, stanza XV (Berlin: Deutscher Klassiker Verlag, 2010). The original German runs thus: "Wer nicht von dreitausend Jahren / Sich weiß Rechenschaft zu geben, / Bleib in Dunkeln unerfahren, / Mag von Tag zu Tage leben." Balthasar presents this passage from Goethe as the epigraph to his great *Trilogy*.

CHAPTER 2. Plotinus on Freedom as Generative Perfection

1. If there is one figure in the interim centuries about whose interpretation of freedom one could make the case that it rises to the same level, it would be Maximus the Confessor, as we will see in our study of him below.

2. Plotinus did not start writing until he was forty-eight, after having studied and then taught philosophy for decades, and so all of his treatises may be said to come from his maturity. Nevertheless, according to Porphyry, this text was the thirty-ninth he composed out of fifty-four, and so represents a middle stage of his writing, when his thoughts had reached a more complete form, and before a certain decline. In Porphyry's words, the *Enneads* "produced in his middle period reveal his power at its height: these are of the highest perfection"; *On the Life of Plotinus and the Order of His Books*, in *Plotinus*, ed. A. H. Armstrong, vol. 1, Loeb Classical Library (Cambridge, MA: Harvard University Press, 1966), 25.

3. Heraclitus, DK B40. Heraclitus is here criticizing the "eclecticism" of Hesiod, Pythagoras, and so forth. Though Plotinus comments on virtually all of the thinkers we know from the early period, the classic period, and the Hellenistic period of Greek philosophy, he is not eclectic insofar as he orders all of the insights he discovers from others in relation to the Good. In this chapter, we will consider one example of this integration, namely, the notion of freedom.

4. Hans Urs von Balthasar presents Plotinus as the figure who sums up the thinking of the old world (the Greeks) and hands it over to the new (the Christians); *GL*4, 280–81.

5. It is generally accepted that the text to which Plotinus was most immediately responding was the Peripatetic Alexander of Aphrodisias's *On Fate*, which raises the question of the freedom of the gods and the freedom of man it entails. Alexander presents here an excellent foil for the position Plotinus will

develop, insofar as he subordinates the gods' freedom to their nature and subsequently interprets the world as ultimately "deterministic." See R. W. Sharples, *Alexander of Aphrodisias, On Fate* (London: Duckworth, 1983).

6. We will be referring to analogy throughout this book as the proper approach to these fundamental questions, in contrast to univocity or equivocity. The notion of analogy that we take for granted is that of a Thomist sort, illuminated by the Christian Neoplatonic tradition, formulated by Erich Przywara, but deepened (and in a certain respect corrected) by Hans Urs von Balthasar and the Thomistic metaphysics of Gustav Siewerth and Ferdinand Ulrich. See Erich Przywara, *Analogia Entis: Metaphysics — Original Structure and Universal Rhythm* (Grand Rapids, MI: Eerdmans, 2014); Gustav Siewerth, *Analogie des Seienden*, 2nd ed. (Freiburg: Johannes Verlag Einsiedeln, 2003); Georges De Schrijver, *Le merveilleux accord de l'homme et de Dieu: Etude de l'analogie de l'être chez Hans Urs von Balthasar* (Louvain: Peeters, 1983); and Ulrich, *Homo Abyssus*, 201–22. For a complementary sense of analogy, see William Desmond, *The Intimate Strangeness of Being* (Washington, DC: Catholic University of America Press, 2012), 231–59.

7. All citations are to Armstrong's edition (Plotinus, *Enneads*, vol. 7 [Cambridge, MA: Harvard University Press, 1988]), and we will follow his translation (unless explicitly indicating Corrigan and Turner's) but will frequently modify as necessary without always indicating that fact.

8. This general articulation of the structure, though not explicitly indicated in the text, is universally recognized among scholars. Georges Leroux helpfully breaks down the second part even further into three subsections, which reveal a certain similarity between Plotinus's approach and traditional analogy: (1) chapters 7–12, an abstraction from predication (*via negativa*); (2) chapters 13–18, a positive "theology" of the will, in which Plotinus interprets God, so to speak, directly "from himself"; and (3) chapters 19–21, conclusions and spiritual prescriptions. See Georges Leroux, ed. and trans., *Traité sur la liberté et la volonté de l'Un*, by Plotinus (Paris: Vrin, 1990), 92.

9. Deep in the treatise, Plotinus refers to God's being carried in love into his own interior (εἰς τὸ εἴσω, *Ennead* 6.8.16.13), which is not a perspective one can find, for example, in Plato.

10. See also Plotinus's treatise on act and potency, *Ennead* 2.5, which is essentially a speculative elaboration of Aristotle's discussion of the notions in his *Metaphysics*. As we will discuss below, these terms appear regularly in his work and reveal the extent to which he has "interiorized" Aristotle.

11. In his in-depth discussion of the concepts in Plotinus, Hans Buchner contrasts Plotinus too starkly to Aristotle, a result, it seems, of a too simplistically passive reading of Aristotle's notion of potency; *Plotins Möglichkeitslehre*

(Munich: Anton Pustet, 1970), 50–51. Nevertheless, he offers an excellent account of Plotinus's enrichment of the terms (see 56–57), which will represent a pivotal part of our own argument.

12. See *Ennead* 6.8.1.1. Plotinus begins by asking what is in the gods' power but approaches this fundamental question by first asking, more modestly, what is in *our* power (6.8.1.16), recognizing—according to analogy—that the meaning of the phrase will necessarily be radically different in the two cases. The phrase "in one's power" was first used philosophically by Aristotle, but it was first systematically developed in Chrysippus. See Erik Eliasson, *The Notion of That Which Depends on Us in Plotinus and Its Background* (Leiden: Brill, 2008), 5. The phrase is used extensively in philosophical literature, especially by the Stoics. It is arguably the governing phrase, for example, in Epictetus's *Enchiridion*, in which it appears in the first sentence as establishing the distinction that presents the principle for every subsequent judgment.

13. See *Ennead* 6.8.3.20 and 22.

14. As my former colleague Thomas W. Smith used to say, potency of this sort is empty the way a stomach is empty, not the way a box is empty.

15. See our presentation of Locke's notion of power in chapter 1 of *FFR*, 13–63.

16. The very notion of an "axiom" illustrates the classical principle. The word comes from the Greek *axios*, meaning "worthy" or "of great value." An axiom is best because it governs the whole of what follows from it, and it governs the whole of what follows from it because it is best.

17. We see this, for example, in Locke, as we discussed in *FFR* (44–45). As for Hellenistic thinkers, it is illuminating to consider, for example, how little reference Epictetus makes to the Good in his long meditations on the *eph' hēmin*. In fact, for Epictetus, the Good finally *reduces* to that over which we have control; see chapter 19 of the *Enchiridion*, where he says the essence of the Good consists in being in one's power. This is the perfect opposite of the position taken by Plotinus, who cannot say two sentences about power without introducing the Good. To be sure, the Stoics were insistent on the role of *logos*, but as we will see later in this book (in the chapters on Anselm and Scotus), such an insistence tends to a kind of immanentistic reduction when separated from the Good. In general, themes such as impulse, consent, reason, and deliberation, which receive significant development in Stoic thought, remain entirely formal and so do not suffice for an account of freedom. On the significance of the Stoics in the development of a theory of "free will," see Kahn, "Discovering the Will," 233–59, and Sarah Byers, *Perception, Sensibility, and Moral Motivation in Augustine: A Stoic-Platonic Synthesis* (Cambridge: Cambridge University Press, 2013). The most thorough presentation of Stoic ideas on this score

can be found in Brad Inwood, *Ethics and Human Action in Early Stoicism* (Oxford: Clarendon Press, 1985).

18. See Leroux, "Human Freedom in the Thought of Plotinus," in *The Cambridge Companion to Plotinus*, ed. Lloyd Gerson (Cambridge: Cambridge University Press, 1996), 308.

19. *FFR*, 300–306.

20. See Sophocles, *Oedipus Tyrannus*, lines 790–98.

21. For an extensive discussion of goodness as entailing a radical shifting of horizons, see my book *Plato's Critique of Impure Reason* (Washington, DC: Catholic University of America Press, 2008), chap. 2, "A Logic of Violence," 41–84.

22. For Sophocles's sense of the ambiguity of *sophia* as "skill," see the famous choral ode from *Antigone*, lines 332–83. In *Oedipus Tyrannus*, the king is referred to simply as the "most powerful of all" (κράτιστον πᾶσιν), line 40. He is called "wise" at 365, and this is connected to skill and art, which can be used for good or ill.

23. *FFR*, 311–13.

24. See his explicit references to, and systematic refutations of, these accounts in the relatively brief *Ennead* 3.1.

25. On the history of Judaism and early Christianity in the Hellenistic age, see Helmet Koester, *Introduction to the New Testament*, vol. 1, *History, Culture, and Religion of the Hellenistic Age*, and vol. 2, *History and Literature of Early Christianity*, 2nd ed. (New York: Walter de Gruyter, 1995, 2000).

26. It is worth signaling that Scotus will raise this very question a thousand years later (we will address this directly in chapter 11), but, whereas Plotinus goes on to show that Intellect is *more* free, Scotus gives the exact opposite answer. Clearly, the very meaning of freedom, and the conception of reality behind the conception of freedom, has changed in the meantime.

27. Such a subjection to nature is clearly evident in the traditional hierarchy of being at the level of the elements. For a more detailed account of this point, and the contribution (i.e., the *good*) it makes to the hierarchy, see my essay "*Analogia Naturae*: What Does Inanimate Matter Contribute to the Meaning of Life?," *Communio* 38 (Winter 2010): 657–80.

28. The term αὐτεξούσιον became in the Hellenistic and early Christian thinkers a principal term for freedom. Alexander of Aphrodisias was the first to connect it with having things immediately "in our power" (Eliasson, *Notion*, 9). It is found in Epictetus and, as we can see, Plotinus, while Tertullian connected it explicitly with "free will" (Kahn, "Discovering the Will," 250–51). For Gregory of Nyssa, who connected it explicitly with the power to choose, it is our most precious gift (Dihle, *Theory of Will*, 119).

29. Though the main part of the treatise "On the Good or the One" comes after the treatise on freedom in Porphyry's published arrangement, it was written early (number 9). In any event, the theme is a constant reference in virtually all of the *Enneads* from start to finish.

30. We discussed this point in *FFR*, 341.

31. According to the classical tradition, goodness is defined as *desirability*. We will see that it begins to take on the predominant sense of moral duty in Scotus, though seeds of this shift can be found already in Anselm (and one might say even earlier in the Stoics).

32. This form is captured, for example, in Plotinus's description of the soul's "natural movement" (κατὰ φύσιν κίνησις): "a circle around something, something not outside but a center, and the center is that from which the circle derives, then [the soul] will move around this from which it is and will depend on this, bringing itself into accord with that which all souls ought to, and the souls of the gods always do; and it is by bringing themselves into accord with it that they are gods" (*Ennead* 6.9.8.3–8).

33. There are two adjustments we make to the Greek here, both following the suggestions from Corrigan and Turner's translation (Plotinus, *Ennead VI.6: On the Voluntary and on the Free Will of the One* [Las Vegas, NV: Parmenides, 2017], 191–92): they reject Kirchhoff's amendment of ὁρώμενον as ὁρμώμενον because ὁρώμενον is in the manuscript and because it is a more common term in Plotinus. (Neither of these reasons is finally determinative, but we keep the original principally because it is easier to translate the passage thus, though we note that ὁρμώμενον, "the rushing toward," sets the movement of the *pros auto, ex autou* more clearly into relief. However that may be, our interpretation of this passage does not directly depend on this particular term, so we do not need to resolve the issue.) We also remove the first occurrence of the phrase εἴπερ πρὸς αὐτὸ, as most scholars do, because it is repeated again in the second line, and the repetition does not add anything to the sense. It appears to be a copy error.

34. "If then [the intellect] is active according to the Good, it would be still more in its own power, for it has already what goes from itself to it, and in itself what would be better for it, being in it, if it is directed towards it." We note that Armstrong accepts Kirchhoff's amendment of ὁρώμενον as ὁρμώμενον, which he translates here as "what goes."

35. In the line above (*Ennead* 6.8.4.35–36), Plotinus identifies being in one's own power and being free (*kai to eleuthero*). We add it here in brackets just to make the point clear.

36. *Ennead* 6.8.4.37–40, trans. Corrigan and Turner, 88.

37. Not only is this the case grammatically, since the "it" is unspecified, but it makes sense logically and philosophically: If I participate in the Good, am

I in it or is it in me? The answer is clearly both; in this case, my moving from it is its moving from me, and my moving toward it is its moving toward me.

38. So as not to belabor the discussion here, we refer the reader to the more elaborate presentation of just this point in the treatment of Aristotle; *FFR*, 325–39.

39. *FFR*, 352.

40. We will see that Plotinus's reflection on the Good itself will radically reverse this claim, though without in the least denying its basic and abiding truth.

41. In *Ennead* 3.1, "On Fate," a treatise in direct dialogue with the Stoics, Epicureans, and Hellenistic astrologers, Plotinus shows that materialism is inescapably slavery (3.1.2.17 ff.).

42. See our assessment of Locke on this particular point (*FFR*, 63). Contemporary discussions of freedom in analytic philosophy tend to assume that these three options are exhaustive (one need only consider the presentations in recent surveys of what the authors or editors take to cover the entire field: Robert Kane, *A Contemporary Introduction to Free Will* [Oxford: Oxford University Press, 2005]; Gary Watson, ed., *Free Will, Oxford Readings in Philosophy*, 2nd ed. [Oxford: Oxford University Press, 2003]; Michael McKenna and Derk Pereboom, eds., *Free Will: A Contemporary Introduction* [New York: Routledge, 2016]), but Plotinus shows that, considered from a deeper metaphysical point of view, these various positions are not fundamentally different from each other. Instead, they present all together an alternative to *genuine* freedom.

43. The *material* logos or soul of the Stoics does not permit freedom, because freedom requires a transcendence of the corporeal (*Ennead* 3.1.8.9–12). Plotinus's criticism is true regardless of how noble or "spiritual" matter may happen to be. The Stoic metaphysics makes the dilemma simply inevitable. For Plotinus's succinct criticism of even a sophisticated form of materialism, such as that found in the Stoics, see *Ennead* 6.1.25–28.

44. See Leroux, *Traité*, 35, 49–50.

45. Klaus Kremer points to *this* sort of freedom as the essential one in Christianity and then goes on to show that Plotinus is more similar to Christian thought on this score than is often assumed: "Das 'Warum' der Schöpfung: '*Quia Bonus*' vel/et '*Quia Voluit*'? Ein Beitrag zum Verhältnis von Neuplatonismus und Christentum an Hand des Prinzips '*Bonum Est Diffusivum Sui*,'" in *Parusia: Studien zur Philosophie Platons und zur Problemgeschichte des Platonismus*, ed. Kurt Flasch (Frankfurt: Minerva, 1965), 241–64. It remains the case, however, that this "freedom *ad extra*" is finally a *secondary* question for Plotinus and needs to be approached in light of the primary question.

46. *Ennead* 5.1.7.7.

47. Plotinus criticizes Aristotle for failing to appreciate this point, even though he recognizes the transcendence of the first principle (see *Ennead* 5.1.9.7–9), which is why Aristotle remains intracosmic and does not have an unambiguously metaphysical conception of God. See also *Ennead* 5.6 for a full argument devoted to just this point. In this respect, Aristotle is more vulnerable to the "onto-theological" critique than, for example, Thomas Joseph White appreciates; *Wisdom in the Face of Modernity* (Naples, FL: Sapientia Press, 2009).

48. *Ennead* 6.8.8.3 and 10.

49. Plotinus uses the word *hoion* six times, for example, in one (admittedly long) sentence; see *Ennead* 6.8.7.46–54.

50. See *Ennead* 6.8.13.5, trans. Corrigan and Turner, 288.

51. A. H. Armstrong is the best-known scholar to argue for a direct Christian influence; see "Two Views of Freedom," *Studia Patristica XVIII: Papers of the Ninth International Conference on Patristic Studies* (Oxford: Pergamon Press, 1982), 397–406. See also the earlier position of John Rist, *Human Value: A Study in Ancient Philosophical Ethics* (Leiden: Brill, 1982), 99, 108, 111–12, cited by Asger Ousager, *Plotinus on Selfhood, Freedom, and Politics* (Aarhus, Denmark: University of Aarhus Press, 2004), 137–38n217.

52. Leroux, *Traité*, 30; Ousager, *Plotinus on Selfhood*, 139.

53. To take an example, even the surprising description of the One more or less as "Father of the Logos" (in *Ennead* 5.1.6, he presents *Nous* as the "first image of God" and, as such, the "begotten offspring" of the One), though it might immediately suggest Christian influence, can be traced back to Plato's *Letter* VI, 323d, in which this description explicitly appears. Some ancient thinkers suggested Plato had encountered the Jewish tradition, and the reference to his having met the "prophets" in Egypt is certainly intriguing (see Dionysius Laertius, *Lives of the Eminent Philosophers* III.6, trans. R. D. Hicks [Cambridge, MA: Harvard University Press, 1972], 1:280–83), but Plato's letter, even if a forgery, was written before the coming of Christ.

54. Rist, *Augustine Deformed*, 70–71. As for the question regarding consistency with Plotinus's philosophy, Rist had originally presented the philosophy of freedom in *Ennead* 6.8 as a foreign intrusion on Plotinus, which is even in some sense *contradictory* to its basic impulse. Laura Westra, by contrast, claims that the freedom expounded in *Ennead* 6.8 represents the culmination of Plotinus's philosophy. *Plotinus and Freedom: A Study of Ennead 6.8* (Lewiston, NY: Edwin Mellen, 1990), 63.

55. Vincenzo Cilento, *Saggi su Plotino* (Milan: University of Mursia, 1973), 119.

56. Plato raises the question specifically in terms of the gods' love of the pious (*Euthyphro* 10a).

57. See Kremer, "'Warum' der Schöpfung," who claims that some integration of these two claims was present from the beginning (241–42). Robert-Henri Cousineau pointedly suggests that, in Augustine at least, the "Deus-Amor" of revelation synthesizes the otherwise separate "Deus-Bonus" and "Deus-Volens"; "Creation and Freedom: An Augustinian Problem," *Recherches Augustiniennes et Patristiques* 2 (1962): 253. The supposed opposition between the Deus-Bonus and the Deus-Volens is the essence of Strauss's *tertium non datur*, which we discussed in chapter 1.

58. This is not to say that there is no tension here, but just that it is not the governing principle of early Christian thought. While there are figures such as Tertullian, for example, who embrace the opposition and attempt to make clear the distinction between God's self-revelation in Christ and other views of God and the world, the predominant effort is to show the *sense* of Christianity: consider Origen's monumental *Contra Celsum*, for instance. On all of this, see Robert Louis Wilken, *The Spirit of Early Christian Thought* (New Haven, CT: Yale University Press, 2003).

59. Aristotle, *Metaph.* 12.7.1072b14–30.

60. Plotinus distinguishes clearly between "nature" and "being" (which does not preclude his using "nature" in an analogous sense to speak of the One, for example); *Ennead* 6.8.8.18–19. Intellect and being are absolutely correlated to each other; see *Ennead* 5.1.4.21–33. If Aristotle does not work out this distinction, it is nevertheless not a distortion of his thought. Once we see the distinction, we recognize that it had been implicit in Aristotle.

61. *Ennead* 5.1.8.7–10 and 5.1.4.29–30. Plotinus is explicit in his critique of the Peripatetic philosophers on this point (5.3.12).

62. The difference between reason and desire that Aristotle admits on the surface, as it were (see *De anima* 3.10.433a21–26), nevertheless gets resolved in the depths: the primary objects of desire and thought are the same (*Metaph.* 12.7.1072a26–27), which is why the highest actuality can be described simply as self-thinking thought. Note, however, that Aristotle does not *exclude* desire from thought here, which is why his notion can be so readily "taken up," as it were, into the Good and not simply contradicted.

63. In fact, he elaborates the activity of θέλησις precisely as both a kind of βούλησις and a kind of αἵρεσις (*Ennead* 6.8.13.52), using the very terms that dominate Aristotle's analysis of action as both willing the end and choosing the best means to that end. Cf. also *Ennead* 6.8.21.9–19.

64. See Dihle's thorough discussion of these terms in *Theory of Will*, Appendix I, 145–49.

65. All of this will require qualification, as we will show in the next chapter on Augustine.

66. Leroux, *Traité*, 34. It is notable that Charles Kahn, in his otherwise illuminating essay "Discovering the Will," simply leaves Plotinus out of the picture. For Kahn, it is ultimately Aquinas who manages finally to gather up the various elements that had been glimpsed and identified throughout the centuries into a unified theory of will (241). But Plotinus arguably anticipates a significant amount of this. To suggest that Plotinus may be the "discoverer" of will is not to deny the elements that arise in Hellenistic philosophy among the various schools—see Inwood on the Stoics (*Ethics and Human Action*), Tim O'Keefe on Epicurus and the atomists (*Epicurus on Freedom* [Cambridge: Cambridge University Press, 2005]), and Sharples on the Peripatetics (*Alexander of Aphrodisias*)—but only to point out that these elements require a suprarational (and not merely irrational or nonrational) principle to represent actual freedom.

67. Jean Trouillard, *La procession plotinienne* (Paris: Presses universitaires de France, 1955), 77–79.

68. See Dihle's discussion, *Theory of Will*, 1–19, esp. 12.

69. G. K. Chesterton saw this with his usual profundity: see chaps. 2 and 3 from *Orthodoxy* (Nashville, TN: Sam Torode Book Arts, 2009), 9–40.

70. We have made a lengthy case for this claim in *Plato's Critique*, especially chap. 2 (85–138).

71. Ernst Benz presents Plotinus as the first to overcome Greek intellectualism by positing will as the *substance* of God in *Marius Victorinus und die Entwicklung der abendländischen Willensmetaphysik* (Stuttgart: W. Kohlhammer, 1932), 301, while Christoph Horn has more recently argued that Plotinus, even in *Ennead* 6.8, remains resolutely within the horizon of Greek intellectualism; see "The Concept of Will in Plotinus," in *Reading Ancient Texts: Essays in Honor of Denis O'Brien*, vol. 2, *Aristotle and Neoplatonism*, ed. Suzanne Stern-Gillet and Kevin Corrigan (Leiden: Brill, 2007), 153–78. (For a discussion of these positions, see Plotinus, *Ennead VI.6*, trans. Corrigan and Turner, 49–50.) In a sense, we are arguing that both interpretations are correct, but this implies that both are in a certain respect wrong: Horn is right to reject all arbitrariness from Plotinus's sense of will but wrong to subordinate Plotinus's will finally to reason (see "Concept of Will," 177). Benz is right that will transcends reason but wrong to make it an irrational force. It is rather the transcendence of reason in the Good, the very origin of order, that *founds* reason in the fullness of its integrity.

72. This is of course a large claim, and we cannot work out all of the details in the present context (again, we refer to an extensive argument on Platonic terms in *Plato's Critique*, chap. 2), but we may at least indicate a couple of ultimate "instances" of this point in metaphysics: *esse* transcends essence and therefore is not opposed to essence as something over against it but is "superessential"

as the "actuality of all acts"; similarly, the world is not something over against God as a thing to which God is opposed but must lie in some sense *within* God—not in the sense of "pantheism" but more in the sense of "panentheism," properly understood—which is why the only thing *opposed* to God, namely, *sin*, has traditionally been understood not as a positive reality but as a "privation." If the transcendent principle excludes what it transcends, or some part of what it transcends, then it represents an opposition that implies a reduction of it to the same order, juxtaposed, as it were, to that with which it now enters into competition. For an example of this insight, see Robert Spaemann, "Nature," in *The Robert Spaemann Reader* (Oxford: Oxford University Press, 2015), 35–36, who explains that nature can be transcended only if it is simultaneously "recollected" in its fullness.

73. "And [the Good] must be understood as infinite [ἄπειρον] not because its size and number cannot be measured or counted but because its power cannot be comprehended. For when you think of him as intellect or God, he is more" (*Ennead* 6.9.6.11–14). For a thorough argument on this point, see Eric Perl, *Thinking Being: Introduction to Metaphysics in the Classical Tradition* (Leiden: Brill, 2014), 111–23.

74. Aristotle, *Metaph.* 12.7.1072b19–22.

75. At *Ennead* 6.8.8.15–16, Plotinus rejects the notion that the Good acts "according to the way it is by nature," because nature comes after the Good. On the other hand, however, he *does* later refer to the nature of the Good (ἡ ἀγαθοῦ φύσις) in what we might call an analogous sense (6.8.13.38).

76. For Plotinus, life is defined by soul, which mediates intellect to the world extended in time and space (i.e., the "physical" world).

77. The absoluteness of the "self" here is not at all an absolute self-ishness. Quite to the contrary, for Plotinus, the One is not in the first place, or indeed at all, good *for itself*, so it is not self-seeking but good for everything else (as Plotinus says in so many words; *Ennead* 6.9.6.41–42). It is thus not opposed to all things as if it were "outside" them; rather, all things are "inside" the One, or, more adequately, inside and outside are the same. The One encompasses all things (*Ennead* 6.8.18.3–5).

78. We note that Plotinus presents one of the clearest statements of the "essence" of divine freedom in the very first chapter he considers it (the end of chapter 7). The rest is an unfolding of the occasionally surprising implications of this insight. Here we have an exhibition of one of the methods that corresponds to the classical philosophy, one that represents a counterpart to the *anagogē*.

79. *Ennead* 6.8.7.11. There is a great deal of scholarly discussion about the source of the "bold discourse" to which Plotinus responds (see the presentation of the spectrum of interpretations in *Ennead VI.6*, trans. Corrigan and Turner,

40–43). Such discussion, however, seems to suppose that the position is so to speak just randomly introduced. But in fact it is a *perfect* foil, and so, from a philosophical perspective, it does not matter whence it comes, however important the question may be from the perspective of intellectual history.

80. See *Ennead* 6.8.11.8–13.

81. For "happening to be," see *Ennead* 6.8.8.24. For chance, see 6.8.8.26–27.

82. In *this* respect, one can affirm Paul Henry's claim that Plotinus is seeking above all to save human freedom ("Le problème de la liberté chez Plotin," *Revue Philosophique de Louvain* 29–31 (1931): 50–79, 180–215, 318–39). It is indeed the case that Plotinus is concerned to save human freedom (as we will see below), but he is in the first place concerned to do justice to God.

83. Henry, "Problème de la liberté," 320. See Leroux, introduction to *Traité*, 94–98, who criticizes Henry's proposal.

84. In the *Timaeus*, Plato directly contrasts intelligibility and necessity and explains that the material world is made up of both, which is why it does not represent perfect order (see *Tim.* 47e–48a).

85. *Ennead* 6.8.21.8. Cf. Balthasar's presentation of beauty as lying beyond contingency and necessity in *Glaubhaft ist nur Liebe* (Einsiedeln: Johannes Verlag, 1963), 34–35.

86. Werner Beierwaltes, *Das Wahre Selbst: Studien zu Plotins Begriff des Geistes und des Einen* (Frankfurt: Klostermann, 2001), especially the two chapters "*Causa Sui*: Plotins Begriff des Einen als Ursprung des Gedankens der Selbstursächlichkeit" and "Plotins Gedanken in Schelling." Beierwaltes takes Plotinus to be the originator of the vision that comes to fruition in this radical current of modern philosophy. We contest that interpretation here but will suggest at the end of the chapter how a latent ambiguity in Plotinus on this point would lead to this view if it is not taken up into a Christian vision. In other words, our suggestion is going to be that this irrationalism will come about to the extent that the Christian appropriation of this classical insight fails. Leroux claims that modern philosophy represents a subjectivistic reduction of the genuinely novel point Plotinus here introduces (introduction to *Traité*, 86–87).

87. For example, *Ennead* 6.8.21.1 and 6.8.15.9.

88. All of this is presented in relatively succinct fashion in the collection of texts found in Heidegger, *End of Philosophy*.

89. See *Ennead* 5.2.1.8–10.

90. This is the principal argument of *Ennead* 3.8, "On Nature and the Contemplation of the One."

91. In addition to ἔρως, Plotinus also uses in the subsequent chapter the verbal form of ἀγαπή three times to describe God's self-relation (*Ennead* 6.8.16.14–16).

92. It is worth noting that the Greek verb "to love," ἐράω, does not take a direct object (accusative) but a genitive object: the object is not what the subject *acts on* but rather what it *receives from* ("genitive of the end desired"; see Herbert Weir Smythe, *A Greek Grammar for Colleges* [Cambridge, MA: Harvard University Press, 1956], 1349). This grammatical form expresses a profound metaphysical truth: the good ("end desired") always precedes action as internal to it; it is never simply an external object of that action.

93. Plato, *Symp.* 202c–d.

94. In the earlier discussion, he had used the usual word ὄρεξις, while here he uses the more violent and aggressive ἔφεσις, but both refer to the same thing, namely, desire as appetite.

95. Plotinus is fully aware of the contradiction this appears to imply: in *Ennead* 6.8.7.26–27, he presents self-making as a self-evident impossibility.

96. We see an example of this sort of argument in Aquinas's treatise *On the Eternity of the World*, which thus demonstrates that there is no contradiction in holding *both* that the world is eternal *and* that it is created out of nothing.

97. See *Ennead* 6.8.8.13–14. It should be noted that to affirm the Good as subsisting "before eternity" or "before being" or "before logic" is not an explanation, if "to explain" means to demonstrate how this condition fits into the given categories of being and logic—which would of course not be an explanation in the present case but a performative self-refutation. The statement that the Good is "before eternity" in itself is a *kind* of explanation in the negative and indirect sense of the exhibition of the self-contradictory implication of the denial of the claim. But the first principle of all thought and being cannot be itself explained (on the basis of something that therefore precedes it); it can only be acknowledged, though in such a way that thinking finds itself solidified and confirmed (see my *Plato's Critique*, 158–59). As Chesterton put it, "The whole secret is this: that man can understand everything by the help of what he does not understand. The morbid logician seeks to make everything lucid, and succeeds in making everything mysterious. The mystic allows one thing to be mysterious, and everything else becomes lucid" (*Orthodoxy*, 23).

98. *FFR*, 325–31.

99. As Aristotle shows, act precedes potency in every sense but one, namely, in the chronological order of individual beings, in which potency precedes act; see *Metaph.* 9.8.

100. On this, see Buchner, *Möglichkeitslehre*, 32–34, 50–51. Buchner claims that Plotinus reverses Aristotle, but he seems to oversimplify Aristotle's view of potency as sheer passivity. In *FFR*, we argued for a richer, more dynamic view. Plotinus *affirms* Aristotle's view of the priority of actuality over potency, which we will show below. There is thus more continuity between

the views of Aristotle and Plotinus than Buchner allows, though he is right that the absolute transcendence of the good is the key here.

101. See, for example, *Ennead* 6.1.26.1–7: "For it is not possible for what is in potency ever to come to actuality if the potential holds the rank of principle among beings: for it certainly will not bring itself to actuality, but the actual must be before it, and then this potential will no longer be a principle."

102. "If actuality is more perfect than substance, and the first is most perfect, then the first will be actuality" (*Ennead* 6.8.20.14–16).

103. Of course, for reasons that become clear, he later on *denies* that the Good is determinate in this way. See *Ennead* 6.8.9.44: the Good is now ἀόριστον.

104. Heidegger observes, for example, that the limit, for Greeks, is what forms a thing so that it can open up and begin to be what it will be; "Question Concerning Technology," in *Basic Writings* (San Francisco: Harper Perennial, 2008), 315. He nevertheless offers a reading of *apeiron* as the openness of Being; see his discussions in *The Beginning of Western Philosophy: Interpretations of Anaximander and Parmenides* (Bloomington: Indiana University Press, 2015).

105. *Ennead* 6.8.20.14–16.

106. Activity, as the bringing about of something, happens according to the Good, or in other words refers to a higher principle (*Ennead* 6.8.9.22–23).

107. Aristotle, *Metaph.* 14.1.1087b1–5.

108. Again, see the clear statement in *Ennead* 6.9.6.11–14; cf. 6.8.9.40. According to Norris Clarke, Plotinus is the first philosopher explicitly to recognize infinity as a perfection. "The Limitation of Act by Potency in St. Thomas: Aristotelianism or Neoplatonism?," in *Explorations in Metaphysics* (Notre Dame, IN: University of Notre Dame Press, 1994), 65–88.

109. See Buchner, *Möglichkeitslehre*, 99–102. As we will explain, Plotinus generally privileges the name δύναμις πάντων but uses *actuality* for the One in *Ennead* 6.8. It may be true that the Scholastic tradition has tended to describe God as "pure act," while the Greek tradition has tended more to the language of potency—see Michel Barnes, *The Power of God: Dynamis in Gregory of Nyssa's Trinitarian Theology* (Washington, DC: Catholic University of America Press, 2016)—but the difference ought not to be exaggerated, since the notions are not ultimately opposed in a simplistic manner. We will see the importance of potency in Aquinas's interpretation in the chapter below, and we see already here how Plotinus himself uses *both* potency and act to describe God. Barnes's judgment that the act-potency distinction played a much smaller role in Neoplatonic thought than is typically assumed (18) is simply false. Plotinus refers to *energeia*, for example, much more often even than Aristotle does (the term appears 768 times in Plotinus's much smaller corpus, compared to 537 times in Aristotle; see Curtis L. Hancock, "Energeia in the

Enneads of Plotinus: A Reaction to Plato and Aristotle" [PhD diss., Loyola University of Chicago, 1984], 1n3).

110. In *Ennead* 6.8.16.30 ff., Plotinus specifies that the actuality of the One is not so much an accomplishment as a kind of "being awake" or "wakefulness" (ἐγρήγορσις), which is more like an abiding openness than a final, once-and-for-all closure.

111. In *Ennead* 5.1.7.12–14, Plotinus says that intellect *itself* has the power to produce *being* and "by its own means [δι' αὐτὸν] even defines its being for itself by the power that comes from the One." The image is of the higher giving power, which enables the lower to enact itself. On all of this, see Brandon Zimmerman, "Plotinian Emanation as a Dynamic of Procession and Return" (MA thesis, Catholic University of America, 2009).

112. See *Ennead* 5.3.15.32–34, in which Plotinus denies that the One can be an actuality (which peaks, we might say, at the level of intellect) but has to be (a unique kind of) *potency*. Cf. Buchner, *Möglichkeitslehre*, 99.

113. See *Ennead* 2.4.16. It is wrongly assumed that Plotinus thus condemns the material world, but the inference is too simple. If he considers matter evil, it is because it is nonbeing, and all being is good. Thus, if matter, as a principle of unreality, is evil, material things are not. For an impassioned case on this point, see Plotinus's treatise "Against the Gnostics," *Ennead* 2.9. This is an early articulation of the classical *privatio boni* theory of evil, generally accepted by the Christian tradition. Nevertheless, there are certain ambiguities on this point that we will address in our discussions of Augustine and Dionysius.

114. See *Ennead* 2.4.15.20. From this perspective, we note an ambiguity in the notion of actuality, which corresponds to the ambiguity of (divine or material) potency: it can mean either *higher perfection* (with respect to potency as lower) or *mere fact* (with respect to potency as higher). See Buchner, *Möglichkeitslehre*, 34, 137n37.

115. See 5 *Ennead* 4.2. Buchner, *Möglichkeitslehre*, 105.

116. See *Ennead* 6.8.14.32–33. It is to be noted that Plotinus uses the verb here "to give" (διδόναι). He refers to existence elsewhere as a "gracious gift" (ἐν χάριτα δόντος); *Ennead* 4.8.6.23.

117. The intellect is not "dead" actuality: "In intellect, there is desire, and it is always desiring and always attaining" (*Ennead* 3.8.10.23–25). Plotinus also describes the knowing of the intellect as simultaneously "a certain longing for, and a certain discovery of, what one is seeking" (*Ennead* 5.3.10.49–51). Note that we are *not* saying Aristotle is *opposed* to this claim, only that it remains implicit in his description. What Plotinus elaborates here is not altogether different from Gregory of Nyssa's celebrated notion of *epektasis*. Cilento (*Saggi su Plotino*, 100) describes Plotinian freedom as an eternal power of renewal.

118. But in fact, as we suggested earlier, the One's radical introversion is simultaneously a radical extroversion; inside and outside are in a certain respect the same, though this does not in the least imply a *dependence* of the One on the things that follow upon it. For an example of a simplistic reading of Plotinus on this score, as radically self-related and cut off from all that is other, one might consult Brendan Thomas Sammon, *The God Who Is Beauty* (Eugene, OR: Pickwick, 2013), 185–203.

119. One cannot help but think here of Nietzsche's line from the preface to the second edition of *The Gay Science*: "'Is it true that God is present everywhere?' a little girl asked her mother; 'I think that's indecent'—a hint for philosophers! One should have more respect for the bashfulness with which nature has hidden behind riddles and iridescent uncertainties" (38). We might add: one should have more respect for finite freedom. Note that we are not in the least denying God's omnipresence, only a crass interpretation of that omnipresence.

120. Buchner, *Möglichkeitslehre*, 52–54. The One produces by giving a shapeless energy that the recipient *forms* (εἰδοποιεῖτο) by actively turning to the source (*Ennead* 3.4.1.9–10).

121. *Ennead* 2.9.3.6–7, "power beyond measure"; *Ennead* 4.8.6.12, "power beyond saying."

122. Buchner, *Möglichkeitslehre*, 87. See *Ennead* 5.4.2.27–30: "In each and every thing there is an activity which belongs to substance and one which goes out from substance; and that which belongs to substance is the active actuality which is each particular thing, and the other activity derives from that first one, and must in everything be a consequence of it, different from the thing itself."

123. See *Ennead* 2.4. Denis O'Brien offers an elucidation of this point in "Plotinus on Matter and Evil," in *The Cambridge Companion to Plotinus* (Cambridge: Cambridge University Press, 1996), 171–95. Cf. Zimmerman, "Plotinian Emanation," 10. But this does not mean that matter is left out of the picture, so to speak. This is why the soul is required to exercise *particular* providential care, through its *historical action*, on what the One cannot attend to, as it were, on its own. Plotinus refers (*Ennead* 3.4.2.1–4) to Plato for this notion (*Phdr.* 246b).

124. See *Ennead* 5.4.1.32–34: all things "imitate the First Principle as far as they are able by tending to everlastingness and generosity [ἀγαθότητα]." In *Ennead* 2.9.3.8, Plotinus expresses this generosity as a general principle: "It is necessary that each thing should give of itself to an other." For a commentary on this, see John Rist, *Plotinus: The Road to Reality* (Cambridge: Cambridge University Press, 2010), 74, who explains that this is not an absolute but a hypothetical necessity.

125. See *Ennead* 1.1.12 and *Ennead* 4.8.5.10–15. This is a principal point of explanation for Henry, "Problème de liberté." Cf. Leroux, "Human Freedom," 296–97; Balthasar, *GL4*, 285; Rist, *Road to Reality*, 112–29. Rist offers an excellently balanced presentation of Plotinus on this point.

126. Note that this is a deficiency measured against what the One always already is, namely, the productive power of all things, rather than a deficiency measured against the One in itself in *abstraction* from its being the productive power of all things. We observe that Plotinus's reflection begins in and with reality rather than bracketing it and subordinating the world that actually is to an abstraction as a mere "subset" thereof. We will see that this is the *decisive* move of late-medieval nominalism, as we mentioned last chapter (note 108) and will elaborate especially in the discussion of Scotus.

127. Plotinus connects this manifestation of hidden powers with the experience of *wonder* at things (*Ennead* 4.8.5.36–38), which suggests the production of a genuine novelty.

128. We note the extraordinary allusion here to history, but we also note the essentially Greek sense, which is different from the Hebraic sense we discussed last chapter: for Plotinus, history is a revelation specifically *of eternity*.

129. *Ennead* 4.8.7.12–15.

130. It is *indeed* true that—in one respect at least—the soul is *strictly unaffected* by the body, so that its passions are understood as "proceeding from" the soul rather than being imposed on the soul from the outside, which means that all of its experiences are "already" in some sense "precontained." Buchner is therefore right to point this out (31–32), and it remains a crucial point. But we also see that this truth must be qualified and paradoxically integrated with what Plotinus lays out in these chapters of *Ennead* 4.8. He says explicitly that the soul "gives something to [the material world] of what it has in itself and receives something from it in return" (ἀντιλαμβάνειν, *Ennead* 4.8.7.8–9). As we have indicated, the Greek form of freedom is a receiving *as* a proceeding forth, which means a proceeding forth that is *also* a receiving. There is a certain tension here, to be sure, but it may not be prematurely relieved by a unilateral reduction. Instead, we will be arguing that it must be elevated and transformed, which is what a Christian vision allows.

131. This is Armstrong's problematic interpretation; see *The Architecture of the Intelligible Universe: The Philosophy of Plotinus* (Cambridge: Cambridge University Press, 1940), 62–63. Kremer is right to respond to this problem by referring to the absolute generosity of the One, which is not a potency to be actualized ("'Warum' der Schöpfung," 245–46).

132. See *Ennead* 3.1.1.1–2. Cilento, incidentally, observes that Plotinus is the first Greek to recognize the mystery of existence (beyond, that is, the being of substance); *Saggi su Plotino*, 103.

133. Here we see that Plotinus anticipates the notion Arendt celebrates in Augustine: namely, man as *initium* (Augustine preserves *principium* for the absolute creation of the world), that is, capacity *to begin* a series of events in time. Hannah Arendt, *Life of the Mind* (New York: Harcourt and Brace, 1978), 108–10.

134. See, for example, Brown, *Freedom, Philosophy, and Faith*, 50–51.

135. Balthasar rightly says that "Plotinus stands in awe and wonder before the glory of the cosmos" (*GL4*, 282). *Glory* is a quasi-technical term for Balthasar, indicating the "epiphany" of a reality that transcends the material world and its forms. There is thus a certain connection between the "glory" of freedom in Plotinus's vision and his offering something *really like* a theology in *Ennead* 6.8.

136. Leo Sweeney goes so far as to propose that Plotinus is not expressing his own philosophy in *Ennead* 6.8 but instead defending a position different from his own against the Gnostics; see Westra, *Plotinus and Freedom*, 64.

137. See Plotinus's grappling with precisely this dilemma at *Ennead* 5.3.15.1–7. Note that the terms of the dilemma cast here are those of generosity: giving and providing.

138. There is *nothing at all* prior to the divine will (*Ennead* 6.8.21.15).

139. See *Ennead* 5.2.2.1–3. In *Ennead* 5.3.15.8–12, Plotinus argues that the intellect must be *other* than the One, but this means it has to be *either* better *or* worse. Plotinus concludes: "It must be worse."

140. According to Plotinus, the "self" (τὸ αὐτὸ) is absolute and prior to any particular thing (τὶ) (*Ennead* 5.3.12.52–53).

141. See *Ennead* 6.8.21.31–32, where Plotinus says that God is perfect freedom because he is not enslaved even to himself.

142. "Providence ought not to exist in such a way as to make us nothing. If everything was providence and nothing but providence, then providence would not exist; for what would it have to provide for?" (*Ennead* 3.2.9.1–3).

143. *Ennead* 6.9.11.51. This passage was not written last, but Porphyry insightfully placed it last in his published arrangement of the *Enneads*.

CHAPTER 3. Augustine and the Gift of the Power to Choose

1. "There are none who are nearer to us [Christians] than the Platonists." *De civ. Dei* 8.5 (PL 41), trans. Henry Bettenson, *City of God* (New York: Penguin, 1984), 304. Augustine also says in *De ver. rel.* 7 (PL 34), "If [the Platonists] could live their lives again today, with the change of a few words and sentiments, they would become Christian" (trans. J. H. S. Burleigh, *Of True Religion* [Chicago: Henry Regnery, 1959], 9). This accords well with what we have

argued in chapter 1. Let us lay some emphasis on the importance of Augustine's wide reading, which might be passed over too quickly. We do not often think of *reading* as a decisive part of the Christian mission, but this is no doubt partly due to the modern tendency to moralize Christianity: *the* most fundamental task of Christianity, prior to everything else, is to *receive* it as a gift, and the reception of tradition is essential, a reception that happens in a decisive way precisely in education. One thinks of the beautiful tradition in art that depicts Mary—*the* Christian—as *reading*, contemplating the Word of God in scripture. The image is drawn from Luke 2:19.

2. *Conf.* 3.5 (PL 32), trans. R. S. Pine-Coffin, *Confessions* (New York: Penguin, 1961), 60.

3. John Rist, *Augustine: Ancient Thought Baptized* (Cambridge: Cambridge University Press, 1996).

4. Among the many studies in English, see especially John Burnaby, *Amor Dei: A Study of the Religion of St. Augustine* (London: Hodder and Staughton, 1938); Mary Clark, *Augustine, Philosopher of Freedom* (New York: Desclee, 1958); Dihle, *Theory of Will*; Arendt, *Life of the Mind*, vol. 2; T. D. J. Chappell, *Aristotle and Augustine on Freedom: Two Theories of Freedom, Voluntary Action, and Akrasia* (New York: St. Martin's Press, 1995); James Wetzel, *Augustine and the Limits of Virtue* (Cambridge: Cambridge University Press, 1992); Byers, *Perception, Sensibility*; Rist, *Augustine Deformed*.

5. See Sarah Byers, "The Meaning of *Voluntas* in Augustine," *Augustinian Studies* 37.2 (2006): 171–89; Kahn, "Discovering the Will," 255; Rist, *Augustine Deformed*, 27–29.

6. This is the interpretation one finds, for example, in Thomas Williams's introduction to *On Free Choice of the Will* (Bloomington, IN: Hackett, 1993), xi–xix; cf. also O'Keefe, *Epicurus on Freedom*, 160–62; Dihle, *Theology of Will*, 127; Alasdair MacIntyre, *Whose Justice, Which Rationality* (Notre Dame, IN: University of Notre Dame Press, 1988), 156.

7. To demonstrate this is a basic thrust of Wetzel's *Augustine*: "There is no faculty of will, distinct from desire, which we use to determine our actions" (8). Chappell refers to the action of this independent will as giving its "royal assent" (*Aristotle and Augustine*, 202). On the non-Augustinian idea of the will as a separate faculty, see also John Rist, "Love and Will: Around *De Trinitate* XV, 20, 38," in *Gott und Sein Bild*, ed. J. Brachtendorf (Munich: Paderborn, 2000), 205–18.

8. Rist, *Augustine Deformed*, 87. Rist seems to imply that the fate of Western civilization rests on an error in scholarship, namely, that behind the "deformed" conception of freedom that comes to dominate in the West lies an ignorance of Augustine's sources in the reception of Augustine himself. We are proposing to recast this ignorance of sources as essentially a failure to receive

the whole tradition. The cause of this failure ought to be interpreted in as comprehensive a way as possible.

9. *De Trin.* 15.20.38 (PL 42), trans. Edmund Hill, *The Trinity* (New York: New City Press, 1991), 430.

10. See his famous presentation of love as a *weight*; *Conf.* 13.9 (PL 32), trans. Pine-Coffin, 317.

11. Some mistakenly think that Augustine comes to deny this in his *Auseinandersetzung* with Pelagius, but this judgment presupposes a false dichotomy, as we will explain below.

12. Hannah Arendt makes a similar point: see her *Life of the Mind*, 2:102.

13. Rist, *Augustine Deformed*, 27.

14. We are not suggesting that Augustine "first" became Christian, then surveyed the philosophical options and selected certain elements. The movement of the spirit, divine, human, and historical, is of course much more mysterious: one might just as well say it was his attraction to certain elements in philosophy that opened him up to Christian conversion. The point we are making is not a positivistically historical one but a description of the "form" of his thought.

15. Because it is unsystematic, we cannot approach Augustine's notion through the exposition of a single work, as we did with Plotinus. Instead, we have to draw in a somewhat eclectic way on a variety of works, but we hope to bring a certain unity to the chapter by relating these aspects to the theme of Christianity as a synthesis of Greeks and Jews.

16. Lewis Ayres has provided a convincing defense of Augustine as a genuinely "Trinitarian" theologian in *Augustine and the Trinity* (Cambridge: Cambridge University Press, 2012). We will not enter here into the historical debate regarding, for example, the adequacy of Augustine's pneumatology and so forth. Instead, we read him here simply as a representative of orthodox Trinitarian theology.

17. Again, Rist has made this claim; see "Love and Will."

18. Evan Kuehn has drawn attention to this theme in Augustine; see "The Johannine Logic of Augustine's Trinity: A Dogmatic Sketch," *Theological Studies* 68.3 (2007): 572–94.

19. Ayres, *Augustine and the Trinity*, 16. But we must be careful not to oversimplify and thus oppose Plotinus and Augustine.

20. According to Josef Lössl, "Augustine does not abandon his [earlier, Platonic] intellectualism when he increases his use of the Bible"; see his "Intellect with a [Divine] Purpose: Augustine on the Will," in *The Will and Human Action*, ed. Thomas Pink and M. W. F. Stone (New York: Routledge, 2004), 58.

21. Cousineau, "Creation and Freedom," 253.

22. Plato, *Phdr.* 250a.

23. In fact, Augustine is regularly criticized for accepting this, on the grounds that it seems to compromise his interpretation of the *biblical* God who is personally involved with his creation. On this point, see Ronald J. Teske, *To Know God and the Soul: Essays on the Thought of Saint Augustine* (Washington, DC: Catholic University of America Press, 2008), 131–55. For a contemporary defense of God's immutability, see David Bentley Hart, *The Doors of the Sea* (Grand Rapids, MI: Eerdmans, 2011).

24. See *Conf.* 13.1 (PL 32).

25. More precisely, beauty first initiates eros, which is always in that sense *responsive*; but eros nevertheless arises in the human soul rather than being given to it, as it were. To put it simply, Plato would never say that *the Good loves the human soul*.

26. *De catechizandis rudibus* 4.7, cited in Rist, *Augustine: Ancient Thought Baptized*, 158.

27. *De civ. Dei* 12.1 (PL 41), trans. Bettenson, 471. Note that Augustine even proposes thinking of the Trinitarian relations in terms of "friendship"; *De Trin.* 7.6.11 (PL 42), trans. Hill, 232. Augustine's theme of friendship with God integrates the Jewish sense of holy covenant with the Greek sense of friendship in the Good. For a fuller account of his notion of friendship, see J. T. Lienhard, "Friendship with God, Friendship in God: Traces in St. Augustine," in *Augustine: Mystic and Mystagogue*, ed. Frederick von Fleteren, Joseph C. Schnaubelt, and Joseph Reino (New York: Peter Lang, 1994), 207–29.

28. *De civ. Dei* 19.11–14 (PL 41), trans. Bettenson, 865–74.

29. *De civ. Dei* 12.9 (PL 41), trans. Bettenson, 483. On the essentially dialogical character of man's relation to God in Augustine, see Scott J. Roniger, "The Conversation of Ascent: Augustine's *Confessions*, Book IX, Chapter 10," *Communio* 43.4 (Winter 2016): 675–94.

30. *De civ. Dei* 19.5 (PL 41), trans. Bettenson, 858.

31. In *De Trin.* 15.26.47 (PL 42), trans. Hill, 437–38, Augustine describes a kind of "searching appetite" that precedes actual knowledge, even if this is not what he designates as love in the most proper sense. The will, he explains, is *perfected* in love understood as established bond. The verb that Augustine tends to use for love is *coniungere*, to "join together," which is one of the things that distinguishes love from simple desire; see, for example, *De Trin.* 9.5.8 and 9.12.18.

32. See Dihle, *Theory of Will*, 107. The second person is named "Dynamis," the mother of life, who cooperates with Nous, the father. Cf., for example, *Chaldean Oracles*, frag. 4.

33. Pierre Hadot, "L'image de la Trinité dans l'âme chez Victorinus et chez saint Augustin," *Studia Patristica* 6 (1962): 429. Cf. Ayres, *Augustine and the Trinity*, 211n36.

34. See Augustine's commentary on this text in *Love One Another, My Friends: Homilies on the First Letter of John*, trans. John Leinenweber (New York: Harper and Row, 1989), 68–71.

35. *De Trin*. 15.17.29 and 15.19.36 (PL 42), trans. Hill, 422–23, 428–29.

36. Augustine, *Love One Another*, 80.

37. The Holy Spirit is the Person who also Personalizes the divine nature as such: he is Spirit, but God is Spirit; he is Love, but God is love. His representing the divine nature, as it were, is one of the reasons his distinct Personhood was not as obvious in the early stages of reflection on the Trinity.

38. See *De Trin*. 8.10.14 (PL 42), trans. Hill, 257. As Augustine puts it, when you see love, you see the Trinity (8.8.12, trans. Hill, 255). In the last chapter, we saw that Plotinus, too, thinks of God in some sense as lover, beloved, and love between them; but in Plotinus it is a metaphor to describe the One's "self-relation," which is radically different from bond as fully actual Person, in absolute oneness with the Persons of Lover and Beloved.

39. Rist, *Augustine: Ancient Thought Baptized*, 181.

40. See *De Trin*. 5.17.22 (PL 42), trans. Hill, 364: "What greater example of obedience could be given to us, us who had been ruined by disobedience, than God the Son obeying God the Father even to death on the cross (Phil 2:8)?" We are not entering into the subtle distinctions necessary in Trinitarian theology, which were not worked out in any event in their fullness in Augustine's time: i.e., the distinction between the economic and immanent Trinity, the question of the extent to which obedience belongs to the Son specifically as incarnate, the question as to what extent there is an analogy between creaturely obedience and immanent filiality, and so forth.

41. See Kuehn, "Johannine Logic."

42. *De civ. Dei* 14.5 (PL 41), trans. Bettenson, 575: "The retribution for disobedience is simply disobedience itself. For man's wretchedness is nothing but his own disobedience to himself."

43. *Conf*. 3.6.11 (PL 32), trans. Pine-Coffin, 62.

44. This does not mean obedience is given an ulterior motive, so to speak, which would eliminate its obediential character. Such an elimination would be the case only insofar as eros is reduced to self-interest, but this is quite evidently *not* Augustine's conception.

45. We recall that it is the ambiguity on this point that led Mueller to misread Aristotle in a liberal direction; see *FFR*, 309, 443n81. Thus, Augustine's conception clarifies this ambiguity in a positive direction.

46. This is the potential problem in the interpretation by Wetzel (*Augustine*), who attempts to interpret Augustinian will exhaustively in terms of desire.

47. It is sometimes said that Augustine eventually came to reject his strong emphasis on free choice of the will, articulated perhaps most clearly in *De libero arbitrio*, but it is illuminating to see that in his final reassessment of his work at the end of his life he does not disown or even qualify but *defends* his formulations from the earlier period. We will come back to this point at the very end of this chapter, arguing that the mature position on grace and will does not exclude his earlier notions in principle but simply requires a further clarification, which is brought out in the continuing tradition. See his *Retractions*, trans. Sister M. Inez Bogan (Washington, DC: Catholic University of America Press, 1968), 32–40.

48. *SL* 30.52 (PL 44), trans. Holmes.

49. *SL* 2.4 (PL 44), trans. Holmes.

50. This is the problem in Sarah Byers's judgment regarding an "evolution" in Augustine's thought, from grace as operating interiorly to its operating extrinsically, which she claims is a trajectory Augustine follows twice (!), having forgotten his first resolution and thus retracing steps he had made previously (see *Perception, Sensibility*, 208–12). This is a strange and speculative interpretation and depends on a sense that interior and exterior help are either-or alternatives, which is just the point we are contesting. Byers seems to fall into a Pelagian assumption that one has to negotiate between divine and human freedom. (Wetzel is much more satisfying on this point, though he does not do sufficient justice to the active, self-moving dimension of obedience, which we mentioned above.) All of this being said, we can still speak of a shift of emphasis, and even an eventual imbalance in formulation, which we will explain at the end of this chapter.

51. *SL* 9.15 (PL 44), trans. Holmes.

52. *SL* 2.2 (PL 44), trans. Holmes, my emphasis.

53. Byers, "Meaning of *Voluntas*," 171. Brad Inwood discusses the difficulty of translating the notion of *hormē* in the Stoics; see his *Ethics and Human Action*, 45.

54. This is not to say that there is no moral content; it turns out that one has control finally only over what is *rational*, which is to say what is according to nature, or indeed even according to the will of God; see Inwood, *Ethics and Human Action*, 194–215.

55. *De civ. Dei* 14.6 (PL 41), trans. Bettenson, 555.

56. See *De Trin.* 11.5.9 (PL 42), trans. Hill, 312–13.

57. See R. A. Gauthier, "Maxime le Confesseur et la psychologie de l'acte humaine," *Recherches de Théologie Ancienne et Médiévale* 21 (1954): 90–91. Cf. Richard Sorabji, "Freedom and Will: Graeco-Roman Origins," in *Selfhood and the Soul: Essays on Ancient Thought and Literature in Honour of Christo-*

pher Gill, ed. Richard Seaford, John Wilkins, and Matthew Wright (Oxford: Oxford University Press, 2017), 49–66. For Augustine's notion of consent, see *SL* 34.60 (PL 44), trans. Holmes. Simo Knuuttila, "The Emergence of the Logic of Will in Medieval Thought," in *The Augustinian Tradition*, ed. Gareth B. Matthews (Berkeley: University of California Press, 1998), 209 (cf. 210–11), explains that passions for Augustine, in contrast to the Stoics who made them agitations of soul prior to judgment, are already *evaluative*, which implies that the soul is already actively engaged, so to speak. Simon Harrison observes that Augustine's conversion coincides with a shift from a more passive to a more active sense of action (see *Conf.* 7.3.5 [PL 32]); "Do We Have a Will? Augustine's Way into the Will," in Matthews, *Augustinian Tradition*, 209. We recall that Plotinus also had argued that passions proceed *from* the soul; see Buchner, *Plotins Möglichkeitslehre*, 31.

58. To be sure, Augustine does describe the prelapsarian state as the complete subjection of the passions of the body to reason, so that even the impulse for sexual intercourse would arrive altogether at command (see *De civ. Dei* 14.23 [PL 41], trans. Bettenson, 585–87). This does indeed suggest a Stoic privileging of rational control, but it should be noted he is speaking here of the subjection of the body to the soul and not about the soul's self-relation.

59. See Chappell, *Aristotle and Augustine*, 155, and Lössl, "Intellect." Wetzel refers to Augustine's view of freedom as "maximally intellectualist," though he is relentless in his critique of a view of freedom that would reduce it to that over which we have deliberate control (*Augustine*, 231).

60. See *Conf.* 10.8 (PL 32), trans. Pine-Coffin, 214–16, and *De Trin.*, bk. 14 (PL 42).

61. Arendt remarks that this insight into memory is precisely what marks Augustine as a *Roman* thinker, as distinct from the Greeks; it is interesting to note that *memoria* tended to disappear in the medieval accounts of the *imago Trinitatis*, which presented the powers of the soul. See Arendt, "What Is Authority?," 126.

62. In *SL* 34.60 (PL 44), trans. Holmes, Augustine says that there is no consent that is not an act of will but that *all* of it is a gift from God: "To yield our consent, indeed, to God's summons, or to withhold it, is (as I have said) the function of our own will. And this not only does not invalidate what is said, 'For what do you have that you did not receive?' [1 Cor 4:7] but it really confirms it. For the soul cannot receive and possess these gifts, which are here referred to, except by yielding its consent. And thus whatever it possesses, and whatever it receives, is from God; and yet the act of receiving and having belongs, of course, to the receiver and possessor." There is clearly a paradox here, but this is to be expected, one might say (with some irony), since we are dealing

with two *radically different* causal orders. The paradox turns into a contradiction only when we negotiate between the orders as two causal forces operating within the same order.

63. Aristotle, *Phys.* 7.1.241b25–242a16.

64. This is not a turning of attention, which would be reduced to one (unmoved) part acting on another (moved) part, but a revolution, so to speak, in the soul precisely as a whole. Note that Plato sought to describe just this in the soul's ultimate relation to the Good (*Rep.* 518c).

65. Augustine, *Conf.* 8.5 (PL 32), trans. Pine-Coffin, 164.

66. Plato, *Phdr.* 82d.

67. For a more ample discussion of this problem, see my essay "Freedom beyond Our Choosing: Augustine on the Will and Its Objects," *Communio* 29.4 (Winter 2002): 618–53.

68. The Manichee psychology, Augustine shows, is fundamentally incoherent; see *Conf.* 8.10 (PL 32), trans. Pine-Coffin, 172–75. Cf. his sustained critique in *Of Two Souls: Against the Manichees*.

69. *Conf.* 8.10 (PL 32), trans. Pine-Coffin, 175.

70. *Conf.* 8.8 (PL 32), trans. Pine-Coffin, 170.

71. This is not to say that Augustine "invented" the private space of introspection, as Phillip Cary argues in *Augustine's Invention of the Inner Self: The Legacy of a Christian Platonist* (Oxford: Oxford University Press, 2000). See Michael Hanby's critique of the central thesis in *Augustine and Modernity* (New York: Routledge, 2002), 181–82n4.

72. *Conf.* 8.9 (PL 32), trans. Pine-Coffin, 172.

73. We will not elaborate the point here, but this is how Augustine avoids the problem of freedom and divine foreknowledge: God knows the will, and causes it, but he knows and causes it specifically as will. This means he knows the will in the full integrity of its nature, which is to be the self-initiating source of action. We will return to this briefly below. See *De civ. Dei* 5.9–10 (PL 41), trans. Bettenson, 190–95, and *De lib. arb.* 3.2–4 (PL 32), trans. Thomas Williams, *On Free Choice of the Will* (Bloomington, IN: Hackett, 1993), 73–78.

74. See note 47 above. To be sure, in his last writings Augustine does indeed deny that the will is in its own power and instead asserts that the will is completely and totally in God's power; see his *GLA* 20.41 and 21.43 (PL 44), trans. Holmes et al. But subtlety is required here: even in this forceful statement he includes the will's own agency. He in fact explains that his purpose in what was nearly his final text (apparently written in AD 427), is specifically to show that grace and freedom are not in competition—rather than to show, for example, that radicalizing grace makes freedom unnecessary; see *GLA* 1.1.

75. It is interesting to note that the Hebrews tended to see the drama of individual sin, slavery, and deliverance as an image of the more real and funda-

mental drama of Israel's liberation from Egypt; see Matthew Tsakanikas, "Unmasking the Pharaoh in the Garden of Eden: A Canonical Reading of Genesis 2–3," *Communio* 47.1 (Spring 2020): 190–212.

76. Augustine's concern for the *future* of this history comes to expression in his wrestling with the theme of "persevering grace," the details of which we will not unfold here.

77. Rist has described this well in *Augustine Deformed*, 17. We are considering the point here, however, not most basically from a moral perspective, as he does, but from a metaphysical perspective.

78. This is Locke's sense of law, which we discussed in the last book (*FFR*, 66–73). It is worth highlighting this point, which is especially misunderstood today, insofar as we generally take for granted a libertarian notion of the nature of freedom, regardless of whether we are more liberal or conservative regarding its proper use.

79. This does not mean man would not have sinned if the angels had not sinned first; the fall of the angels is not necessarily the only thing that could have made it possible.

80. *De civ. Dei* 12.7 (PL 41), trans. Bettenson, 479–80.

81. Associating efficient causality with power is not meant to imply that efficient causality is the exertion of force as a quantity of energy, as we see in the typical modern interpretation. Rather, we mean efficient causality, and the power associated with it, in classical, *qualitative* terms. For a fuller account of the classical sense of efficient causality (as the communication of form), see my *Catholicity of Reason* (Grand Rapids, MI: Eerdmans, 2013), 137–62.

82. See his decisive statement, in this regard, in *De lib. arb.* 3.17 (PL 32), trans. Williams, 104–5.

83. Etienne Gilson, *Introduction à l'étude de saint Augustin* (Paris: Vrin, 1949), 318.

84. Analogy implies both similarity and difference: even the sinful act is to a certain extent a reality that is efficiently caused—to the extent that it is *an act*. There is no such thing as pure evil. But this does not mean a sinful act is generally good but has a little part that is evil. Rather, it is evil as a whole even if not wholly evil, which means that the positive elements are per-verted, turned against their natural order. In this sense, we can even speak of a certain positive evil, even though evil is thoroughly an *absence* of good.

85. *De civ. Dei* 14.11 (PL 41), trans. Bettenson, 569.

86. *Conf.* 1.1 (PL 32), trans. Pine-Coffin, 21.

87. This raises the question of Aristotle's "vicious man," who sins without internal resistance: such spontaneous sinning, for Augustine, would nevertheless represent, not a wholehearted willing, but a fragmentation that has become habitual. Wetzel gets at this problem in distinguishing between voluntary and

involuntary sin and shows why "voluntary" sin, though more difficult to account for, still fits Augustine's notion, because the final measure for Augustine is not internal coherence but the *objective* measure of what is good (*Augustine*, 216–18). But this, while true, can eclipse a crucial point: even what Wetzel calls "voluntary" sin can never be completely wholehearted. One ought to reflect here on Augustine's musings regarding the cheerful drunkard; *Conf.* 6.6 (PL 32), trans. Pine-Coffin, 118–20. Augustine says here, "I yet know that it does matter why a man is happy."

88. *De civ. Dei* 12.8 (PL 41), trans. Bettenson, 480.

89. The famous text opposing love of God and love of self is *De civ. Dei* 14.28 (PL 41), trans. Bettenson, 593. In *Sermon* 96, Augustine says, "The primal destruction of man was self-love." Cited in Oliver O'Donovan, *The Problem of Self-Love in St. Augustine* (Eugene, OR: Wipf and Stock, 2006), 96.

90. See, for example, *De civ. Dei* 12.1 (PL 41), trans. Bettenson, 471, where Augustine describes the fallen angels as those who refused to delight in the *good* that God is but "were delighted rather with their own power, as though they themselves were their own good." This is a precise statement of what we called the "diabolical" in *FFR*: the angels are here replacing actual goodness with their as-yet unrealized power. In *De lib. arb.* 3.25 (PL 32), trans. Williams, 122, Augustine describes the act of sin as one in which a person "takes pleasure in himself and wills to enjoy his own power in perverse imitation of God." On all of this, see O'Donovan, *Problem of Self-Love*, 96–98.

91. The classic instance of this is Nygren's interpretation, which resolves the tension ingeniously by showing Augustine's view to be *essentially* self-centered, but in such a way that this self-centered desire can be directed toward two different objects: the highest, God, in which case the soul is happy, or the lowest, the self, in which case the soul languishes. Nygren takes all of this to be evidence that Augustine's notion of love has been adulterated by pagan influences; see his *Agape and Eros*, 458–63 (see also 464–562).

92. This does not imply that his concern is not in an important way a moral one.

93. Chappell, *Aristotle and Augustine*, 177–78. We discussed this in both Plato and Aristotle (*FFR*, 303–4, 346–47).

94. *De civ. Dei* 22.30 (PL 41), trans. Bettenson, 1088–89.

95. *Homily 7* on *First Letter of John*, in *Love One Another*, 73.

96. *De civ. Dei* 22.30 (PL 41), trans. Bettenson, 1088. Emphasis mine. Augustine is describing not an unmoving state but a harmony that is gracious enough to include spontaneous activity, even something analogous to locomotion, within its *beautiful form*.

97. Chappell, *Aristotle and Augustine*, 121–207; Arendt, *Life of the Mind*, 2:84–110, and "What Is Freedom?," 165–69.

98. Chappell, *Aristotle and Augustine*, 202.

99. Ibid.

100. Arendt, "What Is Freedom?," 165–66.

101. Chappell, *Aristotle and Augustine*, 203–4.

102. Along these lines, Aristotle says that the good that moves the appetite (and so the will) "must be good that can be brought into being by action; and only what can be otherwise than it is can thus be brought into being," *De anima* 3.10.433a27–30, trans. J. A. Smith, in *The Basic Works*, rev. ed., ed. Richard McKeon (New York: Modern Library, 2001), 598.

103. We will lay out a more substantial case for this in our chapter on Aquinas.

104. *Conf.* 8.11 (PL 32), trans. Pine-Coffin, 174–75. After listing several good actions that were possible, Augustine says: "All these different desires are good, yet they are in conflict with each other until he chooses a single course to which the will may apply itself as a single whole, so that it is no longer split into several different wills."

105. See *De civ. Dei* 5.2 (PL 41), trans. Bettenson, 181–82. Augustine says that the different outcomes in the lives of the twins who were brought up in identical circumstances "arise not from physical temperament but from deliberate choice." Cf. Wilhelm Kahl, *Die Lehre vom Primat des Willens bei Augustin, Duns Scotus, und Descartes* (Strassburg: K. J. Trübner, 1886), 21ff.

106. We do not want to burden the presentation with too much detail, but it needs to be pointed out that we do not mean to say that the will is an indeterminate power that stands outside of two otherwise determinate goods, the exercise of which belongs to itself alone. In other words, there are two goods before me, X and Y, either of which is good enough to warrant choice, but whichever I end up choosing is simply up to me *and not determined by any goodness*. This interpretation would separate the causality of the good (and so of God) and that of the will, as two halves that constitute a whole. It also leads to the infinite regression we discussed at great length in Locke in volume 1 (*FFR*, 51–63): I can always come up with some reason for having made the choice I did, etc. The point is that the determination of the good (and God) and the will's own determination are *coincident* and inseparable in this way in any good choice. This is why the choice is a real novelty but at the same time wholly radiant with intelligibility. We intend to unfold this point further in relation to God's providence and also the principle of sufficient reason in our projected third volume.

107. Gabriel Marcel famously elaborates this distinction between "problem" and "mystery" in his essay "On the Ontological Mystery," in *The Philosophy of Existentialism* (New York: Citadel, 1984), 9–46.

108. We recall that Plotinus made the very same point, perhaps even more directly than Augustine (cf. *Ennead* 3.1.8.6–7), though he did not think through

its implications at any length. The point remains that Augustine is not introducing here something simply foreign to, or in clear tension with, Plotinus—and therefore the classical tradition. We should note, too, that in speaking of the operation of the will, we do not mean to make it a separate "faculty," juxtaposed to other faculties, as so many "parts" under the control of the soul.

109. *FFR*, 138–47. This is even more evident in Locke; both in any event think of power as separate ontologically from the good, which moves precisely by attraction.

110. This is not to say that this point is *excluded* by Plotinus; quite to the contrary, we mean to offer a reading whereby Augustine brings about something implicit in this classical tradition that culminates in Plotinus.

111. Kahn, "Discovering the Will," 252–54.

112. One need only consider Rousseau's account of his greatest love affair, which has to be with a woman he invented in his imagination, and with whom he nevertheless carried on very much in public; see his account of the origin of his novel *Julie, or La Nouvelle Héloïse*, in his *Confessions*, bk. 9, trans. Angela Scholar (Oxford: Oxford University Press, 2008), 417–21. Our point here, however, is not to make a personal assessment of Rousseau but to draw attention to the objective "narcissism" of his work, in contrast to the essential, and even constitutive, dialogical nature of Augustine.

113. See Bernd Goebel, *Rectitudo, Wahrheit und Freiheit bei Anselm von Canterbury* (Munster: Aschendorff, 2001), 322. We mentioned in the last volume (*FFR*, 417n42) Thomas Prufer's observation that, in Augustine, we have not the invention of the private self but its definitive overcoming.

114. Rist, *Augustine: Ancient Thought Baptized*, 159ff. For a beautiful statement of this, see *Love One Another*, 104–5.

115. The classic formulation of this critique is Gregory Vlastos's essay "The Individual as an Object of Love in Plato," in *Platonic Studies* (Princeton, NJ: Princeton University Press, 1981), 3–34. Cf. my critique of this position in "Plato and the Problem of Love: On the Nature of Eros in the *Symposium*," *Apeiron* 40.3 (2007): 199–220, which offers an attempt to defend Plato against a simplistic version of this critique, though a profound criticism remains, as we are suggesting here.

116. Rist insists on this point in *Augustine: Ancient Thought Baptized*, 163. Cf. the notorious judgment of Nygren on this score, who interprets any trace of eros as a corruption of the biblical vision and so has no appreciation for Augustine's synthesis, much less for the notion of freedom (*Agape and Eros*, 512–32).

117. *Love One Another*, 102.

118. Roniger, "Conversation of Ascent," 675–94.

119. *De civ. Dei* 22.30 (PL 41), trans. Bettenson, 1091: "For what is our end but to reach that kingdom which is without end."

120. *De civ. Dei* 22.30 (PL 41), trans. Bettenson, 1089. See Dihle, *Theology of Will*, 129.

121. Hegel famously critiques Schelling's undifferentiated infinite by citing the proverb regarding cows (*Phenomenology of Spirit* [Oxford: Oxford University Press, 1977], 9), which seems to be derived from a similar proverb regarding cats; see Goethe, *Faust*, part II.1, trans. Leopold J. Bernays (London: Sampson Low, 1839), 9.

122. We recall the Jewish "corporate" sense of will discussed in chapter 1. Cf. the Greek sense of corporate freedom we argued for in *FFR*, 316–22, 356–58.

123. It remains true, as Karl Löwith observed, that "we cannot expect from Augustine a detailed interest in secular history as such" (*Meaning in History* [Chicago: University of Chicago Press, 1959], 171).

124. To be sure, there is very good reason to criticize it as *an inadequate* theology of history for having eclipsed the reality of the world in relation to the eschaton. We do not mean, here, to justify Augustine's conception, but simply to point out his establishing of the importance of history in a novel way *in principle*.

125. Löwith claims that the aim of Christianity is "to refute the classical notion of time as an eternal cycle" (*Meaning in History*, 160). Cf. Jacques Le Goff, who presents Christianity as introducing a more linear sense of history, which took the place of the remnants of pagan naturalism, and thus opening up to the secular sense of time at the foundation of capitalism; "Merchant's Time and Church's Time in the Middle Ages," *Time, Work, and Culture in the Middle Ages* (Chicago: University of Chicago Press, 1980), 29–42. Nietzsche's championing of the "eternal return," which he presented as his most significant insight, ought to be understood as an attempt to overcome the biblical sense of history, and therefore a recovery of the Greeks, which is a principal part of what he understood to be his intellectual mission. We need an interpretation of Nietzsche in the light of the mission of Christianity as the unity of Greeks and Jews.

126. The Jews also have a sense of absolute primacy of divine perfection, which means that they will not have a merely "progressive" sense of history. In chapter 1, we qualified the usual observation that Israel introduced history into the West—if it did, this is nevertheless not the modern notion of history. According to Arendt, "The modern concept of process pervading history and nature alike separates the modern age from the past more profoundly than any other single idea. To our modern way of thinking nothing is meaningful in and by itself, not even history or nature taken each as a whole, and certainly not particular occurrences in the physical order or specific historical events" ("The Concept of History: Ancient and Modern," in *Between Past and Future*, 63).

Ernest Fortin also challenges the view that Augustine is the father of modern historical consciousness in "Augustine's *City of God* and the Modern Historical Consciousness," *Review of Politics* 41.3 (1979): 323–43. For a more substantial argument on Augustine's difference from the modern forms of thought of which he is often said to be the father, see Hanby, *Augustine and Modernity*.

127. *De civ. Dei* 5.9 (PL 41), trans. Bettenson, 190–94.

128. Augustine was the first to interpret the days of creation as ages in history; see his *De catechizandis rudibus* 22 (PL 40).

129. Godescalc of Orbais articulated this doctrine and was condemned in 849. See Rist, *Augustine Deformed*, 85.

130. Rist makes a similar observation; ibid., 52.

131. At a certain level, a connection is maintained between divine freedom and the good in the insistence on justice, however unsatisfying that may be from a more comprehensive perspective.

132. One can hardly deny that Augustine himself encourages such an oversimplification in some of his late writings against the Pelagians; see, for example, one of his last, *De gratia et libero arbitrio* (*On Grace and Free Will*) which emphasizes relentlessly the fact that it is God who is ultimately in "control" of the final outcome.

133. Augustine, *De doctrina Christiana*, bk. 1.

134. The stark character requires a radical separation of ends and means, which is foreign to Augustine; he speaks in the book of *loving* the means and not merely "using" them, for instance, which implies that they do indeed present an end-like character, i.e., an *analogy* to the absolute end even if they are not the absolute end themselves. For a discussion of *use* in terms of genuine love, see Helmut David Baer, "The Fruit of Charity: Using the Neighbor in *De doctrina Christiana*," *Journal of Religious Ethics* 24.1 (Spring 1996): 47–64.

135. Note that the problem is not a shift from internal to external aid (as Byers suggests) or from will as self-causing to will as caused by God, which would imply a remedy of "balancing" God's power with that of human will. There is no contradiction in principle between the absoluteness of God's power and the will's being fundamentally self-causing (in fact, one could argue, as we have, that the latter requires the former). Instead, we are suggesting that the issue turns more basically on the role of mediating goods, which implies a different sort of "remedy" to the problem of predestination as divine "control."

136. He does this in Simon Harrison, *Augustine's Way into the Will: The Theological and Philosophical Significance of De libero arbitrio* (Oxford: Oxford University Press, 2006).

137. Note that, in his discussion with Evodius in *De lib. arb.* (PL 32), bk. 1, before answering the question regarding *whether* we have free will, he wants

to know whether Evodius *wants to know* the answer, and, when Augustine hears he is unsure, he refuses to continue (*De lib. arb.* 1.12, trans. Williams, 18–19). The will to discuss the will is required to discuss it properly, i.e., to come to an understanding of it.

CHAPTER 4. Perfectly Natural Freedom in Dionysius the Areopagite

1. We refer to him thus, rather than as "Pseudo-Dionysius," not to dispute the standard position regarding authenticity, but simply for the sake of euphony. The best succinct discussion of the problem of authenticity is Placid Spearritt, "A Philosophical Enquiry into Dionysian Mysticism" (PhD diss., University of Fribourg, Switzerland, 1968), 93–110, but compare the very interesting arguments made by John Parker in his introduction to *The Works of Dionysius the Areopagite* (n.p.: Veritatis Splendor, 2013), 35–41.

2. The word appears very rarely in the *Corpus Dionysiacum*. See, for example, *DN* 12.2.969B, ed. B. R. Suchla, *Corpus Dionysiacum*, vol. 1 (Berlin: De Gruyter, 1990) (all subsequent citations of *DN* are to this edition), trans. C. E. Rolt, *The Divine Names and Mystical Theology* (London: Society for the Propagation of Christian Knowledge, 1920), 181, where he defines holiness as "freedom from defilement"; *DN* 7.4.873A3, trans. Rolt, 154, where he presents freedom as resting in truth; and *CH* 8.1.237C4, ed. G. Heil and A. M. Ritter, *Corpus Dionysiacum*, vol. 2 (Berlin: De Gruyter, 1991) (all subsequent citations of *CH* are to this edition), trans. John Parker, *The Works of Dionysius the Areopagite* (London: Parker Publications, 1897), 287, where he describes the lordship of the middle ranks of angels as free rather than slavish. It is significant that, unlike Plotinus, for example, Dionysius does not make "freedom" a central attribute of God, by listing it as one of the divine names, for example.

3. The closest he comes is the adjective he uses to describe the contemplative angelic spirits in the *Ecclesial Hierarchy* (*EH* 2.Contemplation.3.400A1–2, ed. Heil and Ritter, *Corpus Dionysiacum*, vol. 2 [all subsequent citations of *EH* are to this edition], trans. Parker, *Works of Dionysius*, 334), namely, *authairetos*, meaning something like "self-choosing." We will discuss this below.

4. *DN* 4.1.693B5–6, trans. Rolt, 87. We will come back to this point at the end of the chapter.

5. Martin Luther, *The Babylonian Captivity* (1520) (WA 6:562). Of course, Luther himself could not escape the Dionysian influence. See Knute Alfsvåg, "Luther as Reader of Dionysius the Areopagite," *Studia Theologica: Nordic Journal of Theology* 65.2 (2011): 101–14.

6. As we argued in chapter 1, Christianity is not in any simplistic way a "religion of the book."

7. This position is ultimately incoherent, of course, for a variety of reasons, not the least of which is that the hunt for Hellenistic influences leads into the heart of scripture itself, so that one is compelled to excise even John and Paul. We see just this, for example, in Anders Nygren's judgment regarding St. John; *Agape and Eros*, 151–59.

8. He also explicitly casts his project as nothing but an interpretation of scripture; *DN* 2.2.637D1–640B3, trans. Rolt, 67–68. Most of the divine names on which he reflects are drawn from the Old Testament, and in the *Divine Names* he cites scripture as virtually the only authority, apart from references to Irenaeus and Clement, and several to Hierotheus, whom he presents as a Christian thinker. In other words, though his thinking is clearly suffused with Greek philosophy, it is important to recognize that he never cites any philosopher as an authority. Andrew Louth makes a similar observation; *Denys the Areopagite* (London: Geoffrey Chapman, 1989), 21.

9. These are especially evident in *EH*, but their presence is felt throughout the corpus.

10. According to Eusebius, Dionysius, the convert of St. Paul, was the first bishop of Athens; the old tradition holds that he served there until being sent to Gaul, where, after a brief stint in Arles, he was bishop of Paris until his death in 119. This is the personage adopted by the writer of the corpus. Along these lines, the healthiest approach to the question of authenticity would seem to be that followed by Christian Schäfer, *The Philosophy of Dionysius the Areopagite: An Introduction to the Structure and the Content of the Treatise On the Divine Names* (Leiden: Brill, 2006), 18–19, who accepts modern scholarship but takes the historical personage to be essential to the meaning of the corpus precisely because the author intended to write "as him." For another "internal" reading approach to the authorship question, see Charles M. Stang, *Apophasis and Pseudonymity in Dionysius the Areopagite: "No Longer I"* (Oxford: Oxford University Press, 2012).

11. The preceding chapters of *DN* elucidated names that fall more obviously in the philosophical tradition, while chapters 8–12 present names more obviously connected with the Jewish tradition (apart from the peculiarly placed chapter 9, which treats of names similar to what Plato referred to as the Great Forms). For a general discussion of various attempts to outline a structure to *DN*, see Schäfer, *Philosophy of Dionysius*, especially the appendix, 177–80. Schäfer mentions that the names "Salvation" and "Redemption" from chapter 8 are unusual in that they do not have an obvious ontological sense but align more exclusively with scripture (99).

12. *DN* 8.9.896D4–897A10, trans. Rolt, 160–61, italics added. We will in general modify the translation as necessary without indicating that fact.

13. We find a powerful reinforcement of this point at *DN* 6.2.856D1–857A9, trans. Rolt, 145, where Dionysius shows that God grants a *gratuitous* transformation by elevating us to eternal life, which is indeed in a certain respect "above nature" (ὑπὲρ φύσιν). On the other hand, contrary to the ancients, who, as Dionysius observes, thought this meant it was "contrary to nature," this transformation remains in some respect "according to nature." For Dionysius, as we will show, there is *nothing* that is ultimately contrary to nature apart from evil, because nature represents God's definitive and unsurpassable gift.

14. See *EH* 2.4.400B8–400C2, where he speaks of the return to the proper vision of nature as the first sacred gift. For Dionysius, "The redemption is seen more as a continuation of the outflow of God's creating, sustaining, and perfecting His cosmos"; William Riordan, *Divine Light: The Theology of Dionysius the Areopagite* (San Francisco: Ignatius Press, 2008), 154. Riordan insists, nevertheless, that Dionysius's view can be harmonized with that of Augustine and Aquinas on nature and grace.

15. René Roques presents *order* as the fundamental theme of Dionysius's thought and shows how it persists essentially even amid the disorder of sin; *L'univers dionysien: Structure hiérarchique du monde selon le Pseudo-Denys* (Paris: Aubier, 1954), esp. 81–88.

16. See Robert Spaemann's discussion of this point in "Nature," 26–29.

17. At the opening of chapter 3, Dionysius identifies "the Good" as the highest name, which contains in itself all the other names (*DN* 3.1.680B1–4, trans. Rolt, 81). Leo Strauss (who as we mentioned in chapter 1 overlooks the particularly Christian element in his interpretation of history) is not correct that, whenever a premodern author presents a list, the middle item is the most important one; for a Christian writer, the *beginning* also possesses a special status.

18. *DN* 8.2.899D5–7, trans. Rolt, 155.

19. At *DN* 4.32.733A1, trans. Rolt, 128, Dionysius describes the divine goodness as "ἐνδύναμον," which could be translated literally as "empowering," i.e., inserting power *into* some other thing.

20. *DN* 8.3.892B2–3, trans. Rolt, 156.

21. *DN* 8.3.892B3–5, trans. Rolt, 156. This extension to "to be" (*to einai*) seems to allow Dionysius to include *matter*, which lies outside of essential being (*ousia*) but is nonetheless related to "to be" itself. It has a kind of "nonessential" reality. See *DN* 4.3.697A1–7, trans. Rolt, 89–90, and 4.7.704B4–6, trans. Rolt, 97. This extension represents a decisive move beyond Plotinus, for whom (as we saw in chapter 2) matter is evil.

22. *DN* 8.2.892A6–9.

23. *DN* 8.5.892C5–8, trans. Rolt, 156.

24. This intercommunion becomes especially clear in the presentation of the name "Beauty"; *DN* 4.7.704A5–704B3, trans. Rolt, 96–97.

25. Dionysius expresses the "living" reality of even material elements beautifully; *DN* 8.5.892D5–893A6, trans. Rolt, 157.

26. The contrast with Locke could not be clearer; see *FFR*, 16–18.

27. See Spaemann's discussion of this shift in "Nature," 29.

28. *DN* 4.30.732A4, trans. Rolt, 126.

29. *DN* 4.32.732D1, trans. Rolt, 127.

30. It produces no being or becoming: οὐδεμίαν οὐσίαν ἢ γένεσιν ποιεῖ, *DN* 4.20.717B5–6, trans. Rolt, 113.

31. *DN* 4.26.728C1, trans. Rolt, 123.

32. One of the more popular translations of Dionysius can give just this impression: "But it can happen that intelligent beings, because of their free will, can fall away from the light of the mind, and can so desire what is evil that they close off that vision, with its natural capacity for illumination" (*EH* 2.Contemplation.3.400A1–2, trans. Colm Luibheid, *Pseudo-Dionysius: Complete Works* [New York: Paulist Press, 1987], 205). But in fact the text ascribes "free will" to the intelligences in their act of contemplation—specifically, referring to the "self-choosing self-sufficiency of the contemplators" (ἡ τῶν νοερῶν αὐθαίρετος αὐτεξουσιότης), as Parker more accurately translates it (334)—and attributes the Fall to the closing off of illumination through love of evil. In other words, it is precisely the completion of the act of contemplation that presents the power of choice, i.e., "freedom," and so the Fall does not occur *by virtue of* freedom but is in fact a fall *from freedom*. In short, the popular translation conveys exactly the opposite meaning of the text.

33. *DN* 4.33.733B8–9, trans. Rolt, 128.

34. Dionsyius states categorically that "all things in all causation desire the beautiful and the good"; *DN* 4.7.704B1–2, trans. Rolt, 97. Insofar as the will is a cause at all, it causes through desire for the beautiful and good, which is why the beautiful and good represent the more comprehensive cause of the will's own causality. This is what we identified as the fundamental insight of the Western tradition initiated by Plato; *FFR*, 295–322.

35. God does not move a will unwillingly; *DN* 4.33.733B8, trans. Rolt, 129. Moreover, Dionysius explains that God's providence sustains the creature's self-moving *precisely as* self-moving; *DN* 4.33.733B10, trans. Rolt, 128.

36. See *DN* 4.30.732A3–5, trans. Rolt, 126.

37. *DN* 4.32.733A1–2, trans. Rolt, 128.

38. *DN* 4.32.732C4–5, trans. Rolt, 127.

39. *DN* 4.20.720A10–11, trans. Rolt, 115. Also see the list of qualities at *DN* 4.32.732C8–732D8, trans. Rolt, 127.

40. See *DN* 4.21.724A9, in which Dionysius says that God's goodness and his substance (ὕπαρξις) are the same (trans. Rolt, 119).

41. On Dionysius's notion of God as "causality of all causes," and its implications for the structure of being, see my "Giving Cause to Wonder," chap. 7 of *Catholicity of Reason*, 203–19.

42. κατὰ τὴν . . . ἀναλογίαν; *DN* 4.2.696C7, trans. Rolt, 89.

43. In *Ennead* 6.9.9 (ed. Armstrong, 335–39), Plotinus argues that the *being* of things *is* their turning toward and abiding with the good, and names this movement toward the good "eros."

44. *DN* 4.1.696A2–6, trans. Rolt, 87–88. Note the reference to the Jewish theme of the "Divine Law," which one does not find in Plotinus and Proclus, for example. The Greek in fact is not νόμος but θέσμος, which emphasizes the positing of the will (θέσις) rather than organic custom. With this reference to conformity to a positing will from the other, Dionysius can be said to integrate eros and obedience just as does Augustine.

45. For an excellent presentation of this point, see Eric Perl, *Theophany: The Neoplatonic Philosophy of Dionysius the Areopagite* (Albany, NY: SUNY Press, 2007), 35–52.

46. *DN* 4.10.708A6–11, trans. Rolt, 101.

47. Perl is right to affirm the continuity between Dionysius and Neoplatonic thinking (*Theophany*, 44), but he does not sufficiently recognize the supreme perfection of receptivity that Dionysius introduces beyond Plotinus in his identification of goodness and eros as names of God, and the implications of this point. We recall that Plotinus was led in this direction by the logic of the matter but ultimately said that the language of eros in relation to God in himself could only be metaphor (and indeed *false*).

48. He distinguishes between the movements of (the angelic) spirit (section 8) and (the human) soul (section 9), but, formally speaking, the difference amounts to little more than the order of the three constitutive motions: for spirit, it is circular, linear, and then spiral, while for soul it is circular, spiral, and then linear. The difference is due to the relation to matter in the two cases, though we cannot spell that out here. In any event, both are distillations, in the end, of the movement that characterizes the "shape" of being simply.

49. The word he uses is περαίνοντες, which means "bringing to completion or to an end."

50. *DN* 4.8.704D1–705A2, trans. Rolt, 98.

51. For a discussion of the significance of the threefold motion (and its implications for the Neoplatonic sense of contemplation), see Spearritt, *Philosophical Enquiry*, 93–110.

52. This is a point we discussed last chapter, with reference to Rist, *Augustine: Ancient Thought Baptized*, 159 ff.

53. We are not suggesting that God as *exclusive* end necessarily undermines the immanent exercise of love. There is, in other words, no problem in principle with Augustine's *uti/frui* distinction, as we will point out again at the end of this chapter. Our point is simply that it entails an ambiguity that requires clarification.

54. Dionysius insists on this point in *DN* 4.11 and 12.

55. Cf. Benedict XVI, *Deus caritas est*, nos. 9–10, www.vatican.va/content/benedict-xvi/en/encyclicals/documents/hf_ben-xvi_enc_20051225_deus-caritas-est.html.

56. See, for example, *Love One Another*, 70.

57. It turns out that the relation to the world is also *not ad extra*, because God can never exceed himself. This is how Dionysius "solves" the problem of God's actual dramatic interaction with the world without denying his perfect immutability, as we will explain below.

58. Our ongoing argument has been that Christian revelation does not in principle *contradict* pagan philosophy but that if it reverses some of that philosophy's basic axioms, the reversal turns out to effect at a deeper level a fulfillment, which retrospectively sets into relief dimensions that may not have been seen or appreciated otherwise but are no less essential for all that.

59. The verb he uses here is *epistrephei*, which means "turns around," i.e., "converts." The *conversio* is not a simple reversal of nature but implies a transcendence beyond, which nevertheless remains part of the intrinsic meaning of nature. This is an expression of the Dionysian paradox.

60. *DN* 4.10.708A12–708B5, trans. Rolt, 101–2.

61. Nygren, *Agape and Eros*, 75–81, in which Nygren characterizes agape in absolute opposition to eros, as a love that gives in total indifference to the goodness and beauty of the recipient. For a more elaborate critique of this view, see my "Redemption of Eros."

62. Which is inseparable from his *own* beauty; see *DN* 4.13.712A10–712B4, trans. Rolt, 106. We will come back to this point.

63. The phrase he uses is δι' ὑπερβολὴν τῆς ἐρωτικῆς ἀγαθότητος (*DN* 712A11–712B1, trans. Rolt, 106), literally, "through the hyperbole of his erotic goodness."

64. The actual phrase here is "the most novel of all novelties": τὸ πάντων καινῶν καινότατον. Note that the reference to novelty manifests the historicity of the event, its taking place in time.

65. *DN* 2.10.648D3–649A5, trans. Rolt, 78, emphasis added.

66. See, again, *DN* 4.13.712A10–712B4, trans. Rolt, 106.

67. See also Barnes, *Power of God*, which explains the predominance of this notion in the Eastern tradition, as we discussed in chapter 2.

68. *DN* 4.33.732D6, trans. Rolt, 127. It is worth remarking that the word Dionysius uses to describe evil, the "indeterminate," is the one Plotinus used to describe God. But in this latter case it was not opposed to perfect actuality, as we explained in chapter 2.

69. *DN* 10.1.937A5-9, trans. Rolt, 169. Note the reference to the will as *thelesis*. It is interesting that this rare use of the word *thelesis* comes especially in reference to the theme of obedience. Dionysius also uses the term in his discussion of the divine ideas, which he characterizes specifically as "wills" (*thelēmata*, 5.8).

70. See *De pot.* 7.10ad4. Isaac Newton made the same observation, and in response to this, Schelling decided that because God *is* (essentially) Lord, he can *only be* creator (i.e., creating the world belongs to the essence of God); see his *Der System der Weltalter: Münchner Vorlesung 1827/28 in einer Nachschrift von Ernst von Lasaulx*, ed. Sigbert Peetz (Frankfurt: Klostermann, 1991), 105. Dionysius resolves the problem in the opposite direction: because God *is* Lord, lordship cannot *principally* mean "power over the other."

71. τὸ κῦρος can mean "certainty" or "validity"; τὸ κύριον can mean what is "fixed" or "appointed"; τὸ κυριεῦον can refer to that which is established by authority.

72. *DN* 12.2.969B7-9, trans. Rolt, 181. Note that God is unsurpassable precisely *as* good, beautiful, and true.

73. *FFR*, 264-69.

74. Dionysius attributes this objection to "Elymas the sorcerer," a Jew who opposed Paul and was blinded as a result (Acts 13:8); see *DN* 8.6.893B1-893D2, trans. Rolt, 157-58.

75. Dionysius often refers to God as "supernatural" (ὑπερφυὴς) (e.g., *DN* 2.10.649A3-4), but if God is "supernatural," it means specifically that he is "above the visible order of nature around us, not as being above the omnipotence of divine life [i.e., nature]. For in relation to this life (since it is the nature of all forms of life and especially of those that are most divine) no form of life is unnatural or supernatural" (*DN* 6.2.857A1-3, trans. Rolt, 145). Again, we see that Dionysius glorifies nature, so to speak, even more than Plotinus, who gives primacy to God's will over his nature, even in their coincidence.

76. The Greek word for "perfect," τέλειος, contains the word τέλος, "end," which means the perfect is defined, circumscribed by a proper boundary (so to speak).

77. We say "seems to" because he does not explicitly exclude potency but only insists on God's perfect actuality (*Metaph.* 12.7), which would imply the absence of potency only if we opposed the two notions. In fact, however, in this famous passage Aristotle describes that perfect actuality precisely as

understanding and *life*, two activities that Plato observed necessarily entail something like movement and yet are perfections, which means that God must be posited, not as rest in contrast to movement, but as transcending both and including what is perfect in each; see *Sophist* 248e–249d.

78. This is why (*pace* White, *Wisdom*) there is a danger of the "pure act" conception of God degenerating into "onto-theology."

79. Dionysius says, paradoxically, that God is both unmoving and eternally moving; *DN* 10.2.937B4–5.

80. *DN* 10.2.937B1–2, trans. Rolt, 169–70.

81. Eros is described as "good and beautiful": this is already an indication of the transformation Dionysius effects in a nutshell.

82. *DN* 4.13.712A10–712B4, trans. Rolt, 106. Dionysius here connects God's eros for the world with the Jewish notion of God as "jealous," which we might compare to the Platonic notion that God is wholly without envy (*Tim.* 29e). Dionysius does not deny the Greek tradition here but deepens it through an integration of the Jewish theme.

83. *DN* 4.13.712B1, trans. Rolt, 106.

84. *DN* 10.1.936D5–937A5, trans. Rolt, 169.

85. *DN* 7.4.873A3, trans. Rolt, 154.

86. The best exposition of this theme in Dionysius is chapter 2 of Perl's *Theophany*, entitled "Being as Theophany," 17–34.

87. See *Letter 3*, to Gaius, in which Dionysius affirms that God becomes *even more mysterious*, not "beyond" the flesh, but *precisely in the Incarnation*; 1069B, ed. Heil and Ritter, *Corpus Dionysiacum*, vol. 2, trans. Parker, *Works of Dionysius*, 174.

88. Granted, he is not working out an anthropology in this text (or in any of his texts). It is quite natural to deny choice in God; the Neoplatonic tradition generally affirms *freedom* of God, but not in the form of choice among preexisting alternatives, insofar as this would appear to circumscribe God within a temporal horizon. Dionysius is simply giving this standard notion a particular interpretation. We noted his other reference to choice (in the form of "self-choosing," *authairesis*, *EH* 2.Contemplation.3.400A1–2), which is his articulation of the activity of contemplation.

89. *DN* 4.1.693B5–9, trans. Rolt, 87.

90. His eros *did not allow him* (οὐκ εἴασεν αὐτὸν) to remain in himself; God is thus *moved* (ἐκίνησε); *DN* 4.10.708B3–4, trans. Rolt, 102.

CHAPTER 5. Maximus the Confessor

1. Maximus's principal philosophical sources are Aristotle, the Stoics, and the Greek commentaries on Aristotle, though he does not seem to have read Ar-

istotle directly. R.-A. Gauthier has argued that he received what he knows of Aristotle through Nemesius; see Gauthier, "Maxime le Confesseur," 71.

2. See R.-A. Gauthier, *Aristote: L'éthique à Nicomaque*, vol. 1, pt. 1, *Introduction*, 2nd ed. (Louvain: Publications universitaires, 1970), 266. The judgment arises from the fact that Maximus manages to gather up the various elements that had appeared before in Aristotle and the Stoics under a single concept, *thelēsis*, and thus to unify them as expressions of a single human power.

3. This is Kahn's word; see his "Discovering the Will," 238.

4. We have done so elsewhere; see the chapter entitled "Philosophy and Theology" in my *Catholicity of Reason*, 305–32, and "Metaphysics as Praeparatio Evangelica," in my *Companion to Ferdinand Ulrich's Homo Abyssus* (Washington, DC: Humanum Academic Press, 2019), 89–112.

5. From Gregory of Nazianzen, *Letter* 101, in *Cyril of Jerusalem, Gregory Nazianzen*, vol. 7 of *Nicene and Post-Nicene Fathers*, Second Series, 440, cited in Maximus the Confessor, *The Disputation with Pyrrhus*, trans. and annot. Joseph P. Farrell [Waymart, PA: St. Tikhon's Seminary Press, 1990], 99n85).

6. He championed what came to be known as "diatheletism," which affirmed two wills in Christ (divine and human), in an age in which "monotheletism" (a single will), if not "monophysitism" (a single nature), held sway among the ruling elite. He was persecuted and eventually sent into exile with his tongue cut out and his right hand cut off, so that he could not spread this teaching. Eventually, however, it was *his* position that came to be recognized as orthodox.

7. As we discussed in chapter 3, Augustine does not seem to affirm the will as a distinct faculty but tends to use the term to refer to the whole soul in its appetitive or impulsive aspect, even if he describes this aspect in terms that make it irreducible to any other aspect.

8. *DP* (PG 91:293B), ed. Marcel Doucet, "Dispute de Maxime le Confesseur avec Pyrrhus" (PhD diss., University of Montreal, 1972) (all subsequent citations of *DP* are to this edition, which uses PG numbering), trans. Farrell, *Disputation with Pyrrhus*, 63. Aristotle determined that *choice* (ἡ προαίρεσις) is either appetitive thinking or thoughtful appetite (ἡ ὀρεκτικὸς νοῦς . . . ἢ ὄρεξις διανοητική) (*NE* 6.3.1139b5–6), but he does not have an explicit doctrine of the will.

9. *DP* (PG 91:293B–C), trans. Farrell, 63–64. It is worth pointing out that some of the acts Maximus lists as belonging to the will are ones people today would be more inclined to include under the auspices, so to speak, of intellect: for example, inquiring, examining, deliberating, and judging. We will look at these in more detail when we discuss Scotus below.

10. Whether this picture does justice to the Greek father or is rather more Origenist than Origen himself we leave aside here. For a succinct account of

this reversal, see Sotiris Mitralexis, *Ever-Moving Repose: A Contemporary Reading of Maximus the Confessor's Theory of Time* (Eugene, OR: Cascade Books, 2017), 111, 111n12.

11. See Paul M. Blowers and Robert Louis Wilken, introduction to *On the Cosmic Mystery of Jesus Christ: Selected Writings from St. Maximus the Confessor* (Crestwood, NY: St. Vladimir's Seminary Press, 2003), 24.

12. *Ad Thal.* 65 (CCSG 27:285, 546). Mitralexis describes this as the "deification" of the creature, the creature's most complete participation in God; see *Ever-Moving Repose*, 192–213.

13. *Amb.* 67 (PG 91:1401A), *Ad Thal.* 59 (CCSG 22:53, 131), and *Ad Thal.* 65 (CCSG 22:285, 545–46), all cited in Blowers and Wilken, introduction to *On the Cosmic Mystery*, 42.

14. *Amb.* 7, in Maximus the Confessor, *On the Difficulties of the Church Fathers*, ed. and trans. Nicholas Constas (Cambridge, MA: Harvard University Press, 2014), 1:87–89.

15. *Amb.* 65, ed. and trans. Constas, 2:277.

16. Ibid.

17. We will come back to the significance of this important term later. See *Amb.* 7, ed. and trans. Constas, 1:87, where Maximus distinguishes the being that is "according to nature" from the well-being that is "according to gnomie."

18. *Amb.* 85, ed. and trans. Constas, 2:277.

19. Ibid.

20. *Amb.* 7, ed. and trans. Constas, 1:87.

21. The *gnomie* is a disposition that differs from natural desire in that it is acquired by the creature in its historical enactment of its existence; see Gauthier, "Acte humaine," 80. See also Adrian Walker, "The Freedom of Christ: Notes on 'Gnomie' in Maximus the Confessor," *Communio* 43.1 (Spring 2016): 32.

22. *Amb.* 7, ed. and trans. Constas, 1:87.

23. We note that Maximus makes a distinction between actuality and eternity, which is analogous to the distinction we saw in both Plotinus and Dionysius between eternal actuality and God's transcendence of this eternity and serves a similar purpose. Though he admits that Maximus is unsystematic in his usage, Mitralexis proposes a term to capture this transcendence of *both* potency and actuality and the time and eternity that corresponds to it: αἰδιότης, which may perhaps be translated as "beyond eternity"; Mitralexis, *Ever-Moving Repose*, 132–33.

24. *Amb.* 65, ed. and trans. Constas, 2:275–81: "The seventh day and Sabbath is the passage through all the modes pertaining to virtue and all the principles of knowledge pertaining to contemplation. But the eighth day is the true transformation by grace in relation to the beginning and cause of whatever has been accomplished by practice and understood by contemplation" (281).

25. *Amb.* 65, ed. and trans. Constas, 281. The Greek word *akatalutos* means "incorruptible" and thus indicates a mode of being that transcends the movement of coming to be and passing away that characterizes time. On all of this, see Mitralexis, *Ever-Moving Repose*, 210–11.

26. This is one of the revisions Maximus makes in his appropriation of Gregory of Nyssa's notion of *epektasis*. See Paul M. Blowers, "Maximus the Confessor, Gregory of Nyssa, and the Concept of Perpetual Progress," *Vigiliae Christianae* 46 (1992): 151–77.

27. This is simply a more directly theological formulation of the "standard" Platonic insight that what all things desire is not simply happiness, i.e., the fulfillment of desire, but *goodness itself*, which of course is *also* a fulfillment of desire (see my "Plato and the Problem of Love").

28. *Amb.* 7, ed. and trans. Constas, 1:91.

29. *Amb.* 10, ed. and trans. Constas, 1:167–69.

30. *Amb.* 7, ed. and trans. Constas, 1:103. See *Amb.* 7, trans. Constas, 1:114–15. Significantly, Maximus presents this transformation, not as the deed of the creaturely agent, but as the effect of *passion* as an *ecstatic power*. In this sense, the doing, while being *fully* active, nevertheless remains fully passive, a mode of being moved.

31. See Ian McFarland, "'Naturally and by Grace': Maximus the Confessor on the Operation of the Will," *Scottish Journal of Theology* 58.4 (2005): 415. Maximus's reflections on freedom culminate in a definition of the natural will as "the power that longs for what is natural." *Opus.* 3 (PG 91:45D), cited in McFarland, "'Naturally and by Grace,'" 421.

32. McFarland makes a strong case for this ("'Naturally and by Grace,'" 423). Maximus says, "For nothing that is natural can be opposed to God in any way, not even with respect to gnomie," *Opus.* 3 (PG 91:48D–49A), cited in "'Naturally and by Grace,'" 194.

33. See *DP* (PG 91:345D), trans. Farrell, 120, where Maximus lays out an argument that when Paul says, "Behold all things have become new" in grace, he does not mean they acquire a new nature, for even in their transformation they remain the same (and even become more fully the same).

34. In the *Opus.*, Maximus describes the natural will as the "essential desire of things according to nature" (PG 91:153A–B).

35. Plato, *Symp.* 200a–204b.

36. See Walker, "Freedom of Christ," 47.

37. See *Amb.* 7, ed. and trans. Constas, 1:89.

38. *Amb.* 7, ed. and trans. Constas, 1:87.

39. On this, see McFarland, "'Naturally and by Grace,'" 423–24.

40. All of this is presented in *DP* (PG 91:293A), trans. Farrell, 62 ff. Of course, Aquinas makes the well-known distinction between three kinds of

necessity, of nature, of ends, and of coercion, and says only the last is incompatible with freedom (*ST* I.82.1 [Leon. 5]). We will discuss this in the chapter on Aquinas.

41. Mitralexis thus distinguishes Maximus's sense of nature from that of (one reading of) Aristotle as always a "returning motion," specifically a returning to God (*Ever-Moving Repose*, 123–240).

42. *DP* (PG 91:312A–B), trans. Farrell, 86.

43. *DP* (PG 91:329C–D), trans. Farrell, 103–4. The extent to which the problematic aspect of *gnomie* is due to its connection to the sinful condition of man's hypostatic existence or simply to its finite, temporal character remains ambiguous. We will return to this briefly at the end.

44. *This* is what Maximus defines as the essence of the will, and claims as the sense given by the Fathers; see *DP* (PG 91:304C), trans. Farrell, 77; cf. *DP* (PG 91:301C and 324 C–D), trans. Farrell, 75 and 98.

45. We find such a thing, for example, in Hegel; see our discussion in *Perfection of Freedom*, 361–63.

46. Perhaps the closest would be Aristotle, whose highest actuality is eternal self-thinking thought, though one could certainly draw on aspects of his thinking that push against a unilateral reduction to this principle. (We attempted to bring out some of these aspects, for example, in *FFR*, 339–48.)

47. We might recall Arendt's vivid sense of the "natality" of human freedom, which opens up in principle unending lines of consequences that cannot simply be contained in Greek *form*. Arendt associates this sense of political action with the Romans, and for good reason, but we are connecting it in our context with the *Jews*, who (curiously) have little place in her interpretation of this theme.

48. One aspect of this insight that needs to be developed further is the role of Mary's fiat, which indicates the need for a human act of will, not as exercised simply *by* a divine Person, as in Christ, but specifically *in response* to God. In this case, we have the inclusion of the human in the divine, but *also* the inclusion of the divine in the human: Mary's fiat is the acceptance of God in her womb. On this, see the profound essay by Fr. Paolo Prosperi "'Fixed End.'"

49. See *Opus*. 6, "On the Two Wills of Christ in the Agony of Gethsemane," in *Cosmic Mystery*, trans. Blowers and Wilken, 173–76.

50. See Jonathan Bieler, "Maximus the Confessor on Christ's Human Will," *Communio* 43 (Spring 2016): 55–82. Cf. McFarland, "'Naturally and by Grace,'" 424–26.

51. In *DP* (PG 91:292C), trans. Farrell, 60–61, Maximus explains how we speak of the saints as having "one will" with God in the sense of having an identical object of will.

52. *Amb*. 1, ed. and trans. Constas, 1:11.

53. Ibid.

54. *Amb.* 1, ed. and trans. Constas, 1:15.

55. It also implies that this order is not a necessary one in any simplistic sense: it *includes* freedom, which means it allows the drama.

56. See Hans Urs von Balthasar, *Cosmic Liturgy: The Universe According to Maximus the Confessor* (San Francisco: Ignatius Press, 2003), 153–54.

57. See, e.g., *Ad Thal.* 1, "On the Utility of the Passions," in *Cosmic Mystery*, trans. Blowers and Wilken, 97–98.

58. See Paul M. Blowers, "Gentiles of the Soul: Maximus the Confessor on the Substance and Transformation of the Human Passions," *Journal of Early Christian Studies* 4 (1996): 57–85.

59. We have argued in another context that the triumphant recapitulation of order in a way that magnanimously embraces what appears to be an unexpected intrusion of disorder is the heart of what Plato means by "beauty"; see "Disclosing Beauty: On Order and Disorder in the *Symposium*," in *Beauty and the Good: Recovering the Classical Tradition from Plato to Duns Scotus*, ed. Alice Ramos (Washington, DC: Catholic University of America Press, 2020), 19–48.

60. See McFarland, who reflects on Maximus's affirmation of the ultimate transformation of man in Christ as "all-encompassing, natural, and by grace" (from *Expositio in Psalmum* 59 [PG 91: 857A], in "'Naturally and by Grace,'" 410 ff.

61. *Amb.* 7, *Amb.* 1, ed. and trans. Constas, 1:107–9; cf. *DN* 5.8.824C. On this point, see Mitralexis, *Ever-Moving Repose*, 80–82.

62. See his "Commentary on the Our Father" (PG 90). Cf. Blowers and Wilken, introduction to *Cosmic Mystery*, 37.

63. *DP* (PG 91:309C–D), trans. Farrell, 82, 83. See *DP* (PG 91:329D), trans. Farrell, 103–4. See Lars Thunberg, *Microcosm and Mediation: The Theological Anthropology of Maximus the Confessor*, 2nd ed. (Chicago: Open Court Press, 1995), 216. This is not to deny that his thinking developed in the ways often described. The point is that the way he formulates gnomic will in the mature writing does not exclude other senses of *gnomie* that would be, or at the very least could be, interpreted in an altogether positive sense, which is what we propose below.

64. Joseph Farrell is one of the scholars who has given the strongest defenses of the *ultimacy* of free choice in Maximus: as he shows in his book *Free Choice in Maximus the Confessor* (Waymart, PA: St. Tikhon's Seminary Press, 1989), Maximus clearly separates the phenomenon of choice from the moral dilemma of good and evil (to which Farrell claims with some justification Augustine tends to reduce the issue of choice). In the end, there is free choice even among the saints in the eschaton: there is no motion of a rational soul without

choice, and no life without motion; as eternal life, heaven must therefore include the act of free choice (111), though Farrell explains that these choices are perfectly certain, free from any "better or worse," and made without deliberation, since they are occupied exclusively with the equally good "divine energies" (179). What remains ambiguous even in Farrell's defense is the question whether deliberation can itself be good, i.e., not a sign of a lack of resolve to do what is best, and whether there can be altogether good opposition (as in the dramatic reciprocity of persons in their interrelation).

CHAPTER 6. St. Anselm

1. To point out a certain thematic continuity is not at all to suggest that Anselm was in any direct way familiar with Maximus. There has been some suggestion that Anselm was at least superficially familiar with John Scotus Eriugena (815–77), who had translated parts of Maximus's *Ambigua* and *Quaestiones ad Thalassium* into Latin; see Deno J. Geanakoplos, "Some Aspects of the Influence of the Byzantine Maximos the Confessor on the Theology of East and West," *Church History* 38.2 (June 1969): 150–63, and Dermot Moran, *The Philosophy of John Scottus Eriugena: A Study of Idealism in the Middle Ages* (Cambridge: Cambridge University Press, 2004), 272, but as many scholars have observed, apart from Augustine, whom Anselm mentions explicitly (*Monologion*, Preface, 2), and Aristotle in Boethius's translation (*CDH* 2.17 [Schmitt 2:125]), any other influence can be determined only speculatively. It is clear from his general references to "holy Fathers" (*CDH*, Commendation [Schmitt 3:39], trans. H/R, 295), or to "celebrated debates" (*CD* 21 [Schmitt 1:266], trans. H/R, 251) that he was aware of an intellectual tradition and continuing conversation, but this does not receive direct attention in his work. We will come back to this point in the end.

2. It is to be noted, however, that Anselm does not present the matter in these terms, except in the argument in *CDH* for the necessity of Christ's sacrifice for the restoration of justice, which, as we will see, is a condition of human freedom. In his specific discussions of the nature of freedom, however, there is little explicit reference to Christ, and nothing that would evidently touch on the substance of the matter.

3. As we will see, below, this does not mean that there is no reference to God's freedom; instead, the point is that God's freedom is referenced principally to make sense of human freedom rather than being a theme unfolded in its own right.

4. C. G. Normore has argued "that Anselm . . . begins the process of freeing us" from the Aristotelian model, which sees the will as a "moved mover,"

though this process comes to completion only in the later Franciscan thinkers; see C. G. Normore, "Picking and Choosing: Anselm and Ockham on Choice," *Vivarium* 36.1 (1998): 39.

5. G. R. Evans observes that Anselm did not publish a work until he was completely certain of the argument, so did not have to modify his views at any point in a substantial sense: he wrote no "Retractiones," for example, as did Augustine. See G. R. Evans, "Anselm's Life, Works, and Immediate Influences," in *The Cambridge Companion to Anselm*, ed. Brian Davies and Brian Leftow (Cambridge: Cambridge University Press, 2004), 11. In his last completed work, *De concordia*, Anselm himself explains that he is taking there for granted the view of freedom he expounded in the two earlier texts, *De veritate* and *De libertate arbitrii*; C 1.6 (Schmitt 2:256), trans. H/R, 542.

6. LA 3 (Schmitt 1:212), trans. H/R, 197.

7. V 12 (Schmitt 1:194), trans. H/R, 184.

8. This is an expression found in Augustine's early work—*De actis cum felice manichaeo* 2.3 and *De lib. arb.* 1.16.35—and was widely accepted as Augustine's view, though as we have seen in our study of Augustine the formulation is hardly adequate to his mature understanding. See Stanley G. Kane, "Anselm's Definition of Freedom," *Religious Studies* 9.3 (September 1973): 299.

9. "Although the free choice of men differs from that of God and of the good angels, nevertheless the definition of this freedom ought to be the same in both cases, in accordance with the name 'freedom'"; LA 1 (Schmitt 1:208), trans. H/R, 192. Here we see a tendency toward a certain univocity, which we will discuss below.

10. LA 2 (Schmitt 1:210), trans. H/R, 194.

11. Ibid.

12. S. Kane, "Anselm's Definition of Freedom," 301. Kane observes that, when it is necessary to explain that one's sins are one's own, Anselm uses the adverb *sponte* rather than *libre*.

13. One of the differences between analogy and univocity is that univocity represents an abstraction that is able to cover the whole range of difference without essential modification, while analogy represents a unity that is different from the ground up in every realization.

14. C 3.11 (Schmitt 2:279–80), trans. H/R, 565–66.

15. Rist is correct to say that Anselm introduces the notion of will as a distinct *faculty*, separate from other parts of the soul and essentially intelligible as such, which is not found in Augustine (though as we have seen there is something like a distinct faculty in Maximus). See his *Augustine Deformed*, 32, 87, 92.

16. LA 7 (Schmitt 1:219), trans. H/R, 204–5.

17. LA 7 (Schmitt 1:219), trans. H/R, 204. Note that this is what we would call a univocal, in contrast to an analogical, conception of will.

18. *LA* 7 (Schmitt 1:219), trans. H/R, 205. Indeed, he goes on to argue in the subsequent chapter that to the extent that it is free—i.e., wills justice—even the strictly omnipotent God cannot overcome the creature's will (because to do so would imply a self-contradiction, which is the only thing impossible to God).

19. Katherin S. Rogers, *Anselm on Freedom* (Oxford: Oxford University Press, 2008), presents this as an astonishingly "radical power" (101). We will return to a discussion of this point at the end.

20. *CD* 27 (Schmitt 1:275), trans. H/R, 260.

21. This is something like a "habitus" in Scholastic thought, or indeed like *gnomie* in Maximus. But whereas such things were understood as achieved in history through action, what Anselm has in mind here is "infused" directly by God. This is significant because of the relative absence in his thought of the habit of "virtue," which we will discuss below.

22. *CD* 12 (Schmitt 1:254), trans. H/R, 238.

23. *C* 3.12 (Schmitt 2:284), trans. H/R, 569.

24. *CD* 12 (Schmitt 1:252), trans. H/R, 236. Note that the reason the inclination must be supplied by God is that a pure potency cannot bring *itself* into any actuality at all. Anselm thus retains, in a certain respect at least, the Aristotelian tradition, which subordinates potency to act.

25. Consider the contrast with the classical sense of potency, which we discussed in relation to Augustine: Is it possible to conceive, even hypothetically, the power to walk, for example, separate from reference to the activity of walking to which it is ordered? It is difficult even to express the point because it is simply unintelligible. We cannot think of this power in itself first, to which the aptitude for walking would be added afterward.

26. *CD* 16 (Schmitt 1:254), trans. H/R, 243.

27. *LA* 3 (Schmitt 1:211–12), trans. H/R, 196.

28. See our discussion of Plato in *FFR*, 295–321.

29. See Plato, *Rep.* 505d–e; *Symp.* 206a.

30. Sandra Visser and Thomas Williams, "Anselm's Account of Freedom," in B. Davies and Leftow, *Cambridge Companion to Anselm*, 179–203.

31. Rogers (*Anselm on Freedom*) is one of the principal defenders of the libertarian interpretation of freedom in English (though she has been criticized for reading modern notions into Anselm and departing significantly from the constraints of the text; see Thomas Williams's review in *Notre Dame Philosophical Reviews: An Electronic Journal*, February 11, 2009). For a more balanced account, see Goebel, *Rectitudo*.

32. Visser and Williams, "Anselm's Account of Freedom," 180.

33. *CD* 12 (Schmitt 1:251), trans. H/R, 235. This is a classic point, found not only in Augustine, but also in a very different context in Aristotle, who explains that the principle of the motion in the soul is not reason but the principle

of reason itself, namely, God; *Eudemian Ethics* 8.2 (1248a 25–30). Aquinas refers to this principle in *ST* I.82.4ad3 (Leon. 5), which we will discuss in chapter 9.

34. *CD* 12 (Schmitt 1:254), trans. H/R, 238.

35. Ibid.

36. We will discuss the significance of the phrase *per se* in more detail below. It is a decisive one for Anselm.

37. *C* 3.10 (Schmitt 2:278), trans. H/R, 565. See Kristell Trego, *L'essence de la liberté: La refondation de l'éthique dans l'oeuvre de saint Anselm de Cantérbéry* (Paris: Vrin, 2010), 243. She argues that there is no "weakness of will" in Anselm; if I sin, it is not because I lacked the power to do good but because I did not use the power that remained present. See also Rist, *Augustine Deformed*, 93.

38. Significantly, Anselm uses the language of *will* even for such creatures, which means he does not think of will as rational appetite (as Maximus defines it); see Trego, *Essence*, 205. Even Augustine, who does not yet have this definition, resists such language. There is no doubt a connection between this and the interpretation of will as an instrument even apart from inclination and appetite. Note that, as Trego explains, will is separate from both intellect and appetite, rather than being in some sense their unity (206).

39. See *CD* 14 (Schmitt 1:258), trans. H/R, 242. Anselm seems to imply that justice requires the capacity to do otherwise. If a being had *only* the will-for-justice, it would not be just even in willing fitting things, "since it would have received this capability in such a way that it would not have been able to will otherwise." At the very least, *merit* is required, which implies an achievement of some sort and so the possibility of failure.

40. *CD* 14 (Schmitt 1:258), trans. H/R, 242.

41. *CD* 27 (Schmitt 1:275), trans. H/R, 259–60.

42. To the student's question why the angel willed what it ought not to have willed, Anselm says simply: "Only because he willed [it]. For this willing had no other cause by which in any respect to be driven or drawn; rather, it was an efficient cause of itself—if this can be said—and its own effect." *CD* 27 (Schmitt 1:275), trans. H/R, 260. There is something *absolute* about freedom, something un-get-behind-able.

43. See *Monologion* 3–6 (Schmitt 1:15–20), trans. H/R, 9–15.

44. He is explicit about this in the preface: "This book goes on to prove by rational necessity—Christ being removed from sight, as if there had never been anything known about Him—that no man can possibly be saved without Him." *CDH* preface (Schmitt 2:42), trans. H/R, 296.

45. John Paul II, *Fides et ratio* (1998), no. 42, www.vatican.va/content/john-paul-ii/en/encyclicals/documents/hf_jp-ii_enc_14091998_fides-et-ratio.html. See Victor Roberts, "The Relation of Faith and Reason in St. Anselm of Canterbury," *American Benedictine Review* 25 (1974): 494–512. Cf. Marilyn

McCord Adams, "Anselm on Faith and Reason," in B. Davies and Leftow, *Cambridge Companion to Anselm*, 32–60.

46. This is one of the implications of Dionysius's describing God's self-gift as occurring without choice: it is therefore absolute rather than one of many possibilities determined on the basis of something more absolute.

47. W. J. Courtenay explains that Anselm reasons *from* the nature of God *to* revelation in scripture and then *to* the content of natural claims, which would otherwise be purely formal; see Courtenay, "Necessity and Freedom," 49. Note that there is a certain parallel in this move to Anselm's isolating the potential instrument from the (now extrinsic) actualizing reality. We will discuss this parallel below.

48. *CDH* 1.12 (Schmitt 2:70), trans. H/R, 320–21; cf. *Meditatio* (Schmitt 3:86), trans. H/R, 421. Anselm, however, insists that God's will not transgress his *dignity*, which suggests that there is a standard in God to which his will must conform.

49. *Proslogion* 7 (Schmitt 1:105–6), trans. H/R, 96–97.

50. *CDH* 2.17 (Schmitt 2:122), trans. H/R, 376.

51. Courtney makes this basic point, though he uses terms that are slightly different from the ones we use here; "Necessity and Freedom," 58.

52. *CDH* 1.24 (Schmitt 2:93), trans. H/R, 345–46.

53. *CDH* 1.12 (Schmitt 2:70), trans. H/R, 321.

54. *CDH* 1.12 (Schmitt 2:70), trans. H/R, 321, and 1.24 (Schmitt 2:93), trans. H/R, 346. In *Meditatio* (Schmitt 3:86), trans. H/R, 421, he says, regarding the act of Redemption, "He acted of His own will; and because His will is always good, He acted out of goodness alone."

55. Hans Urs von Balthasar, "La *Concordantia libertatis* chez saint Anselme," in *L'homme devant Dieu* (Paris: Editions Montaignes, 1964), 32–33.

56. Courtenay, "Necessity and Freedom," 58.

57. *CDH* 2.5 (Schmitt 2:99–100), trans. H/R, 352–53. Anselm had illustrated this point in the preceding text by analogy to making a vow. Courtenay explains that the idea of promise that we see here became decisive for nominalism; "Necessity and Freedom," 54–61. See our discussion of this in the context of covenant in chapter 1.

58. We mean this *paradoxically*, not in a one-sidedly linear way: the will precedes the nature *and* the nature precedes the will. The full mystery requires the embrace of both of these aspects at once.

59. See Balthasar's reflections along these lines in *TD2*, 258–61.

60. We recall that something of this point was already somewhat visible in the Jewish tradition. See Robert R. Williams, *Recognition: Fichte and Hegel on the Other* (Albany, NY: SUNY Press, 1992).

61. He also refers to this as a distinction between *aliquid* and *propter quod*. *V* 12 (Schmitt 1:193–94), trans. H/R, 183; cf. *LA* 3 (Schmitt 1:210–12), trans. H/R, 195–97.

62. Plato, *Grg.* 467d. See our discussion in *FFR*, 205–8, 264–69.

63. See Kahn, "Discovering the Will," 252–54, and Trego, *Essence*, 20.

64. See *C* 3.11 (Schmitt 2:279), trans. H/R, 567.

65. Rogers, *Anselm on Freedom*, 66–67.

66. The *propter hoc* is not necessarily the *finis*, the practical goal of the particular means chosen. I might choose the means of sawing in order to build a house (*finis*), but I can build a house either to increase my own honor or for the greater glory of God. Note here that Aristotle insists that the *end* is precisely never itself an aspect of choice, while Anselm is making the reason the ultimate matter of choice.

67. Nietzsche, *Beyond Good and Evil*, §32 (New York: Vintage, 1989), 43–45. This is not far from the classic, though of course too simplistically drawn, distinction between a *shame* culture and a *guilt* culture; see the classic text in E. R. Dodds, *The Greeks and the Irrational* (Berkeley: University of California Press, 1951), 28–63.

68. As Goebel explains in *Rectitudo*, for Anselm the will is *causally determined* to will advantage but is *self-caused* as morally good; these two aspects can be affirmed at once (381–82). A comparison can be drawn between this perspective and the one we find, for example, in the Stoic tradition that a causally determined event still permits a purely interior self-determination as to one's attitude to that event.

69. *C* 3.11 (Schmitt 2:280–82), trans. H/R, 567–68.

70. In fact, *intention* is not the best word, insofar as Anselm also says that the affection need not be something of which one is consciously aware, while of course *intention* implies awareness; see *C* 3.11 (Schmitt 2:281), trans. H/R, 568. Only *use* is necessarily conscious.

71. *CD* 6 (Schmitt 1:244), trans. H/R, 227.

72. Goebel, *Rectitudo*, 323, explains that Christianity introduces a notion of good that exceeds the will's *intrinsic capacity*, which is what appears here in Anselm, why the justice that represents the condition of freedom is not something the will can achieve on its own, but only something the will can preserve once it is given.

73. *C* 3.12 (Schmitt 2:284), trans. H/R, 569; cf. *LA* 7 (Schmitt 1:219), trans. H/R, 204.

74. In *CDH*, Anselm connects justice with the good and then with the *greater good*. *CDH* 2.1 (Schmitt 2:97–98), trans. H/R, 349.

75. *LA* 8 (Schmitt 1:220), trans. H/R, 205.

76. See my *Plato's Critique*, 88–93 and passim, and also my "Plato and the Problem of Love."

77. As we will point out below, he *does* still present justice as the Supreme Good, which is meant to be enjoyed and as bringing happiness; *CDH* 2.1 (Schmitt, 2:97–98), trans. H/R, 349–50. In other words, we are yet still far from a deontological ethics. But cf. Balthasar, "*Concordantia libertatis*," 34, who says that Anselm avoids the Augustinian language of *delectatio spiritualis* and privileges instead the language of obedience.

78. Balthasar, "*Concordantia libertatis*," 34.

79. Ibid.

80. We ought to contrast this, for example, with Maximus, who, as we saw in the previous chapter, interprets spontaneous self-movement most specifically in terms of desire.

81. Balthasar, "*Concordantia libertatis*," 35–36.

82. The fundamental argument seeks to show that there is a harmony (*concordia*) between the self-determining freedom of the human will and the absolute priority of God implied in the concepts of foreknowledge, predestination, and grace.

83. The purpose of our rational nature is to "do just works by loving and choosing the Supreme Good," namely, the will of God; *CDH* 2.1 (Schmitt 2:97–98), trans. H/R, 350.

84. Here we see a need to qualify Balthasar's judgment about the essential *analogy of freedom* in Anselm ("*Concordantia libertatis*," 30 and 36). To be sure, there is something like an analogy in the unity-in-difference of the reciprocity of divine and human wills, but there is no analogy in the sense of a reverberation down into the lowest ground of nature. The relation is an essentially "spiritual" or personal one.

85. This idea emerges from the line of argument in *De conceptu virginem* 1–3 (Schmitt 2:140–43), trans. H/R, 429–33. It is a drift, we note, rather than a precisely formulated position on the matter.

86. In fact, this emphasis tends to undo Maximus's achievement: if will belongs to person rather than to nature, there would not be two wills in Christ but only one.

87. Trego, *L'essence de la liberté: La refondation de l'éthique dans l'oeuvre de saint Anselme de Cantorbéry* (Paris: Vrin, 2010). It should be noted that Trego overlooks the positive contribution of the *personal* element and the correlative *personal* dimension of goodness as love, which we have just discussed. This is an important point, which must be kept in mind even alongside the critique.

88. She uses the term for his interpretation of *matter* most directly, but it seems fitting as a characterization of the whole (ibid., 51).

89. This is not to say that Anselm falls into the problem of "ontotheology" as it is often conceived, namely, as the reduction of God to *a* being, which is infinite, over against other, finite beings. Anselm has a much more subtle sense of the relation between God and the spiritual soul, which are not for him opposed beings. For a profound exploration of this, see Ferdinand Ulrich, "Cur non video praesentem? Zur Implikation der griechischen und lateinischen Denkform bei Anselm und Scotus Erigena," *Freiburger Zeitschrift für Philosophie und Theologie* 1–2 (1975): 70–170.

90. For a profound reflection on the *ontological* sense of interiority implicit within the classical metaphysical tradition, see Kenneth Schmitz, "The First Principle of Personal Becoming," *Review of Metaphysics* 47.4 (1994): 757–74.

91. To be sure, as Trego notes, Augustine had already proposed translating *ousia* as *essentia* rather than *substantia* (*De Trin.* 5.8.9), but she goes on to explain that Augustine nevertheless understood the creature's dependence on God as providing an ontological foundation. Anselm, by contrast, relates the *properties* to God and posits the substrate as a reality for the properties; Trego, *Essence*, 68–69.

92. Trego, *Essence*, 184.

93. Ibid., 187. As we are seeing, the locus of the self in Anselm shifts to the will in abstraction from the concrete being of the agent as a whole.

94. A metaphysics of gift worked out along these lines can be found in Kenneth Schmitz, *The Gift: Creation* (Milwaukee, WI: Marquette University Press, 1982), and even more radically in Ferdinand Ulrich, *Homo Abyssus: The Drama of the Question of Being* (Washington, DC: Humanum Academic Press, 2017).

95. Trego, *Essence*, 181. Compare an actual ruling power to one's having the capacity or potential to rule, whether that potency is actualized or not. Trego discusses the difference in much greater depth in *L'impuissance du possible: Emergence et développement du possible, d'Aristote à l'aube des temps moderns* (Paris: Vrin, 2019).

96. Trego, *Essence*, 9, 24.

97. God causes everything *by which* the will acts, but this is not the same; we will return to this point below. See *C* 3.11 (Schmitt 2:284), trans. H/R, 569, and *CD* 27 (Schmitt 1:275), trans. H/R, 260.

98. There is some important ambiguity on this point, which Trego also observes (*Essence*, 24), and which we will explain in (3) below.

99. Kane objects that this entails a contradiction at the heart of Anselm's vision of freedom, since it amounts to saying that one who has lost an ability still has that ability (S. Kane, "Anselm's Definition of Freedom," 306). Cf. Goebel, who argues that, just because a power is not used (because the external

conditions are absent) does not mean it is not present: being in total darkness is not the same as being blind (*Rectitudo*, 483–85). He admits a problem that will come to plague the modern conception of freedom: Is the mere possession of the power the essential meaning of freedom (487–88)? We discussed just this problem at great length in *FFR*. The fact that Anselm insists on the devil's *ignorance* of the consequences of his decision as a precondition for free choice, however, implies that for him a limit has to be placed on the attraction the good causes in order to allow freedom. *CD* 23 (Schmitt 1:270), trans. H/R, 255.

100. *LA* 3 (Schmitt 1:213), trans. H/R, 197–98.
101. Plato, *Rep*. 518c.
102. See *FFR*, 300–308.
103. *LA* 7 (Schmitt 1:219–20), trans. H/R, 205.
104. *LA* 5 (Schmitt 1:216), trans. H/R, 202. Balthasar writes, "This need for a created freedom to conquer itself by its own power [*forces*] is one of Anselm's major contributions, and governs his entire doctrine of freedom" ("*Concordantia libertatis*," 31).
105. *C* 3.13 (Schmitt 2:286), trans. H/R, 571.
106. *C* 2.1 (Schmitt 2:260), trans. H/R, 349–50; cf. *CD* 15 (Schmitt 1:259), trans. H/R, 243.
107. *V* 12 (Schmitt 1:194), trans. H/R, 186.
108. *LA* 8 (Schmitt 1:220), trans. H/R, 205.
109. See my "Plato and the Problem of Love." Anselm would not dispute this point, as we have seen, insofar as he insists on the happiness of the just. The difference is a very subtle one, and there is an ambiguity. There is a certain "moreness" in Plato's sense of desire, which entails in the end an expropriation; that is why even he posits an obedience that transcends desire as part of the intrinsic meaning of goodness in its highest sense (see my argument on this point, based on Platonic texts, in *Plato's Critique*, 199–216). To distinguish the two thinkers we might say that in Plato the transcendence occurs within an analogy, while in Anselm there is a more abrupt discontinuity.
110. Here again we see that the difference is quite subtle: Plato also "takes away the seeming" (*Rep*. 361c) in a kind of thought experiment in order to set the "in-itself" quality of justice into relief, or in other words he dramatically requires a movement beyond the terms of reward and punishment, but this is not a veiling of the goodness that attracts; instead, it is something like an *isolation* of the "in-itself" aspect of goodness.
111. For a profound interpretation of faith as personal trust in just this sense, see Paolo Prosperi, "Believing and Seeing," *Theological Studies* 78.4 (2017): 905–29.

112. *De conceptu virginem* 4 (Schmitt 2:143–45), trans. H/R, 433–36.

113. Maximus had observed that it is possible for the saints and God to have *one will* in the sense of object or purpose, and yet have distinct wills in the sense of faculty; see *DP* (PG 91:292C), trans. Farrell, 60–61.

114. In the *De concordia* (Schmitt 2:287), trans. H/R, 573, Anselm affirms the classical tradition, which we have witnessed in Augustine and Dionysius, for example, that God causes man's good works but not the aspect of evil in man's evil works, but his explanation is radically different from the classical metaphysical interpretation: "In the case of good works God causes both the fact that they are good with respect to their being and that they are good with respect to their justice." He does not say—as, for example, Maximus said before him and Aquinas will say after him—that God causes the actual act of will itself. As we recall, for Anselm, the cause of the will in its acts is ultimately the will itself. It is interesting to note that Rogers brings out the ambiguity here: in one respect, Anselm wants to give the will "a very modest contribution" (*Anselm on Freedom*, 101), but at the very same time this turns out to be a "radiant power," a "power so tremendous that great medieval thinkers like Augustine and Aquinas insisted that a created agent could not possibly possess such a thing" (101). W. Matthews Grant, in a review of Rogers's book, argues that Rogers misreads Anselm because she takes him to be denying either God's omnipotence as creator *ex nihilo* or the classical view, implied in this, of evil as *privatio boni*. W. Matthews Grant, "Anselm on Freedom: A Defense of Rogers' Project, a Critique of Her Reconciliation of Libertarian Freedom with God the Creator Omnium," *Saint Anselm Journal* 8.1 (Fall 2012): 1–10. While Grant's arguments are much more compelling taken in themselves as a metaphysical account, it is not obvious that he offers a more accurate interpretation of Anselm. One must note a problematic ambiguity in Anselm. While he wants to avoid a "competitive" relation between the wills by saying that God in some sense gives even a bad use of the will (*CD* 28 [Schmitt 1:276], trans. H/R, 261), that God's permitting the will's causality is in a sense causing its acts (see *CD* 18 [Schmitt 1:263], trans. H/R, 247), and that God causes the will's movement by being the cause of everything by which it moves itself (*C* 3.11 [Schmitt 2:284], trans. H/R, 569), this is more like an attempt to replace a genuine paradox and compensate by as near a likeness as a new set of terms allows.

115. *CD* 23–24 (Schmitt 1:269–72), trans. H/R, 254–56.

116. As Trego argues, Anselm ironically posits a fundamental indifference in the will precisely in his effort to affirm a normative conception (*Essence*, 259–60).

117. Ibid., 32–34.

118. Bonnie Kent recounts this reconception of ethics principally in the thirteenth century, but we see it has a seed planted already in Anselm. See her *Virtues of the Will: The Transformation of Ethics in the Late Thirteenth Century* (Washington, DC: Catholic University of America Press, 1995), which we will be consulting frequently in our discussion of Bonaventure and Scotus.

119. Balthasar, "*Concordantia libertatis*," 39–40. Justice concerns the *interiority* of the will, as we recall; it is meant actually to *become* good and *delight* in goodness. There is a profound intimacy here with God and not a mere imputation of justice that never really "takes" ontologically.

120. Maximus, *Opus*. 1 (PG 91:25A–B), cited in David Bradshaw, "St. Maximus on the Will," in *A Saint for East and West: Maximus the Confessor's Contribution to Eastern and Western Christian Theology*, ed. Daniel Haynes (Eugene, OR: Wipf and Stock, 2019), 104.

121. Trego, *Essence*, 30–32. To be sure, there are a variety of ways to understand this point. Aquinas, too, affirms that an agent exists in some sense for the sake of its operations, but this does not require an instrumentalist interpretation of course.

122. It is not an accident that Anselm does not foreground his sources, the authorities he cites. Instead, he cites only scripture directly as an authority, along with the relatively autonomous power of reasoning.

123. See Courtenay, "Necessity and Freedom," esp. 63, and Julia Gauss, "Die Auseinandersetzung mit Judentum und Islam bei Anselm," in *Die Wirkungsgeschichte Anselm von Canterburys: Akten der ersten internationalen Anselm-Tagung in Bad Wimpfen, 13.–16.9.1970*, ed. Helmut Kohlenberger (Frankfurt: Minerva, 1975), 101–9. Gauss mentions explicitly Saadja Fajumi among the Jews and Al-Ghazzali, Avicenna, and Alfarabi among the Muslims (101). These all considered their faith superior to that of the Christians because theirs was not contrary to reason, as the Christian faith appeared to be.

124. See *Monologion*, preface (1): there is no reference to scriptural authority, only arguments by means of rational necessity.

125. John Marenbon, for example, observes that, while Plato's *Timaeus* was widely available in Latin translation in Anselm's time, that work "seems not to have interested" him. John Marenbon, *Anselm's Proslogion* (Montreal: McGill-Queen's University Press, 2005), 170.

126. It arises, of course, many centuries later, but one may consider Henry Veatch's classic argument regarding the sort of logic that develops outside of a grasp of being articulated in a basic way in terms of substance and accidents. Henry Veatch, *Two Logics* (Evanston, IL: Northwestern University Press, 1969).

CHAPTER 7. Bernard of Clairvaux

1. Michel Corbin judges that Bernard gathers everything good from Anselm's work from the *De libertate* to the *De concordia*; see *La grace et la liberté chez saint Bernard de Clairvaux* (Paris: Cerf, 2002), 28. Jacques Leclercq explains that Bernard received his understanding of free will from Anselm, though Leclercq also mentions Origen, Gregory of Nyssa, and especially Basil of Caesarea as influences; see "General Introduction to the Works of Saint Bernard (III)," *Cistercian Studies Quarterly* 40.4 (November 2005): 365–93. Etienne Gilson says that Bernard was acquainted with Dionysius, Maximus, and possibly even Eriugena; see *The History of Christian Philosophy in the Middle Ages* (New York: Random House, 1955), 164. For a general account of sources and influence, see Ulrich Faust, "Bernhards 'Liber de Gratia et Libero Arbitrio': Bedeutung, Quellen, und Einfluss," in *Analecta Monastica: Textes et études sur la vie des moines au Moyen Age*, ed. Ulrich Faust, Studia Anselmiana 50 (Rome: Centro Studi S. Anselmo, 1962), 6:35–52. Bernard lived in a time in which reception of tradition as authority was paramount; see Alois Dempf, *Die Hauptform mittelalterlichen Weltanschauung* (Munich: Oldenbourg, 1925), 61 ff. As Dempf puts it, between 600 and 1200 the dominant intellectual ethos was "traditionalistic," taking the form of a "pure receptivity." Bernard himself is known above all for his argument *against* the introduction of novelties (which is evident above all in his famous dispute with Abelard). One of the distinctive features of Bernard's age, with respect to previous ones, was nonetheless the inclusion of recent predecessors among the *auctoritates*; see Artur Michael Landgraf, "Bernards Verhältnis zur Theologie des 12. Jahrhunderts," in *Bernhard von Clairvaux: Mönch und Mystiker*, ed. Joseph Lortz (Wiesbaden: Franz Steiner, 1955), 44–62. But it is curious that Bernard, with such a broad cultural and theological formation, makes virtually no direct use of sources outside of scripture in his discussion of free will. We will come back to this point at the end.

2. Etienne Gilson, *The Mystical Theology of Saint Bernard* (Kalamazoo, MI: Cistercian Publications, 1990), 33.

3. This is a point on which Corbin also insists (*Grace et la liberté*, 120).

4. More specifically, the end is entry into Trinitarian life; see Gilson, *Mystical Theology*, 98–99.

5. Ibid., 94.

6. Aimé Forest, "Das Erlebnis des consensus voluntatis beim hl. Bernhard," in Lortz, *Bernhard von Clairvaux*, 124.

7. Gilson, *Mystical Theology*, 55–56.

8. Bernard delivered more than eighty sermons on the biblical epithalamium the Song of Songs, at the center of which, according to the mystical tradition, lies the unity between the soul and God.

9. According to Goffredo Venuta, Bernard's treatise on grace and free choice is the "basis and foundation" for his treatise on the love of God. *Libero arbitrio e libertà della grazia nel pensiero di S. Bernardo* (Rome: F. Ferrari, 1953), 17.

10. See Bernard McGinn, introduction to *On Grace and Free Choice* (Kalamazoo, MI: Cistercian Publications, 1977), 4.

11. *GLA* 14.47 (Leclercq 3:198), trans. Bernard McGinn, *On Grace and Free Choice*, 106.

12. Gilson seems to tend in this direction: the union Bernard intends here "is neither a confusion of the two substances in general nor a confusion of the substances of the will in particular; but it is their perfect accord, the coincidence of two willings... in which intention and object coincide to such an extent that one is a perfect image of the other" (*Mystical Theology*, 123).

13. It is worth pointing out that the word thus designates an activity that is both intellectual and voluntary at once. The old Indo-European root *sent-* means "to go," a meaning reflected in the Old High German *sinnan*, "to go, travel, strive after, have in mind"; the word *con-sentire* would thus indicate traveling together along a particular path.

14. "Free judgment" is probably closer, and Bernard himself will connect *arbitrium* with *judicium*; *GLA* 4.11 (Leclercq 3:173), trans. McGinn, 67. Moreover, Bernard eventually argues that choice in the sense of deciding between possible alternatives is not essential to *liberum arbitrium*; see *GLA* 10.35 (Leclercq 3:190), trans. McGinn, 90–91. But "free judgment" is not a normal English expression.

15. Venuta, *Libero arbitrio*, 60–61. Whether *liberum arbitrium* is a habitus in the Aristotelian sense will become a major question in the Scholastic world. We will look at two different answers in the next two chapters and consider their implications.

16. *GLA* 2.4 (Leclercq 3:3, 168–69), trans. McGinn, 58–59. Cf. *Sermon* 81 on the Song of Songs in *St. Bernard's Sermons on the Canticle of Canticles*, vol. 2 (Dublin: Browne and Nolan, 1920), 465–66.

17. *GLA* 1.2 (Leclercq 3:167), trans. McGinn, 55.

18. Toward the end of the treatise (*GLA* 14.46 [Leclercq 3:199], trans. McGinn, 105), in describing the interaction between man and God, Bernard presents the activity of thinking as something God works in us without us, *preceding* our activity, while willing is an activity he works in us *with* us.

19. See Venuta's succinct discussion of this problem in *Libero arbitrio*, 54–56.

20. "Instruction, not destruction" is his way of putting it; *GLA* 2.4 (Leclercq 3:168), trans. McGinn, 58.

21. *GLA* 3.6 (Leclercq 3:170), trans. McGinn, 61. We will not attempt to decide whether the judgment belongs to the will itself or the reason. It remains ambiguous; see Venuta's discussion in *Libero arbitrio*, 61.

22. See *GLA* 4.11 (Leclercq 3:173), trans. McGinn, 66. To be sure, he speaks of the *will* judging here, but he previously attributed the will's capacity to judge to reason. A less significant role is its proposing an option to the will without im-posing it. In this role it precedes the will, while in the other, more distinctively characteristic, it follows the will.

23. Venuta explains that there are two senses of *liberum arbitrium* in Bernard, one in which the *arbitrium* is a function of the *liberum*, and the other in which the *liberum* is a function of the *arbitrium*, but he determines that the former is clearly dominant in Bernard's thought (*Libero arbitrio*, 68–69).

24. Jean-Luc Marion interprets the moral indifference of the will as the essential feature of Bernard's doctrine; see "L'image de la liberté," in *Saint Bernard et la philosophie*, ed. Rémi Brague (Paris: Presses universitaires de France, 1993), 54–55, referring to it as an "irreal indeterminacy." Michel Corbin criticizes Marion on this point (*Grace et la liberté*, 67) because he insists that for Bernard the will can never be taken in abstraction but must always be determined with respect to its particular concrete context. We will come back to this point at the end.

25. *GLA* 4.9 (Leclercq 3:172), trans. McGinn, 66.

26. *GLA* 4.9 (Leclercq 3:172), trans. McGinn, 65.

27. See Venuta, *Libero arbitrio*, 99–100.

28. *GLA* 4.9 (Leclercq 3:172–73), trans. McGinn, 66. Cf. Marion, "Image," 56–57. It is worth pointing out that Bernard in fact associates the will, as such an invincible and inalienable power, with the absoluteness of God himself; *GLA* 9.28 (Leclercq 3:185), trans. McGinn, 84.

29. Bernard tends to emphasize the *exclusivity* of scripture. Pieper refers to him as saying, "What do I care about philosophy? 'My teachers are the apostles.... They have taught me to live. Do you think it a little thing, to know how to live?'" *Sermones*, PL 183:1187 ff., cited in Josef Pieper, *Scholasticism* (South Bend, IN: St. Augustine's Press, 2001), 89. Forest also observes the apparent refusal of ancient sources in Bernard beside the Bible ("Erlebnis," 120).

30. See McGinn, introduction to *On Grace and Free Choice*, 39–40.

31. It is often observed that Bernard's interpretation of the relation between image and likeness does not remain consistent through his work; see, for example, Venuta, *Libero arbitrio*, 38–43. Bernard himself explicitly admits this but leaves it to his audience to choose which interpretation they prefer; see *Sermon* 81, in *St. Bernard's Sermons*, 472. The question of which interpretation is best does not bear on our present theme.

32. *GLA* 3.6–8 (Leclercq 3:170–72), trans. McGinn, 61–64.

33. *GLA* 4.11 (Leclercq 3:173–74), trans. McGinn, 67.

34. This fact sets into relief its strictly univocal character.

35. *GLA* 7.21 (Leclercq 3:182), trans. McGinn, 79. Here we have an implicit reference to the famous formulation from Augustine in *Of Correction and Grace* 33 [12]. It is to be noted nevertheless that the description still remains stuck, as it were, to potency, the *capacity* to bring about or to resist something, rather than an *actual* condition. One wonders which is more basic, the inability to be disturbed or the pleasure, i.e., joy. Are these in fact equivalent? If they are taken to be equivalent, what are the implications?

36. See *GLA* 4.9 (Leclercq 3:172–73), trans. McGinn, 66, and cf. 6.19 (Leclercq 3:180), trans. McGinn, 75, where he speaks of the highest freedom as one in which the will is "plene . . . bona, et bene plena" (fully good and goodly full), as it were. Is the will, then, *always* full, regardless of its condition, as he says in the earlier passage, or only in its perfected state? Corbin admits that this looks like a contradiction but insists the contradiction falls away when we begin from the perspective of grace (*Grace et la liberté*, 115–16). Whether this is an adequate resolution we will consider at the end.

37. Corbin says this explicitly: the pure capacity to will, without content, is *nothing, no substance*, because there is no real will except in the concrete activity of willing the good or the bad (*Grace et la liberté*, 118). This is for him essentially why the question of the will immediately points us to the concrete context.

38. Venuta, *Libero arbitrio*, 151.

39. *GLA* 6.16 (Leclercq 3:178), trans. McGinn, 72, italics added.

40. *GLA* 6.18 (Leclercq 3:179), trans. McGinn, 74.

41. Ibid.

42. Venuta explains this point well (*Libero arbitrio*, 94).

43. *GLA* 6.18 (Leclercq 3:179), trans. McGinn, 74.

44. As Corbin puts it, in criticism of R. Javelet's interpretation of Bernard, to isolate this essence is to confuse gospel freedom with metaphysical freedom (*Grace et la liberté*, 84).

45. Sermon 83, on the Song of Songs, cited in Pierre Rousselot, *The Problem of Love in the Middle Ages* (Milwaukee, WI: Marquette University Press, 2002), 197. We must nonetheless recognize the limits of this explanation, which is in the end too generous. Bernard explicitly rejects the idea that the will is genuinely free only in charity when he says that the will is equally free whether in sin or in goodness: "Freedom of choice belongs to everyone who has the use of reason; no less, essentially, to the bad than to the good; as fully in this life as in the next." *GLA* 5.15 (Leclercq 3:177), trans. McGinn, 71.

46. Gilson, *Mystical Theology*, 90.

47. As Corbin argues, for Bernard the will has always already been preceded by a Yes from God and so never stands outside as a pure indeterminacy in an abstract sense (*Grace et la liberté*, 61–62, 85, 113).

48. Forest, "Erlebnis," 120–21.

49. Gilson observes that Bernard seems to have gotten his beloved word *excessus* from Maximus's sense of motion as *ecstasis* in and toward the good (*Mystical Theology*, 26).

50. *GLA* 12.40 (Leclercq 3:194–95), trans. McGinn, 97–98.

51. Gilson, *Mystical Theology*, 33: "We shall be able to perceive [the truth of his idea] only if we begin where St. Bernard himself begins, that is to say with the question about what love ought to be, rather than what it is."

52. Bernard does not appear to recognize that his interpretation of the will requires him to give an account of the indefectibility of the saints and the absolute goodness of God. Showing that freedom can be reconciled with permanent goodness is insufficient here, insofar as one needs to show why the saints, for example, are indefectible de jure and not only de facto.

53. In this sense, there is something quite ominous in Bernard's presenting *liberum arbitrium*, in its *inamissibilitas*, as like the omnipotence of God (*GLA* 9.28 [Leclercq 3:185]), because it implies at least by way of insinuation that God is like the will, interpreted specifically with respect to its perfectly indifferent essence: the "evil genius" of Descartes is a half step away, and in between lies the "reification" of the divine *potentia absoluta* in Scotus, as we will see in chapter 11.

54. Gilson, *Mystical Theology*, 42.

55. See Gilson's discussion, ibid., 55–57. Cf. Venuta, *Libero arbitrio*, 73, who says that for Bernard natural appetite runs in opposition to God because it is subject to *necessity* rather than being *free*. We saw this position, so evidently contrary to the classical tradition, emerge in Anselm, and we shall see it expressed quite forcefully in Scotus.

56. When Venuta explains what he claims to be the *positive* sense of freedom in Bernard, namely, *spontaneity*, he clarifies the technical meaning of spontaneity as *the contrary of the natural* (*Libertà della Grazia*, 79). In *Sermon* 81, on the Song of Songs, Bernard writes: "Man is the only mortal who can resist the coercive power of nature" (*St. Bernard's Sermons*, 466).

57. For a more detailed analysis of the Aristotelian notion of life as implying from its roots a relation to what is other than the self, see my "*Analogia Naturae*: What Does Inanimate Matter Contribute to the Meaning of Life?," *Communio* (Winter 2011): 657–80.

58. According to Bernard, life "is an internal and natural movement, having existence only within the confines of the body [*vigens tantum intrinsecus*]";

GLA 2.3 (Leclercq 3:167), trans. McGinn, 57. Note that, if life is a motion wholly circumscribed within the body, any movement beyond—such as love— would have to move in a direction essentially opposed to the natural movement of life.

59. Here we see the insight of Rousselot's description of love in Bernard, in which he raises a question about the "anti-natural" aspect, which makes love at the same time *essentially* irrational; see *Problem of Love*, 169, 189.

CHAPTER 8. Bonaventure on the Trinitarian Origin of Freedom

1. Sixtus V, *Triumphantis Hierusalem* (1588), para. 13, www.papal encyclicals.net/sixtus05/triumph.htm, citing Rev 11:4. Leo XIII refers approvingly to Sixtus's characterization of the two great luminaries in *Aeterni Patris* (1879), paras. 14–16, www.vatican.va/content/leo-xiii/en/encyclicals/documents/hf_l-xiii_enc_04081879_aeterni-patris.html. Cf. Leo XIII's Allocution from October 11, 1890, in which he recommends Bonaventure as the authority in mystical theology.

2. Gilson, *The Philosophy of St. Bonaventure* (New York: Sheed and Ward, 1938), 495. It is worth observing that this highlighting of two complementary but irreducibly different figures rather than a single one to represent the Christian interpretation of existence resonates with a basic methodological principle of this book: no one figure captures the whole because of the nature of tradition, which is a whole greater than the sum of its parts. This wholeness is expressed in a symbolically fruitful way in polarity: a double vision, which allows the perception of *depth*.

3. See ibid., 32–33. Bonaventure begins his *Hexaemeron* by saying, "Our intent is to show that in Christ are hidden all the treasures of wisdom and knowledge, and that he is the central point of all understanding." Cited in Kevin Hughes, "Bonaventure *contra Mundum*? The Catholic Theological Tradition Revisited," *Theological Studies* 74 (2013): 387.

4. Kevin Hughes has made a similar suggestion in "Bonaventure *contra Mundum*." Ferdinand Ulrich's interpretation of Christian metaphysics and anthropology in terms of the paradoxical simultaneity of wealth and poverty will turn out to be the key; see his *Homo Abyssus*, but also the reflection on tradition in part 1 of *Gegenwart der Freiheit* (Freiburg: Johannes Verlag Einsiedeln, 1974), 11–72.

5. Gilson represents this older tradition, presenting Bonaventure as opting for Plato *rather* than Aristotle; *Philosophy of St. Bonaventure*, 96. Balthasar, by contrast, presents Bonaventure as integrating Plato and Aristotle (*GL2*, 284).

Bonnie Kent discusses the shift regarding the supposed clash between Augustinians and Aristotelians in scholarship in *Virtues of the Will*, 1–93. The crux would be distinguishing between a hostility toward Aristotle and a resistance to reading Aristotle in independence from the Christian tradition.

     6. See Ernst Stadter, *Psychologie und Metaphysik der menschlichen Freiheit: Die ideengeschichtliche Entwecklung zwischen Bonaventura und Duns Scotus* (Munich: Ferdinand Schöningen, 1971), 29. Stadter explains that Bonaventure approaches the question of freedom from a psychological perspective (the experience of freedom) rather than a metaphysical perspective (what accounts for the reduction of potency to actuality in a given act). But this, while illuminating, is insufficient to explain the difference of interpretation.

     7. See William G. Thompson, "The Doctrine of Liberum Arbitrium in Saint Bonaventure" (Master's thesis, Loyola University Chicago, 1956), 5–6.

     8. The most direct discussion is found in distinctions 24 and 25 of the *Commentary on the Sentences*, book 2, which, as Stadter has observed (*Psychologie und Metaphysik*, 29), was written before the controversies emerged regarding Aristotle's anthropology and psychology. Beyond the *Sentences* commentary, there are significant passing observations regarding the will and freedom in other works, perhaps most notably the *Itinerarium*, the *Breviloquium*, and the *Hexaemeron*, plus the *Disputed Questions on the Mystery of the Trinity*.

     9. In his words, "Emanatio personae non attenditur secundum rationem bonitatis essentiae, sed magis fecunditatis personae." *I Sent.* d. 19, p. 1, q. 2, sol. 3 (Quar. 1:345b).

     10. Dennis Bray has recently sought to demonstrate the justice of Ewert Cousins's determination that Bonaventure's Trinitarian conception of God is the key to his entire theological synthesis and that it has an essential philosophical dimension in "Bonaventure's *I Sentence* Argument for the Trinity from Beatitude," *American Catholic Philosophical Quarterly*, prepublished July 29, 2021, https://doi.org/10.5840/acpq2021728234. Cousins expresses this judgment in his essay "God as Dynamic in Bonaventure and Contemporary Thought," in *Thomas and Bonaventure: A Septicentenary Commemoration*, ed. G. F. McLean, O.M.I. (Washington, DC: Catholic University of America Press, 1974), 138.

     11. See, for example, Cilento, *Saggi su Plotino*.

     12. See Zachary Hayes, introduction to *Disputed Questions on the Mystery of the Trinity* (St. Bonaventure, NY: Franciscan Institute, 1979), 41–43.

     13. Bonaventure derives the idea of two modes of emanation from Augustine but at the same time from Aristotle: *Metaph.* 8.7 (1032a12–13) and *Phys.* 2.5. Note the traditional connection between intellect and nature, which both represent a principle of immanent actuality (in-stasis); the will and liberality, by contrast, point to an *ecstasis*, or actualizing beyond oneself.

14. For his beautiful interpretation of "Word," which reveals a fuller sense of *embodiment* implied therein than we find in Aquinas, see his *Commentary on John* c. 1, p. 1, q. 1 (Quar. 6:247a–b), cited in Hayes, introduction to *Disputed Questions*, 51–53.

15. Balthasar, *GL2*, 290; cf. Gilson, *Philosophy of St. Bonaventure*, 146.

16. Balthasar, *TL2*, 163. We will discuss this point, and its implications, more fully in our final chapter.

17. The Son proceeds "per modum naturae, nihilominus ut dilectus"; *I Sent.* d. 6, a. 1, q. 2 (Quar. 1:128a). Cf. *Itin.* c. 6, 2 and 3 (Quar. 5:310b), where Bonaventure distinguishes the procession of the Son as *naturalis* from that of the spirit as *voluntaria* but insists on their radical consubstantiality, so that the Son is named *dilectus* in himself, and not only with respect to the Spirit.

18. According to Bonaventure, nature is the principle of the generation of the Son, but with the concurrence of will ("natura est principium concomitante voluntate") and the will is the principle of the spiration of the Spirit, but with the concurrence of nature ("voluntas est principium concomitante natura"); *I Sent.* d. 6, a. 1, q. 2, resp. (Quar. 1:128a–b). On the significance of this point, see Balthasar, *GL2*, 288.

19. See *Hex.* 11.8 (Quar. 5:381a–b); *Trin.* q. 2, a. 2, fund. 6 (Quar. 5:64a–b). Cf. Hayes, introduction to *Disputed Questions*, 36.

20. This comes to expression especially in his Joachimite interpretation of history and his particular reading of the "dynamic" nature of the divine ideas. For a discussion of Schelling and the sources of his thinking, see Xavier Tilliette, *Schelling: Une philosophie en devenir* (Paris: Vrin, 1992).

21. See my discussion of this theme from Schelling's positive "philosophy of revelation" in the chapter "Creation as Theogony," in *Perfection of Freedom*, 207–26.

22. Schelling, *Philosophical Investigations into the Essence of Human Freedom* (Albany, NY: SUNY Press, 2007).

23. On Bonaventure's appropriation of the distinction between *potentia absoluta* and *potentia ordinata*, see Lawrence Moonan, *The Medieval Power Distinction up to Its Adoption by Albert, Bonaventure, and Aquinas* (Oxford: Clarendon Press, 1994), 193–228. Moonan remarks that Bonaventure did not make much use of the distinction compared to others at the time (228). Gilson observes that Bonaventure criticizes the exaggeration of divine power in Peter Damian and Gilbert de la Poirée (*Philosophy of St. Bonaventure*, 168–69).

24. Aristotle, *Phys.* 3.7. See also Balthasar, *GL2*, 292; cf. *Brev.*, in which Bonaventure observes that the divine power is completely ordered; *Brev.* 1.7 (Quar. 5:215a–216a). Bonaventure refers here to the impossibility for God to make an actual infinity, but he is referring to an actuality in the created order.

25. *Trin.* q. 4, a. 2, concl. (Quar. 5:85b).
26. *I Sent.* d. 6, a. 1, q. 3 (Quar. 1:129b).
27. See Richard of St. Victor, *On the Trinity*, trans. Ruben Angelici (Eugene, OR: Cascade Books, 2011), especially book 3.
28. See Gilson's observations on this score in *Philosophy of St. Bonaventure*, 159–60.
29. Bonaventure of course received the influence of Plotinus and Maximus indirectly: Plotinus through the general stream of Neoplatonism (Augustine, Dionysius, and the Victorines) and Maximus through John Damascene. It is worth pointing out that we are not claiming that Bonaventure "deduced" his notion of human freedom from the Trinity; in fact, he does not draw explicit attention to the connection himself. But he does present the perfection of "liberality" in God as a perfection of freedom, and his anthropology is obviously worked out within this horizon.
30. This becomes clear in the Franciscans after Bonaventure, especially Peter Olivi and William of Ockham, and even, between these figures, in Scotus, who attempts to recover a deeper integration with reason, as we will see. But the real harvest of the move is no doubt in the modern tradition that begins with Schelling.
31. Kent, *Virtues of the Will*, 95–96. Perhaps in the end, we could speak of a "libertism" or "amorism," to coin awkward terms. Gilson rightly says that for Bonaventure what is highest is in the end not the will but simply God, in whom all attributes coincide in perfect unity (*Philosophy of St. Bonaventure*, 182).
32. This is what Bonaventure means by insisting on the need for "merit" in the achievement of blessedness; *Brev.* 2.9.2 (Quar. 5:227a). Cf. Marianne Schlosser, *Cognitio et amor: Zum kognitiven und voluntativen Grund der Gotteserfahrung nach Bonaventura* (Munich: Ferdinand Schöningh, 1990), 63–64.
33. See *Brev.* 2.9.1 (Quar. 5:226b); Schlosser, *Cognitio et amor*, 64.
34. We will discuss this below. See Tilman Anselm Ramelow, "Der Begriff des Willens in seiner Entwicklung von Boethius bis Kant," *Archiv für Begriffsgeschichte* 46 (2004): 42.
35. *II Sent.* d. 25, p. 2, dub. 2 (Quar. 2:625a–626a). Bonaventure refers explicitly to Bernard in this passage. See Schlosser, *Cognitio et amor*, 64.
36. See Stadter, *Psychologie und Metaphysik*, 30. The difference is subtle: rather than presenting the will as a *potentia*, in the Aristotelian sense of a capacity to be filled, Bonaventure presents it in the more directly Augustinian and Anselmian sense as a *potestas*, a superabundance of ability; but whereas Anselm interpreted this *potestas* as a quantity of force, Bonaventure will emphasize its real achievement.

37. For more detail, see Antonio San Cristóbal-Sebastián, *Controversias acerca de la voluntad desde 1270 a 1300* (Madrid: Coculsa, 1958), and the classic work by Odon Lottin, *Psychologie et morale aux XIIe et XIIIe siècles*, 6 vols., 2nd ed. (Louvain: Abbaye du Mont César, 1942–60).

38. *II Sent.* d. 38, p. 2, q. 2 (Quar. 2:893a–b); this image will be taken up by Scotus, specifically in relation to the act of generation, as we will discuss in chapter 10.

39. *II Sent.* d. 25, p. 2, q. 3 (Quar. 2:599b). Lottin, *Psychologie et morale*, 1:176n2, observes that this interpretation of *facultas* as *facilitas* is unique to Bonaventure.

40. *II Sent.* d. 25, p. 2, q. 3 (Quar. 2:599a).

41. We might compare this to Aquinas, who affirms that, whenever two principles come together in a substantial unity, one must be active and the other passive; see *In VIII Meta.* lect. 5, 1759, ed. Raimondo Spiazzi, *In duodecim libros Metaphysicorum Aristotelis expositio* (Rome: Marietti, 1950); cf. *De spir. creat.* q. un., a. 1 (Leon. 24/2).

42. For a discussion of this, see Kent, *Virtues of the Will*, 133; Stadter, *Psychologie und Metaphysik*, 179–80; Bonnie Kent, "Our Inalienable Ability to Sin: Peter Olivi's Rejection of Asymmetrical Freedom," *British Journal of the History of Philosophy* 25.6 (June 2017): 1073–92.

43. *I Sent.* d. 3, p. 2, a. 1, q. 3 (Quar. 1:86a); cf. Thompson, "Doctrine," 16–22.

44. Aquinas proposes the notion of "proper accidents," which flow immediately from the substance without being identical to it, so that if one were to think away all accidents, one would think away the faculties (*ST* I.77.1 ad 6 [Leon 5]).

45. The word is used loosely here; there is evidently not a numerical plurality in the sense that would compromise God's absolute simplicity.

46. *I Sent.* d. 3, p. 2, a. 1, q. 3 (Quar. 1:86a), my translation; see also *II Sent.* d. 24, p. 1, a. 2, q. 1 (Quar. 2:558a–563b).

47. Thompson, "Doctrine," 21. See *II Sent.* d. 24, p. 1, a. 2, q. 1 (Quar. 2:560a–b).

48. More specifically, the soul is not present in the faculties as a universal whole (so that each part would be named after the substance), or as an integral whole (so that the parts would combine to form the whole), but as a *totum potestativum* (in the sense that the whole of the soul's power is present in each part). (For this distinction, see, for example, Aquinas, *ST* I.77.1 ad 1 [Leon. 5].)

49. "Intention" is central to Bonaventure, but he takes it in an objective, etymological sense (rather than a modern subjectivistic sense): the total directedness of the soul (*in-*) to possession (*tentio*) of its object. See Schlosser, who

translates *intentio* as "Aufgespanntheit auf den Besitz des Anderen" (*Cognitio et amor*, 71–72). Bonaventure also affirms the "typical" sense of *intentio*: "Intentio proprie accepta, secundum quod dicit lumen, per quod est collatio et tendentia in Deum, attenditur circa animae supremum" (*II Sent.* d. 38, a. 2, q. 2 [Quar. 2:890b–891a]).

50. *II Sent.* d. 25, p. 1, a. un., q. 6, ad 2 (Quar. 2:605a–b), my translation.

51. Gilson observes that the principal *end* of the will, and thus of man simply, is *love*, which is interpreted as generosity; see Gilson, *Philosophy of St. Bonaventure*, 413–15. The root of the coincidence of love and will for Bonaventure is of course the Holy Spirit, who bears the names Love, Will — and Liberality. On love in Bonaventure, see Robert Prentice, *The Psychology of Love According to St. Bonaventure* (St. Bonaventure, NY: Franciscan Institute, 1957).

52. Balthasar, *GL2*, 316; *Brev.* 2.9 (Quar. 5:227b).

53. See Balthasar's extensive discussion of the theme of beauty in Bonaventure, in *GL2*, 260–362, esp. 333–52.

54. Dionysius famously accords a certain privilege to the "lower" names of God over the more evidently metaphysical names, insofar as the lower names preserve the essential mystery of God than do these latter, which are more conceptual; see *Mystical Theology*, chap. 3, and *DN* 4.12. Aquinas observes (citing Dionysius) that love specifically as *passion* (*amor*) brings one closer to God than reason or reasoned love (*dilectio*); *ST* I-II.26.3 ad 4 (Leon. 6).

55. *II Sent.* d. 34, p. 2, q. 3, fund. 6 (Quar. 2:814a).

56. St. Francis was of course the paradigm of this phenomenon for Bonaventure in his reception of the stigmata; see *The Life of Francis* (*Legenda Maior*), prologue 1–2.

57. *II Sent.* d. 25, p. 1, un. 1, resp. (Quar. 2:593a), my translation; see John F. Quinn, C.S.B., "The Moral Philosophy of St. Bonaventure," *Southwestern Journal of Philosophy* 5.2 (Summer 1974): 53.

58. Lottin, *Psychologie et morale*, 1:176, my translation.

59. See Quinn, "Moral Philosophy," 52.

60. *II Sent.* d. 25, p. 1, a. 1, q. 6 ad 2 (Quar. 2:605b), my translation.

61. Note that dominion in Bonaventure is not that of the Roman sense of property, namely, *ius utendi et abutendi*, but is *always related* to the good (*II Sent.* d. 25, p. 2, a. 1, q. 3 concl. [Quar. 2:614b]). In this respect, Bonaventure retains what we might call a normative sense of freedom (more fully than Bernard does, for example). On the connection between the will and goodness, see Thompson, "Doctrine," 66–68.

62. God gave a twofold command at creation, one corresponding to nature (to preserve the good that was *given*), the other to discipline (to merit the

good that was *promised*); merit occurs through "pure obedience." *Brev.* 2.11.5 (Quar. 5:229b).

63. *II Sent.* d. 25, p. 1, q. 6., dub. 1 (Quar. 2:607a–b). We will see that for Aquinas the act of command belongs to *intellect* (moving under the power of the will). This is a significant issue because the authority to command comes from what is highest.

64. It is interesting to note that Bonaventure refers explicitly to Anselm and his sense of the will as instrument on this point: "Sicut dicit Anselmus, 'voluntas est instrumentum se ipsum movere.'" The passage he refers to in Anselm is *C* 3.11.

65. *II Sent.* d. 25, p. 1, a. un., q. 3 (Quar. 2:599a).

66. This is not to say that "self-reflexivity" is essential to intellect but not to will. For Bonaventure, both faculties have this capacity, because both are matters of spirit: "cum enim tam ratio quam voluntas sit nata super se reflecti" (*II Sent.* d. 25, p. 1, a. 1, q. 2 [Quar. 2:596b]).

67. "For in spiritual beings *moving* and *being moved* do not have to differ according to substance"; *II Sent* d. 25, p. 1, a. un., q. 2, resp. (Quar. 2:596b). Bonaventure accepts the Aristotelian axiom that "whatever moves is moved by another" (*Phys.* 7.1.241b24) but only for material being (see *Itin.* 2.5 [Quar. 5:300b]), which is another fundamental point of difference with Aquinas.

68. *II Sent.* d. 25, p. 1, a. un., q. 3, resp. (Quar. 2:593a–b), my translation.

69. As Bonaventure says, "Affectio praesupponit cognitionem" (*Myst. Trin.* q. 1, a. 1, f. 3 [Quar. 5:45b], and *II Sent.* d. 25, p. 1, a. 1, q. 6 [Quar. 2:605a]). Cf. Thompson, "Doctrine," 41.

70. We might compare this to *synderesis*, which is also a *natural* ordination to God; but *synderesis* concerns the will considered in itself, while *intentio* concerns the whole soul in the act of the *liberum arbitrium* (see Schlosser, *Cognitio et amor*, 74).

71. *II Sent.* d. 38, a. 2, q. 2 (Quar. 2:893a), my translation.

72. *II Sent.* d. 25, p. 1, a. 1, q. 3 (Quar. 2:599b), my translation.

73. *II Sent.* d. 38, a. 2, q. 2 (Quar. 2:893a), my translation.

74. We do not mean to suggest that the two distinctions are exactly the same; they are not. But we do not have the room here to make a detailed comparison. To mention just one point of difference, Maximus means by *gnomic* a kind of acquired tendency, whereas Bonaventure has in mind the mode of operation in a discrete act. But Bonaventure insists that the natural will and the deliberate will are not two different faculties but one and the same (*II Sent.* d. 24, p. 1, a. 2, q. 3 [Quar. 2:566b]). Bonaventure inherited the terminology, which ultimately originated in Maximus, through the mediation of John Damascus; see Ramelow, "Begriff des Willens," 42.

75. *II Sent.* d. 24, p. 1, a. 2, q. 3 (Quar. 2:566a). Note that Bonaventure identifies synderesis with will, whereas Aquinas will identify it with the (practical) intellect (*ST* I.79.12 [Leon. 5]).

76. See the discussion of merit in *Brev.* 2.9 (Quar. 5:227a).

77. We note that "synderesis" is the soul's natural ordering to the good. See *II Sent.* d. 39, a. 2, q. 1 (Quar. 2:910a), where Bonaventure explains that synderesis is the natural weight innate to the will, which inclines it *ad bonum honestum*; cf. *Itin.*, where he says that synderesis is the "*apex mentis*" (Quar. 5:297b) and that the deliberate will is true to itself only if it cooperates with this natural element. Moreover, Bonaventure affirms God's capacity to *intervene* in the soul's acts, so to speak, without compromising the soul's freedom (see Thompson, "Doctrine," 74). There is thus no competition in principle between God's freedom and the creature's freedom.

78. If Jakob Schmutz ("The Medieval Doctrine of Causality and the Theology of Pure Nature," in *Surnaturel: A Controversy at the Heart of Twentieth-Century Thomist Thought*, ed. Serge-Thomas Bonino [Naples, FL: Ave Maria Press, 2007], 203–50) has a point in raising the question whether Bonaventure introduces a kind of *concursus* in the relationship between God and the creature, which ultimately threatens to turn into a reduction of grace and nature to activities within the same order and therefore potentially in competition, one might also point to the danger of eliminating the reciprocity altogether, rendering God's activity too transcendental, so to speak, so that it is always already simply presupposed in nature's own activities. In this case, nature would be, as it were, always already graced precisely in its natural activity, which implies that there is ultimately no need to refer to anything at all beyond the natural order. Here we see the danger of "transcendental Thomism." There must be an entry of grace *into* the natural order as other—i.e., some sort of cooperative reciprocity—without surrendering the genuine transcendence of grace and the integrity of nature.

79. Though we cannot explore it here, it is worth pointing out that Bonaventure makes the practical order higher, ultimately, than the speculative in the order of man's relation to God; see Quinn, "Moral Philosophy," 39. Hughes helpfully qualifies this point by observing that, if Aquinas arrives at a different conclusion regarding the question of the highest science, it is because he is asking a different question: for Aquinas the question is objective, concerning the object of the science, while for Bonaventure the question is subjective, concerning the purpose of the science (namely, to make us good); see Hughes, "Bonaventure *contra Mundum*." But one nevertheless needs to ask, further, why the two thinkers interpret the question differently.

80. Thompson, "Doctrine," 85.

81. See Ignatius Brady, "Beatitude and Psychology: A Problem in the Philosophy of St. Bonaventure," *Franciscan Studies* 2.4 (December 1942): 411–27.

82. See Gilson, *Philosophy of St. Bonaventure*, 431–69, and especially Schlosser, *Cognitio et amor*, 247–62.

83. See *II Sent*. d. 25, p. 2, a. 1, q. 4, *sed contra* 4 (Quar. 2:616a); *Brev*. 2.4.4 (Quar. 5:221b). Cf. Stadter, *Psychologie und Metaphysik*, 29, and Thompson, "Doctrine," 74.

84. Stadter, *Psychologie und Metaphysik*, 30. It is a curious paradox that the teaching regarding "most high poverty" would coincide with a sense of the human soul as predominantly *full*, though the paradox is no doubt due to the potential implication in extreme poverty of separating from all mediation in separating from the connection to the world simply.

85. Gilson, *Philosophy of St. Bonaventure*, 347.

86. See *II Sent*. d. 25, p. 2, a. 1, q. 3, ad 4 (Quar. 2:594a), my translation.

87. See Gilson, *Philosophy of St. Bonaventure*, 179–80: "From the point of view of Christian Aristotelianism, the soul in its essence considered separately does not contain the sufficient conditions for any of its acts, while from the Augustinian point of view as interpreted by St. Bonaventure, it is sufficient to explain and produce them." Gilson goes on to explain that, in Bonaventure's thought, goodness is both the productive and the final cause. This marks a fundamental difference from Aristotle, for whom things move in order to achieve good essentially as end. For Bonaventure, the achievement of good brings about production—"The will is the productivity of a good which is its own rule" (180). Note that we return to a point in Plotinus again here, namely, the emphasis on movement *out* of perfection rather than *toward* perfection.

88. *II Sent*. d. 25, p. 1, a. 1, q. 6 (Quar. 2:605b), where Bonaventure explains that the "facultas, quae dicitur liberum arbitrium, in ratione inchoatur et in voluntate consummatur."

89. Bonaventure explains the Trinitarian taxis in terms of the logic of the faculties; *Brev*. 1.6 (Quar. 5:215b): "Will presupposes knowledge, and both will and knowledge presuppose power and strength, because 'the capacity to know is a certain power'" (quoting Richard of St. Victor here, *De Trin*. 6.15 [PL 196:979D]).

90. Lottin, *Psychologie et morale*, 1:179.

91. We recall that, for Bernard, reason is not "part" of the *liberum arbitrium* but instead presents an extrinsic check on what is otherwise wholly an act of will.

92. *II Sent*. d. 25, p. 1, a. 1, q. 3, ad 5 (Quar. 2:599b), my translation.

93. See *II Sent*. d. 25, p. 2, a. un., q. 4 (Quar. 2:616b) and q. 5 (Quar. 2:619b). One might wonder whether there is a connection between the radical

poverty of the Franciscans, which implies a renunciation of any fundamental and abiding bond with the world beyond the "incidental" contact through discrete use, and the notion of will as having a kind of uncontested and uncontestable power over things: *dominium* is transferred from indicating an embodied condition of being to a quality of the soul's activity considered in itself.

94. "Rursus, quia discretio veri est cognitio, fuga et appetitus est affectio; idea tota anima dividitur in cognitivam et affectivam"; *Brev.* 2.9 (Quar. 5:227b). Note that appetite is a species of *affectio*, which also comprises its opposite, *fuga*. Cf. *II Sent.* d. 25, p. 1, a. 1, q. 2 (Quar. 2:596b); Thompson, "Doctrine," 22.

95. Schlosser, *Cognitio et amor*, 65n42.

96. *Itin.* 1.14 (Quar. 5:299a), my translation.

97. John Milbank insightfully raises this question in "The Franciscan Conundrum," *Communio* 42 (Fall 2015): 472. We might think here of the appearance of the "creche." The urgent question is whether *imitatio* thus interpreted flattens out the analogy, and whether it tends to eclipse the fundamental receptivity in the relation to God: Do we *first* (and abidingly) receive God's action on our behalf, or do we enact the reality for ourselves according to God's model?

98. *Hex.* 2.2 (Quar. 5:336b); *II Sent.* d. 1, p. 1, q. 1, ad 2 (Quar. 2:17b).

99. Gilson, *Philosophy of St. Bonaventure*, 428–29. The point is not to pit Bonaventure and Aquinas against each other as opposites but to highlight a difference that makes them at least potentially complementary in the manner we have suggested.

100. Bonaventure maintains that the movement from the lower to the higher is not possible unless there is a prior, active disposition; see *Hex.* 4.10 (Quar. 5:351a). In other words, what comes after must already have been anticipated. This is a point we have repeatedly identified as essential to the meaning of freedom, but it is only half of the full paradox, which turns into a distortion if separated from the other half, namely, the novelty introduced from above.

101. Bonaventure wrote of course of the reduction of all arts to theology because Christ is the divine art, so to speak (*De sc. chr.* 4c [Quar. 5:23b]), or the *ars Patris* (*De red. art.* 20 [Quar. 5:324b]). Cf. Balthasar, *GL2*, 292–93.

102. We say "inchoate" in order to preserve the ambiguity: The centrality of Christ—in whom there is no Greek or Jew—does not *necessarily* imply the exclusion of the Greek tradition, but it does to the extent that one insists Aristotle (and all he represents) can contribute nothing to what is already there.

103. See the essay regarding Bonaventure's influence on Franciscan aesthetics by Christopher M. Cullen, S.J., "Bonaventure's Aesthetic Imperative: *Pulcherrimum Carmen*," in *Beauty and the Good: Recovering the Classical Tradition from Plato to Duns Scotus*, ed. Alice Ramos (Washington, DC: Catholic University of America Press, 2020), 251–68.

104. See Balthasar, *GL2*, 319–26.

105. Although Bonaventure says that body and soul represent the maximum difference possible within the genus of substance (matter and spirit), he insists that God has united them in man through his supreme power; *Brev.* 2.10 (Quar. 5:228a). See Brady, "Beatitude and Psychology," 427, and Thompson, "Doctrine," 14.

106. As Bonaventure puts it, "Completio vero naturae requirit, ut homo constet simul ex corpore et anima tamquam ex materia et forma, quae mutuum habent appetitum et inclinationem mutuum"; *Brev.* 7.5 (Quar. 5:286b).

107. Kent, *Virtues of the Will*, 215.

108. Ibid., 212–16.

109. We recall here that the human ideal for Bonaventure is the *Poverello*. See Balthasar's discussion in *GL2*, 326–33.

110. This is a point made forcefully by Alexander Gerken, *Theologie des Wortes: Das Verhältnis von Schöpfung und Inkarnation bei Bonaventura* (Dusseldorf: Patmos, 1963), cited in Balthasar, *GL2*, 360.

111. Consider the fact that love is not just gratuity but also *bond* (*I Sent.* d. 11, a. 1, q. 1 [Quar. 1:210–11]): "Because [God's] infinity includes every form of completion, it does not exclude the perfection of power, order, union, beatitude, representation, and inhabitation" (*Trin.*, q. 4, a. 2, concl. [Quar. 5:85b]). Bonaventure explains that dominion is a sign of perfection only when the action is distinct from the agent, which is the case in human action but not in the Trinitarian processions; *Trin.*, q. 7, a. 2 ad 2 (Quar. 5:111b). One may nevertheless ask whether the lack of dominion—taking *dominion* here to mean standing above and outside—is *also* a perfection. We hope to take up this line of reflection in the projected third volume of our study of the nature of freedom.

112. Lottin, *Psychologie et morale*, 1:174.

113. See, e.g., Kent, *Virtues of the Will*, and Stadter, *Psychologie und Metaphysik*.

114. *II Sent.* d. 25, p. 2, a. un., q. 2 (Quar. 2:612a–b, 613a).

CHAPTER 9. Thomas Aquinas

1. For a similar observation, see Gustav Siewerth, *Die menschliche Willensfreiheit* (Dusseldorf: L. Schwann, 1954), 11–12.

2. The term *unprethinkable* (*unvordenklich*) was famously coined by Schelling in his constantly repeated, and frustrated, efforts to achieve a complete philosophy of freedom; see D. C. Schindler, *Perfection of Freedom*, 113 et passim.

3. The point is that the poverty of tradition *coincides* with the first clear inadequacies in the conception of freedom. Nevertheless, we do not mean to make a facile judgment; Christianity is *essentially* traditional, and tradition passes fruitfully through these figures even if they do not consciously appropriate it in full. But the response to this relative poverty is to see that part of properly understanding the meaning of a notion and passing it on is ensuring the transmission of the proper conditions. (So, for example, the preservation of a library is, even in its status as "material culture," part of what it means to try to understand a theme, and so forth.)

4. On the significance of this text, see Philipp W. Rosemann, *The Story of a Great Medieval Book: Peter Lombard's Sentences* (Peterborough, ON: Broadview Press, 2007): the *Sentences* "folded the tradition back into a unity that it needed in the twelfth century: a highly differentiated unity, in which the voices of the Bible itself, of its earliest interpreters—the Fathers of the Church—and of the medieval theologians retained their distinctiveness while being woven into a harmonious composition of systematic theology" (17). To be sure, Lombard's book is composed almost entirely of passages from Augustine, but the point is that it represents, and enacts, an effort to see the tradition as an integrated body of wisdom.

5. M.-D. Chenu, *Nature, Man, and Society in the Twelfth Century* (Chicago: University of Chicago Press, 1968), 1–48.

6. According to Olivier Boulnois, the practice of commentary on the *Sentences* is precisely what distinguishes the Scholastic period from the monastic one; *La puissance et son ombre* (Paris: Aubier, 1994), 14.

7. *ST* I.6.4 (Leon. 4).

8. *De pot.* 3.7, ed. Raimondo Spiazzi, *Quaestiones disputatae* (Turin: Marietti, 1953) (all citations of *De pot.* are to this edition), trans. English Dominican Fathers, *On the Power of God* (Westminster, MD: Newman Press, 1952). Translations in this chapter are given with occasional slight modifications.

9. *SCG* 3.85.4 (Leon. 14).

10. *ST* III.18.4ad1 (Leon. 11). Aquinas is explicitly addressing Damascene here, but it is through Damascene that he received the influence of Maximus; see Gauthier, "Maxime le Confesseur," 52 and 57. We also have Aquinas's appropriation of the distinction between the natural and the gnomic will, with the priority of the natural; *ST* I.60.4 (Leon. 5).

11. *De ver.* 23.6 ad 1 (Leon. 22/3). Moreover, Aquinas affirms Anselm's statement that freedom in man (and angels) must be similar to freedom in God, but he introduces the notion of analogy, which allows nevertheless a radical difference; *De ver.* 24.3 (Leon. 22/3).

12. See *De ver.* 22.5 and 14 (Leon. 22/3).

13. *ST* I-II.9.3 (Leon. 6).

14. Gustav Siewerth, *Das Gute als bewegender Grund der Freiheit* (Freiburg: Gustav-Siewerth-Gesellschaft, 2011), which is a commentary on *ST* I-II.10.1–3 (Leon. 6).

15. For a magisterial summation of Aquinas's teaching on the freedom of the will, which is based on the *De veritate* but addresses Aquinas's entire development, albeit in a concise way, see Anselm Ramelow's substantial afterword to his translation of questions from *De veritate*: *Über die Wahrheit*, vol. 5 of the *Quaestiones disputatae* series (Hamburg: Felix Meiner, 2013), 311–99. See also Yul Kim, *Selbstbewegung des Willens bei Thomas von Aquin* (Berlin: Akademie Verlag, 2007); David M. Gallagher, "Free Choice and Free Judgment in Thomas Aquinas," *Archiv für Geschichte der Philosophie* 76 (1994): 247–77.

16. *SCG* 1.78.1–7 (Leon. 13).

17. The principal argument Aquinas gives for God having a will is that will is *included within* intellect (*SCG* 1.72.2 [Leon. 13]; cf. *ST* I.19.1 [Leon. 4]). It is impossible, according to Aquinas, to have an intellect without having a will. Maximus had already implied this in his account of the will as rational appetite. We will see Aquinas's reasoning as we proceed.

18. *ST* I.19.3 ad 6 (Leon. 4), trans. Fathers of the English Dominican Province [hereafter FEDP], *Summa Theologica* (New York: Benziger Bros., 1947–48); see also *De ver.* 22.3 ad 4 (Leon. 22/3) and *ST* I.60.2 (Leon. 5).

19. In human knowers this mode of existence is likeness, in God it is the reality itself but presupposes the will; see *SCG* 1.72.3 (Leon. 13).

20. See *ST* I.6.4 *sed contra* (Leon. 4).

21. It is crucial to note that the *end* of God's creative will—as distinct from the end of his will *simpliciter*, which is of course his own good—is not simply the properties of things (as Trego argued tends to be the case in Anselm, as we saw) and indeed not only the substance of things, but the *subsisting* substance, the very act of being of things, which is most intimate and formal (*ST* I.8.1 [Leon. 4]); it is not simply the good as property, or even good as substance, but good *simpliciter*. We will elaborate this point below.

22. See *ST* I.19.4 (Leon. 4) and *SCG* 1.75.7 (Leon. 13). An illuminating presentation of the relation between the divine intellect and will in creation, which demonstrates a sensitivity to the problematic implications of common misinterpretations, can be found in James Ross, "Aquinas's Exemplarism; Aquinas's Voluntarism," *American Catholic Philosophical Quarterly* 64.2 (1990): 171–98.

23. *I Sent.* 37.1.1c, in *Opera omnia* (Parma: Fiaccadori, 1852–73), vol. 6; all subsequent cites to this work are to this edition. See also *Super Evangelium S. Ioannis lectura* c. 1, l. 5, n133.

24. *SCG* 1.75.3 (Leon. 13), trans. Anton C. Pegis et al., *On the Truth of the Catholic Faith* (New York: Hanover House, 1955–57).

25. *ST* I.5.1 ad 3 (Leon. 4). Aquinas affirms, furthermore, that goodness is not only the actual form of things but also everything precedes and follows from it; *ST* I.5.5 (Leon. 4).

26. By this word, I mean to indicate the fact that the will to the good is a will to its *increase*, which means that the very ordering to the good turns out also in some respect to exceed it. As we will see, this will be key to the depth dimension of freedom.

27. *SCG* 1.81.4 (Leon. 13): "God, in willing His own goodness, wills things other than Himself to be in so far as they participate in His goodness. But, since the divine goodness is infinite, it can be participated in in infinite ways, and in ways other than it is participated in by the creatures that now exist. If, then, as a result of willing His own goodness, God necessarily willed the things that participate in it, it would follow that He would will the existence of an infinity of creatures participating in His goodness in an infinity of ways. This is patently false, because, if He willed them, they would be, since His will is the principle of being for things. . . . Therefore, God does not necessarily will even the things that now exist" (trans. Pegis et al.). The impossibility is due to the fact that an actual infinity cannot exist. In *ST* I.32.1 ad 2 (Leon. 4), Aquinas affirms that creation *ex nihilo* is already itself an expression of the *infinity* of God's power, because there is an infinite difference between being and nothing. He concludes from this that we do not need to posit an infinite effect, beyond this, but only that the recipient receives the goodness according to its own mode. Nevertheless, our argument is not that the effect needs to be (univocally) infinite itself but that it will necessarily reflect the infinity of its cause in a manner fitting to it—i.e., analogously. In other words, it would be unfitting—which is *not* to say strictly impossible, unless we measure possibility by God's goodness—for God to have a created a single finite reality from nothing: though this single finite reality would display the infinity of God's power in one respect, having been brought into being from nothing, in another respect in its singularity it would give a radically deficient expression of that infinity in comparison to a teeming cosmos. The world ought to reflect the infinity of God's power and goodness not only in the sheer fact of existing, but also, analogously, in the content of what exists (God is, so to speak, the species of the form of things; *De pot*. 6.6 ad 5).

28. *SCG* 1.75 and 1.76 (Leon. 13). It is important to keep in mind the distinction between the necessary and the contingent, which is reflected in the distinction between the divine *voluntas* and the divine *liberum arbitrium*.

29. Which is not to say there is no otherness. Plotinus famously criticizes Aristotle for failing to see that the difference that necessarily accompanies intellect implies a unity that transcends intellect as its principle; *Ennead* 5.1.4.

30. See *ST* I.19.2 ad 1 (Leon. 4): "For when we say that God exists, no relation to any other is implied, as we do imply when we say that God wills" (trans. FEDP). This also means when God wills himself. To feel the provocation of this point, we might simply ask: If the divine will is omnipotent, can we say that God is omnipotent with respect to himself, with respect to his own essence? What would this mean for the meaning of will, of essence, of power—in short, of freedom?

31. For a more extensive exploration of this particular theme than is possible here, see my essay "What's the Difference? On the Metaphysics of Participation in Plato, Plotinus, and Aquinas," *Nova et Vetera* 5 (2007): 583–618.

32. See Plotinus, *Ennead* 6.8.13. We discussed this in chapter 2.

33. *ST* I.28.3, I.30.3 (Leon. 4). Cf. my discussion of this point in "What's the Difference?"

34. *De pot.* 2.1. It is important to note that, while Aquinas affirms that the generation of the Son is *willed* by the Father, he categorically denies that the will can be in any way a *principle* of generation (*De pot.* 2.3). We will reflect on the implications of this point at the end. The question of whether the essential generativity of God offers the possibility of a rational demonstration of the Trinity is profoundly interesting, but we cannot follow it out here.

35. *SCG* 1.72.9 (Leon. 13): "He is therefore not only the appetible end, but also the seeker of Himself as the end, so to speak" (trans. Pegis et al.).

36. *ST* I.32.1 ad 3 (Leon. 4); cf. *ST* I.45.6 ad 1 (Leon. 4).

37. This is not to say that only Christians have ever conceived creation as an act of freedom, but only that, for that conception to be able to be sustained, a Trinitarian notion of God would eventually be necessary. For a subtle assessment of this point, see Burrell, *Freedom and Creation in Three Traditions*, e.g., 96 and 166. The argument Thomas sketched in *ST* I.32.1 ad 3 (Leon. 4) can be filled out by the discussion in *De pot.* 2.3 and *SCG* 1.88 (Leon. 13). Essentially, the argument would run thus: just as will as *liberum arbitrium* presupposes *voluntas* (or freedom *ut natura*), so too does the freedom of the creative act, which Aquinas explicitly compares to *liberum arbitrium*, presuppose a perfect act of will already in itself: *voluntas*, which is the procession *per modum voluntatis* (i.e., the procession of the Spirit) that in turn presupposes the procession *per modum intellectus* (i.e., the procession of the Son).

38. Aquinas makes this point explicitly in *SCG* 1.76.8 (Leon. 13); cf. *SCG* 2.6.6 (Leon. 13), *ST* I.44.3 (Leon. 4), which affirms exemplarity, and *ST* I.44.4 (Leon. 4), which draws the inference regarding created things' appetite in relation to their own goodness.

39. There is nothing *accidental* in God, strictly speaking; *SCG* 1.82.2 (Leon. 13); *ST* I.3.6 (Leon. 4).

40. *De pot.* 3.15 ad 20: "God's will is his essence: wherefore his working by his will does not prevent his working by his essence. God's will is not an intention in addition to his essence, but is his very essence" (trans. English Dominican Fathers). *De ver.* 22.2 (Leon. 22/3): "Created existence is itself a likeness to the divine goodness. So in desiring to be, things implicitly desire a likeness to God and God Himself" (trans. Robert W. Mulligan et al., *Truth* [Chicago: Henry Regnery, 1952–54]).

41. Note that we do not mean infinity in the extensive sense here, which would entail the affirmation that God's omnipotence would imply an *omnivolens* in the sense of God's willing exhaustively every possible thing into infinity. That omnipotence does not mean *omnivolens* in this sense is clear; *De ver.* 25.3 ad 1 (Leon. 22/3).

42. *De ver.* 23.5 (Leon. 22/3).

43. *ST* I.25.6 (Leon. 4). Cf. *De pot.* 1.5 ad 8.

44. Or more accurately it is the supreme *penultimate* form: the ultimate form is the relation between the Persons and the essence of God, or in fact the relation between the Persons.

45. For the origin of the *potentia absoluta/ordinata* distinction, see W. J. Courtenay, *Covenant and Causality in Medieval Thought* (London: Variorum Reprints, 1984), Essay IV, 2. In fact, the original putting of the question was quite concrete according to Courtenay: it began at a dinner in 1067, in a discussion between Peter Damian and Desiderius, the abbot of Monte Cassino. Aquinas does refer to the distinction between *potentia ordinata* and *potentia absoluta* but explains that this distinction is not real; it applies only to our understanding (see *SCG* 1.87.6 [Leon. 13] and *De pot.* 1.5 ad 5). Burrell insists on the "relentlessly *actual* character of God's presence to the world" (*Freedom and Creation in Three Traditions*, 105) and the radical priority of actuality over possibility in Christian thought (111–18). Fr. Anselm Ramelow has shown that something like what is later called *possibile logicum* can be found in Aquinas (see, for example, *ST* I.25.3 [Leon. 4], in which Aquinas articulates a sense of absolute possibility, defined by the compatibility of predicates with a particular subject); Ramelow, *Gott, Freiheit, Weltanwahl* (Leiden: Brill, 1997), 8–31. But even this, Ramelow goes on to show, remains a possibility *relative* to God as an actual agent and to the finality of a subject considered as a perfected substance—or in other words, relative to a more fundamental actuality.

46. It would imply a capacity to change, and it would deny God as total cause of all things; *ST* I.19.6 ad 7 (Leon. 4). As we mentioned above, Aquinas distinguishes God's omnipotence from his being actually *omnivolens* (*De ver.* 23.3 ad 1 [Leon. 22/3]); we are raising a question about the logic and ground of this distinction.

47. We recall that the question of the nature of power arose in the Bible; see our discussion in chapter 1. This point should be connected to our discussion of freedom as "dominion," "power *over*," which we explored at the end of the previous chapter.

48. For a general account of the transformation of the meaning of possibility/potency over the course of the Middle Ages, and its implications, see Boulnois, *Puissance et son ombre*, and Trego, *Impuissance du possible*.

49. See *ST* I.7 (Leon. 4).

50. As Burrell notes, the idea of a preexistent set of possibilities in the divine mind is a projection of pagan ideas onto a Jewish-Christian-Muslim canvas; *Freedom and Creation in Three Traditions*, 111. We will discuss this further in our chapter on Scotus below. Aquinas does allow a kind of "incomplete" sort of idea of things God has no intention of ever making, but these are, first of all, secondary in relation to complete ideas (which are or will be real) and, second, are not objects to be known in a theoretical mode but forms lying implicit in the power of an actual maker; *De pot.* 1.5 ad 11. It is *not* the case that God *first* has a set of possibles as objects of intellect, from which he subsequently selects. Note, too, that the actual world is thus measured, not against the infinity of possible worlds, but against the infinity of God's goodness, which *enforces* the world's actuality.

51. The "therefore" references the previous point: we might know something that does not yet exist. In this case, "Although at that moment the thing does not exist save only in the intellect, the relation following upon the apprehension is to the thing, not as it exists in the knower, but as it is in its own nature, which the one apprehending apprehends" (*SCG* 1.79.7 [Leon. 13], trans. Pegis et al.).

52. *SCG* 1.79.8 (Leon. 13), trans. Pegis et al.

53. As Aquinas explains, it is possible for God to will an infinity as long as we see that infinity unfolding successively in time, which means that, with respect to what is now, the infinity remains potential rather than actual; see *ST* I.7.3 ad 4 (Leon. 4).

54. The fact that he does not do so is significant and concerns the ambiguity in his thought that we will highlight at the end of this chapter.

55. In taking this approach, we are skipping over, so to speak, a solution to the problem outlined in detail in Ramelow's *Gott, Freiheit, Weltanwahl*. As Ramelow shows, Aquinas does indeed posit a sphere of "logical possibility," which is an absolute possibility considered in itself, and not only in relation to divine power, as an implication of the *freedom* of God's act of creation. He shows, however, that this sphere differs from that of Scotus insofar as Aquinas approaches the question as one of the "compossibility" of predicates in a subject (and not the pure formality of predicates in their interrelation) and relative

to God's actual will. Moreover, the measure of compossibility takes its bearings from the subject considered as a perfected substance. In this regard, it is embedded in the orienting context of actuality, even if this differs from empirical reality. Affirming all of this, we are taking a step further, considering the perfection of substance in relation specifically to the actuality of *esse*, the perfection of all perfections. In other words, Aquinas places a certain teleological constraint on logic, and we are interpreting this point as ultimately ordered to *esse*: the teleology is not an abstract ideal but the actuality of being.

56. *ST* I.47.2 (Leon. 4); cf. *SCG* 1.77 (Leon. 13).

57. See *SCG* 1.85 (Leon. 13).

58. Hannah Arendt is therefore wrong to say that "Scotus is the only thinker for whom the word 'contingent' has no derogatory association" (*Life of the Mind*, 134).

59. We borrow the term *superdeterminacy* from Yves Simon, who uses it to describe the human will, which is ordered to universal goodness and so not necessarily determined to any one thing in particular; see Yves Simon, *Freedom of Choice* (New York: Fordham University Press, 1969). We will discuss this point below, but it is crucial to see that what Simon calls the superdeterminacy of the will has its roots in the superdeterminacy of being.

60. This is why Aquinas insists that, even if God acts beyond nature in things, it is never *against nature*, which means it will always turn out to be a fulfillment of given, actual natural principles; *ST* I.105.6 (Leon. 5).

61. Note, this is a necessity *ex hypothesi*, one resulting from the inner determination of the artist's will, rather than imposed from without.

62. For a somewhat trivial but still illuminating illustration of the point, one might consider how the power of a film fades when one is "treated" to "alternate endings" in the collector's edition DVD. Rather than enhancing the beauty of the film, the experience of which arrives with a sense of necessity, a sense that it could not have ended any other way, these alternate endings tend to make the actual ending finally chosen seem arbitrary. The dramatic interest of the film tends to dissipate.

63. The position Burrell adopts, which we cited earlier (*Freedom and Creation in Three Traditions*, 111–18), is reinforced by Ross's interpretation of the divine ideas ("Aquinas's Exemplarism").

64. *ST* I.45.2 ad 2 (Leon. 4).

65. Note we are not saying that God can create *only* the world that exists in an empirical sense and that there is no infinite (and world-transcending) potency in God's will, but only in creatures, which now possess infinite possibilities of their own, subject to their own power alone. This is a complete misunderstanding of the argument, which assumes a kind of competition between

God's power and that belonging to creatures. We will elaborate below that the superdeterminacy lies most basically in the order of *esse*, which is itself always limited by the finite natures that participate in it, without for all that being subsumed simply into that finitude. This line of thinking has been inspired by Ulrich, *Homo Abyssus*.

66. See Brian J. Shanley, O.P., "Divine Causation and Human Freedom in Aquinas," *American Catholic Philosophical Quarterly* 72.1 (1998): 99–122. Cf. Steven A. Long, "Providence, Freedom, and Natural Law," *Nova et Vetera* 4.3 (2006): 557–606.

67. Etienne Gilson, *The Philosophy of St. Thomas Aquinas* (New York: Dorset, 1948), 197.

68. Note that the eternal "foreknowledge," which of course belongs to God, does not mean a determination that temporally precedes the act. To think it does is to reduce eternity to a temporal order, and so to put God's eternity into competition with the actuality of history. Burrell notes the difference in Aquinas between "providence" and "predestination" along these lines; *Freedom and Creation in Three Traditions*, 120–22.

69. Gilson, *Philosophy of St. Thomas Aquinas*, 196. Nature may seem to be *essentially* determined (*ad unum*), which is what distinguishes it from freedom. But this does not imply a necessary determinism; see James Weisheipl, "Aristotle's Concept of Nature: Avicenna and Aquinas," in *Approaches to Nature in the Middle Ages*, ed. L. D. Roberts (Binghamton, NY: Center for Medieval and Early Renaissance Studies, 1982). Note, we cite this essay, not to endorse Weisheipl's interpretation of Avicenna on its own merits, but rather to affirm the view of Aquinas, to which the other is a foil. If nature is an *internal* principle, it can be determined *ad unum* without eliminating the contingency of its accomplishment of that end, in its concrete interaction with the rest of the cosmos.

70. The statement "Prima rerum creatorum est esse" is from the *Liber de causis*. See *ST* I.45.4 (Leon. 4). Rudi te Velde explains that Aquinas affirms a *self-transcending* sense of nature because nature is understood specifically as a participating *in being*; "*Natura in Seipsa Recurva Est*: Duns Scotus and Aquinas on the Relationship between Nature and Will," in *John Duns Scotus: Renewal of Philosophy. Acts of the Third Symposium Organized by the Dutch Society for Medieval Philosophy Medium Aevum*, ed. E. P. Bos (Amsterdam: Rodopi, 1998), 160–61. Gustav Siewerth justly observes that the reason the classical tradition reaches its perfection in Aquinas is that he gathers the various Christian insights into the nature and importance of freedom and interprets them specifically on the basis of *being*; *Menschliche Willensfreiheit*, 16.

71. See Etienne Gilson, *Being and Some Philosophers* (Toronto: Pontifical Institute of Medieval Studies, 2016), 71–73.

72. *I Sent.* 37.1.1. Aquinas says that *to give* is to hand over in a definitive way; *ST* I.38.2 (Leon. 4).

73. Gilson, *Philosophy of St. Thomas Aquinas*, 197. Let us note a point we will return to below, namely, that freedom is first of all a matter of goodness rather than power, and that so conceived it may properly be described as love.

74. The point is *not*, as Jean-Luc Marion supposes, principally because of the privileging of conceptuality, even if Aquinas does indeed affirm that being is the first thing known, and so forth; see Jean-Luc Marion, *God without Being* (Chicago: University of Chicago Press, 1991), 53–107.

75. It is helpful to recall, here, the problems that arise when one does not affirm the concrete *substance* as the terminus of God's creative act, which we discussed in the chapter on Anselm.

76. *ST* I.4.1 ad 3 (Leon. 4), trans. FEDP; John Wippel, "Thomas Aquinas and Participation," in *Studies in Medieval Philosophy*, ed. John Wippel (Washington, DC: Catholic University of America Press, 1987), 123.

77. In *ST* I.103.4 (Leon. 5), trans. FEDP, Aquinas explains that the effects of God's providence are "without number."

78. See *ST* I.45.2 ad 3 (Leon. 4); this is sometimes referred to as *creatio continua*, a phrase that can be affirmed only if it is not taken to imply that the act of creation is something like an "ongoing process." Instead, it has to be affirmed as complete in every moment.

79. This is not in the least a denial of the *immanence* of the act of will; see the discussion of this point in my short piece "A Deeper Unity: Response to Professor Feingold on the Psychological Analogy for the Trinity," *Nova et Vetera* 17.2 (2019): 533–43.

80. *ST* I.44.4 ad 1 (Leon. 4). Notice that Aquinas refers to God's *freedom*, i.e., his "liberality," in giving in this way. Cf. *SCG* 1.75.5 and 6 (Leon. 13).

81. In *De ver.* 1.1 (Leon. 22/1), Aquinas identifies the *other*, to which being considered universally is ordered, as the human soul.

82. *De ver.* 22.2 (Leon. 22/3), which identifies goodness with the act of being that all things seek for themselves.

83. *ST* I.5.2 and 4 (Leon. 4).

84. With this, we connect with the notion of God's will as "covenantal," which we described in chapter 1. Here, we are desiring God's communication of goodness, and so synthesizing the Jewish and Greek senses of divine power.

85. Note that when Aquinas affirms that God has free choice, *liberum arbitrium*, he explains that this does not mean God makes a selection from pregiven alternatives to which his will would stand in potency (see the argument he offers in *SCG* 1.82.2 and the response he gives in 1.82.6 [Leon. 13]). Note that Aquinas thus presents a certain "twist" on the meaning of *liberum arbitrium*: it

is not free (i.e., contingent) *principally* because it is faced by a series of options, but it is free (i.e., contingent) because it is relative to the end of God's absolute goodness. The possibility does not *precede* the actuality as a *possibile logicum* that is opposed to actual reality but coincides with the (super-)actuality of what God actually wills. We might say instead that the phrase in this context indicates in the first place the creation of finite "infinities," full of perfect contingencies, in each thing individually and in the cosmos as a whole. In this case, we could say that *liberum arbitrium* means the capacity to fill a finite reality with infinite significance. God's creative will (*liberum arbitrium*) is an *ad extra* expression of his simple will of himself (*voluntas*), and so the creature will necessarily reflect something of God's infinite goodness (*SCG* 1.76.8 [Leon. 13]; cf. *SCG* 1.88.4 [Leon. 13]). We already questioned at length the opposition between a "free" creation and a "necessary" emanation in our discussion of Plotinus and Dionysius in previous chapters above.

86. Aquinas explains the meaning of "active power" in *De pot.* 1.1.

87. See our discussion in *FFR*, 56–60. We will see a forerunner of this notion in Scotus, in chapter 11 below.

88. It is worth noting, in view of a longer discussion that would have to take place elsewhere, that Aquinas affirms a kind of indeterminacy in God (*ST* I.19.4 [Leon. 4]), though this is not at all a potency in need of determination, but already a perfection (*ST* I.9.1 [Leon. 4]); even the generation of the Son is not a change from potency to act (*SCG* 4.14.3 [Leon. 15]). But this perfection is not a reduction of God to an actuality of the finite, essential order, which is why these affirmations can be reconciled with the indeterminacy in God. Aquinas can be said to integrate Plotinus and Aristotle on this score: with Plotinus he affirms an infinite potency, which is to that extent indeterminate, and with Aristotle he affirms the complete *perfection* of God as pure act. We see that Aquinas offers the possibility of a nuanced response to the problem with God as pure act elaborated in Barnes, *Power of God*.

89. Siewerth, *Menschliche Willensfreiheit*, 30.

90. A subtle but profound expression of this point can be seen in the comparison between Aristotle's notion of form, which he says cannot desire itself in any respect but can only be the unmoved object of the desire of matter (see *Phys.* 1.9.192a16–22), and Aquinas's highlighting of the *actual subsistence* of form, which does not remain unmoved in itself but pours itself out and returns to itself (*De ver.* 2.2.2 [Leon. 22/1]), a "transcendental" sort of movement, which *includes* the movement of matter to form and the emanation of the substance in its accidents, and which comes to light specifically in the relation between essence and *esse*.

91. *De pot.* 3.7; *ST* I.105.5 (Leon. 4); *SCG* 3.69 and 70 (Leon. 14).

92. See Norris Clarke's classic essay "Action as the Self-Revelation of Being: A Central Theme in the Thought of St. Thomas," in *Explorations in Metaphysics* (Notre Dame, IN: University of Notre Dame Press, 1994), 45–64.

93. *De pot.* 2.1.

94. *SCG* 3.64 (Leon. 14).

95. This is not to say that Aristotle positively excludes this dimension, which is why we can "reread" him and not just set him aside.

96. See *ST* I.19.2 (Leon. 4): "For natural things have a natural inclination not only towards their own proper good, to acquire it if not possessed, and, if possessed, to rest therein; but also to spread abroad their own good amongst others, so far as possible" (trans. FEDP). In *SCG* 3.24.8 (Leon. 14), Aquinas affirms the simultaneity of things tending *to God*, to give good generously *to others*, and to seek their *own perfection*. Cf. *De ver.* 2.2.2 (Leon. 22/1), where he connects the self-relation of subsistence with the movement outward that *perfects* the other.

97. Plato, *Tim.* 29e. Hegel adopted this point in Plato as central to his own philosophy; see his *Lectures on the History of Philosophy* (Lincoln: University of Nebraska Press, 1995), 72–73.

98. According to Daniel J. Pierson, the phrase "Omne agens agit sibi simile" occurs over 220 times in the Thomistic corpus; "Thomas Aquinas on the Principle *Omne Agens Agit Sibi Simile*" (PhD diss., Catholic University of America, 2015).

99. *SCG* 3.69 (Leon. 14). See Petr Dvořak, "The Concurrentism of Thomas Aquinas," *Philosophia* 41.3 (2013): 617–34.

100. *ST* I.60.4 (Leon. 5), trans. FEDP. Emphasis added.

101. This seems to be Plotinus's view; he appeals to the evident fruitfulness of perfection as an explanation for the productivity of the One (*Ennead* 6.1.6).

102. There is a fascinating anticipation of this point in Aristotle's notion of luck (*tychē*), which is a kind of gratuitous achievement of ends, a causality that exceeds the intrinsic dimension of nature without for all that relativizing nature; see *Phys.* 2.4–6 and Weisheipl, "Aristotle's Concept of Nature," 80.

103. He explains that *creation*, i.e., the giving of *esse*, does not occur outside of the order of nature because it does not belong to the order of nature (and so cannot be opposed to it); *ST* I.105.7 ad 1 (Leon. 5). Peter Damian, by contrast, interpreted *creatio ex nihilo* as *contra naturam*; see Boulnois, *Puissance et son ombre*, 24.

104. *ST* I.19.2 (Leon. 4), trans. FEDP. This is ultimately why the supposed opposition between eros and agape (see Nygren, *Agape and Eros*) is a later invention, which presupposes a nominalist metaphysics. The principle

cited in Aquinas is an echo of a central theme in the Christian Neoplatonist tradition. For a presentation of this central notion, see our discussion of Dionysius above and in *Catholicity of Reason*, 203–19.

105. *De ver.* 5.8 (Leon. 22/1). See also *Compendium theologiae*, chap. 103, where Aquinas says things desire to communicate their own being as far as they are perfect, in imitation of divine causality.

106. This Greek form characterized *spirit* (νοῦς) above all; here we see an analogous extension of this form all the way through to the bottom of nature.

107. *De ver.* 22.1 (Leon. 22/3).

108. One sees this interpretation of appetitive desire, for example, in José Ortega y Gassett, who therefore opposes it to the other-directed movement of love, claiming that Aquinas was simply confused on this point; *On Love* (New York: Meridian Books, 1957), 7–18.

109. "Whatever is found in reality is called a nature." *De ver.* 22.5 (Leon. 22/3).

110. *De ver.* 1.1 (Leon. 22/1).

111. *ST* I-II.26.1 (Leon. 6).

112. *De pot.* 2.1.

113. *ST* I.19.2 (Leon. 4).

114. *ST* I.80.1 (Leon. 5).

115. *ST* I.80.2 (Leon. 5).

116. *De ver.* 22.1 (Leon. 22/1).

117. *De ver.* 22.4 (Leon. 22/3).

118. *ST* I.78.1 (Leon. 5).

119. *De ver.* 22.1.3 (Leon. 22/3).

120. *ST* I.5.5 (Leon. 4): "Upon the form follows an inclination to the end, or to an action, or something of that sort; for everything, in so far as it is in act, acts and tends towards that which is in accordance with its form" (trans. FEDP) (note the coincidence of acting and tending toward indicated here). *In. divin. nom.* iv.10.13–25, ed. C. Pera, *In librum Beati Dionysii De divinis nominibus expositio* (Turin: Marietti, 1950), my translation: "The relation of appetite to something as to its own good is called love. But all that is ordained to something as to its own good has in a certain sense that thing present and united to itself according to a certain similitude, at least of proportion, just as form is in some way in matter in that matter has an aptitude and order to form."

121. See our discussion of Aristotle in these terms in *FFR*, 323–58.

122. Hegel does not have *esse* as a principle; his interpretation of being as pure indeterminacy in the opening pages of the *Science of Logic* is not unrelated to his interpretation of philosophical movement as essentially dialectical.

123. This is not to deny the distinction between them formally, only to say that they inevitably interpenetrate in the concrete order.

124. *De malo* 6 ad 7 (Leon. 23), trans. Richard Regan, *On Evil* (Oxford: Oxford University Press, 2003). See Ramelow, afterword to *De veritate*, 347.

125. *ST* I.60.2 (Leon. 5), trans. FEDP. A general theme in Aquinas's thought is the *prioritas naturae*; see Josef Pieper, *The Silence of St. Thomas* (Chicago: Regnery, 1965). The affirmation of the absoluteness of nature is meant, not to deny the higher order of grace, but only to observe that nature remains an inviolable reference point even in relation to the higher orders of grace and glory; *ST* I.1.8 ad 2 and *ST* I.2.2 ad 1 (Leon. 4).

126. Jean-Paul Sartre, "Existentialism," in *Existentialism and Human Emotions* (New York: Philosophical Library, 1957), 9–51. There is a devastating contradiction at the heart of Sartre's theory: our choices are meant to be infinitely dramatic, and filled with the weight of responsibility, because we are deciding about the whole in each moment, which we only have ourselves to answer for. But if that meaning is, as it were, "up for grabs" at each moment, no decision bears on anything at all but itself and so has *no* significance beyond the moment in which it is made. We discussed this self-undermining character, which is to say the diabolical character, of freedom so conceived, in *FFR*, 185–88.

127. Ulrich helpfully explains that the priority of *esse* can nevertheless coincide (in fact *cannot but coincide*) with its presupposed essence; see *Homo Abyssus*, 61–96b.

128. Note that when Aquinas elevates "love of choice" (*dilectio electiva*) over "natural love" (*dilectio naturalis*), as a kind of love possessed by rational creatures, he nevertheless indicates that this love of choice concerns *means*, which are loved for the sake of the end loved by nature; *ST* I.60.4 (Leon. 5), trans. FEDP.

129. *ST* I.84.1 ad 3 (Leon. 5); *ST* I.82.1 (Leon. 4).

130. We will address this point more directly and extensively in volume 3, where we will discuss the work of Ferdinand Ulrich, who has reflected on this no doubt more profoundly than anyone else.

131. See David M. Gallagher, "Thomas Aquinas on the Will as Rational Appetite," *Journal of the History of Philosophy* 24.4 (October 1991): 559–84. Gallagher describes the discursive activity of the will, but Aquinas is clear that the will is more fundamentally *intellectual* than *rational*; see *ST* I.82.1 ad 2 (Leon. 5).

132. In a sense this is a tautology, but of course the matter is not simple: the most fundamental truths cannot be derived from something more basic but may nevertheless may be confirmed and in that sense illuminated by what follows from them.

133. *ST* I.80.2 ad 3 and *ST* I.82.5 (Leon. 5). There is an important difference between goodness in its universal sense and the universal good, i.e., God, which we will discuss below.

134. As we recall from our discussion in chapter 6, Anselm has to isolate the power of the will from any given inclination in order to make room, so to speak, for two opposed affections.

135. Walter Hoeres helpfully characterizes the will in Aquinas essentially as a "haben wollen," a desire to possess, which thus comes to completion, not in the gratuitous affirmation of the other in friendship, as it will do in Scotus, but principally in *enjoyment*: *Der Wille als reine Vollkommenheit nach Duns Scotus* (Salzburg: A. Pustet, 1962), 222–25. We will nevertheless qualify this observation below, showing how love does indeed fit into Aquinas's conception, even if he does not thematize this point in his own *ex professo* discussion of the will's freedom.

136. *SCG* 1.72.3 (Leon. 13), trans. Pegis et al. We might interpret this "containment" of will in intellect by analogy to the body that is contained in the soul; *ST* I.76.3 (Leon. 5). Moreover, the intellect and will share the same complete universality in their object, though under different aspects: "As an example of simple infinity, we have the act *to understand*, of which the object is *the true*, and the act *to will*, of which the object is *the good*; each of which is convertible with being; and so, to understand and to will, of themselves, bear relation to all things, and each receives its species from its object" (*ST* I.54.2 [Leon. 5], trans. FEDP).

137. *ST* I.59.2 (Leon. 5), trans. FEDP.

138. *ST* I.78.1 (Leon. 5): "Now, since whatever operates must in some way be united to the object about which it operates, it follows of necessity that this something extrinsic, which is the object of the soul's operation, must be related to the soul in a twofold manner. First, inasmuch as this something extrinsic has a natural aptitude to be united to the soul, and to be by its likeness in the soul. In this way there are two kinds of powers—namely, the 'sensitive' in regard to the less common object—the sensible body; and the 'intellectual,' in regard to the most common object—universal being. Secondly, forasmuch as the soul itself has an inclination and tendency to the something extrinsic. And in this way there are again two kinds of powers in the soul: one—the 'appetitive'—in respect of which the soul is referred to something extrinsic as to an end, which is first in the intention; the other—the 'locomotive' power—in respect of which the soul is referred to something extrinsic as to the term of its operation and movement; for every animal is moved for the purpose of realizing its desires and intentions" (trans. FEDP).

139. *De ver.* 1.1 (Leon. 22/1).

140. We saw this sense of reason as constraint on will in Bernard.

141. As Aquinas explains, the lower powers of the soul "proceed from" the higher powers—in this case, the will from the intellect—which is just to

say that the soul's relation to the world in the will always takes place through the medium of the intellect; *ST* I.77.7 (Leon. 5).

142. See Long, "Providence, Freedom."

143. Simon, *Freedom of Choice*, 106.

144. We recall that this is the fundamental insight of Plato (see *FFR*, 300–308), though he did not have the differentiation of ideas that we now see in Aquinas.

145. It is significant that this is a late text in Aquinas and so includes the "voluntarist" dimension that some say evolved in his thought by virtue of the debates that culminated in the condemnations of 1270 and 1277.

146. This is why Aquinas thinks of the will as in a certain sense "composed," to which Scotus will eventually object; see Johannes Auer, *Die Menschliche Willsensfreiheit im Lehrsystem des Thomas von Aquin und Johannes Duns Scotus* (Munich: M. Hüber, 1938), 45–46.

147. Aquinas mentions the planets because of the prevalence of astrology in accounts of human freedom. Setting aside the theme of astrology, the point made here is actually far more interesting and important than it may initially seem, since it arguably concerns the presence of the whole cosmos in its arrangement in the act of freedom. A similar point is made in Aquinas's discussion of fate in *SCG* 3.93 (Leon. 14). To be sure, Aquinas insists that the wise men who alone are truly free oppose their will to such cosmic influences—but one can affirm this point without going on to read this in the (ancient) Stoic or (modern) libertarian sense of isolating the will and its freedom over against the body and all it implies.

148. *ST* I.83.1 ad 3 (Leon. 5).

149. Again, we observe that this bearing is quite distant and indirect; Aquinas explains that a material force can affect an intellectual power only through the bodily dispositions, and that it subverts the soul and its freedom if it is made determinative; *ST* I-II.9.5 (Leon. 6). In a modern context, we might "apply" what Aquinas says about the planets to the "natural determinants" of human behavior, such as genetic makeup and physiological disposition, not to mention the analogous "social, cultural, or environmental determinants," such as one's ethnic background, familial relationships, economic conditions, political context, and so forth. Aquinas himself makes a reference to such things in principle in comparing the cosmic influences to one's being disposed by one's "natural complexion" (*ex complexione naturali*); *ST* I-II.9.5 ad 3 (Leon. 6). These various elements dispose freedom but do not determine it.

150. *ST* I-II.8.1 (Leon. 6).

151. In *De ver.* 5.8 ad 5 (Leon. 22/1), Aquinas specifies that this outpouring is not simply the divine nature but most fundamentally the divine will.

152. See *SCG* 3.86.12 and 13 and *SCG* 3.97.10 (Leon. 14). Aquinas affirms that the *order* of the cosmos is thus referred not simply to divine *reason* but finally to the divine *will* (*SCG* 3.97.14 [Leon. 14]).

153. "The end is called the cause of causes" (*ST* I.5.2 ad 1 [Leon. 4], trans. FEDP); goodness is principally end but includes the other causes (*ST* I.5.4 [Leon. 4]). Cf. *De principiis naturae* 1.29.

154. In our account here, we are taking for granted a consistent position in Aquinas, following Daniel Westberg, "Did Aquinas Change His Mind about the Will?," *The Thomist* 58.1 (January 1994): 41–60, and Yul Kim, "A Change in Thomas Aquinas's Theory of the Will: Solutions to a Long-Standing Problem," *American Catholic Philosophical Quarterly* 82.2 (2008): 221–36, as opposed to the classic thesis of development proposed by Lottin. We will address further down the controverted question of development in Aquinas on this point.

155. On this question, see Daniel Shields, "Aquinas on Will, Happiness and God: The Problem of Love and Aristotle's *Liber de Bona Fortuna*," *American Catholic Philosophical Quarterly* 91:1 (Winter 2017): 113–42. Aquinas more often describes this in Aristotelian terms as a desire for happiness (beatitude) rather than in Platonic terms as a desire for the good in its fullness, which is decidedly *not* the same thing, however inseparable they may be in reality. But the reason Aquinas posits *happiness* as the last end (rather than God simply) is that it indicates the end, not simply considered in itself (which is indeed God), but considered *as attained*, which means the end considered as the final destination, or resting point, of the movement; see *ST* I-II.3.1 ad 2 and ad 3 (Leon. 6).

156. See *ST* I.60.5 (Leon. 5) ("Everything naturally loves God more than itself," ad 5, trans. FEDP). Timothy Noone has drawn attention to the late text in the *De malo* in which, Noone claims, Aquinas appears to depart from his normal position (e.g., *ST* I.82.2 [Leon. 5]) that man necessarily wills the vision of God and ends with a position similar to the one Scotus will take, namely, that even this ultimate need is not willed by necessity (*De malo* 6 ad 7 [Leon. 23]); Timothy Noone, "Nature, Freedom, and Will," *American Catholic Philosophical Quarterly* 81 (2008): 1–23. We will discuss Scotus at length in the second to last chapter of this book, but it is important to point out that Aquinas is not thus making the will to happiness an arbitrary option, under the control of the will. Instead, when reading the *De malo* text, we have to keep in mind that, for Aquinas, the will can only will anything at all under the aspect of goodness (*ST* I.82.2 ad 1 [Leon. 5]), and this means in relation to goodness in its truth. Thus, the will always wills God implicitly in every act of will; even when the will "avoids thinking about happiness" explicitly, it remains a will to ultimate

happiness in its depth. This is why in his late text, *ST* I-II.10.2 (Leon. 6), Aquinas says that the will *necessarily* wills the universal good "if it wills anything at all" and explains that one wills the last end in everything one wills, so that, even when one is not explicitly thinking of this end, the "virtue" of it remains in all of one's acts; *ST* I-II.1.6 ad 3 (Leon. 6), trans. FEDP. This can be harmonized with the *De malo* text simply by saying that the will does not necessarily have to will perfect happiness because it does not have to will *simpliciter*. Nevertheless, there is indeed an ambiguity in Aquinas's texts, which we will discuss at the end of this chapter.

157. We made this argument in relation to Plato; see *FFR*, 308–13.

158. Again, see Simon, *Freedom of Choice*, 152–53; Siewerth, *Menschliche Willensfreiheit*, 24.

159. *ST* I-II.10.2 (Leon. 6).

160. See *ST* I-II.10.2 ad 3 (Leon. 6). This affirmation does not mean that one cannot, at least from a more superficial perspective, choose *against* such goods: for example, it is possible for a person to choose to end his own life.

161. This is what Aquinas has in mind when he says that no particular good, as particular, provides a sufficient causality to move the will by necessity simply; *ST* I-II.10.2 (Leon. 6). We will come back to this point below.

162. *ST* I-II.8.3 (Leon. 6). This does not mean that one cannot choose which end to pursue in a given case (see, e.g., *ST* I-II.11.2 ad 2 [Leon. 6]), but only that, when one does so, it will inevitably be in relation to a more ultimate end taken as given. In every act of choice, there is some end presupposed as absolute to which the alternative means are relative.

163. According to Aquinas, the perfection of spirit, which is both intellect and will, does not exclude the open multiplicity of means to an end; *ST* I.60.2 (Leon. 5).

164. *ST* I.83.4 (Leon. 5).

165. *ST* I-II.8.3 (Leon. 6); cf. *ST* I.83.4 (Leon. 6). We recall that, by contrast, Bernard interpreted free will as a power that operated according to its own principles, not informed by intellect, but regulated extrinsically.

166. For a discussion of this point in Aquinas, see Long, "Providence, Freedom."

167. *ST* I-II.8.1 (Leon. 6).

168. We will have to wait until volume 3 to develop the broader cultural implications of this point, namely, that the provision of freedom requires opening the horizon to the whole truth, the ultimate truth, of man.

169. *ST* I-II.1.6 (Leon. 6). Chesterton is popularly supposed to have once said that the young man who rings the doorbell at the brothel is unconsciously looking for God.

170. For a good overview of the discussion, see Kim, "Change," 221–23.

171. For an account of Aquinas in these terms, see, for example, P. S. Eardley, "Thomas Aquinas and Giles of Rome on the Will," *Review of Metaphysics* 56.4 (June 2003): 832–62.

172. The classic proposal of this thesis comes from Lottin, *Psychologie et morale*, vol. 1.

173. Ramelow, afterword to *De veritate*, 350.

174. See *ST* I.82.4 ad 1 (Leon. 5); cf. *De ver.* 22.12 (Leon. 22/3).

175. *ST* I-II.9.1 ad 3 (Leon. 6). We might contrast this "reciprocal causality" thus to the image Bonaventure uses, namely, that of two men lifting a rock, since the two men are agents in the same order.

176. *ST* I-II.10.2 (Leon. 6). In the earlier texts, he presents the will as governing the order of efficient causality and the intellect the order of final causality; in the later texts, by contrast, he identifies *will* with the order of final causality, and the intellect with formal causality. These characterizations are not simply opposed, however much they may shift the points of emphasis, insofar as there is a connection between efficient and final causality on the one hand and between formal and final causality on the other.

177. *ST* I-II.10.2 (Leon. 6). This is a strange way to put the argument: Can one in fact *see* anything at all without color? The strangeness is worth reflecting on, but the illustration may be interpreted in a simple way: glass can in some sense be seen, or darkness, without color. The image nevertheless seems to foreground the essential role of the intellect in the activity of the will.

178. *De malo* 6.15 (Leon. 23), trans. Regan.

179. *ST* I.82.4 ad 3 (Leon. 5), trans. FEDP.

180. Laurence Dewan, "St. Thomas and the Causes of Free Choice," *Acta Philosophica* 8.1 (1999): 87–96.

181. This is one of the central arguments in Shanley, "Divine Causation." Note that we are not suggesting here that the simultaneity of the acts of intellect and will suffices without reference to God to avoid the infinite regress, but only that God's absolute priority does not imply a simple temporal succession of causality. For a subtle treatment of this issue, see Ramelow, afterword to *De veritate*, 366–70.

182. See Gallagher, "Free Choice." Westberg likewise insists that the reciprocity is not successive but a simultaneous dependence; "Did Aquinas Change," 51–52.

183. Gallagher, "Free Choice."

184. This is one of the concluding insights of his dissertation, "Thomas Aquinas on the Causes of Human Choice" (PhD diss., Catholic University of America, 1989). Gallagher thus tries to justify the "nonrational" aspects of our

choices. But the fact that a choice does not have a reason that temporally precedes it does not mean it is without reason, as we will explain below.

185. See *ST* I.82.4 ad 3 (Leon. 5). Aquinas says that every act of will is preceded by an apprehension, though the first apprehension is preceded only by God.

186. In *ST* I.20.1 ad 1 (Leon. 4), Aquinas insists that "the cognitive faculty does not move except through the medium of the appetite" (trans. FEDP). It seems true to say that, even if the intellect is absolutely prior to the will, it never acts alone. It may be the case that God plants thoughts directly in the intellect (see *SCG* 3.89 [Leon. 14]; *De malo* 3.3 ad 11 [Leon. 23]; *ST* I-II.109.2 ad 1 [Leon. 7]), but presumably even these, to the extent they are *actually thought* at all, inevitably involve the operation of the will.

187. When Aquinas says that the "object moves the will," he explains that it does so precisely through the intellect, since it moves the will by determining the act *formally*; *ST* I-II.9.1 (Leon. 6), trans. FEDP.

188. It is not enough to say, as Yul Kim does, for example ("Change," 226–27), that the actuality of the will in its first act is able to actualize the second act (operation) because of the reflexivity of the will. All of this is true, but we have to ask how the will is actual in its first act. It ultimately must be due to a communication of goodness and the presence of God, as we will see below. Scotus will answer the question in a decisively different way.

189. See *ST* I.82.3 ad 2 (Leon. 5). Aquinas draws a clear connection between the priority of intellect over the will and the priority of act over potency. Indeed, it is also the particular good apprehended in relation to the ultimate good, a relation that has a certain "gratuity" to it, that is the indeterminacy that ultimately belongs to the will.

190. Kim, "Change," 227.

191. Actually, two long essays, written in the early years of the twentieth century, which were later gathered together in a single volume: Rousselot, *The Eyes of Faith* (New York: Fordham University Press, 1990).

192. Essentially, Rousselot argues that the perception of the credibility of faith and the assent the soul gives to it are one and the same act, which means that the love (assent) is the condition of possibility for the knowledge (perception of its truth) at the very same time that the perception of truth is the condition of possibility for the assent. These are irreducibly different aspects but are simultaneous in the real, concrete act of faith. We are proposing something analogous in the act of freedom: the reason for the choice presents itself most properly *in* the choosing, even as that reason suffices for the choice made.

193. *De malo* 6 (Leon. 23): "And so a good, if it is presented to us as good but not as suitable, will not move the will" (trans. Regan).

194. This affirmation does not eliminate the great variety of ways choices are made: some after long deliberation, some after coming to a decision about the right thing to do and then working up the courage to carry the decision through, some through a kind of leap of faith without much of a sense of what one is doing, and so forth. All of these would nevertheless reveal a simultaneity of intellect and will in analogous fashion.

195. As we pointed out above, this paradox is implied in the simultaneity of reciprocity between intellect and will, as distinct moments of a single act, which other authors affirm, without, however, making clear how paradoxical the point is.

196. This point introduces a *temporal* paradox, which requires reflection in order to deal fully with the question of freedom. Aquinas does not elaborate the significance of this point but notes that the actuality of an operation, which achieves a proper completion, is not a mere moment in a series but transcends time: "The act of something perfect, i.e., of something existing in act, e.g., to understand, to feel, and to will and such like . . . is not successive, nor is it of itself in time" (*ST* I-II.31.2 ad 1 [Leon. 6], trans. FEDP). We are going to leave a full discussion of this matter for volume 3.

197. As we will see, it is just this point that distinguishes Aquinas's account from that given by Scotus, who begins with the discrete powers of the soul *first* in themselves and then fits them together in their acts; see Auer, *Menschliche Willensfreiheit*, 58–59, and Hoeres, *Wille als reine Vollkommenheit*, 247.

198. As Siewerth explains, for Aquinas, being determines acts, not the reverse; *Menschliche Willensfreiheit*, 21.

199. *De ver.* 22.1 ad 3 (Leon. 22/3): There has to be a form *already* in the soul, or it would not be able to pursue it, since potency depends on act. But the form cannot be *completely* actual, or there will be repose rather than desire. So it must be *present* indeed, but in an *incomplete* way.

200. In *Sententia libri De anima* 3.10, lectio 15, para. 827, my translation. Aquinas goes on to observe that this good "always changes, just as do all things that are subject to our actions."

201. In fact, he explicitly rejects truth qua true as moving the soul; *De ver.* 22.12 (Leon. 22/3). Intriguingly, he identifies as responsible for the final cause both the intellect and, in the later text, the *will*. Rather than say he "changed his mind" in the interim, it is more adequate to say *both* the intellect and the will are responsible for final causality in different respects: we are proposing to see the simultaneity as a matter of the perception of *beauty*.

202. We recall that, in *De malo* 6 (Leon. 23), Aquinas says that a good does not move the soul unless I recognize it as *suitable to me* in particular, and it is the will that is occupied with particulars. To say that we have to "feel" the

good for it to move us does not mean that the concupiscible passion must necessarily be aroused for action to take place: Aquinas explicitly affirms the contrary (*ST* I-II.10.3 ad 3 [Leon. 6]), saying we can act *in spite of* our passions, from choice alone. Nevertheless, there is still a reception of the desirability of the thing to be done in this case, and not "only" of its truth.

203. A striking exception to the neglect of the fundamental role love plays in freedom can be found in Klaus Riesenhuber, *Die Transzendenz der Freiheit zum Guten: Der Wille in der Anthropologie und Metaphysik des Thomas von Aquin* (Munich: Berchmanskolleg Verlag, 1971), 95–122 and passim. Riesenhuber sees the importance of love no doubt precisely because he approaches freedom, not simply as a matter of the will, but from the deeper perspective of anthropology and metaphysics.

204. For example, when he raises the question about the bearing of the passions—of which love is the first (*ST* I-II.25.2 [Leon. 6])—on the will's operation, he does not mention love directly; *ST* I-II.9.2 (Leon. 6). Moreover, in his analysis of the basic structure of human action, the word *love* does not seem to appear, except indirectly in relation to enjoyment (*ST* I-II.11.1 [Leon. 6]).

205. *De ver.* 24.2 (Leon. 22/3). Aquinas cites Damascene, Gregory, and Augustine, all saying that reason is the cause of free choice.

206. It also reveals why making love the root does not imply the displacement of reason as the root of freedom, as we will see.

207. *ST* I.20.1 (Leon. 4).

208. One might think that the desire for happiness suffices for particular choices, which seems to be the case in some formulations, such as *ST* I-II.9.3 (Leon. 6): "The will, through its volition of the end, moves itself to will the means" (trans. FEDP). The *movement* of appetite ends, not in the intellectual apprehension, but *in the thing itself* (*ST* I.81.1 [Leon. 5]), which means that the movement *begins from* the thing and not simply from the apprehension. We ought to say it begins *from* the thing, *through* the apprehension. The *real object* moves the will *by means of* the intentional presence in the intellect. As Aquinas explains, "When the object of the will is distinct from the will itself, the *object really moves the will*" (*De ver.* 23.1 ad 7 [Leon. 22/3], emphasis added). Moreover, "The appetible object moves the appetite, introducing itself, as it were, into its intentions, while the appetite moves towards the realization of the appetible object, so that the movement ends where it began" (*ST* I-II.26.2 [Leon. 6], trans. FEDP). Thus, "The being which desires a good does not seek to have the good according to its intentional existence, as it is had by one who knows it, but according to its essential or real existence" (*De ver.* 22.3 ad 4 [Leon. 22/3]). What all of this means is that it is not the *apprehension* of the good that moves the will, but the good itself that makes its presence felt, so

to speak, in the apprehension. There is an interesting analogy between this point and Aquinas's argument that the concept is not what one knows but that *by* which or *through* which the soul knows the thing itself; *ST* I.85.2 *sed contra* (Leon. 5).

209. This again is why the intellectual apprehension does not itself possess motive force in the way of efficient causality (*De ver.* 22.12 [Leon. 22/3]).

210. *ST* I-II.26.2 (Leon. 6).

211. Because "love is the first movement of the will and of every appetitive faculty" (*ST* I.20.1 [Leon. 4], trans. FEDP), and because the *act* of apprehension, insofar as it is an *act*, is exercised by the will, it would seem to follow that love is itself the "apprehension" that moves the appetite, which is to say it is not an apprehension preceded by some other apprehension. See *ST* I.20.1 ad 1 (Leon. 4), where Aquinas affirms that the cognitive faculty operates only through the medium of the appetitive.

212. *De malo* 6 ad 13 (Leon. 23): "Amor dicitur transformare amantem in amatum, inquantum per amorem movetur amans ad ipsam rem amatum."

213. In *ST* I-II.27.2 (Leon. 6), Aquinas explains that love requires the apprehension of the good and connects this explicitly with beauty. For a more substantial argument on Thomistic grounds for the essential connection between love and beauty, see my "Love and Beauty, the Forgotten Transcendental, in Thomas Aquinas," *Communio* 44 (Summer 2017): 334–56, and "Beauty and Love," in *Love and the Postmodern Predicament*, 85–117.

214. *ST* I-II.26.1 (Leon. 6).

215. *De ver.* 1.1 (Leon. 22/1). Aquinas also says that love exists "universally in all things: because as Dionsius says . . . beauty and goodness are beloved by all things; since each single thing has a connaturalness with that which is naturally suitable [*conveniens*] to it" (*ST* I-II.26.1 ad 3 [Leon. 6], trans. FEDP).

216. *ST* I-II.25.2 (Leon. 6).

217. *ST* I.20.1 (Leon. 4); and *ST* I-II.26.4 (Leon. 6) on the division of the one love (*amor*) into friendship and desire.

218. "As an example of simple infinity, we have *to understand*, of which the object is *the true*, and the act *to will*, of which the object is *the good*; each of which is convertible with being; and so, to understand and to will, of themselves, bear relation to all things, and each receives its species from its object"; *ST* I.54.2 (Leon. 4), trans. FEDP.

219. See, e.g., *De ver.* 1.2 (Leon. 22/1).

220. Again, see *De malo* 6 ad 13 (Leon. 23).

221. Aquinas is certainly ambiguous on this point, and we are proposing a distinct reading here. The alternative would be to see love as simply a means

to an end, or in other words a station (the point of departure) on the way to joy; see *ST* I-II.25.2 ad 3 (Leon. 6): the union that is love *precedes* desire. But cf. *ST* I-II.25.2 ad 3 (Leon. 6): the intention of the pleasure to be achieved is a cause of love. This alternative is a common one and has ample support in the texts (which is why Aquinas is generally thought to embrace a "possessive" sense of love and a reductively "eudaimonistic" vision of happiness), but we are suggesting this understanding is in itself problematic and leaves out a crucial dimension that Aquinas himself opens up, even if he does not follow it fully explicitly.

222. Again, see my essays "Beauty and Love" and "Love and Beauty" for a more thorough argument on this point.

223. Aquinas explains that "nothing can be desired except being [*esse*], and consequently nothing is good except being" (*ST* I.5.2 ad 4 [Leon. 4], trans. FEDP).

224. We recall that, for Aquinas, men, and indeed *all* created things, *naturally* love God more than themselves: there is no "private self-interest" anywhere in the created world (*ST* I.60.5, I.60.1, and I.60.1 ad 3 [Leon. 5]). As te Velde explains, for Aquinas (in contrast to Anselm, as we saw, and to Scotus, as we will see), the will does not require a special superadded virtue to be ordered to the good; "Natura in Seipsa Recurva Est," 165.

225. *ST* I-II.26.4 (Leon. 6).

226. In his *Commentary on the Divine Names*, Aquinas connects love for a subsisting good with *amor benevolentiae*, in contrast to love for an accidental good (such as health); *In divin. nomin.* c.iv.1.ix.n.404, ed. Pera. He affirms quite clearly that love, as such, is directed, not simply to the thing in relation to me, but to the thing *in itself*, which is why he says it regards things whether or not they are possessed in actuality (*ST* I.20.1 [Leon. 4]) and suggests that love extends beyond actual knowledge (but importantly *not* beyond knowledge in principle—again, because it is the *truth* of the good): "Love is in the appetitive power, which regards a thing as it is in itself: wherefor it suffices, for the perfection of love, that a thing be loved according as it is known in itself" (*ST* I-II.27.2ad2 [Leon. 6], trans. FEDP). We might recall here Pieper's famous description of the meaning of love in Aquinas: an affirmation, "It is good that you exist!"; *Faith–Hope–Love* (San Francisco: Ignatius Press, 1997), 187–206. According to Aquinas, "He who wills a thing for its own sake, wills it to last forever, for the very reason that he wills it for itself. . . . Wherefore from the very fact that God made creatures it is to be inferred that he willed them to last forever, and seeing that his will is unchangeable the opposite will never happen"; *De pot.* 5.4, trans. English Dominican Fathers.

227. *ST* I.5.1 (Leon. 4).

228. This line of reflection is very much inspired by the metaphysics of Ferdinand Ulrich; see *Homo Abyssus*, esp. 463–87.

229. See *De ver.* 22.1 ad 7 (Leon. 22/3). It is in and through its accidents that a being connects with what is outside of itself: *De ver.* 21.5 (Leon. 22/3). For an illuminating exploration of the revelation of being in and through accidents, see Clarke, "Action."

230. This is not to say that their existence simply *depends on* or *results from* their interactions.

231. A fascinating dialogue would open up here between Aquinas and the German Idealism that arises from Kant's aesthetics.

232. "The object that moves the appetite is an apprehended good. Now if a thing is perceived to be beautiful as soon as it is apprehended (*in ipsa apprehensione*), it is taken to be something becoming and good (*conveniens et bonum*)"; *ST* II-II.145.2 ad 1 (Leon. 10), trans. FEDP.

233. Aquinas observes that what exists outside the human soul "has a natural aptitude to be united to the soul, and to be by its likeness in the soul"; *ST* I.78.1 (Leon. 5), trans. FEDP.

234. This is why there is not only a (Greek) justice at the basis of the will but at the very same time a (Jewish) mercy or gratuitous love.

235. *Hyperbolic* is meant here in the sense of Dionysius, who uses the term, as we saw, to express the ecstatic, erotic *goodness* of God that gives in such a way as to be able to *receive*.

236. Esther Lightcap Meek, inspired by Michael Polanyi, has written at length about the intimation of "indeterminate future manifestations," which is the indication of a genuine encounter with a thing, a genuine contact with reality; see chaps. 5–7 especially of *Contact with Reality: Michael Polanyi's Realism, and Why It Matters* (Eugene, OR: Cascade Books, 2017), 64–107.

237. Again, this is the paradox of the soul's "inborn" *convenientia* with all things; *De ver.* 1.1 (Leon. 22/1).

238. To illustrate Aquinas's distinction between love of desire and love of friendship, one often points to the wine that one loves, and the beloved friend with whom one drinks it. But there is a certain abstraction in this cursory observation: we also appreciate the wine in itself and even take care to preserve it, not in the same way as a person, of course, but nevertheless as something of intrinsic value. There are more analogies than we tend to recognize here. For a deep reflection on some of these issues, see Robert Spaemann, "What Does It Mean to Say 'Art Imitates Nature'?" in *The Spaemann Reader* (Oxford: Oxford University Press, 2015), 192–210.

239. *ST* II-II.27.2 (Leon. 8). For a more substantial argument regarding love as an affective bond, giving rise to a "quasi-substance," see my essay "Crisis of Marriage."

240. On the connection between love and being, see my essay "Love and Being," in *Love and the Postmodern Predicament*, 118–45.

241. A classic statement of this point can be found in Plotinus, *Ennead* 3.5.1, ed. Armstrong, 167–69. The priority of love to knowledge does not at all imply an irrationalism, as is clear in Plotinus, who of course follows Plato (the point of the *Phaedrus* is to present a suprarational transcendence [divine mania] precisely in *contrast* to the subrational view of love of the sophists).

242. There has been a renewal of interest in the role of the *vis cogitativa* or *ratio particularis* in Aquinas's theory of knowledge, which gives greater weight to the often-marginalized moment of *perception* than standard neo-Thomist rationalism tends to do; see, e.g., Anthony J. Lisska, *Aquinas's Theory of Perception* (Oxford: Oxford University Press, 2016), Mark Barker, "The Cogitative Power: Objects and Terminology" (PhD diss., University of St. Thomas, Houston, TX, 2007), and Daniel de Haan, "Perception and the Vis Cogitativa," *American Catholic Philosophical Quarterly* 88.3 (2014): 397–437. Cornelio Fabro remains the one who saw the importance of this aspect first; see "The Intensive Hermeneutics of Thomistic Philosophy: The Notion of Participation," in *Selected Works of Cornelio Fabro*, vol. 1, *Selected Articles on Metaphysics and Participation* (Chillum, MD: IVE Press, 2015), 91 (Fabro himself refers to his exposition of the teaching in *Percezione e pensiero*, 2nd ed. [Brescia: Morcelliana, 1962], 198 ff., 222 ff., 234 ff., 238 ff.). It seems that something analogous is needed in Aquinas's theory of freedom and action: namely, an enriching of the *vis aestimativa*, which is connected with imagination (see *ST* I.78.4 [Leon. 5]), through a recollection of the place of *love* as *coaptatio* and *complacentia*. In this case, the *intentio* that transcends simple sense experience can be understood nevertheless as being born, so to speak, from within that experience, that is, as the revelation of a possibility toward which the soul is disposed to move (*in-tentio*), from the actuality of what is given but as a result of the interactuality of the soul and its object. Aquinas suggests that the *vis aestimativa* is proper to animals and is replaced in human beings by the *vis cogitativa*, which is a perception according to a universal essence and thus supposes reason (*ST* I.78.4 [Leon. 5]: "The power which in other animals is called the natural estimative, in man is called the cogitative" [trans. FEDP]). But there has to be a rational perception (i.e., imagination) that lies, not simply in the order of understanding and the true, but in the order of action and the good. If the cogitative power perceives the particular *sub specie universalis*, we ought to say that the specifically rational mode of the *vis aestimativa* would be a perception of the particular *sub specia boni universali*, or at least *ad hoc finem*. In other words, it would have to be a vision of the thing specifically in the light of the universal good, which is the only one that can move the human will, as the best way to realize this here and now: something is appetible for the human

will only as likeness to the divine goodness (*De ver.* 22.3 ad 1). The fact that Aquinas simply *substitutes* the *vis cogitativa* for the *vis aestimativa* in man, rather than deepening the *vis aestimativa* in the human soul in addition to the *vis cogitativa*, seems to be evidence of the one-sided rationalism that we will discuss at the end of this chapter. It is significant, incidentally, that Daniel de Haan is able to connect the *vis cogitativa* with the perception of beauty: see his essay "Beauty and Aesthetic Perception in Thomas Aquinas," in *Beauty and the Good: Recovering the Classical Tradition from Plato to Duns Scotus*, ed. Alice Ramos (Washington, DC: Catholic University of America Press, 2020), 288–318.

243. *ST* I-II.9.1 ad 2 (Leon. 6), trans. FEDP. Aquinas goes on to say, following Aristotle, that "it is not the speculative intellect that moves, but the practical intellect." This is not adequate. One can grasp *that* something is desirable without being actually moved by the desirability. Our suggestion is that this latter corresponds to the imaginative reception of the beautiful form in the appetite, or in other words: to love. It is significant, in this respect, that Aquinas connects the perception of suitability in a certain (not fully elaborated) respect with the will, since the will relates to particulars (*De malo* 6 [Leon. 23]). As Aquinas puts it, it is not the intentional object in the soul under the aspect of truth that moves the soul, because efficient causality requires substantial reality (see *De ver.* 22.12 [Leon. 22/3]). Thus, "The will is referred to things as subject to nature, but not the intellect." This moment of the will requires a communication of that nature, i.e., that principle of motion, and so grasps things in their actual giving of themselves concretely in their accidents.

244. *ST* I.78.4 (Leon. 5).

245. According to Aquinas, the proper object of the human intellect is the "quiddity of a material thing, which comes under the action of the senses and the imagination" (*ST* I.85.5 ad 3 [Leon. 5], trans. FEDP), and this is because it is proper to the human soul to be united to the body (*ST* I.76.1 ad 5 [Leon. 5]).

246. According to Aquinas, "In us the intellect is not the only motive principle. The imagination is also such, and by its means, the universal knowledge of the intellect is applied to some particular thing to be done" (*De ver.* 2.6.2 [Leon. 22/1]). Moreover, "Since the same thing considered under different conditions can be made either pleasurable or repulsive by means of the imagination, reason lays a particular thing before sensuality under the aspect of the pleasurable or the disagreeable as it appears to reason; and so sensuality is moved to joy or sorrow" (*De ver.* 25.4 [Leon. 22/3]).

247. We are setting the distinction between these terms into greater relief than Aquinas does, and we do so by analogy to the distinction Aquinas draws between subsistent being itself and common being; *De pot.* 7.2 ad 6. See also *ST* I.6.4 *sed contra* (Leon. 4).

248. *ST* I.93.1 (Leon. 5).

249. This is evident in the importance he gives not only to the will/love but also to the procession of the word in understanding, which is not so obviously foregrounded in Aristotle's interpretation of the intellect; see *ST* I.27.1 (Leon. 4).

250. *ST* I.93.4 and *ST* I.93.8 (Leon. 5). Aquinas does not say that, just as God knows and loves himself, so too does man know and love himself (an *analogia proporionalitatis*); instead, the image is constituted most basically because man knows and loves *God*, just as God does. See also *ST* I.93.7 (Leon. 5).

251. *ST* I.105.3 (Leon. 5). Aquinas says that God moves the intellect immediately in every act of understanding, both subjectively and objectively, but this is not "illuminationism" because it includes the actual and effective encounter of mind and object as a secondary cause.

252. *ST* I.105.5 ad 3 (Leon. 5): "God not only gives things their form, but He also preserves them in existence, and applies them to act, and is moreover the end of every action, as above explained" (trans. EDFP). Cf. *De pot.* 3.7, where he makes a similarly comprehensive statement.

253. *ST* I.105.4 (Leon. 5), trans. EDFP.

254. Note, the transcendence of the good in relation to human nature would seem to be the *supernatural* good of grace in contrast to the natural good belonging to human nature as such, and so as lying within "unaided" human power. But this is too simplistic because Aquinas affirms the will's *natural* ordination to the *universal good*, which is also in some sense beyond human capacity; see *ST* I-II.109.2 ad 1 (Leon. 7): "The mind of man still unweakened [by original sin] is not so much master of its act that it does not need to be moved by God" (trans. EDFP).

255. God acts in every agent (*ST* I.105.5 [Leon. 5]). Again, God's causality is comprehensive, embracing the efficient, formal, and final dimensions. Steven Long makes a similar observation but ends up inferring from this an insufficiently qualified support for Bañez in the famous controversy and so posits a kind of unilateral determinism with respect to salvation. We cannot enter into this debate here but intend to take it up in volume 3. See Long, "Providence, Freedom."

256. See *ST* I-II.9.6 ad 3 (Leon. 6): Aquinas presents grace here *as an instance* of particular movement, not the sole case. The editor's allusion to *ST* I-II.109.2 ad 1 (Leon. 7) strengthens the point regarding God's causal activity in the natural operation of the human will in general. On this point, see Shields, "Aquinas on Will."

257. See *ST* I-II.17.5 ad 3 and *ST* I-II.9.4 (Leon. 6). The point seems to be that, in man, while the will always operates subsequently upon the intellect, reason does not have to be first moved by the will but is dependent on what transcends the human soul simply and so remains absolutely prior *in* the soul.

258. More specifically the *Liber de bona fortuna*, which was a pair of chapters selected by the Latin translator, William of Moerbeck, from Aristotle's *Eudemian Ethics* and his *Magna moralia*. This book had a significant presence in Scholastic discussions.

259. *ST* I-II.9.4 (Leon. 6).

260. Cornelio Fabro, "Le 'Liber de bona fortuna' de l'"Ethique à Eudème' d'Aristote et la dialectique de la divine Providence chez saint Thomas," in "L'être, la liberté, et l'église aux XXe siècle," ed. Cornelio Fabro, special issue, *Revue Thomiste* 111 (2011): 157.

261. We might say that Aquinas takes Anselm's insight into the need for a "First Will," given by God, as the foundation for all other acts of will and makes it immanent in every human act in such a way that God's First Will coincides in a certain sense with the creature's self-willing.

262. Thus, his causality is not and in fact *cannot be* violent but always makes nature more natural and the will more volitional. This is not a moral point but an ontological one. See *ST* I.105.6 ad 1 (Leon. 5). Shanley makes this point clearly in "Divine Causation," 122.

263. *ST* I.5.4 ad 1 (Leon. 4).

264. *ST* I-II.110.1 (Leon. 7). Aquinas says here that the human will is moved by the "preexisting" good in things, which however implies that its *actual existing* will be in some sense (also) due to the will itself that chooses it. Thus, Aquinas does not simply deny that the will produces goodness, only that it does so *wholly*.

265. "Choice is only of possible things"; *ST* I-II.13.5 (Leon. 6), trans. EDFP.

266. *De pot.* 7.2. In this respect there is a genuine *analogy* between natural causes and free ones, insofar as all causes bring something *into being* that was not there before, and so all causes introduce some novelty. The concreteness and contingency of this bringing into being are what accounts for the (relative) unpredictability of things even in nature.

267. "If, therefore, God has made [creatures] like unto Himself by giving them existence, He has consequently made them like unto Himself by giving them causal efficacy, that is to say, by granting them the power to exert causal actions of their own. Such is the reason why, although no finite being can create existence, each of them can at least impart it. In any relation of efficient causality, something of the *esse* (to be) of the cause is somehow imparted to its effect" (Gilson, *Being and Some Philosophers*, 185).

268. "See" is meant, not in the sense of physical vision, of course, or even simply intellectual insight without further qualification, but as the reality presents itself in my imagination. Nietzsche has a profound insight into this appar-

ent coincidence of necessity and freedom, above all in the creativity of the artist, who at his best and freest does *nothing* "arbitrarily"; *Beyond Good and Evil*, no. 213. But Nietzsche ends up *eliminating* freedom and the reason that is its necessary condition; see the text on the "Four Great Errors" in *Twilight of the Idols*, in *The Portable Nietzsche*, ed. Walter Kaufmann (New York: Penguin, 1982), 492–501.

269. Dante, *Paradiso* 5.1.4–6: "If I flame at you . . . / do not wonder, for this is the result of perfect vision, which, even as it apprehends, moves its foot toward the apprehended good."

270. Gustav Siewerth observes that, for Aquinas, we cannot know a good except through our striving toward it (*Menschliche Willensfreiheit*, 66).

271. This, again, is a regular theme in the work of Ferdinand Ulrich.

272. Though natural movement is not sufficient for acts of freedom (*SCG* 3.85.4 and 6 [Leon. 14]), it remains the case that nature is the abiding foundation of freedom (*De ver.* 22.5 [Leon. 22/3]). The special transcendence and reflexivity of spirit is not something over against nature but represents the perfection of the principle of motion and rest that defines nature: thus, "Person signifies what is most perfect in all nature" (*ST* I.29.3 [Leon. 4], trans. EDFP). The human person represents the analogy of freedom and nature even more perfectly than the angel because of the relation between soul and body, spirit and material nature, that constitutes his personhood.

273. God is not the highest being but is outside every genus and so is said to exceed, or transcend, all things (*ST* I.6.2 ad 3 [Leon. 4]).

274. Vernon Bourke, *Will in Western Thought* (New York: Sheed and Ward, 1964), 88.

275. Cornelio Fabro makes a different judgment: "It can be agreed, then, that in Saint Thomas, the Aristotelian and Christian formulas of freedom seem to fit together; however, it is really the Christian election of the ultimate existential end which takes the central place in consciousness." "Orizzontalità e verticalità nella dialettica della libertà," in *Riflessioni sulla libertà* (Rimini: Maggioli Editore, 1983), 51. But Fabro is referring here to what he calls the "theological and mystical plane"; we are concerned by contrast with the natural level, or better, with human freedom as a created and constitutive reality. It is not enough to complement a natural rationalism with a supernatural voluntarism.

276. Siewerth notes that the primacy Aquinas accords to the intellect is surprising given the interpretation of the two powers in the full actuality of the person implied in his thought; *Menschliche Willensfreiheit*, 125–26.

277. *ST* I.82.3 ad 2 (Leon. 5).

278. *De ver.* 24.2 (Leon. 22/3): "Totius libertatis radix est in ratione constituta."

279. *ST* I.82.3 (Leon. 5): "Absolutely, however, the intellect is nobler than the will" (trans. EDFP); cf. *De ver.* 21.1.3 *sed contra* (Leon. 22/3).

280. *ST* I-II.17.1 (Leon. 6).

281. *ST* I-II.17.1 (Leon. 6).

282. *ST* I-II.17.3 ad 3 (Leon. 6). Note, the reciprocity he alludes to here would open up to the paradox we have tried to unfold.

283. *ST* I-II.17.6 and *ST* I-II.17.5 (Leon. 6).

284. *ST* I-II.3.4 (Leon. 6).

285. *ST* I-II.3.5 (Leon. 6), trans. EDFP.

286. See my critique of Aquinas on this point in *Catholicity of Reason*, 85–115. Aquinas gives priority to the speculative intellect because "the practical intellect is ordered to the good which is outside of it" (*ST* I-II.3.5 ad 2 [Leon. 6], trans. EDFP), even though in the next reply he describes God as "outside of man" but still says we relate to him through the speculative intellect. There is clearly a tension here. Aquinas's discussion here ought to be compared with the striking text from the *SCG* 3.62.9 (Leon. 14): "Nothing that is contemplated with wonder can be tiresome, since as long as the thing remains in wonder it continues to stimulate desire. But the divine substance is always viewed with wonder by any created intellect, since no created intellect comprehends it. So, it is impossible for an intellectual substance to become tired of this vision. And thus, it cannot, of its own will, desist from this vision" (trans. Pegis et al.).

287. See D. C. Schindler, "Beauty and Love," 116–17, and *Catholicity of Reason*, 85–115.

288. To be sure, as we noted above, Aquinas insists that freedom accomplishes acts beyond the inclination of nature; but it remains the case that it does so within the horizon set by nature. Thus, as he argues in *De pot.* 2.3 ad 3, the intellect as natural must be the absolute first act, and this is because nature is *logically* prior to will (2.3 ad 6). Moreover, in *ST* I.60.4 (Leon. 5), he distinguishes "love of choice," as belonging specifically to rational beings, from the "natural love" that belongs to all but indicates that the love of choice concerns means, which are necessarily ordered to the end that is loved naturally (trans. FEDP).

289. This is why Aquinas can describe the beatific vision as a state of permanent wonder, as we saw in the passage quoted above from *SCG* 3.62.9 (Leon. 14).

290. *De pot.* 2.3 ad 9.

291. We would have to note, here, that this would imply a need to recover Maximus's *Christological* resolution of the reconciliation of nature and history and to integrate this more completely into a Trinitarian theology. At the heart of this is the great question of eternal predestination and the hope for universal salvation, and how this fits into the meaning of the inner-Trinitarian life.

Clearly, the relation between human freedom and the procession of the Persons in God goes well beyond what the thinkers we are considering treat directly and becomes an explicit theme only in twentieth-century theology. We will engage it in our third volume.

292. Aquinas himself describes the will as an active principle (*ST* I-II.10.4 [Leon. 6]), and he can do this without contradicting his more general characterization of the will as *principally* passive, insofar as it is an intellectual appetite. In fact, Aquinas admits that, in a certain respect, the will is *more* active than the intellect because it is the "principle of the exterior action" and that the principle of such action is specifically the existence of things in themselves; *ST* I-II.22.2 ad 2 (Leon. 6), trans. FEDP.

293. Lawrence Feingold has recently attempted to introduce the notion of will as self-gift into Thomistic thought by drawing on other authors from the tradition, for example, St. John of the Cross; see "The Word Breathes Forth Love: The Psychological Analogy for the Trinity and the Complementarity of Intellect and Will," *Nova et Vetera* 17.2 (Spring 2019): 501–32.

294. *ST* I.19.2 (Leon. 4).

CHAPTER 10. Godfrey of Fontaines

1. The precise dates are uncertain. He was likely born shortly before 1250, and the date of his death falls between 1306 and 1309. See John Wippel, "Godfrey of Fontaines," in *The Stanford Encyclopedia of Philosophy*, Winter 2018 ed., ed. Edward N. Zalta, Plato.Stanford.edu/entries/godfrey.

2. Wippel has suggested that his obscurity in intellectual history, given the prominence he appears to have held in his own age, is possibly due to his not belonging to a religious order, and thus his having no community to promote his cause for sanctity (in fact, Godfrey was a critic of the mendicant orders).

3. On this, see Ruedi Imbach, "L'averroïsme latin du XIIIe siècle," in *Gli studi di filosfia medievale fra otto e novecento*, ed. R. Imbach and A. Maierù (Rome: Ed. di Storia e Letteratura 1991), 191–208.

4. Msgr. John Wippel, "Godfrey of Fontaines and the Act-Potency Axiom," *Journal of the History of Philosophy* 11 (1973): 299–317.

5. Georges de Lagarde writes: "Godfrey of Fontaines is ... a convinced Aristotelian, who wishes to achieve as complete an adaptation of Aristotelianism to Christianity as possible." "La philosophie sociale d'Henri de Gand et Godefroid de Fontaines," *Archives d'Histoire Doctrinale et Littéraire du Moyen Age* 18 (1943): 73–142.

6. If he references Aquinas in his explanations of the nature of freedom and the relation between the intellect and will, it is implicit rather than explicit:

consider, for example, his unattributed verbatim quoting of Aquinas (*ST* I-II.6.2) in Q 8, q. 16 (PB 4:146) (pointed out by Michael Szlachta in "A Defense of Intellectualism: Will, Intellect, and Control in Late Thirteenth-Century Philosophy" [PhD diss., University of Toronto, 2019], 112). François-Xavier Putallaz judges that, "regarding the theme of the liberum arbitrium, Godfrey is not a Thomist; he borrows many elements [instead] from the doctrine of Siger of Brabant." *Insolente liberté: Controverses et condamnations au XIIIe siècle* (Paris: Cerf, 1995), 251. But his general esteem for Aquinas is clear: in Q 12, q. 5 (PB 5:100–102), he refers to the teachings of Aquinas as the highest heights achieved in the church's thought since the fathers. Whether Godfrey is faithful to the inheritance of the thought of Aquinas is a question we will consider at the end.

7. Q 15, q. 4 (PB 14:24–25). On this point, see Lottin, *Psychologie et morale*, 1:327. To be sure, Aquinas also ascribes something like efficient causality to the object, insofar as he affirms Aristotle's notion that the appetible object moves the appetite in the mode of an "unmoved mover." Lottin claims that, in contrast to Godfrey, Aquinas never accords efficient causality to the object of will (1:334), but this is true only if we interpret efficient causality in an exclusive and singular sense. What *is* certainly true is that Aquinas never denies the will's own (self-moving) efficient causality in its action.

8. See Godfrey's discussion in Q 9, q. 19 (PB 4:277).

9. In other words, when I will an object, my will is really related to the object, but the object is not really related to my will, in the sense that whether or not I will the object has no bearing on the object in any ontological sense.

10. The language of intentionality, though not Godfrey's, is helpfully proposed by Szlachta, "Defense of Intellectualism," 120–23.

11. Q 9, q. 19 (PB 4:277): "What has the nature of a terminus with respect to some act is, in some way, passive with respect to it, and *simpliciter*, that which 'looks to another' as to a terminus seems to be, in some way, active with respect to it" (cited in, and translated by, Szlachta in "Defense of Intellectualism," 120).

12. On this, see Jamie Anne Spiering, "'Liber Est Causa Sui': Thomas Aquinas and the Maxim 'The Free Is the Cause of Itself,'" *Review of Metaphysics* 65.2 (December 2011): 351–76. Spiering explains that Aquinas does not mean the phrase *causa sui* in the radical sense of self-creation, but she does give it an efficient sense, which Szlachta does not acknowledge. Szlachta is right to criticize Gallagher's voluntaristic interpretation ("Defense of Intellectualism," 53–55) but takes it to be a simple dichotomy, which is just what we rejected.

13. Q 15, q. 4 (PB 14:30–31), trans. Neil Lewis, "Selections from Quodlibet 15, Question 4," in "Godfrey of Fontaines and the Freedom of the Will," 2016, http://lewis.georgetown.domains/godfrey-of-fontaines-quodlibet-8-question-6/#Selections_from_Quodlibet_15_Question_4.

14. Q 8, q. 16 (PB 4:173).
15. Q 6, q. 7 (PB 3:171).
16. Q 6, q. 7 (PB 3:171); see Szlachta, "Defense of Intellectualism," 108.
17. Q 8, q. 16 (PB 4:173).
18. Q 8, q. 16 (PB 4:173).
19. A great deal of the medieval debate concerning freedom implicated this principle from Aristotle's *Physics* (8.5) (Stadter, *Psychologie und Metaphysik*, 309). See Johannes Staffler, S.J., "Der hl. Thomas und das Axiom: Omne quod movetur ab alio movetur," *Zeitschrift für katholische Theologie* 47.3 (1923): 369–90; Roy R. Effler, O.F.M., *John Duns Scotus and the Principle "Omne Quod Movetur ab Alio Movetur"* (St. Bonaventure, NY: Franciscan Institute, 1962); Kent, *Virtues of the Will*, passim.
20. Wippel speaks of Godfrey's absolutely "unbending application" of the principle in "Act-Potency Axiom," 302.
21. Strictly speaking, the object and the intellect act as one and the same on the will: the object (*obiectum applicatum*) as the "immediate" cause and the intellect (*obiectum applicans*) as the "remote" cause; see Szachta, "Defense of Intellectualism," 107–8.
22. See Kent, *Virtues of the Will*, 137–43.
23. See Roland J. Teske, S.J., "Henry of Ghent on the Freedom of the Human Will," in *A Companion to Henry of Ghent*, ed. Gordon Wilson (Leiden: Brill, 2010), 315–35.
24. See Q 8, q. 1 (PB 4:19), my translation: "Item, actus et potentia sunt contraria; quare non possunt eisdem secundum idem convenire; quod enim est in potentia receptiva, cum sic illo sit carens, non potest esse in actu secundum illud sive habens. Et quod est in actu secundum aliquid et sic illud habens, non potest esse in potentia receptiva respectu illius, illo scilicet carens." Cf. Wippel, "Act-Potency Axiom," 306–7.
25. Q 13, q. 3 (PB 5:193): "Et qui dicit contrarium hoc non probat et manifeste dicit contraria et contradicit primis principiis generalissimis fundatis super terminos generalissimos, scilicet super ens et non ens, et super actuam et potentiam." See Wippel, "Act-Potency Axiom," 317.
26. John Wippel presents this point in detail in *The Metaphysical Thought of Godfrey of Fontaines* (Washington, DC: Catholic University of America Press, 1981), 173–207.
27. Cf. Aquinas, *ST* I.77.6.
28. For a succinct account of Godfrey's epistemology, see John Wippel, "The Role of the Phantasm in Godfrey of Fontaines's Theory of Intellection," in *L'homme et son univers au moyen age: Actes du 7. Congrès Internat. de Philosophie Médiévale (30 Aug–4 Sept, 1982)*, ed. C. Wenin (Louvain-la-Neuve: Institut Supérieur de Philosophie, 1986), 2:573–82.

29. Siger of Brabant is also a relatively pure "intellectualist"—but he is a pure Aristotelian, in contrast to Godfrey, who wants to incorporate Aristotle into the Christian tradition, so to speak, rather than affirm him alongside it. On Siger, see Putallaz, *Insolente liberté*, 15–49. Other prominent intellectualists, apart from Aquinas of course, who would not qualify as "pure," are Giles of Rome (who was explicitly condemned) and Thomas of Sutton. But Giles and Thomas of Sutton are in fact not as pure as Godfrey: Giles gives the will the power to withhold itself from assent to what the intellect presents (while Godfrey insists that, if it does so, it is always for a reason, and so as subordinate to intellect), and Thomas of Sutton affirms that will at least moves itself in the order of exercise (like Aquinas).

30. "Volo quia volo; hoc enim est dictum puerorum"; Q 10, q. 13 (PB 4:371), my translation.

31. Lottin, *Psychologie et morale*, 1:323.

32. Bonnie Kent, for instance, takes essentially this position in *Virtues of the Will*. Szlachta, by contrast, is right to defend the core idea in intellectualism, but his interpretation is one-sided, for reasons we are attempting to show.

33. For a presentation of the list, see David Piché and Claude Lafleur, *La condamnation parisienne de 1277* (Paris: Vrin, 1999).

34. Lottin, *Psychologie et morale*, 1:322.

35. Godfrey *affirms* that the reason can very well be a culpable one; Q 15, q. 4 (PB 14:30). See Szlachta's discussion of this point in "Defense of Intellectualism," 110–18.

36. Q 8, q. 16 (PB 4:166–68). It is interesting to note that Godfrey clearly takes Bernard to be an authority, which thus requires such a demonstration of harmony between his position and that of Bernard.

37. See Q 8, q. 16 (PB 4:150).

38. *Not* that he rejects this simply; in fact, he insists that man is free because he possesses a certain *dominium* (Q 8, q. 16 [PB 4:147]). Thus, for Godfrey, the will is free without having "power over" itself.

39. He refers to Aristotle's *Metaph.* (1.1.2 [982b]) and *Politics* (1.1.5 [1254b]) in Q 8, q. 16 (PB 4:145), interpreting the phrase *causa sui* (or more specifically in the cited text, the statement that the free man is one who "suimet et non alterius causa est") in ontological terms as one's existing for one's own sake, rather than in dynamic terms as actualizing itself in the mode of efficient causality. On all of this, see Szlachta, "Defense of Intellectualism," 63–65.

40. To be sure, Godfrey does not in fact emphasize the normative language of truth but speaks principally of judgment. The position he takes is more subjective, and more able to coincide with voluntarism, than it initially appears. We will come back to this point at the end of this chapter.

41. Though Bernard, as we saw, strongly emphasizes the independence of the will from reason, he nevertheless clearly affirms a "normative" sense of freedom in the end: his "freedom from suffering" is a freedom more perfect than the freedom from sin or the freedom from coercion.

42. Q 15, q. 4 (PB 14:29–31).

43. See Q 8, q. 16 (PB 4:146).

44. This position is ultimately quite similar to the classical "intellectualist" one Socrates presents in Plato's *Protagoras*, though as we argued in *FFR*, Plato presented the argument prior to the conceptual differentiation of the two spiritual faculties, intellect and will, which took place later in the tradition (*FFR*, 300–303).

45. See Plato, *Laws* 645a. We discuss the Platonic tradition of freedom using the metaphor of the golden thread in *FFR*, 295–322.

46. Lottin, *Psychologie et morale*, 1:337; Wippel, *Metaphysical Thought*, 201.

47. Q 8, q. 6 (PB 4:173), trans. Lewis.

48. He notes that the position he describes accords with the saints and with the Philosopher.

49. Q 10, q. 11 (PB 4:352–53). The end forms the basis of the practical syllogism in a willed act, so the will precedes the intellectual grasp of the proper means, which precedes the choice.

50. Q 8, q. 16 (PB 4:173): "Et sic est causa talis actus effectiva moventis et impellentis quasi ad exercitum actus."

51. In fact, Godfrey says the intellect and will are so perfectly conjoined in the act of choice that it is impossible to tell which power is the principal one in the act; Q 8, q. 16 (PB 4:175).

52. Q 6, q. 7 (PB 3:170), trans. Szlachta in "Defense of Intellectualism," 109.

53. As Yul Kim has shown, Godfrey rejected this point by arguing that, if it were true, then wood would be able in principle to set itself on fire; see "Why Does the Wood Not Ignite Itself? Duns Scotus's Defense of the Will's Self-Motion," *American Catholic Philosophical Quarterly* 95.1 (2021): 49–68.

54. In spite of his saying here that the two powers act "simul tempore," he insists elsewhere on the importance of recognizing that the intellect acts *first* (*primo*), and the will *follows* (*deinde*) (Q 8, q. 16 [PB 4:154]), even in those acts in which they appear to occur at the same time, such as decisions made suddenly: *subreptitiam*.

55. To be sure, Godfrey does indeed say that the action of the intellect and will is "simul tempore," but while a metaphysical dependence is possible in a single temporal moment, a *reciprocal* dependence requires a principle that transcends the temporal order simply.

56. As we mentioned above, Szachta assumes that, if the will is caused by another, it is not caused by the self, but we showed in the last chapter that such a simple dichotomy is a false one.

57. Plato, *Sophist* 249d. Plato here asks whether reality in its highest sense is moving or unmoving and says it has to be both, even if these seem contradictory. Arguably, his point here is not only similar to but the very same as the one we are seeking to make.

58. See, for example, *ST* I.82.4 ad 3.

59. This is the basic argument made at length in a variety of contexts in D. C. Schindler, *Hans Urs von Balthasar*.

60. Wippel, *Metaphysical Thought*, 39–99, esp. 89–99.

61. Q 8, q. 1 (PB 4:19).

62. See, e.g., his use of the distinction in Q 6, q. 1 (PB 3:94–95). Thomas Osborne Jr. observes that, in invoking this distinction to respond to a question (in this case whether it is possible to know God and not to love him), Godfrey shows more affinity with voluntarism than intellectualism; see Thomas Osborne Jr., "Giles of Rome, Henry of Ghent, and Godfrey of Fontaines on Whether to See God Is to Love Him," *Recherches de Théologie et Philosophie Médiévale* 80.1 (2013): 73–75.

63. See Disputed Question 12, in "Disputed Questions 9, 10 and 12," *Franciscan Studies* 33 (2973): 351–72, ed. Wippel.

64. To be sure, Godfrey himself insists that the object is the efficient cause of all spiritual acts, but the logic of his view tends to undermine this causal energy because it deprives the object of any capacity genuinely to *communicate* itself to the soul: thus, when it transfers its causal energy, we might say that the energy takes on a new actuality inside the soul, which is necessarily different from the actuality it has in reality. Therefore, it turns out in the end that, strictly speaking, it is not the object that moves the soul but the soul's idea of the object that moves the soul.

65. Q 8, q. 16 (PB 4:174–75).

66. To put the matter in technical terms, Godfrey explains that, while the specification or determination of the will is traced back to the object, the *exercise* of the act is more properly traced back to the intellect, which is able to "indifferently apply *this* or *that* [to the will]"; Q 15, q. 2 (PB 14:10), my translation. In a sense, one might suggest that, if he absorbs the proper act of the will into the intellect, it carries with it a certain arbitrary power.

67. See the similar judgment of Lagarde, who presents Godfrey as having hardened the Thomistic-Aristotelian synthesis, and Henry of Ghent as having opened the way to Scotus and Ockham by restricting Aristotle's relevance to natural philosophy and opening up what at least seems on the surface to be a purely Christian metaphysics; "Philosophie sociale," 140.

CHAPTER 11. John Duns Scotus and the Radicalizing of Potency

1. As we recall, there is a symphony of co-causes, which is why Aquinas's philosophy implies a sense of agency as always embedded.

2. For a time, it was thought that Scotus's philosophy of freedom was introduced from out of the blue, but scholars such as Stadter (*Psychologie und Metaphysik*) have shown how much some of the basic insights were already anticipated by earlier figures, such as Walter of Bruges or Henry of Ghent. This does not diminish the achievement of Scotus, who gave this movement a paradigmatic expression.

3. William A. Frank, preface to *Duns Scotus on the Will and Morality*, trans. Allan B. Wolter, ed. William A. Frank (Washington, DC: Catholic University of America Press, 1997), ix. Cf. A. Vos Jaczn et al., introduction to *Contingency and Freedom: Lectura I 39, Introduction, Translation, and Commentary* (Boston: Kluwer, 1994), 27–28. The authors discuss Scotus's insights into freedom as due ultimately to God's love, and especially its Trinitarian character.

4. According to Gustav Siewerth, "In his metaphysics, Scotus's thinking is theological from start to finish"; *Das Schicksal der Metaphysik von Thomas zu Heidegger* (Freiburg: Johannesverlag-Einsiedeln, 2003), 119. On the question of Scotus's alleged "theologism," see Allan Wolter, "The 'Theologism' of Duns Scotus," in *The Philosophical Theology of John Duns Scotus*, ed. Marilyn McCord Adams (Ithaca, NY: Cornell University Press, 1990), 209–53. Wolter reduces this question to that of whether Scotus offered a strictly rationally demonstrable proof for the existence of God.

5. Etienne Gilson, *John Duns Scotus: Introduction to His Fundamental Positions* (London: T&T Clark, 2019), 18–20. Boulnois points out that, because philosophy is limited by the horizon of nature, theology, which introduces a higher perspective, represents a principle of constant innovation; see *Puissance et son ombre*, 15–16.

6. While we cannot enter into the complex question of the relation between theology and philosophy in Scotus, it may suffice within the strictures of our discussion to observe that, contrary to some who judge that Scotus seeks to *invalidate* non-Christian thought (for example, see Vos Jaczn et al., introduction to *Contingency and Freedom*, 5), the more adequate view is that Scotus sought to recuperate a discussion of pagan thought that harmonizes with the Christian view of freedom. This is, for example, the general argument advanced by Kent in *Virtues of the Will*. Scotus was not against Aristotle per se but only against a particular interpretation of Aristotle, to which he opposed an alternative interpretation, which foregrounded texts that were neglected by the other, more common interpretation.

7. See the discussion of all the controversies surrounding the condemnation in 1277 of naturalist tendencies, above all in anthropology and cosmology; Putallaz, *Insolente liberté*.

8. Ludger Honnefelder, "Die Kritik des Johannes Duns Scotus am kosmologischen Nezessitarismus der Araber: Ansätze zu einem neuen Freiheitsbegriff," in *Die abendländische Freiheit vom 10. zu 14. Jahrhundert*, ed. Johannes Fried (Ostfildern: Jan Thorbecke, 1991), 249–63.

9. Scotus argues against both Godfrey (see *Lectura* and *Reportatio* II, d. 25, nn. 28–37, in *Opera omnia*, ed. Carolus Balić et al. [Vatican City: Typis Polyglottis Vaticanis, 1950–2013], 19:236–40) and Aquinas (*Lectura* and *Reportatio* II, d. 25, nn. 40–50, ed. Balić et al., 19:241–44). The editors of the Vatican edition note that Scotus has both Aquinas and Godfrey in mind in his critique of the notion that the intellect's object would exercise efficient causality with respect to the will (ed. Balić et al., 19:235, notes to lines 1–2), though as we have seen in our discussion Aquinas's position on this point is complex. Scotus assumes that to move the will is to impose a force on the will from the outside, which is the very assumption we have attempted to call into question regularly in the present book (and in the discussion of Plato and Aristotle in volume 1). On this matter in Scotus, see the definitive study by Stephen Dumont, "Did Duns Scotus Change His Mind on the Will?," in *Nach der Verurteiling von 1277: Philosophie und Theologie an der Universität von Paris im letzten Viertel des 13. Jahrhunderts*, ed. J. A. Aertsen, K. Emergy, and A. Speer (New York: Walter de Gruyter, 2001), 744–45nn81–83.

10. Honnefelder, "Kritik," 255, 260. Honnefelder observes that Aquinas follows Aristotle in attributing deviations from necessity to matter, but this is already to put the issue in Scotus's terms. Aristotle's notion of chance is an accidental deviation from a principal causal account, but this is not the same thing as a disturbance of an otherwise predetermined causal chain, which would require quite a different metaphysical interpretation of the basic notions in play. In any event, it is interesting to consider that Plato already attributed necessity essentially to the "mechanical" force of matter rather than to form; see *Tim.* 47e ff.

11. Aristotle, *Metaph.* 12.7.1072b14–30.

12. We find an echo of this same perspective centuries later in Spinoza, who no doubt works out the details of this system for the first time in a genuinely systematic way in his *Ethics*. In his plea for the *salto mortale* to secure Christian freedom over against this deterministic naturalism, and therefore what he for the first time names "nihilism," Friedrich Heinrich Jacobi might be said to play Scotus to Spinoza's Averroes; see his *Concerning the Doctrine of Spinoza in Letters to Herr Moses Mendelssohn* (Breslau: Gottlieb Löwe, 1785) and *The Spinoza Conversations between Lessing and Jacobi: Text with Excerpts from the Ensuing Controversy* (Lanham, MD: University Press of America,

1988). The difference here is the radicalizing of Jacobi's judgment, which makes the fall into determinism essential to human reason per se unless it is redeemed by faith. A deeper comparison between the two, Scotus and Jacobi, would be quite illuminating.

13. Honnefelder, "Kritik," 254.

14. See Stadter, *Psychologie und Metaphysik*, 337–43. Scotus is not an *opponent* of Aristotle (as, for example, Walter of Bruges and Henry of Ghent more obviously are) but rereads him in a novel way.

15. As is generally recognized now, Scotus is not a "voluntarist" in the sense of absolutizing the will as a purely arbitrary power (see Milbank, afterword to Gilson, *John Duns Scotus*, 557–58, who says that the issue is not whether Scotus is a voluntarist in this simplistic sense but concerns the way in which he separates intellect and will). Mary Beth Ingham insists that Scotus does not even separate the intellect and will in the manner some believe, since in fact he seeks increasingly over the course of the evolution of his thinking to "integrate rationality into willing"; see "Re-situating Scotus's Thought," *Modern Theology* 21.4 (October 2005): 615. What Ingham, and others such as Tobias Hoffmann and those who similarly emphasize the *rationality* of the will in Scotus, do not sufficiently recognize in making this claim is that Scotus changes the meaning of rationality from the order that arises from an intuitive grasp of truth to order that arises from the capacity to choose between alternatives and so express a preference.

16. As we saw in the earlier chapter, Bonaventure drew on Aristotle's distinction between natural and voluntary emanations in *Metaph*. 7.7.1032a12–13 and *Phys*. 2.5.

17. We discussed this in *FFR*, 325–31.

18. The principal text in this regard is Scotus's discussion of the theme of actuality and potency in Aristotle in *Q. in Meta*. IX, q. 15, ed. G. Etzkorn et al., *Opera philosophica*, 5 vols. (St. Bonaventure, NY: Franciscan Institute, 1997–2006), 4:675–99, trans. Wolter, *Duns Scotus*, 136–49.

19. What distinguishes Scotus from Aquinas, according to Johannes Auer, is the interpretation of the will as essentially active versus the will as essentially passive; see Auer, *Menschliche Willensfreiheit*, 46–48.

20. See *Q. in Meta*. IX, q. 15 ad 2, n. 7: "The intellect does not suffice to qualify as a rational potency" (ed. Etzkorn et al., 4:697, trans. Wolter, *Duns Scotus*, 149.

21. See Wolter's discussion of this in "Duns Scotus on the Will as Rational Potency," in Adams, *Philosophical Theology*, 163–80.

22. Note here a kind of simultaneously metaphysical and moral transcendence: goodness "beyond" nature, a kind of radical gratuity that in fact establishes nature. We will discuss this point briefly in the General Conclusion.

23. See Auer, *Menschliche Willensfreiheit*, 247–49. Hoeres says that the coincidence of freedom and necessity "is the decisive position of the entire teaching on the will and freedom of the subtle Doctor" (*Wille als reine Vollkommenheit*, 78).

24. QQ 16.32, ed. Felix Alluntis, *Obras del Doctor Sutil Juan Duns Escoto: Cuestiones Cuodlibetales* (Madrid: Biblioteca de Autores Cristianos, 1963) (all subsequent citations are to this edition), trans. Felix Alluntis and Allan B. Wolter, *God and Creatures: The Quodlibetal Questions* (Princeton, NJ: Princeton University Press, 1975), 378. Scotus concedes that it is not possible to *explain* the coincidence of freedom and necessity (QQ 16.33, trans. Wolter, *God and Creatures*, 379), but we simply recognize the fact of this coincidence in God.

25. Anselm and Bernard did posit a certain freedom outside of the bounds of nature but did not give the point a properly metaphysical grounding. Bonaventure moved in the direction of a theory of being but did not develop the notion of freedom at length at this level.

26. We recall that Aquinas interprets God's will in himself as *voluntas* rather than *liberum arbitrium*, which preserves its natural necessity even while distinguishing it from nature simply.

27. *Ordinatio* II, d. 17, ed. Balić et al., vol. 8, trans. Wolter, *Duns Scotus*, 155. Hoeres explains that the decisive opposition for Scotus is that between nature and will (*Wille als reine Vollkommenheit*, 80); Wolter says that the opposition between the natural and the free is fundamental for the whole of Scotus's thought ("Native Freedom of the Will as Key to the Ethics of Scotus," in Adams, *Philosophical Theology*, 149).

28. Scotus distinguishes between the communication of the divine essence to the Holy Spirit and God's act of loving himself (which belongs properly to the Holy Spirit); see the note Scotus added to his manuscript of the *Quaestiones Quodlibetales* in *Obras del doctor sutil Juan Duns Escoto* (Madrid: Biblioteca de Autores Cristianos, 1968). This passage is cited in QQ 16.42.15, trans. Alluntis and Wolter, *God and Creatures*, 379–80n23.

29. QQ 16.41.14, trans. Alluntis and Wolter, *God and Creatures*, 384: Scotus explains that, just as the Son (intellect) is begotten by the Father (memory) as principle, and yet according to what he is in himself we say he is produced *per modum naturae*, so too the Spirit is generated by nature and yet considered in himself proceeds *per modum voluntatis*.

30. As Scotus puts it, the natural necessity is "something consecutive, annexed to the will, something with the assistance of which the will itself by its power as will and as free is able to elicit its notional act, an act it could not elicit without its assistance"; QQ q. 16, a. 3, trans. Alluntis and Wolter, *God and Creatures*, 381.

31. As Stadter explains, for Scotus the act of will does not presuppose a prior determining act; rather, the determining act occurs in the positing of the act itself (*in positione actus*); *Psychologie und Metaphysik*, 302.

32. QQ 16.35, trans. Alluntis and Wolter, *God and Creatures*, 381. Note that, in this context, nature is reduced to a kind of (effective) energy—"natural force"—rather than a formal principle. See William Frank, "Duns Scotus's Concept of Willing Freely: What Divine Freedom beyond Choice Teaches Us," *Franciscan Studies* 42 (1982): 80; Gilson, *Scotus*, 198.

33. QQ 16.50, trans. Alluntis and Wolter, *God and Creatures*, 387.

34. Hoeres, *Wille als reine Vollkommenheit*, 80–84.

35. QQ 16.34, trans. Alluntis and Wolter, *God and Creatures*, 379.

36. See Joseph Incandela, "Duns Scotus and the Experience of Human Freedom," *The Thomist* 56.2 (April 1992): 252; cf. Frank, "Duns Scotus' Concept," 68–89.

37. QQ 16.35, trans. Alluntis and Wolter, *God and Creatures*, 381.

38. We saw that the Christian notion of Trinity introduces a more complex view, insofar as the traditional taxis recognizes a certain priority of the Son's procession with respect to the procession of the Spirit; Aquinas is thus able in principle to affirm a more genuine analogy between divine and human freedom. The question is whether the absolute priority of the Father needs to be reflected on more deeply in relation to this particular question, which will be one of our tasks in volume 3.

39. See Cruz Gonzalez-Ayesta, "Es la voluntad un apetito o un poder?," *Anuario Filosofico* 47.1 (2014): 81. Scotus does not simply reject the definition of will as "rational appetite," but he insists that the will is an appetite only generically (see John Boler, "Transcending the Natural: Duns Scotus on the Two Affections of the Will," *American Catholic Philosophical Quarterly* 67.1 [1993]: 111; cf. Gilson, *John Duns Scotus*, 455); what specifies it is its active power to move itself. Thus, as Bonnie Kent explains, he tends (like Bonaventure, as we saw in the earlier chapter) to present the will more typically in Anselm's terms as *affectio justitiae* (Kent, *Virtues of the Will*, 197). Nevertheless, even *affectio* is not used here principally in the normal moral sense; Tobias Hoffmann, "Freedom beyond Practical Reason: Duns Scotus on Will-Dependent Relations," *British Journal for the History of Philosophy* 21.6 (2013): 1079n28.

40. QQ 16.6, trans. Alluntis and Wolter, *God and Creatures*, 370–71.

41. More specifically, Scotus recognizes the perfection of a will ordered to what is prior or a higher good but cannot harmonize that with the total perfection of God and so finds a compromise by making the will and its object *equal*: "It implies concomitant perfection to be so determined by what is on a par with it" (QQ 16.34, trans. Alluntis and Wolter, *God and Creatures*, 379). Note that

this is an *alternative* to the "supraeternity" we have affirmed in Plotinus, Dionysius, and Maximus, which is able to preserve a taxis even as it renders that taxis radically paradoxical. To summarize the transformation that occurs here in Scotus, Auer says that the will's relation to the good is no longer "natural," as it is in Aquinas, but now "ideal and ethical"; *Menschlich Willsensfreiheit*, 123. Cf. Hoffmann, "Freedom beyond Practical Reason," 1081; Hoeres, *Wille als reine Vollkommenheit*, 117.

42. *Ordinatio* III, d. 26 (ed. Balić et al., 10:35–36), trans. Wolter, *Duns Scotus*, 153. See Wolter, "Native Freedom," 152.

43. According to Aquinas, "The essence of goodness consists in this, that it is in some way desirable"; *ST* I.5.1 (Leon. 4). For Scotus, to define goodness thus would improperly naturalize the cosmos.

44. Milbank, afterword to Gilson, *John Duns Scotus*, 567.

45. Hoeres, *Wille als reine Vollkommenheit*, 222.

46. Ibid., 225.

47. There is of course a significant amount of debate surrounding the question of the relationship between desire for happiness and love of friendship in Aquinas. One of the more prominent lines of argument can be found in David Gallagher, "Desire for Beatitude and Love of Friendship in Thomas Aquinas," *Mediaeval Studies* 58 (1996): 1–47, and "Thomas Aquinas on Self-Love as the Basis for Love of Others," *Acta Philosophica* 8 (1999): 23–44. A classical presentation of the theme is Rousselot, *Problem of Love*. Rudi te Velde has argued that the problem of relating self-love to love of the other arises in Scotus only because of an essentially self-centered concept of nature, which is not to be found in Aquinas; "'*Natura in Seipsa Recurvata Est*,'" 155–70. I have proposed that reading love specifically in connection with *beauty* (rather than simply the good) in Aquinas opens up precisely this "other-centered" dimension *within* happiness; see "Love and Beauty."

48. As Gilson has shown, Scotus is decidedly *not* a voluntarist in this sense; the "legend" of his being such seems to have begun with an influential mischaracterization by Ferdinand Christian Bauer in 1842 (see Gilson, *John Duns Scotus*, 452).

49. Scotus affirms that the will "is naturally posterior to the intellect"; *Lectura*, prol. pars. 4, qq. 1–2, ed. Balić et al., 17:47, my translation. We will see, below, how it is possible to affirm this and yet, as Hoffmann asserts, claim that the will acts in complete independence of the intellect ("Freedom beyond Practical Reason," 1071).

50. Dumont has demonstrated that Scotus nevertheless seems to have shifted to a more "voluntarist" position toward the end; "Did Duns Scotus Change His Mind?"

51. Ontologically, not chronologically, of course, since God does not operate in time.

52. *Ordinatio* I, d. 38, ed. Balić et al., 6:305.

53. As Scotus puts it, "For if the intellect understands something to be done or to be produced before an act of the will, does the will then will this necessarily or not? If necessarily, then it is necessitated to produce that; if it does not necessarily will, then it wills against the dictate of the intellect and then it would be evil, since that dictate can only be right"; *Lectura* I, 43, trans. Vos Jaczyn et al., *Contingency and Freedom*, 104. See the commentary in this edition, 107.

54. Because Scotus makes the divine ideas indifferent to actuality, Kristell Trego writes: "The divine knowledge therefore does not refer to being [*n'est alors pas indexée sur l'être*]"; *Impuissance du possible*, 261.

55. The phrases are essentially interchangeable, according to Scotus; see *Lectura* I, d. 35, q. un. 30, ed. Balić et al., 17:455; *Lectura* I, d. 35, q. un. 40, ed. Balić et al., 17:460; and *Reportatio* IA, d. 36, qq. 1–2.57, ed. Timothy Noone, "Scotus on Divine Ideas: Reportatio Paris. I–A, d. 36," *Medioevo* 24 (1998): 419. On this point, see Martin Tweedale, "Representation in Scholastic Epistemology," in *Representation and Objects of Thought in Medieval Philosophy*, ed. Henrik Lagerlund (London: Routledge, 2016), 73–74. See also Gilson, *John Duns Scotus*, 223–24.

56. *Reportatio* IA, d. 38, q. 1–2.37, ed. Joachim R. Söder, *Johannes Duns Scotus. Reportatio Parisiensis examinata I 38–44 = Pariser Vorlesungen über Wissen und Kontingenz: Lateinisch, deutsch*, Herders Bibliothek der Philosophie des Mittelalters 4 (Freiburg im Breisgau: Herder, 2005), 233–34.

57. *Ordinatio* I, d. 36, q. un., 60–61, ed. Balić et al., 6:296.

58. *Ordinatio* I, d. 3, p. 1, q. 4, ed. Balić et al., 3:162–63, and *Ordinatio* II, d. 1, q. 1, ed. Balić et al., 7:16.

59. *Reportatio* IA, d. 36, q. 3, ed. Noone, 430.

60. Hoffmann, "Freedom beyond Practical Reason," 1085; see commentary, ed. Vos Jaczyn et al., *Contingency and Freedom*, 107.

61. Hoffmann argues that the possibles are neither arbitrary nor wholly dependent on God; "Duns Scotus on the Origin of the Possibles in the Divine Intellect," in *Philosophical Debates at Paris in the Early Fourteenth Century*, ed. S. Brown, T. Dewender, and T. Kobusch (Leiden: Brill, 2009), 359–79.

62. This is the heart of the "essentialism" that Gilson says characterizes Scotus's thought most fundamentally (*John Duns Scotus*, 493).

63. As Ludger Honnefelder explains, in Scotus, the "nothingness" out of which God creates is transformed into the "purely formal" possibility of things in themselves ("Kritik," 262). Ferdinand Ulrich has argued that this

is the decisive move in Scotus that paradoxically returns his thought to a pagan—i.e., "Platonizing"—context. See Marine de la Tour's exposition of Ulrich's interpretation of Scotus on this point; *Gabe im Anfang: Grundzüge des metaphysischen Denkens von Ferdinand Ulrich* (Stuttgart: Kohlhammer, 2016), 83–100.

64. In fact, as Wolter has observed, it is the relation to the will that makes the intellect (thus only accidentally) rational ("Native Freedom," 149).

65. *Ordinatio* II, d. 6, 1n19, ed. Balić et al., 8:32–33.

66. *Ordinatio* I, d. 3, p. 3, q. 2, Balić et al., 3:297, cited in Emmanuel Perrier, "Duns Scotus Facing Reality: Between Absolute Contingency and Unquestionable Consistency," *Modern Theology* 21:4 (October 2005): 531.

67. QQ 13.39, trans. Alluntis and Wolter, *God and Creatures*, 294.

68. Perrier, "Duns Scotus Facing Reality," 632.

69. See Catherine Pickstock, "Duns Scotus: His Historical and Contemporary Significance," *Modern Theology* 21.4 (October 2005): 566–67.

70. Scotus expounds this notion in *Lectura* I, 39. It was dubbed "synchronic contingency" by A. Vos Jaczn, and its importance for the history of thought seems to have been discovered more or less simultaneously in 1981 by two scholars working independently, A. Vos Jaczn and S. Knuutila. For an account of the emergence of this concept in scholarship, see Vos Jaczn et al., introduction to *Contingency and Freedom*, 1–2. See also Stephen Dumont, "The Origin of Scotus's Theory of Synchronic Contingency," *Modern Schoolman* 72.2–3 (1995): 149–67.

71. Aristotle, *De interpretatione* 9.18b1–4.

72. In fact, it also presents a problem for the angels, who, as spiritual, make an eternal decision in the very moment of their creation, which raises the question: Is this decision a free one? If freedom requires the ability to be otherwise, then to say "yes" would seem to require something like "synchronic contingency."

73. Vos Jaczyn et al., commentary to *Contingency and Freedom*, 129.

74. Not that he is absolutely first, but that the notion is most basically associated with him. Stephen Dumont has observed that others had an intuition of this point prior to Scotus, most obviously Peter Olivi (Dumont, "Origin of Scotus's Theory," 150–51).

75. Note: we have shown how the classical tradition that absolutizes nature does not necessarily enclose it in itself. The question of the "closure" of nature will turn out to be one of the most significant in the end for one's interpretation of freedom, and we will return to it in our General Conclusion.

76. *Q. in Meta.* IX, q. 15, ed. Etzkorn et al., 4:694, trans. Wolter, *Duns Scotus*, 147. The decisive texts that reveal this fundamental shift in Scotus are *Lec-*

tura I, d. 39, and *Q. in Meta.* IX, q. 15, ed. Etzkorn et al., 4:675–99, trans. Wolter, *Duns Scotus*, 136–50. In this latter text, Scotus wants to argue for the possibility of a thing being *actually contingent* (i.e., contingent as actual), and in its very actuality: "Neither, then, is an effect actually contingent, unless the cause actually causing it has the power to do the opposite at the very moment that it is causing the other"; *Q. in Meta.* IX, q. 15, ed. Etzkorn et al., 4:694, trans. Wolter, *Duns Scotus*, 147.

77. See, again, Hoffman's "Origin of the Possibles."

78. Simo Knuutila, "Duns Scotus' Criticism of the 'Statistical' Interpretation of Modality," in *Sprache und Erkenntnis im Mittelalter* (Boston: Kluwer, 1981), 441–50, and "Time and Modality in Scholasticism," in *Reforging the Great Chain of Being: Studies of the History of Modal Theories*, ed. S. Knuutila (Boston: Kluwer, 1981), 163–257.

79. See Gilson, *John Duns Scotus*, 177–78.

80. See Emmanuel Perrier, "Scotus Facing Reality," 629–32. In the face of the growing criticism of Scotus on univocity, Thomas Williams has argued that Scotus's teaching on univocity is a *semantic* theory, not a directly *ontological* one, and as such is more or less compatible with an analogy of being, but this distinction itself already betrays the decisive point (insofar as the separation of thought and being that constitutes the theory of univocity is what allows one to think a semantic theory and an ontological theory are essentially independent). Thomas Williams, "The Doctrine of Univocity Is True and Salutary," *Modern Theology* 21.4 (October 2005): 575–85. Gustav Siewerth demonstrates this convincingly in *Analogie des Seienden*, 2nd ed. (Freiburg: Johannesverlag Einsiedeln, 2003), 85–111.

81. Ludger Honnefelder, "Metaphysik als *scientia transcendens*: Johannes Duns Scotus und der zweite Anfang der Metaphysik," in *New Essays on Metaphysics as "Scientia Transcendens,"* ed. Roberto Hofmeister Pich (Porto Alegre: Brepol, 2006), 1–16.

82. Siewerth, *Schicksal der Metaphysik*, 119.

83. Henri Veldhuis, "Ordained and Absolute Power in Scotus' *Ordinatio I 44*," *Vivarium* 38.2 (2000): 222–30.

84. See Courtenay, *Covenant and Causality*, essay IV, 9. A certain qualification is necessary, since the distinction itself can express the superabundant fullness of God, as we saw in our discussion of Aquinas.

85. See the discussion in Scotus, *Ordinatio* I, d. 44., trans. Wolter, *Duns Scotus*, 192.

86. Scotus, *Ordinatio* III, suppl., d. 37, ed. Luke Wadding, *Opera omnia* (Paris: Apud Ludovicum Vivès, 1891–95), 15:741–42, 783–84, 785–86, 825–27, 843–45, 851, trans. Wolter, *Duns Scotus*, 198–207.

87. See *Ordinatio* I, d. 44, ed. Balić et al., 6:363–69, trans. Wolter, *Duns Scotus*, 191–94. As Hoeres has argued, Scotus has a powerful sense of the pure spontaneity of the divine will, and therefore its sovereignty, but insists that sovereignty in this case is not pure, arbitrary power; rather, it is power always determined by God's own perfection (*Wille als reine Vollkommenheit*, 97). Allan Wolter observes, moreover, that God never acts arbitrarily because he cannot but act with perfect justice; "Native Freedom," 61.

88. Allan B. Wolter, introduction to *Duns Scotus on the Will and Morality*, by John Duns Scotus, trans. Allan B. Wolter, O.F.M., and ed. William A. Frank (Washington, DC: Catholic University of America Press, 1997), 47.

89. *Ordinatio* I, d. 3, p. 3, q. 2, ed. Balić et al., 3:305.

90. The classic study of this notion in Scotus is Effler, *John Duns Scotus*. See the observation regarding the universalizing of the principle on page 168.

91. See Yul Kim's account in "Why Does the Wood Not Ignite Itself?"

92. As William Frank puts it in his preface to *Duns Scotus*, ix: "Freedom is the glue of the universe."

93. Scotus says that the indeterminacy of the will represents a "surpassing perfection and power" (*Q. in Meta.* IX, q. 15, ed. Etzkorn et al., 4:684, trans. Wolter, *Duns Scotus*, 141), and "The will with respect to the intellect is the superior agent" (*Opus Oxoniense* II, d. 42, qq. 1–4, nn. 10–11, ed. Wadding, 13:461, trans. Wolter, *Duns Scotus*, 151). Mary Beth Ingham observes that if, "in its most generic sense, *voluntarism* refers to any position that favors the will over the intellect," then "Scotus can never be anything but a voluntarist." "Did Scotus Modify His Position on the Relationship of Intellect and Will?," *Recherches de Théologie et Philosophie Médiévales* 69.1 (2002): 103–4. She goes on to explain, nevertheless, that the will supplants the intellect only as it simultaneously becomes "rationalized."

94. "Anything that is in potency to a certain act 'formally' speaking and yet at the same time possesses the actuality 'virtually'—as is the case when a thing moves itself—is in a certain respect unlimited [*aliqualiter illimitatum*]"; *Ordinatio* I, d. 3, p. 3, q. 2, ed. Balić et al., 3:309, my translation. But the human will is the paradigm case of such an unlimited power. See Wolter, "Duns Scotus," 176–78. Kim observes, referring to *Q. in Meta.* IX, q. 15, that, for Scotus, "despite its finitude as a created being, the will shares a kind of extraordinary similarity with God. Scotus refers to it as an 'indeterminacy of a superabundant sufficiency'" ("Why Does the Wood Not Ignite Itself?").

95. As Hoeres puts it, "The creaturely will is what the divine will is, but to an infinitely weak degree" (*Wille als reine Vollkommenheit*, 113). Moreover, unlike in God, in the embodied creature the will has to move from potency to act and is thus subject to the concrete conditions of this movement. See the dis-

cussion of Scotus's description of three kinds of freedom, with respect to act, to objects, and to effects, by which he compares and contrasts divine and human freedom, in Frank, "Duns Scotus' Concept," 77.

96. "In every agent acting intelligently and voluntarily that can act in conformity with an upright or just law but does not have to do so of necessity, one can distinguish between its ordained power and its absolute power"; *Ordinatio* I, d. 44, ed. Balić et al., 6:364, trans. Wolter, *Duns Scotus*, 191. See Veldhuis, "Ordained and Absolute Power," 225.

97. Frank, "Duns Scotus' Concept," 89.

98. Scotus, *Q. in Meta.* IX, q. 15, n. 31, ed. Etzkorn et al., 4:683, trans. Wolter, *Duns Scotus*, 140.

99. The active power to choose either of two opposites is what constitutes the will's "innate freedom" (*libertas ingenita*); *Ordinatio* III, d. 26, ed. Balić et al., 10:35–36; trans. Wolter, *Duns Scotus*, 153. See also Stadter, *Psychologie und Metaphysik*, 288. This is not to deny that the will is essentially ordered to the good; it is only to say that the will does not *receive* its superabundant sufficiency from the effective presence of goodness to it (Hoffmann, "Freedom beyond Practical Reason," 1081).

100. As Scotus puts it, the will is a *potentia* that is not determined by anything other than itself; *Q. in Meta.* IX, q. 15, ed. Etzkorn et al., 4:686–88, trans. Wolter, *Duns Scotus*, 142–43.

101. See Gonzalez-Ayesta, "Es la voluntad," 92, where the author explains that the will virtually contains in itself the acts it produces.

102. See Scotus, *Ordinatio* III, d. 26, ed. Balić et al., 10:35–36, trans. Wolter, *Duns Scotus*, 153. According to Frank, "Scotus is under the sway of a single idea: *Liberality—the freedom that is generosity—has its own order*"; preface to *Duns Scotus*, xi.

103. Scotus, *Ordinatio* III, d. 26, ed. Balić et al., 10:35–36, trans. Wolter, *Duns Scotus*, 153.

104. Maximus defined the will as rational appetite, but the notion was clearly operative in Augustine and in some sense already in Aristotle.

105. This is the point of the work of Kent, *Virtues of the Will*, among others.

106. Scotus explains that this capacity to "self-actualize," as it were, distinguishes the will in some respect from every other potency in the cosmos: *Q. in Meta.* IX, q. 15, ed. Etzkorn et al., 4:687–88, trans. Wolter, *Duns Scotus*, 143: "The will is an active principle distinct from the whole class of active principles which are not the will." On the other hand, as we observed above, Scotus eventually comes to hold that all potencies nevertheless have a kind of self-motion (Yul Kim, "Why Does the Wood Not Ignite Itself?"). What distinguishes the

will is not self-motion per se but the *rationality* of that self-motion, which is equally capable of opposite effects and so renders every act essentially contingent even in its actual being. On the distinctiveness of the will in relation to other potencies, see Boler, "Transcending the Natural," 112, and Stadter, *Psychologie und Metaphysik*, 289.

107. Dumont's important study shows that, contrary to previous judgments (even by the Vatican editors of the critical edition of Scotus's works), Scotus actually moved *closer* to the "voluntarist" position of Henry of Ghent that he had initially criticized, namely, that which reduced the intellect's role in choice to a mere "sine qua non" causality, than away from it: "Scotus's mature position is . . . more, rather than less, open to a thoroughgoing voluntarism of the sort found in Henry of Ghent" ("Did Scotus Change His Mind?," 794). Dumont's judgment has recently been confirmed, and further refined, by work on the forthcoming critical edition of the *Collationes parisienses*; see Guido Allinez, "Quando Duns Scotus ha cambiato idea sulla volontà? La causa del volere secondo la Quaestio 6 delle *Collactiones Parisienses*," forthcoming in *Noctua* but currently available online at www.academia.edu/42772664/QUANDO_DUNS _SCOTO_HA_CAMBIATO_IDEA_SULLA_VOLONTÀ. While this increasingly absolute move toward voluntarism is evidently true, we recall the point alluded to above, namely, that as Mary Beth Ingham has pointed out, Scotus is fundamentally different from radical voluntarists such as Henry insofar as he sought to integrate rationality *into* the will precisely to the extent that he separated the will's operation from that of the intellect. Nevertheless, confusion continues to exist in scholarship over whether Scotus reduced the intellect's role to that of "sine qua non" causality. Witness, for example, the various affirmations and negations in the following accounts: Patrick Lee says that Scotus developed his thought beyond the affirmation of intellect as mere sine qua non ("The Relation between Intellect and Will in Free Choice According to Aquinas and Scotus," *The Thomist* 49.3 [July 1985]: 321–42), as do Kent in *Virtues of the Will*, 147, Eef Dekker in "Scotus's Freedom of the Will Revisited," in Bos, *John Duns Scotus*, 116, and Gilson in *John Duns Scotus*, 465, while Hoeres says that Scotus comes back to sine qua non causality (*Wille als reine Vollkommenheit*, 208). That confusion is itself revealing: as the wording of Dumont's conclusion itself shows, Scotus may have become more inclined to one position over the other, but he did not come to a final judgment on the matter—and the reason, we are proposing, is that an absolute self-actualizing power simply cannot be integrated with anything else except in an extrinsic, i.e., superficial, manner. Note that, when Kent simply affirms Scotus's conception of a cooperation between the effective power of the object, grasped through the intellect, and the effective power of the will, she simply sidesteps this metaphysical issue (*Virtues of the Will*, 147).

108. Gloria Frost shows that Scotus wrestled with the question of the relation between the operations of the divine and human will in human choice, rejecting and then accepting different positions over the course of his career, and finally appearing to incline toward a position that affirms the independence of the human will—a position he nevertheless proceeds to reject in another context because it appears to compromise the possibility of God's perfect foreknowledge of human choice. In short, this question, like the prior one, cannot be resolved within the terms established. "Duns Scotus on How God Causes the Created Will's Volitions," in *Interpreting Duns Scotus: Critical Essays*, ed. Giorgio Pini (Cambridge: Cambridge University Press, forthcoming).

109. Gilson, *John Duns Scotus*, 414. Note that, like Bonaventure, Scotus denies a real distinction between the essence of the soul and its powers and posits instead a formal distinction (*II Sent.*, d. 16, q. 1, n. 17, ed. Luke Wadding, *Opera omnia* [Paris: Apud Ludovicum Vivès, 1891–95], 13:43 ff.); see Allan Wolter, "Duns Scotus on the Natural Desire for the Supernatural," in Adams, *Philosophical Theology*, 133. It is important to note that whatever integration he eventually affirms occurs in an "additive" way in the objective act rather than in any intrinsic sense in the operation. On the will and intellect as autonomous co-causes, see Dekker, "Scotus's Freedom," 116.

110. *Lectura* I, d. 3, nn. 366–68, ed. Balić et al., 16:367–68, and *Ordinatio* I, d. 3, p. 3, q. 2, ed. Balić et al., 3:293–94. William Frank judges this to be one of the most basic distinctions in Scotus's thought. See "Duns Scotus on Autonomous Freedom and Divine Co-causality," *Medieval Philosophy and Theology* 2 (1992): 153n28.

111. *Lectura* II, d. 2.25, and *Ordinatio* I, d. 3, q. 2, ed. Balić et al., 3:293–94. See Frank, "Duns Scotus on Autonomous Freedom," 154.

112. Frank, "Duns Scotus on Autonomous Freedom," 155 (see also 142, 143–44n2, 152, where Frank explains the meaning of "immediate, partial cause"). Or so it seems in the end, though Scotus also seems to have considered for a time an affirmation of God as total mediate cause and the human will as total immediate cause, which he says is less plausible, finally, because it seems to undermine God's perfect foreknowledge of human acts. Frost draws attention to a third type of cooperation (which she says Frank missed; manuscript page 12), in which each of the two cooperating causes can be considered a *total* cause in its own order; see *Lectura* II, d. 35–37, q. 5, nn. 124–26, ed. Balić et al., 19:358. In the end, even this total causality assumes an extrinsic cooperation of essentially separate agents, and so the integration problem remains.

113. We note that, even if Scotus is taken to come back in the end to a reduction of the intellect's contribution to mere "sine qua non" causality, this is not a significant development with respect to the basic argument we seek to make here: if the will is absolutely self-determining of its essence (which is

undeniable in Scotus), whatever cooperation may be posited with respect to the intellect can only be incidental.

114. Hoeres discusses this term as originating with Scotus in *Wille als reine Vollkommenheit*, 269–71. Stadter points out that, contrary to what some think (like Auer, *Menschliche Willensfreiheit*, 264), Scotus did not himself coin the term, because it can already be found in Olivi; see *Psychologie und Metaphysik*, 311–12.

115. *Opus Oxoniense* II, d. 42, qq. 1–4, nn. 10–11, ed. Wadding, 13:460–61, trans. Wolter, *Duns Scotus*, 150–51.

116. *Ordinatio* IV, d. 46, ed. Balić et al., 14:208, trans. Wolter, *Duns Scotus*, 189.

117. Kent observes that this was a favored image among voluntarists, from William de la Mare and Henry of Ghent, to Scotus and Richard of Middleton (*Virtues of the Will*, 122).

118. The operation of "command" belongs naturally to what is highest. As Auer has pointed out, while Aquinas, for example, ascribes this operation to the intellect, Scotus ascribes it to the will (*Menschliche Willensfreiheit*, 105–6).

119. Scotus posits the "active potency" of the will as *not* a relation but "an absolute nature (*natura absoluta*), which represents the proper foundation for several relationships toward opposite effects." *Q. in Meta.* IX, q. 15, a. 1, ed. Etzkorn et al., 4:678, trans. Wolter, *Duns Scotus*, 136.

120. We recall the list of cooperative causes, each of which has an article in itself, in *ST* I-II.9.

121. Scotus discusses these in *Ordinatio* III, d. 26, ed. Balić et al., 10:35–36, trans. Wolter, *Duns Scotus*, 153. See Wolter, "Native Freedom," 150. Cf. Walter Hoeres, "Naturtendenz und Freiheit nach Duns Scotus," *Salzburger Jahrbuch für Philosophie* 2 (1958): 95–139.

122. As Ludger Honnefelder observes, Scotus's observation that the will *has* a nature but does not act in a *natural way* implies a new status of nature ("Kritik," 255).

123. As Hoeres explains, we cannot say strictly speaking that the will acts according to its nature, but instead that the natural inclination is taken up and made to accord with the will (*Wille als reine Vollkommenheit*, 162–63).

124. *Ordinatio* III, d. 17, ed. Balić et al., 9:565–66, trans. Wolter, *Duns Scotus*, 154–55.

125. Ibid., and *Reportatio parisiensia* II, d. 6, q. 2, n. 9 (XXVII), 27:621a–22a, ed. Wadding, *Opera omnia*, vol. 22. John Boler presents this as the key to the *unity* of the will, noting that Henry of Ghent had already hit on this way of interpreting Anselm; "An Image for the Unity of the Will in Duns Scotus," *Journal of the History of Philosophy* 32.1 (1994): 25n5.

126. *Ordinatio* IV, suppl., d. 49, qq. 9–10, a. 1, Codex A ff. 281va–82va, trans. Wolter, *Duns Scotus*, 156: "The natural appetite is no more an elicited act of will than is the natural appetite in a stone."

127. *Ordinatio* II, d. 6, q. 2, ed. Balić et al., 8:49, trans. Wolter, *Duns Scotus*, 298–99, emphasis added. It is worth pointing out that Scotus comes to a conclusion that is more or less perfectly opposed to that of Maximus, who identifies freedom with the natural will and the possibility of sin with the gnomic will, precisely because it is exercised in some sense beyond the givenness of nature. On this difference, see Wolter, introduction to *Duns Scotus*, 41–42.

128. As Scotus puts it: "Nor is every object of the will an end, but only that which has what the will wills, and for the sake of which it wills. When the will and object concur at the same time, the object moves efficiently in so far as it is that which the will wills." This is a text reported by Scotus's pupil, William of Alnwick: *Magnae Additiones*, ed. Charles Balić, in *Les commentaires de Jean Duns Scot sur les quatre livres des Sentences* (Louvain: Bureau de la Revue, 1927), 285, quoted in Incandela, "Duns Scotus." As Incandela summarizes, for Scotus, "Freedom goes all the way down to the will's choice of its ends" (239). See Auer, *Menschliche Willensfreiheit*, 126–27; Lee, "Relation," 327; and Hoffmann, "Freedom beyond Practical Reason," 1077.

129. *Ordinatio* IV, suppl., d. 49, qq. 9–10, a. 2, Codex A ff. 281va–82va, trans. Wolter, *Duns Scotus*, 160–61: "As for the reason given to support the other view, namely, that the will must necessarily love whatever possesses no aspect of evil or lack of good, I say that this is false, for the will is free with respect to any act of volition or notion, and no object necessitates it."

130. Incandela argues that Scotus and Aquinas are totally at odds on this point, so that we can say it marks what is most distinctive about Scotus ("Duns Scotus," 229–30). We discussed this matter in chapter 9 above.

131. As Wolter explains, the "natural appetite for beatitude" is for Scotus purely *metaphorical* precisely because appetite is not an act or operation at all; "Duns Scotus on the Natural Desire," 140–41.

132. Frank, "Duns Scotus' Concept," 85.

133. *Faust*, 329 (lines 11573–76), trans. Walter Arndt, 2nd ed. (New York: Norton, 2001).

134. Robert Spaemann echoes something of this; see *Persons: The Difference between Someone and Something*, trans. Oliver O'Donovan (Oxford: Oxford University Press, 2006).

135. As we will explore in the General Conclusion, the affirmation of freedom at the core of being has been implicit in the tradition but was not emphasized in a direct way.

136. This is not to suggest a simple, direct line from Scotus to Locke and the other moderns. Instead, there are quite a few mediating figures: Ockham, Suarez, Molina, Bañez, Petrarch, Luther, Erasmus, Calvin, and so forth. The point is that the basic form that we see in modern thought has received a first paradigmatic articulation in Scotus.

137. For Gilson, this essentialism is the distinctive core of Scotus's thought (*John Duns Scotus*, xxx and 297).

138. Ibid., 494–95.

139. We refer again here to the essay by Frost, "Duns Scotus," in which she shows Scotus's evolving attempts to integrate divine and human freedom in a way that does full justice to both, but is never able to resolve the conundra that arise precisely because of his assumption of freedom as *total* spontaneity that cannot but be absolute in itself—and so incapable of integration.

140. Joke Spruyte explains that the key difference between Scotus and Henry of Ghent is that Scotus complements the radical theory of will with a new theory of *being*; "Duns Scotus's Criticism of Henry of Ghent's Notion of Free Will," in Bos, *John Duns Scotus*, 140. As Hoeres puts it, Scotus radicalizes the *libertas exerciti* to such an extent that the capacity to posit an act or not belongs even to the blessed in heaven (*Wille als reine Vollkommenheit*, 119).

141. The highest instance of this is, as we saw above, no doubt Scotus's separating the Holy Spirit as nature, and as free act, which aspects are subsequently affirmed together; see Alluntis and Wolter's commentary in Scotus, *God and Creatures*, 381.

142. Trego, *Impuissance du possible*, 262.

143. Scotus, *Q. in Meta.* IX, q. 15, ed. Etzkorn et al., 4:697, trans. Wolter, *Duns Scotus*, 149; cf. Boler, "Transcending the Natural," 114.

144. Aquinas, *SCG* 1.72.2.

145. Aquinas, *ST* I.78.1.

146. Aquinas, *ST* I.29.3.

147. Boulnois, *Puissance et son ombre*, 64.

148. We might compare it to the stability of a marriage that is due on the one hand to the *actual reality* of the sacrament and on the other hand only to the sincerity of the active commitment of the two spouses.

149. Hoeres, in *Wille als reine Vollkommenheit*, explains that for Scotus the highest act of the will lies in its binding itself with its object but observes that in the end the ground is the *operatio* and not the *relatio*: this implies that the will's activity terminates, not in an object, but in its own activity (301–2).

150. Kent, *Virtues of the Will*, 196.

151. See Wolter, "Duns Scotus and the Natural Desire," 147.

152. It is instructive to consider Hegel's project in light of this point. For Hegel, the fundamental problem of modern religiosity (which inevitably has a

philosophical and a political expression) is a failure to recognize *revealedness* to be the very *essence* of spirit—which is why Christianity, founded on the *ontological* self-revelation of God in Christ, and then by extension (through the Holy Spirit) in the church, is the *consummate* religion. This is why he is able to articulate one of the most profound alternatives to the modern conception of freedom, namely, freedom as the perfect actuality of social order: being *with* oneself *in* another. But as we have argued at length elsewhere, Hegel overshoots the mark by insisting that God's perfect self-revelation necessarily ends with the final surrender of all mystery. This notion is behind his notorious insistence that philosophy give way to pure science and his even more notorious tendencies to totalitarianism in the political order. Hegel's failure in this regard nevertheless does not imply the success of liberalism. What Hegel lacks is the analogy of being. On all of this, see D. C. Schindler, *Perfection of Freedom*, 238–372.

CHAPTER 12. The Givenness of Freedom

1. As Anselm Ramelow puts it, in the Franciscan tradition that Scotus brings to a certain completion, "The will itself here becomes a sort of '*bonum diffusivum sui*': it produces its own object" (afterword to Aquinas's *De veritate*, 332).

2. We might also compare Dionysius's judgment that, even if God is "supranatural" in himself, it is nevertheless precisely the *divine nature* that transcends nature, and so nature remains the unsurpassable horizon of all things, to Scotus's judgment that if we allow nature to be the unsurpassable horizon, we have definitively eliminated the possibility of freedom and definitively excluded God's Trinitarian reality and his free self-revelation in Christ.

3. For a reference to the family as a "spiritual womb" (*utero spiritualis*), see Aquinas, *ST* II-II.10.12 (Leon. 8).

4. Balthasar, *TD4*, 52–53.

BIBLIOGRAPHY

Sources for Principal Authors

Anselm

Complete Philosophical and Theological Treatises. Translated by Jasper Hopkins and Herbert Richardson. Minneapolis, MN: Arthur J. Banning Press, 2000.
Opera omnia. Edited by Franciscus Salesius Schmitt. 6 vols. Stuttgart-Bad Cannstatt: Friedrich Fromann, 1968.

Aquinas, Thomas

Commentary on the Book of Causes. Translated by Richard C. Taylor. Washington, DC: Catholic University of America Press, 1996.
Commentary on the Gospel of St. John. Translated by James A. Weisheipl, O.P. Albany, NY: Magi Books, 1998.
In duodecim libros Metaphysicorum Aristotelis expositio. Edited by Raimondo Spiazzi. Rome: Marietti, 1950.
In librum Beati Dionysii De divinis nominibus expositio. Edited by C. Pera. Turin: Marietti, 1950.
On Evil (Questiones disputatae de malo). Translated by Richard Regan. Oxford: Oxford University Press, 2003.
On the Power of God (Quaestiones disputatae de potentia dei). Translated by the English Dominican Fathers. Westminster, MD: Newman Press, 1952.
On the Truth of the Catholic Faith (Summa contra Gentiles). Translated by Anton C. Pegis, James F. Anderson, Vernon J. Bourke, and Charles J. O'Neil. New York: Hanover House, 1955–57.
Opera omnia. Parma: Fiaccadori, 1852–73.
Quaestiones disputatae. Edited by Raimondo Spiazzi. Turin: Marietti, 1953.
Sancti Thomae de Aquino Opera omnia. Leonine ed. Multiple volumes. Rome: Ex Typographia Polyglotta S.C. de Propaganda Fide, 1882 ff.

The Summa Theologica. Translated by the Fathers of the English Dominican Province. New York: Benziger Bros., 1947–48.
Super librum de causis expositio. Edited by H. D. Suffrey. 2nd ed. Paris: Vrin, 2002.
Truth: A Translation of Questiones disputatae de veritate. Translated by Robert W. Mulligan, S.J., James V. McGlynn, S.J., and Robert W. Schmidt, S.J. Chicago: Henry Regnery, 1952–54.

Augustine

The City of God. Translated by Henry Bettenson. New York: Penguin, 1984.
Confessions. Translated by R. S. Pine-Coffin. New York: Penguin, 1961.
Love One Another, My Friends: St. Augustine's Homilies on the First Letter of John. Translated by John Leinenweber. New York: Harper and Row, 1989.
Of True Religion. Translated by J. H. S. Burleigh. Chicago: Henry Regnery, 1959.
On Free Choice of the Will. Translated by Thomas Williams. Bloomington: Hackett, 1993.
On Grace and Free Will. Translated by Peter Holmes and Robert Ernest Wallis and revised by Benjamin B. Warfield, with additional revision for New Advent by Kevin Knight. From *St. Augustine: Anti-Pelagian Writings*, vol. 5 of *Nicene and Post-Nicene Fathers*, First Series, edited by Philip Schaff. Buffalo, NY: Christian Literature Publishing, 1887. www.newadvent.org/fathers/1510.htm.
On the Spirit and the Letter. Translated by Peter Holmes. In *St. Augustine: Anti-Pelagian Writings*, vol. 5 of *Nicene and Post-Nicene Fathers*, First Series, edited by Philip Schaff. Buffalo, NY: Christian Literature Publishing, 1887. www.newadvent.org/fathers/1502.htm.
Opera omnia. PL 32–45.
Retractions. Translated by Sister M. Inez Bogan. Washington, DC: Catholic University of America Press, 1968.
Sermons (148–183). Translated by Edmund Hill. The Works of Saint Augustine: A Translation for the 21st Century, part III, vol. 5. New Rochelle, NY: New City Press, 1990.
The Trinity. Translated by Edmund Hill. New York: New City Press, 1991.

Bernard of Clairvaux

On Grace and Free Choice. Translated by Bernard McGinn. Kalamazoo, MI: Cistercian Publications, 1977.

Sancti Bernardi Opera. 8 vols. Edited by Jean Leclercq, Charles H. Talbot, and Henri Marie Rochais. Rome: Éditions cisterciennes, 1957–77.

St. Bernard's Sermons on the Canticle of Canticles. Dublin: Browne and Nolan, 1920.

Bonaventure

Collations on the Hexaemeron. Edited by Jay M. Hammond. St. Bonaventure, NY: Franciscan Institute Publications, 2018.

Opera omnia. 9 vols. Edited by the Fathers of the Collegii S. Bonaventura. Florence: Quaracchi, 1882–1902.

Dionysius the Areopagite

Corpus Dionysiacum. Vol. 1. *De divinis nominibus*. Edited by B. R. Suchla. Berlin: De Gruyter, 1990.

Corpus Dionysiacum. Vol. 2. *De coelesti hierarchia; De ecclesiastica hierarchia; De mystica theologia; Epistulae*. Edited by G. Heil and A. M. Ritter. Berlin: De Gruyter, 1991.

The Divine Names and Mystical Theology. Translated by C. E. Rolt. London: Society for the Propagation of Christian Knowledge, 1920.

Pseudo-Dionysius: Complete Works. Translated by Colm Luibheid. New York: Paulist Press, 1987.

The Works of Dionysius the Areopagite. Translated by John Parker. London: Parker Publications, 1897.

Godfrey of Fontaines

"Disputed Questions 9, 10 and 12." Edited by Msgr. John Wippel. *Franciscan Studies* 33 (1973): 351–72.

Le huitième Quodlibet, Le neuvième Quodlibet, Le dixième Quodlibet. Edited by J. Hoffmans. Les Philosophes Belges, vol. 4. Louvain: Institut Supérieur de Philosophie de l'Université, 1924, 1928, 1931.

Les quatres premiers Quodlibets de Godefroid de Fontaines. Edited by M. De Wulf and A. Pelzer. Les Philosophes Belges, vol. 2. Louvain: Institut Supérieur de Philosophie de l'Université, 1904.

Le Quodlibet XV et trois Questions ordinaires de Godefroid de Fontaines. Edited by O. Lottin. Les Philosophes Belges, vol. 14. Louvain: Institut Supérieur de Philosophie de l'Université, 1937.

Les Quodlibets cinq, six et sept. Edited by M. De Wulf and J. Hoffmans. Les Philosophes Belges, vol. 3. Louvain: Institut Supérieur de Philosophie de l'Université, 1914.

Les Quodlibets onze et douze, Les Quodlibets treize et quatorze. Edited by J. Hoffmans. Les Philosophes Belges, vol. 5. Louvain: Institut Supérieur de Philosophie de l'Université, 1932, 1935.

"Selections from Quodlibet 15, Question 4." In "Godfrey of Fontaines and the Freedom of the Will." Translated by Neil Lewis. 2016. http://lewis.georgetown.domains/godfrey-of-fontaines-quodlibet-8-question-6/#Selections_from_Quodlibet_15_Question_4.

Maximus the Confessor

Ad Thalassium. CCSG 22 and 27.

The Disputation with Pyrrhus. Translated by Joseph P. Farrell. Waymart, PA: St. Tikhon's Seminary Press, 1990.

"Dispute de Maxime le Confesseur avec Pyrrhus." Greek text with French translation. Edited, annotated, and translated by Marcel Doucet. PhD diss., University of Montreal, 1972.

On Difficulties in the Church Fathers: The Ambigua. Two volumes. Greek text with English translation by Nicholas Constas. Cambridge, MA: Harvard University Press, 2014.

On the Cosmic Mystery of Jesus Christ: Selected Writings from St. Maximus the Confessor. Translated by Paul M. Blowers and Robert Louis Wilken. Crestwood, NY: St. Vladimir's Seminary Press, 2003.

Opera omnia. PG 90 and 91.

Plotinus

Ennead VI.6: On the Voluntary and on the Free Will of the One. Translated by Kevin Corrigan and John D. Turner. Las Vegas, NV: Parmenides, 2017.

Enneads. 7 vols. Greek text with English translation by A. H. Armstrong. Loeb Classical Library. Cambridge, MA: Harvard University Press, 1968–88.

Scotus, John Duns

Contingency and Freedom: Lectura I 39. Translated by A. Vos Jaczn, H. Veldhuis, A. A. Looman-Graaskamp, E. Dekker, and N. W. Den Bok. Dordrecht: Kluwer, 1994.

Duns Scotus on the Will and Morality. Translated by Allan B. Wolter, O.F.M. Edited by William A. Frank. Washington, DC: Catholic University of America Press, 1997.

The Examined Report of the Paris Lecture: Reportatio I-A. Edited and translated by Allan B. Wolter, O.F.M., and Oleg V. Bychkov. St. Bonaventure, NY: Franciscan Institute, 2004.

God and Creatures: The Quodlibetal Questions. Translated by Felix Alluntis and Allan B. Wolter, O.F.M. Washington, DC: Catholic University of America Press, 1975.

Noone, Timothy. "Scotus on Divine Ideas: Reportatio Paris. I-A, d. 36." *Medioevo* 24 (1998): 359–453.

"Notabilia Scoti super Metaphysicam: Una testimonianza ritrovata dell'insegnamento di Duns Scoto sulla Metafisica." Edited by Giorgio Pini. *Archivum Franciscanum Historicum* 89 (1996): 137–80.

Obras del Doctor Sutil Juan Duns Escoto: Cuestiones Cuodlibetales. Edited by Felix Alluntis. Madrid: Biblioteca de Autores Cristianos, 1963.

Opera omnia. Edited by Carolus Balić et al. 20 vols. Vatican City: Typis Polyglottis Vaticanis, 1950–2013.

Opera omnia. Edited by Luke Wadding. Paris: Apud Ludovicum Vivès, 1891–95.

Opera philosophica. Edited by G. Etzkorn et al. 5 vols. St. Bonaventure, NY: Franciscan Institute, 1997–2006.

The Report of the Paris Lecture: Reportatio IV-A. Edited and translated by Oleg B. Bychkov and Trent Pomplun. St. Bonaventure, NY: Franciscan Institute, 2016.

Söder, Joachim R., ed. *Johannes Duns Scotus. Reportatio Parisiensis examinata I 38–44 = Pariser Vorlesungen über Wissen und Kontingenz: Lateinisch, deutsch.* Herders Bibliothek der Philosophie des Mittelalters 4. Freiburg im Breisgau: Herder, 2005.

OTHER SOURCES

Adams, Marilyn McCord. "Anselm on Faith and Reason." In B. Davies and Leftow, *Cambridge Companion to Anselm*, 32–60.

———, ed. *The Philosophical Theology of John Duns Scotus.* Ithaca, NY: Cornell University Press, 1990

Alfsvåg, Knute. "Luther as Reader of Dionysius the Areopagite." *Studia Theologica: Nordic Journal of Theology* 65.2 (2011): 101–14.

Allinez, Guido. "Quando Duns Scotus ha cambiato idea sulla volontà? La causa del volere secondo la Quaestio 6 delle *Collactiones Parisienses*." Forthcoming in *Noctua*, but currently available online at www.academia.edu/42772664/QUANDO_DUNS_SCOTO_HA_CAMBIATO_IDEA_SULLA_VOLONTÀ.

Alter, Robert. *The Art of Biblical Narrative.* 2nd ed. New York: Basic Books, 2011.

Arendt, Hannah. *Between Past and Future.* New York: Penguin, 2006.

———. "The Concept of History: Ancient and Modern." In *Between Past and Future*, 41–90.
———. *The Human Condition*. 2nd ed. Chicago: University of Chicago Press, 1998.
———. *Life of the Mind*. New York: Harcourt and Brace, 1978.
———. "What Is Authority?" In *Between Past and Future*, 91–141.
———. "What Is Freedom?" In *Between Past and Future*, 142–69.
Aristotle. *Aristotelis opera*. Edited by Immanuel Bekker. Berlin: Berolini, 1831–70.
———. *De anima*. Translated by J. A. Smith. In *The Basic Works*, rev. ed., edited by Richard McKeon. New York: Modern Library, 2001.
Armstrong, A. H. *The Architecture of the Intelligible Universe: The Philosophy of Plotinus*. Cambridge: Cambridge University Press, 1940.
———. "Two Views of Freedom." In *Studia Patristica XVIII: Papers of the Ninth International Conference on Patristic Studies*, 397–406. Oxford: Pergamon Press, 1982.
Atkinson, Joseph. *Biblical and Theological Foundations of the Family: Domestic Church*. Washington, DC: Catholic University of America Press, 2014.
Auer, Johannes. *Die menschliche Willensfreiheit im Lehrsystem des Thomas von Aquin und Johannes Duns Scotus*. Munich: M. Hüber, 1938.
Ayres, Lewis. *Augustine and the Trinity*. Cambridge: Cambridge University Press, 2012.
Baer, Helmut David. "The Fruit of Charity: Using the Neighbor in De doctrina Christiana." *Journal of Religious Ethics* 24.1 (Spring 1996): 47–64.
Balthasar, Hans Urs von. "La *Concordantia libertatis* chez saint Anselme." In *L'homme devant Dieu*, 29–45. Paris: Editions Montaignes, 1964.
———. *Cosmic Liturgy: The Universe According to Maximus the Confessor*. San Francisco: Ignatius Press, 2003.
———. *Glaubhaft ist nur Liebe*. Einsiedeln: Johannes Verlag, 1963.
———. *Glory of the Lord*. Vol. 4, *The Realm of Metaphysics in Antiquity*. San Francisco: Ignatius Press, 1989.
———. *Glory of the Lord*. Vol. 6, *Theology: The Old Covenant*. San Francisco: Ignatius Press, 1991.
———. *Theo-Drama*. 5 vols. San Francisco: Ignatius Press, 1988–98.
———. *Theo-Logic*. 3 vols. San Francisco: Ignatius Press, 2001–5.
Barker, Mark. "The Cogitative Power: Objects and Terminology." PhD diss., University of St. Thomas, Houston, TX, 2007.
Barnes, Michel. *The Power of God: Dynamis in Gregory of Nyssa's Trinitarian Theology*. Washington, DC: Catholic University of America Press, 2016.

Barth, Karl. *Church Dogmatics*. Vol. 3, pt. 1, *The Doctrine of Creation*. Edinburgh: T&T Clark, 2004.

Begrich, Joachim. "Berit: Ein Beitrag zur Erfassung einer alttestamentlichen Denkform." *Zeitschrift für die alttestamentliche Wissenschaft* 60 (1944): 1–11.

Beierwaltes, Werner. *Das Wahre Selbst: Studien zu Plotins Begriff des Geistes und des Einen*. Frankfurt: Klostermann, 2001.

Benedict XVI. *Deus caritas est*. 2005. www.vatican.va/content/benedict-xvi/en/encyclicals/documents/hf_ben-xvi_enc_20051225_deus-caritas-est.html.

Benz, Ernst. *Marius Victorinus und die Entwicklung der abendländischen Willensmetaphysik*. Stuttgart: W. Kohlhammer, 1932.

Bieler, Jonathan. "Maximus the Confessor on Christ's Human Will." *Communio* 43 (Spring 2016): 55–82.

Blowers, Paul. "Gentiles of the Soul: Maximus the Confessor on the Substance and Transformation of the Human Passions." *Journal of Early Christian Studies* 4 (1996): 57–85.

———. "Maximus the Confessor, Gregory of Nyssa, and the Concept of Perpetual Progress." *Vigiliae Christianae* 46 (1992): 151–77.

Blowers, Paul M., and Robert Louis Wilken. Introduction to *On the Cosmic Mystery of Jesus Christ: Selected Writings from St. Maximus the Confessor*. Crestwood, NY: St. Vladimir's Seminary Press, 2003.

Boler, John. "An Image for the Unity of Will in Duns Scotus." *Journal of the History of Philosophy* 32.1 (1994): 23–44.

———. "Transcending the Natural: Duns Scotus on the Two Affections of the Will." *American Catholic Philosophical Quarterly* 67.1 (1993): 109–26.

Bos, E. P., ed. *John Duns Scotus: Renewal of Philosophy. Acts of the Third Symposium Organized by the Dutch Society for Medieval Philosophy Medium Aevum*. Amsterdam: Rodopi, 1998.

Boulnois, Olivier. *La puissance et son ombre*. Paris: Aubier, 1994.

Bourke, Vernon. *Will in Western Thought*. New York: Sheed and Ward, 1964.

Bradshaw, David. "St. Maximus on the Will." In *A Saint for East and West: Maximus the Confessor's Contribution to Eastern and Western Christian Theology*, edited by Daniel Haynes, 102–14. Eugene, OR: Wipf and Stock, 2019.

Brady, Ignatius. "Beatitude and Psychology: A Problem in the Philosophy of St. Bonaventure." *Franciscan Studies* 2.4 (December 1942): 411–27.

Brague, Rémi. "Athens, Jerusalem, Mecca: Leo Strauss's Muslim Understanding of Greek Philosophy." *Poetics Today* 19.2 (1998): 235–59.

———. "The Biblical Roots of the Western Idea of Liberty." In *Christianity and Freedom*, edited by Timothy Shah and Allen Hertzke, 391–402. Cambridge: Cambridge University Press, 2016.

———. *Eccentric Culture: A Theory of Western Civilization.* South Bend, IN: St. Augustine's Press, 2002.

———. *On the God of the Christians (and on One or Two Others).* South Bend, IN: St. Augustine's Press, 2013.

Bray, Dennis. "Bonaventure's *I Sentence* Argument for the Trinity from Beatitude." *American Catholic Philosophical Quarterly,* prepublished July 29, 2021. https://doi.org/10.5840/acpq2021728234.

Brown, Montague. *Freedom, Philosophy, and Faith.* Lanham, MD: Lexington Books, 2011.

Brueggemann, W. "The Covenanted Family: A Zone for Humanness." *Journal of Current Social Issues* 14 (1977): 18–23.

Buchner, Hans. *Plotins Möglichkeitslehre.* Munich: Anton Pustet, 1970.

Burnaby, John. *Amor Dei: A Study of the Religion of St. Augustine.* London: Hodder and Staughton, 1938.

Burrell, David. *Freedom and Creation in the Abrahamic Traditions.* Washington, DC: Center for Muslim-Christian Understanding, 1995.

———. *Freedom and Creation in Three Traditions.* Notre Dame, IN: University of Notre Dame Press, 1993.

Byers, Sarah. "The Meaning of *Voluntas* in Augustine." *Augustinian Studies* 37.2 (2006): 171–89.

———. *Perception, Sensibility, and Moral Motivation in Augustine: A Stoic-Platonic Synthesis.* Cambridge: Cambridge University Press, 2012.

Cary, Phillip. *Augustine's Invention of the Inner Self: The Legacy of a Christian Platonist.* Oxford: Oxford University Press, 2000.

Chaldean Oracles. Translated by Thomas Taylor. Vancouver, BC: Kshetra Books, 2015.

Chappell, T. D. J. *Aristotle and Augustine on Freedom: Two Theories of Freedom, Voluntary Action, and Akrasia.* New York: St. Martin's Press, 1995.

Chenu, Marie-Dominique. *Nature, Man, and Society in the Twelfth Century.* Chicago: University of Chicago Press, 1968.

Chesterton, G. K. *Orthodoxy.* Nashville, TN: Sam Torode Book Arts, 2009.

Cilento, Vincenzo. *Saggi su Plotino.* Milan: University of Mursia, 1973.

Clark, Mary. *Augustine, Philosopher of Freedom.* New York: Desclee, 1958.

Clarke, Norris. "Action as the Self-Revelation of Being: A Central Theme in the Thought of St. Thomas." In *Explorations in Metaphysics,* 45–64. Notre Dame, IN: University of Notre Dame Press, 1994.

———. "The Limitation of Act by Potency in St. Thomas: Aristotelianism or Neoplatonism?" In *Explorations in Metaphysics,* 65–88. Notre Dame, IN: University of Notre Dame Press, 1994.

Clement of Alexandria. *Stromateis, Books 1–3*. Translated by John Ferguson. Washington, DC: Catholic University of America Press, 1991.

Corbin, Michel. *La grace et la liberté chez saint Bernard de Clairvaux*. Paris: Cerf, 2002.

Courtenay, W. J. *Covenant and Causality in Medieval Thought*. London: Variorum Reprints, 1984.

———. "The Critique on Natural Causality in the Mutakallimum and Nominalism." *Harvard Theological Review* 66 (1973): 77–94.

———. "The Dialectic of Divine Omnipotence." In *Covenant and Causality in Medieval Thought*, chap. 5. London: Variorum Reprints, 1984.

———. "Necessity and Freedom in Anselm's Conception of God." In *Die Wirkungsgeschichte Anselms von Canterbury, Analecta Anselmiana* 4/2, edited by Helmut Kohlenberger, 39–64. Frankfurt: Minerva, 1975.

Cousineau, Robert-Henri. "Creation and Freedom: An Augustinian Problem." *Recherches Augustiniennes et Patristiques* 2 (1962): 253–72.

Cousins, Ewert. "God as Dynamic in Bonaventure and Contemporary Thought." In *Thomas and Bonaventure: A Septicentenary Commemoration*, edited by G. F. McLean, O.M.I., 136–48. Washington, DC: Catholic University of America, 1974.

Cross, Frank Moore. "Kinship and Covenant in Ancient Israel." In *From Epic to Canon: History and Literature in Ancient Israel*, 3–21. Baltimore: Johns Hopkins University Press, 1998.

Cullen, Christopher M., S.J. "Bonaventure's Aesthetic Imperative: *Pulcherrimum Carmen*." In *Beauty and the Good: Recovering the Classical Tradition from Plato to Duns Scotus*, edited by Alice Ramos, 251–68. Washington, DC: Catholic University of America Press, 2020.

Culley, Robert C. *Themes and Variations: A Study of Action in Biblical Narrative*. Atlanta, GA: Scholars Press, 1992.

Damrosch, David. *The Narrative Covenant: Transformations of Genre in the Growth of Biblical Literature*. San Francisco: Harper and Row, 1987.

Dante Alighieri. *Paradiso*. New York: Modern Library, 2007.

Daube, David. *The Exodus Pattern in the Bible*. London: Faber and Faber, 1963.

Davies, Brian, and Brian Leftow, eds. *The Cambridge Companion to Anselm*. Cambridge: Cambridge University Press, 2004

Davies, J. A. *A Royal Priesthood*. London: T&T Clark, 2004.

Dekker, Eef. "Scotus's Freedom of the Will Revisited." In Bos, *John Duns Scotus*, 113–22.

De la Tour, Marine. *Gabe im Anfang: Grundzüge des metaphysischen Denkens von Ferdinand Ulrich*. Stuttgart: Kohlhammer, 2016.

Dempf, Alois. *Die Hauptform mittelalterlichen Weltanschauung.* Munich: Oldenbourg, 1925.
Descartes, René. *Discourse on Method and Meditations on First Philosophy.* 4th ed. Indianapolis: Hackett, 1998.
De Schrijver, Georges. *Le merveilleux accord de l'homme et de Dieu: Etude de l'analogie de l'être chez Hans Urs von Balthasar.* Louvain: Peeters, 1983.
Desmond, William. *The Intimate Strangeness of Being.* Washington, DC: Catholic University of America Press, 2012.
Dewan, Laurence. "St. Thomas and the Causes of Free Choice." *Acta Philosophica* 8.1 (1999): 87–96.
Dihle, Albrecht. *The Theory of Will in Classical Antiquity.* Berkeley: University of California Press, 1982.
Dodds, E. R. *The Greeks and the Irrational.* Berkeley: University of California Press, 1951.
Dumbrell, William J. *Covenant and Creation: A Theology of Old Testament Covenants.* New York: Thomas Nelson, 1984.
Dumont, Stephen. "Did Duns Scotus Change His Mind on the Will?" In *Nach der Verurteilung von 1277: Philosophie und Theologie an der Universität von Paris im letzten Viertel des 13. Jahrhunderts*, edited by J. A. Aertsen, K. Emergy, and A. Speer, 719–94. New York: Walter de Gruyter, 2001.
———. "The Origin of Scotus's Theory of Synchronic Contingency." *Modern Schoolman* 72.2–3 (1995): 149–67.
Dvořak, Petr. "The Concurrentism of Thomas Aquinas." *Philosophia* 41.3 (2013): 617–34.
Eardley, P. S. "Thomas Aquinas and Giles of Rome on the Will." *Review of Metaphysics* 56.4 (June 2003): 832–62.
Effler, Roy R., O.F.M. *John Duns Scotus and the Principle "Omne Quod Movetur ab Alio Movetur."* St. Bonaventure, NY: Franciscan Institute, 1962.
Eichrodt, Walther. *Theology of the Old Testament.* 2 vols. Translated by J. A. Baker. Philadelphia: Westminster Press, 1961.
Eliade, Mircea. *The Sacred and the Profane.* New York: Harcourt Brace, 1958.
Eliasson, Erik. *The Notion of That Which Depends on Us in Plotinus and Its Background.* Leiden: Brill, 2008.
Epictetus. *Discourses and Selected Writings.* New York: Penguin Classics, 2008.
Evans, G. R. "Anselm's Life, Works, and Immediate Influences." In B. Davies and Leftow, *Cambridge Companion to Anselm*, 5–31.
Fabro, Cornelio. "The Intensive Hermeneutics of Thomistic Philosophy: The Notion of Participation." In *Selected Works of Cornelio Fabro*, vol. 1, *Selected Articles on Metaphysics and Participation*, 65–103. Chillum, MD: IVE Press, 2015.

———. "Le 'Liber de bona fortuna' de l'"Ethique à Eudème' d'Aristote et la dialectique de la divine Providence chez saint Thomas." In "L'être, la liberté, et l'église aux XXe siècle," edited by Cornelio Fabro, special issue, *Revue Thomiste* 111 (2011): 151–70.

———. "Orizzontalità e verticalità nella dialettica della libertà." In *Riflessioni sulla libertà*, 41–52. Rimini: Maggioli Editore, 1983.

———. *Percezione e pensiero*. 2nd ed. Brescia: Morcelliana, 1962.

Farrell, Joseph. *Free Choice in Maximus the Confessor*. Waymart, PA: St. Tikhon's Seminary Press, 1989.

Faust, Ulrich. "Bernhards 'Liber de Gratia et Libero Arbitrio': Bedeutung, Quellen, und Einfluss." In *Analecta Monastica: Textes et études sur la vie des moines au Moyen Age*, edited by Ulrich Faust, 6:35–52. Studia Anselmiana 50. Rome: Centro Studi S. Anselmo, 1962.

Feingold, Lawrence. "The Word Breathes Forth Love: The Psychological Analogy for the Trinity and the Complementarity of Intellect and Will." *Nova et Vetera* 17.2 (Spring 2019): 501–32.

Forest, Aimé. "Das Erlebnis des consensus voluntatis beim hl. Bernhard." In *Bernhard von Clairvaux: Mönch und Mystiker*, edited by Joseph Lortz, 120–27. Wiesbaden: Franz Steiner, 1955.

Fortin, Ernest. "Augustine's *City of God* and the Modern Historical Consciousness." *Review of Politics* 41.3 (1979): 323–43.

Frank, William A. "Duns Scotus on Autonomous Freedom and Divine Co-causality." *Medieval Philosophy and Theology* 2 (1992): 142–64.

———. "Duns Scotus's Concept of Willing Freely: What Divine Freedom beyond Choice Teaches Us." *Franciscan Studies* 42 (1982): 68–89.

———. Preface to *John Duns Scotus on the Will and Morality*, edited by Allan B. Wolter. Washington, DC: Catholic University of America Press, 1997.

Frost, Gloria. "Duns Scotus on How God Causes the Created Will's Volitions." In *Interpreting Duns Scotus: Critical Essays*, edited by Giorgio Pini. Cambridge: Cambridge University Press, forthcoming.

Galen. *On the Usefulness of the Parts of the Human Body*. Edited by Georg Helmreich. Leipzig: Tuebneri, 1907–9.

Gallagher, David M. "Desire for Beatitude and Love of Friendship in Thomas Aquinas." *Mediaeval Studies* 58 (1996): 1–47.

———. "Free Choice and Free Judgment in Thomas Aquinas." *Archiv für Geschichte der Philosophie* 76 (1994): 247–77.

———. "Thomas Aquinas on Self-Love as the Basis for Love of Others." *Acta Philosophica* 8 (1999): 23–44.

———. "Thomas Aquinas on the Causes of Human Choice." PhD diss., Catholic University of America, 1989.

———. "Thomas Aquinas on the Will as Rational Appetite." *Journal of the History of Philosophy* 24.4 (October 1991): 559–84.

Gauss, Julia. "Die Auseinandersetzung mit Judentum und Islam bei Anselm." In *Die Wirkungsgeschichte Anselm von Canterburys: Akten der ersten internationalen Anselm-Tagung in Bad Wimpfen, 13.–16.9.1970*, edited by Helmut Kohlenberger, 601–9. Frankfurt: Minerva, 1975.

Gauthier, R. A. *Aristote: L'éthique à Nicomaque*. Vol. 1, pt. 1, *Introduction*. 2nd ed. Louvain: Publications universitaires, 1970.

———. "Maxime le Confesseur et la psychologie de l'acte humaine." *Recherches de Théologie Ancienne et Médiévale* 21 (1954): 51–100.

Geanakoplos, Deno J. "Some Aspects of the Influence of the Byzantine Maximos the Confessor on the Theology of East and West." *Church History* 38.2 (June 1969): 150–63.

Gerken, Alexander. *Theologie des Wortes: Das Verhältnis von Schöpfung und Inkarnation bei Bonaventura*. Dusseldorf: Patmos, 1963.

Gilson, Etienne. *Being and Some Philosophers*. Toronto: Pontifical Institute of Medieval Studies, 2016.

———. *The History of Christian Philosophy in the Middle Ages*. New York: Random House, 1955.

———. *Introduction à l'étude de saint Augustin*. Paris: Vrin, 1949.

———. *John Duns Scotus: Introduction to His Fundamental Positions*. London: T&T Clark, 2019.

———. *The Mystical Theology of Saint Bernard*. Kalamazoo, MI: Cistercian Publications, 1990.

———. "Notes pour l'histoire de la cause efficiente." *Archives d'Histoire Doctrineale et Littéraire du Moyen Age* 37 (1962): 7–31.

———. *The Philosophy of St. Bonaventure*. New York: Sheed and Ward, 1938.

———. *The Philosophy of St. Thomas Aquinas*. New York: Dorset, 1948.

———. *The Unity of Philosophical Experience*. New York: Scribner, 1950.

Goebel, Bernd. *Rectitudo, Wahrheit und Freiheit bei Anselm von Canterbury*. Munster: Aschendorff, 2001.

Goethe. *Faust*. Translated by Leopold J. Bernays. London: Sampson Low, 1839.

———. *Faust*. Translated by Walter Arndt. 2nd ed. New York: Norton, 2001.

———. *West-Oestliche Divan*. Berlin: Deutscher Klassiker Verlag, 2010.

Gonzalez-Ayesta, Cruz. "Es la voluntad un apetito o un poder?" *Anuario Filosofico* 47.1 (2014): 77–102.

Grant, W. Matthews. "Anselm on Freedom: A Defense of Rogers' Project, a Critique of Her Reconciliation of Libertarian Freedom with God the Creator Omnium." *Saint Anselm Journal* 8.1 (Fall 2012): 1–10.

Gregory, Brad. *The Unintended Reformation: How a Religious Revolution Secularized Society*. Cambridge, MA: Harvard University Press, 2015.

Gregory Nazianzen. *Letter 101*. Nicene and Post-Nicene Fathers, 2nd ser., vol. 7, 440.

Haan, Daniel de. "Beauty and Aesthetic Perception in Thomas Aquinas." In *Beauty and the Good: Recovering the Classical Tradition from Plato to Duns Scotus*, edited by Alice Ramos, 288–318. Washington, DC: Catholic University of America Press, 2020.

———. "Perception and the Vis Cogitativa." *American Catholic Philosophical Quarterly* 88.3 (2014): 397–437.

Hadot, Pierre. "L'image de la Trinité dans l'âme chez Victorinus et chez saint Augustin." *Studia Patristica* 6 (1962): 409–42.

Hahn, Scott. *Kinship by Covenant: A Canonical Approach to the Fulfillment of God's Saving Promises*. New Haven, CT: Yale University Press, 2009.

Hanby, Michael. *Augustine and Modernity*. New York: Routledge, 2003.

Hancock, Curtis L. "Energeia in the Enneads of Plotinus: A Reaction to Plato and Aristotle." PhD diss., Loyola University of Chicago, 1984.

Harris, R. Laird, Gleason L. Archer, and Bruce K. Waltke. *Theological Wordbook of the Old Testament*. Chicago: Moody, 1980.

Harrison, Simon. *Augustine's Way into the Will: The Theological and Philosophical Significance of De libero arbitrio*. Oxford: Oxford University Press, 2006.

———. "Do We Have a Will? Augustine's Way into the Will." In *The Augustinian Tradition*, edited by G. B. Matthews, 195–205. Berkeley: University of California Press, 1999.

Hart, David Bentley. *The Doors of the Sea*. Grand Rapids, MI: Eerdmans, 2011.

Hayes, Zachary. Introduction to *Disputed Questions on the Mystery of the Trinity*. St. Bonaventure, NY: Franciscan Institute, 1979.

Hegel, Georg Wilhelm Friedrich. *Elements of the Philosophy of Right*. Cambridge: Cambridge University Press, 2011.

———. *Lectures on the History of Philosophy*. Lincoln: University of Nebraska Press, 1995.

———. *Phenomenology of Spirit*. Oxford: Oxford University Press, 1977.

———. *Philosophy of History*. New York: Dover, 1956.

Heidegger, Martin. *The Beginning of Western Philosophy: Interpretations of Anaximander and Parmenides*. Bloomington: Indiana University Press, 2015.

———. *The End of Philosophy*. New York: Harper and Row, 1973.

———. "Plato's Doctrine of Truth." In *Pathmarks*, 155–82. Cambridge: Cambridge University Press, 1998.

———. "Question Concerning Technology." In *Basic Writings*, 307–42. San Francisco: Harper Perennial, 2008.

Henry, Paul. "Le problème de la liberté chez Plotin." *Revue Philosophique de Louvain* 29–31 (1931): 50–79, 180–215, 318–39.

Heraclitus. *Fragments*. Translated by Brooks Haxton. New York: Penguin, 2003.

Heschel, Abraham Joshua. *The Sabbath*. New York: Farrar, Strauss, and Giroux, 2005.

Hoeres, Walter. "Naturtendenz und Freiheit nach Duns Scotus." *Salzburger Jahrbuch für Philosophie* 2 (1958): 95–139.

———. *Der Wille als reine Vollkommenheit nach Duns Scotus*. Salzburg: A. Pustet, 1962.

Hoffmann, Tobias. "Duns Scotus on the Origin of the Possibles in the Divine Intellect." In *Philosophical Debates at Paris in the Early Fourteenth Century*, edited by S. Brown, T. Dewender, and T. Kobusch, 359–79. Leiden: Brill, 2009.

———. "Freedom beyond Practical Reason: Duns Scotus on Will-Dependent Relations." *British Journal for the History of Philosophy* 21.6 (2013): 1071–90.

Honnefelder, Ludger. "Die Kritik des Johannes Duns Scotus am kosmologischen Nezessitarismus der Araber: Ansätze zu einem neuen Freiheitsbegriff." In *Die abendländische Freiheit vom 10. zu 14. Jahrhundert*, edited by Johannes Fried, 249–63. Ostfildern: Jan Thorbecke, 1991.

———. "Metaphysik als *scientia transcendens*: Johannes Duns Scotus und der zweite Anfang der Metaphysik." In *New Essays on Metaphysics as "Scientia Transcendens,"* edited by Roberto Hofmeister Pich, 1–16. Porto Alegre: Brepol, 2006.

Horn, Christoph. "The Concept of Will in Plotinus." In *Reading Ancient Texts: Essays in Honor of Denis O'Brien*. Vol. 2, *Aristotle and Neoplatonism*, edited by Suzanne Stern-Gillet and Kevin Corrigan, 153–78. Leiden: Brill, 2007.

Hugenberger, G. P. *Marriage as a Covenant*. Leiden: Brill, 1994.

Hughes, Kevin. "Bonaventure *contra Mundum*? The Catholic Theological Tradition Revisited." *Theological Studies* 74 (2013): 372–98.

Imbach, Ruedi. "L'averroïsme latin du XIIIe siècle." In *Gli studi di filosfia medievale fra otto e novecento*, edited by R. Imbach and A. Maierù, 191–208. Rome: Ed. di Storia e Letteratura, 1991.

Incandela, Joseph. "Duns Scotus and the Experience of Human Freedom." *The Thomist* 56.2 (April 1992): 229–56.

Ingham, Mary Beth. "Did Scotus Modify His Position on the Relationship of Intellect and Will?" *Recherches de Théologie et Philosophie Médiévales* 69.1 (2002): 88–116.

———. "Re-situating Scotus's Thought." *Modern Theology* 21.4 (October 2005): 609–18.

Inwood, Brad. *Ethics and Human Action in Early Stoicism.* Oxford: Clarendon Press, 1985.
Jacobi, Friedrich Heinrich. *Concerning the Doctrine of Spinoza in Letters to Herr Moses Mendelssohn.* Breslau: Gottlieb Löwe, 1785.
———. *The Spinoza Conversations between Lessing and Jacobi: Text with Excerpts from the Ensuing Controversy.* Lanham, MD: University Press of America, 1988.
John Paul II. *Fides et ratio.* 1998. www.vatican.va/content/john-paul-ii/en/encyclicals/documents/hf_jp-ii_enc_14091998_fides-et-ratio.html.
Kahl, Wilhelm. *Die Lehre vom Primat des Willens bei Augustin, Duns Scotus, und Descartes.* Strassburg: K. J. Trübner, 1886.
Kahn, Charles. "Discovering the Will: From Aristotle to Augustine." In *The Question of "Eclecticism": Studies in Later Greek Philosophy*, edited by John M. Dillon and A. A. Long, 234–59. Berkeley: University of California Press, 1988.
Kane, Robert. *A Contemporary Introduction to Free Will.* Oxford: Oxford University Press, 2005.
Kane, Stanley G. "Anselm's Definition of Freedom." *Religious Studies* 9.3 (September 1973): 297–306.
Kant, Immanuel. *Schriften zur Ethik und Religionsphilosophie.* Vol. 4 of *Kants Werke in sechs Bände.* Wiesbaden: Insel, 1956.
Kent, Bonnie. "Our Inalienable Ability to Sin: Peter Olivi's Rejection of Asymmetrical Freedom." *British Journal of the History of Philosophy* 25.6 (June 2017): 1073–92.
———. *Virtues of the Will: The Transformation of Ethics in the Late Thirteenth Century.* Washington, DC: Catholic University of America Press, 1995.
Kim, Yul. "A Change in Thomas Aquinas's Theory of the Will: Solutions to a Long-Standing Problem." *American Catholic Philosophical Quarterly* 82.2 (2008): 221–36.
———. *Selbstbewegung des Willens bei Thomas von Aquin.* Berlin: Akademie Verlag, 2007.
———. "Why Does the Wood Not Ignite Itself? Duns Scotus's Defense of the Will's Self-Motion." *American Catholic Philosophical Quarterly* 95.1 (2021): 49–68.
Knuuttila, Simo. "Duns Scotus' Criticism of the 'Statistical' Interpretation of Modality." In *Sprache und Erkenntnis im Mittelalter*, 441–50. Boston: Kluwer, 1981.
———. "The Emergence of the Logic of Will in Medieval Thought." In *The Augustinian Tradition*, edited by Gareth B. Matthews, 206–21. Berkeley: University of California Press, 1998.

———. "Time and Modality in Scholasticism." In *Reforging the Great Chain of Being: Studies of the History of Modal Theories*, edited by Simo Knuuttila, 163–257. Boston: Kluwer, 1981.

Koester, Helmet. *Introduction to the New Testament*. Vol. 1, *History, Culture, and Religion of the Hellenistic Age*. Vol. 2, *History and Literature of Early Christianity*. 2nd ed. New York: Walter de Gruyter, 1995, 2000.

Kremer, Klaus. "Das 'Warum' der Schöpfung: *Quia Bonus Vel/et Quia Voluit?* Ein Beitrag zum Verhältnis von Neuplatonismus und Christentum an Hand des Prinzips 'Bonum Est Diffusivum Sui.'" In *Parusia: Studien zur Philosophie Platons und zur Problemgeschichte des Platonismus*, edited by Kurt Flasch, 241–64. Frankfurt: Minerva, 1965.

Kuehn, Evan. "The Johannine Logic of Augustine's Trinity: A Dogmatic Sketch." *Theological Studies* 68.3 (2007): 572–94.

Laertius, Dionysius. *Lives of the Eminent Philosophers*. Vol. 1. Translated by R. D. Hicks. Cambridge, MA: Harvard University Press, 1972.

Lagarde, Georges de. "La philosophie sociale d'Henri de Gand et Godefroid de Fontaines." *Archives d'Histoire Doctrinale et Littéraire du Moyen Age* 18 (1943): 73–142.

Landgraf, Michael. "Bernards Verhältnis zur Theologie des 12. Jahrhunderts." In *Bernhard von Clairvaux: Mönch und Mystiker*, edited by Joseph Lortz, 44–62. Wiesbaden: Franz Steiner, 1955.

Leclercq, Jacques. "General Introduction to the Works of Saint Bernard (III)." *Cistercian Studies Quarterly* 40.4 (November 2005): 365–93.

Lee, Patrick. "The Relation between Intellect and Will in Free Choice According to Aquinas and Scotus." *The Thomist* 49.3 (July 1985): 321–42.

Le Goff, Jacques. "Merchant's Time and Church's Time in the Middle Ages." In *Time, Work, and Culture in the Middle Ages*, 29–42. Chicago: University of Chicago Press, 1980.

Leo XIII. *Aeterni Patris*. 1879. www.vatican.va/content/leo-xiii/en/encyclicals/documents/hf_l-xiii_enc_04081879_aeterni-patris.html.

Leroux, Georges. "Human Freedom in the Thought of Plotinus." In *The Cambridge Companion to Plotinus*, edited by Lloyd Gerson, 292–314. Cambridge: Cambridge University Press, 1996.

———, ed. and trans. *Traité sur la liberté et la volonté de l'Un*. By Plotinus. Paris: Vrin, 1990.

Levenson, Jon D. *Sinai and Zion: An Entry into the Jewish Bible*. San Francisco: Harper, 1985.

Lienhard, J. T. "Friendship with God, Friendship in God: Traces in St. Augustine." In *Augustine: Mystic and Mystagogue*, edited by Frederick von Fleteren, Joseph C. Schnaubelt, and Joseph Reino, 207–29. New York: Peter Lang, 1994.

Lisska, Anthony J. *Aquinas's Theory of Perception*. Oxford: Oxford University Press, 2016.

Locke, John. *Two Treatises of Government*. Cambridge: Cambridge University Press, 1988.

Long, Steven A. "Providence, Freedom, and Natural Law." *Nova et Vetera* 4.3 (2006): 557–606.

Lössl, Josef. "Intellect with a [Divine] Purpose: Augustine on the Will." In *The Will and Human Action*, edited by Thomas Pink and M. W. F. Stone, 53–77. New York: Routledge, 2004.

Lottin, Odon. *Psychologie et morale aux XIIe et XIIIe siècles*. 6 vols. Louvain: Abbaye du Mont César, 1942–60.

Louth, Andrew. *Denys the Areopagite*. London: Geoffrey Chapman, 1989.

Löwith, Karl. *Meaning in History*. Chicago: University of Chicago Press, 1959.

Lucretius. *On the Nature of the Universe*. Oxford: Oxford University Press, 2009.

Luther, Martin. *The Babylonian Captivity of the Church*. Minneapolis, MN: Fortress Press, 2016.

———. *The Bondage of the Will: A New Translation of De Servo Arbitrio (1525), Martin Luther's Reply to Erasmus of Rotterdam*. Old Tappan, NJ: Fleming H. Revell, 1957.

———. *D. Martin Luthers Werke*. 127 vols. Weimarer Ausgabe. Weimar: Böhlau, then Hermann Böhlaus Nachfolger, 1883–2009.

MacIntyre, Alasdair. *Whose Justice, Which Rationality*. Notre Dame, IN: University of Notre Dame Press, 1988.

Marcel, Gabriel. "On the Ontological Mystery." In *The Philosophy of Existentialism*, 9–46. New York: Citadel, 1984.

Marenbon, John. *Anselm's Proslogion*. Montreal: McGill-Queen's University Press, 2005.

Marion, Jean-Luc. *God without Being*. Chicago: University of Chicago Press, 1991.

———. "L'image de la liberté." In *Saint Bernard et la philosophie*, edited by Rémi Brague, 49–72. Paris: Presses universitaires de France, 1993.

McFarland, Ian. "'Naturally and by Grace': Maximus the Confessor on the Operation of the Will." *Scottish Journal of Theology* 58.4 (2005): 410–33.

McGinn, Bernard. Introduction to *On Grace and Free Choice*. Kalamazoo, MI: Cistercian Publications, 1977.

McKenna, Michael, and Derk Pereboom, eds. *Free Will: A Contemporary Introduction*. New York: Routledge, 2016.

Meek, Esther Lightcap. *Contact with Reality: Michael Polanyi's Realism, and Why It Matters*. Eugene, OR: Cascade Books, 2017.

Milbank, John. Afterword to *John Duns Scotus: Introduction to His Fundamental Positions*, by Etienne Gilson, 538–76. London: T&T Clark, 2019.
———. "The Franciscan Conundrum." *Communio* 42 (Fall 2015): 466–92.
Milgrom, Jacob. "Covenants: The Sinaitic and Patriarchal Covenants in the Holiness Code (Leviticus 17–24)." In *Sefer Moshe: The Moshe Weinfeld Jubilee Volume*, edited by C. Cohen, A. Hurvitz, and S. M. Paul, 91–101. Winona Lake, IN: Eisenbrauns, 2004.
Mitralexis, Sotiris. *Ever-Moving Repose: A Contemporary Reading of Maximus the Confessor's Theory of Time*. Eugene, OR: Cascade Books, 2017.
Monteiro Pacheco, M. C. "Les transformations du concept de *natura* aux XIIe siècle." In *L'élaboration du vocabulaire philosophique au Moyen Age*, edited by J. Harnesse and C. Steel, 280–92. Tournhout, Belgium: Brepols, 2000.
Moonan, Lawrence. *The Medieval Power Distinction up to Its Adoption by Albert, Bonaventure, and Aquinas*. Oxford: Clarendon Press, 1994.
Moran, Dermot. *The Philosophy of John Scottus Eriugena: A Study of Idealism in the Middle Ages*. Cambridge: Cambridge University Press, 2004.
Muller, H. J. *Freedom in the Ancient World*. New York: Harper and Row, 1961.
Nietzsche, Friedrich. *Beyond Good and Evil*. New York: Vintage, 1989.
———. *The Gay Science*. New York: Vintage Books, 1974.
———. *Genealogy of Morals*. New York: Vintage, 1989.
———. *Twilight of the Idols*. In *The Portable Nietzsche*, edited by Walter Kaufmann, 463–564. New York: Viking Penguin, 1982.
Noone, Timothy. "Nature, Freedom, and Will." *American Catholic Philosophical Quarterly* 81 (2008): 1–23.
Normore, C. G. "Picking and Choosing: Anselm and Ockham on Choice." *Vivarium* 36.1 (1998): 23–39.
Nygren, Anders. *Agape and Eros*. Philadelphia: Westminster Press, 1953.
O'Brien, Denis. "Plotinus on Matter and Evil." In *The Cambridge Companion to Plotinus*, edited by Lloyd Gerson, 171–95. Cambridge: Cambridge University Press, 1996.
O'Donovan, Oliver. *The Problem of Self-Love in St. Augustine*. Eugene, OR: Wipf and Stock, 2006.
O'Keefe, Tim. *Epicurus on Freedom*. Cambridge: Cambridge University Press, 2005.
Onians, Richard. *The Origins of European Thought about the Body, the Mind, the Soul, the World, Time, and Fate*. Cambridge: Cambridge University Press, 1951.
Origen. *Contra Celsum*. Translated by Henry Chadwick. Cambridge: Cambridge University Press, 1980.

———. *On First Principles*. Edited by G. W. Butterworth. New York: Harper, 1966.

Ortega y Gassett, José. *On Love*. New York: Meridian Books, 1957.

Osborne, Thomas, Jr. "Giles of Rome, Henry of Ghent, and Godfrey of Fontaines on Whether to See God Is to Love Him." *Recherches de Théologie et Philosophie Médiévale* 80.1 (2013): 57–76.

Ousager, Asger. *Plotinus on Selfhood, Freedom, and Politics*. Aarhus, Denmark: University of Aarhus Press, 2004.

Oz-Salzberger, Fania. "The Jewish Roots of Western Freedom." *Azure* 13 (Summer 2002): 88–132.

Parker, John. Introduction to *The Works of Dionysius the Areopagite*. n.p.: Veritatis Splendor, 2013.

Pederson, Johannes. *Israel: Its Life and Culture*. 2 vols. London: Oxford University Press, 1926.

Perl, Eric. *Theophany: The Neoplatonic Philosophy of Dionysius the Areopagite*. Albany, NY: SUNY Press, 2007.

———. *Thinking Being: Introduction to Metaphysics in the Classical Tradition*. Leiden: Brill, 2014.

Perrier, Emmanuel. "Duns Scotus Facing Reality: Between Absolute Contingency and Unquestionable Consistency." *Modern Theology* 21.4 (October 2005): 619–43.

Piché, David, and Claude Lafleur. *La condamnation parisienne de 1277*. Paris: Vrin, 1999.

Pickstock, Catherine. "Duns Scotus: His Historical and Contemporary Significance." *Modern Theology* 21.4 (October 2005): 543–74.

Pieper, Josef. *Faith–Hope–Love*. San Francisco: Ignatius Press, 1997.

———. *Scholasticism*. South Bend, IN: St. Augustine's Press, 2001.

———. *The Silence of St. Thomas*. Chicago: Regnery, 1965.

Pierson, Daniel J. "Thomas Aquinas on the Principle *Omne Agens Agit Sibi Simile*." PhD diss., Catholic University of America, 2015.

Plato. *Complete Works*. Edited by John Cooper. Indianapolis: Hackett, 1997.

———. *Platonis opera*. 5 vols. Edited by John Burnett. Oxford: Oxford University Press, 1961.

Polanyi, Michael. *The Tacit Dimension*. Chicago: University of Chicago Press, 2009.

Porphyry. *On the Life of Plotinus and the Order of His Books*. In *Plotinus*, edited by A. H. Armstrong, Loeb Classical Library, 1:1–89. Cambridge, MA: Harvard University Press, 1966.

Prentice, Robert. *The Psychology of Love according to St. Bonaventure*. St. Bonaventure, NY: Franciscan Institute, 1957.

Prosperi, Fr. Paolo. "Believing and Seeing." *Theological Studies* 78.4 (2017): 905–29.

———. "'Fixed End of the Eternal Plan': Rereading Cabasilas's 'Homily on the Annunciation.'" *Communio* 46.2 (Summer 2019): 207–36.

Przywara, Erich. *Analogia Entis: Metaphysics—Original Structure and Universal Rhythm*. Grand Rapids, MI: Eerdmans, 2014.

Putallaz, François-Xavier. *Insolente liberté: Controverses et condamnations au XIIIe siècle*. Paris: Cerf, 1995.

Quash, Ben. "Drama and the End of Modernity." In *Balthasar at the End of Modernity*, edited by Lucy Gardner and David Moss, 139–71. Edinburgh: T&T Clark, 1999.

Quinn, John F., C.S.B. "The Moral Philosophy of St. Bonaventure." *Southwestern Journal of Philosophy* 5.2 (Summer 1974): 39–70.

Ramelow, Tilman Anselm. Afterword to *De veritate: Über die Wahrheit*, 311–99. Hamburg: Felix Meiner, 2013.

———. "Der Begriff des Willens in seiner Entwicklung von Boethius bis Kant." *Archiv für Begriffsgeschichte* 46 (2004): 29–67.

———. *Gott, Freiheit, Weltanwahl*. Leiden: Brill, 1997.

Richard of St. Victor. *On the Trinity*. Translated by Ruben Angelici. Eugene, OR: Cascade Books, 2011.

Riesenhuber, Klaus. *Die Transzendenz der Freiheit zum Guten: Der Wille in der Anthropologie und Metaphysik des Thomas von Aquin*. Munich: Berchmanskolleg Verlag, 1971.

Riordan, William. *Divine Light: The Theology of Dionysius the Areopagite*. San Francisco: Ignatius Press, 2008.

Rist, John. *Augustine: Ancient Thought Baptized*. Cambridge: Cambridge University Press, 1996.

———. *Augustine Deformed: Love, Sin and Freedom in the Western Moral Tradition*. Cambridge: Cambridge University Press, 2014.

———. *Human Value: A Study in Ancient Philosophical Ethics*. Leiden: Brill, 1982.

———. "Love and Will: Around *De Trinitate* XV, 20, 38." In *Gott und Sein Bild*, 205–18. Edited by J. Brachtendorf. Munich: Paderborn, 2000.

———. *Plotinus: The Road to Reality*. Cambridge: Cambridge University Press, 2010.

Roberts, Victor. "The Relation of Faith and Reason in St. Anselm of Canterbury." *American Benedictine Review* 25 (1974): 494–512.

Rogers, Katherin S. *Anselm on Freedom*. Oxford: Oxford University Press, 2008.

Roniger, Scott J. "The Conversation of Ascent: Augustine's *Confessions*, Book IX, Chapter 10." *Communio* 43.4 (Winter 2016): 675–94.

Roques, René. *L'univers dionysien: Structure hiérarchique du monde selon le Pseudo-Denys.* Paris: Aubier, 1954.

Rosemann, Philipp W. *The Story of a Great Medieval Book: Peter Lombard's Sentences.* Peterborough, ON: Broadview Press, 2007.

Ross, James. "Aquinas's Exemplarism; Aquinas's Voluntarism." *American Catholic Philosophical Quarterly* 64.2 (1990): 171–98.

Roth, Sol. "Two Concepts of Freedom." *Tradition: A Journal of Orthodox Jewish Thought* 13.2 (1972): 59–70.

Rousseau, Jean-Jacques. *Confessions.* Translated by Angela Scholar. Oxford: Oxford University Press, 2008.

———. *La nouvelle Héloise.* University Park: Pennsylvania State University Press, 1986.

Rousselot, Pierre. *The Eyes of Faith.* New York: Fordham University Press, 1990.

———. *The Problem of Love in the Middle Ages.* Milwaukee, WI: Marquette University Press, 2002.

Sammon, Brendan Thomas. *The God Who Is Beauty.* Eugene, OR: Pickwick, 2013.

San Cristóbal-Sebastián, Antonio. *Controversias acerca de la voluntad desde 1270 a 1300.* Madrid: Coculsa, 1958.

Sartre, Jean-Paul. *Existentialism and Human Emotions.* New York: Philosophical Library, 1957.

Schäfer, Christian. *The Philosophy of Dionysius the Areopagite: An Introduction to the Structure and the Content of the Treatise "On the Divine Names."* Leiden: Brill, 2006.

Schelling, Friedrich Wilhelm Joseph von. *On the History of Modern Philosophy.* Cambridge: Cambridge University Press, 1994.

———. *Philosophical Investigations into the Essence of Human Freedom.* Albany, NY: SUNY Press, 2007.

———. *Der System der Weltalter: Münchner Vorlesung 1827/28 in einer Nachschrift von Ernst von Lasaulx.* Edited by Sigbert Peetz. Frankfurt: Klostermann, 1991.

Schindler, D. C. "*Analogia Naturae*: What Does Inanimate Matter Contribute to the Meaning of Life?" *Communio* 38 (Winter 2010): 657–80.

———. "Beauty and Love." In *Love and the Postmodern Predicament*, 85–117.

———. "Being and God." In *Love and the Postmodern Predicament*, 149–66.

———. *Catholicity of Reason.* Grand Rapids, MI: Eerdmans, 2013.

———. "The Crisis of Marriage as a Crisis of Meaning: On the Sterility of the Modern Will." *Communio* 41 (Summer 2014): 331–71.

———. "A Deeper Unity: Response to Professor Feingold on the Psychological Analogy for the Trinity." *Nova et Vetera* 17.2 (2019): 533–43.

———. "Disclosing Beauty: On Order and Disorder in the *Symposium*." In *Beauty and the Good: Recovering the Classical Tradition from Plato to Duns Scotus*, edited by Alice Ramos, 19–48. Washington, DC: Catholic University of America Press, 2020.

———. "Freedom beyond Our Choosing: Augustine on the Will and Its Objects." *Communio* 29.4 (Winter 2002): 618–53.

———. *Freedom from Reality: The Diabolical Character of Modern Liberty*. Notre Dame, IN: University of Notre Dame Press, 2018.

———. *Hans Urs von Balthasar and the Dramatic Structure of Truth*. New York: Fordham University Press, 2004.

———. "Love and Beauty, the Forgotten Transcendental, in Thomas Aquinas." *Communio* 44 (Summer 2017): 334–56.

———. "Love and Being." In *Love and the Postmodern Predicament*, 118–45.

———. *Love and the Postmodern Predicament*. Eugene, OR: Cascade Books, 2018.

———. "Metaphysics as Praeparatio Evangelica." In *A Companion to Ferdinand Ulrich's "Homo Abyssus,"* by D. C. Schindler, 89–112. Washington, DC: Humanum Academic Press, 2019.

———. *The Perfection of Freedom*. Eugene, OR: Cascade Books, 2012.

———. "Plato and the Problem of Love: On the Nature of Eros in the *Symposium*." *Apeiron* 40.3 (2007): 199–220.

———. *Plato's Critique of Impure Reason*. Washington, DC: Catholic University of America Press, 2008.

———. *The Politics of the Real: The Church between Liberalism and Integralism*. Steubenville, OH: New Polity Press, 2021.

———. "The Redemption of Eros: Philosophical Reflections on Benedict XVI's First Encyclical." *Communio* 33 (Fall 2006): 375–99.

———. "What's the Difference? On the Metaphysics of Participation in Plato, Plotinus, and Aquinas." *Nova et Vetera* 5 (2007): 583–618.

Schindler, David L. "Is Truth Ugly? Moralism and the Convertibility of Being and Love." *Communio* 27 (Winter 2000): 701–28.

———. "Toward a Culture of Life: The Eucharist, the 'Restoration' of Creation, and the 'Worldly' Task of the Laity in Liberal Societies." *Communio* 29 (Fall 2002): 679–90.

———. "Trinity, Creation, and the Order of Intelligence in the Modern Academy." *Communio* 28.3 (Fall 2001): 406–28.

Schlosser, Marianne. *Cognitio et amor: Zum kognitiven und voluntativen Grund der Gotteserfahrung nach Bonaventura*. Munich: Ferdinand Schöningh, 1990.

Schmitz, Kenneth. "The First Principle of Personal Becoming." *Review of Metaphysics* 47.4 (1994): 757–74.

———. *The Gift: Creation*. Milwaukee, WI: Marquette University Press, 1982.

Schmutz, Jakob. "The Medieval Doctrine of Causality and the Theology of Pure Nature." In *Surnaturel: A Controversy at the Heart of Twentieth-Century Thomist Thought*, edited by Serge-Thomas Bonino, 203–50. Naples, FL: Ave Maria Press, 2007.

Shanley, Brian J., O.P. "Divine Causation and Human Freedom in Aquinas." *American Catholic Philosophical Quarterly* 72.1 (1998): 99–122.

Sharples, R. W. *Alexander of Aphrodisias, On Fate*. London: Duckworth, 1983.

Shestov, Lev. "The Bull of Phalaris." In *Athens and Jerusalem*, 2nd ed., 127–206. Athens: Ohio University Press, 2016.

———. "Parmenides in Chains." In *Athens and Jerusalem*, 2nd ed., 69–126. Athens: Ohio University Press, 2016.

Shields, Daniel. "Aquinas on Will, Happiness and God: The Problem of Love and Aristotle's *Liber de Bona Fortuna*." *American Catholic Philosophical Quarterly* 91.1 (Winter 2017): 113–42.

Siewerth, Gustav. *Die Analogie des Seienden*. 2nd ed. Freiburg: Johannesverlag Einsiedeln, 2003.

———. *Das Gute als bewegender Grund der Freiheit*. Freiburg: Gustav-Siewerth-Gesellschaft, 2011.

———. *Die menschliche Willensfreiheit*. Dusseldorf: L. Schwann, 1954.

———. *Das Schicksal der Metaphysik von Thomas zu Heidegger*. Freiburg: Johannesverlag-Einsiedeln, 2003.

Simon, Yves. *Freedom of Choice*. New York: Fordham University Press, 1969.

Singer, Isidore, ed. *The Jewish Encyclopedia: A Descriptive Record*, edited by Isidore Singer. New York: Funk and Wagnalls, 1906.

Sixtus V. *Triumphantis Hierusalem*. 1588. www.papalencyclicals.net/sixtus05/triumph.htm.

Smythe, Herbert Weir. *A Greek Grammar for Colleges*. Cambridge, MA: Harvard University Press, 1956.

Sophocles. *The Three Theban Plays*. New York: Penguin, 2000.

Sorabji, Richard. "The Concept of Will from Plato to Maximus the Confessor." In *The Will and Human Action: From Antiquity to the Present Day*, edited by Thomas Pink and M. W. F. Stone, 6–28. New York: Routledge, 2004.

———. "Freedom and Will: Graeco-Roman Origins." In *Selfhood and the Soul: Essays on Ancient Thought and Literature in Honour of Christopher Gill*, edited by Richard Seaford, John Wilkins, and Matthew Wright, 49–66. Oxford: Oxford University Press, 2017.

Spaemann, Robert. "Nature," in *The Robert Spaemann Reader*, edited by D. C. Schindler and Jeanne Heffernan Schindler, 22–36. Oxford: Oxford University Press, 2015.

———. *Persons: The Difference between Someone and Something.* Translated by Oliver O'Donovan. Oxford: Oxford University Press, 2006.

———. "What Does It Mean to Say 'Art Imitates Nature'?" In *The Spaemann Reader*, edited by D. C. Schindler and Jeanne Heffernan Schindler, 192–210. Oxford: Oxford University Press, 2015.

Spearritt, Placid. "A Philosophical Enquiry into Dionysian Mysticism." PhD diss., University of Fribourg, Switzerland, 1968.

Spiering, Jamie Anne. "'Liber Est Causa Sui': Thomas Aquinas and the Maxim 'The Free Is the Cause of Itself.'" *Review of Metaphysics* 65.2 (December 2011): 351–76.

Spinoza, Baruch de. *Ethics.* Indianapolis: Hackett, 1992.

Spruyte, Joke. "Duns Scotus's Criticism of Henry of Ghent's Notion of Free Will." In Bos, *John Duns Scotus*, 139–54.

Stadter, Ernst. *Psychologie und Metaphysik der menschlichen Freiheit: Die ideengeschichtliche Entwecklung zwischen Bonaventura und Duns Scotus.* Munich: Ferdinand Schöningen, 1971.

Staffler, Johannes, S.J. "Der hl. Thomas und das Axiom: Omne quod movetur ab alio movetur." *Zeitschrift für katholische Theologie* 47.3 (1923): 369–90.

Stang, Charles M. *Apophasis and Pseudonymity in Dionysius the Areopagite: "No Longer I."* Oxford: Oxford University Press, 2012.

Strauss, Leo. "Reason and Revelation." In *Leo Strauss and the Theologico-Political Problem.* Cambridge: Cambridge University Press, 2006.

Szlachta, Michael. "A Defense of Intellectualism: Will, Intellect, and Control in Late Thirteenth-Century Philosophy." PhD diss., University of Toronto, 2019.

Tertullian. *Prescription against Heretics.* In *Early Latin Theology*, edited by S. L. Greenslade, 19–64. Louisville, KY: Westminster Press, 1956.

Teske, Ronald J. "Henry of Ghent on the Freedom of the Human Will." In *A Companion to Henry of Ghent*, edited by Gordon Wilson, 315–35. Leiden: Brill, 2010.

———. *To Know God and the Soul: Essays on the Thought of Saint Augustine.* Washington, DC: Catholic University of America Press, 2008.

te Velde, Rudi. "*Natura in Seipsa Recurva Est*: Duns Scotus and Aquinas on the Relationship between Nature and Will." In Bos, *John Duns Scotus*, 155–69.

Thompson, William G. "The Doctrine of Liberum Arbitrium in Saint Bonaventure." Master's thesis, Loyola University Chicago, 1956.

Thunberg, Lars. *Microcosm and Mediation: The Theological Anthropology of Maximus the Confessor.* 2nd ed. Chicago: Open Court Press, 1995.

Tilliette, Xavier. *Schelling: Une philosophie en devenir.* Paris: Vrin, 1992.

Trego, Kristell. *L'essence de la liberté: La refondation de l'éthique dans l'oeuvre de saint Anselm de Canterbéry.* Paris: Vrin, 2010.

———. *L'impuissance du possible: Emergence et développement du possible, d'Aristote à l'aube des temps moderns*. Paris: Vrin, 2019.

Trouillard, Jean. *La procession plotinienne*. Paris: Presses universitaires de France, 1955.

Tsakanikas, Matthew. "Unmasking the Pharaoh in the Garden of Eden: A Canonical Reading of Genesis 2–3." *Communio* 47.1 (Spring 2020): 190–212.

Tweedale, Martin. "Representation in Scholastic Epistemology." In *Representation and Objects of Thought in Medieval Philosophy*, edited by Henrik Lagerlund, 64–82. London: Routledge, 2016.

Ulrich, Ferdinand. "Cur non video praesentem? Zur Implikation der griechischen und lateinischen Denkform bei Anselm und Scotus Erigena." *Freiburger Zeitschrift für Philosophie und Theologie* 1–2 (1975): 70–170.

———. *Gabe und Vergebung*. Freiburg: Johannes Verlag Einsiedeln, 2006.

———. *Gegenwart der Freiheit*. Freiburg: Johannes Verlag Einsiedeln, 1974.

———. *Homo Abyssus: The Drama of the Question of Being*. Translated by D. C. Schindler. Washington, DC: Humanum Academic Press, 2017.

———. *Leben in der Einheit von Leben und Tod*. Freiburg: Johannes Verlag Einsiedeln, 1999.

Veatch, Henry. *Two Logics*. Evanston, IL: Northwestern University Press, 1969.

Veldhuis, Henri. "Ordained and Absolute Power in Scotus' *Ordinatio I 44*." *Vivarium* 38.2 (2000): 222–30.

Venuta, Goffredo. *Libero arbitrio e libertà della grazia nel pensiero di S. Bernardo*. Rome: F. Ferrari, 1953.

Visser, Sandra, and Thomas Williams. "Anselm's Account of Freedom." In B. Davies and Leftow, *Cambridge Companion to Anselm*, 179–203.

Vlastos, Gregory. "The Individual as an Object of Love in Plato." In *Platonic Studies*, 3–34. Princeton, NJ: Princeton University Press, 1981.

Voegelin, Eric. *Order and History*. Vol. 1, *Israel and Revelation*. Baton Rouge: Louisiana State University Press, 1956.

von Rad, Gerhard. *Old Testament Theology*. New York: Harper and Row, 1965.

Vos Jaczn, A., H. Veldhuis, A. A. Looman-Graaskamp, E. Dekker, and N. W. Den Bok. Introduction to *Contingency and Freedom: Lectura I 39*, 1–41. Dordrecht: Kluwer, 1994.

Walker, Adrian. "The Freedom of Christ: Notes on 'Gnomie' in Maximus the Confessor." *Communio* 43.1 (Spring 2016): 32.

Watson, Gary, ed. *Free Will, Oxford Readings in Philosophy*. 2nd ed. Oxford: Oxford University Press, 2003.

Weisheipl, James. "Aristotle's Concept of Nature: Avicenna and Aquinas." In *Approaches to Nature in the Middle Ages*, edited by L. D. Roberts, 137–60. Binghamton, NY: Center for Medieval and Early Renaissance Studies, 1982.

Westberg, Daniel. "Did Aquinas Change His Mind about the Will?" *The Thomist* 58.1 (January 1994): 41–60.
Westra, Laura. *Plotinus and Freedom: A Study of Ennead 6.8*. Lewiston, NY: Edwin Mellen, 1990.
Wetzel, James. *Augustine and the Limits of Virtue*. Cambridge: Cambridge University Press, 1992.
White, Thomas Joseph. *Wisdom in the Face of Modernity*. Naples, FL: Sapientia Press, 2009.
Wilken, Robert Louis. *The Spirit of Early Christian Thought*. New Haven, CT: Yale University Press, 2003.
Williams, Robert R. *Recognition: Fichte and Hegel on the Other*. Albany, NY: SUNY Press, 1992.
Williams, Thomas. "The Doctrine of Univocity Is True and Salutary." *Modern Theology* 21.4 (October 2005): 575–85.
———. Introduction to *On Free Choice of the Will*, by Augustine, xi–xix. Bloomington: Hackett, 1993.
———. Review of Katherin Rogers' *Anselm on Freedom*. *Notre Dame Philosophical Reviews: An Electronic Journal*, February 11, 2009.
Wippel, John. "Godfrey of Fontaines." In *The Stanford Encyclopedia of Philosophy*, Winter 2018 ed, edited by Edward N. Zalta. Plato.Stanford.edu/entries/godfrey.
———. "Godfrey of Fontaines and the Act-Potency Axiom." *Journal of the History of Philosophy* 11 (1973): 299–317.
———. *The Metaphysical Thought of Godfrey of Fontaines*. Washington, DC: Catholic University of America Press, 1981.
———. "The Role of the Phantasm in Godfrey of Fontaines's Theory of Intellection." In *L'homme et son univers au moyen age: Actes du 7. Congrès Internat. de Philosophie Médiévale (30 Aug–4 Sept, 1982)*, edited by C. Wenin, 2:573–82. Louvain-la-Neuve: Institut Supérieur de Philosophie, 1986.
———. "Thomas Aquinas and Participation." In *Studies in Medieval Philosophy*, edited by John Wippel. Washington, DC: Catholic University of America Press, 1987.
Wolter, Allan B. "Duns Scotus on the Natural Desire for the Supernatural." In Adams, *Philosophical Theology*, 125–47.
———. "Duns Scotus on the Will as Rational Potency." In Adams, *Philosophical Theology*,163–80.
———. Introduction to *On the Will and Morality*, by John Duns Scotus, translated by Allan B. Wolter, O.F.M., and edited by William A. Frank. Washington, DC: Catholic University of America Press, 1997.
———. "Native Freedom of the Will as Key to the Ethics of Scotus." In Adams, *Philosophical Theology*, 148–62.

———. "The 'Theologism' of Duns Scotus." In *The Philosophical Theology of John Duns Scotus*, edited by Marilyn McCord Adams, 209–53. Ithaca, NY: Cornell University Press, 1990.

Wright, G. Ernest. *God Who Acts.* London: SCM Press, 1952.

———. *The Old Testament against Its Environment.* London: SCM Press, 1950.

———. *The Old Testament and Theology.* New York: Harper and Row, 1969.

Wu, John. *Beyond East and West.* Notre Dame, IN: University of Notre Dame Press, 2018.

Zimmerman, Brandon. "Plotinian Emanation as a Dynamic of Procession and Return." Master's thesis, Catholic University of America, 2009.

INDEX

Abelard, Peter, 362n109
Abraham, 25, 35
actuality (or act), 65, 67; and
 potency, 6, 29, 44, 52–54, 73–76,
 100, 130, 143–46, 152, 166,
 182–83, 204, 236, 257–58, 260,
 263, 274, 371n173, 374n10,
 384n99, 385n109, 386n114,
 388n131, 418n24, 430n35,
 475n20, 481n18
adoption, 38, 41–42
affection, 220–21, 483n39; for
 advantage or justice, 163,
 167–69, 178
agape, 126–27, 132, 383n91, 453n104.
 See also love
akrasia, 349n5
Alexander of Aphrodisias, 373n5
anagogē, 53–55, 57, 59, 65, 73,
 382n78
Anselm, xii, 97, 163–88, 189–90,
 193–94, 198, 208–10, 214, 220,
 226, 258, 263, 416nn1–4,
 417n12, 418n24, 418n31,
 419n37, 419n39, 419n42,
 420n48, 420n57, 421n66,
 421n72, 421n74, 422n77,
 423n89, 423n91, 423n99,
 424n109, 425n114, 425n116,
 426n122, 427n1, 431n55,
 435n36, 438n64, 443n11,
 444n21, 456n134, 470n261,
 482n25, 483n39, 492n125
appetite, 93, 215, 243–45, 247, 261,
 431n55, 454n108, 454n120,
 463n208
Aquinas, Thomas, xii, 45, 51, 74, 97,
 120, 129, 194, 203–5, 211, 213,
 215, 218–20, 222, 225–77, 347n1,
 352n31, 366n132, 370n168,
 384n96, 385n109, 413n40,
 418n33, 425n114, 426n121,
 436n41, 436n44, 436n48, 437n54,
 438n63, 438n67, 439n75, 439n79,
 441n99, 443nn10–11, 444n17,
 445n27, 446n34, 446nn37–38,
 447n46, 448n53, 448n55, 449n60,
 450nn69–70, 451n74, 451n77,
 451nn80–81, 451n85, 452n88,
 452n90, 453n96, 454n105,
 455n124, 455n128, 456n135,
 456n141, 457nn144–51, 458n152,
 458nn154–56, 459n161, 459n163,
 461nn185–89, 462nn196–97,
 462n202, 463n208, 464n211,
 464nn213–15, 464n221, 465n224,
 466n238, 467n242, 468n243,
 468nn245–47, 469nn250–51,
 469n256, 470n261, 470n264,
 471n276, 472n286, 472nn288–89,
 473n292, 473n6 (chap. 10),
 474n7, 474n12, 479n1,

Aquinas, Thomas (*cont.*)
  480nn9–10, 481n19, 482n26,
  483n38, 484n43, 484n47, 487n84,
  492n118, 493n130
Arendt, Hannah, 27, 103–5, 350n12,
  364n121, 389n133, 395n61,
  401n126, 414n47, 449n58
Aristotle, 10–11, 44, 52, 59–60,
  64–65, 67–68, 70, 74–77, 81,
  94, 96, 140, 149, 176, 181, 204,
  220, 228, 240–41, 256, 269,
  352n27, 352nn30–31, 353n35,
  358n80, 374n10, 379n47,
  380n60, 380nn62–63,
  384nn99–100, 397n87, 399n102,
  409n77, 410n1, 411n2, 411n8,
  414n41, 414n46, 416n1, 416n4,
  418n33, 421n66, 428n15,
  431n57, 432n5, 433n8, 438n67,
  440n87, 452n88, 452n90,
  453n95, 458n155, 468n243,
  469n249, 470n258, 474n7,
  476n29, 478n67, 479n6,
  480n10, 481n14, 489n104;
  as representative of classical
  tradition, ix, 34, 43
Atkinson, Joseph, 23, 359n88,
  360n91, 360n96, 361n98,
  363n113
Auer, Johannes, 481n19, 483n41,
  492n118
Augustine, xi, 82–112, 122–24, 126,
  128–29, 134–35, 139, 141, 148,
  153, 155, 165–66, 171, 176, 183,
  209, 212, 226–28, 348n3, 391n11,
  391nn14–15, 392n23, 392n27,
  393n40, 394n47, 395nn61–62,
  396n68, 396n71, 396n74, 397n76,
  398n90, 398n96, 399nn104–5,
  399n108, 400n110, 402n132,
  402n137, 407n44, 411n7, 416n1,
  417n8, 417n15, 418n25, 418n33,
  419n38, 422n77, 423n91,
  425n114, 430n35, 443n4,
  489n104
authority, 350n12
Ayres, Lewis, 85, 391n16

Balthasar, Hans Urs von, 28, 174,
  178–79, 351n23, 357n74,
  365n124, 369n157, 373n186,
  373n4, 374n6, 389n135, 422n77,
  422n84, 424n104
Bañez, Domingo, 469n255
Barnes, Michel, 408n67, 452n88
Barth, Karl, 364n115
Bauer, Ferdinand Christian,
  484n48
beauty, 261, 265, 392n25, 398n96,
  406n24, 437n53, 462n201,
  464n213
Begrich, Joachim, 359n87
Beierwaltes, Werner, 383n86
being (*esse*), 120, 229, 236, 246, 271,
  381n72, 405n21, 448n55,
  449n65, 452n90, 453n103,
  454n122, 455n127
Benz, Ernst, 381n71
Bernard of Clairvaux, xii, 189–200,
  209–10, 219, 226, 258, 427n1,
  427n8, 428n12, 429n29,
  429n31, 430nn44–45, 431n49,
  431nn52–56, 431n58, 437n61,
  456n140, 459n165, 476n36,
  482n25
Bieler, Jonathan, 155
Boler, John, 489n106, 492n125
Bonaventure, xiii, 8, 203–24, 226,
  432n1, 432n3, 432n5, 433n13,
  434nn17–18, 434n24,

Index 525

435nn29–32, 435nn35–36, 436n49, 437n56, 437n61, 438n64, 438nn66–67, 438n74, 439n75, 439nn77–79, 440nn87–89, 441nn100–101, 441n103, 442nn105–6, 442n109, 442n111, 481n16, 482n25, 483n39
boulēsis, 61, 66, 124, 380n63
Boulnois, Olivier, 443n6, 448n48, 479n5
Brague, Rémi, 18, 349n10, 362n109, 364n119, 366n135
Bray, Dennis, 433n10
Buchner, Hans, 374n11, 384n100, 388n130
Burrell, David, 33, 355n44, 355n51, 361n105, 362n109, 368n145, 447n45, 448n50, 449n63, 450n68
Byers, Sarah, 93, 394n50

Calvin, John, 348n4
causa sui, 70, 250, 284, 288, 474n12, 476n39
Chaldean Oracles, 88
Chappell, Tim, 101–5
Chesterton, G. K., 384n97, 459n169
choice. *See* power: to choose
Christ, Jesus, 8, 37, 40–41, 154, 159, 220, 414n48, 416n2, 419n44, 494–95n152
Christianity, 3–4, 9, 45, 63, 116, 403n6; and freedom, 6–7, 64; as synthesizing Greek, Roman, and Jewish form, 31–42, 84, 133, 138, 155, 158, 187–88, 268, 367n141, 391n15, 401n125, 441n102; as tradition, 8, 38
Cicero, 369n156
Cilento, Vincenzo, 64, 386n117, 388n132

Clarke, Norris, 241, 385n108, 453n92
Clement of Alexandria, 367n137
compatibilism, 61
condilectio, 207
consent, 92, 94, 191–92, 195, 216, 394n57, 395n62
contingency, 69, 234–35, 238, 253, 486n76; synchronic, 235, 486n70, 486n72
Corbin, Michel, 427n1, 429n24, 430nn36–37, 430n44, 431n47
Courtenay, W.J., 362n108, 420n47, 420n51, 420n57, 447n45
Cousineau, Robert-Henri, 86, 380n57
Cousins, Ewert, 433n10
covenant, 20–28, 36–39, 88–89, 116, 190, 266, 356n54, 359n83, 360n96, 362n109, 363n114, 365n128, 370n159, 370n161, 392n27, 451n84; and contract, 39
Cross, Frank Moore, 20, 370n167

Damian, Peter, 447n45, 453n103
Dante, 271, 471n269
Davies, J.A., 21
deficient causality, 98–100, 104, 166, 171
deprecation, 155–56
Descartes, 367n143, 431n53
desire, 58, 71, 85, 91, 96, 129, 141, 146, 195, 377n31, 380n62, 393n46, 413n27, 424n109, 447n40, 456n135, 458n155, 462n199, 463n208, 472n286, 484n43
desubstratalization, 180–81, 185
determinism, 61, 277, 480n10, 480n12

diabolical conception of freedom, 6, 9, 129, 168, 398n90
diatheletism, 411n6, 422n86
Dihle, Albrecht, 103, 358n76, 364n117, 369n156
Dionysius the Areopagite, xii, 115–36, 137, 139, 142, 144–45, 148–49, 153–54, 158, 173, 178, 208, 213, 226, 403n2, 404n10, 405n14, 405n19, 405n21, 406nn34–35, 407nn40–41, 407n44, 407n47, 408n57, 408n59, 409n69, 409nn74–75, 410n82, 410nn87–88, 420n46, 425n114, 437n54, 464n215, 495n2; as "Pseudo-Dionysius," 403n1
dominion, 129, 213–23, 284, 288, 292, 313, 327, 437n61, 440n93, 442n111, 448n47, 476n38
Dumbrell, William J., 363n114
Dumont, Stephen, 484n50, 486n74, 490n107

Eichrodt, Walther, 24, 355n51, 357n75, 359n82, 360n96, 361n107, 363n110, 371n172
election, 13
Eliade, Mircea, 355n47, 357n73
Eliot, T. S., 156
epektasis, 413n26
eph'hēmin, 53, 55, 83, 252, 375n12, 376n28
Epictetus, 375n17, 376n28
Eriugena, John Scotus, 416n1
eros, 71, 87, 89–97, 99, 107, 117, 123–32, 135, 383n91, 393n44, 400n116, 407nn43–44, 407n47, 410nn81–82, 410n90, 453n104
eternity, 109–10; "before (or beyond) eternity," 72, 276, 384n97, 412n23

Euthyphro dilemma, 64, 86, 131, 135, 172, 174, 176
Evans, G. R., 417n5
event, 17, 154
evil, 5, 98–104, 122, 133–34, 157, 386n113, 405n13, 409n68, 425n114
exitus, and *reditus*, 11, 27, 124
expressio, 206, 213
Eusebius, 108, 404n10

Fabro, Cornelio, 471n275
fall of the devil, 165–66, 177
Farrell, Joseph, 415n64
fate, 78. *See also* determinism
Feingold, Lawrence, 473n293
Fichte, 176
fidelity, 29
force, 184, 198
Forest, Aimé, 429n29
Francis of Assisi, 437n56
Frank, William, 488n92, 491n110, 491n112
freedom, as liberation from, 18, 29–30, 133, 195, 371n169; as capacity for justice, 165
friendship, 37, 87, 392n27
Frost, Gloria, 491n108, 491n112, 494n139

Galen, 19
Gallagher, David, 256, 258, 274, 455n131, 460n184, 474n12
Gauss, Julia, 426n123
Gauthier, R.-A., 137–38, 410n1
gift, 7, 33, 45–47, 89, 92, 95, 105–6, 110, 112, 118–19, 133, 141, 168, 175, 178, 181, 269–72, 386n116, 395n62, 405n13
Giles of Rome, 476n29

Gilson, Etienne, 98, 189, 198–99,
203, 237, 362n109, 427n1,
428n12, 431n49, 432n5, 434n23,
435n31, 437n51, 440n87,
470n267, 479n5, 484n48,
485n62, 490n107
gnomie, 144–45, 151, 159, 412n17,
412n21, 413n32, 414n43,
418n21, 438n74, 443n10
God, 14, 16, 20, 36, 40, 64, 100, 108,
136, 145–46, 149–50, 171, 229,
407n47, 469n250; as absolutely
simple, 436n45; as absolutely
transcendent, 17, 90–91,
471n273; and freedom, 4–5, 51,
55, 62–63, 69, 71, 73, 111, 150,
185, 231, 374n9, 385n109,
402n132, 406n35, 410n88,
416n3, 425n114, 431n52;
intellect of, 444n22, 458n152;
and Israel, 21; power of, 25, 92,
119, 128, 232, 409n70, 418n18,
418n24, 445n27, 447n41,
447n46; will of, 15, 19, 22, 26,
68, 70, 80, 86, 110, 131, 135,
230–33, 236, 238, 420n48,
422n83, 444n22, 446n30,
451n85, 457n151, 482n26
Godescale of Orbais, 402n129
Godfrey of Fontaines, xiii, 473n6,
474n7, 474n9, 475n28,
476nn35–36, 476n40, 477n51,
477n53, 477n55, 478n62,
478n64, 478nn66–67, 480n9
Goebel, Berndt, 421n72, 423n99
Goethe, 373n186
Good, 11–13, 30, 34–35, 40, 52–53,
55–68, 70–74, 87, 92–95, 104–6,
110, 119, 122–23, 128, 225–26,
237, 375n17, 377n37,
382nn73–75, 384n92, 384n97,
385n103, 392n25, 399n102,
407n43, 422n77, 458n155,
463n208, 469n254
grace, 89–91, 97, 146, 164, 183,
190–91, 221, 372n183, 394n47,
396n74, 397n76, 413n33, 422n82,
455n125, 469n254, 469n256
Grant, W. Matthews, 425n114
Greeks, 116; in relation to Jews and/or
Romans, 8–10, 13, 26–31, 37, 43,
46, 84–85, 108, 117, 125, 133, 153,
179, 187–88, 227, 241–43
Gregory, Brad, 372n185
Gregory of Nyssa, xii-xiii, 376n28,
386n117, 413n26

Hadot, Pierre, 88
Hahn, Scott, 359n86, 363n112,
365n128
Hanby, Michael, 396n71
Harrison, Simon, 111, 394n57
Hart, David Bentley, 392n23
heart, 356n60
Hegel, 53, 176, 206, 365n122,
368n150, 401n121, 414n45,
453n97, 454n122, 494–95n152
Heidegger, 13, 73, 353n35, 385n104
Henry, Paul, 383n82
Henry of Ghent, 478n67, 492n125
Heraclitus, 51, 353n33, 373n3
Heschel, Abraham Joshua, 351n22,
357n73, 364n119
history, 15, 77, 96–97, 108–9, 136,
153–57, 183, 269–70, 387n123,
388n128, 401nn125–26
Hoeres, Walter, 456n135, 482n23,
488n87, 488n95, 490n107,
492n114, 492n123, 494n140,
494n149

Hoffman, Tobias, 481n15, 484n49, 485n61
holy, 14–15, 18, 154, 357n71
Honnefelder, Ludger, 480n10, 485n63, 492n122
Horn, Christoph, 381n71
Hughes, Kevin, 432n4, 439n79

illuminationism, 469n251
imagination, 266, 468n246
Incandela, Joseph, 493n128, 493n130
Incarnation, 33, 36, 41, 44, 128, 138, 205, 410n87
Ingham, Mary Beth, 481n15, 488n93, 490n107
intellect, 58–59, 65, 73–74, 86, 386n117; and will, 94, 96–97, 193, 210–11, 229, 248–49, 255, 257–58, 433n13, 438n66, 444n17, 456n136, 456n141, 458n156, 460n176, 461nn185–93, 462n195, 462n201, 468n243, 469n257, 473n6, 477n44, 477n51, 477n54, 478n66, 484n49, 485n53, 486n64, 488n93, 491n109
intellectualism, xii–xiii, 28, 66, 142, 152, 193, 209, 254, 273–74, 395n59, 471n275, 476n29, 477n44, 478n62
intention, 177, 186, 216, 421n70, 436n49, 438n70, 467n242
intentionality, 474n9
Inwood, Brad, 394n53

Jacobi, Friedrich Heinrich, 480n12
Jaczn, A. Vos, 486n70
Jews, 13–31, 420n60. *See also* Greeks
Joachim di Fiore, 434n20

Kahn, Charles, 106, 352n31
Kane, Stanley, 165, 417n12, 423n99
Kant, 105, 112, 168
Kent, Bonnie, 426n118, 432n5, 476n32, 479n6, 483n39, 489n105, 490n107, 492n117
Knuuttila, Simo, 394n57
Kim, Yul, 254, 257, 461n188, 477n53
Kremer, Klaus, 378n45, 380n57, 388n131
Kuehn, Evan, 391n18

Lagarde, Georges de, 473n5, 478n67
law, 91
Lee, Patrick, 490n107
Le Goff, Jacques, 401n125
Leroux, Georges, 52, 63, 66, 374n8, 383n86
Levenson, Jon D., 17, 356n58, 361n99, 366n133
libertarianism, 61, 95, 98, 277, 397n78, 418n31, 457n147
Liberty: as liberality, 10, 115, 205–7, 218, 239, 433n13, 437n51; as modern, ix
liberum arbitrium, 101, 191–93, 209–219, 223–24, 226–27, 250, 394n47, 428nn14–15, 429n23, 431n53, 438n70, 440n88, 440n91, 451n85, 473n6; and *voluntas*, 445n28, 446n37, 482n26
Locke, John, ix, 149, 239, 375n17, 378n42, 397n78, 399n106, 400n109, 406n26
logos, 34–35, 55
Lombard, Peter, 226, 443n4
Long, Steven, 469n255
Lössel, Josef, 391n20
Lottin, Odon, 213, 458n154, 474n7
Louth, Andrew, 404n8

love, 70, 84–90, 93–94, 100, 105, 107–8, 111, 125–26, 132, 169, 188, 196–200, 208, 218, 227–29, 237, 259–72, 274, 361n107, 374n9, 384n92, 392n31, 398n91, 408n53, 432n59, 437n51, 442n111, 454n120, 455n128, 463n206, 464n211, 464n213, 465n226, 467n242, 472n288; as passion, 437n54, 463n204. *See also* eros

Löwith, Karl, 109, 401n123, 401n125

Lucretius, 369n156

Luther, Martin, 116, 348n4, 364n116, 403n5

Marcel, Gabriel, x

Marenbon, John, 426n125

Marion, Jean-Luc, 194, 429n24, 451n74

marriage (or nuptial mystery), 21, 180, 190, 494n148

Mary, 34, 41, 370n160, 370n162, 389n1, 414n48

Maximus the Confessor, xii, 137–60, 163–64, 170, 173, 178–80, 182, 186, 189, 209, 226, 240, 373n1, 410n1, 411n2, 411n9, 412n23, 413n26, 413nn30–34, 414n41, 414n44, 414n51, 415n60, 415n64, 416n1, 417n15, 418n21, 422n80, 422n86, 425n113, 431n49, 435n29, 438n74, 472n291, 489n104, 493n127

Meek, Esther Lightcap, 466n236

Milbank, John, 441n97, 481n15

Mitralexis, Sotiris, 411n10, 412n12, 412n23, 414n41

monotheletism or monophysitism, 411n6

Moonan, Lawrence, 434n23

Moses, 19, 21, 223

nature, 11–13, 40, 67–68, 117–25, 138–39, 149–50, 156, 180–82, 186, 228, 242, 246, 270, 380n60, 405n13, 434n18, 449n60, 455n125, 481n22, 483n32, 484n47, 486n75, 492n122, 494n141; and freedom, 9, 151–52, 200, 275, 420n58, 471n272, 479n5, 482n25, 482n30; and God, 15; and supernature, 409n75, 495n2

Newton, Isaac, 409n70

Nietzsche, Friedrich, 3, 69, 106, 177, 347n1, 353n34, 372n181, 387n119, 401n125, 421n67, 470n268

nihilism, 5, 95, 480n12

Noone, Timothy, 458n156

nominalism, 388n126, 453n104

Normore, C. G., 416n4

Nygren, Anders, 127, 361n107, 398n91, 400n116, 404n7, 408n61

obedience, 90–93, 99, 107, 129, 159, 185, 393n40, 393n44, 394n50, 407n44, 422n77

Ockham, William of, 478n67

Odysseus, 107

Oedipus, 56–57

Olivi, Peter, 211, 223, 486n74

Onians, Richard, 354n37

ontotheology, 423n89

options, 101–2, 173

Origen, xiii, 140, 144, 358n77, 411n10

Ortega y Gassett, José, 454n108
Osborne, Thomas, Jr., 478n62
Ousager, Asger, 63–64
Oz-Salzberger, Fania, 358n78

Pacheco, Monteiro, 351n18
Parker, John, 403n1
participation, 12
passions, 93, 96, 158, 250, 261, 394n57, 395n58, 462n202
Paul, 25, 32, 40, 132, 157–58, 194, 350n15, 363n112, 366n136, 367n140, 370n165
Pederson, Johannes, 23, 361n101
Pelagius, 391n11, 394n50, 402n132
Perl, Eric, 407n47
person, 15, 39–40, 87, 106, 188, 370n168
Philo, 32
Pieper, Josef, 429n29, 465n226
Plato, 12, 63, 65, 71, 73, 75, 83, 86, 95, 109, 149, 169, 178, 183–84, 225, 352n25, 353n35, 354n38, 368n148, 379n53, 379n56, 389n1, 392n25, 396n64, 400n115, 404n11, 409n77, 410n82, 424nn109–10, 432n5, 457n144, 458n155, 478n57, 480n10; as representative of classical tradition, ix, 34, 43, 406n34, 413n27
Plotinus, xi-xii, 43–45, 51–81, 82, 85–86, 88, 90, 92, 106, 108–9, 122–24, 127, 130, 134, 138, 144–45, 153, 158, 172, 205, 225–26, 231, 373nn2–3, 374nn8–11, 375n12, 375n17, 376n26, 376n28, 377nn32–35, 378nn41–43, 378n45, 379n47, 379n49, 379n54, 380nn60–61, 381n66, 381n71, 382nn75–79, 383n86, 383n91, 384n95, 384n100, 385nn108–9, 386nn110–13, 386nn116–17, 387n118, 387nn123–24, 388nn125–27, 388n130, 388n132, 389n133, 389nn136–41, 391n15, 394n57, 399n108, 400n110, 403n2, 407n44, 407n47, 409n68, 409n75, 435n29, 440n87, 445n29, 451n85, 452n88, 453n101, 467n241
poiēsis, 11, 80, 124
Polanyi, Michael, 42
Porphyry, 51, 373n2, 377n29, 389n143
possibilia, 307–8, 318, 448n50, 485n61
potentia absoluta and/or *ordinata*, 207, 223, 232, 362n108, 431n53, 434n23, 447n45, 489n96
power, 24, 98, 100, 119–20, 128–29, 167, 184–85, 232, 269, 387n121; as active, 239, 492n119; as arbitrary, 488n87; to choose, 84, 97–106, 135–36, 142, 145, 147–48, 150, 154, 159–60, 165, 167, 171, 176, 192, 196, 209–10, 216, 369n158, 406n32, 411n8, 415n64, 417n9, 418n24, 459n162, 463n205, 477n51; as (logical) possibility, 447n45, 448n55, 449n65, 451n85; and potency, 80, 109, 151; as *potestas*, 182, 435n36, 436n48. *See also* actuality
praxis, 11, 79
prayer, 19
predestination, 5–6, 33, 38, 40, 164, 327, 348nn3–4, 371n174,

396n73, 402n135, 422n82,
    450n68, 472n291, 491n108
Proclus, 352n26
promise, 29, 174
Promised Land, 30, 38, 223
Prosperi, Paolo, 350n12, 370n160,
    414n48, 424n111
providence, 109, 124, 387n123,
    389n142
Prufer, Thomas, 400n113
Przywara, Erich, 44, 374n6
Putallaz, François-Xavier, 473n6

Quash, Ben, 365n123

Rad, Gerhard von, 370n161
Ramelow, Anselm, 254, 444n15,
    447n45, 448n55, 495n1
rational (or intellectual) appetite,
    139, 141, 218–19, 247–48, 251,
    263, 419n38, 473n292, 483n39,
    489n104
reditio completa, 11
Richard of St. Victor, 207
Riesenhuber, Klaus, 463n203
Riordan, William, 405n14
Rist, John, 63, 83, 89, 107, 379n54,
    387n124, 390n8, 397n77,
    400n116, 417n15
Rogers, Katherin S., 418n19, 418n31,
    425n114
Roniger, Scott, 108
Roques, René, 405n15
Rosemann, Philipp W., 443n4
Ross, James, 449n63
Roth, Sol, 354n43, 355n44
Rousseau, Jean-Jacques, 107,
    400n112, 484n47
Rousselot, Pierre, 257, 432n59,
    461nn191–92

Salvation, 117, 119, 133
Sartre, Jean-Paul, 69, 246, 455n126
Schäfer, Christian, 404nn10–11
Schelling, 69, 206–7, 365n122,
    401n121, 409n70, 434n20,
    435n30, 442n1
Schindler, David L., 368n144
Schlosser, Marianne, 212, 436n49
Schmitz, Kenneth, 423n90, 423n94
Schmutz, Jakob, 439n78
Schopenhauer, 69
Scotus, John Duns, xiii, 45, 148, 168,
    178, 223, 235, 376n26, 431n55,
    435n30, 448n50, 448n55,
    456n135, 457n146, 458n156,
    461n188, 462n197, 478n67,
    479nn2–4, 479n6, 480nn9–12,
    481nn14–15, 481nn18–19,
    482n24, 482nn27–28, 482n30,
    483n31, 483n41, 484n43,
    484nn47–50, 485nn53–54,
    485n63, 486n70, 486n76,
    487n80, 488n87, 488nn93–95,
    489n100, 489n106, 490n107,
    491nn108–10, 491nn112–13,
    492nn118–19, 492n122,
    493n128, 493nn130–31,
    494n136, 494nn139–41,
    494n149, 495n2
Shestov, Lev, 358n78
Siewerth, Gustav, 450n70, 471n270,
    471n276, 479n4
Siger of Brabant, 473n6, 476n29
Simon, Yves, 249, 449n59
sin, and freedom, 4, 38, 98–100, 103,
    140, 151, 157, 160, 165, 194,
    347n2, 348n3, 396n75, 397n79,
    397n84, 397n87, 398n90,
    469n254
Sixtus V, 432n1

Smith, Thomas W., 375n14
Socrates, 354n39
Sophocles, 56–57, 376n22
Sorabji, Richard, 349n7
soul, 76–77, 86, 94, 356n61; as form of the body, 221–22, 266, 395n58; as a whole, 84, 208
Spaemann, Robert, 405n16, 493n134
Spinoza, 70, 121, 358nn78–79, 480n12
Spearitt, Placid, 407n51
Spiering, Jamie Anne, 474n12
Spruyte, Joke, 494n140
Stadter, Ernst, 433n6, 433n8, 479n2, 483n31, 492n114
Strauss, Leo, 8–9, 110, 358n79, 405n17
Stoics, 52–53, 83, 93–95, 97, 106, 137, 140, 158, 176, 252, 348n4, 369n151, 375n12, 375n17, 378n43, 394n53, 395n58, 410n1, 411n2, 421n68, 457n147
superabundant sufficiency, 315–16, 327, 488n94, 489n99
superdeterminacy, 235–36, 249, 253, 264, 449n59, 449n65
Sweeney, Leo, 389n136
synderesis, 438n70, 439n77
Szlachta, Michael, 474n12, 476n32, 476n35, 478n56

thelēsis, 66–67, 139, 158, 380n63
Tertullian, 8, 376n28, 380n58
Thomas of Sutton, 476n29
Tour, Marine de la, 486n63
tradition, x, 47, 51, 54, 187, 203, 225–26, 443n3

Trego, Kristell, 180–81, 186, 419nn37–38, 422n87, 423n91, 423n95, 423n98, 425n116, 448n48, 485n54
Trinity, 33, 40, 44, 85–89, 107, 125–26, 128, 137, 148, 156, 205–9, 211, 219, 222, 224–25, 228, 231, 276–77, 372n184, 393nn37–38, 393n40, 427n4, 434n17, 435n29, 440n89, 442n111, 446n37, 472n291, 482n29, 483n38, 495n2
Tsakanikas, Matthew, 396n75

Ulrich, Ferdinand, 423n89, 423n94, 432n4, 449n65, 455n127, 455n130, 466n228, 471n271, 485n63

Veatch, Henry, 426n126
Velde, Rudi te, 450n70, 465n224, 484n47
Venuta, Goffredo, 192–95, 428n9, 428n19, 429n23, 431n56
Victorinus, 88
vis cogitativa, 467n242
Visser, Sandra, 169, 172, 178
Voegelin, Eric, 15, 356n57
voluntarism, xii, 28, 66, 98, 142, 174, 196, 205, 208–9, 254, 273–74, 457n145, 471n275, 474n12, 476n40, 478n62, 481n15, 484n48, 484n50, 488n93, 490n107

Walker, Adrian, 412n21
Weisheipl, James, 450n69
Westra, Laura, 379n54
Wetzel, James, 390n7, 394n50, 395n59, 397n87

will, 9, 92, 95; as bond, 19, 23, 88–89, 227, 392n31; as common, 23, 190–91, 198; as faculty, 139, 166–67, 186, 210, 347n2, 390n7, 436n39, 436n44; as natural, 148–49, 152, 154, 156, 163, 167, 170, 182, 216–17, 413n34, 438n74, 443n10, 493n127; in Old Testament, 13–19; and power or *potentia*, 21, 186. *See also* intellect

William of Moerbeck, 470n258

Williams, Thomas, 169, 172, 178, 487n80

Wippel, John, 473n2, 475n20, 475n26

Wolter, Allan, 479n4, 486n64, 488n87, 493n131

Wu, John, 366n136

D. C. SCHINDLER
is professor of metaphysics and anthropology at the John Paul II Institute, Washington, DC. He is the author of eleven books, including *Freedom from Reality: The Diabolical Character of Modern Liberty* (University of Notre Dame Press, 2017).

www.ingramcontent.com/pod-product-compliance
Lightning Source LLC
Chambersburg PA
CBHW021413300426
44114CB00010B/481